AMERICAN POETRY:
THE NINETEENTH CENTURY

AMERICAN POETRY:
THE NINETEENTH CENTURY

THE LIBRARY OF AMERICA

Some of the material in this volume is reprinted by
permission of the holders of copyright and publication rights.
Acknowledgments will be found in the Note on the Texts.

Distributed in the United States
by Penguin Books USA Inc
and in Canada by Penguin Books Canada Ltd.

Library of Congress Catalog Number: 96–8927
For cataloging information, see end of Index.
ISBN 1–883011–36–1
―――――
Originally published in hardcover in a two-volume unabridged edition
by The Library of America in 1993.

First Library of America College Edition
October 1996

Contents

FOLK SONGS AND SPIRITUALS

PHILIP FRENEAU
(1752–1832)

On the Great Western Canal
of the State of New York

Meliusne sylvas ire per longas
Fuit, an recentes carpere undas?
—HORACE.

i. e. which was best—to travel through tedious,
dreary forests, or to sail on these recent waters?

The nation true to honor's cause,
To *equal rights* and *equal laws*,
Is well secured, and well released
From the proud monarchs of the east.

Thus *Holland* rose from *Spain's* controul,
And thus shall rise from pole to pole
Those systems formed on reason's plan
That vindicate the *Rights of man.*—

Nature, herself, will change her face,
And arts fond arms the world embrace;
In works of peace mankind engage,
And close the despot's iron age.

And *here* behold a work progress,
Advancing through the wilderness,
A work, so recently began,
Where Liberty enlightens man:
Her powerful voice, at length, awakes
Imprisoned seas and bounded lakes.

The great idea to pursue,
To lead the veins the system through;
Such glorious toils to emulate,
Should be the task of every *State.*

I

From *Erie's* shores to *Hudson's* stream
The unrivalled work would endless seem;
Would *millions* for the work demand,
And half depopulate the land.

To *Fancy's* view, what years must run,
What ages, till the task is done!
Even *truth*, severe would seem to say,
One hundred years must pass away:—

The sons might see what sires began,
Still unperformed the mighty plan,
The impeded barque, in durance held,
By hills confined, by rocks repelled.—

Not *China's* wall, though grand and strong,
Five hundred leagues it towers along,
Not China's wall, though stretching far,
Which this vast object can compare,

With such gigantic works of old
This proud *Canal* may be enrolled,
Which to our use no tyrant gave
Nor owes its grandeur to one Slave.—

If kings their object tribes compell'd
With toil immense, such walls to build,
A *new Republic* in the west
(A great example to the rest)
Can seas unite, and *here* will shew
What Freedom's nervous sons can do.

See Commerce *here* expand her sail,
And distant shores those waters hail,
As wafting to Manhattan's coast
The products that new regions boast.

And hence our fleets transport their freights
To jealous kings and sister states,
And spread her fame from shore to shore,
Where suns ascend, or billows roar,

To make the purpose all complete,
Before they bid *two oceans* meet;
Before the task is finished, all,
What rocks must yield, what forests fall?

Three years elapsed, behold it done!
A work from Nature's *chaos* won;
By hearts of oak and hands of toil
The Spade inverts the rugged soil
A work, that may remain secure
While suns exist and Moon's endure.

With patient step I see them move
O'er many a plain, through many a grove;
Herculean strength disdains the sod
Where tigers ranged or *Mohawks* trod;
The powers that can the soil subdue
Will see the mighty project through.

Ye patrons of this bold design
Who *Erie* to the *Atlantic* join,
To you be every honour paid—
No time shall see your fame decayed:—
Through gloomy groves you traced the plan,
The rude abodes of savage man.

Ye Prompters of a work so vast
That may for years, for centuries last;
Where Nature toiled to bar the way
You mark'd her steps, but changed her sway.

Ye Artists, who, with skillful hand,
Conduct such rivers through the land,
Proceed!—and in your bold carreer
May every Plan as wise appear,
As *this*, which joins to *Hudson's* wave
What Nature to *St. Lawrence* gave.

JOEL BARLOW
(1754–1812)

Advice to a Raven in Russia

December, 1812

Black fool, why winter here? These frozen skies,
Worn by your wings and deafen'd by your cries,
Should warn you hence, where milder suns invite,
And day alternates with his mother night.
You fear perhaps your food will fail you there,
Your human carnage, that delicious fare
That lured you hither, following still your friend
The great Napoleon to the world's bleak end.
You fear, because the southern climes pour'd forth
Their clustering nations to infest the north,
Barvarians, Austrians, those who Drink the Po
And those who skirt the Tuscan seas below,
With all Germania, Neustria, Belgia, Gaul,
Doom'd here to wade thro slaughter to their fall,
You fear he left behind no wars, to feed
His feather'd canibals and nurse the breed.
Fear not, my screamer, call your greedy train,
Sweep over Europe, hurry back to Spain,
You'll find his legions there; the valliant crew
Please best their master when they toil for you.
Abundant there they spread the country o'er
And taint the breeze with every nation's gore,
Iberian, Lussian, British widely strown,
But still more wide and copious flows their own.
Go where you will; Calabria, Malta, Greece,
Egypt and Syria still his fame increase,
Domingo's fatten'd isle and India's plains
Glow deep with purple drawn from Gallic veins.
No Raven's wing can stretch the flight so far
As the torn bandrols of Napoleon's war.
Choose then your climate, fix your best abode,
He'll make you deserts and he'll bring you blood.

4

How could you fear a dearth? have not mankind,
Tho slain by millions, millions left behind?
Has not CONSCRIPTION still the power to weild
Her annual faulchion o'er the human field?
A faithful harvester! or if a man
Escape that gleaner, shall he scape the BAN?
The triple BAN, that like the hound of hell
Gripes with three joles, to hold his victim well.
   Fear nothing then, hatch fast your ravenous brood,
Teach them to cry to Bonaparte for food;
They'll be like you, of all his suppliant train,
The only class that never cries in vain.
For see what mutual benefits you lend!
(The surest way to fix the mutual friend)
While on his slaughter'd troops your tribes are fed,
You cleanse his camp and carry off his dead.
Imperial Scavenger! but now you know
Your work is vain amid these hills of snow.
His tentless troops are marbled thro with frost
And change to crystal when the breath is lost.
Mere trunks of ice, tho limb'd like human frames
And lately warm'd with life's endearing flames,
They cannot taint the air, the world impest,
Nor can you tear one fiber from their breast.
No! from their visual sockets, as they lie,
With beak and claws you cannot pluck an eye.
The frozen orb, preserving still its form,
Defies your talons as it braves the storm,
But stands and stares to God, as if to know
In what curst hands he leaves his world below.
   Fly then, or starve; tho all the dreadful road
From Minsk to Moskow with their bodies strow'd
May count some Myriads, yet they can't suffice
To feed you more beneath these dreary skies.
Go back, and winter in the wilds of Spain;
Feast there awhile, and in the next campaign
Rejoin your master; for you'll find him then,
With his new million of the race of men,
Clothed in his thunders, all his flags unfurl'd,
Raging and storming o'er the prostrate world.

War after war his hungry soul requires,
State after State shall sink beneath his fires,
Yet other Spains in victim smoke shall rise
And other Moskows suffocate the skies,
Each land lie reeking with its people's slain
And not a stream run bloodless to the main.
Till men resume their souls, and dare to shed
Earth's total vengeance on the monster's head,
Hurl from his blood-built throne this king of woes,
Dash him to dust, and let the world repose.

MANOAH BODMAN

(1765–1850)

from *An Oration on Death*

What rich profusion here,
  Is scatter'd all abroad,
To make us love and fear,
   Obey and worship God.
    And sound his praise,
      Through every clime,
    In constant lays,
      Till end of time.

The huge leviathan,
  The oyster and the eel,
The lion and the lamb,
  Each in their nature feel.
    And go abroad,
      In quest of food,
    Depend on God,
      For every good.

These shining crumbs of clay,
  With yellow, green and gold,
March on their lucid way,
  And day in night unfold.
    And shine so bright,
      And please themselves,
    And fill'd with light,
      They quit their cells.

———————

Is dull conformity
    Confin'd to spirits alone,
Who all so clearly see
    The Great, the Three in One?
        Forbid it sense,
            It cannot be:
        In heaven's immense,
            They different see.

JOHN QUINCY ADAMS

(1767–1848)

To the Sun-Dial

Under the Window of the Hall of the House of
Representatives of the United States

Thou silent herald of Time's silent flight!
   Say, could'st thou speak, what warning voice were thine?
   Shade, who canst only show how others shine!
Dark, sullen witness of resplendent light
In day's broad glare, and when the noontide bright
   Of laughing fortune sheds the ray divine,
   Thy ready favors cheer us—but decline
The clouds of morning and the gloom of night.
Yet are thy counsels faithful, just, and wise;
   They bid us seize the moments as they pass—
Snatch the retrieveless sunbeam as it flies,
   Nor lose one sand of life's revolving glass—
Aspiring still, with energy sublime,
By virtuous deeds to give eternity to Time.

To Sally

"Integer vitæ, scelerisque purus
Non eget Mauris jaculis, neque arcu."

The man in righteousness array'd,
   A pure and blameless liver,
Needs not the keen Toledo blade,
   Nor venom-freighted quiver.
What though he wind his toilsome way
   O'er regions wild and weary—
Through Zara's burning desert stray;
   Or Asia's jungles dreary:

9

What though he plough the billowy deep
   By lunar light, or solar,
Meet the resistless Simoon's sweep,
   Or iceberg circumpolar.
In bog or quagmire deep and dank,
   His foot shall never settle;
He mounts the summit of Mont Blanc,
   Or Popocatapetl.

On Chimborazo's breathless height,
   He treads o'er burning lava;
Or snuffs the Bohan Upas blight,
   The deathful plant of Java.
Through every peril he shall pass,
   By Virtue's shield protected;
And still by Truth's unerring glass
   His path shall be directed.

Else wherefore was it, Thursday last,
   While strolling down the valley
Defenceless, musing as I pass'd
   A canzonet to Sally;
A wolf, with mouth protruding snout,
   Forth from the thicket bounded—
I clapped my hands and raised a shout—
   He heard—and fled—confounded.

Tangier nor Tunis never bred
   An animal more crabbed;
Nor Fez, dry nurse of lions, fed
   A monster half so rabid.
Nor Ararat so fierce a beast
   Has seen, since days of Noah;
Nor strong, more eager for a feast,
   The fell constrictor boa.

Oh! place me where the solar beam
    Has scorch'd all verdure vernal;
Or on the polar verge extreme,
    Block'd up with ice eternal—
Still shall my voice's tender lays
    Of love remain unbroken;
And still my charming SALLY praise,
    Sweet smiling and sweet spoken.

JAMES KIRKE PAULDING

(1778–1860)

from *The Backwoodsman*

Neglected Muse! of this our western clime,
How long in servile, imitative rhyme,
Wilt thou thy stifled energies impart,
And miss the path that leads to every heart?
How long repress the brave decisive flight,
Warm'd by thy native fires, led by thy native light?
Thrice happy he who first shall strike the lyre,
With homebred feeling, and with homebred fire;
He need not envy any favour'd bard,
Who Fame's bright meed, and Fortune's smiles reward;
Secure, that wheresoe'er this empire rolls,
Or east, or west, or tow'rd the firm fixed poles,
While Europe's ancient honours fade away,
And sink the glories of her better day,
When, like degenerate Greece, her former fame
Shall stand contrasted with her present shame,
And all the splendours of her bright career
Shall die away, to be relighted here,
A race of myriads will the tale rehearse,
And love the author of the happy verse.
Come then, neglected Muse! and try with me
The untrack'd path—'tis death or victory;
Let Chance or Fate decide, or critics will,
No fame I lose—I am but nothing still.

Book I, lines 17–40

In truth it was a landscape wildly gay
That 'neath his lofty vision smiling lay;
A sea of mingling hills, with forests crown'd,
E'en to their summits, waving all around,
Save where some rocky steep aloft was seen,
Frowning amid the wild romantic scene,

Around whose brow, where human step ne'er trode,
Our native Eagle makes his high abode;
Oft in the warring of the whistling gales,
Amid the scampering clouds, he bravely sails,
Without an effort winds the loftiest sky,
And looks into the Sun with steady eye:
Emblem and patron of this fearless land,
He mocks the might of any mortal hand,
And, proudly seated on his native rock,
Defies the World's accumulated shock.
Here, mid the piling mountains scatter'd round,
His winding way majestic Hudson found,
And as he swept the frowning ridge's base,
In the pure mirror of his morning face,
A lovelier landscape caught the gazer's view,
Softer than nature, yet to nature true.
Now might be seen, reposing in stern pride,
Against the mountain's steep and rugged side,
High PUTNAM's battlements, like tow'r of old,
Haunt of night-robbing baron, stout and bold,
Scourge of his neighbour, Nimrod of the chase,
Slave of his king, and tyrant of his race.
Beneath its frowning brow, and far below,
The weltering waves, unheard, were seen to flow
Round West Point's rude and adamantine base,
That call'd to mind old ARNOLD's deep disgrace,
ANDRE's hard fate, lamented, though deserv'd,
And men, who from their duty never swerv'd—
The HONEST THREE—the pride of yeomen bold,
Who sav'd the country which they might have sold;
Refus'd the proffer'd bribe, and, sternly true,
Did what the man that doubts them ne'er would do.
Yes! if the Scroll of never-dying Fame,
Shall tell the truth, 'twill bear each lowly name;
And while the wretched man, who vainly tried
To wound their honour, and his Country's pride,
Shall moulder in the dirt from whence he came,
Forgot, or only recollected to his shame,
Quoted shall be these gallant, honest men,
By many a warrior's voice, and poet's pen,

To wake the sleeping spirit of the land,
And nerve with energy the patriot band.
Beyond, on either side the river's bound,
Two lofty promontories darkly frown'd,
Through which, in times long past, as learned say,
The pent up waters forc'd their stubborn way;
Grimly they frown'd, as menacing the wave
That storm'd their bulwarks with its current brave,
And seem'd to threaten from their shatter'd brow,
To crush the vessels all becalm'd below,
Whose white sails, hanging idly at the mast,
O'er the still waves a deep reflexion cast.
Still farther off, the Kaatskill, bold and high,
Kiss'd the pure concave of the arched sky,
Mingled with that its waving lines of blue,
And shut the world beyond from mortal view.

Book II, lines 61 –122

'Tis true—yet 'tis no pity that 'tis true,
Many fine things they neither felt nor knew.
Unlike the sons of Europe's happier clime,
They never died to music's melting chime,
Or groan'd, as if in agonizing pain,
At some enervate, whining, sickly strain;
Nor would they sell their heritage of rights,
For long processions, fetes, and pretty sights,
Or barter for a bauble, or a feast,
All that distinguishes the man from beast.
With them, alas! the fairest masterpiece,
Of beggar'd Italy, or rifled Greece,
A chisell'd wonder, or a thing of paint,
A marble godhead, or a canvass saint,
Were poor amends for cities wrapt in flame,
A ruin'd land and deep dishonour'd name;
Nor would they mourn Apollo sent away,
More than the loss of Freedom's glorious day;
Among them was no driv'ling princely race,
Who'd beggar half a state, to buy a vase,
Or starve a province nobly to reclaim,

From mother Earth, a thing without a name,
Some mutilated trunk decay'd and worn,
Of head bereft, of legs and arms all shorn,
Worthless, except to puzzle learned brains,
And cause a world of most laborious pains,
To find if this same headless, limbless thing,
A worthless godhead was, or worthless king.

Book III, lines 499 –526

CLEMENT MOORE

(1779–1863)

A Visit from St. Nicholas

'Twas the night before Christmas, when all through
    the house
Not a creature was stirring, not even a mouse;
The stockings were hung by the chimney with care,
In hopes that ST. NICHOLAS soon would be there;
The children were nestled all snug in their beds,
While visions of sugar-plums danced in their heads;
And Mamma in her 'kerchief, and I in my cap,
Had just settled our brains for a long winter's nap;
When out on the lawn there arose such a clatter,
I sprang from the bed to see what was the matter.
Away to the window I flew like a flash,
Tore open the shutters and threw up the sash.
The moon on the breast of the new-fallen snow,
Gave the lustre of mid-day to objects below,
When, what to my wondering eyes should appear,
But a miniature sleigh, and eight tiny rein-deer,
With a little old driver, so lively and quick,
I knew in a moment it must be St. Nick.
More rapid than eagles his coursers they came,
And he whistled, and shouted, and called them by name;
"Now, *Dasher*! now, *Dancer*! now, *Prancer* and *Vixen*!
On, *Comet*! on, *Cupid*! on, *Donder* and *Blitzen*!
To the top of the porch! to the top of the wall!
Now dash away! dash away! dash away all!"
As dry leaves that before the wild hurricane fly,
When they meet with an obstacle, mount to the sky;
So up to the house-top the coursers they flew,
With the sleigh full of Toys, and St. Nicholas too.
And then, in a twinkling, I heard on the roof,
The prancing and pawing of each little hoof—
As I drew in my head, and was turning around,
Down the chimney St. Nicholas came with a bound.

He was dressed all in fur, from his head to his foot,
And his clothes were all tarnished with ashes and soot;
A bundle of Toys he had flung on his back,
And he look'd like a pedlar just opening his pack.
His eyes—how they twinkled! his dimples how merry!
His cheeks were like roses, his nose like a cherry!
His droll little mouth was drawn up like a bow,
And the beard of his chin was as white as the snow;
The stump of a pipe he held tight in his teeth,
And the smoke it encircled his head like a wreath;
He had a broad face and a little round belly,
That shook when he laughed, like a bowlfull of jelly.
He was chubby and plump, a right jolly old elf,
And I laughed when I saw him, in spite of myself,
A wink of his eye and a twist of his head,
Soon gave me to know I had nothing to dread;
He spoke not a word, but went straight to his work,
And fill'd all the stockings; then turned with a jerk,
And laying his finger aside of his nose,
And giving a nod, up the chimney he rose;
He sprang to his sleigh, to his team gave a whistle,
And away they all flew like the down of a thistle.
But I heard him exclaim, ere he drove out of sight,
"Happy Christmas to all, and to all a good night."

FRANCIS SCOTT KEY

(1779–1843)

Defence of Fort Mᶜ Henry

O! say can you see, by the dawn's early light,
　What so proudly we hail'd at the twilight's last gleaming,
Whose broad stripes and bright stars through the perilous
　　　　fight,
　　O'er the ramparts we watch'd, were so gallantly
　　　　streaming?
　　　And the rockets' red glare, the bombs bursting in air,
　　　Gave proof through the night that our flag was still
　　　　there—
　　　　O! say, does that star-spangled banner yet wave
　　　　O'er the land of the free, and the home of the brave?

On the shore, dimly seen through the mists of the deep,
　Where the foe's haughty host in dread silence reposes,
What is that which the breeze o'er the towering steep,
　　As it fitfully blows, half conceals, half discloses?
　　　Now it catches the gleam of the morning's first beam,
　　　In full glory reflected now shines on the stream—
　　　　'Tis the star-spangled banner, O! long may it wave
　　　　O'er the land of the free, and the home of the brave.

And where is that band who so vauntingly swore
　That the havock of war and the battle's confusion
A home and a country should leave us no more?
　　Their blood has wash'd out their foul foot-steps'
　　　　pollution.
　　　No refuge could save the hireling and slave,
　　　From the terror of flight or the gloom of the grave;
　　　　And the star-spangled banner in triumph doth wave
　　　　O'er the land of the free, and the home of the brave.

O! thus be it ever when freemen shall stand
  Between their lov'd home, and the war's desolation,
Blest with vict'ry and peace, may the heav'n-rescued land
  Praise the power that hath made and preserv'd us a
            nation!
    Then conquer we must, when our cause it is just,
    And this be our motto—"In God is our trust!"
      And the star-spangled banner in triumph shall wave
      O'er the land of the free, and the home of the brave.

WASHINGTON ALLSTON

(1779–1843)

On a Falling Group in the Last Judgement of Michael Angelo, in the Cappella Sistina

How vast, how dread, o'erwhelming is the thought
Of Space interminable! to the soul
A circling weight that crushes into nought
Her mighty faculties! a wond'rous whole,
Without or parts, beginning, or an end!
How fearful then on desp'rate wings to send
The fancy e'en amid the waste profound!
Yet, born as if all daring to astound,
Thy giant hand, oh Angelo, hath hurl'd
E'en human forms, with all their mortal weight,
Down the dread void—fall endless as their fate!
Already now they seem from world to world
For ages thrown; yet doom'd, another past,
Another still to reach, nor e'er to reach the last!

On the Group of the Three Angels Before the Tent of Abraham, by Raffaelle, in the Vatican

Oh, now I feel as though another sense
From Heaven descending had inform'd my soul;
I feel the pleasurable, full control
Of Grace, harmonious, boundless, and intense.
In thee, celestial Group, embodied lives
The subtle mystery; that speaking gives
Itself resolv'd: the essences combin'd
Of Motion ceaseless, Unity complete.
Borne like a leaf by some soft eddying wind,
Mine eyes, impell'd as by enchantment sweet,
From part to part with circling motion rove,

Yet seem unconscious of the power to move;
From line to line through endless changes run,
O'er countless shapes, yet seem to gaze on One.

On Rembrant; Occasioned by His Picture of Jacob's Dream

As in that twilight, superstitious age
When all beyond the narrow grasp of mind
Seem'd fraught with meanings of supernal kind,
When e'en the learned philosophic sage,
Wont with the stars thro' boundless space to range,
Listen'd with rev'rence to the changeling's tale;
E'en so, thou strangest of all beings strange!
E'en so thy visionary scenes I hail;
That like the ramblings of an idiot's speech,
No image giving of a thing on earth,
Nor thought significant in Reason's reach,
Yet in their random shadowings give birth
To thoughts and things from other worlds that come,
And fill the soul, and strike the reason dumb.

On the Luxembourg Gallery

There is a Charm no vulgar mind can reach,
No critick thwart, no mighty master teach;
A Charm how mingled of the good and ill!
Yet still so mingled that the mystick whole
Shall captive hold the struggling Gazer's will,
'Till vanquish'd reason own its full control.
And such, oh Rubens, thy mysterious art,
The charm that vexes, yet enslaves the heart!
Thy lawless style, from timid systems free,
Impetuous rolling like a troubled sea,
High o'er the rocks of reason's lofty verge
Impending hangs; yet, ere the foaming surge
Breaks o'er the bound, the refluent ebb of taste
Back from the shore impels the wat'ry waste.

America to Great Britain

All hail! thou noble Land,
  Our Fathers' native soil!
O stretch thy mighty hand,
  Gigantic grown by toil,
O'er the vast Atlantic wave to our shore:
  For thou with magic might
  Canst reach to where the light
  Of Phœbus travels bright
    The world o'er!

The Genius of our clime,
  From his pine-embattled steep,
Shall hail the guest sublime;
  While the Tritons of the deep
With their conchs the kindred league shall proclaim.
  Then let the world combine—
  O'er the main our Naval Line
  Like the milky way shall shine
    Bright in fame!

Though ages long have past
  Since our Fathers left their home,
Their pilot in the blast,
  O'er untravell'd seas to roam,
Yet lives the blood of England in our veins!
  And shall we not proclaim
  That blood of honest fame
  Which no tyranny can tame
    By its chains?

While the language free and bold
  Which the Bard of Avon sung,
In which our Milton told
  How the vault of Heaven rung
When Satan, blasted, fell with his host;
  While this, with rev'rence meet,
  Ten thousand echoes greet,
  From rock to rock repeat
    Round our coast;

While the manners, while the arts,
   That mould a nation's soul,
Still cling around our hearts—
   Between let ocean roll,
Our joint communion breaking with the Sun:
   Yet still from either beach
   The voice of blood shall reach,
   More audible than speech,
      'We are One.'

Coleridge

And thou art gone most loved, most honor'd friend!
No—never more thy gentle voice shall blend
With air of earth its pure ideal tones—
Binding in one, as with harmonious zones,
The heart and intellect. And I no more
Shall with thee gaze on that unfathom'd deep,
The Human Soul; as when, push'd off the shore,
Thy mystic bark would thro' the darkness sweep—
Itself the while so bright! For oft we seem'd
As on some starless sea—all dark above,
All dark below—yet, onward as we drove,
To plough up light that ever round us stream'd.
But he who mourns is not as one bereft
Of all he loved: thy living Truths are left.

Art

O Art, high gift of Heaven! how oft defamed
When seeming praised! To most a craft that fits,
By dead, prescriptive Rule, the scattered bits
Of gathered knowledge; even so misnamed
By some who would invoke thee; but not so
By him,—the noble Tuscan,—who gave birth
To forms unseen of man, unknown to Earth,
Now living habitants; he felt the glow
Of thy revealing touch, that brought to view
The invisible Idea; and he knew,

E'en by his inward sense, its form was true:
'T was life to life responding,—highest truth!
So, through Elisha's faith, the Hebrew Youth
Beheld the thin blue air to fiery chariots grow.

Rubens

Thus o'er his art indignant Rubens reared
His mighty head, nor critic armies feared.
His lawless style, from vain pretension free,
Impetuous rolling like a troubled sea,
High o'er the rocks of Reason's ridgy verge
Impending hangs; but, ere the foaming surge
Breaks o'er the bound, the under-ebb of taste
Back from the shore impels the watery waste.

JOHN PIERPONT

(1785–1866)

The Fugitive Slave's Apostrophe to the North Star

Star of the North! though night winds drift
　　The fleecy drapery of the sky
Between thy lamp and me, I lift,
　　Yea, lift with hope, my sleepless eye
To the blue heights wherein thou dwellest,
And of a land of freedom tellest.

Star of the North! while blazing day
　　Pours round me its full tide of light,
And hides thy pale but faithful ray,
　　I, too, lie hid, and long for night:
For night;—I dare not walk at noon,
Nor dare I trust the faithless moon,—

Nor faithless man, whose burning lust
　　For gold hath riveted my chain;
Nor other leader can I trust,
　　But thee, of even the starry train;
For, all the host around thee burning,
Like faithless man, keep turning, turning.

I may not follow where they go:
　　Star of the North, I look to thee
While on I press; for well I know
　　Thy light and truth shall set me free;—
Thy light, that no poor slave deceiveth;
Thy truth, that all my soul believeth.

They of the East beheld the star
　　That over Bethlehem's manger glowed;
With joy they hailed it from afar,

And followed where it marked the road,
Till, where its rays directly fell,
They found the Hope of Israel.

Wise were the men who followed thus
    The star that sets man free from sin!
Star of the North! thou art to us,—
    Who 're slaves because we wear a skin
Dark as is night's protecting wing,—
Thou art to us a holy thing.

And we are wise to follow thee!
    I trust thy steady light alone:
Star of the North! thou seem'st to me
    To burn before the Almighty's throne,
To guide me, through these forests dim
And vast, to liberty and HIM.

Thy beam is on the glassy breast
    Of the still spring, upon whose brink
I lay my weary limbs to rest,
    And bow my parching lips to drink.
Guide of the friendless negro's way,
I bless thee for this quiet ray!

In the dark top of southern pines
    I nestled, when the driver's horn
Called to the field, in lengthening lines,
    My fellows at the break of morn.
And there I lay, till thy sweet face
Looked in upon "my hiding-place."

The tangled cane-brake,—where I crept
    For shelter from the heat of noon,
And where, while others toiled, I slept
    Till wakened by the rising moon,—
As its stalks felt the night wind free,
Gave me to catch a glimpse of thee.

Star of the North! in bright array
   The constellations round thee sweep,
Each holding on its nightly way,
   Rising, or sinking in the deep,
And, as it hangs in mid heaven flaming,
The homage of some nation claiming.

This nation to the Eagle cowers;
   Fit ensign! she 's a bird of spoil;—
Like worships like! for each devours
   The earnings of another 's toil.
I 've felt her talons and her beak,
And now the gentler Lion seek.

The Lion, at the Virgin's feet
   Crouches, and lays his mighty paw
Into her lap!—an emblem meet
   Of England's Queen and English law:—
Queen, that hath made her Islands free!
Law, that holds out its shield to me!

Star of the North! upon that shield
   Thou shinest!—O, for ever shine!
The negro, from the cotton-field,
   Shall then beneath its orb recline,
And feed the Lion couched before it,
Nor heed the Eagle screaming o'er it!

SAMUEL WOODWORTH

(1785–1842)

The Bucket

Air — The Flower of Dumblane

How dear to this heart are the scenes of my childhood,
   When fond recollection presents them to view!
The orchard, the meadow, the deep-tangled wild-wood,
   And every loved spot which my infancy knew!
The wide-spreading pond, and the mill that stood by it,
   The bridge, and the rock where the cataract fell,
The cot of my father, the dairy-house nigh it,
   And e'en the rude bucket that hung in the well—
The old oaken bucket, the iron-bound bucket,
The moss-covered bucket which hung in the well.

That moss-covered vessel I hail'd as a treasure,
   For often at noon, when return'd from the field,
I found it the source of an exquisite pleasure,
   The purest and sweetest that nature can yield.
How ardent I seized it, with hands that were glowing,
   And quick to the white-pebbled bottom it fell;
Then soon, with the emblem of truth overflowing,
   And dripping with coolness, it rose from the well—
The old oaken bucket, the iron-bound bucket,
The moss-covered bucket, arose from the well.

How sweet from the green mossy brim to receive it,
   As poised on the curb it inclined to my lips!
Not a full blushing goblet could tempt me to leave it,
   The brightest that beauty or revelry sips.
And now, far removed from the loved habitation,
   The tear of regret will intrusively swell,
As fancy reverts to my father's plantation,
   And sighs for the bucket that hangs in the well—
The old oaken bucket, the iron-bound bucket,
The moss-covered bucket that hangs in the well!

RICHARD HENRY DANA

(1787–1879)

The Dying Raven

Come to these lonely woods to die alone?
It seems not many days since thou wast heard,
From out the mists of spring, with thy shrill note,
Calling unto thy mates—and their clear answers.
The earth was brown, then; and the infant leaves
Had not put forth to warm them in the sun,
Or play in the fresh air of heaven. Thy voice,
Shouting in triumph, told of winter gone,
And prophesying life to the seal'd ground,
Did make me glad with thoughts of coming beauties.
And now they 're all around us;—offspring bright
Of earth,—a mother, who, with constant care,
Doth feed and clothe them all.—Now o'er her fields,
In blessed bands, or single, they are gone,
Or by her brooks they stand, and sip the stream;
Or peering o'er it,—vanity well feign'd—
In quaint approval seem to glow and nod
At their reflected graces.—Morn to meet,
They in fantastic labours pass the night,
Catching its dews, and rounding silvery drops
To deck their bosoms.—There, on tall, bald trees,
From varnish'd cells some peep, and the old boughs
Make to rejoice and dance in the unseen winds.
Over my head the winds and they make music;
And grateful, in return for what they take,
Bright hues and odours to the air they give.

Thus mutual love brings mutual delight—
Brings beauty, life;—for love is life—hate, death.

Thou Prophet of so fair a revelation!
Thou who abod'st with us the winter long,
Enduring cold or rain, and shaking oft,

From thy dark mantle, falling sleet or snow—
Thou, who with purpose kind, when warmer days
Shone on the earth, midst thaw and steam, cam'st forth
From rocky nook, or wood, thy priestly cell,
To speak of comfort unto lonely man—
Didst say to him,—though seemingly alone
'Midst wastes and snows, and silent, lifeless trees,
Or the more silent ground—that 't was not death,
But nature's sleep and rest, her kind repair;—
That Thou, albeit unseen, did'st bear with him
The winter's night, and, patient of the day,
And cheer'd by hope, (instinct divine in Thee,)
Waitedst return of summer.

                    More Thou saidst,
Thou Priest of Nature, Priest of God, to man!
Thou spok'st of Faith, (than instinct no less sure,)
Of Spirits near him, though he saw them not:
Thou bad'st him ope his intellectual eye,
And see his solitude all populous:
Thou showd'st him Paradise, and deathless flowers;
And didst him pray to listen to the flow
Of living waters.

                    Preacher to man's spirit!
Emblem of Hope! Companion! Comforter!
Thou faithful one! is this thine end? 'T was thou,
When summer birds were gone, and no form seen
In the void air, who cam'st, living and strong,
On thy broad, balanced pennons, through the winds.
And of thy long enduring, this the close!
Thy kingly strength brought down, of storms
Thou Conqueror!

                    The year's mild, cheering dawn
Upon thee shone a momentary light.
The gales of spring upbore thee for a day,
And then forsook thee. Thou art fallen now;
And liest amongst thy hopes and promises—

Beautiful flowers, and freshly springing blades,
Gasping thy life out.—Here for thee the grass
Tenderly makes a bed; and the young buds
In silence open their fair, painted folds—
To ease thy pain, the one—to cheer thee, these.
But thou art restless; and thy once keen eye
Is dull and sightless now. New blooming boughs,
Needlessly kind, have spread a tent for thee.
Thy mate is calling to the white, piled clouds,
And asks for thee. No answer give they back.
As I look up to their bright angel faces,
Intelligent and capable of voice
They seem to me. Their silence to my soul
Comes ominous. The same to thee, doom'd bird,
Silence or sound. For thee there is no sound,
No silence.—Near thee stands the shadow, Death;—
And now he slowly draws his sable veil
Over thine eyes. Thy senses soft he lulls
Into unconscious slumbers. The airy call
Thou 'lt hear no longer. 'Neath sun-lighted clouds,
With beating wing, or steady poise aslant,
Thou 'lt sail no more. Around thy trembling claws
Droop thy wings' parting feathers. Spasms of death
Are on thee.

　　　　　Laid thus low by age? Or is 't
All-grudging man has brought thee to this end?
Perhaps the slender hair, so subtly wound
Around the grain God gives thee for thy food,
Has proved thy snare, and makes thine inward pain!

　I needs must mourn for thee. For I, who have
No fields, nor gather into garners—I
Bear thee both thanks and love, not fear nor hate.

　And now, farewell! The falling leaves ere long
Will give thee decent covering. Till then,
Thine own black plumage, which will now no more
Glance to the sun, nor flash upon my eyes,

Like armour of steel'd knight of Palestine,
Must be thy pall. Nor will it moult so soon
As sorrowing thoughts on those borne from him, fade
In living man.

Who scoffs these sympathies,
Makes mock of the divinity within;
Nor feels he gently breathing through his soul
The universal spirit.—Hear it cry,
"How does thy pride abase thee, man, vain man!
How deaden thee to universal love,
And joy of kindred, with all humble things,—
God's creatures all!"

And surely it is so.
He who the lily clothes in simple glory,
He who doth hear the ravens cry for food,
Hath on our hearts, with hand invisible,
In signs mysterious, written what alone
Our *hearts* may read.—Death bring thee rest, poor Bird.

The Pleasure Boat

I.

Come, hoist the sail, the fast let go!
They 're seated all aboard.
Wave chases wave in easy flow:
The bay is fair and broad.

II.

The ripples lightly tap the boat.
Loose!—Give her to the wind!
She flies ahead:—They 're all afloat:
The strand is far behind.

III.

No danger reach so fair a crew!
Thou goddess of the foam,
I 'll pay thee ever worship due,
If thou wilt bring them home.

IV.

Fair ladies, fairer than the spray
The prow is dashing wide,
Soft breezes take you on your way,
Soft flow the blessed tide!

V.

O, might I like those breezes be,
And touch that arching brow,
I 'd toil for ever on the sea
Where ye are floating now.

VI.

The boat goes tilting on the waves;
The waves go tilting by;
There dips the duck;—her back she laves;
O'er head the sea-gulls fly.

VII.

Now, like the gull that darts for prey,
The little vessel stoops;
Then, rising, shoots along her way,
Like gulls in easy swoops.

VIII.

The sun-light falling on her sheet,
It glitters like the drift,
Sparkling, in scorn of summer 's heat,
High up some mountain rift.

IX.

The winds are fresh—she 's driving fast.
Upon the bending tide,
The crinkling sail, and crinkling mast,
Go with her side by side.

X.

Why dies the breeze away so soon?
Why hangs the pennant down?
The sea is glass—the sun at noon.—
—Nay, lady, do not frown;

XI.

For, see, the winged fisher 's plume
Is painted on the sea.
Below 's a cheek of lovely bloom.
Whose eyes look up at thee?

XII.

She smiles; thou need'st must smile on her.
And, see, beside her face
A rich, white cloud that doth not stir.—
What beauty, and what grace!

XIII.

And pictured beach of yellow sand,
And peaked rock, and hill,
Change the smooth sea to fairy land.—
How lovely and how still!

XIV.

From yonder isle the thrasher 's flail
Strikes close upon the ear;
The leaping fish, the swinging sail
Of that far sloop sound near.

XV.

The parting sun sends out a glow
Across the placid bay,
Touching with glory all the show.—
— A breeze!—Up helm!—Away!

XVI.

Careening to the wind, they reach,
With laugh and call, the shore.
They 've left their foot-prints on the beach.
And shall I see them more?

XVII.

Goddess of Beauty, must I now
Vow 'd worship to thee pay?
Dear goddess, I grow old, I trow:—
My head is growing gray.

RICHARD HENRY WILDE

(1789–1847)

The Lament of the Captive

My life is like the summer rose
  That opens to the morning sky,
And, ere the shades of evening close,
  Is scattered on the ground to die:
Yet on that rose's humble bed
The softest dews of night are shed;
As if she wept such waste to see—
But none shall drop a tear for me!

My life is like the autumn leaf
  That trembles in the moon's pale ray,
Its hold is frail—its date is brief—
  Restless, and soon to pass away:
Yet when that leaf shall fall and fade,
The parent tree will mourn its shade,
The wind bewail the leafless tree,
But none shall breathe a sigh for me!

My life is like the print, which feet
  Have left on TAMPA's desert strand,
Soon as the rising tide shall beat,
  Their track will vanish from the sand:
Yet, as if grieving to efface
All vestige of the human race,
On that lone shore loud moans the sea,
But none shall thus lament for me!

To the Mocking-Bird

Winged mimic of the woods! thou motley fool,
Who shall thy gay buffoonery describe?
Thine ever-ready notes of ridicule
Pursue thy fellows still with jest and gibe;

Wit, sophist, songster, Yorick of thy tribe,
Thou sportive satirist of Nature's school,
To thee the palm of scoffing we ascribe,
Arch mocker, and mad abbot of misrule!
For such thou art by day; but all night long
Thou pour'st a soft, sweet, solemn, pensive strain,
As if thou didst, in this thy moonlight song,
Like to the melancholy Jaques complain,
Musing on falsehood, violence, and wrong,
And sighing for thy motley coat again!

from *Hesperia*

Across the Prairie's silent waste I stray,
A fertile, verdant, woodless, boundless plain;
Shadeless it lies beneath the glare of day,
But gentle breezes sweep the grassy main,
Over whose surface, as they rest or play,
The waving billows sink or rise again;
While some far distant lonely hut or tree
Looms like a solitary sail at sea!

What is yon rude and overhanging steep
That frowns on Illinois' unmurmuring tide, —
Fortress, or cliff, or Pharos of the deep?
Stern Nature's monument of savage pride,
The Sioux's tower of hunger! — Pisa's keep,
Amid whose horrors Ugolino died,
Before that rock of famine well might quail,
Did but an Indian Dante tell its tale.

Wouldst thou receive of Superstition's power
And man's credulity astounding proof,
Behold the modern saint and prophet's bower,
The city of Nauvoo. All grave reproof
Were lost upon such folly: — hour by hour,
Wall upon wall ascends, and roof on roof,
And soon the Impostor's temple will arise,
As if to flout the lightning of the skies.

This in the nineteenth century!—So blind
Are they who deem the mighty triumph wrought,
And point us boldly to "the march of mind,"
As though the world were near perfection brought,
And the Millennium reached, or left behind,
Because scarce worthy of a second thought:
Sages, Philosophers, and Sophists, you
Who praise all things as good, laud great NAUVOO!

Savage Leucadia! to thy steep repair
The pilgrims of a faith,—the bleeding heart;
Sacred thy shrine to Love and to Despair,
And wanting only Sappho's lyric art
To give imprisoned echoes to the air,
Till Oolaïtha's gentle ghost should start,
Wondering to see a pale-face at her grave,
Calling her name and spirit from the wave!

Hast thou forgot our Indian friend's abode,
Our welcome, and the scenes we witnessed there?
The wigwam floor with robes and peltry strewed,—
The calumet of Peace that all must share,—
The council-fire,—the conjurer's tricks it showed,—
The Medicine dance,—the wolf,—the moose,—the bear,—
And the great ball-play, with the dawn begun,
And hardly finished by the set of sun.

How keen, how active is the mimic strife!
What grace of form and motion they display!
Hundred of Grecian statues sprung to life
Would not have seemed of more immortal clay,
Or more Apollo-like. The angry knife
Is laid aside,—or sport might turn to fray,
So fierce the struggle between bands that watch
To stop or urge the ball, or turn, or catch.

Not Angelo's nor Donatello's skill
In folds more graceful human form could twine;
Nor his—my countryman—who, if he will,
May rival yet the artist called "Divine."

Sinews and muscles twist and swell,—veins fill,—
Hither and thither waving groups incline,
Till the live mass crashes confused to earth,
And the ball springs like Discord's apple forth!

Sons of the Forest!—yet not wholly rude,
Children of Nature, eloquent are they,
By their Great Spirit taught in solitude,
To boast o'er pain a more than stoic sway;
Their pastime war affords, the chase their food;
No foe they pardon, and no friend betray;
Admiring nothing,—men without a tear,—
Strangers to falsehood, pity, mirth, and fear.

Here Chastellux and Chateaubriand found
Matter to point a moral or a tale;
This was Atala's consecrated ground,
Ample the canvas—if the colors fail.
Yet should a trump of more exalted sound
The Christian genius and the Martyr hail:
To the fallen monarchs of the vainly free,
"Faithful among the faithless," only he!

Behold the sinking mountain! year by year,
Lower and lower still, the boatman thinks,
Its rudely castellated cliffs appear,
And he is sure that in the stream it sinks.
Gazing in wonder, not unmixed with fear
To see how fast its rocky basis shrinks,
He murmurs to himself in lower tone,
"What does the Devil do with all this stone?"

Superior! shall I call thee lake or sea?
Thou broad Atlantic of the Western waters,
Whose ocean-depths and spring-like purity,
Unstained by civilized or savage slaughters,
Proclaim thee worthiest of streams to be
The bath and mirror of Hesperia's daughters,
Their Caspian thou! alike to freeze or shine,
And every Caspian beauty matched by thine!

Beside thy beach stern Nature's tablets rise,
Her pictured rocks, eternal and sublime,
Mountains her canvass, framed in sea and skies,—
Her colors air and water, earth and time.
Fata Morgana's magic landscape flies,
Even with the mists that o'er Messina climb;
But this endures,—traced on creation's youth,
It will outlive all earthly things save TRUTH!

Colossal wall and column, arch and dome,
O'erhanging cliff and cavern, and cascade,
Ruins like those of Egypt, Greece, or Rome,
And towers that seem as if by giants made;
Surpassing beauty—overwhelming gloom—
Masses of dazzling light and blinding shade,—
All that can awe, delight, o'erpower, amaze,
Rises for leagues on leagues to our bewildered gaze!

Ozolapaida! Helen of the West,
Whose fatal beauty and adulterous joy
Two nations with the scourge of war opprest
Twice tenfold longer than the siege of Troy:
Assiniboin and Sioux both confessed
Such prize well worth the struggle to destroy
A kindred people; but no Homer kept
The memory of thy charms, and so they slept.

Canto IV, stanzas 91–105

FITZ-GREENE HALLECK

(1790–1867)

On the Death of Joseph Rodman Drake

Of New-York, Sept. 1820

Green be the turf above thee,
    Friend of my better days!
None knew thee but to love thee,
    Nor named thee but to praise.

Tears fell, when thou wert dying,
    From eyes unused to weep,
And long, where thou art lying,
    Will tears the cold turf steep.

When hearts, whose truth was proven,
    Like thine, are laid in earth,
There should a wreath be woven
    To tell the world their worth,

And I, who woke each morrow
    To clasp thy hand in mine,
Who shared thy joy and sorrow,
    Whose weal and woe were thine;

It should be mine to braid it
    Around thy faded brow,
But I've in vain essayed it,
    And feel I cannot now.

While memory bids me weep thee,
    Nor thoughts nor words are free,
The grief is fixed too deeply
    That mourns a man like thee.

Marco Bozzaris

At midnight, in his guarded tent,
   The Turk was dreaming of the hour
When Greece, her knee in suppliance bent,
   Should tremble at his power:
In dreams, through camp and court, he bore
The trophies of a conqueror;
   In dreams his song of triumph heard;
Then wore his monarch's signet ring:
Then pressed that monarch's throne—a king;
As wild his thoughts, and gay of wing,
   As Eden's garden bird.

At midnight, in the forest shades,
   Bozzaris ranged his Suliote band,
True as the steel of their tried blades,
   Heroes in heart and hand.
There had the Persian's thousands stood,
There had the glad earth drunk their blood
   On old Platæa's day;
And now there breathed that haunted air
The sons of sires who conquered there,
With arm to strike, and soul to dare,
   As quick, as far as they.

An hour passed on—the Turk awoke;
   That bright dream was his last;
He woke—to hear his sentries shriek,
"To arms! they come! the Greek! the Greek!"
He woke—to die midst flame, and smoke,
And shout, and groan, and sabre stroke,
   And death shots falling thick and fast
As lightnings from the mountain cloud;
And heard, with voice as trumpet loud,
   Bozzaris cheer his band:
"Strike—till the last armed foe expires;
Strike—for your altars and your fires;
Strike—for the green graves of your sires;
   God—and your native land!"

They fought—like brave men, long and well;
　　They piled that ground with Moslem slain,
They conquered—but Bozzaris fell,
　　Bleeding at every vein.
His few surviving comrades saw
His smile when rang their proud hurrah,
　　And the red field was won;
Then saw in death his eyelids close
Calmly, as to a night's repose,
　　Like flowers at set of sun.

Come to the bridal chamber, Death!
　　Come to the mother's, when she feels,
For the first time, her first-born's breath;
　　Come when the blessed seals
That close the pestilence are broke,
And crowded cities wail its stroke;
Come in consumption's ghastly form,
The earthquake shock, the ocean storm;
Come when the heart beats high and warm,
　　With banquet song, and dance, and wine;
And thou art terrible—the tear,
The groan, the knell, the pall, the bier;
And all we know, or dream, or fear
　　Of agony, are thine.

But to the hero, when his sword
　　Has won the battle for the free,
Thy voice sounds like a prophet's word;
And in its hollow tones are heard
　　The thanks of millions yet to be.
Come, when his task of fame is wrought—
Come, with her laurel-leaf, blood-bought—
　　Come in her crowning hour—and then
Thy sunken eye's unearthly light
To him is welcome as the sight
　　Of sky and stars to prisoned men:
Thy grasp is welcome as the hand
Of brother in a foreign land;
Thy summons welcome as the cry

That told the Indian isles were nigh
  To the world-seeking Genoese,
When the land wind, from woods of palm,
And orange groves, and fields of balm,
  Blew o'er the Haytian seas.

Bozzaris! with the storied brave
  Greece nurtured in her glory's time,
Rest thee—there is no prouder grave,
  Even in her own proud clime.
She wore no funeral weeds for thee,
  Nor bade the dark hearse wave its plume,
Like torn branch from death's leafless tree
In sorrow's pomp and pageantry,
  The heartless luxury of the tomb:
But she remembers thee as one
Long loved, and for a season gone;
For thee her poet's lyre is wreathed,
Her marble wrought, her music breathed;
For thee she rings the birthday bells;
Of thee her babes' first lisping tells;
For thine her evening prayer is said
At palace couch and cottage bed;
Her soldier, closing with the foe,
Gives for thy sake a deadlier blow;
His plighted maiden, when she fears
For him, the joy of her young years,
Thinks of thy fate, and checks her tears:
  And she, the mother of thy boys,
Though in her eye and faded cheek
Is read the grief she will not speak,
  The memory of her buried joys,
And even she who gave thee birth,
Will, by their pilgrim-circled hearth,
  Talk of thy doom without a sigh:
For thou art Freedom's now, and Fame's;
One of the few, the immortal names,
  That were not born to die.

from *Connecticut*

I.

They burnt their last witch in CONNECTICUT
   About a century and a half ago;
They made a school-house of her forfeit hut,
   And gave a pitying sweet-briar leave to grow
Above her thankless ashes; and they put
   A certified description of the show
Between two weeping willows, craped with black,
On the last page of that year's almanac.

II.

Some warning and well-meant remarks were made
   Upon the subject by the weekly printers;
The people murmured at the taxes laid
   To pay for jurymen and pitch-pine splinters,
And the sad story made the rose-leaf fade
   Upon young listeners' cheeks for several winters,
When told at fire-side eves by those who saw
Executed—the lady and the law.

III.

She and the law found rest: years rose and set;
   That generation, cottagers and kings,
Slept with their fathers, and the violet
   Has mourned above their graves a hundred springs:
Few persons keep a file of the Gazette,
   And almanacs are sublunary things,
So that her fame is almost lost to earth,
As if she ne'er had breathed; and of her birth,

IV.

And death, and lonely life's mysterious matters,
   And how she played, in our forefathers' times,
The very devil with their sons and daughters;
   And how those "delicate Ariels" of her crimes,
The spirits of the rocks, and woods, and waters,

Obeyed her bidding when, in charméd rhymes,
She muttered, at deep midnight, spells whose power
Woke from brief dream of dew the sleeping summer flower.

V.

And hushed the night-bird's solitary hymn,
    And spoke in whispers to the forest-tree,
Till his awed branches trembled, leaf and limb,
    And grouped her church-yard shapes of fantasie
Round merry moonlight's meadow-fountain's brim,
    And, mocking for a space the dread decree,
Brought back to dead, cold lips the parted breath,
And changed to banquet-board the bier of death,

VI.

None knew—except a patient, precious few,
    Who've read the folios of one COTTON MATHER,
A chronicler of tales more strange than true,
    New-England's chaplain, and her history's father;
A second Monmouth's GEOFFRY, a new
    HERODOTUS, their laurelled victor rather,
For in one art he soars above them high:
The Greek or Welshman does not always lie.

VII.

Know ye the venerable COTTON? He
    Was the first publisher's tourist on this station;
The first who made, by libelling earth and sea,
    A huge book, and a handsome speculation:
And ours was then a land of mystery,
    Fit theme for poetry's exaggeration,
The wildest wonder of the month; and there
He wandered freely, like a bird or bear,

VIII.

And wove his forest dreams into quaint prose,
    Our sires his heroes, where, in holy strife,
They treacherously war with friends and foes;

Where meek Religion wears the assassin's knife,
And 'bids the desert blossom like the rose,'
  By sprinkling earth with blood of Indian life,
And rears her altars o'er the indignant bones
Of murdered maidens, wives, and little ones.

JOHN HOWARD PAYNE

(1791–1852)

Home, Sweet Home!

'Mid pleasures and palaces though we may roam,
Be it ever so humble, there's *no* place like home.
A charm from the sky seems to hallow us there,
Which, seek through the *world*, is ne'er met with elsewhere.
  Home! sweet home!
  There's no place like home!

An exile from home, splendour dazzles in vain!
Oh! give me my lowly thatch'd cottage again!
The birds singing gaily that came at my call,
Give me *them*, with the *peace of mind* DEARER than all!
  Home! sweet home!
  There's no place like home!

LYDIA HUNTLEY SIGOURNEY

(1791–1865)

Indian Names

*"How can the red men be forgotten, while so many of
our states and territories, bays, lakes and rivers, are
indelibly stamped by names of their giving?"*

Ye say they all have passed away,
    That noble race and brave,
That their light canoes have vanished
    From off the crested wave;
That 'mid the forests where they roamed
    There rings no hunter shout,
But their name is on your waters,
    Ye may not wash it out.

'Tis where Ontario's billow
    Like Ocean's surge is curled,
Where strong Niagara's thunders wake
    The echo of the world.
Where red Missouri bringeth
    Rich tribute from the west,
And Rappahannock sweetly sleeps
    On green Virginia's breast.

Ye say their cone-like cabins,
    That clustered o'er the vale,
Have fled away like withered leaves
    Before the autumn gale,
But their memory liveth on your hills,
    Their baptism on your shore,
Your everlasting rivers speak
    Their dialect of yore.

Old Massachusetts wears it,
  Within her lordly crown,
And broad Ohio bears it,
  Amid his young renown;
Connecticut hath wreathed it
  Where her quiet foliage waves,
And bold Kentucky breathed it hoarse
  Through all her ancient caves.

Wachuset hides its lingering voice
  Within his rocky heart,
And Alleghany graves its tone
  Throughout his lofty chart;
Monadnock on his forehead hoar
  Doth seal the sacred trust,
Your mountains build their monument,
  Though ye destroy their dust.

Ye call these red-browed brethren
  The insects of an hour,
Crushed like the noteless worm amid
  The regions of their power;
Ye drive them from their father's lands,
  Ye break of faith the seal,
But can ye from the court of Heaven
  Exclude their last appeal?

Ye see their unresisting tribes,
  With toilsome step and slow,
On through the trackless desert pass,
  A caravan of woe;
Think ye the Eternal's ear is deaf?
  His sleepless vision dim?
Think ye the *soul's blood* may not cry
  From that far land to him?

JOHN NEAL
(1793–1876)

from *The Battle of Niagara*

There's a fierce gray Bird, with a bending beak,
With a glittering eye and a piercing shriek,
That nurses her brood where the cliff-flowers blow
On the precipice top—in perpetual snow—
Where the fountains are mute or in secrecy flow:
A BIRD that is first to worship the sun,
When he gallops in light—till the cloud-tides run
In billows of fire as his course is done:
Above where the torrent is forth in its might—
Above where the fountain is gushing in light—
Above where the silvery flashing is seen
Of streamlets that bend o'er the rich mossy green,
Emblazed with the tint of the young morning's eye—
Like ribbons of flame—or the bow of the sky:
Above that dark torrent—above that bright stream,
Her voice may be heard with its clear wild scream,
As she chants to her God and unfolds in his beam;
While her young are all laid in his rich red blaze,
And their winglets are fledged in his hottest rays:
Proud Bird of the Cliff! where the barren yew springs:
Where the sunshine stays, and the wind-harp sings;
And the heralds of battle are pluming their wings:
That BIRD is abroad over hill top and flood—
Over valley and rock, over mountain and wood—
Sublimely she sails with her storm-cleaving brood!

Canto I, lines 1–25

Ontario of the woods! may no broad sail
Ever unfold upon thy mountain gale!
Thy waters were thus spread—so fresh and blue
But for thy white fowl and the light canoe.
Should once the smooth dark lustre of thy breast

With mightier burthens, ever be oppressed—
Farewell to thee! and all thy loveliness!
Commerce will rear her arks—and Nature's dress
Be scattered to the winds: thy shores will bloom,
Like dying flow'rets sprinkled o'er a tomb;
The feverish, fleeting lustre of the flowers
Burst into life in Art's unnatural bowers;
Not the green—graceful—wild luxuriance
Of Nature's garlands, in their negligence:
The clambering jassimine, and flushing rose
That in the wilderness their hearts disclose:
The dewy violet, and the bud of gold,
Where drooping lilies on the wave unfold;
Where nameless flowers hang fainting on the air,
As if they breathed their lovely spirits there;
Where heaven itself is bluer, and the light
Is but a coloured fragrance—floating—bright;
Where the sharp note—and whistling song is heard,
Of many a golden beak, and sunny sparkling bird:

  There the tame honeysuckle will arise;
The gaudy hot-house plant will spread its dyes,
In flaunting boldness to the sunny skies:
And sickly buds, as soon as blown, will shed
Their fainting leaves o'er their untimely bed;
Unnatural violets in the blaze appear—
With hearts unwet by youthful Flora's tear:
And the loose poppy with its sleepy death,
And flashy leaf: the warm and torpid breath
Of lazy garlands, over crawling vines;
The tawdry wreath that Fashion intertwines
To deck her languid brow: the streamy gold,
And purple flushing of the tulip's fold;
And velvet buds, of crimson, and of blue,
Unchangeable and lifeless, as the hue
Of Fashion's gaudy wreaths, that ne'er were wet with dew.

Canto II, lines 140–180

CARLOS WILCOX

(1794–1827)

from *The Age of Benevolence*

A sultry noon, not in the summer's prime
When all is fresh with life, and youth, and bloom,
But near its close when vegetation stops,
And fruits mature, stand ripening in the sun,
Sooths and enervates with its thousand charms,
Its images of silence and of rest,
The melancholy mind. The fields are still;
The husbandman has gone to his repast,
And, that partaken, on the coolest side
Of his abode, reclines, in sweet repose.
Deep in the shaded stream the cattle stand,
The flocks beside the fence, with heads all prone
And panting quick. The fields for harvest ripe,
No breezes bend in smooth and graceful waves,
While with their motion, dim and bright by turns,
The sun-shine seems to move; nor e'en a breath
Brushes along the surface with a shade,
Fleeting and thin, like that of flying smoke.
The slender stalks, their heavy bended heads
Support as motionless, as oaks their tops.
O'er all the woods the top-most leaves are still,
E'en the wild poplar leaves, that, pendant hung
By stems elastic, quiver at a breath,
Rest in the general calm. The thistle down
Seen high and thick, by gazing up beside
Some shading object, in a silver shower
Plumb down, and slower than the slowest snow,
Through all the sleepy atmosphere descends;
And where it lights, though on the steepest roof,
Or smallest spire of grass, remains unmoved.
White as a fleece, as dense and as distinct
From the resplendent sky, a single cloud
On the soft bosom of the air becalmed,

53

Drops a lone shadow as distinct and still,
On the bare plain, or sunny mountain's side;
Or in the polished mirror of the lake,
In which the deep reflected sky appears
A calm sublime immensity below.

*   *   *   *   *   *   Beneath a sun
That crowns the centre of the azure cope,
A blaze of light intense o'erspreads the whole
Of nature's face; and he that overlooks,
From some proud eminence, the champaign round,
Notes all the buildings, scattered far and near,
Both great and small, magnificent and mean,
By their smooth roofs of shining silver white,
Spangling with brighter spots the bright expanse.
No sound, nor motion, of a living thing
The stillness breaks, but such as serve to soothe
Or cause the soul to feel the stillness more.
The yellow-hammer by the way-side picks,
Mutely, the thistle's seed; but in her flight,
So smoothly serpentine, her wings outspread
To rise a little, closed to fall as far,
Moving like sea-fowl o'er the heaving waves,
With each new impulse chimes a feeble note.
The russet grasshopper, at times, is heard,
Snapping his many wings, as half he flies,
Half hovers in the air. Where strikes the sun
With sultriest beams, upon the sandy plain,
Or stony mount, or in the close deep vale,
The harmless locust of this western clime,
At intervals, amid the leaves unseen,
Is heard to sing with one unbroken sound,
As with a long-drawn breath, beginning low,
And rising to the midst with shriller swell,
Then in low cadence dying all away.
Beside the stream collected in a flock,
The noiseless butterflies, though on the ground,
Continue still to wave their open fans
Powder'd with gold; while on the jutting twigs
The spindling insects that frequent the banks,

Rest, with their thin transparent wings outspread
As when they fly. Oft times, though seldom seen,
The cuckoo, that in summer haunts our groves,
Is heard to moan, as if at every breath
Panting aloud. The hawk in mid-air high,
On his broad pinions sailing round and round,
With not a flutter, or but now and then,
As if his trembling balance to regain,
Utters a single scream but faintly heard,
And all again is still.

WILLIAM CULLEN BRYANT

(1794–1878)

Thanatopsis

To him who in the love of nature holds
Communion with her visible forms, she speaks
A various language; for his gayer hours
She has a voice of gladness, and a smile
And eloquence of beauty, and she glides
Into his darker musings, with a mild
And gentle sympathy, that steals away
Their sharpness, ere he is aware. When thoughts
Of the last bitter hour come like a blight
Over thy spirit, and sad images
Of the stern agony, and shroud, and pall,
And breathless darkness, and the narrow house,
Make thee to shudder, and grow sick at heart;—
Go forth, under the open sky, and list
To Nature's teachings, while from all around—
Earth and her waters, and the depths of air,—
Comes a still voice—Yet a few days, and thee
The all-beholding sun shall see no more
In all his course; nor yet in the cold ground,
Where thy pale form was laid, with many tears,
Nor in the embrace of ocean shall exist
Thy image. Earth, that nourished thee, shall claim
Thy growth, to be resolved to earth again;
And, lost each human trace, surrendering up
Thine individual being, shalt thou go
To mix forever with the elements,
To be a brother to the insensible rock
And to the sluggish clod, which the rude swain
Turns with his share, and treads upon. The oak
Shall send his roots abroad, and pierce thy mould.
Yet not to thy eternal resting place
Shalt thou retire alone—nor couldst thou wish
Couch more magnificent. Thou shalt lie down

With patriarchs of the infant world—with kings,
The powerful of the earth—the wise, the good,
Fair forms, and hoary seers of ages past,
All in one mighty sepulchre.—The hills
Rock-ribbed and ancient as the sun,—the vales
Stretching in pensive quietness between;
The venerable woods—rivers that move
In majesty, and the complaining brooks
That make the meadows green; and poured round all,
Old ocean's gray and melancholy waste,—
Are but the solemn decorations all
Of the great tomb of man. The golden sun,
The planets, all the infinite host of heaven,
Are shining on the sad abodes of death,
Through the still lapse of ages. All that tread
The globe are but a handful to the tribes
That slumber in its bosom.—Take the wings
Of morning—and the Barcan desert pierce,
Or lose thyself in the continuous woods
Where rolls the Oregan, and hears no sound,
Save his own dashings —yet—the dead are there,
And millions in those solitudes, since first
The flight of years began, have laid them down
In their last sleep—the dead reign there alone.
So shalt thou rest—and what if thou shalt fall
Unheeded by the living—and no friend
Take note of thy departure? All that breathe
Will share thy destiny. The gay will laugh
When thou art gone, the solemn brood of care
Plod on, and each one as before will chase
His favorite phantom; yet all these shall leave
Their mirth and their employments, and shall come,
And make their bed with thee. As the long train
Of ages glide away, the sons of men,
The youth in life's green spring, and he who goes
In the full strength of years, matron, and maid,
And the sweet babe, and the gray-headed man,—
Shall one by one be gathered to thy side,
By those, who in their turn shall follow them.
So live, that when thy summons comes to join

The innumerable caravan, that moves
To that mysterious realm, where each shall take
His chamber in the silent halls of death,
Thou go not, like the quarry-slave at night,
Scourged to his dungeon, but sustained and soothed
By an unfaltering trust, approach thy grave,
Like one who wraps the drapery of his couch
About him, and lies down to pleasant dreams.

To a Waterfowl

Whither, 'midst falling dew,
While glow the heavens with the last steps of day
Far, through their rosy depths, dost thou pursue
        Thy solitary way?

Vainly the fowler's eye
Might mark thy distant flight to do thee wrong,
As, darkly painted on the crimson sky,
        Thy figure floats along.

Seek'st thou the plashy brink
Of weedy lake, or marge of river wide,
Or where the rocking billows rise and sink
        On the chafed ocean side?

There is a Power whose care
Teaches thy way along that pathless coast,—
The desert and illimitable air,—
        Lone wandering, but not lost.

All day thy wings have fanned,
At that far height, the cold thin atmosphere,
Yet stoop not, weary, to the welcome land,
        Though the dark night is near.

And soon that toil shall end,
Soon shalt thou find a summer home, and rest,
And scream among thy fellows; reeds shall bend,
        Soon, o'er thy sheltered nest.

Thou'rt gone, the abyss of heaven
Hath swallow'd up thy form; yet, on my heart
Deeply hath sunk the lesson thou hast given,
And shall not soon depart.

He, who, from zone to zone,
Guides through the boundless sky thy certain flight,
In the long way that I must tread alone,
Will lead my steps aright.

Inscription for the Entrance to a Wood

Stranger, if thou hast learnt a truth which needs
No school of long experience, that the world
Is full of guilt and misery, and hast seen
Enough of all its sorrows, crimes, and cares,
To tire thee of it, enter this wild wood
And view the haunts of Nature. The calm shade
Shall bring a kindred calm, and the sweet breeze
That makes the green leaves dance, shall waft a balm
To thy sick heart. Thou wilt find nothing here
Of all that pained thee in the haunts of men
And made thee loathe thy life. The primal curse
Fell, it is true, upon the unsinning earth,
But not in vengeance. God hath yoked to guilt
Her pale tormentor, misery. Hence, these shades
Are still the abodes of gladness, the thick roof
Of green and stirring branches is alive
And musical with birds, that sing and sport
In wantonness of spirit; while below
The squirrel, with raised paws and form erect,
Chirps merrily. Throngs of insects in the shade
Try their thin wings and dance in the warm beam
That waked them into life. Even the green trees
Partake the deep contentment; as they bend
To the soft winds, the sun from the blue sky
Looks in and sheds a blessing on the scene.
Scarce less the cleft-born wild-flower seems to enjoy
Existence, than the winged plunderer

That sucks its sweets. The massy rocks themselves,
And the old and ponderous trunks of prostrate trees
That lead from knoll to knoll a causey rude
Or bridge the sunken brook, and their dark roots,
With all their earth upon them, twisting high,
Breathe fixed tranquillity. The rivulet
Sends forth glad sounds and tripping o'er its bed
Of pebbly sands, or leaping down the rocks,
Seems, with continuous laughter, to rejoice
In its own being. Softly tread the marge,
Lest from her midway perch thou scare the wren
That dips her bill in water. The cool wind,
That stirs the stream in play, shall come to thee,
Like one that loves thee nor will let thee pass
Ungreeted, and shall give its light embrace.

Green River

When breezes are soft and skies are fair,
I steal an hour from study and care,
And hie me away to the woodland scene,
Where wanders the stream with waters of green;
As if the bright fringe of herbs on its brink,
Had given their stain to the wave they drink;
And they, whose meadows it murmurs through,
Have named the stream from its own fair hue.

Yet pure its waters—its shallows are bright
With colored pebbles and sparkles of light,
And clear the depths where its eddies play,
And dimples deepen and whirl away,
And the plane-tree's speckled arms o'ershoot
The swifter current that mines its root,
Through whose shifting leaves, as you walk the hill,
The quivering glimmer of sun and rill,
With a sudden flash on the eye is thrown,
Like the ray that streams from the diamond stone.
Oh, loveliest there the spring days come,
With blossoms, and birds, and wild-bees' hum;

The flowers of summer are fairest there,
And freshest the breath of the summer air;
And sweetest the golden autumn day
In silence and sunshine glides away.

Yet fair as thou art, thou shun'st to glide,
Beautiful stream! by the village side;
But windest away from haunts of men,
To quiet valley and shaded glen;
And forest, and meadow, and slope of hill,
Around thee, are lonely, lovely, and still.
Lonely—save when, by thy rippling tides,
From thicket to thicket the angler glides;
Or the simpler comes with basket and book,
For herbs of power on thy banks to look;
Or haply, some idle dreamer, like me,
To wander, and muse, and gaze on thee.
Still—save the chirp of birds that feed
On the river cherry and seedy reed,
And thy own mild music gushing out
With mellow murmur and fairy shout,
From dawn, to the blush of another day,
Like traveller singing along his way.

That fairy music I never hear,
Nor gaze on those waters so green and clear,
And mark them winding away from sight,
Darkened with shade or flashing with light,
While o'er them the vine to its thicket clings,
And the zephyr stoops to freshen his wings,
But I wish that fate had left me free
To wander these quiet haunts with thee,
Till the eating cares of earth should depart,
And the peace of the scene pass into my heart;
And I envy thy stream, as it glides along,
Through its beautiful banks in a trance of song.

Though forced to drudge for the dregs of men,
And scrawl strange words with the barbarous pen,
And mingle among the jostling crowd,

Where the sons of strife are subtle and loud —
I often come to this quiet place,
To breathe the airs that ruffle thy face,
And gaze upon thee in silent dream,
For in thy lonely and lovely stream,
An image of that calm life appears,
That won my heart in my greener years.

Summer Wind

It is a sultry day; the sun has drank
The dew that lay upon the morning grass,
There is no rustling in the lofty elm
That canopies my dwelling, and its shade
Scarce cools me. All is silent, save the faint
And interrupted murmur of the bee,
Settling on the sick flowers, and then again
Instantly on the wing. The plants around
Feel the too potent fervors; the tall maize
Rolls up its long green leaves; the clover droops
Its tender foliage, and declines its blooms.
But far in the fierce sunshine tower the hills,
With all their growth of woods, silent and stern,
As if the scorching heat and dazzling light
Were but an element they loved. Bright clouds,
Motionless pillars of the brazen heaven; —
Their bases on the mountains — their white tops
Shining in the far ether — fire the air
With a reflected radiance, and make turn
The gazer's eye away. For me, I lie
Languidly in the shade, where the thick turf,
Yet virgin from the kisses of the sun,
Retains some freshness, and I woo the wind
That still delays its coming. Why so slow,
Gentle and voluble spirit of the air?
Oh, come and breathe upon the fainting earth
Coolness and life. Is it that in his caves
He hears me? See, on yonder woody ridge,
The pine is bending his proud top, and now,

Among the nearer groves, chesnut and oak
Are tossing their green boughs about. He comes!
Lo, where the grassy meadow runs in waves!
The deep distressful silence of the scene
Breaks up with mingling of unnumbered sounds
And universal motion. He is come,
Shaking a shower of blossoms from the shrubs,
And bearing on their fragrance; and he brings
Music of birds, and rustling of young boughs,
And sound of swaying branches, and the voice
Of distant waterfalls. All the green herbs
Are stirring in his breath; a thousand flowers,
By the road-side and the borders of the brook,
Nod gaily to each other; glossy leaves
Are twinkling in the sun, as if the dew
Were on them yet, and silver waters break
Into small waves and sparkle as he comes.

Autumn Woods

Ere, in the northern gale,
The summer tresses of the trees are gone,
The woods of Autumn, all around our vale,
Have put their glory on.

The mountains that infold
In their wide sweep, the colored landscape round,
Seem groups of giant kings, in purple and gold,
That guard the enchanted ground.

I roam the woods that crown
The upland, where the mingled splendors glow,
Where the gay company of trees look down
On the green fields below.

My steps are not alone
In these bright walks; the sweet southwest, at play,
Flies, rustling, where the painted leaves are strown
Along the winding way.

And far in heaven, the while,
The sun, that sends that gale to wander here,
Pours out on the fair earth his quiet smile,—
    The sweetest of the year.

Where now the solemn shade,
Verdure and gloom where many branches meet;
So grateful, when the noon of summer made
    The valleys sick with heat?

Let in through all the trees
Come the strange rays; the forest depths are bright;
Their sunny-colored foliage, in the breeze,
    Twinkles, like beams of light.

The rivulet, late unseen,
Where bickering through the shrubs its waters run,
Shines with the image of its golden screen,
    And glimmerings of the sun.

But 'neath yon crimson tree,
Lover to listening maid might breathe his flame,
Nor mark, within its roseate canopy,
    Her blush of maiden shame.

Oh, Autumn! why so soon
Depart the hues that make thy forests glad;
Thy gentle wind and thy fair sunny noon,
    And leave thee wild and sad!

Ah! 'twere a lot too blest
Forever in thy colored shades to stray;
Amidst the kisses of the soft southwest
    To rove and dream for aye;

And leave the vain low strife
That makes men mad—the tug for wealth and power,
The passions and the cares that wither life,
    And waste its little hour.

To an American Painter Departing for Europe

Thine eyes shall see the light of distant skies:
  Yet, Cole! thy heart shall bear to Europe's strand
  A living image of thy native land,
Such as on thy own glorious canvass lies.
Lone lakes—savannahs where the bison roves—
  Rocks rich with summer garlands—solemn streams—
  Skies, where the desert eagle wheels and screams—
Spring bloom and autumn blaze of boundless groves.
Fair scenes shall greet thee where thou goest—fair,
  But different—every where the trace of men,
  Paths, homes, graves, ruins, from the lowest glen
To where life shrinks from the fierce Alpine air.
  Gaze on them, till the tears shall dim thy sight,
  But keep that earlier, wilder image bright.

To the Fringed Gentian

Thou blossom bright with autumn dew,
And colored with the heaven's own blue,
That openest, when the quiet light
Succeeds the keen and frosty night.

Thou comest not when violets lean
O'er wandering brooks and springs unseen,
Or columbines, in purple drest,
Nod o'er the ground bird's hidden nest.

Thou waitest late, and com'st alone,
When woods are bare and birds are flown,
And frosts and shortening days portend
The aged year is near its end.

Then doth thy sweet and quiet eye
Look through its fringes to the sky,
Blue—blue—as if that sky let fall
A flower from its cerulean wall.

I would that thus, when I shall see
The hour of death draw near to me,
Hope, blossoming within my heart,
May look to heaven as I depart.

The Prairies

These are the Gardens of the Desert, these
The unshorn fields, boundless and beautiful,
For which the speech of England has no name—
The Prairies. I behold them for the first,
And my heart swells, while the dilated sight
Takes in the encircling vastness. Lo! they stretch
In airy undulations, far away,
As if the ocean, in his gentlest swell,
Stood still, with all his rounded billows fixed,
And motionless for ever.—Motionless?—
No—they are all unchained again. The clouds
Sweep over with their shadows, and, beneath,
The surface rolls and fluctuates to the eye;
Dark hollows seem to glide along and chase
The sunny ridges. Breezes of the South!
Who toss the golden and the flame-like flowers,
And pass the prairie-hawk that, poised on high,
Flaps his broad wings, yet moves not—ye have played
Among the palms of Mexico and vines
Of Texas, and have crisped the limpid brooks
That from the fountains of Sonora glide
Into the calm Pacific—have ye fanned
A nobler or a lovelier scene than this?
Man hath no part in all this glorious work:
The hand that built the firmament hath heaved
And smoothed these verdant swells, and sown their slopes
With herbage, planted them with island groves,
And hedged them round with forests. Fitting floor
For this magnificent temple of the sky—
With flowers whose glory and whose multitude
Rival the constellations! The great heavens
Seem to stoop down upon the scene in love,—

A nearer vault, and of a tenderer blue,
Than that which bends above the eastern hills.
    As o'er the verdant waste I guide my steed,
Among the high rank grass that sweeps his sides,
The hollow beating of his footstep seems
A sacrilegious sound. I think of those
Upon whose rest he tramples. Are they here —
The dead of other days? — and did the dust
Of these fair solitudes once stir with life
And burn with passion? Let the mighty mounds
That overlook the rivers, or that rise
In the dim forest crowded with old oaks,
Answer. A race, that long has passed away,
Built them; — a disciplined and populous race
Heaped, with long toil, the earth, while yet the Greek
Was hewing the Pentelicus to forms
Of symmetry, and rearing on its rock
The glittering Parthenon. These ample fields
Nourished their harvests, here their herds were fed,
When haply by their stalls the bison lowed,
And bowed his maned shoulder to the yoke.
All day this desert murmured with their toils,
Till twilight blushed and lovers walked, and wooed
In a forgotten language, and old tunes,
From instruments of unremembered form,
Gave the soft winds a voice. The red man came —
The roaming hunter tribes, warlike and fierce,
And the mound-builders vanished from the earth.
The solitude of centuries untold
Has settled where they dwelt. The prairie wolf
Hunts in their meadows, and his fresh-dug den
Yawns by my path. The gopher mines the ground
Where stood their swarming cities. All is gone —
All — save the piles of earth that hold their bones —
The platforms where they worshipped unknown gods —
The barriers which they builded from the soil
To keep the foe at bay — till o'er the walls
The wild beleaguerers broke, and, one by one,
The strongholds of the plain were forced, and heaped
With corpses. The brown vultures of the wood

Flocked to those vast uncovered sepulchres,
And sat, unscared and silent, at their feast.
Haply some solitary fugitive,
Lurking in marsh and forest, till the sense
Of desolation and of fear became
Bitterer than death, yielded himself to die.
Man's better nature triumphed. Kindly words
Welcomed and soothed him; the rude conquerors
Seated the captive with their chiefs; he chose
A bride among their maidens, and at length
Seemed to forget,—yet ne'er forgot,—the wife
Of his first love, and her sweet little ones
Butchered, amid their shrieks, with all his race.

Thus change the forms of being. Thus arise
Races of living things, glorious in strength,
And perish, as the quickening breath of God
Fills them, or is withdrawn. The red man too—
Has left the blooming wilds he ranged so long,
And, nearer to the Rocky Mountains, sought
A wider hunting-ground. The beaver builds
No longer by these streams, but far away,
On waters whose blue surface ne'er gave back
The white man's face—among Missouri's springs,
And pools whose issues swell the Oregan,
He rears his little Venice. In these plains
The bison feeds no more. Twice twenty leagues
Beyond remotest smoke of hunter's camp,
Roams the majestic brute, in herds that shake
The earth with thundering steps—yet here I meet
His ancient footprints stamped beside the pool.

Still this great solitude is quick with life.
Myriads of insects, gaudy as the flowers
They flutter over, gentle quadrupeds,
And birds, that scarce have learned the fear of man,
Are here, and sliding reptiles of the ground,
Startlingly beautiful. The graceful deer
Bounds to the wood at my approach. The bee,
A more adventurous colonist than man,
With whom he came across the eastern deep,
Fills the savannas with his murmurings,

And hides his sweets, as in the golden age,
Within the hollow oak. I listen long
To his domestic hum, and think I hear
The sound of that advancing multitude
Which soon shall fill these deserts. From the ground
Comes up the laugh of children, the soft voice
Of maidens, and the sweet and solemn hymn
Of Sabbath worshippers. The low of herds
Blends with the rustling of the heavy grain
Over the dark-brown furrows. All at once
A fresher wind sweeps by, and breaks my dream,
And I am in the wilderness alone.

The Painted Cup

The fresh savannas of the Sangamon
Here rise in gentle swells, and the long grass
Is mixed with rustling hazels. Scarlet tufts
Are glowing in the green, like flakes of fire;
The wanderers of the prairie know them well,
And call that brilliant flower the Painted Cup.

Now, if thou art a poet, tell me not
That these bright chalices were tinted thus
To hold the dew for fairies, when they meet
On moonlight evenings in the hazel bowers,
And dance till they are thirsty. Call not up,
Amid this fresh and virgin solitude,
The faded fancies of an elder world;
But leave these scarlet cups to spotted moths
Of June, and glistening flies, and humming-birds,
To drink from, when on all these boundless lawns
The morning sun looks hot. Or let the wind
O'erturn in sport their ruddy brims, and pour
A sudden shower upon the strawberry plant,
To swell the reddening fruit that even now
Breathes a slight fragrance from the sunny slope.

But thou art of a gayer fancy. Well—
Let then the gentle Manitou of flowers,
Lingering amid the bloomy waste he loves,
Though all his swarthy worshippers are gone—
Slender and small, his rounded cheek all brown
And ruddy with the sunshine; let him come
On summer mornings, when the blossoms wake,
And part with little hands the spiky grass;
And touching, with his cherry lips, the edge
Of these bright beakers, drain the gathered dew.

MARIA GOWEN BROOKS

(1794?–1845)

from *Zophiël, or the Bride of Seven*

Canto the Third: Palace of the Gnomes

I.

'Tis now the hour of mirth, the hour of love,
  The hour of melancholy: Night, as vain
Of her full beauty, seems to pause above,
  That all may look upon her ere it wane.

II.

The heavenly angel watched his subject star
  O'er all that's good and fair benignly smiling;
The sighs of wounded love he hears, from far;
  Weeps that he cannot heal, and wafts a hope beguiling.

III.

The nether earth looks beauteous as a gem;
  High o'er her groves in floods of moonlight laving,
The towering palm displays his silver stem,
  The while his plumy leaves scarce in the breeze are waving.

IV.

The nightingale among his roses sleeps;
  The soft-eyed doe in thicket deep is sleeping;
The dark green myrrh her tears of fragrance weeps,
  And, every odorous spike in limpid dew is steeping.

V.

Proud prickly cerea, now thy blossom 'scapes
  Its cell; brief cup of light; and seems to say,
"I am not for gross mortals: blood of grapes—
  And sleep for them! Come spirits, while ye may!"

VI.

A silent stream winds darkly through the shade,
  And slowly gains the Tigris, where 'tis lost;
By a forgotten prince, of old, 'twas made,
  And, in its course, full many a fragment crost

Of marble fairly carved; and by its side
  Her golden dust the flaunting lotos threw
O'er her white sisters, throned upon the tide,
  And queen of every flower that loves perpetual dew.

VII.

Gold-sprinkling lotos, theme of many a song
  By slender Indian warbled to his fair!
Still tastes the stream thy rosy kiss, though long
  Has been but dust the hand that placed thee there.

VIII.

The little temple where its relics rest,
  Long since has fallen; its broken columns lie
Beneath the lucid wave, and give its breast
  A whitened glimmer as 'tis stealing by.

IX.

Here, cerea, too, thy clasping mazes twine
  The only pillar time has left erect;
Thy serpent arms embrace it, as 'twere thine,
  And roughly mock the beam it should reflect.

X.

An ancient prince, in happy madness blest,
  Was wont to wander to this spot; and deem'd
A water nymph came to him, and carest
  And loved him well; haply he only dream'd;

But on the spot a little dome arose,
   And flowers were set that still in wildness bloom;
And the cold ashes that were him, repose,
   Carefully shrined in this lone ivory tomb.

XI.

It is a place so strangely wild and sweet,
   That spirits love to come; and now, upon
A moonlight fragment, Zophiël chose his seat,
   In converse close with soft Phraërion;

XII.

Who, on the moss, beside him lies reclining,
   O'erstrewn with leaves, from full-blown roses shaken,
By nightingales, that on their branches twining,
   The live-long night to love and music waken.

Composed at the Request of a Lady, and Descriptive of Her Feelings

She Returned to the North, and Died Soon After

Adieu, fair isle! I love thy bowers,
   I love thy dark-eyed daughters there;
The cool pomegranate's scarlet flowers
   Look brighter in their jetty hair.

They praised my forehead's stainless white;
   And when I thirsted, gave a draught
From the full clustering cocoa's height,
   And smiling, blessed me as I quaff'd.

Well pleased, the kind return I gave,
   And, clasped in their embraces' twine,
Felt the soft breeze, like Lethe's wave,
   Becalm this beating heart of mine.

Why will my heart so wildly beat?
  Say, Seraphs, is my lot too blest,
That thus a fitful, feverish heat
  Must rifle me of health and rest?

Alas! I fear my native snows—
  A clime too cold, a heart too warm—
Alternate chills—alternate glows—
  Too fiercely threat my flower-like form.

The orange-tree has fruit and flowers;
  The grenadilla, in its bloom,
Hangs o'er its high, luxuriant bowers,
  Like fringes from a Tyrian loom.

When the white coffee-blossoms swell,
  The fair moon full, the evening long,
I love to hear the warbling bell,
  And sun-burnt peasant's wayward song.

Drive gently on, dark muleteer,
  And the light seguidilla frame;
Fain would I listen still, to hear
  At every close thy mistress' name.

Adieu, fair isle! the waving palm
  Is pencilled on thy purest sky;
Warm sleeps the bay, the air is balm,
  And, soothed to languor, scarce a sigh

Escapes for those I love so well,
  For those I've loved and left so long,
On me their fondest musings dwell,
  To them alone my sighs belong.

On, on, my bark! blow southern breeze!
  No longer would I lingering stay;
'Twere better far *to die* with these
  Than *live in pleasure* far away.

JOSEPH RODMAN DRAKE

(1795–1820)

The Mocking-Bird

Early on a pleasant day,
In the poets' month of May;
Field and forest look'd so fair,
So refreshing was the air,
That, despite of morning dew,
Forth I walk'd where, tangling grew,
Many a thorn and briery bush,
Where the red-breast and the thrush,
Gaily rais'd their early lay,
Thankful for returning day;
Every thicket, bush, and tree,
Swell'd the grateful harmony.
As it sweetly swept along,
Echo seem'd to catch the song;
But the plain was wide and clear,
Echo never whisper'd there.
From a neighb'ring mocking-bird
Came the answering note I heard;
Near a murmuring streamlet's side,
Perch'd on branch extending wide.
Low, and soft, the song began;
Scarce I caught it, as it ran
Through the ring dove's plaintive wail,
Chattering jay, and whistling quail,
Twittering sparrow, cat-bird's cry,
Red-bird's whistle, robin's sigh,
Black-bird, blue-bird, swallow, lark;
Each his native note might mark.
Oft he tried the lesson o'er,
Each time louder than before;
Burst at length the finish'd song:
Loud and clear it pour'd along.
All the choir in silence heard,

Hush'd before the wondrous bird.
All transported and amaz'd,
Scarcely breathing, long I gaz'd.
Now it reach'd the loudest swell;
Lower, lower, now it fell;
Lower, lower, lower still,
Scarce it sounded o'er the rill.
Now the warbler ceas'd to sing;
And I saw him spread his wing;
And I saw him take his flight,
Other regions to delight.
Then, in most poetic wise,
I began to moralize.
    In this bird can fancy trace
An emblem of the rhyming race.
Ere with heaven's immortal fire,
Loud they strike the quivering wire;
Ere in high, majestic song,
Thundering wars the verse along;
Soft and low each note they sing,
Soft they try each varied string;
Till each power is tried and known;
Then the kindling spark is blown.
Thus, perchance, has Maro sung;
Thus, his harp has Milton strung;
Thus, immortal Avon's child;
Thus, O Scott! thy witch-notes wild;
Thus, has Pope's melodious lyre
Rung each note with Homer's fire;
Thus, did Campbell's war-blast roar
Round the cliffs of Elsinore;
Thus, he dug the soldier's grave,
Iser! by thy purpled wave.

The National Painting

Awake! ye forms of verse divine—
  Painting! descend on canvass wing,
And hover ov'r my head, Design!
  Your son, your glorious son, I sing!
At T*******'s name I break my sloth,
  To load him with poetic riches;
The Titian of a tablecloth!
  The Guido of a pair of breeches!

Come star-eyed maid—Equality!
  In thine adorers' praise I revel;
Who brings, so fierce, his love to thee—
  All forms and faces to a level:
Old, young—great, small—the grave, the gay;
  Each man might swear the next his brother;
And there they stand in dread array,
  To fire their votes at one another.

How bright their buttons shine! how straight
  Their coat-flaps fall in plaited grace;
How smooth the hair on every pate;
  How vacant each immortal face!
And then thy tints—the shade—the flush—
  (I wrong them with a strain too humble)
Not mighty S*****d's strength of brush
  Can match thy glowing hues, my T——l.

Go on, great painter! dare be dull;
  No longer after nature dangle;
Call rectilinear beautiful;
  Find grace and freedom in an angle:
Pour on the red—the green—the yellow—
  Paint till a horse may mire upon it,
And while I've strength to write or bellow,
  I'll sound your praises in a sonnet.

The American Flag

I.

When Freedom from her mountain height
   Unfurled her standard to the air,
She tore the azure robe of night,
   And set the stars of glory there.
She mingled with its gorgeous dyes
The milky baldric of the skies,
And striped its pure celestial white,
With streakings of the morning light;
Then from his mansion in the sun
She called her eagle bearer down,
And gave into his mighty hand,
   The symbol of her chosen land.

II.

Majestic monarch of the cloud,
   Who rear'st aloft thy regal form,
To hear the tempest trumpings loud
   And see the lightning lances driven,
When strike the warriors of the storm,
   And rolls the thunder-drum of heaven,
Child of the sun! to thee 'tis given
   To guard the banner of the free,
To hover in the sulphur smoke,
To ward away the battle stroke,
And bid its blendings shine afar,
Like rainbows on the cloud of war,
   The harbingers of victory!

III.

Flag of the brave! thy folds shall fly,
   The sign of hope and triumph high,
When speaks the signal trumpet tone,
   And the long line comes gleaming on.
Ere yet the life-blood, warm and wet,
   Has dimm'd the glistening bayonet,

Each soldier eye shall brightly turn
  To where thy sky-born glories burn;
And as his springing steps advance,
  Catch war and vengeance from the glance.
And when the cannon-mouthings loud
  Heave in wild wreaths the battle shroud,
And gory sabres rise and fall
Like shoots of flame on midnight's pall;
  Then shall thy meteor glances glow,
And cowering foes shall shrink beneath
  Each gallant arm that strikes below
That lovely messenger of death.

IV.

Flag of the seas! on ocean wave
  Thy stars shall glitter o'er the brave;
When death, careering on the gale,
  Sweeps darkly round the bellied sail,
And frighted waves rush wildly back
  Before the broadside's reeling rack,
Each dying wanderer of the sea
  Shall look at once to heaven and thee,
  And smile to see thy splendours fly
  In triumph o'er his closing eye.

V.

Flag of the free heart's hope and home!
  By angel hands to valour given;
Thy stars have lit the welkin dome,
  And all thy hues were born in heaven.
Forever float that standard sheet!
  Where breathes the foe but falls before us,
With Freedom's soil beneath our feet,
  And Freedom's banner streaming o'er us?

Bronx

I sat me down upon a green bank-side,
  Skirting the smooth edge of a gentle river,
Whose waters seemed unwillingly to glide,
  Like parting friends who linger while they sever;
Enforced to go, yet seeming still unready,
  Backward they wind their way in many a wistful eddy.

Grey o'er my head the yellow-vested willow
  Ruffled its hoary top in the fresh breezes,
Glancing in light, like spray on a green billow,
  Or the fine frost-work which young winter freezes;
When first his power in infant pastime trying,
Congeals sad autumn's tears on the dead branches lying.

From rocks around hung the loose ivy dangling,
  And in the clefts sumach of liveliest green,
Bright ising-stars the little beach was spangling,
  The gold-cup sorrel from his gauzy screen
Shone like a fairy crown, enchased and beaded,
Left on some morn, when light flashed in their eyes
      unheeded.

The hum-bird shook his sun-touched wings around,
  The bluefinch caroll'd in the still retreat;
The antic squirrel capered on the ground
  Where lichens made a carpet for his feet:
Through the transparent waves, the ruddy minkle
Shot up in glimmering sparks his red fin's tiny twinkle.

There were dark cedars with loose mossy tresses,
  White powdered dog-trees, and stiff hollies flaunting
Gaudy as rustics in their May-day dresses,
  Blue pelloret from purple leaves upslanting
A modest gaze, like eyes of a young maiden
Shining beneath dropt lids the evening of her wedding.

The breeze fresh springing from the lips of morn,
  Kissing the leaves, and sighing so to lose 'em,

The winding of the merry locust's horn,
    The glad spring gushing from the rock's bare bosom:
Sweet sights, sweet sounds, all sights, all sounds excelling,
Oh! 'twas a ravishing spot formed for a poet's dwelling.

And did I leave thy loveliness, to stand
    Again in the dull world of earthly blindness?
Pained with the pressure of unfriendly hands,
    Sick of smooth looks, agued with icy kindness?
Left I for this thy shades, where none intrude,
To prison wandering thought and mar sweet solitude?

Yet I will look upon thy face again,
    My own romantic Bronx, and it will be
A face more pleasant than the face of men.
    Thy waves are old companions, I shall see
A well-remembered form in each old tree,
And hear a voice long loved in thy wild minstrelsy.

JAMES GATES PERCIVAL
(1795–1856)

The Coral Grove

Deep in the wave is a coral grove,
Where the purple mullet, and gold-fish rove,
Where the sea-flower spreads its leaves of blue,
That never are wet with falling dew,
But in bright and changeful beauty shine,
Far down in the green and glassy brine.
The floor is of sand, like the mountain drift,
And the pearl shells spangle the flinty snow;
From coral rocks the sea plants lift
Their boughs, where the tides and billows flow;
The water is calm and still below,
For the winds and waves are absent there,
And the sands are bright as the stars that glow
In the motionless fields of upper air:
There with its waving blade of green,
The sea-flag streams through the silent water,
And the crimson leaf of the dulse is seen
To blush, like a banner bathed in slaughter:
There with a light and easy motion,
The fan-coral sweeps through the clear deep sea;
And the yellow and scarlet tufts of ocean,
Are bending like corn on the upland lea:
And life, in rare and beautiful forms,
Is sporting amid those bowers of stone,
And is safe, when the wrathful spirit of storms,
Has made the top of the wave his own:
And when the ship from his fury flies,
Where the myriad voices of ocean roar,
When the wind-god frowns in the murky skies,
And demons are waiting the wreck on shore;
Then far below in the peaceful sea,
The purple mullet, and gold-fish rove,
Where the waters murmur tranquilly,
Through the bending twigs of the coral grove.

GEORGE MOSES HORTON

(1798? – 1883?)

On Liberty and Slavery

Alas! and am I born for this,
　　To wear this slavish chain?
Deprived of all created bliss,
　　Through hardship, toil and pain!

How long have I in bondage lain,
　　And languished to be free!
Alas! and must I still complain—
　　Deprived of liberty.

Oh, Heaven! and is there no relief
　　This side the silent grave—
To soothe the pain—to quell the grief
　　And anguish of a slave?

Come Liberty, thou cheerful sound,
　　Roll through my ravished ears!
Come, let my grief in joys be drowned,
　　And drive away my fears.

Say unto foul oppression, Cease:
　　Ye tyrants rage no more,
And let the joyful trump of peace,
　　Now bid the vassal soar.

Soar on the pinions of that dove
　　Which long has cooed for thee,
And breathed her notes from Afric's grove,
　　The sound of Liberty.

Oh, Liberty! thou golden prize,
　　So often sought by blood—
We crave thy sacred sun to rise,
　　The gift of nature's God!

Bid Slavery hide her haggard face,
   And barbarism fly:
I scorn to see the sad disgrace
   In which enslaved I lie.

Dear Liberty! upon thy breast,
   I languish to respire;
And like the Swan unto her nest,
   I'd to thy smiles retire.

Oh, blest asylum—heavenly balm!
   Unto thy boughs I flee—
And in thy shades the storm shall calm,
   With songs of Liberty!

On Hearing of the Intention of a Gentleman to Purchase the Poet's Freedom

When on life's ocean first I spread my sail,
I then implored a mild auspicious gale;
And from the slippery strand I took my flight,
And sought the peaceful haven of delight.

Tyrannic storms arose upon my soul,
And dreadful did their mad'ning thunders roll;
The pensive muse was shaken from her sphere,
And hope, it vanish'd in the clouds of fear.

At length a golden sun broke thro' the gloom,
And from his smiles arose a sweet perfume—
A calm ensued, and birds began to sing,
And lo! the sacred muse resumed her wing.

With frantic joy she chaunted as she flew,
And kiss'd the clement hand that bore her thro'
Her envious foes did from her sight retreat,
Or prostrate fall beneath her burning feet.

'Twas like a proselyte, allied to Heaven—
Or rising spirits' boast of sins forgiven,

Whose shout dissolves the adamant away
Whose melting voice the stubborn rocks obey.

'Twas like the salutation of the dove,
Borne on the zephyr thro' some lonesome grove,
When Spring returns, and Winter's chill is past,
And vegetation smiles above the blast.

'Twas like the evening of a nuptial pair,
When love pervades the hour of sad despair—
'Twas like fair Helen's sweet return to Troy,
When every Grecian bosom swell'd with joy.

The silent harp which on the osiers hung,
Was then attuned, and manumission sung:
Away by hope the clouds of fear were driven,
And music breathed my gratitude to heaven.

Hard was the race to reach the distant goal,
The needle oft was shaken from the pole:
In such distress, who could forbear to weep?
Toss'd by the headlong billows of the deep!

The tantalizing beams which shone so plain,
Which turn'd my former pleasures into pain—
Which falsely promised all the joys of fame,
Gave way, and to a more substantial flame.

Some philanthropic souls as from afar,
With pity strove to break the slavish bar;
To whom my floods of gratitude shall roll,
And yield with pleasure to their soft control.

And sure of Providence this work begun—
He shod my feet this rugged race to run;
And in despite of all the swelling tide,
Along the dismal path will prove my guide.

Thus on the dusky verge of deep despair,
Eternal Providence was with me there;
When pleasure seemed to fade on life's gay dawn,
And the last beam of hope was almost gone.

SAMUEL HENRY DICKSON

(1798–1872)

Song — Written at the North

I sigh for the land of the Cypress and Pine,
Where the Jessamine blooms, and the gay Woodbine;
Where the moss droops low from the green Oak tree,
Oh! that sunbright land is the land for me.

The snowy flower of the Orange there,
Sheds its sweet fragrance through the air—
And the Indian rose delights to 'twine
Its branches with the laughing vine.

There the Humming-bird of rainbow plume,
Hangs over the scarlet creeper's bloom,
While midst the leaves his varying dies,
Sparkle like half-seen fairy eyes.

There the deer leaps light through the open glade,
Or hides him far in the forest shade,
When the woods resound in the dewy morn,
With the clang of the merry hunter's horn.

There the echoes ring through the livelong day,
With the Mockbird's changeful roundelay,
And at night when the scene is calm and still,
With the moan of the plaintive Whip-poor-Will.

Oh! I sigh for the land of the Cypress and Pine,
Of the Laurel, the Rose, and the gay Woodbine;
Where the long grey moss decks the rugged Oak tree,
That sunbright land is the land for me.

A. BRONSON ALCOTT

(1799–1888)

Sonnet XIV

"Ye blessed creatures, I have heard the call
Ye to each other make: I see
The heavens laugh with you in your jubilee;
My heart is at your festival,
My head hath its coronal,
The fulness of your bliss I feel—I feel it all."
WORDSWORTH.

Not Wordsworth's genius, Pestalozzi's love,
The stream have sounded of clear infancy.
Baptismal waters from the Head above
These babes I foster daily are to me;
I dip my pitcher in these living springs
And draw, from depths below, sincerity;
Unsealed, mine eyes behold all outward things
Arrayed in splendors of divinity.
What mount of vision can with mine compare?
Not Roman Jove nor yet Olympian Zeus
Darted from loftier ether through bright air
One spark of holier fire for human use.
Glad tidings thence these angels downward bring,
As at their birth the heavenly choirs do sing.

THOMAS COLE

(1801–1848)

A Painter

I know 'tis vain ye mountains, and ye woods,
To strive to match your wild, and wondrous hues,
Ye rocks and lakes, and ever rolling floods,
Gold-cinctur'd eve, or morn begemm'd with dews—

Yes, day by day & year by year Ive toild
In the lone chamber, and the sunny field
To match your beauty; but I have been foil'd:
I cannot conquer; but I will not yield—

How oft have I, where spread the pictur'd scene
Wrought on the canvas with fond, anxious care,
Deem'd I had equalled Natures, forests green,
Her lakes, her rocks, and e'en the ambient air.

Vain unpious thought! such feverish fancies sweep
Swift from the brain—when Nature's landscapes break
Upon the thrilling sense—O I could weep
Not that *she* is so beautiful; but *I* so weak—

O! for a power to snatch the living light
From heaven, & darkness from some deep abyss,
Made palpable: with skill to mingle right
Their mystery of beauty! then mine would be bliss!

Lines Suggested by Hearing Music on the Boston Common at Night

Music it was I heard, and music too
Of mortal utterance; but it did sound
Unto my Fancy's ear like that of spirits;
Spirits that dwell within the vasty caves

Near the earths center—
                              Silence dwelt around.
Then came soft sounds slowly, with pauses 'twixt
Like sighs of sleepers in deep distant caves
They sank and list'ning silence reign'd again.

Then rose a voice, a single voice but shrill
It rent the sable curtains of the gloom
And pierc'd the confines of each echoing cave,
And ev'ry spirit rais'd his sleepy head
From the cold pillow of the dripping rock—
Again the single voice, rung with a shriller tone,
Each spirit answer'd from his hidden nook—
Some voices came from distant winding clifts
And sought the ear like Angel whisperings.
From the deep arches of the rocky roof
Tones rich as those of heav'ns own trumpets burst.
From out the dark profound abysms arose
Sounds as of earthquake, thunder, or the roar
Of booming cataracts—Silence again—

Hark! they have met within the giant hall:
Whose roof is pillar'd by huge mountain tops,
And voices shrill, and deep in concord loudly join.
The heaving harmony sweeps to and fro
Surge over surge and fills the ample place.
Ocean of sound sublime!! The tides contend,
Augment, higher, yet higher; Earth cannot
Contain; it yields—tis riven—and falling rocks
And tottering pinnacles join their dread voices
In the tumultuous and astounding roar—

'Tis past. And nought now strikes the waiting ear
Save the soft echoes ling'ring on their way.
Soft! They have ceas'd to whisper, having found
The cave of silence their eternal tomb.

from *The Voyage of Life, Part 2nd*

As the broad mountain where the shadows flit
Of clouds dispersing in the summer-breeze;
Or like the eye of one who high does sit
On Taòrmìnas' antique height & sees
The fiery Mount afar, the Ruin near at hand,
The flowers, the purple waves that wash the golden strand.

So changed my thought from light to shade;
At times exulting in the glow of hope, at times
In darkness cast by what my soul had said;
'Till sunk in reverie her words seemed chimes
From some far tower, that tell of nuptial joy,
Or knell that fills the air as with a lingering sigh.

Again I raised my downcast eyes to look
Upon the scene so beautiful when lo!
The stream no longer from the cavern took
Its gentle way 'tween flowery banks & low
But through a landscape varied, rich & vast
Beneath a sky that dusky cloud had surely never passed.

Wide was the river; with majestic flow
And pomp & power it swept the curving banks
Like some great conqueror whose march is slow
Through tributary lands; while the abasèd ranks,
Shrinking give back on either hand o'erawed
As though their hearts confirmed the presence of a God.

And like some Wizard's mirror, that displays
The Macrocosm, it did reflect the sky,
Rocks, lawns & mountains with their purple haze,
And living things, the filmy butterfly,
The trembling fawn that drinks, the fluttering dove
And the triumphant eagle soaring far above.

And trees like those which spread their pleasant shade
Oer the green slopes of Eden, & the bowers

Of the once sinless pair, soft, intermingling made
Stood on each shore with branches lifted high
And caught eolian strains that wandered from the sky.

Far, far away the shining river sped
Towards the etherial mountains which did close
Fold beyond fold until they vanishèd
In the horizon's silver, whence uprose
A structure strangely beautiful & vast
Which every earthly fane Egyptian, Gothic, Greek,
    surpassed.

It seemed a gorgeous palace in the sky
Such as the glad sun builds above the Deep
On summer-eve & lighteth dazzlingly,
Where towering clouds climb up the azure steep
And pinnacles on pinnacles fantastic rise
And ever-changing charm the wondering eyes.

There, rank oer rank that climbed the crystal air
In horizontal majesty, were crossed
The multitudinous shafts, or ranged afar
Till in the blue perspective they were lost,
And arches linked with arches stretched along
Like to the mystic measures of an antique song.

An antique song whose half-discovered sense
Seems to spring forth from depths, as yet, unknown
And fills the heart with wonder & suspense
Until to thrilling rapture it is grown;
Breathless we listen to each wandering strain
And when the numbers cease we listen still again.

Above the columned pile sublimely rose
A Dome stupendous, like the moon it shone
When first upon the orient sky she glows
And moves along the Ocean's verge alone;
And yet beyond, above, another sphere
And yet another, vaster, dimly did appear.

As though the blue supernal space were filled
With towers & temples, which the eye intent
Piercing the filmy atmosphere that veiled,
From glorious dome to dome rejoicing went,
And the deep folds of ether were unfurled
To show the splendors of a higher world.

stanzas 1 –12

The Dial

Gray hairs, unwelcome monitors, begin
To mingle with the locks that shade my brow
And sadly warn me that I stand within
That pale uncertain called the middle age.
Upon the billows head which soon must bow
I reel; and gaze into the depths where rage
No more the wars 'twixt Time & Life as now,
And gazing swift, descend towards that great Deep
Whose secrets the Almighty One doth keep.

I am as one on mighty errand bound
Uncertain is the distance — fixed the hour;
He stops to gaze upon the Dial's round
Trembling & earnest; when a rising cloud
Casts its oblivious shadow & no more
The gnomon tells what he would know and loud
Thunders are heard & gathering tempests lower.
Lamenting mispent time he hastes away
And treads again the dim & dubious way.

Lago Maggiore

O sky & earth! How ye are linked together
Upon the bosom of this gentle lake;
The wild & wandering breeze is doubtful whether
It may your calm & sweet communion break.
'Tis thus within my silent bosom mingle
The memory of distant scenes — my home
And these enchanting prospects; whilst I, single
And silently in pensive thought do roam.
 The distant & the present sometimes meet
 In dream-like hues; but dark thoughts quickly rise
 And mar the mirror of the vision sweet,
 And truth oerwhelmeth with a sad surprise;
 'Twixt me & those I love an ocean lies
 And all the glory of the landscape dies.

EDWARD COOTE PINKNEY

(1802–1828)

Italy

I.

Know'st thou the land which lovers ought to choose?
Like blessings there descend the sparkling dews;
In gleaming streams the chrystal rivers run,
The purple vintage clusters in the sun;
Odours of flowers haunt the balmy breeze,
Rich fruits hang high upon the vernant trees;
And vivid blossoms gem the shady groves,
Where bright-plumed birds discourse their careless loves.
Beloved!—speed we from this sullen strand
Until thy light feet press that green shore's yellow sand.

II.

Look seaward thence, and nought shall meet thine eye
But fairy isles like paintings on the sky;
And, flying fast and free before the gale,
The gaudy vessel with its glancing sail;
And waters glittering in the glare of noon,
Or touched with silver by the stars and moon,
Or flecked with broken lines of crimson light
When the far fisher's fire affronts the night.
Lovely as loved! towards that smiling shore
Bear we our household gods, to fix for evermore.

III.

It looks a dimple on the face of earth,
The seal of beauty, and the shrine of mirth;
Nature is delicate and graceful there,
The place's genius, feminine and fair:
The winds are awed, nor dare to breathe aloud;
The air seems never to have borne a cloud,

Save where volcanoes send to heav'n their curled
And solemn smokes, like altars of the world.
Thrice beautiful!—to that delightful spot
Carry our married hearts, and be all pain forgot.

IV.

There Art too shows, when Nature's beauty palls,
Her sculptured marbles, and her pictured walls;
And there are forms in which they both conspire
To whisper themes that know not how to tire:
The speaking ruins in that gentle clime
Have but been hallowed by the hand of Time,
And each can mutely prompt some thought of flame
—The meanest stone is not without a name.
Then come, beloved!—hasten o'er the sea
To build our happy hearth in blooming Italy.

The Voyager's Song

"A tradition prevailed among the natives of Puerto Rico, that in the Isle of Bimini, one of the Lucayos, there was a fountain of such wonderful virtue, as to renew the youth and recal the vigour of every person who bathed in its salutary waters. In hopes of finding this grand restorative, Ponce de Leon and his followers, ranged through the islands, searching with fruitless solicitude for the fountain, which was the chief object of the expedition."

—ROBERTSON'S AMERICA.

I.

Sound trumpets, ho!—weigh anchor—loosen sail—
The seaward flying banners chide delay;
As if 'twere heaven that breathes this kindly gale,
Our life-like bark beneath it speeds away.
Flit we, a gliding dream, with troublous motion,
Across the slumbers of uneasy ocean;
And furl our canvass by a happier land,
So fraught with emanations from the sun,
That potable gold streams through the sand
Where element should run.

II.

Onward, my friends, to that bright, florid isle,
The jewel of a smooth and silver sea,
With springs on which perennial summers smile
A power of causing immortality.
For Bimini;—in its enchanted ground,
The hallowed fountains we would seek, are found;
Bathed in the waters of those mystic wells,
The frame starts up in renovated truth,
And, freed from Time's deforming spells,
Resumes its proper youth.

III.

Hail, better birth!—once more my feelings all
A graven image to themselves shall make,
And, placed upon my heart for pedestal,
That glorious idol long will keep awake
Their natural religion, nor be cast
To earth by Age, the great Iconoclast.
As from Gadara's founts they once could come,
Charm-called, from these Love's genii shall arise,
And build their perdurable home,
Miranda, in thine eyes.

IV.

By Nature wisely gifted, not destroyed
With golden presents, like the Roman maid,—
A sublunary paradise enjoyed,
Shall teach thee bliss incapable of shade;—
An Eden ours, nor angry gods, nor men,
Nor star-clad Fates, can take from us again.
Superiour to animal decay,
Sun of that perfect heaven, thou'lt calmly see
Stag, raven, phenix, drop away
With *human* transiency.

V.

Thus rich in being,—beautiful,—adored,
Fear not exhausting pleasure's precious mine;
The wondrous waters we approach, when poured
On passion's lees, supply the wasted wine:
Then be thy bosom's tenant prodigal,
And confident of termless carnival.
Like idle yellow leaves afloat on time,
Let others lapse to death's pacific sea,—
We'll fade nor fall, but sport sublime
In green eternity.

VI.

The envious years, which steal our pleasures, thou
May'st call at once, like magic memory, back,
And, as they pass o'er thine unwithering brow,
Efface their footsteps ere they form a track.
Thy bloom with wilful weeping never stain,
Perpetual life must not belong to pain.
For me,—this world has not yet been a place
Conscious of joys so great as will be mine,
Because the light has kissed no face
Forever fair as thine.

Serenade

Look out upon the stars, my love,
And shame them with thine eyes,
On which, than on the lights above,
There hang more destinies.
Night's beauty is the harmony
Of blending shades and light;
Then, Lady, up,—look out, and be
A sister to the night!—

Sleep not!—thine image wakes for aye,
Within my watching breast:
Sleep not!—from her soft sleep should fly,

Who robs all hearts of rest.
Nay, Lady, from thy slumbers break,
And make this darkness gay,
With looks, whose brightness well might make
Of darker nights a day.

The Widow's Song

I burn no incense, hang no wreath,
    On this, thine early tomb:
Such cannot cheer the place of death,
    But only mock its gloom.
Here odorous smoke and breathing flower
    No grateful influence shed;
They lose their perfume and their power,
    When offered to the dead.

And if, as is the Afghaun's creed,
    The spirit may return,
A disembodied sense to feed,
    On fragrance, near its urn—
It is enough, that she, whom thou
    Did'st love in living years,
Sits desolate beside it now,
    And falls these heavy tears.

GEORGE POPE MORRIS

(1802–1864)

The Oak

Woodman, spare that tree!
  Touch not a single bough!
In youth it sheltered me,
  And I'll protect it now.
'Twas my forefather's hand
  That placed it near his cot;
There, woodman, let it stand,
  Thy axe shall harm it not!

That old familiar tree,
  Whose glory and renown
Are spread o'er land and sea,
  And wouldst thou hack it down?
Woodman, forbear thy stroke!
  Cut not its earth-bound ties;
Oh, spare that aged oak,
  Now towering to the skies!

When but an idle boy
  I sought its grateful shade;
In all their gushing joy
  Here too my sisters played.
My mother kiss'd me here;
  My father press'd my hand—
Forgive this foolish tear,
  But let that old oak stand!

My heart-strings round thee cling,
  Close as thy bark, old friend!
Here shall the wild-bird sing,
  And still thy branches bend.
Old tree! the storm still brave!
  And, woodman, leave the spot;
While I've a hand to save,
  Thy axe shall harm it not.

LYDIA MARIA CHILD

(1802–1880)

The New-England Boy's Song
About Thanksgiving Day

Over the river, and through the wood,
　　To grandfather's house we go;
　　　The horse knows the way,
　　　To carry the sleigh,
　　Through the white and drifted snow.

Over the river, and through the wood,
　　To grandfather's house away!
　　　We would not stop
　　　For doll or top,
　　For 't is Thanksgiving day.

Over the river, and through the wood,
　　Oh, how the wind does blow!
　　　It stings the toes,
　　　And bites the nose,
　　As over the ground we go.

Over the river, and through the wood,
　　With a clear blue winter sky,
　　　The dogs do bark,
　　　And children hark,
　　As we go jingling by.

Over the river, and through the wood,
　　To have a first-rate play—
　　　Hear the bells ring
　　　Ting a ling ding,
　　Hurra for Thanksgiving day!

Over the river, and through the wood—
　　No matter for winds that blow;

Or if we get
The sleigh upset,
Into a bank of snow.

Over the river, and through the wood,
To see little John and Ann;
We will kiss them all,
And play snow-ball,
And stay as long as we can.

Over the river, and through the wood,
Trot fast, my dapple grey!
Spring over the ground,
Like a hunting hound,
For 't is Thanksgiving day!

Over the river, and through the wood,
And straight through the barn-yard gate;
We seem to go
Extremely slow,
It is so hard to wait.

Over the river, and through the wood—
Old Jowler hears our bells;
He shakes his pow,
With a loud bow wow,
And thus the news he tells.

Over the river, and through the wood—
When grandmother sees us come,
She will say, Oh dear,
The children are here,
Bring a pie for every one.

Over the river, and through the wood—
Now grandmother's cap I spy!
Hurra for the fun!
Is the pudding done?
Hurra for the pumpkin pie!

RALPH WALDO EMERSON

(1803–1882)

To Rhea

Thee, dear friend, a brother soothes,
Not with flatteries, but truths,
Which tarnish not, but purify
To light which dims the morning's eye.
I have come from the spring-woods,
From the fragrant solitudes;—
Listen what the poplar-tree
And murmuring waters counselled me.

If with love thy heart has burned;
If thy love is unreturned;
Hide thy grief within thy breast,
Though it tear thee unexpressed;
For when love has once departed
From the eyes of the false-hearted,
And one by one has torn off quite
The bandages of purple light;
Though thou wert the loveliest
Form the soul had ever dressed,
Thou shalt seem, in each reply,
A vixen to his altered eye;
Thy softest pleadings seem too bold,
Thy praying lute will seem to scold;
Though thou kept the straightest road,
Yet thou errest far and broad.

But thou shalt do as do the gods
In their cloudless periods;
For of this lore be thou sure,—
Though thou forget, the gods, secure,
Forget never their command,
But make the statute of this land.
As they lead, so follow all,

Ever have done, ever shall.
Warning to the blind and deaf,
'Tis written on the iron leaf,
Who drinks of Cupid's nectar cup
Loveth downward, and not up;
Therefore, who loves, of gods or men,
Shall not by the same be loved again;
His sweetheart's idolatry
Falls, in turn, a new degree.
When a god is once beguiled
By beauty of a mortal child,
And by her radiant youth delighted,
He is not fooled, but warily knoweth
His love shall never be requited.
And thus the wise Immortal doeth.—
'Tis his study and delight
To bless that creature day and night;
From all evils to defend her;
In her lap to pour all splendor;
To ransack earth for riches rare,
And fetch her stars to deck her hair:
He mixes music with her thoughts,
And saddens her with heavenly doubts:
All grace, all good his great heart knows,
Profuse in love, the king bestows:
Saying, 'Hearken! Earth, Sea, Air!
This monument of my despair
Build I to the All-Good, All-Fair.
Not for a private good,
But I, from my beatitude,
Albeit scorned as none was scorned,
Adorn her as was none adorned.
I make this maiden an ensample
To Nature, through her kingdoms ample,
Whereby to model newer races,
Statelier forms, and fairer faces;
To carry man to new degrees
Of power, and of comeliness.
These presents be the hostages
Which I pawn for my release.

See to thyself, O Universe!
Thou art better, and not worse.'—
And the god, having given all,
Is freed forever from his thrall.

Uriel

It fell in the ancient periods,
    Which the brooding soul surveys,
Or ever the wild Time coined itself
    Into calendar months and days.

This was the lapse of Uriel,
Which in Paradise befell.
Once, among the Pleiads walking,
SAID overheard the young gods talking;
And the treason, too long pent,
To his ears was evident.
The young deities discussed
Laws of form, and metre just,
Orb, quintessence, and sunbeams,
What subsisteth, and what seems.
One, with low tones that decide,
And doubt and reverend use defied,
With a look that solved the sphere,
And stirred the devils everywhere,
Gave his sentiment divine
Against the being of a line.
'Line in nature is not found;
Unit and universe are round;
In vain produced, all rays return;
Evil will bless, and ice will burn.'
As Uriel spoke with piercing eye,
A shudder ran around the sky;
The stern old war-gods shook their heads;
The seraphs frowned from myrtle-beds;
Seemed to the holy festival
The rash word boded ill to all;
The balance-beam of Fate was bent;

The bounds of good and ill were rent;
Strong Hades could not keep his own,
But all slid to confusion.
A sad self-knowledge, withering, fell
On the beauty of Uriel;
In heaven once eminent, the god
Withdrew, that hour, into his cloud;
Whether doomed to long gyration
In the sea of generation,
Or by knowledge grown too bright
To hit the nerve of feebler sight.
Straightway, a forgetting wind
Stole over the celestial kind,
And their lips the secret kept,
If in ashes the fire-seed slept.
But now and then, truth-speaking things
Shamed the angels' veiling wings;
And, shrilling from the solar course,
Or from fruit of chemic force,
Procession of a soul in matter,
Or the speeding change of water,
Or out of the good of evil born,
Came Uriel's voice of cherub scorn,
And a blush tinged the upper sky,
And the gods shook, they knew not why.

Hamatreya

Minott, Lee, Willard, Hosmer, Meriam, Flint
Possessed the land which rendered to their toil
Hay, corn, roots, hemp, flax, apples, wool, and wood.
Each of these landlords walked amidst his farm,
Saying, ' 'Tis mine, my children's, and my name's:
How sweet the west wind sounds in my own trees!
How graceful climb those shadows on my hill!
I fancy these pure waters and the flags
Know me, as does my dog: we sympathize;
And, I affirm, my actions smack of the soil.'
Where are these men? Asleep beneath their grounds;

And strangers, fond as they, their furrows plough.
Earth laughs in flowers, to see her boastful boys
Earth-proud, proud of the earth which is not theirs;
Who steer the plough, but cannot steer their feet
Clear of the grave.
They added ridge to valley, brook to pond,
And sighed for all that bounded their domain.
'This suits me for a pasture; that's my park;
We must have clay, lime, gravel, granite-ledge,
And misty lowland, where to go for peat.
The land is well,—lies fairly to the south.
'Tis good, when you have crossed the sea and back,
To find the sitfast acres where you left them.'
Ah! the hot owner sees not Death, who adds
Him to his land, a lump of mould the more.
Hear what the Earth says:—

EARTH-SONG.

'Mine and yours;
Mine, not yours.
Earth endures;
Stars abide—
Shine down in the old sea;
Old are the shores;
But where are old men?
I who have seen much,
Such have I never seen.

'The lawyer's deed
Ran sure,
In tail,
To them, and to their heirs
Who shall succeed,
Without fail,
Forevermore.

'Here is the land,
Shaggy with wood,
With its old valley,
Mound, and flood.

But the heritors?
Fled like the flood's foam,—
The lawyer, and the laws,
And the kingdom,
Clean swept herefrom.

'They called me theirs,
Who so controlled me;
Yet every one
Wished to stay, and is gone.
How am I theirs,
If they cannot hold me,
But I hold them?'

When I heard the Earth-song,
I was no longer brave;
My avarice cooled
Like lust in the chill of the grave.

The Rhodora:

On Being Asked, Whence Is the Flower?

In May, when sea-winds pierced our solitudes,
I found the fresh Rhodora in the woods,
Spreading its leafless blooms in a damp nook,
To please the desert and the sluggish brook.
The purple petals, fallen in the pool,
Made the black water with their beauty gay;
Here might the red-bird come his plumes to cool,
And court the flower that cheapens his array.
Rhodora! if the sages ask thee why
This charm is wasted on the earth and sky,
Tell them, dear, that if eyes were made for seeing,
Then Beauty is its own excuse for being:
Why thou wert there, O rival of the rose!
I never thought to ask, I never knew;
But, in my simple ignorance, suppose
The self-same Power that brought me there brought you.

The Humble-Bee

Burly, dozing, humble-bee,
Where thou art is clime for me.
Let them sail for Porto Rique,
Far-off heats through seas to seek;
I will follow thee alone,
Thou animated torrid-zone!
Zigzag steerer, desert cheerer,
Let me chase thy waving lines;
Keep me nearer, me thy hearer,
Singing over shrubs and vines.

Insect lover of the sun,
Joy of thy dominion!
Sailor of the atmosphere;
Swimmer through the waves of air;
Voyager of light and noon;
Epicurean of June;
Wait, I prithee, till I come
Within earshot of thy hum,—
All without is martyrdom.

When the south wind, in May days,
With a net of shining haze
Silvers the horizon wall,
And, with softness touching all,
Tints the human countenance
With a color of romance,
And, infusing subtle heats,
Turns the sod to violets,
Thou, in sunny solitudes,
Rover of the underwoods,
The green silence dost displace
With thy mellow, breezy bass.

Hot midsummer's petted crone,
Sweet to me thy drowsy tone
Tells of countless sunny hours,
Long days, and solid banks of flowers;

Of gulfs of sweetness without bound
In Indian wildernesses found;
Of Syrian peace, immortal leisure,
Firmest cheer, and bird-like pleasure.

Aught unsavory or unclean
Hath my insect never seen;
But violets and bilberry bells,
Maple-sap, and daffodels,
Grass with green flag half-mast high,
Succory to match the sky,
Columbine with horn of honey,
Scented fern, and agrimony,
Clover, catchfly, adder's tongue,
And brier roses, dwelt among;
All beside was unknown waste,
All was picture as he passed.

Wiser far than human seer,
Yellow-breeched philosopher!
Seeing only what is fair,
Sipping only what is sweet,
Thou dost mock at fate and care,
Leave the chaff, and take the wheat.
When the fierce north-western blast
Cools sea and land so far and fast,
Thou already slumberest deep;
Woe and want thou canst outsleep;
Want and woe, which torture us,
Thy sleep makes ridiculous.

The Snow-Storm

Announced by all the trumpets of the sky,
Arrives the snow, and, driving o'er the fields,
Seems nowhere to alight: the whited air
Hides hills and woods, the river, and the heaven,
And veils the farm-house at the garden's end.

The sled and traveller stopped, the courier's feet
Delayed, all friends shut out, the housemates sit
Around the radiant fireplace, enclosed
In a tumultuous privacy of storm.

    Come see the north wind's masonry.
Out of an unseen quarry evermore
Furnished with tile, the fierce artificer
Curves his white bastions with projected roof
Round every windward stake, or tree, or door.
Speeding, the myriad-handed, his wild work
So fanciful, so savage, nought cares he
For number or proportion. Mockingly,
On coop or kennel he hangs Parian wreaths;
A swan-like form invests the hidden thorn;
Fills up the farmer's lane from wall to wall,
Maugre the farmer's sighs; and, at the gate,
A tapering turret overtops the work.
And when his hours are numbered, and the world
Is all his own, retiring, as he were not,
Leaves, when the sun appears, astonished Art
To mimic in slow structures, stone by stone,
Built in an age, the mad wind's night-work,
The frolic architecture of the snow.

from *Woodnotes II*

    Once again the pine-tree sung:—
'Speak not thy speech my boughs among;
 Put off thy years, wash in the breeze;
 My hours are peaceful centuries.
 Talk no more with feeble tongue;
 No more the fool of space and time,
 Come weave with mine a nobler rhyme.
 Only thy Americans
 Can read thy line, can meet thy glance,
 But the runes that I rehearse
 Understands the universe;

The least breath my boughs which tossed
Brings again the Pentecost,
To every soul it soundeth clear
In a voice of solemn cheer,—
"Am I not thine? Are not these thine?"
And they reply, "Forever mine!"
My branches speak Italian,
English, German, Basque, Castilian,
Mountain speech to Highlanders,
Ocean tongues to islanders,
To Fin, and Lap, and swart Malay,
To each his bosom secret say.
   Come learn with me the fatal song
Which knits the world in music strong,
Whereto every bosom dances,
Kindled with courageous fancies.
Come lift thine eyes to lofty rhymes,
Of things with things, of times with times,
Primal chimes of sun and shade,
Of sound and echo, man and maid,
The land reflected in the flood,
Body with shadow still pursued.
For Nature beats in perfect tune,
And rounds with rhyme her every rune,
Whether she work in land or sea,
Or hide underground her alchemy.
Thou canst not wave thy staff in air,
Or dip thy paddle in the lake,
But it carves the bow of beauty there,
And the ripples in rhymes the oar forsake.
The wood is wiser far than thou;
The wood and wave each other know.
Not unrelated, unaffied,
But to each thought and thing allied,
Is perfect Nature's every part,
Rooted in the mighty Heart.
But thou, poor child! unbound, unrhymed,
Whence camest thou, misplaced, mistimed?
Whence, O thou orphan and defrauded?
Is thy land peeled, thy realm marauded?

Who thee divorced, deceived, and left?
Thee of thy faith who hath bereft,
And torn the ensigns from thy brow,
And sunk the immortal eye so low?
Thy cheek too white, thy form too slender,
Thy gait too slow, thy habits tender
For royal man;—they thee confess
An exile from the wilderness,—
The hills where health with health agrees,
And the wise soul expels disease.
Hark! in thy ear I will tell the sign
By which thy hurt thou may'st divine.
When thou shalt climb the mountain cliff,
Or see the wide shore from thy skiff,
To thee the horizon shall express
Only emptiness and emptiness;
There is no man of Nature's worth
In the circle of the earth;
And to thine eye the vast skies fall,
Dire and satirical,
On clucking hens, and prating fools,
On thieves, on drudges, and on dolls.
And thou shalt say to the Most High,
"Godhead! all this astronomy,
And fate, and practice, and invention,
Strong art, and beautiful pretension,
This radiant pomp of sun and star,
Throes that were, and worlds that are,
Behold! were in vain and in vain;—
It cannot be,—I will look again;
Surely now will the curtain rise,
And earth's fit tenant me surprise;—
But the curtain doth *not* rise,
And Nature has miscarried wholly
Into failure, into folly."

'Alas! thine is the bankruptcy,
Blessed Nature so to see.
Come, lay thee in my soothing shade,
And heal the hurts which sin has made.

I will teach the bright parable
Older than time,
Things undeclarable,
Visions sublime.
I see thee in the crowd alone;
I will be thy companion.
Let thy friends be as the dead in doom,
And build to them a final tomb;
Let the starred shade that nightly falls
Still celebrate their funerals,
And the bell of beetle and of bee
Knell their melodious memory.
Behind thee leave thy merchandise,
Thy churches, and thy charities;
And leave thy peacock wit behind;
Enough for thee the primal mind
That flows in streams, that breathes in wind.
Leave all thy pedant lore apart;
God hid the whole world in thy heart.
Love shuns the sage, the child it crowns,
And gives them all who all renounce.
The rain comes when the wind calls;
The river knows the way to the sea;
Without a pilot it runs and falls,
Blessing all lands with its charity;
The sea tosses and foams to find
Its way up to the cloud and wind;
The shadow sits close to the flying ball;
The date fails not on the palm-tree tall;
And thou,—go burn thy wormy pages,
Shalt outsee seers, and outwit sages.
Oft didst thou thread the woods in vain
To find what bird had piped the strain;—
Seek not, and the little eremite
Flies gayly forth and sings in sight.

'Hearken once more!
I will tell thee the mundane lore.
Older am I than thy numbers wot;
Change I may, but I pass not.

Hitherto all things fast abide,
And anchored in the tempest ride.
Trenchant time behoves to hurry
All to yean and all to bury:
All the forms are fugitive,
But the substances survive.
Ever fresh the broad creation,
A divine improvisation,
From the heart of God proceeds,
A single will, a million deeds.
Once slept the world an egg of stone,
And pulse, and sound, and light was none;
And God said, "Throb!" and there was motion,
And the vast mass became vast ocean.
Onward and on, the eternal Pan,
Who layeth the world's incessant plan,
Halteth never in one shape,
But forever doth escape,
Like wave or flame, into new forms
Of gem, and air, of plants, and worms.
I, that to-day am a pine,
Yesterday was a bundle of grass.
He is free and libertine,
Pouring of his power the wine
To every age, to every race;
Unto every race and age
He emptieth the beverage;
Unto each, and unto all,
Maker and original.
The world is the ring of his spells,
And the play of his miracles.
As he giveth to all to drink,
Thus or thus they are and think.
He giveth little or giveth much,
To make them several or such.
With one drop sheds form and feature;
With the second a special nature;
The third adds heat's indulgent spark;
The fourth gives light which eats the dark;
In the fifth drop himself he flings,

And conscious Law is King of kings.
Pleaseth him, the Eternal Child,
To play his sweet will, glad and wild;
As the bee through the garden ranges,
From world to world the godhead changes;
As the sheep go feeding in the waste,
From form to form he maketh haste;
This vault which glows immense with light
Is the inn where he lodges for a night.
What recks such Traveller if the bowers
Which bloom and fade like meadow flowers
A bunch of fragrant lilies be,
Or the stars of eternity?
Alike to him the better, the worse,—
The glowing angel, the outcast corse.
Thou metest him by centuries,
And lo! he passes like the breeze;
Thou seek'st in globe and galaxy,
He hides in pure transparency;
Thou askest in fountains and in fires,
He is the essence that inquires.
He is the axis of the star;
He is the sparkle of the spar;
He is the heart of every creature;
He is the meaning of each feature;
And his mind is the sky,
Than all it holds more deep, more high.'

Fable

The mountain and the squirrel
Had a quarrel;
And the former called the latter 'Little Prig.'
Bun replied,
'You are doubtless very big;
But all sorts of things and weather
Must be taken in together,
To make up a year
And a sphere.

And I think it no disgrace
To occupy my place.
If I'm not so large as you,
You are not so small as I,
And not half so spry.
I'll not deny you make
A very pretty squirrel track;
Talents differ; all is well and wisely put;
If I cannot carry forests on my back,
Neither can you crack a nut.'

Ode, Inscribed to W. H. Channing

Though loath to grieve
The evil time's sole patriot,
I cannot leave
My honied thought
For the priest's cant,
Or statesman's rant.

If I refuse
My study for their politique,
Which at the best is trick,
The angry Muse
Puts confusion in my brain.

But who is he that prates
Of the culture of mankind,
Of better arts and life?
Go, blindworm, go,
Behold the famous States
Harrying Mexico
With rifle and with knife!

Or who, with accent bolder,
Dare praise the freedom-loving mountaineer?
I found by thee, O rushing Contoocook!
And in thy valleys, Agiochook!
The jackals of the negro-holder.

The God who made New Hampshire
Taunted the lofty land
With little men;—
Small bat and wren
House in the oak:—
If earth-fire cleave
The upheaved land, and bury the folk,
The southern crocodile would grieve.
Virtue palters; Right is hence;
Freedom praised, but hid;
Funeral eloquence
Rattles the coffin-lid.

What boots thy zeal,
O glowing friend,
That would indignant rend
The northland from the south?
Wherefore? to what good end?
Boston Bay and Bunker Hill
Would serve things still;—
Things are of the snake.

The horseman serves the horse,
The neatherd serves the neat,
The merchant serves the purse,
The eater serves his meat;
'Tis the day of the chattel,
Web to weave, and corn to grind;
Things are in the saddle,
And ride mankind.

There are two laws discrete,
Not reconciled,—
Law for man, and law for thing;
The last builds town and fleet,
But it runs wild,
And doth the man unking.

'Tis fit the forest fall,
The steep be graded,

The mountain tunnelled,
The sand shaded,
The orchard planted,
The glebe tilled,
The prairie granted,
The steamer built.

Let man serve law for man;
Live for friendship, live for love,
For truth's and harmony's behoof;
The state may follow how it can,
As Olympus follows Jove.

    Yet do not I invite
The wrinkled shopman to my sounding woods,
Nor bid the unwilling senator
Ask votes of thrushes in the solitudes.
Every one to his chosen work;—
Foolish hands may mix and mar;
Wise and sure the issues are.
Round they roll till dark is light,

Sex to sex, and even to odd;—
The over-god
Who marries Right to Might,
Who peoples, unpeoples,—
He who exterminates
Races by stronger races,
Black by white faces,—
Knows to bring honey
Out of the lion;
Grafts gentlest scion
On pirate and Turk.

The Cossack eats Poland,
Like stolen fruit;
Her last noble is ruined,
Her last poet mute:
Straight, into double band

The victors divide;
Half for freedom strike and stand;—
The astonished Muse finds thousands at her side.

Astræa

Himself it was who wrote
His rank, and quartered his own coat.
There is no king nor sovereign state
That can fix a hero's rate;
Each to all is venerable,
Cap-a-pie invulnerable,
Until he write, where all eyes rest,
Slave or master on his breast.

I saw men go up and down,
In the country and the town,
With this prayer upon their neck,—
'Judgment and a judge we seek.'
Not to monarchs they repair,
Nor to learned jurist's chair;
But they hurry to their peers,
To their kinsfolk and their dears;
Louder than with speech they pray,—
'What am I? companion, say.'
And the friend not hesitates
To assign just place and mates;
Answers not in word or letter,
Yet is understood the better;
Is to his friend a looking-glass,
Reflects his figure that doth pass.
Every wayfarer he meets
What himself declared repeats,
What himself confessed records,
Sentences him in his words;
The form is his own corporal form,
And his thought the penal worm.

Yet shine forever virgin minds,
Loved by stars and purest winds,
Which, o'er passion throned sedate,
Have not hazarded their state;
Disconcert the searching spy,
Rendering to a curious eye
The durance of a granite ledge
To those who gaze from the sea's edge.
It is there for benefit;
It is there for purging light;
There for purifying storms;
And its depths reflect all forms;
It cannot parley with the mean,—
Pure by impure is not seen.
For there's no sequestered grot,
Lone mountain tarn, or isle forgot,
But Justice, journeying in the sphere,
Daily stoops to harbor there.

Give All to Love

Give all to love;
Obey thy heart;
Friends, kindred, days,
Estate, good-fame,
Plans, credit, and the Muse,—
Nothing refuse.

'Tis a brave master;
Let it have scope:
Follow it utterly,
Hope beyond hope:
High and more high
It dives into noon,
With wing unspent,
Untold intent;
But it is a god,
Knows its own path,
And the outlets of the sky.

It was not for the mean;
It requireth courage stout,
Souls above doubt,
Valor unbending;
Such 'twill reward,—
They shall return
More than they were,
And ever ascending.

Leave all for love;
Yet, hear me, yet,
One word more thy heart behoved,
One pulse more of firm endeavor,—
Keep thee to-day,
To-morrow, forever,
Free as an Arab
Of thy beloved.

Cling with life to the maid;
But when the surprise,
First vague shadow of surmise
Flits across her bosom young
Of a joy apart from thee,
Free be she, fancy-free;
Nor thou detain her vesture's hem,
Nor the palest rose she flung
From her summer diadem.

Though thou loved her as thyself,
As a self of purer clay,
Though her parting dims the day,
Stealing grace from all alive;
Heartily know,
When half-gods go,
The gods arrive.

Merlin I

Thy trivial harp will never please
Or fill my craving ear;
Its chords should ring as blows the breeze,
Free, peremptory, clear.
No jingling serenader's art,
Nor tinkle of piano strings,
Can make the wild blood start
In its mystic springs.
The kingly bard
Must smite the chords rudely and hard,
As with hammer or with mace;
That they may render back
Artful thunder, which conveys
Secrets of the solar track,
Sparks of the supersolar blaze.
Merlin's blows are strokes of fate,
Chiming with the forest tone,
When boughs buffet boughs in the wood;
Chiming with the gasp and moan
Of the ice-imprisoned flood;
With the pulse of manly hearts;
With the voice of orators;
With the din of city arts;
With the cannonade of wars;
With the marches of the brave;
And prayers of might from martyrs' cave.

Great is the art,
Great be the manners, of the bard.
He shall not his brain encumber
With the coil of rhythm and number;
But, leaving rule and pale forethought,
He shall aye climb
For his rhyme.
'Pass in, pass in,' the angels say,
In to the upper doors,
Nor count compartments of the floors,
But mount to paradise
By the stairway of surprise.

Blameless master of the games,
King of sport that never shames,
He shall daily joy dispense
Hid in song's sweet influence.
Things more cheerly live and go,
What time the subtle mind
Sings aloud the tune whereto
Their pulses beat,
And march their feet,
And their members are combined.

By Sybarites beguiled,
He shall no task decline;
Merlin's mighty line
Extremes of nature reconciled, —
Bereaved a tyrant of his will,
And made the lion mild.
Songs can the tempest still,
Scattered on the stormy air,
Mould the year to fair increase,
And bring in poetic peace.

He shall not seek to weave,
In weak, unhappy times,
Efficacious rhymes;
Wait his returning strength.
Bird, that from the nadir's floor
To the zenith's top can soar,
The soaring orbit of the muse exceeds that journey's length.
Nor profane affect to hit
Or compass that, by meddling wit,
Which only the propitious mind
Publishes when 'tis inclined.
There are open hours
When the God's will sallies free,
And the dull idiot might see
The flowing fortunes of a thousand years; —
Sudden, at unawares,
Self-moved, fly-to the doors
Nor sword of angels could reveal
What they conceal.

Merlin II

The rhyme of the poet
Modulates the king's affairs;
Balance-loving Nature
Made all things in pairs.
To every foot its antipode;
Each color with its counter glowed;
To every tone beat answering tones,
Higher or graver;
Flavor gladly blends with flavor;
Leaf answers leaf upon the bough;
And match the paired cotyledons.
Hands to hands, and feet to feet,
Coeval grooms and brides;
Eldest rite, two married sides
In every mortal meet.
Light's far furnace shines,
Smelting balls and bars,
Forging double stars,
Glittering twins and trines.
The animals are sick with love,
Lovesick with rhyme;
Each with all propitious time
Into chorus wove.

Like the dancers' ordered band,
Thoughts come also hand in hand;
In equal couples mated,
Or else alternated;
Adding by their mutual gage,
One to other, health and age.
Solitary fancies go
Short-lived wandering to and fro,
Most like to bachelors,
Or an ungiven maid,
Not ancestors,
With no posterity to make the lie afraid,
Or keep truth undecayed.
Perfect-paired as eagle's wings,

Justice is the rhyme of things;
Trade and counting use
The self-same tuneful muse;
And Nemesis,
Who with even matches odd,
Who athwart space redresses
The partial wrong,
Fills the just period,
And finishes the song.

Subtle rhymes, with ruin rife,
Murmur in the house of life,
Sung by the Sisters as they spin;
In perfect time and measure they
Build and unbuild our echoing clay,
As the two twilights of the day
Fold us music-drunken in.

Bacchus

Bring me wine, but wine which never grew
In the belly of the grape,
Or grew on vine whose tap-roots, reaching through
Under the Andes to the Cape,
Suffered no savor of the earth to scape.

Let its grapes the morn salute
From a nocturnal root,
Which feels the acrid juice
Of Styx and Erebus;
And turns the woe of Night,
By its own craft, to a more rich delight.

We buy ashes for bread;
We buy diluted wine;
Give me of the true,—
Whose ample leaves and tendrils curled
Among the silver hills of heaven,
Draw everlasting dew;

Wine of wine,
Blood of the world,
Form of forms, and mould of statures,
That I intoxicated,
And by the draught assimilated,
May float at pleasure through all natures;
The bird-language rightly spell,
And that which roses say so well.

Wine that is shed
Like the torrents of the sun
Up the horizon walls,
Or like the Atlantic streams, which run
When the South Sea calls.

Water and bread,
Food which needs no transmuting,
Rainbow-flowering, wisdom-fruiting
Wine which is already man,
Food which teach and reason can.

Wine which Music is,—
Music and wine are one,—
That I, drinking this,
Shall hear far Chaos talk with me;
Kings unborn shall walk with me;
And the poor grass shall plot and plan
What it will do when it is man.
Quickened so, will I unlock
Every crypt of every rock.

I thank the joyful juice
For all I know;—
Winds of remembering
Of the ancient being blow,
And seeming-solid walls of use
Open and flow.

Pour, Bacchus! the remembering wine;
Retrieve the loss of me and mine!

Vine for vine be antidote,
And the grape requite the lote!
Haste to cure the old despair,—
Reason in Nature's lotus drenched,
The memory of ages quenched;
Give them again to shine;
Let wine repair what this undid;
And where the infection slid,
A dazzling memory revive;
Refresh the faded tints,
Recut the aged prints,
And write my old adventures with the pen
Which on the first day drew,
Upon the tablets blue,
The dancing Pleiads and eternal men.

Merops

What care I, so they stand the same,—
　　Things of the heavenly mind,—
How long the power to give them name
　　Tarries yet behind?

Thus far to-day your favors reach,
　　O fair, appeasing presences!
Ye taught my lips a single speech,
　　And a thousand silences.

Space grants beyond his fated road
　　No inch to the god of day;
And copious language still bestowed
　　One word, no more, to say.

Saadi

Trees in groves,
Kine in droves,
In ocean sport the scaly herds,

Wedge-like cleave the air the birds,
To northern lakes fly wind-borne ducks,
Browse the mountain sheep in flocks,
Men consort in camp and town,
But the poet dwells alone.

God, who gave to him the lyre,
Of all mortals the desire,
For all breathing men's behoof,
Straitly charged him, 'Sit aloof;'
Annexed a warning, poets say,
To the bright premium,—
Ever, when twain together play,
Shall the harp be dumb.

Many may come,
But one shall sing;
Two touch the string,
The harp is dumb.
Though there come a million,
Wise Saadi dwells alone.

Yet Saadi loved the race of men,—
No churl, immured in cave or den;
In bower and hall
He wants them all,
Nor can dispense
With Persia for his audience;
They must give ear,
Grow red with joy and white with fear;
But he has no companion;
Come ten, or come a million,
Good Saadi dwells alone.

Be thou ware where Saadi dwells;
Wisdom of the gods is he,—
Entertain it reverently.
Gladly round that golden lamp
Sylvan deities encamp,
And simple maids and noble youth

Are welcome to the man of truth.
Most welcome, they who need him most,
They feed the spring which they exhaust;
For greater need
Draws better deed:
But, critic, spare thy vanity,
Nor show thy pompous parts,
To vex with odious subtlety
The cheerer of men's hearts.

Sad-eyed Fakirs swiftly say
Endless dirges to decay,
Never in the blaze of light
Lose the shudder of midnight;
Pale at overflowing noon
Hear wolves barking at the moon;
In the bower of dalliance sweet
Hear the far Avenger's feet;
And shake before those awful Powers,
Who in their pride forgive not ours.
Thus the sad-eyed Fakirs preach:
'Bard, when thee would Allah teach,
And lift thee to his holy mount,
He sends thee from his bitter fount
Wormwood,—saying, "Go thy ways,
Drink not the Malaga of praise,
But do the deed thy fellows hate,
And compromise thy peaceful state;
Smite the white breasts which thee fed;
Stuff sharp thorns beneath the head
Of them thou shouldst have comforted;
For out of woe and out of crime
Draws the heart a lore sublime." '
And yet it seemeth not to me
That the high gods love tragedy;
For Saadi sat in the sun,
And thanks was his contrition;
For haircloth and for bloody whips,
Had active hands and smiling lips;
And yet his runes he rightly read,

And to his folk his message sped.
Sunshine in his heart transferred
Lighted each transparent word,
And well could honoring Persia learn
What Saadi wished to say;
For Saadi's nightly stars did burn
Brighter than Dschami's day.

Whispered the Muse in Saadi's cot:
'O gentle Saadi, listen not,
Tempted by thy praise of wit,
Or by thirst and appetite
For the talents not thine own,
To sons of contradiction.
Never, son of eastern morning,
Follow falsehood, follow scorning.
Denounce who will, who will deny,
And pile the hills to scale the sky;
Let theist, atheist, pantheist,
Define and wrangle how they list,
Fierce conserver, fierce destroyer,—
But thou, joy-giver and enjoyer,
Unknowing war, unknowing crime,
Gentle Saadi, mind thy rhyme;
Heed not what the brawlers say,
Heed thou only Saadi's lay.

'Let the great world bustle on
With war and trade, with camp and town:
A thousand men shall dig and eat;
At forge and furnace thousands sweat;
And thousands sail the purple sea,
And give or take the stroke of war,
Or crowd the market and bazaar;
Oft shall war end, and peace return,
And cities rise where cities burn,
Ere one man my hill shall climb,
Who can turn the golden rhyme.
Let them manage how they may,
Heed thou only Saadi's lay.

Seek the living among the dead,—
Man in man is imprisoned;
Barefooted Dervish is not poor,
If fate unlock his bosom's door,
So that what his eye hath seen
His tongue can paint as bright, as keen;
And what his tender heart hath felt
With equal fire thy heart shall melt.
For, whom the Muses smile upon,
And touch with soft persuasion,
His words like a storm-wind can bring
Terror and beauty on their wing;
In his every syllable
Lurketh nature veritable;
And though he speak in midnight dark,—
In heaven no star, on earth no spark,—
Yet before the listener's eye
Swims the world in ecstasy,
The forest waves, the morning breaks,
The pastures sleep, ripple the lakes,
Leaves twinkle, flowers like persons be,
And life pulsates in rock or tree.
Saadi, so far thy words shall reach:
Suns rise and set in Saadi's speech!'

And thus to Saadi said the Muse:
'Eat thou the bread which men refuse;
Flee from the goods which from thee flee;
Seek nothing,—Fortune seeketh thee.
Nor mount, nor dive; all good things keep
The midway of the eternal deep.
Wish not to fill the isles with eyes
To fetch thee birds of paradise:
On thine orchard's edge belong
All the brags of plume and song;
Wise Ali's sunbright sayings pass
For proverbs in the market-place;
Through mountains bored by regal art,
Toil whistles as he drives his cart.
Nor scour the seas, nor sift mankind,

A poet or a friend to find:
Behold, he watches at the door!
Behold his shadow on the floor!
Open innumerable doors
The heaven where unveiled Allah pours
The flood of truth, the flood of good,
The Seraph's and the Cherub's food:
Those doors are men: the Pariah hind
Admits thee to the perfect Mind.
Seek not beyond thy cottage wall
Redeemers that can yield thee all:
While thou sittest at thy door
On the desert's yellow floor,
Listening to the gray-haired crones,
Foolish gossips, ancient drones,
Saadi, see! they rise in stature
To the height of mighty Nature,
And the secret stands revealed
Fraudulent Time in vain concealed,—
That blessed gods in servile masks
Plied for thee thy household tasks.'

Xenophanes

By fate, not option, frugal Nature gave
One scent to hyson and to wall-flower,
One sound to pine-groves and to waterfalls,
One aspect to the desert and the lake.
It was her stern necessity: all things
Are of one pattern made; bird, beast, and flower,
Song, picture, form, space, thought, and character,
Deceive us, seeming to be many things,
And are but one. Beheld far off, they differ
As God and devil; bring them to the mind,
They dull its edge with their monotony.
To know one element, explore another,
And in the second reappears the first.
The specious panorama of a year
But multiplies the image of a day,—

A belt of mirrors round a taper's flame;
And universal Nature, through her vast
And crowded whole, an infinite paroquet,
Repeats one note.

Blight

Give me truths;
For I am weary of the surfaces,
And die of inanition. If I knew
Only the herbs and simples of the wood,
Rue, cinquefoil, gill, vervain, and agrimony,
Blue-vetch, and trillium, hawkweed, sassafras,
Milkweeds, and murky brakes, quaint pipes, and sundew,
And rare and virtuous roots, which in these woods
Draw untold juices from the common earth,
Untold, unknown, and I could surely spell
Their fragrance, and their chemistry apply
By sweet affinities to human flesh,
Driving the foe and stablishing the friend, —
O, that were much, and I could be a part
Of the round day, related to the sun
And planted world, and full executor
Of their imperfect functions.
But these young scholars, who invade our hills, *intellectual &c*
Bold as the engineer who fells the wood,
And travelling often in the cut he makes,
Love not the flower they pluck, and know it not,
And all their botany is Latin names.
The old men studied magic in the flowers,
And human fortunes in astronomy,
And an omnipotence in chemistry,
Preferring things to names, for these were men,
Were unitarians of the united world,
And, wheresoever their clear eye-beams fell,
They caught the footsteps of the SAME. Our eyes
Are armed, but we are strangers to the stars,
And strangers to the mystic beast and bird,
And strangers to the plant and to the mine.

The injured elements say, 'Not in us;'
And night and day, ocean and continent,
Fire, plant, and mineral say, 'Not in us,'
And haughtily return us stare for stare.
For we invade them impiously for gain;
We devastate them unreligiously,
And coldly ask their pottage, not their love.
Therefore they shove us from them, yield to us
Only what to our griping toil is due;
But the sweet affluence of love and song,
The rich results of the divine consents
Of man and earth, of world beloved and lover,
The nectar and ambrosia, are withheld;
And in the midst of spoils and slaves, we thieves
And pirates of the universe, shut out
Daily to a more thin and outward rind,
Turn pale and starve. Therefore, to our sick eyes,
The stunted trees look sick, the summer short,
Clouds shade the sun, which will not tan our hay,
And nothing thrives to reach its natural term;
And life, shorn of its venerable length,
Even at its greatest space is a defeat,
And dies in anger that it was a dupe;
And, in its highest noon and wantonness,
Is early frugal, like a beggar's child;
With most unhandsome calculation taught,
Even in the hot pursuit of the best aims
And prizes of ambition, checks its hand,
Like Alpine cataracts frozen as they leaped,
Chilled with a miserly comparison
Of the toy's purchase with the length of life.

Hymn:
Sung at the Completion of the Concord Monument
April 19, 1836

By the rude bridge that arched the flood,
  Their flag to April's breeze unfurled,
Here once the embattled farmers stood,
  And fired the shot heard round the world.

The foe long since in silence slept;
  Alike the conqueror silent sleeps;
And Time the ruined bridge has swept
  Down the dark stream which seaward creeps.

On this green bank, by this soft stream,
  We set to-day a votive stone;
That memory may their deed redeem,
  When, like our sires, our sons are gone.

Spirit, that made those heroes dare
  To die, or leave their children free,
Bid Time and Nature gently spare
  The shaft we raise to them and thee.

Brahma

If the red slayer think he slays,
  Or if the slain think he is slain,
They know not well the subtle ways
  I keep, and pass, and turn again.

Far or forgot to me is near;
  Shadow and sunlight are the same;
The vanished gods to me appear;
  And one to me are shame and fame.

They reckon ill who leave me out;
  When me they fly, I am the wings;
I am the doubter and the doubt,
  And I the hymn the Brahmin sings.

The strong gods pine for my abode,
  And pine in vain the sacred Seven;
But thou, meek lover of the good!
  Find me, and turn thy back on heaven.

Mottoes from the Essays

Nature (1836)

A subtle chain of countless rings
The next unto the farthest brings;
The eye reads omens where it goes,
And speaks all languages the rose;
And, striving to be man, the worm
Mounts through all the spires of form.

Compensation

I.

The wings of Time are black and white,
Pied with morning and with night.
Mountain tall and ocean deep
Trembling balance duly keep.
In changing moon and tidal wave
Glows the feud of Want and Have.
Gauge of more and less through space,
Electric star or pencil plays,
The lonely Earth amid the balls
That hurry through the eternal halls,
A makeweight flying to the void,
Supplemental asteroid,
Or compensatory spark,
Shoots across the neutral Dark.

II.

Man's the elm, and Wealth the vine;
Stanch and strong the tendrils twine:
Though the frail ringlets thee deceive,
None from its stock that vine can reave.
Fear not, then, thou child infirm,
There's no god dare wrong a worm;
Laurel crowns cleave to deserts,
And power to him who power exerts.

Hast not thy share? On winged feet,
Lo! it rushes thee to meet;
And all that Nature made thy own,
Floating in air or pent in stone,
Will rive the hills and swim the sea,
And, like thy shadow, follow thee.

Circles

Nature centres into balls,
And her proud ephemerals,
Fast to surface and outside,
Scan the profile of the sphere;
Knew they what that signified,
A new genesis were here.

Experience

The lords of life, the lords of life,—
I saw them pass,
In their own guise,
Like and unlike,
Portly and grim,—
Use and Surprise,
Surface and Dream,
Succession swift and spectral Wrong,
Temperament without a tongue,
And the inventor of the game
Omnipresent without name;—
Some to see, some to be guessed,
They marched from east to west:
Little man, least of all,
Among the legs of his guardians tall,
Walked about with puzzled look.
Him by the hand dear Nature took,
Dearest Nature, strong and kind,
Whispered, 'Darling, never mind!
To-morrow they will wear another face,
The founder thou; these are thy race!'

Nature (*1844*)

The rounded world is fair to see,
Nine times folded in mystery:
Though baffled seers cannot impart
The secret of its laboring heart,
Throb thine with Nature's throbbing breast,
And all is clear from east to west.
Spirit that lurks each form within
Beckons to spirit of its kin;
Self-kindled every atom glows,
And hints the future which it owes.

"*Who knows this or that*"

Who knows this or that
Hark in the wall to the rat
Since the world was, he has gnawed;
Of his wisdom of his fraud
What dost thou know
In the wretched little beast
Is life & heart
Child & parent
Not without relation
To fruitful field & sun & moon
What art thou? his wicked eye
Is cruel to thy cruelty

Maia

Illusion works impenetrable,
Weaving webs innumerable,
Her gay pictures never fail,
Crowds each on other, veil on veil,
A charmer who will be believed
By Man who thirsts to be deceived.

SARAH HELEN WHITMAN

(1803–1878)

To ——

Vainly my heart had with thy sorceries striven:
It had no refuge from thy love,—no Heaven
But in thy fatal presence;—from afar
It owned thy power and trembled like a star
O'erfraught with light and splendor. Could I deem
How dark a shadow should obscure its beam?—
Could I believe that pain could ever dwell
Where thy bright presence cast its blissful spell?
Thou wert my proud palladium;—could I fear
The avenging Destinies when thou wert near?—
Thou wert my Destiny;—thy song, thy fame,
The wild enchantments clustering round thy name,
Were my soul's heritage, its royal dower;
Its glory and its kingdom and its power!

NATHANIEL HAWTHORNE

(1804–1864)

"I left my low and humble home"

I left my low and humble home,
Far from my Father's fields to roam.
My peaceful cot no more had charms,
My only joy was War's alarms.
I panted for the field of fight,
I gaz'd upon the deathless light,
Which o'er the Hero's grave is shed,
The glorious memory of the dead.
Ambition show'd a distant star,
That shed its radience bright and far,
And pointed to a path which led
O'er heaps of dying and of dead;
Onward I press'd with eager feet,
And War's dread thunder still would greet
My reckless ears. Where'er I trod,
I saw the green and verdant sod,
Turn red with blood of slaughter'd foes,
And Fury veil'd in smoke arose.
I gain'd the envied height, and there,
I sigh'd for that lone cottage, where
The early hours of life flew by,
On wings of youthful ecstacy.
Too late I found that Glory's ray,
Could never bring one happy day.

NATHANIEL PARKER WILLIS

(1806–1867)

January 1, 1829

Winter is come again. The sweet south west
Is a forgotten wind, and the strong earth
Has laid aside its mantle to be bound
By the frost fetter. There is not a sound
Save of the skaiter's heel, and there is laid
An icy finger on the lip of streams,
And the clear icicle hangs cold and still,
And the snow-fall is noiseless as a thought.
Spring has a rushing sound, and Summer sends
Many sweet voices with its odors out,
And Autumn rustleth its decaying robe
With a complaining whisper. Winter's dumb!
God made his ministry a silent one,
And he has given him a foot of steel
And an unlovely aspect, and a breath
Sharp to the senses — and we know that He
Tempereth well, and hath a meaning hid
Under the shadow of his hand. Look up!
And it shall be interpreted — Your home
Hath a temptation now. There is no voice
Of waters with beguiling for your ear,
And the cool forest and the meadows green
Witch not your feet away; and in the dells
There are no violets, and upon the hills
There are no sunny places to lie down.
You must go in, and by your cheerful fire
Wait for the offices of love, and hear
Accents of human tenderness, and feast
Your eye upon the beauty of the young.
It is a season for the quiet thought,
And the still reckoning with thyself. The year
Gives back the spirits of its dead, and time
Whispers the history of its vanished hours;

And the heart, calling its affections up,
Counteth its wasted ingots. Life stands still
And settles like a fountain, and the eye
Sees clearly through its depths, and noteth all
That stirred its troubled waters. It is well
That Winter with the dying year should come!

Unseen Spirits

The shadows lay along Broadway,
  'Twas near the twilight-tide—
And slowly there a lady fair
  Was walking in her pride.
Alone walk'd she; but, viewlessly,
  Walk'd spirits at her side.

Peace charm'd the street beneath her feet,
  And Honor charm'd the air;
And all astir look'd kind on her,
  And call'd her good as fair—
For all God ever gave to her
  She kept with chary care.

She kept with care her beauties rare
  From lovers warm and true—
For her heart was cold to all but gold,
  And the rich came not to woo—
But honor'd well are charms to sell
  If priests the selling do.

Now walking there was one more fair—
  A slight girl, lily-pale;
And she had unseen company
  To make the spirit quail—
'Twixt Want and Scorn she walk'd forlorn,
  And nothing could avail.

No mercy now can clear her brow
  For this world's peace to pray;

For, as love's wild prayer dissolved in air,
   Her woman's heart gave way!—
But the sin forgiven by Christ in heaven
   By man is cursed alway!

The Lady in the White Dress, Whom I Helped Into the Omnibus

I know her not! Her hand has been in mine,
And the warm pressure of her taper arm
Has thrill'd upon my fingers, and the hem
Of her white dress has lain upon my feet,
Till my hush'd pulse, by the caressing folds,
Was kindled to a fever! I, to her,
Am but the undistinguishable leaf
Blown by upon the breeze—yet I have sat,
And in the blue depths of her stainless eyes,
(Close as a lover in his hour of bliss,
And steadfastly as look the twin stars down
Into unfathomable wells,) have gazed!
And I have felt from out its gate of pearl
Her warm breath on my cheek, and while she sat
Dreaming away the moments, I have tried
To count the long dark lashes in the fringe
Of her bewildering eyes! The kerchief sweet
That enviably visits her red lip
Has slumber'd, while she held it, on my knee,—
And her small foot has crept between mine own—
And yet, she knows me not!

                  Now, thanks to heaven
For blessings chainless in the rich man's keeping—
Wealth that the miser cannot hide away!
Buy, if they will, the invaluable flower—
They cannot store its fragrance from the breeze!
Wear, if they will, the costliest gem of Ind—
It pours its light on every passing eye!
And he who on this beauty sets his name—
Who dreams, perhaps, that for his use alone

Such loveliness was first of angels born—
Tell him, oh whisperer at his dreaming ear,
That I too, in her beauty, sun my eye,
And, unrebuked, may worship her in song—
Tell him that heaven, along our darkling way,
Hath set bright lamps with loveliness alight—
And all may in their guiding beams rejoice;
But he—as 'twere a watcher by a lamp—
Guards but this bright one's shining.

WILLIAM GILMORE SIMMS

(1806–1870)

The Lost Pleiad

I.

Not in the sky,
Where it was seen—
Nor, on the white tops of the glistering wave—
Nor in the mansions of the hidden deep—
However green,
In its enamell'd caves of mystery—
Shall the bright watcher have
A place—nor once again proud station keep!

II.

Gone, gone!
O! never more, to cheer
The mariner, who hold his course alone,
On the Atlantic, thro' the weary night,
When the waves turn to watchers, and do sleep—
Shall it appear—
With the sweet fixedness of certain light,
Shining upon the shut eye of the blue deep!

III.

O! when the shepherd on Chaldea's hills,
Watching his flocks;
Looks forth, in vain for thy first light to come,
Warning him home—
From his deep sleep, among the sky-kiss'd rocks—
How shall he wake, when dewy silence fills
The scene, to wonder at the weight of night,
Without the one strong beam, whose blessed light,
As to the wandering child, his native rills,
Was natural to his sight!

IV.

Vain, vain!
O! less than vain, shall he look forth—
The sailor from his barque—
(Howe'er the North,
Doth raise his certain lamp, when tempests lower)
To catch the light of the lost star again—
The weary hour,
To him, shall be more weary, when the dark
Displays not the lost planet on her tower.

V.

And lone
Where its first splendor, shone—
Shall be that pleasant company of stars:—
How should they know that death,
The happy glory of the immortal, mars,
When like the Earth, and all its common breath,
Extinguish'd are the pure beams of the sky,
Fallen from on high—
And their concerted springs of harmony
Snapt rudely, and all pleasant music, gone.

VI.

A strain—a mellow strain,
Of parting music, fill'd the earth and sky—
The stars lamenting, in unborrowed pain,
That one of the selectest one's, must die—
The brightest of their train!
Alas! it is the destiny—
The dearest hope is that which first is lost,
The tenderest flower is soonest nipt by frost—
Are not the shortest-lived, the loveliest—
And like the wandering orb that leaves the sky,
Look they not brightest, when about to fly,
The desolate spot they blest?

By the Swanannoa

Is it not lovely, while the day flows on
　　Like some unnoticed water through the vale,
　　Sun-sprinkled,—and, across the fields, a gale,
　　Ausonian, murmurs out an idle tale,
Of groves deserted late, but lately won.
How calm the silent mountains, that, around,
　　Bend their blue summits, as if grouped to hear
Some high ambassador from foreign ground,—
To hearken, and, most probably confound!
　　While, leaping onward, with a voice of cheer,
Glad as some schoolboy ever on the bound,
　　The lively Swanannoa sparkles near;—
A flash and murmur mark him as he roves,
Now foaming white o'er rocks, now glimpsing soft
　　　　through groves.

HENRY WADSWORTH LONGFELLOW

(1807–1882)

The Spirit of Poetry

There is a quiet spirit in these woods,
That dwells where'er the gentle south wind blows,
Where, underneath the white-thorn, in the glade,
The wild flowers bloom, or, kissing the soft air,
The leaves above their sunny palms outspread.
With what a tender and impassioned voice
It fills the nice and delicate ear of thought,
When the fast-ushering star of morning comes
O'er-riding the gray hills with golden scarf;
Or when the cowled and dusky-sandaled Eve,
In mourning weeds, from out the western gate,
Departs with silent pace! That spirit moves
In the green valley, where the silver brook,
From its full laver, pours the white cascade;
And, babbling low amid the tangled woods,
Slips down through moss-grown stones with endless laughter.
And frequent, on the everlasting hills,
Its feet go forth, when it doth wrap itself
In all the dark embroidery of the storm,
And shouts the stern, strong wind. And here, amid
The silent majesty of these deep woods,
Its presence shall uplift thy thoughts from earth,
As to the sunshine, and the pure bright air,
Their tops the green trees lift. Hence gifted bards
Have ever loved the calm and quiet shades.
For them there was an eloquent voice in all
The sylvan pomp of woods, the golden sun,
The flowers, the leaves, the river on its way,
Blue skies, and silver clouds, and gentle winds,—
The swelling upland, where the sidelong sun
Aslant the wooded slope, at evening, goes,—

Groves, through whose broken roof the sky looks in,
Mountain, and shattered cliff, and sunny vale,
The distant lake, fountains,—and mighty trees,
In many a lazy syllable, repeating
Their old poetic legends to the wind.

   And this is the sweet spirit, that doth fill
The world; and, in these wayward days of youth,
My busy fancy oft embodies it,
As a bright image of the light and beauty
That dwell in nature,—of the heavenly forms
We worship in our dreams, and the soft hues
That stain the wild bird's wing, and flush the clouds
When the sun sets. Within her eye
The heaven of April, with its changing light,
And when it wears the blue of May, is hung,
And on her lip the rich, red rose. Her hair
Is like the summer tresses of the trees,
When twilight makes them brown, and on her cheek
Blushes the richness of an autumn sky,
With ever-shifting beauty. Then her breath,
It is so like the gentle air of Spring,
As, from the morning's dewy flowers, it comes
Full of their fragrance, that it is a joy
To have it round us,—and her silver voice
Is the rich music of a summer bird,
Heard in the still night, with its passionate cadence.

A Psalm of Life

What the Heart of the Young Man Said to the Psalmist

   Tell me not, in mournful numbers,
     Life is but an empty dream!
  For the soul is dead that slumbers,
     And things are not what they seem.

Life is real! Life is earnest!
　　And the grave is not its goal;
Dust thou art, to dust returnest,
　　Was not spoken of the soul.

Not enjoyment, and not sorrow,
　　Is our destined end or way;
But to act, that each to-morrow
　　Find us farther than to-day.

Art is long, and Time is fleeting,
　　And our hearts, though stout and brave,
Still, like muffled drums, are beating
　　Funeral marches to the grave.

In the world's broad field of battle,
　　In the bivouac of Life,
Be not like dumb, driven cattle!
　　Be a hero in the strife!

Trust no Future, howe'er pleasant!
　　Let the dead Past bury its dead!
Act,—act in the living Present!
　　Heart within, and God o'erhead!

Lives of great men all remind us
　　We can make our lives sublime,
And, departing, leave behind us
　　Footprints on the sands of time;

Footprints, that perhaps another,
　　Sailing o'er life's solemn main,
A forlorn and shipwrecked brother,
　　Seeing, shall take heart again.

Let us, then, be up and doing,
　　With a heart for any fate;
Still achieving, still pursuing,
　　Learn to labor and to wait.

Hymn to the Night

’Ασπασίη, τρίλλιστος.

I heard the trailing garments of the Night
    Sweep through her marble halls!
I saw her sable skirts all fringed with light
    From the celestial walls!

I felt her presence, by its spell of might,
    Stoop o’er me from above;
The calm, majestic presence of the Night,
    As of the one I love.

I heard the sounds of sorrow and delight,
    The manifold, soft chimes,
That fill the haunted chambers of the Night,
    Like some old poet’s rhymes.

From the cool cisterns of the midnight air
    My spirit drank repose;
The fountain of perpetual peace flows there,—
    From those deep cisterns flows.

O holy Night! from thee I learn to bear
    What man has borne before!
Thou layest thy finger on the lips of Care,
    And they complain no more.

Peace! Peace! Orestes-like I breathe this prayer!
    Descend with broad-winged flight,
The welcome! the thrice-prayed for! the most fair!
    The best-beloved Night!

The Wreck of the Hesperus

It was the schooner Hesperus,
  That sailed the wintry sea;
And the skipper had taken his little daughtèr,
  To bear him company.

Blue were her eyes as the fairy-flax,
  Her cheeks like the dawn of day,
And her bosom white as the hawthorn buds,
  That ope in the month of May.

The skipper he stood beside the helm,
  His pipe was in his mouth,
And he watched how the veering flaw did blow
  The smoke now West, now South.

Then up and spake an old Sailòr,
  Had sailed the Spanish Main,
"I pray thee, put into yonder port,
  For I fear a hurricane.

"Last night, the moon had a golden ring,
  And to-night no moon we see!"
The skipper, he blew a whiff from his pipe,
  And a scornful laugh laughed he.

Colder and louder blew the wind,
  A gale from the Northeast;
The snow fell hissing in the brine,
  And the billows frothed like yeast.

Down came the storm, and smote amain,
  The vessel in its strength;
She shuddered and paused, like a frighted steed,
  Then leaped her cable's length.

"Come hither! come hither! my little daughtèr,
  And do not tremble so;
For I can weather the roughest gale,
  That ever wind did blow."

He wrapped her warm in his seaman's coat
    Against the stinging blast;
He cut a rope from a broken spar,
    And bound her to the mast.

"O father! I hear the church-bells ring,
    O say, what may it be?"
" 'T is a fog-bell on a rock-bound coast!"—
    And he steered for the open sea.

"O father! I hear the sound of guns,
    O say, what may it be?"
"Some ship in distress, that cannot live
    In such an angry sea!"

"O father! I see a gleaming light,
    O say, what may it be?"
But the father answered never a word,
    A frozen corpse was he.

Lashed to the helm, all stiff and stark,
    With his face turned to the skies,
The lantern gleamed through the gleaming snow
    On his fixed and glassy eyes.

Then the maiden clasped her hands and prayed
    That savèd she might be;
And she thought of Christ, who stilled the wave
    On the Lake of Galilee.

And fast through the midnight dark and drear,
    Through the whistling sleet and snow,
Like a sheeted ghost, the vessel swept
    Towards the reef of Norman's Woe.

And ever the fitful gusts between
    A sound came from the land;
It was the sound of the trampling surf,
    On the rocks and the hard sea-sand.

The breakers were right beneath her bows,
　　She drifted a dreary wreck,
And a whooping billow swept the crew
　　Like icicles from her deck.

She struck where the white and fleecy waves
　　Looked soft as carded wool,
But the cruel rocks, they gored her side
　　Like the horns of an angry bull.

Her rattling shrouds, all sheathed in ice,
　　With the masts went by the board;
Like a vessel of glass, she stove and sank,
　　Ho! ho! the breakers roared!

At daybreak, on the bleak sea-beach,
　　A fisherman stood aghast,
To see the form of a maiden fair,
　　Lashed close to a drifting mast.

The salt-sea was frozen on her breast,
　　The salt tears in her eyes;
And he saw her hair, like the brown sea-weed,
　　On the billows fall and rise.

Such was the wreck of the Hesperus,
　　In the midnight and the snow!
Christ save us all from a death like this,
　　On the reef of Norman's Woe!

The Village Blacksmith

Under a spreading chestnut tree
　　The village smithy stands;
The smith, a mighty man is he,
　　With large and sinewy hands;
And the muscles of his brawny arms
　　Are strong as iron bands.

His hair is crisp, and black, and long,
  His face is like the tan;
His brow is wet with honest sweat,
  He earns whate'er he can,
And looks the whole world in the face,
  For he owes not any man.

Week in, week out, from morn till night,
  You can hear his bellows blow;
You can hear him swing his heavy sledge,
  With measured beat and slow,
Like a sexton ringing the village bell,
  When the evening sun is low.

And children coming home from school
  Look in at the open door;
They love to see the flaming forge,
  And hear the bellows roar,
And catch the burning sparks that fly
  Like chaff from a threshing floor.

He goes on Sunday to the church,
  And sits among his boys;
He hears the parson pray and preach,
  He hears his daughter's voice,
Singing in the village choir,
  And it makes his heart rejoice.

It sounds to him like her mother's voice,
  Singing in Paradise!
He needs must think of her once more,
  How in the grave she lies;
And with his hard, rough hand he wipes
  A tear out of his eyes.

Toiling,—rejoicing,—sorrowing,
  Onward through life he goes;
Each morning sees some task begin,
  Each evening sees it close;
Something attempted, something done,
  Has earned a night's repose.

Thanks, thanks to thee, my worthy friend,
    For the lesson thou hast taught!
Thus at the flaming forge of life
    Our fortunes must be wrought;
Thus on its sounding anvil shaped
    Each burning deed and thought!

Mezzo Cammin

Boppard on the Rhine. August 25, 1842.

Half of my life is gone, and I have let
    The years slip from me and have not fulfilled
    The aspiration of my youth, to build
    Some tower of song with lofty parapet.
Not indolence, nor pleasure, nor the fret
    Of restless passions that would not be stilled,
    But sorrow, and a care that almost killed,
    Kept me from what I may accomplish yet;
Though, half-way up the hill, I see the Past
    Lying beneath me with its sounds and sights,—
    A city in the twilight dim and vast,
With smoking roofs, soft bells, and gleaming lights,—
    And hear above me on the autumnal blast
    The cataract of Death far thundering from the heights.

The Day Is Done

The day is done, and the darkness
    Falls from the wings of Night,
As a feather is wafted downward
    From an eagle in his flight.

I see the lights of the village
    Gleam through the rain and the mist,
And a feeling of sadness comes o'er me,
    That my soul cannot resist:

A feeling of sadness and longing,
　　That is not akin to pain,
And resembles sorrow only
　　As the mist resembles the rain.

Come, read to me some poem,
　　Some simple and heartfelt lay,
That shall soothe this restless feeling,
　　And banish the thoughts of day.

Not from the grand old masters,
　　Not from the bards sublime,
Whose distant footsteps echo
　　Through the corridors of Time.

For, like strains of martial music,
　　Their mighty thoughts suggest
Life's endless toil and endeavour;
　　And to-night I long for rest.

Read from some humbler poet,
　　Whose songs gushed from his heart,
As showers from the clouds of summer,
　　Or tears from the eyelids start;

Who, through long days of labor,
　　And nights devoid of ease,
Still heard in his soul the music
　　Of wonderful melodies.

Such songs have power to quiet
　　The restless pulse of care,
And come like the benediction
　　That follows after prayer.

Then read from the treasured volume
　　The poem of thy choice,
And lend to the rhyme of the poet
　　The beauty of thy voice.

And the night shall be filled with music,
   And the cares, that infest the day,
Shall fold their tents, like the Arabs,
   And as silently steal away.

Seaweed

When descends on the Atlantic
   The gigantic
Storm-wind of the equinox,
Landward in his wrath he scourges
   The toiling surges,
Laden with seaweed from the rocks:

From Bermuda's reefs; from edges
   Of sunken ledges,
In some far-off, bright Azore;
From Bahama, and the dashing,
   Silver-flashing
Surges of San Salvador;

From the tumbling surf, that buries
   The Orkneyan skerries,
Answering the hoarse Hebrides;
And from wrecks of ships, and drifting
   Spars, uplifting
On the desolate, rainy seas;—

Ever drifting, drifting, drifting
   On the shifting
Currents of the restless main;
Till in sheltered coves, and reaches
   Of sandy beaches,
All have found repose again.

So when storms of wild emotion
   Strike the ocean
Of the poet's soul, ere long

From each cave and rocky fastness,
　　In its vastness,
Floats some fragment of a song:

From the far-off isles enchanted,
　　Heaven has planted
With the golden fruit of Truth;
From the flashing surf whose vision
　　Gleams Elysian
In the tropic clime of Youth;

From the strong Will, and the Endeavour
　　That for ever
Wrestles with the tides of Fate;
From the wreck of Hopes far-scattered,
　　Tempest-shattered,
Floating waste and desolate;—

Ever drifting, drifting, drifting
　　On the shifting
Currents of the restless heart;
Till at length in books recorded,
　　They, like hoarded
Household words, no more depart.

Couplet: February 24, 1847

In Hexameter sings serenely a Harvard Professor;
In Pentameter him damns censorious Poe.

Fragment: December 18, 1847

Soft through the silent air descend the feathery snow-flakes;
White are the distant hills, white are the neighboring fields;
Only the marshes are brown, and the river rolling among
　　them
Weareth the leaden hue seen in the eyes of the blind.

The Fire of Drift-Wood

We sat within the farm-house old,
    Whose windows, looking o'er the bay,
Gave to the sea-breeze, damp and cold,
    An easy entrance, night and day.

Not far away we saw the port,—
    The strange, old-fashioned, silent town,—
The light-house,—the dismantled fort,—
    The wooden houses, quaint and brown.

We sat and talked until the night,
    Descending, filled the little room;
Our faces faded from the sight,
    Our voices only broke the gloom.

We spake of many a vanished scene,
    Of what we once had thought and said,
Of what had been, and might have been,
    And who was changed, and who was dead;

And all that fills the hearts of friends,
    When first they feel, with secret pain,
Their lives thenceforth have separate ends,
    And never can be one again;

The first slight swerving of the heart,
    That words are powerless to express,
And leave it still unsaid in part,
    Or say it in too great excess.

The very tones in which we spake
    Had something strange, I could but mark;
The leaves of memory seemed to make
    A mournful rustling in the dark.

Oft died the words upon our lips,
    As suddenly, from out the fire
Built of the wreck of stranded ships,
    The flames would leap and then expire.

And, as their splendor flashed and failed,
    We thought of wrecks upon the main,—
Of ships dismasted, that were hailed
    And sent no answer back again.

The windows, rattling in their frames,—
    The ocean, roaring up the beach,—
The gusty blast,—the bickering flames,—
    All mingled vaguely in our speech;

Until they made themselves a part
    Of fancies floating through the brain,—
The long-lost ventures of the heart,
    That send no answers back again.

O flames that glowed! O hearts that yearned!
    They were indeed too much akin,
The drift-wood fire without that burned,
    The thoughts that burned and glowed within.

from *Evangeline*

This is the forest primeval. The murmuring pines and the
    hemlocks,
Bearded with moss, and in garments green, indistinct in the
    twilight,
Stand like Druids of eld, with voices sad and prophetic,
Stand like harpers hoar, with beards that rest on their
    bosoms.
Loud from its rocky caverns, the deep-voiced neighbouring
    ocean
Speaks, and in accents disconsolate answers the wail of the
    forest.

This is the forest primeval; but where are the hearts that
    beneath it
Leaped like the roe, when he hears in the woodland the
    voice of the huntsman?

Where is the thatch-roofed village, the home of Acadian
    farmers,—
Men whose lives glided on like rivers that water the
    woodlands,
Darkened by shadows of earth, but reflecting an image of
    heaven?
Waste are those pleasant farms, and the farmers forever
    departed!
Scattered like dust and leaves, when the mighty blasts of
    October
Seize them, and whirl them aloft, and sprinkle them far
    o'er the ocean.
Naught but tradition remains of the beautiful village
    of Grand-Pré.

lines 1–15

The Jewish Cemetery at Newport

How strange it seems! These Hebrews in their graves,
    Close by the street of this fair seaport town,
Silent beside the never-silent waves,
    At rest in all this moving up and down!

The trees are white with dust, that o'er their sleep
    Wave their broad curtains in the south-wind's breath,
While underneath such leafy tents they keep
    The long, mysterious Exodus of Death.

And these sepulchral stones, so old and brown,
    That pave with level flags their burial-place,
Seem like the tablets of the Law, thrown down
    And broken by Moses at the mountain's base.

The very names recorded here are strange,
    Of foreign accent, and of different climes;
Alvares and Rivera interchange
    With Abraham and Jacob of old times.

"Blessed be God! for he created Death!"
   The mourners said, "and Death is rest and peace";
Then added, in the certainty of faith,
   "And giveth Life that never more shall cease."

Closed are the portals of their Synagogue,
   No Psalms of David now the silence break,
No Rabbi reads the ancient Decalogue
   In the grand dialect the Prophets spake.

Gone are the living, but the dead remain,
   And not neglected; for a hand unseen,
Scattering its bounty, like a summer rain,
   Still keeps their graves and their remembrance green.

How came they here? What burst of Christian hate,
   What persecution, merciless and blind,
Drove o'er the sea—that desert desolate—
   These Ishmaels and Hagars of mankind?

They lived in narrow streets and lanes obscure,
   Ghetto and Judenstrass, in mirk and mire;
Taught in the school of patience to endure
   The life of anguish and the death of fire.

All their lives long, with the unleavened bread
   And bitter herbs of exile and its fears,
The wasting famine of the heart they fed,
   And slaked its thirst with marah of their tears.

Anathema maranatha! was the cry
   That rang from town to town, from street to street;
At every gate the accursed Mordecai
   Was mocked and jeered, and spurned by Christian feet.

Pride and humiliation hand in hand
   Walked with them through the world where'er they went;
Trampled and beaten were they as the sand,
   And yet unshaken as the continent.

For in the background figures vague and vast
　　Of patriarchs and of prophets rose sublime,
And all the great traditions of the Past
　　They saw reflected in the coming time.

And thus for ever with reverted look
　　The mystic volume of the world they read,
Spelling it backward, like a Hebrew book,
　　Till life became a Legend of the Dead.

But ah! what once has been shall be no more!
　　The groaning earth in travail and in pain
Brings forth its races, but does not restore,
　　And the dead nations never rise again.

from *The Song of Hiawatha*

from XXII: HIAWATHA'S DEPARTURE

　　Heavy with the heat and silence
Grew the afternoon of Summer;
With a drowsy sound the forest
Whispered round the sultry wigwam,
With a sound of sleep the water
Rippled on the beach below it;
From the corn-fields shrill and ceaseless
Sang the grasshopper, Pah-puk-keena;
And the guests of Hiawatha,
Weary with the heat of Summer,
Slumbered in the sultry wigwam.
　　Slowly o'er the simmering landscape
Fell the evening's dusk and coolness,
And the long and level sunbeams
Shot their spears into the forest,
Breaking through its shields of shadow,
Rushed into each secret ambush,
Searched each thicket, dingle, hollow;
Still the guests of Hiawatha
Slumbered in the silent wigwam.

From his place rose Hiawatha,
Bade farewell to old Nokomis,
Spake in whispers, spake in this wise,
Did not wake the guests, that slumbered:
"I am going, O Nokomis,
On a long and distant journey,
To the portals of the Sunset,
To the regions of the home-wind,
Of the Northwest wind, Keewaydin.
But these guests I leave behind me,
In your watch and ward I leave them;
See that never harm comes near them,
See that never fear molests them,
Never danger nor suspicion,
Never want of food or shelter,
In the lodge of Hiawatha!"

Forth into the village went he,
Bade farewell to all the warriors,
Bade farewell to all the young men,
Spake persuading, spake in this wise:
"I am going, O my people,
On a long and distant journey;
Many moons and many winters
Will have come, and will have vanished,
Ere I come again to see you.
But my guests I leave behind me;
Listen to their words of wisdom,
Listen to the truth they tell you,
For the Master of Life has sent them
From the land of light and morning!"

On the shore stood Hiawatha,
Turned and waved his hand at parting;
On the clear and luminous water
Launched his birch canoe for sailing,
From the pebbles of the margin
Shoved it forth into the water;
Whispered to it, "Westward! westward!"
And with speed it darted forward.

And the evening sun descending
Set the clouds on fire with redness,

Burned the broad sky, like a prairie,
Left upon the level water
One long track and trail of splendor,
Down whose stream, as down a river,
Westward, westward Hiawatha
Sailed into the fiery sunset,
Sailed into the purple vapors,
Sailed into the dusk of evening.
    And the people from the margin
Watched him floating, rising, sinking,
Till the birch canoe seemed lifted
High into that sea of splendor,
Till it sank into the vapors
Like the new moon slowly, slowly
Sinking in the purple distance.
    And they said, "Farewell for ever!"
Said, "Farewell, O Hiawatha!"
And the forests, dark and lonely,
Moved through all their depths of darkness,
Sighed, "Farewell, O Hiawatha!"
And the waves upon the margin
Rising, rippling on the pebbles,
Sobbed, "Farewell, O Hiawatha!"
And the heron, the Shuh-shuh-gah,
From her haunts among the fen-lands,
Screamed, "Farewell, O Hiawatha!"
    Thus departed Hiawatha,
Hiawatha the Beloved,
In the glory of the sunset,
In the purple mists of evening,
To the regions of the home-wind,
Of the Northwest wind Keewaydin,
To the Islands of the Blessed,
To the kingdom of Ponemah,
To the land of the Hereafter!

My Lost Youth

Often I think of the beautiful town
　　That is seated by the sea;
Often in thought go up and down
The pleasant streets of that dear old town,
　　And my youth comes back to me.
　　　　And a verse of a Lapland song
　　　　Is haunting my memory still:
　　"A boy's will is the wind's will,
And the thoughts of youth are long, long thoughts."

I can see the shadowy lines of its trees,
　　And catch, in sudden gleams,
The sheen of the far-surrounding seas,
And islands that were the Hesperides
　　Of all my boyish dreams.
　　　　And the burden of that old song,
　　　　It murmurs and whispers still:
　　"A boy's will is the wind's will,
And the thoughts of youth are long, long thoughts."

I remember the black wharves and the slips,
　　And the sea-tides tossing free;
And Spanish sailors with bearded lips,
And the beauty and mystery of the ships,
　　And the magic of the sea.
　　　　And the voice of that wayward song
　　　　Is singing and saying still:
　　"A boy's will is the wind's will,
And the thoughts of youth are long, long thoughts."

I remember the bulwarks by the shore,
　　And the fort upon the hill;
The sun-rise gun, with its hollow roar,
The drum-beat repeated o'er and o'er,
　　And the bugle wild and shrill.
　　　　And the music of that old song
　　　　Throbs in my memory still:
　　"A boy's will is the wind's will,
And the thoughts of youth are long, long thoughts."

I remember the sea-fight far away,
    How it thundered o'er the tide!
And the dead captains, as they lay
In their graves, o'erlooking the tranquil bay,
    Where they in battle died.
        And the sound of that mournful song
        Goes through me with a thrill:
    "A boy's will is the wind's will,
And the thoughts of youth are long, long thoughts."

I can see the breezy dome of groves,
    The shadows of Deering's Woods;
And the friendships old and the early loves
Come back with a sabbath sound, as of doves
    In quiet neighborhoods.
        And the verse of that sweet old song,
        It flutters and murmurs still:
    "A boy's will is the wind's will,
And the thoughts of youth are long, long thoughts."

I remember the gleams and glooms that dart
    Across the schoolboy's brain;
The song and the silence in the heart,
That in part are prophecies, and in part
    Are longings wild and vain.
        And the voice of that fitful song
        Sings on, and is never still:
    "A boy's will is the wind's will,
And the thoughts of youth are long, long thoughts."

There are things of which I may not speak;
    There are dreams that cannot die;
There are thoughts that make the strong heart weak,
And bring a pallor into the cheek,
    And a mist before the eye.
        And the words of that fatal song
        Come over me like a chill:
    "A boy's will is the wind's will,
And the thoughts of youth are long, long thoughts."

Strange to me now are the forms I meet
　　When I visit the dear old town;
But the native air is pure and sweet,
And the trees that o'ershadow each well-known
　　　　street,
　　As they balance up and down,
　　　Are singing the beautiful song,
　　Are sighing and whispering still:
　"A boy's will is the wind's will,
And the thoughts of youth are long, long thoughts."

And Deering's Woods are fresh and fair,
　　And with joy that is almost pain
My heart goes back to wander there,
And among the dreams of the days that were,
　　I find my lost youth again.
　　　And the strange and beautiful song,
　　The groves are repeating it still:
　"A boy's will is the wind's will,
And the thoughts of youth are long, long thoughts."

The Children's Hour

　Between the dark and the daylight,
　　When the night is beginning to lower,
　Comes a pause in the day's occupations,
　　That is known as the Children's Hour.

　I hear in the chamber above me
　　The patter of little feet,
　The sound of a door that is opened,
　　And voices soft and sweet.

　From my study I see in the lamplight,
　　Descending the broad hall stair,
　Grave Alice, and laughing Allegra,
　　And Edith with golden hair.

A whisper, and then a silence:
    Yet I know by their merry eyes
They are plotting and planning together
    To take me by surprise.

A sudden rush from the stairway,
    A sudden raid from the hall!
By three doors left unguarded
    They enter my castle wall!

They climb up into my turret
    O'er the arms and back of my chair;
If I try to escape, they surround me;
    They seem to be everywhere.

They almost devour me with kisses,
    Their arms about me entwine,
Till I think of the Bishop of Bingen
    In his Mouse-Tower on the Rhine!

Do you think, O blue-eyed banditti,
    Because you have scaled the wall,
Such an old moustache as I am
    Is not a match for you all!

I have you fast in my fortress,
    And will not let you depart,
But put you down into the dungeon
    In the round-tower of my heart.

And there will I keep you forever,
    Yes, forever and a day,
Till the walls shall crumble to ruin,
    And moulder in dust away!

from *Tales of a Wayside Inn*

The Landlord's Tale: Paul Revere's Ride

Listen, my children, and you shall hear
Of the midnight ride of Paul Revere,
On the eighteenth of April, in Seventy-five;
Hardly a man is now alive
Who remembers that famous day and year.

He said to his friend, "If the British march
By land or sea from the town to-night,
Hang a lantern aloft in the belfry arch
Of the North Church tower as a signal light,—
One, if by land, and two, if by sea;
And I on the opposite shore will be,
Ready to ride and spread the alarm
Through every Middlesex village and farm,
For the country-folk to be up and to arm."

Then he said, "Good night!" and with muffled oar
Silently rowed to the Charlestown shore,
Just as the moon rose over the bay,
Where swinging wide at her moorings lay
The Somerset, British man-of-war;
A phantom ship, with each mast and spar
Across the moon like a prison bar,
And a huge black hulk, that was magnified
By its own reflection in the tide.

Meanwhile, his friend, through alley and street,
Wanders and watches with eager ears,
Till in the silence around him he hears
The muster of men at the barrack door,
The sound of arms, and the tramp of feet,
And the measured tread of the grenadiers,
Marching down to their boats on the shore.

Then he climbed the tower of the Old North Church,
By the wooden stairs, with stealthy tread,
To the belfry-chamber overhead,
And startled the pigeons from their perch
On the sombre rafters, that round him made
Masses and moving shapes of shade, —
By the trembling ladder, steep and tall,
To the highest window in the wall,
Where he paused to listen and look down
A moment on the roofs of the town,
And the moonlight flowing over all.

Beneath, in the churchyard, lay the dead,
In their night-encampment on the hill,
Wrapped in silence so deep and still
That he could hear, like a sentinel's tread,
The watchful night-wind, as it went
Creeping along from tent to tent,
And seeming to whisper, "All is well!"
A moment only he feels the spell
Of the place and the hour, and the secret dread
Of the lonely belfry and the dead;
For suddenly all his thoughts are bent
On a shadowy something far away,
Where the river widens to meet the bay, —
A line of black that bends and floats
On the rising tide, like a bridge of boats.

Meanwhile, impatient to mount and ride,
Booted and spurred, with a heavy stride
On the opposite shore walked Paul Revere.
Now he patted his horse's side,
Now gazed at the landscape far and near,
Then, impetuous, stamped the earth,
And turned and tightened his saddle-girth;
But mostly he watched with eager search
The belfry-tower of the Old North Church,
As it rose above the graves on the hill,
Lonely and spectral and sombre and still.
And lo! as he looks, on the belfry's height

A glimmer, and then a gleam of light!
He springs to the saddle, the bridle he turns,
But lingers and gazes, till full on his sight
A second lamp in the belfry burns!

A hurry of hoofs in a village street,
A shape in the moonlight, a bulk in the dark,
And beneath, from the pebbles, in passing, a spark
Struck out by a steed flying fearless and fleet:
That was all! And yet, through the gloom and the light,
The fate of a nation was riding that night;
And the spark struck out by that steed, in his flight,
Kindled the land into flame with its heat.

He has left the village and mounted the steep,
And beneath him, tranquil and broad and deep,
Is the Mystic, meeting the ocean tides;
And under the alders, that skirt its edge,
Now soft on the sand, now loud on the ledge,
Is heard the tramp of his steed as he rides.

It was twelve by the village clock
When he crossed the bridge into Medford town.
He heard the crowing of the cock,
And the barking of the farmer's dog,
And felt the damp of the river fog,
That rises after the sun goes down.

It was one by the village clock,
When he galloped into Lexington.
He saw the gilded weathercock
Swim in the moonlight as he passed,
And the meeting-house windows, blank and bare,
Gaze at him with a spectral glare,
As if they already stood aghast
At the bloody work they would look upon.

It was two by the village clock,
When he came to the bridge in Concord town.
He heard the bleating of the flock,

And the twitter of birds among the trees,
And felt the breath of the morning breeze
Blowing over the meadows brown.
And one was safe and asleep in his bed
Who at the bridge would be first to fall,
Who that day would be lying dead,
Pierced by a British musket-ball.

You know the rest. In the books you have read,
How the British Regulars fired and fled,—
How the farmers gave them ball for ball,
From behind each fence and farm-yard wall,
Chasing the red-coats down the lane,
Then crossing the fields to emerge again
Under the trees at the turn of the road,
And only pausing to fire and load.

So through the night rode Paul Revere;
And so through the night went his cry of alarm
To every Middlesex village and farm,—
A cry of defiance and not of fear,
A voice in the darkness, a knock at the door,
And a word that shall echo forevermore!
For, borne on the night-wind of the Past,
Through all our history, to the last,
In the hour of darkness and peril and need,
The people will waken and listen to hear
The hurrying hoof-beats of that steed,
And the midnight message of Paul Revere.

Snow-Flakes

Out of the bosom of the Air,
    Out of the cloud-folds of her garments shaken,
Over the woodlands brown and bare
    Over the harvest-fields forsaken,
        Silent, and soft, and slow
        Descends the snow.

Even as our cloudy fancies take
   Suddenly shape in some divine expression,
Even as the troubled heart doth make
   In the white countenance confession,
     The troubled sky reveals
     The grief it feels.

This is the poem of the air,
   Slowly in silent syllables recorded;
This is the secret of despair,
   Long in its cloudy bosom hoarded,
     Now whispered and revealed
     To wood and field.

Divina Commedia

I.

Oft have I seen at some cathedral door
   A laborer, pausing in the dust and heat,
   Lay down his burden, and with reverent feet
   Enter, and cross himself, and on the floor
Kneel to repeat his paternoster o'er;
   Far off the noises of the world retreat;
   The loud vociferations of the street
   Become an undistinguishable roar.
So, as I enter here from day to day,
   And leave my burden at this minster gate,
   Kneeling in prayer, and not ashamed to pray,
The tumult of the time disconsolate
   To inarticulate murmurs dies away,
   While the eternal ages watch and wait.

II.

How strange the sculptures that adorn these towers!
   This crowd of statues, in whose folded sleeves
   Birds build their nests; while canopied with leaves
   Parvis and portal bloom like trellised bowers,
And the vast minster seems a cross of flowers!

But fiends and dragons on the gargoyled eaves
   Watch the dead Christ between the living thieves,
   And, underneath, the traitor Judas lowers!
Ah! from what agonies of heart and brain,
   What exultations trampling on despair,
   What tenderness, what tears, what hate of wrong,
What passionate outcry of a soul in pain,
   Uprose this poem of the earth and air,
   This mediæval miracle of song!

III.

I enter, and I see thee in the gloom
   Of the long aisles, O poet saturnine!
   And strive to make my steps keep pace with thine.
   The air is filled with some unknown perfume;
The congregation of the dead make room
   For thee to pass; the votive tapers shine;
   Like rooks that haunt Ravenna's groves of pine
   The hovering echoes fly from tomb to tomb.
From the confessionals I hear arise
   Rehearsals of forgotten tragedies,
   And lamentations from the crypts below;
And then a voice celestial, that begins
   With the pathetic words, "Although your sins
   As scarlet be," and ends with "as the snow."

IV.

With snow-white veil and garments as of flame,
   She stands before thee, who so long ago
   Filled thy young heart with passion and the woe
   From which thy song and all its splendors came;
And while with stern rebuke she speaks thy name,
   The ice about thy heart melts as the snow
   On mountain heights, and in swift overflow
   Comes gushing from thy lips in sobs of shame.
Thou makest full confession; and a gleam,
   As of the dawn on some dark forest cast,
   Seems on thy lifted forehead to increase;
Lethe and Eunoe—the remembered dream
   And the forgotten sorrow—bring at last
   That perfect pardon which is perfect peace.

V.

I lift mine eyes, and all the windows blaze
   With forms of saints and holy men who died,
   Here martyred and hereafter glorified;
   And the great Rose upon its leaves displays
Christ's Triumph, and the angelic roundelays,
   With splendor upon splendor multiplied;
   And Beatrice again at Dante's side
   No more rebukes, but smiles her words of praise.
And then the organ sounds, and unseen choirs
   Sing the old Latin hymns of peace and love,
   And benedictions of the Holy Ghost;
And the melodious bells among the spires
   O'er all the house-tops and through heaven above
   Proclaim the elevation of the Host!

VI.

O star of morning and of liberty!
   O bringer of the light, whose splendor shines
   Above the darkness of the Apennines,
   Forerunner of the day that is to be!
The voices of the city and the sea,
   The voices of the mountains and the pines,
   Repeat thy song, till the familiar lines
   Are footpaths for the thought of Italy!
Thy fame is blown abroad from all the heights,
   Through all the nations, and a sound is heard,
   As of a mighty wind, and men devout,
Strangers of Rome, and the new proselytes,
   In their own language hear thy wondrous word,
   And many are amazed and many doubt.

Belisarius

I am poor and old and blind;
The sun burns me, and the wind
    Blows through the city gate
And covers me with dust
From the wheels of the august
    Justinian the Great.

It was for him I chased
The Persians o'er wild and waste,
    As General of the East;
Night after night I lay
In their camps of yesterday;
    Their forage was my feast.

For him, with sails of red,
And torches at mast-head,
    Piloting the great fleet,
I swept the Afric coasts
And scattered the Vandal hosts,
    Like dust in a windy street.

For him I won again
The Ausonian realm and reign,
    Rome and Parthenope;
And all the land was mine
From the summits of Apennine
    To the shores of either sea.

For him, in my feeble age,
I dared the battle's rage,
    To save Byzantium's state,
When the tents of Zabergan,
Like snow-drifts overran
    The road to the Golden Gate.

And for this, for this, behold!
Infirm and blind and old,
    With gray, uncovered head,
Beneath the very arch
Of my triumphal march,
    I stand and beg my bread!

Methinks I still can hear,
Sounding distinct and near,
   The Vandal monarch's cry,
As, captive and disgraced,
With majestic step he paced,—
   "All, all is Vanity!"

Ah! vainest of all things
Is the gratitude of kings;
   The plaudits of the crowd
Are but the clatter of feet
At midnight in the street,
   Hollow and restless and loud.

But the bitterest disgrace
Is to see forever the face
   Of the Monk of Ephesus!
The unconquerable will
This, too, can bear;--I still
   Am Belisarius!

Chaucer

An old man in a lodge within a park;
  The chamber walls depicted all around
   With portraitures of huntsman, hawk, and hound,
   And the hurt deer. He listeneth to the lark,
Whose song comes with the sunshine through the dark
  Of painted glass in leaden lattice bound;
   He listeneth and he laugheth at the sound,
   Then writeth in a book like any clerk.
He is the poet of the dawn, who wrote
  The Canterbury Tales, and his old age
   Made beautiful with song; and as I read
I hear the crowing cock, I hear the note
  Of lark and linnet, and from every page
   Rise odors of ploughed field or flowery mead.

Choruses from *Kéramos*

Turn, turn, my wheel! Turn round and round
Without a pause, without a sound:
    So spins the flying world away!
This clay, well mixed with marl and sand,
Follows the motion of my hand;
For some must follow, and some command,
    Though all are made of clay!

Turn, turn, my wheel! All things must change
To something new, to something strange;
    Nothing that is can pause or stay;
The moon will wax, the moon will wane,
The mist and cloud will turn to rain,
The rain to mist and cloud again,
    To-morrow be to-day.

Turn, turn, my wheel! All life is brief;
What now is bud will soon be leaf,
    What now is leaf will soon decay;
The wind blows east, the wind blows west;
The blue eggs in the robin's nest
Will soon have wings and beak and breast,
    And flutter and fly away.

Turn, turn, my wheel! This earthen jar
A touch can make, a touch can mar;
    And shall it to the Potter say,
What makest thou? Thou hast no hand?
As men who think to understand
A world by their Creator planned,
    Who wiser is than they.

Turn, turn, my wheel! 'T is nature's plan
The child should grow into the man,
    The man grow wrinkled, old, and gray;
In youth the heart exults and sings,
The pulses leap, the feet have wings;
In age the cricket chirps, and brings
    The harvest home of day.

Turn, turn, my wheel! The human race,
Of every tongue, of every place,
    Caucasian, Coptic, or Malay,
All that inhabit this great earth,
Whatever be their rank or worth,
Are kindred and allied by birth,
    And made of the same clay.

Turn, turn, my wheel! What is begun
At daybreak must at dark be done,
    To-morrow will be another day;
To-morrow the hot furnace flame
Will search the heart and try the frame,
And stamp with honor or with shame
    These vessels made of clay.

Stop, stop, my wheel! Too soon, too soon
The noon will be the afternoon,
    Too soon to-day be yesterday;
Behind us in our path we cast
The broken potsherds of the past,
And all are ground to dust at last,
    And trodden into clay!

Venice

White swan of cities, slumbering in thy nest
   So wonderfully built among the reeds
   Of the lagoon, that fences thee and feeds,
   As sayeth thy old historian and thy guest!
White water-lily, cradled and caressed
   By ocean streams, and from the silt and weeds
   Lifting thy golden filaments and seeds,
   Thy sun-illumined spires, thy crown and crest!
White phantom city, whose untrodden streets
   Are rivers, and whose pavements are the shifting
   Shadows of palaces and strips of sky;
I wait to see thee vanish like the fleets
   Seen in mirage, or towers of cloud uplifting
   In air their unsubstantial masonry.

The Cross of Snow

In the long, sleepless watches of the night,
   A gentle face — the face of one long dead —
   Looks at me from the wall, where round its head
   The night-lamp casts a halo of pale light.
Here in this room she died; and soul more white
   Never through martyrdom of fire was led
   To its repose; nor can in books be read
   The legend of a life more benedight.
There is a mountain in the distant West
   That, sun-defying, in its deep ravines
   Displays a cross of snow upon its side.
Such is the cross I wear upon my breast
   These eighteen years, through all the changing scenes
   And seasons, changeless since the day she died.

The Tide Rises, the Tide Falls

The tide rises, the tide falls,
The twilight darkens, the curlew calls;
Along the sea-sands damp and brown
The traveller hastens toward the town,
    And the tide rises, the tide falls.

Darkness settles on roofs and walls,
But the sea, the sea in the darkness calls;
The little waves, with their soft, white hands,
Efface the footprints in the sands,
    And the tide rises, the tide falls.

The morning breaks; the steeds in their stalls
Stamp and neigh, as the hostler calls;
The day returns, but nevermore
Returns the traveller to the shore,
    And the tide rises, the tide falls.

The Bells of San Blas

What say the Bells of San Blas
To the ships that southward pass
    From the harbor of Mazatlan?
To them it is nothing more
Than the sound of surf on the shore,—
    Nothing more to master or man.

But to me, a dreamer of dreams,
To whom what is and what seems
    Are often one and the same,—
The Bells of San Blas to me
Have a strange, wild melody,
    And are something more than a name.

For bells are the voice of the church;
They have tones that touch and search
    The hearts of young and old;

One sound to all, yet each
Lends a meaning to their speech,
    And the meaning is manifold.

They are a voice of the Past,
Of an age that is fading fast,
    Of a power austere and grand;
When the flag of Spain unfurled
Its folds o'er this western world,
    And the Priest was lord of the land.

The chapel that once looked down
On the little seaport town
    Has crumbled into the dust;
And on oaken beams below
The bells swing to and fro,
    And are green with mould and rust.

"Is, then, the old faith dead,"
They say, "and in its stead
    Is some new faith proclaimed,
That we are forced to remain
Naked to sun and rain,
    Unsheltered and ashamed?

"Once in our tower aloof
We rang over wall and roof
    Our warnings and our complaints;
And round about us there
The white doves filled the air,
    Like the white souls of the saints.

"The saints! Ah, have they grown
Forgetful of their own?
    Are they asleep, or dead,
That open to the sky
Their ruined Missions lie,
    No longer tenanted?

"Oh, bring us back once more
  The vanished days of yore,
      When the world with faith was filled;
  Bring back the fervid zeal,
  The hearts of fire and steel,
      The hands that believe and build.

"Then from our tower again
  We will send over land and main
      Our voices of command,
  Like exiled kings who return
  To their thrones, and the people learn
      That the Priest is lord of the land!"

O Bells of San Blas, in vain
Ye call back the Past again!
      The Past is deaf to your prayer:
Out of the shadows of night
The world rolls into light;
      It is daybreak everywhere.

JOHN GREENLEAF
WHITTIER
(1807–1892)

Ichabod!

So fallen! so lost! the light withdrawn
   Which once he wore!
The glory from his gray hairs gone
   Forevermore!

Revile him not—the Tempter hath
   A snare for all;
And pitying tears, not scorn and wrath,
   Befit his fall!

Oh! dumb be passion's stormy rage,
   When he who might
Have lighted up and led his age,
   Falls back in night.

Scorn! would the angels laugh, to mark
   A bright soul driven,
Fiend-goaded, down the endless dark,
   From hope and heaven!

Let not the land, once proud of him,
   Insult him now,
Nor brand with deeper shame his dim,
   Dishonored brow.

But let its humbled sons, instead,
   From sea to lake,
A long lament, as for the dead,
   In sadness make.

Of all we loved and honored, nought
  Save power remains—
A fallen angel's pride of thought,
  Still strong in chains.

All else is gone; from those great eyes
  The soul has fled:
When faith is lost, when honor dies,
  The man is dead!

Then, pay the reverence of old days
  To his dead fame;
Walk backward, with averted gaze,
  And hide the shame!

Astræa

——"Jove means to settle
Astrea in her seat again,
And let down from his golden chain
An age of better metal."

  BEN JONSON, 1615.

O poet rare and old!
  Thy words are prophecies;
Forward the age of gold,
  The new Saturnian lies.

The universal prayer
  And hope are not in vain;
Rise, brothers! and prepare
  The way for Saturn's reign.

Perish shall all which takes
  From labor's board and can;
Perish shall all which makes
  A spaniel of the man!

Free from its bonds the mind,
    The body from the rod;
Broken all chains that bind
    The image of our God.

Just men no longer pine
    Behind their prison-bars;
Through the rent dungeon shine
    The free sun and the stars.

Earth own, at last, untrod
    By sect, or caste, or clan,
The fatherhood of God,
    The brotherhood of man!

Fraud fail, craft perish, forth
    The money-changers driven,
And God's will done on earth,
    As now in heaven!

The Haschish

Of all that Orient lands can vaunt
    Of marvels with our own competing,
The strangest is the Haschish plant,
    And what will follow on its eating.

What pictures to the taster rise,
    Of Dervish or of Almeh dances!
Of Eblis, or of Paradise,
    Set all aglow with Houri glances!

The poppy visions of Cathay,
    The heavy beer-trance of the Suabian;
The wizard lights and demon play
    Of nights Walpurgis and Arabian!

The Mollah and the Christian dog
  Change place in mad metempsychosis;
The Muezzin climbs the synagogue,
  The Rabbi shakes his beard at Moses!

The Arab by his desert well
  Sits choosing from some Caliph's daughters,
And hears his single camel's bell
  Sound welcome to his regal quarters.

The Koran's reader makes complaint
  Of Shitan dancing on and off it;
The robber offers alms, the saint
  Drinks Tokay and blasphemes the Prophet!

Such scenes that Eastern plant awakes;
  But we have one ordained to beat it,
The Haschish of the West, which makes
  Or fools or knaves of all who eat it.

The preacher eats, and straight appears
  His Bible in a new translation;
Its angels negro overseers,
  And Heaven itself a snug plantation!

The man of peace, about whose dreams
  The sweet millennial angels cluster,
Tastes the mad weed, and plots and schemes,
  A raving Cuban filibuster!

The noisiest Democrat, with ease,
  It turns to Slavery's parish beadle;
The shrewdest statesman eats and sees
  Due southward point the polar needle.

The Judge partakes, and sits ere long
  Upon his bench a railing blackguard;
Decides off-hand that right is wrong,
  And reads the ten commandments backward!

O, potent plant! so rare a taste
  Has never Turk or Gentoo gotten;
The hempen Haschish of the East
  Is powerless to our Western Cotton!

The Barefoot Boy

  Blessings on thee, little man,
Barefoot boy, with cheek of tan!
With thy turned-up pantaloons,
And thy merry whistled tunes;
With thy red lip, redder still
Kissed by strawberries on the hill;
With the sunshine on thy face,
Through thy torn brim's jaunty grace:
From my heart I give thee joy —
I was once a barefoot boy!
Prince thou art — the grown-up man
Only is republican.
Let the million-dollared ride!
Barefoot, trudging at his side,
Thou hast more than he can buy,
In the reach of ear and eye —
Outward sunshine, inward joy:
Blessings on thee, barefoot boy!

  O, for boyhood's painless play,
Sleep that wakes in laughing day,
Health that mocks the doctor's rules,
Knowledge never learned of schools,
Of the wild bee's morning chase,
Of the wild-flower's time and place,
Flight of fowl, and habitude
Of the tenants of the wood;
How the tortoise bears his shell,
How the woodchuck digs his cell,
And the ground-mole sinks his well;
How the robin feeds her young,
How the oriole's nest is hung;

Where the whitest lilies blow,
Where the freshest berries grow,
Where the ground-nut trails its vine,
Where the wood-grape's clusters shine;
Of the black wasp's cunning way,
Mason of his walls of clay,
And the architectural plans
Of gray, hornet artisans! —
For, eschewing books and tasks,
Nature answers all he asks;
Hand in hand with her he walks,
Face to face with her he talks,
Part and parcel of her joy, —
Blessings on the barefoot boy!

O, for boyhood's time of June,
Crowding years in one brief moon,
When all things I heard or saw
Me, their master, waited for.
I was rich in flowers and trees,
Humming-birds and honey-bees;
For my sport the squirrel played,
Plied the snouted mole his spade;
For my taste the blackberry cone
Purpled over hedge and stone;
Laughed the brook for my delight
Through the day and through the night,
Whispering at the garden wall,
Talked with me from fall to fall;
Mine the sand-rimmed pickerel pond,
Mine the walnut slopes beyond,
Mine, on bending orchard trees,
Apples of Hesperides!
Still, as my horizon grew,
Larger grew my riches too;
All the world I saw or knew
Seemed a complex Chinese toy,
Fashioned for a barefoot boy!

O, for festal dainties spread,
Like my bowl of milk and bread,—
Pewter spoon and bowl of wood,
On the door-stone, gray and rude!
O'er me, like a regal tent,
Cloudy-ribbed, the sunset bent,
Purple-curtained, fringed with gold,
Looped in many a wind-swung fold;
While for music came the play
Of the pied frogs' orchestra;
And, to light the noisy choir,
Lit the fly his lamp of fire.
I was monarch: pomp and joy
Waited on the barefoot boy!

Cheerily, then, my little man,
Live and laugh, as boyhood can!
Though the flinty slopes be hard,
Stubble-speared the new-mown sward,
Every morn shall lead thee through
Fresh baptisms of the dew;
Every evening from thy feet
Shall the cool wind kiss the heat:
All too soon these feet must hide
In the prison cells of pride,
Lose the freedom of the sod,
Like a colt's for work be shod,
Made to tread the mills of toil,
Up and down in ceaseless moil:
Happy if their track be found
Never on forbidden ground;
Happy if they sink not in
Quick and treacherous sands of sin.
Ah! that thou couldst know thy joy,
Ere it passes, barefoot boy!

Skipper Ireson's Ride

Of all the rides since the birth of time,
Told in story or sung in rhyme,—
On Apuleius's Golden Ass,
Or one-eyed Calendar's horse of brass,
Witch astride of a human hack,
Islam's prophet on Al-Borák,—
The strangest ride that ever was sped
Was Ireson's, out from Marblehead!
  Old Floyd Ireson, for his hard heart,
   Tarred and feathered and carried in a cart
   By the women of Marblehead!

Body of turkey, head of owl,
Wings a-droop like a rained-on fowl,
Feathered and ruffled in every part,
Skipper Ireson stood in the cart.
Scores of women, old and young,
Strong of muscle, and glib of tongue,
Pushed and pulled up the rocky lane,
Shouting and singing the shrill refrain:
  "Here's Flud Oirson, fur his horrd horrt,
   Torr'd an' futherr'd an' corr'd in a corrt
   By the women o' Morble'ead!"

Wrinkled scolds with hands on hips,
Girls in bloom of cheek and lips,
Wild-eyed, free-limbed, such as chase
Bacchus round some antique vase,
Brief of skirt, with ankles bare,
Loose of kerchief and loose of hair,
With couch-shells blowing and fish-horns' twang,
Over and over the Mænads sang:
  "Here's Flud Oirson, fur his horrd horrt,
   Torr'd an' futherr'd an' corr'd in a corrt
   By the women o' Morble'ead!"

Small pity for him! — He sailed away
From a leaking ship, in Chaleur Bay, —
Sailed away from a sinking wreck,
With his own town's-people on her deck!
"Lay by! lay by!" they called to him.
Back he answered, "Sink or swim!
Brag of your catch of fish again!"
And off he sailed through the fog and rain!
  Old Floyd Ireson, for his hard heart,
  Tarred and feathered and carried in a cart
  By the women of Marblehead!

Fathoms deep in dark Chaleur
That wreck shall lie forevermore.
Mother and sister, wife and maid,
Looked from the rocks of Marblehead
Over the moaning and rainy sea, —
Looked for the coming that might not be!
What did the winds and the sea-birds say
Of the cruel captain who sailed away? —
  Old Floyd Ireson, for his hard heart,
  Tarred and feathered and carried in a cart
  By the women of Marblehead!

Through the street, on either side,
Up flew windows, doors swung wide;
Sharp-tongued spinsters, old wives gray,
Treble lent the fish-horn's bray.
Sea-worn grandsires, cripple-bound,
Hulks of old sailors run aground,
Shook head, and fist, and hat, and cane,
And cracked with curses the hoarse refrain:
  "Here's Flud Oirson, fur his horrd horrt,
  Torr'd an' futherr'd an' corr'd in a corrt
  By the women o' Morble'ead!"

Sweetly along the Salem road
Bloom of orchard and lilac showed.
Little the wicked skipper knew
Of the fields so green and the sky so blue.
Riding there in his sorry trim,

Like an Indian idol glum and grim,
Scarcely he seemed the sound to hear
Of voices shouting far and near:
    "Here's Flud Oirson, fur his horrd horrt,
      Torr'd an' futherr'd an' corr'd in a corrt
      By the women o' Morble'ead!"

"Hear me, neighbors!" at last he cried,—
"What to me is this noisy ride?
What is the shame that clothes the skin
To the nameless horror that lives within?
Waking or sleeping, I see a wreck,
And hear a cry from a reeling deck!
Hate me and curse me,—I only dread
The hand of God and the face of the dead!"
    Said old Floyd Ireson, for his hard heart,
      Tarred and feathered and carried in a cart
      By the women of Marblehead!

Then the wife of the skipper lost at sea
Said, "God has touched him!—why should we?"
Said an old wife mourning her only son,
"Cut the rogue's tether and let him run!"
So with soft relentings and rude excuse,
Half scorn, half pity, they cut him loose,
And gave him a cloak to hide him in,
And left him alone with his shame and sin.
    Poor Floyd Ireson, for his hard heart,
      Tarred and feathered and carried in a cart
      By the women of Marblehead!

My Playmate

The pines were dark on Ramoth hill,
    Their song was soft and low;
The blossoms in the sweet May wind
    Were falling like the snow.

The blossoms drifted at our feet,
    The orchard birds sang clear;

The sweetest and the saddest day
   It seemed of all the year.

For, more to me than birds or flowers,
   My playmate left her home,
And took with her the laughing spring,
   The music and the bloom.

She kissed the lips of kith and kin,
   She laid her hand in mine:
What more could ask the bashful boy
   Who fed her father's kine?

She left us in the bloom of May:
   The constant years told o'er
Their seasons with as sweet May morns,
   But she came back no more.

I walk, with noiseless feet, the round
   Of uneventful years;
Still o'er and o'er I sow the spring
   And reap the autumn ears.

She lives where all the golden year
   Her summer roses blow;
The dusky children of the sun
   Before her come and go.

There haply with her jewelled hands
   She smooths her silken gown,—
No more the homespun lap wherein
   I shook the walnuts down.

The wild grapes wait us by the brook,
   The brown nuts on the hill,
And still the May-day flowers make sweet
   The woods of Follymill.

The lilies blossom in the pond,
   The bird builds in the tree,

The dark pines sing on Ramoth hill
    The slow song of the sea.

I wonder if she thinks of them,
    And how the old time seems,—
If ever the pines of Ramoth wood
    Are sounding in her dreams.

I see her face, I hear her voice:
    Does she remember mine?
And what to her is now the boy
    Who fed her father's kine?

What cares she that the orioles build
    For other eyes than ours,—
That other hands with nuts are filled,
    And other laps with flowers?

O playmate in the golden time!
    Our mossy seat is green,
Its fringing violets blossom yet,
    The old trees o'er it lean.

The winds so sweet with birch and fern
    A sweeter memory blow;
And there in spring the veeries sing
    The song of long ago.

And still the pines of Ramoth wood
    Are moaning like the sea,—
The moaning of the sea of change
    Between myself and thee!

Barbara Frietchie

Up from the meadows rich with corn,
Clear in the cool September morn,

The clustered spires of Frederick stand
Green-walled by the hills of Maryland.

Round about them orchards sweep,
Apple- and peach-tree fruited deep,

Fair as a garden of the Lord
To the eyes of the famished rebel horde,

On that pleasant morn of the early fall
When Lee marched over the mountain wall,—

Over the mountains winding down,
Horse and foot, into Frederick town.

Forty flags with their silver stars,
Forty flags with their crimson bars,

Flapped in the morning wind: the sun
Of noon looked down, and saw not one.

Up rose old Barbara Frietchie then,
Bowed with her fourscore years and ten;

Bravest of all in Frederick town,
She took up the flag the men hauled down;

In her attic-window the staff she set,
To show that one heart was loyal yet.

Up the street came the rebel tread,
Stonewall Jackson riding ahead.

Under his slouched hat left and right
He glanced: the old flag met his sight.

"Halt!"—the dust-brown ranks stood fast.
"Fire!"—out blazed the rifle-blast.

It shivered the window, pane and sash;
It rent the banner with seam and gash.

Quick, as it fell, from the broken staff
Dame Barbara snatched the silken scarf;

She leaned far out on the window-sill,
And shook it forth with a royal will.

"Shoot, if you must, this old gray head,
But spare your country's flag," she said.

A shade of sadness, a blush of shame,
Over the face of the leader came;

The nobler nature within him stirred
To life at that woman's deed and word:

"Who touches a hair of yon gray head
Dies like a dog! March on!" he said.

All day long through Frederick street
Sounded the tread of marching feet:

All day long that free flag tost
Over the heads of the rebel host.

Ever its torn folds rose and fell
On the loyal winds that loved it well;

And through the hill-gaps sunset light
Shone over it with a warm good-night.

Barbara Frietchie's work is o'er,
And the Rebel rides on his raids no more.

Honor to her! and let a tear
Fall, for her sake, on Stonewall's bier.

Over Barbara Frietchie's grave
Flag of Freedom and Union, wave!

Peace and order and beauty draw
Round thy symbol of light and law;

And ever the stars above look down
On thy stars below in Frederick town!

What the Birds Said

The birds against the April wind
    Flew northward, singing as they flew;
They sang, "The land we leave behind
    Has swords for corn-blades, blood for dew."

"O wild-birds, flying from the South,
    What saw and heard ye, gazing down?"
"We saw the mortar's upturned mouth,
    The sickened camp, the blazing town!

"Beneath the bivouac's starry lamps,
    We saw your march-worn children die;
In shrouds of moss, in cypress swamps,
    We saw your dead uncoffined lie.

"We heard the starving prisoner's sighs,
    And saw, from line and trench, your sons
Follow our flight with home-sick eyes
    Beyond the battery's smoking guns."

"And heard and saw ye only wrong
    And pain," I cried, "O wing-worn flocks?"
"We heard," they sang, "the freedman's song,
    The crash of Slavery's broken locks!

"We saw from new, uprising States
    The treason-nursing mischief spurned,
As, crowding Freedom's ample gates,
    The long-estranged and lost returned.

"O'er dusky faces, seamed and old,
    And hands horn-hard with unpaid toil,
With hope in every rustling fold,
    We saw your star-dropt flag uncoil.

"And struggling up through sounds accursed,
    A grateful murmur clomb the air;
A whisper scarcely heard at first,
    It filled the listening heavens with prayer.

"And sweet and far, as from a star,
    Replied a voice which shall not cease,
Till, drowning all the noise of war,
    It sings the blessed song of peace!"

So to me, in a doubtful day
    Of chill and slowly greening spring,
Low stooping from the cloudy gray,
    The wild-birds sang or seemed to sing.

They vanished in the misty air,
    The song went with them in their flight;
But lo! they left the sunset fair,
    And in the evening there was light.

Snow-Bound

The sun that brief December day
Rose cheerless over hills of gray,
And, darkly circled, gave at noon
A sadder light than waning moon.
Slow tracing down the thickening sky
Its mute and ominous prophecy,
A portent seeming less than threat,
It sank from sight before it set.
A chill no coat, however stout,
Of homespun stuff could quite shut out,
A hard, dull bitterness of cold,
    That checked, mid-vein, the circling race
    Of life-blood in the sharpened face,
The coming of the snow-storm told.
The wind blew east: we heard the roar
Of Ocean on his wintry shore,
And felt the strong pulse throbbing there
Beat with low rhythm our inland air.

Meanwhile we did our nightly chores,—
Brought in the wood from out of doors,
Littered the stalls, and from the mows
Raked down the herd's-grass for the cows;

Heard the horse whinnying for his corn;
And, sharply clashing horn on horn,
Impatient down the stanchion rows
The cattle shake their walnut bows;
While, peering from his early perch
Upon the scaffold's pole of birch,
The cock his crested helmet bent
And down his querulous challenge sent.

Unwarmed by any sunset light
The gray day darkened into night,
A night made hoary with the swarm
And whirl-dance of the blinding storm,
As zigzag wavering to and fro
Crossed and recrossed the wingéd snow:
And ere the early bed-time came
The white drift piled the window-frame,
And through the glass the clothes-line posts
Looked in like tall and sheeted ghosts.

So all night long the storm roared on:
The morning broke without a sun;
In tiny spherule traced with lines
Of Nature's geometric signs,
In starry flake, and pellicle,
All day the hoary meteor fell;
And, when the second morning shone,
We looked upon a world unknown,
On nothing we could call our own.
Around the glistening wonder bent
The blue walls of the firmament,
No cloud above, no earth below,—
A universe of sky and snow!
The old familiar sights of ours
Took marvellous shapes; strange domes and towers
Rose up where sty or corn-crib stood,
Or garden wall, or belt of wood;
A smooth white mound the brush-pile showed,
A fenceless drift what once was road;
The bridle-post an old man sat

With loose-flung coat and high cocked hat;
The well-curb had a Chinese roof;
And even the long sweep, high aloof,
In its slant splendor, seemed to tell
Of Pisa's leaning miracle.

A prompt, decisive man, no breath
Our father wasted: "Boys, a path!"
Well pleased, (for when did farmer boy
Count such a summons less than joy?)
Our buskins on our feet we drew;
  With mittened hands, and caps drawn low,
  To guard our necks and ears from snow,
We cut the solid whiteness through.
And, where the drift was deepest, made
A tunnel walled and overlaid
With dazzling crystal: we had read
Of rare Aladdin's wondrous cave,
And to our own his name we gave,
With many a wish the luck were ours
To test his lamp's supernal powers.
We reached the barn with merry din,
And roused the prisoned brutes within.
The old horse thrust his long head out,
And grave with wonder gazed about;
The cock his lusty greeting said,
And forth his speckled harem led;
The oxen lashed their tails, and hooked,
And mild reproach of hunger looked;
The hornéd patriarch of the sheep,
Like Egypt's Amun roused from sleep,
Shook his sage head with gesture mute,
And emphasized with stamp of foot.

All day the gusty north-wind bore
The loosening drift its breath before;
Low circling round its southern zone,
The sun through dazzling snow-mist shone.
No church-bell lent its Christian tone
To the savage air, no social smoke

Curled over woods of snow-hung oak.
A solitude made more intense
By dreary voicéd elements,
The shrieking of the mindless wind,
The moaning tree-boughs swaying blind,
And on the glass the unmeaning beat
Of ghostly finger-tips of sleet.
Beyond the circle of our hearth
No welcome sound of toil or mirth
Unbound the spell, and testified
Of human life and thought outside.
We minded that the sharpest ear
The buried brooklet could not hear,
The music of whose liquid lip
Had been to us companionship,
And, in our lonely life, had grown
To have an almost human tone.

As night drew on, and, from the crest
Of wooded knolls that ridged the west,
The sun, a snow-blown traveller, sank
From sight beneath the smothering bank,
We piled, with care, our nightly stack
Of wood against the chimney-back,—
The oaken log, green, huge, and thick,
And on its top the stout back-stick;
The knotty forestick laid apart,
And filled between with curious art
The ragged brush; then, hovering near,
We watched the first red blaze appear,
Heard the sharp crackle, caught the gleam
On whitewashed wall and sagging beam,
Until the old, rude-furnished room
Burst, flower-like, into rosy bloom;
While radiant with a mimic flame
Outside the sparkling drift became,
And through the bare-boughed lilac-tree
Our own warm hearth seemed blazing free.
The crane and pendent trammels showed,
The Turks' heads on the andirons glowed;

While childish fancy, prompt to tell
The meaning of the miracle,
Whispered the old rhyme: *"Under the tree,*
When fire outdoors burns merrily,
There the witches are making tea."

The moon above the eastern wood
Shone at its full; the hill-range stood
Transfigured in the silver flood,
Its blown snows flashing cold and keen,
Dead white, save where some sharp ravine
Took shadow, or the sombre green
Of hemlocks turned to pitchy black
Against the whiteness at their back.
For such a world and such a night
Most fitting that unwarming light,
Which only seemed where'er it fell
To make the coldness visible.

Shut in from all the world without,
We sat the clean-winged hearth about,
Content to let the north-wind roar
In baffled rage at pane and door,
While the red logs before us beat
The frost-line back with tropic heat;
And ever, when a louder blast
Shook beam and rafter as it passed,
The merrier up its roaring draught
The great throat of the chimney laughed.
The house-dog on his paws outspread
Laid to the fire his drowsy head,
The cat's dark silhouette on the wall
A couchant tiger's seemed to fall;
And, for the winter fireside meet,
Between the andirons' straddling feet,
The mug of cider simmered slow,
The apples sputtered in a row,
And, close at hand, the basket stood
With nuts from brown October's wood.

What matter how the night behaved?
What matter how the north-wind raved?
Blow high, blow low, not all its snow
Could quench our hearth-fire's ruddy glow.
O Time and Change!—with hair as gray
As was my sire's that winter day,
How strange it seems, with so much gone
Of life and love, to still live on!
Ah, brother! only I and thou
Are left of all that circle now,—
The dear home faces whereupon
That fitful firelight paled and shone.
Henceforward, listen as we will,
The voices of that hearth are still;
Look where we may, the wide earth o'er,
Those lighted faces smile no more.
We tread the paths their feet have worn,
    We sit beneath their orchard-trees,
    We hear, like them, the hum of bees
And rustle of the bladed corn;
We turn the pages that they read,
    Their written words we linger o'er,
But in the sun they cast no shade,
No voice is heard, no sign is made,
    No step is on the conscious floor!
Yet Love will dream, and Faith will trust,
(Since He who knows our need is just,)
That somehow, somewhere, meet we must.
Alas for him who never sees
The stars shine through his cypress-trees!
Who, hopeless, lays his dead away,
Nor looks to see the breaking day
Across the mournful marbles play!
Who hath not learned, in hours of faith,
    The truth to flesh and sense unknown,
That Life is ever lord of Death,
    And Love can never lose its own!

We sped the time with stories old,
Wrought puzzles out, and riddles told,

Or stammered from our school-book lore
"The Chief of Gambia's golden shore."
How often since, when all the land
Was clay in Slavery's shaping hand,
As if a trumpet called, I've heard
Dame Mercy Warren's rousing word:
"Does not the voice of reason cry,
    Claim the first right which Nature gave,
From the red scourge of bondage fly,
    Nor deign to live a burdened slave!"
Our father rode again his ride
On Memphremagog's wooded side;
Sat down again to moose and samp
In trapper's hut and Indian camp;
Lived o'er the old idyllic ease
Beneath St. François' hemlock-trees;
Again for him the moonlight shone
On Norman cap and bodiced zone;
Again he heard the violin play
Which led the village dance away,
And mingled in its merry whirl
The grandam and the laughing girl.
Or, nearer home, our steps he led
Where Salisbury's level marshes spread
    Mile-wide as flies the laden bee;
Where merry mowers, hale and strong,
Swept, scythe on scythe, their swaths along
    The low green prairies of the sea.
We shared the fishing off Boar's Head,
    And round the rocky Isles of Shoals
    The hake-broil on the drift-wood coals;
The chowder on the sand-beach made,
Dipped by the hungry, steaming hot,
With spoons of clam-shell from the pot.
We heard the tales of witchcraft old,
And dream and sign and marvel told
To sleepy listeners as they lay
Stretched idly on the salted hay,
Adrift along the winding shores,
When favoring breezes deigned to blow

The square sail of the gundalow
And idle lay the useless oars.
Our mother, while she turned her wheel
Or run the new-knit stocking-heel,
Told how the Indian hordes came down
At midnight on Cochecho town,
And how her own great-uncle bore
His cruel scalp-mark to fourscore.
Recalling, in her fitting phrase,
  So rich and picturesque and free,
  (The common unrhymed poetry
Of simple life and country ways,)
The story of her early days,—
She made us welcome to her home;
Old hearths grew wide to give us room;
We stole with her a frightened look
At the gray wizard's conjuring-book,
The fame whereof went far and wide
Through all the simple country side;
We heard the hawks at twilight play,
The boat-horn on Piscataqua,
The loon's weird laughter far away;
We fished her little trout-brook, knew
What flowers in wood and meadow grew,
What sunny hillsides autumn-brown
She climbed to shake the ripe nuts down,
Saw where in sheltered cove and bay
The ducks' black squadron anchored lay,
And heard the wild-geese calling loud
Beneath the gray November cloud.

Then, haply, with a look more grave,
And soberer tone, some tale she gave
From painful Sewell's ancient tome,
Beloved in every Quaker home,
Of faith fire-winged by martyrdom,
Or Chalkley's Journal, old and quaint,—
Gentlest of skippers, rare sea-saint!—
Who, when the dreary calms prevailed,
And water-butt and bread-cask failed,

And cruel, hungry eyes pursued
His portly presence mad for food,
With dark hints muttered under breath
Of casting lots for life or death,
Offered, if Heaven withheld supplies,
To be himself the sacrifice.
Then, suddenly, as if to save
The good man from his living grave,
A ripple on the water grew,
A school of porpoise flashed in view.
"Take, eat," he said, "and be content;
These fishes in my stead are sent
By Him who gave the tangled ram
To spare the child of Abraham."

Our uncle, innocent of books,
Was rich in lore of fields and brooks,
The ancient teachers never dumb
Of Nature's unhoused lyceum.
In moons and tides and weather wise,
He read the clouds as prophecies,
And foul or fair could well divine,
By many an occult hint and sign,
Holding the cunning-warded keys
To all the woodcraft mysteries;
Himself to Nature's heart so near
That all her voices in his ear
Of beast or bird had meanings clear,
Like Apollonius of old,
Who knew the tales the sparrows told,
Or Hermes, who interpreted
What the sage cranes of Nilus said;
A simple, guileless, childlike man,
Content to live where life began;
Strong only on his native grounds,
The little world of sights and sounds
Whose girdle was the parish bounds,
Whereof his fondly partial pride
The common features magnified,
As Surrey hills to mountains grew

In White of Selborne's loving view,—
He told how teal and loon he shot,
And how the eagle's eggs he got,
The feats on pond and river done,
The prodigies of rod and gun;
Till, warming with the tales he told,
Forgotten was the outside cold,
The bitter wind unheeded blew,
From ripening corn the pigeons flew,
The partridge drummed i' the wood, the mink
Went fishing down the river-brink.
In fields with bean or clover gay,
The woodchuck, like a hermit gray,
Peered from the doorway of his cell;
The muskrat plied the mason's trade,
And tier by tier his mud-walls laid;
And from the shagbark overhead
The grizzled squirrel dropped his shell.

Next, the dear aunt, whose smile of cheer
And voice in dreams I see and hear,—
The sweetest woman ever Fate
Perverse denied a household mate,
Who, lonely, homeless, not the less
Found peace in love's unselfishness,
And welcome wheresoe'er she went,
A calm and gracious element,
Whose presence seemed the sweet income
And womanly atmosphere of home,—
Called up her girlhood memories,
The huskings and the apple-bees,
The sleigh-rides and the summer sails,
Weaving through all the poor details
And homespun warp of circumstance
A golden woof-thread of romance.
For well she kept her genial mood
And simple faith of maidenhood;
Before her still a cloud-land lay,
The mirage loomed across her way;

The morning dew, that dries so soon
With others, glistened at her noon;
Through years of toil and soil and care
From glossy tress to thin gray hair,
All unprofaned she held apart
The virgin fancies of the heart.
Be shame to him of woman born
Who hath for such but thought of scorn.

There, too, our elder sister plied
Her evening task the stand beside;
A full, rich nature, free to trust,
Truthful and almost sternly just,
Impulsive, earnest, prompt to act,
And make her generous thought a fact,
Keeping with many a light disguise
The secret of self-sacrifice.
O heart sore-tried! thou hast the best
That Heaven itself could give thee,—rest,
Rest from all bitter thoughts and things!
  How many a poor one's blessing went
  With thee beneath the low green tent
Whose curtain never outward swings!

As one who held herself a part
Of all she saw, and let her heart
  Against the household bosom lean,
Upon the motley-braided mat
Our youngest and our dearest sat,
Lifting her large, sweet, asking eyes,
  Now bathed within the fadeless green
And holy peace of Paradise.
O, looking from some heavenly hill,
  Or from the shade of saintly palms,
  Or silver reach of river calms,
Do those large eyes behold me still?
With me one little year ago:—
The chill weight of the winter snow
  For months upon her grave has lain;

And now, when summer south-winds blow
  And brier and harebell bloom again,
I tread the pleasant paths we trod,
I see the violet-sprinkled sod
Whereon she leaned, too frail and weak
The hillside flowers she loved to seek,
Yet following me where'er I went
With dark eyes full of love's content.
The birds are glad; the brier-rose fills
The air with sweetness; all the hills
Stretch green to June's unclouded sky;
But still I wait with ear and eye
For something gone which should be nigh,
A loss in all familiar things,
In flower that blooms, and bird that sings.
And yet, dear heart! remembering thee,
  Am I not richer than of old?
Safe in thy immortality,
  What change can reach the wealth I hold?
  What chance can mar the pearl and gold
Thy love hath left in trust with me?
And while in life's late afternoon,
  Where cool and long the shadows grow,
I walk to meet the night that soon
  Shall shape and shadow overflow,
I cannot feel that thou art far,
Since near at need the angels are;
And when the sunset gates unbar,
  Shall I not see thee waiting stand,
And, white against the evening star,
  The welcome of thy beckoning hand?

Brisk wielder of the birch and rule,
The master of the district school
Held at the fire his favored place,
Its warm glow lit a laughing face
Fresh-hued and fair, where scarce appeared
The uncertain prophecy of beard.
He teased the mitten-blinded cat,
Played cross-pins on my uncle's hat,

Sang songs, and told us what befalls
In classic Dartmouth's college halls.
Born the wild Northern hills among,
From whence his yeoman father wrung
By patient toil subsistence scant,
Not competence and yet not want,
He early gained the power to pay
His cheerful, self-reliant way;
Could doff at ease his scholar's gown
To peddle wares from town to town;
Or through the long vacation's reach
In lonely lowland districts teach,
Where all the droll experience found
At stranger hearths in boarding round,
The moonlit skater's keen delight,
The sleigh-drive through the frosty night,
The rustic party, with its rough
Accompaniment of blind-man's-buff,
And whirling plate, and forfeits paid,
His winter task a pastime made.
Happy the snow-locked homes wherein
He tuned his merry violin,
Or played the athlete in the barn,
Or held the good dame's winding yarn,
Or mirth-provoking versions told
Of classic legends rare and old,
Wherein the scenes of Greece and Rome
Had all the commonplace of home,
And little seemed at best the odds
'Twixt Yankee pedlers and old gods;
Where Pindus-born Araxes took
The guise of any grist-mill brook,
And dread Olympus at his will
Became a huckleberry hill.

A careless boy that night he seemed;
    But at his desk he had the look
And air of one who wisely schemed,
    And hostage from the future took
    In trainéd thought and lore of book.

Large-brained, clear-eyed,—of such as he
Shall Freedom's young apostles be,
Who, following in War's bloody trail,
Shall every lingering wrong assail;
All chains from limb and spirit strike,
Uplift the black and white alike;
Scatter before their swift advance
The darkness and the ignorance,
The pride, the lust, the squalid sloth,
Which nurtured Treason's monstrous growth,
Made murder pastime, and the hell
Of prison-torture possible;
The cruel lie of caste refute,
Old forms remould, and substitute
For Slavery's lash the freeman's will,
For blind routine, wise-handed skill;
A school-house plant on every hill,
Stretching in radiate nerve-lines thence
The quick wires of intelligence;
Till North and South together brought
Shall own the same electric thought,
In peace a common flag salute,
And, side by side in labor's free
And unresentful rivalry,
Harvest the fields wherein they fought.

Another guest that winter night
Flashed back from lustrous eyes the light.
Unmarked by time, and yet not young,
The honeyed music of her tongue
And words of meekness scarcely told
A nature passionate and bold,
Strong, self-concentred, spurning guide,
Its milder features dwarfed beside
Her unbent will's majestic pride.
She sat among us, at the best,
A not unfeared, half-welcome guest,
Rebuking with her cultured phrase
Our homeliness of words and ways.
A certain pard-like, treacherous grace

Swayed the lithe limbs and drooped the lash,
Lent the white teeth their dazzling flash;
And under low brows, black with night,
Rayed out at times a dangerous light;
The sharp heat-lightnings of her face
Presaging ill to him whom Fate
Condemned to share her love or hate.
A woman tropical, intense
In thought and act, in soul and sense,
She blended in a like degree
The vixen and the devotee,
Revealing with each freak or feint
    The temper of Petruchio's Kate,
The raptures of Siena's saint.
Her tapering hand and rounded wrist
Had facile power to form a fist;
The warm, dark languish of her eyes
Was never safe from wrath's surprise.
Brows saintly calm and lips devout
Knew every change of scowl and pout;
And the sweet voice had notes more high
And shrill for social battle-cry.

Since then what old cathedral town
Has missed her pilgrim staff and gown,
What convent-gate has held its lock
Against the challenge of her knock!
Through Smyrna's plague-hushed thoroughfares,
Up sea-set Malta's rocky stairs,
Gray olive slopes of hills that hem
Thy tombs and shrines, Jerusalem,
Or startling on her desert throne
The crazy Queen of Lebanon
With claims fantastic as her own,
Her tireless feet have held their way;
And still, unrestful, bowed, and gray,
She watches under Eastern skies,
    With hope each day renewed and fresh,
    The Lord's quick coming in the flesh,
Whereof she dreams and prophesies!

Where'er her troubled path may be,
 The Lord's sweet pity with her go!
The outward wayward life we see,
 The hidden springs we may not know.
Nor is it given us to discern
 What threads the fatal sisters spun,
 Through what ancestral years has run
The sorrow with the woman born,
What forged her cruel chain of moods,
What set her feet in solitudes,
 And held the love within her mute,
What mingled madness in the blood,
 A life-long discord and annoy,
 Water of tears with oil of joy,
And hid within the folded bud
 Perversities of flower and fruit.
It is not ours to separate
The tangled skein of will and fate,
To show what metes and bounds should stand
Upon the soul's debatable land,
And between choice and Providence
Divide the circle of events;
But He who knows our frame is just,
 Merciful, and compassionate,
And full of sweet assurances
And hope for all the language is,
That He remembereth we are dust!

At last the great logs, crumbling low,
Sent out a dull and duller glow,
The bull's-eye watch that hung in view,
Ticking its weary circuit through,
Pointed with mutely-warning sign
Its black hand to the hour of nine.
That sign the pleasant circle broke:
My uncle ceased his pipe to smoke,
Knocked from its bowl the refuse gray
And laid it tenderly away,
Then roused himself to safely cover
The dull red brands with ashes over.

And while, with care, our mother laid
The work aside, her steps she stayed
One moment, seeking to express
Her grateful sense of happiness
For food and shelter, warmth and health,
And love's contentment more than wealth,
With simple wishes (not the weak,
Vain prayers which no fulfilment seek,
But such as warm the generous heart,
O'er-prompt to do with Heaven its part)
That none might lack, that bitter night,
For bread and clothing, warmth and light.

Within our beds awhile we heard
The wind that round the gables roared,
With now and then a ruder shock,
Which made our very bedsteads rock.
We heard the loosened clapboards tost,
The board-nails snapping in the frost;
And on us, through the unplastered wall,
Felt the light sifted snow-flakes fall.
But sleep stole on, as sleep will do
When hearts are light and life is new;
Faint and more faint the murmurs grew,
Till in the summer-land of dreams
They softened to the sound of streams,
Low stir of leaves, and dip of oars,
And lapsing waves on quiet shores.

Next morn we wakened with the shout
Of merry voices high and clear;
And saw the teamsters drawing near
To break the drifted highways out.
Down the long hillside treading slow
We saw the half-buried oxen go,
Shaking the snow from heads uptost,
Their straining nostrils white with frost.
Before our door the straggling train
Drew up, an added team to gain.
The elders threshed their hands a-cold,

Passed, with the cider-mug, their jokes
   From lip to lip; the younger folks
Down the loose snow-banks, wrestling, rolled,
Then toiled again the cavalcade
   O'er windy hill, through clogged ravine,
   And woodland paths that wound between
Low drooping pine-boughs winter-weighed.
From every barn a team afoot,
At every house a new recruit,
Where, drawn by Nature's subtlest law,
Haply the watchful young men saw
Sweet doorway pictures of the curls
And curious eyes of merry girls,
Lifting their hands in mock defence
Against the snow-ball's compliments,
And reading in each missive tost
The charm with Eden never lost.

We heard once more the sleigh-bells' sound;
   And, following where the teamsters led,
The wise old Doctor went his round,
Just pausing at our door to say,
In the brief autocratic way
Of one who, prompt at Duty's call,
Was free to urge her claim on all,
   That some poor neighbor sick abed
At night our mother's aid would need.
For, one in generous thought and deed,
   What mattered in the sufferer's sight
   The Quaker matron's inward light,
The Doctor's mail of Calvin's creed?
All hearts confess the saints elect
   Who, twain in faith, in love agree,
And melt not in an acid sect
   The Christian pearl of charity!

So days went on: a week had passed
Since the great world was heard from last.
The Almanac we studied o'er,
Read and reread our little store,

Of books and pamphlets, scarce a score;
One harmless novel, mostly hid
From younger eyes, a book forbid,
And poetry, (or good or bad,
A single book was all we had,)
Where Ellwood's meek, drab-skirted Muse,
    A stranger to the heathen Nine,
    Sang, with a somewhat nasal whine,
The wars of David and the Jews.
At last the floundering carrier bore
The village paper to our door.
Lo! broadening outward as we read,
To warmer zones the horizon spread;
In panoramic length unrolled
We saw the marvels that it told.
Before us passed the painted Creeks,
    And daft McGregor on his raids
    In Costa Rica's everglades.
And up Taygetos winding slow
Rode Ypsilanti's Mainote Greeks,
A Turk's head at each saddle-bow!
Welcome to us its week-old news,
Its corner for the rustic Muse,
    Its monthly gauge of snow and rain,
Its record, mingling in a breath
The wedding bell and dirge of death;
Jest, anecdote, and love-lorn tale,
The latest culprit sent to jail;
Its hue and cry of stolen and lost,
Its vendue sales and goods at cost,
    And traffic calling loud for gain.
We felt the stir of hall and street,
The pulse of life that round us beat;
The chill embargo of the snow
Was melted in the genial glow;
Wide swung again our ice-locked door,
And all the world was ours once more!

Clasp, Angel of the backward look
    And folded wings of ashen gray

And voice of echoes far away,
The brazen covers of thy book;
The weird palimpsest old and vast,
Wherein thou hid'st the spectral past;
Where, closely mingling, pale and glow
The characters of joy and woe;
The monographs of outlived years,
Or smile-illumed or dim with tears,
   Green hills of life that slope to death,
And haunts of home, whose vistaed trees
Shade off to mournful cypresses
   With the white amaranths underneath.
Even while I look, I can but heed
   The restless sands' incessant fall,
Importunate hours that hours succeed,
Each clamorous with its own sharp need,
   And duty keeping pace with all.
Shut down and clasp the heavy lids;
I hear again the voice that bids
The dreamer leave his dream midway
For larger hopes and graver fears:
Life greatens in these later years,
The century's aloe flowers to-day!

Yet, haply, in some lull of life,
Some Truce of God which breaks its strife,
The worldling's eyes shall gather dew,
   Dreaming in throngful city ways
Of winter joys his boyhood knew;
And dear and early friends — the few
Who yet remain — shall pause to view
   These Flemish pictures of old days;
Sit with me by the homestead hearth,
And stretch the hands of memory forth
   To warm them at the wood-fire's blaze!
And thanks untraced to lips unknown
Shall greet me like the odors blown
From unseen meadows newly mown,
Or lilies floating in some pond,
Wood-fringed, the wayside gaze beyond;

The traveller owns the grateful sense
Of sweetness near, he knows not whence,
And, pausing, takes with forehead bare
The benediction of the air.

from *Among the Hills*

Prelude

Along the roadside, like the flowers of gold
That tawny Incas for their gardens wrought,
Heavy with sunshine droops the golden-rod,
And the red pennons of the cardinal-flowers
Hang motionless upon their upright staves.
The sky is hot and hazy, and the wind,
Wing-weary with its long flight from the south,
Unfelt; yet, closely scanned, yon maple leaf
With faintest motion, as one stirs in dreams,
Confesses it. The locust by the wall
Stabs the noon-silence with his sharp alarm.
A single hay-cart down the dusty road
Creaks slowly, with its driver fast asleep
On the load's top. Against the neighboring hill,
Huddled along the stone wall's shady side,
The sheep show white, as if a snow-drift still
Defied the dog-star. Through the open door
A drowsy smell of flowers—gray heliotrope,
And white sweet-clover, and shy mignonette—
Comes faintly in, and silent chorus lends
To the pervading symphony of peace.

No time is this for hands long overworn
To task their strength; and (unto Him be praise
Who giveth quietness!) the stress and strain
Of years that did the work of centuries
Have ceased, and we can draw our breath once more
Freely and full. So, as yon harvesters
Make glad their nooning underneath the elms
With tale and riddle and old snatch of song,

I lay aside grave themes, and idly turn
The leaves of Memory's sketch-book, dreaming o'er
Old summer pictures of the quiet hills,
And human life, as quiet, at their feet.

And yet not idly all. A farmer's son,
Proud of field-lore and harvest craft, and feeling
All their fine possibilities, how rich
And restful even poverty and toil
Become when beauty, harmony, and love
Sit at their humble hearth as angels sat
At evening in the patriarch's tent, when man
Makes labor noble, and his farmer's frock
The symbol of a Christian chivalry
Tender and just and generous to her
Who clothes with grace all duty; still, I know
Too well the picture has another side, —
How wearily the grind of toil goes on
Where love is wanting, how the eye and ear
And heart are starved amidst the plenitude
Of nature, and how hard and colorless
Is life without an atmosphere. I look
Across the lapse of half a century,
And call to mind old homesteads, where no flower
Told that the spring had come, but evil weeds,
Nightshade and rough-leaved burdock in the place
Of the sweet doorway greeting of the rose
And honeysuckle, where the house walls seemed
Blistering in sun, without a tree or vine
To cast the tremulous shadow of its leaves
Across the curtainless windows from whose panes
Fluttered the signal rags of shiftlessness;
Within, the cluttered kitchen-floor, unwashed
(Broom-clean I think they called it); the best room
Stifling with cellar damp, shut from the air
In hot midsummer, bookless, pictureless
Save the inevitable sampler hung
Over the fireplace, or a mourning-piece,
A green-haired woman, peony-cheeked, beneath
Impossible willows; the wide-throated hearth

Bristling with faded pine-boughs half concealing
The piled up rubbish at the chimney's back;
And, in sad keeping with all things about them,
Shrill, querulous women, sour and sullen men,
Untidy, loveless, old before their time,
With scarce a human interest save their own
Monotonous round of small economies,
Or the poor scandal of the neighborhood;
Blind to the beauty everywhere revealed,
Treading the May-flowers with regardless feet;
For them the song-sparrow and the bobolink
Sang not, nor winds made music in the leaves;
For them in vain October's holocaust
Burned, gold and crimson, over all the hills,
The sacramental mystery of the woods.
Church-goers, fearful of the unseen Powers,
But grumbling over pulpit-tax and pew-rent,
Saving, as shrewd economists, their souls
And winter pork with the least possible outlay
Of salt and sanctity; in daily life
Showing as little actual comprehension
Of Christian charity and love and duty,
As if the Sermon on the Mount had been
Outdated like a last year's almanac:
Rich in broad woodlands and in half-tilled fields,
And yet so pinched and bare and comfortless,
The veriest straggler limping on his rounds,
The sun and air his sole inheritance,
Laughed at a poverty that paid its taxes,
And hugged his rags in self-complacency!

Not such should be the homesteads of a land
Where whoso wisely wills and acts may dwell
As king and lawgiver, in broad-acred state,
With beauty, art, taste, culture, books, to make
His hour of leisure richer than a life
Of fourscore to the barons of old time,
Our yeoman should be equal to his home
Set in the fair, green valleys, purple walled,
A man to match his mountains, not to creep

Dwarfed and abased below them. I would fain
In this light way (of which I needs must own
With the knife-grinder of whom Canning sings,
"Story, God bless you! I have none to tell you!")
Invite the eye to see and heart to feel
The beauty and the joy within their reach,—
Home, and home loves, and the beatitudes
Of nature free to all. Haply in years
That wait to take the places of our own,
Heard where some breezy balcony looks down
On happy homes, or where the lake in the moon
Sleeps dreaming of the mountains, fair as Ruth,
In the old Hebrew pastoral, at the feet
Of Boaz, even this simple lay of mine
May seem the burden of a prophecy,
Finding its late fulfilment in a change
Slow as the oak's growth, lifting manhood up
Through broader culture, finer manners, love,
And reverence, to the level of the hills.

O Golden Age, whose light is of the dawn,
And not of sunset, forward, not behind,
Flood the new heavens and earth, and with thee bring
All the old virtues, whatsoever things
Are pure and honest and of good repute,
But add thereto whatever bard has sung
Or seer has told of when in trance and dream
They saw the Happy Isles of prophecy!
Let Justice hold her scale, and Truth divide
Between the right and wrong; but give the heart
The freedom of its fair inheritance;
Let the poor prisoner, cramped and starved so long,
At Nature's table feast his ear and eye
With joy and wonder; let all harmonies
Of sound, form, color, motion, wait upon
The princely guest, whether in soft attire
Of leisure clad, or the coarse frock of toil.
And, lending life to the dead form of faith,
Give human nature reverence for the sake
Of One who bore it, making it divine

With the ineffable tenderness of God;
Let common need, the brotherhood of prayer,
The heirship of an unknown destiny,
The unsolved mystery round about us, make
A man more precious than the gold of Ophir.
Sacred, inviolate, unto whom all things
Should minister, as outward types and signs
Of the eternal beauty which fulfils
The one great purpose of creation, Love,
The sole necessity of Earth and Heaven!

Burning Drift-Wood

Before my drift-wood fire I sit,
    And see, with every waif I burn,
Old dreams and fancies coloring it,
    And folly's unlaid ghosts return.

O ships of mine, whose swift keels cleft
    The enchanted sea on which they sailed,
Are these poor fragments only left
    Of vain desires and hopes that failed?

Did I not watch from them the light
    Of sunset on my towers in Spain,
And see, far off, uploom in sight
    The Fortunate Isles I might not gain?

Did sudden lift of fog reveal
    Arcadia's vales of song and spring,
And did I pass, with grazing keel,
    The rocks whereon the sirens sing?

Have I not drifted hard upon
    The unmapped regions lost to man,
The cloud-pitched tents of Prester John,
    The palace domes of Kubla Khan?

Did land winds blow from jasmine flowers,
   Where Youth the ageless Fountain fills?
Did Love make sign from rose blown bowers,
   And gold from Eldorado's hills?

Alas! the gallant ships, that sailed
   On blind Adventure's errand sent,
Howe'er they laid their courses, failed
   To reach the haven of Content.

And of my ventures, those alone
   Which Love had freighted, safely sped,
Seeking a good beyond my own,
   By clear-eyed Duty piloted.

O mariners, hoping still to meet
   The luck Arabian voyagers met,
And find in Bagdad's moonlit street
   Haroun al Raschid walking yet,

Take with you, on your Sea of Dreams,
   The fair, fond fancies dear to youth.
I turn from all that only seems,
   And seek the sober grounds of truth.

What matter that it is not May,
   That birds have flown, and trees are bare,
That darker grows the shortening day,
   And colder blows the wintry air!

The wrecks of passion and desire,
   The castles I no more rebuild,
May fitly feed my drift-wood fire,
   And warm the hands that age has chilled.

Whatever perished with my ships,
   I only know the best remains;
A song of praise is on my lips
   For losses which are now my gains.

Heap high my hearth! No worth is lost;
  No wisdom with the folly dies.
Burn on, poor shreds, your holocaust
  Shall be my evening sacrifice!

Far more than all I dared to dream,
  Unsought before my door I see;
On wings of fire and steeds of steam
  The world's great wonders come to me,

And holier signs, unmarked before,
  Of Love to seek and Power to save, —
The righting of the wronged and poor,
  The man evolving from the slave;

And life, no longer chance or fate,
  Safe in the gracious Fatherhood.
I fold o'er-wearied hands and wait,
  In full assurance of the good.

And well the waiting time must be,
  Though brief or long its granted days,
If Faith and Hope and Charity
  Sit by my evening hearth-fire's blaze.

And with them, friends whom Heaven has spared,
  Whose love my heart has comforted,
And, sharing all my joys, has shared
  My tender memories of the dead, —

Dear souls who left us lonely here,
  Bound on their last, long voyage, to whom
We, day by day, are drawing near,
  Where every bark has sailing room.

I know the solemn monotone
  Of waters calling unto me;
I know from whence the airs have blown
  That whisper of the Eternal Sea.

As low my fires of drift-wood burn,
   I hear that sea's deep sounds increase,
And, fair in sunset light, discern
   Its mirage-lifted Isles of Peace.

EDGAR ALLAN POE
(1809–1849)

To Science

Science! true daughter of Old Time thou art!
  Who alterest all things with thy peering eyes.
Why preyest thou thus upon the poet's heart,
  Vulture, whose wings are dull realities?
How should he love thee? or how deem thee wise,
  Who wouldst not leave him in his wandering
To seek for treasure in the jewelled skies,
  Albeit he soared with an undaunted wing?
Hast thou not dragged Diana from her car?
  And driven the Hamadryad from the wood
To seek a shelter in some happier star?
  Hast thou not torn the Naiad from her flood,
The Elfin from the green grass, and from me
The summer dream beneath the tamarind tree?

from *Al Aaraaf*

PART II

High on a mountain of enamell'd head —
Such as the drowsy shepherd on his bed
Of giant pasturage lying at his ease,
Raising his heavy eyelid, starts and sees
With many a mutter'd "hope to be forgiven"
What time the moon is quadrated in Heaven —
Of rosy head, that towering far away
Into the sunlit ether, caught the ray
Of sunken suns at eve — at noon of night,
While the moon danc'd with the fair stranger light —
Uprear'd upon such height arose a pile
Of gorgeous columns on th' unburthen'd air,
Flashing from Parian marble that twin smile
Far down upon the wave that sparkled there,

And nursled the young mountain in its lair.
Of molten stars their pavement, such as fall
Thro' the ebon air, besilvering the pall
Of their own dissolution, while they die—
Adorning then the dwellings of the sky.
A dome, by linked light from Heaven let down,
Sat gently on these columns as a crown—
A window of one circular diamond, there,
Look'd out above into the purple air,
And rays from God shot down that meteor chain
And hallow'd all the beauty twice again,
Save when, between th' Empyrean and that ring,
Some eager spirit flapp'd his dusky wing.
But on the pillars Seraph eyes have seen
The dimness of this world: that greyish green
That Nature loves the best for Beauty's grave
Lurk'd in each cornice, round each architrave—
And every sculptur'd cherub thereabout
That from his marble dwelling peeréd out,
Seem'd earthly in the shadow of his niche—
Achaian statues in a world so rich?
Friezes from Tadmor and Persepolis—
From Balbec, and the stilly, clear abyss
Of beautiful Gomorrah! O, the wave
Is now upon thee—but too late to save!

Sound loves to revel in a summer night:
Witness the murmur of the grey twilight
That stole upon the ear, in Eyraco,
Of many a wild star-gazer long ago—
That stealeth ever on the ear of him
Who, musing, gazeth on the distance dim,
And sees the darkness coming as a cloud—
Is not its form—its voice—most palpable and loud?

lines 1 –47

"Alone"

From childhood's hour I have not been
As others were—I have not seen
As others saw—I could not bring
My passions from a common spring—
From the same source I have not taken
My sorrow—I could not awaken
My heart to joy at the same tone—
And all I lov'd—*I* lov'd alone—
Then—in my childhood—in the dawn
Of a most stormy life—was drawn
From ev'ry depth of good and ill
The mystery which binds me still—
From the torrent, or the fountain—
From the red cliff of the mountain—
From the sun that 'round me roll'd
In its autumn tint of gold—
From the lightning in the sky
As it pass'd me flying by—
From the thunder, and the storm—
And the cloud that took the form
(When the rest of Heaven was blue)
Of a demon in my view—

To Helen

Helen, thy beauty is to me
  Like those Nicéan barks of yore,
That gently, o'er a perfumed sea,
  The weary, way-worn wanderer bore
  To his own native shore.

On desperate seas long wont to roam,
  Thy hyacinth hair, thy classic face,
Thy Naiad airs have brought me home
  To the glory that was Greece,
  And the grandeur that was Rome.

Lo! in yon brilliant window-niche
　　How statue-like I see thee stand,
The agate lamp within thy hand!
　　Ah, Psyche, from the regions which
　　Are Holy-Land!

Israfel

In Heaven a spirit doth dwell
　　"Whose heart-strings are a lute;"
None sing so wildly well
As the angel Israfel,
And the giddy stars (so legends tell)
Ceasing their hymns, attend the spell
　　Of his voice, all mute.

Tottering above
　　In her highest noon,
　　The enamoured moon
Blushes with love,
　　While, to listen, the red levin
　　(With the rapid Pleiads, even,
　　Which were seven,)
　　Pauses in Heaven.

And they say (the starry choir
　　And the other listening things)
That Israfeli's fire
Is owing to that lyre
　　By which he sits and sings—
The trembling living wire
Of those unusual strings.

But the skies that angel trod,
　　Where deep thoughts are a duty—
Where Love's a grown-up God—
　　Where the Houri glances are
Imbued with all the beauty
　　Which we worship in a star.

Therefore, thou art not wrong,
 Israfeli, who despisest
An unimpassioned song;
To thee the laurels belong,
 Best bard, because the wisest!
Merrily live, and long!

The ecstasies above
 With thy burning measures suit—
Thy grief, thy joy, thy hate, thy love,
With the fervour of thy lute—
Well may the stars be mute!

Yes, Heaven is thine; but this
 Is a world of sweets and sours;
  Our flowers are merely—flowers,
And the shadow of thy perfect bliss
 Is the sunshine of ours.

If I could dwell
Where Israfel
 Hath dwelt, and he where I,
He might not sing so wildly well
 A mortal melody,
While a bolder note than this might swell
 From my lyre within the sky.

The City in the Sea

Lo! Death has reared himself a throne
In a strange city lying alone
Far down within the dim West,
Where the good and the bad and the worst and the best
Have gone to their eternal rest.
There shrines and palaces and towers
(Time-eaten towers that tremble not!)
Resemble nothing that is ours.
Around, by lifting winds forgot,
Resignedly beneath the sky
The melancholy waters lie.

No rays from the holy heaven come down
On the long night-time of that town;
But light from out the lurid sea
Streams up the turrets silently—
Gleams up the pinnacles far and free—
Up domes—up spires—up kingly halls—
Up fanes—up Babylon-like walls—
Up shadowy long-forgotten bowers
Of sculptured ivy and stone flowers—
Up many and many a marvellous shrine
Whose wreathéd friezes intertwine
The viol, the violet, and the vine.

Resignedly beneath the sky
The melancholy waters lie.
So blend the turrets and shadows there
That all seem pendulous in air,
While from a proud tower in the town
Death looks gigantically down.

There open fanes and gaping graves
Yawn level with the luminous waves;
But not the riches there that lie
In each idol's diamond eye—
Not the gaily-jewelled dead
Tempt the waters from their bed;
For no ripples curl, alas!
Along that wilderness of glass—
No swellings tell that winds may be
Upon some far-off happier sea—
No heavings hint that winds have been
On seas less hideously serene.

But lo, a stir is in the air!
The wave—there is a movement there!
As if the towers had thrust aside,
In slightly sinking, the dull tide—
As if their tops had feebly given
A void within the filmy Heaven.
The waves have now a redder glow—

The hours are breathing faint and low—
And when, amid no earthly moans,
Down, down that town shall settle hence.
Hell, rising from a thousand thrones,
Shall do it reverence.

The Haunted Palace

In the greenest of our valleys
　　By good angels tenanted,
Once a fair and stately palace—
　　Radiant palace—reared its head.
In the monarch Thought's dominion—
　　It stood there!
Never seraph spread a pinion
　　Over fabric half so fair!

Banners yellow, glorious, golden,
　　On its roof did float and flow—
(This—all this—was in the olden
　　Time long ago)
And every gentle air that dallied,
　　In that sweet day,
Along the ramparts plumed and pallid,
　　A wingéd odor went away.

Wanderers in that happy valley,
　　Through two luminous windows, saw
Spirits moving musically,
　　To a lute's well-tunéd law,
Round about a throne where, sitting,
　　Porphyrogene,
In state his glory well befitting
　　The ruler of the realm was seen.

And all with pearl and ruby glowing
　　Was the fair palace door,
Through which came flowing, flowing, flowing,
　　And sparkling evermore,

A troop of Echoes whose sweet duty
    Was but to sing,
In voices of surpassing beauty,
    The wit and wisdom of their king.

But evil things, in robes of sorrow,
    Assailed the monarch's high estate.
(Ah, let us mourn!—for never morrow
    Shall dawn upon him, desolate!)
And round about his home the glory
    That blushed and bloomed,
Is but a dim-remembered story
    Of the old-time entombed.

And travellers, now, within that valley,
    Through the encrimsoned windows see
Vast forms that move fantastically
    To a discordant melody,
While, like a ghastly rapid river,
    Through the pale door
A hideous throng rush out forever
    And laugh—but smile no more.

Silence

There are some qualities—some incorporate things,
    That have a double life, which thus is made
A type of that twin entity which springs
    From matter and light, evinced in solid and shade.
There is a two-fold *Silence*—sea and shore—
    Body and soul. One dwells in lonely places,
    Newly with grass o'ergrown; some solemn graces,
Some human memories and tearful lore,
Render him terrorless: his name's "No More."
He is the corporate Silence: dread him not!
    No power hath he of evil in himself;
But should some urgent fate (untimely lot!)
    Bring thee to meet his shadow (nameless elf,
That haunteth the lone regions where hath trod
No foot of man,) commend thyself to God!

The Conqueror Worm

Lo! 'tis a gala night
   Within the lonesome latter years!
An angel throng, bewinged, bedight
   In veils, and drowned in tears,
Sit in a theatre, to see
   A play of hopes and fears,
While the orchestra breathes fitfully
   The music of the spheres.

Mimes, in the form of God on high,
   Mutter and mumble low,
And hither and thither fly—
   Mere puppets they, who come and go
At bidding of vast formless things
   That shift the scenery to and fro,
Flapping from out their Condor wings
   Invisible Wo!

That motley drama—oh, be sure
   It shall not be forgot!
With its Phantom chased for evermore,
   By a crowd that seize it not,
Through a circle that ever returneth in
   To the self-same spot,
And much of Madness, and more of Sin,
   And Horror the soul of the plot.

But see, amid the mimic rout
   A crawling shape intrude!
A blood-red thing that writhes from out
   The scenic solitude!
It writhes!—it writhes!—with mortal pangs
   The mimes become its food,
And seraphs sob at vermin fangs
   In human gore imbued.

Out—out are the lights—out all!
   And, over each quivering form,
The curtain, a funeral pall,
   Comes down with the rush of a storm,
While the angels, all pallid and wan,
   Uprising, unveiling, affirm
That the play is the tragedy, "Man,"
   And its hero the Conqueror Worm.

Dream-Land

By a route obscure and lonely,
Haunted by ill angels only,
Where an Eidolon, named NIGHT,
On a black throne reigns upright,
I have reached these lands but newly
From an ultimate dim Thule—
From a wild weird clime that lieth, sublime,
     Out of SPACE—out of TIME.

Bottomless vales and boundless floods,
And chasms, and caves, and Titan woods,
With forms that no man can discover
For the tears that drip all over;
Mountains toppling evermore
Into seas without a shore;
Seas that restlessly aspire,
Surging, unto skies of fire;
Lakes that endlessly outspread
Their lone waters—lone and dead,—
Their still waters—still and chilly
With the snows of the lolling lily.

By the lakes that thus outspread
Their lone waters, lone and dead,—
Their sad waters, sad and chilly
With the snows of the lolling lily,—
By the mountains—near the river
Murmuring lowly, murmuring ever,—
By the grey woods,—by the swamp

Where the toad and the newt encamp,—
By the dismal tarns and pools
    Where dwell the Ghouls,—
By each spot the most unholy—
In each nook most melancholy,—
There the traveller meets, aghast,
Sheeted Memories of the Past—
Shrouded forms that start and sigh
As they pass the wanderer by—
White-robed forms of friends long given,
In agony, to the Earth—and Heaven.

For the heart whose woes are legion
'Tis a peaceful, soothing region—
For the spirit that walks in shadow
'Tis—oh 'tis an Eldorado!
But the traveller, travelling through it,
May not—dare not openly view it;
Never its mysteries are exposed
To the weak human eye unclosed;
So wills its King, who hath forbid
The uplifting of the fringéd lid;
And thus the sad Soul that here passes
Beholds it but through darkened glasses.

By a route obscure and lonely,
Haunted by ill angels only,
Where an Eidolon, named NIGHT,
On a black throne reigns upright,
I have wandered home but newly
From this ultimate dim Thule.

The Raven

Once upon a midnight dreary, while I pondered, weak and
    weary,
Over many a quaint and curious volume of forgotten lore—
While I nodded, nearly napping, suddenly there came a
    tapping,

As of some one gently rapping, rapping at my chamber
        door.
" 'Tis some visiter," I muttered, "tapping at my chamber
        door —
                Only this and nothing more."

Ah, distinctly I remember it was in the bleak December;
And each separate dying ember wrought its ghost upon the
        floor.
Eagerly I wished the morrow;—vainly I had sought to
        borrow
From my books surcease of sorrow—sorrow for the lost
        Lenore—
For the rare and radiant maiden whom the angels name
        Lenore—
                Nameless *here* for evermore.

And the silken, sad, uncertain rustling of each purple
        curtain
Thrilled me—filled me with fantastic terrors never felt
        before;
So that now, to still the beating of my heart, I stood
        repeating
" 'Tis some visiter entreating entrance at my chamber
        door—
Some late visiter entreating entrance at my chamber door;—
                This it is and nothing more."

Presently my soul grew stronger; hesitating then no longer,
"Sir," said I, "or Madam, truly your forgiveness I implore;
But the fact is I was napping, and so gently you came
        rapping,
And so faintly you came tapping, tapping at my chamber
        door,
That I scarce was sure I heard you"—here I opened wide
        the door;——
                Darkness there and nothing more.

Deep into that darkness peering, long I stood there
        wondering, fearing,

Doubting, dreaming dreams no mortal ever dared to dream
  before;
But the silence was unbroken, and the stillness gave no
  token,
And the only word there spoken was the whispered word,
  "Lenore?"
This I whispered, and an echo murmured back the word,
  "Lenore!"
  Merely this and nothing more.

Back into the chamber turning, all my soul within me
  burning,
Soon again I heard a tapping somewhat louder than before.
"Surely," said I, "surely that is something at my window
  lattice;
Let me see, then, what thereat is, and this mystery explore—
Let my heart be still a moment and this mystery explore;—
  'Tis the wind and nothing more!"

Open here I flung the shutter, when, with many a flirt and
  flutter,
In there stepped a stately Raven of the saintly days of yore;
Not the least obeisance made he; not a minute stopped or
  stayed he;
But, with mien of lord or lady, perched above my chamber
  door—
Perched upon a bust of Pallas just above my chamber door—
  Perched, and sat, and nothing more.

Then this ebony bird beguiling my sad fancy into smiling,
By the grave and stern decorum of the countenance it wore,
"Though thy crest be shorn and shaven, thou," I said, "art
  sure no craven,
Ghastly grim and ancient Raven wandering from the
  Nightly shore—
Tell me what thy lordly name is on the Night's Plutonian
  shore!"
  Quoth the Raven "Nevermore."

Much I marvelled this ungainly fowl to hear discourse so
    plainly,
Though its answer little meaning—little relevancy bore;
For we cannot help agreeing that no living human being
Ever yet was blessed with seeing bird above his chamber
    door—
Bird or beast upon the sculptured bust above his chamber
    door,
                With such name as "Nevermore."

But the Raven, sitting lonely on the placid bust, spoke only
That one word, as if his soul in that one word he did
    outpour.
Nothing farther then he uttered—not a feather then he
    fluttered—
Till I scarcely more than muttered "Other friends have
    flown before—
On the morrow *he* will leave me, as my Hopes have flown
    before."
                Then the bird said "Nevermore."

Startled at the stillness broken by reply so aptly spoken,
"Doubtless," said I, "what it utters is its only stock and
    store
Caught from some unhappy master whom unmerciful
    Disaster
Followed fast and followed faster till his songs one burden
    bore—
Till the dirges of his Hope that melancholy burden bore
              Of 'Never—nevermore.' "

But the Raven still beguiling my sad fancy into smiling,
Straight I wheeled a cushioned seat in front of bird, and
    bust and door;
Then, upon the velvet sinking, I betook myself to linking
Fancy unto fancy, thinking what this ominous bird of yore—
What this grim, ungainly, ghastly, gaunt, and ominous bird
    of yore
            Meant in croaking "Nevermore."

This I sat engaged in guessing, but no syllable expressing
To the fowl whose fiery eyes now burned into my bosom's
    core;
This and more I sat divining, with my head at ease reclining
On the cushion's velvet lining that the lamp-light gloated
    o'er,
But whose velvet-violet lining with the lamp-light gloating
    o'er,
                She shall press, ah, nevermore!

Then, methought, the air grew denser, perfumed from an
    unseen censer
Swung by seraphim whose foot-falls tinkled on the tufted
    floor.
"Wretch," I cried, "thy God hath lent thee — by these
    angels he hath sent thee
Respite — respite and nepenthe from thy memories of Lenore;
Quaff, oh quaff this kind nepenthe and forget this lost
    Lenore!"
            Quoth the Raven "Nevermore."

"Prophet!" said I, "thing of evil! — prophet still, if bird or
    devil! —
Whether Tempter sent, or whether tempest tossed thee here
    ashore,
Desolate yet all undaunted, on this desert land enchanted —
On this home by Horror haunted — tell me truly, I implore —
Is there — *is* there balm in Gilead? — tell me — tell me, I
    implore!"
            Quoth the Raven "Nevermore."

"Prophet!" said I, "thing of evil! — prophet still, if bird or
    devil!
By that Heaven that bends above us — by that God we both
    adore —
Tell this soul with sorrow laden if, within the distant
    Aidenn,
It shall clasp a sainted maiden whom the angels name
    Lenore —

Clasp a rare and radiant maiden whom the angels name
  Lenore."
           Quoth the Raven "Nevermore."

"Be that word our sign of parting, bird or fiend!" I shrieked,
  upstarting—
"Get thee back into the tempest and the Night's Plutonian
  shore!
 Leave no black plume as a token of that lie thy soul hath
  spoken!
 Leave my loneliness unbroken!—quit the bust above my
  door!
 Take thy beak from out my heart, and take thy form from
  off my door!"
           Quoth the Raven "Nevermore."

And the Raven, never flitting, still is sitting, *still* is sitting
On the pallid bust of Pallas just above my chamber door;
And his eyes have all the seeming of a demon's that is
  dreaming,
And the lamp-light o'er him streaming throws his shadow
  on the floor;
And my soul from out that shadow that lies floating on the
  floor
           Shall be lifted—nevermore!

Ulalume—A Ballad

The skies they were ashen and sober;
  The leaves they were crispéd and sere—
  The leaves they were withering and sere:
It was night, in the lonesome October
  Of my most immemorial year:
It was hard by the dim lake of Auber,
  In the misty mid region of Weir:—
It was down by the dank tarn of Auber,
  In the ghoul-haunted woodland of Weir.

Here once, through an alley Titanic,
  Of cypress, I roamed with my Soul—
  Of cypress, with Psyche, my Soul.
These were days when my heart was volcanic
  As the scoriac rivers that roll—
  As the lavas that restlessly roll
Their sulphurous currents down Yaanek,
  In the ultimate climes of the Pole—
That groan as they roll down Mount Yaanek,
  In the realms of the Boreal Pole.

Our talk had been serious and sober,
  But our thoughts they were palsied and sere—
  Our memories were treacherous and sere;
For we knew not the month was October,
  And we marked not the night of the year—
  (Ah, night of all nights in the year!)
We noted not the dim lake of Auber,
  (Though once we had journeyed down here)
We remembered not the dank tarn of Auber,
  Nor the ghoul-haunted woodland of Weir.

And now, as the night was senescent,
  And star-dials pointed to morn—
  As the star-dials hinted of morn—
At the end of our path a liquescent
  And nebulous lustre was born,
Out of which a miraculous crescent
  Arose with a duplicate horn—
Astarte's bediamonded crescent,
  Distinct with its duplicate horn.

And I said—"She is warmer than Dian;
  She rolls through an ether of sighs—
  She revels in a region of sighs.
She has seen that the tears are not dry on
  These cheeks where the worm never dies,
And has come past the stars of the Lion,
  To point us the path to the skies—

To the Lethean peace of the skies—
Come up, in despite of the Lion,
   To shine on us with her bright eyes—
Come up, through the lair of the Lion,
   With love in her luminous eyes."

But Psyche, uplifting her finger,
   Said—"Sadly this star I mistrust—
   Her pallor I strangely mistrust—
Ah, hasten!—ah, let us not linger!
   Ah, fly!—let us fly!—for we must."
In terror she spoke; letting sink her
   Wings till they trailed in the dust—
In agony sobbed; letting sink her
   Plumes till they trailed in the dust—
   Till they sorrowfully trailed in the dust.

I replied—"This is nothing but dreaming.
   Let us on, by this tremulous light!
   Let us bathe in this crystalline light!
Its Sibyllic splendor is beaming
   With Hope and in Beauty to-night—
   See!—it flickers up the sky through the night!
Ah, we safely may trust to its gleaming
   And be sure it will lead us aright—
We surely may trust to a gleaming
   That cannot but guide us aright
Since it flickers up to Heaven through the night."

Thus I pacified Psyche and kissed her,
   And tempted her out of her gloom—
   And conquered her scruples and gloom;
And we passed to the end of the vista—
   But were stopped by the door of a tomb—
   By the door of a legended tomb:—
And I said—"What is written, sweet sister,
   On the door of this legended tomb?"
   She replied—"Ulalume—Ulalume!—
   'T is the vault of thy lost Ulalume!"

Then my heart it grew ashen and sober
    As the leaves that were crispéd and sere—
    As the leaves that were withering and sere—
And I cried—"It was surely October,
    On *this* very night of last year,
    That I journeyed—I journeyed down here!—
    That I brought a dread burden down here—
    On this night, of all nights in the year,
    Ah; what demon hath tempted me here?
Well I know, now, this dim lake of Auber—
    This misty mid region of Weir:—
Well I know, now, this dank tarn of Auber—
    This ghoul-haunted woodland of Weir."

Said we, then—the two, then—"Ah, can it
    Have been that the woodlandish ghouls—
    The pitiful, the merciful ghouls,
To bar up our way and to ban it
    From the secret that lies in these wolds—
    From the thing that lies hidden in these wolds—
Have drawn up the spectre of a planet
    From the limbo of lunary souls—
This sinfully scintillant planet
    From the Hell of the planetary souls?"

The Bells

I

    Hear the sledges with the bells—
        Silver bells!
What a world of merriment their melody foretells!
    How they tinkle, tinkle, tinkle,
        In the icy air of night!
    While the stars that oversprinkle
    All the Heavens, seem to twinkle
        With a crystalline delight;
    Keeping time, time, time,
    In a sort of Runic rhyme,

To the tintinabulation that so musically wells
  From the bells, bells, bells, bells,
      Bells, bells, bells—
    From the jingling and the tinkling of the bells.

2

    Hear the mellow wedding bells—
      Golden bells!
What a world of happiness their harmony foretells!
    Through the balmy air of night
    How they ring out their delight!—
      From the molten-golden notes
      And all in tune,
     What a liquid ditty floats
  To the turtle-dove that listens while she gloats
      On the moon!
    Oh, from out the sounding cells
What a gush of euphony voluminously wells!
     How it swells!
     How it dwells
    On the Future!—how it tells
    Of the rapture that impels
   To the swinging and the ringing
    Of the bells, bells, bells!—
  Of the bells, bells, bells, bells,
     Bells, bells, bells—
  To the rhyming and the chiming of the bells!

3

    Hear the loud alarum bells—
      Brazen bells!
What tale of terror, now, their turbulency tells!
    In the startled ear of Night
    How they scream out their affright!
     Too much horrified to speak,
     They can only shriek, shriek,
      Out of tune,
In a clamorous appealing to the mercy of the fire—
In a mad expostulation with the deaf and frantic fire,

Leaping higher, higher, higher,
With a desperate desire
And a resolute endeavor
Now—now to sit, or never,
By the side of the pale-faced moon.
Oh, the bells, bells, bells!
What a tale their terror tells
Of despair!
How they clang and clash and roar!
What a horror they outpour
In the bosom of the palpitating air!
Yet the ear, it fully knows,
By the twanging
And the clanging,
How the danger ebbs and flows:—
Yes, the ear distinctly tells,
In the jangling
And the wrangling,
How the danger sinks and swells,
By the sinking or the swelling in the anger of the bells—
Of the bells—
Of the bells, bells, bells, bells,
Bells, bells, bells—
In the clamor and the clangor of the bells.

4

Hear the tolling of the bells—
Iron bells!
What a world of solemn thought their monody compels!
In the silence of the night
How we shiver with affright
At the melancholy meaning of the tone!
For every sound that floats
From the rust within their throats
Is a groan.
And the people—ah, the people
They that dwell up in the steeple
All alone,
And who, tolling, tolling, tolling,

      In that muffled monotone,
     Feel a glory in so rolling
      On the human heart a stone —
They are neither man nor woman —
They are neither brute nor human,
       They are Ghouls: —
And their king it is who tolls: —
And he rolls, rolls, rolls, rolls
     A Pæan from the bells!
   And his merry bosom swells
     With the Pæan of the bells!
   And he dances and he yells;
Keeping time, time, time,
In a sort of Runic rhyme,
    To the Pæan of the bells —
     Of the bells: —
Keeping time, time, time,
In a sort of Runic rhyme,
   To the throbbing of the bells —
Of the bells, bells, bells —
    To the sobbing of the bells: —
Keeping time, time, time,
   As he knells, knells, knells,
In a happy Runic rhyme,
   To the rolling of the bells —
Of the bells, bells, bells: —
   To the tolling of the bells —
Of the bells, bells, bells, bells,
   Bells, bells, bells —
To the moaning and the groaning of the bells.

Eldorado

    Gaily bedight,
    A gallant knight,
In sunshine and in shadow,
   Had journeyed long,
   Singing a song,
In search of Eldorado.

       But he grew old—
       This knight so bold—
And o'er his heart a shadow
       Fell, as he found
       No spot of ground
That looked like Eldorado.

       And, as his strength
       Failed him at length,
He met a pilgrim shadow—
       'Shadow,' said he,
       'Where can it be—
This land of Eldorado?'

       'Over the Mountains
       Of the Moon,
Down the Valley of the Shadow,
       Ride, boldly ride,'
       The shade replied,—
'If you seek for Eldorado!'

Annabel Lee

It was many and many a year ago,
    In a kingdom by the sea,
That a maiden there lived whom you may know
    By the name of Annabel Lee;—
And this maiden she lived with no other thought
    Than to love and be loved by me.

She was a child and *I* was a child,
    In this kingdom by the sea,
But we loved with a love that was more than love—
    I and my Annabel Lee—
With a love that the wingéd seraphs of Heaven
    Coveted her and me.

And this was the reason that, long ago,
    In this kingdom by the sea,

A wind blew out of a cloud by night
   Chilling my Annabel Lee;
So that her high-born kinsmen came
   And bore her away from me,
To shut her up in a sepulchre
   In this kingdom by the sea.

The angels, not half so happy in Heaven,
   Went envying her and me;
Yes! that was the reason (as all men know,
   In this kingdom by the sea)
That the wind came out of the cloud, chilling
   And killing my Annabel Lee.

But our love it was stronger by far than the love
   Of those who were older than we—
   Of many far wiser than we—
And neither the angels in Heaven above
   Nor the demons down under the sea
Can ever dissever my soul from the soul
   Of the beautiful Annabel Lee:—

For the moon never beams without bringing me dreams
   Of the beautiful Annabel Lee;
And the stars never rise but I see the bright eyes
   Of the beautiful Annabel Lee;
And so, all the night-tide, I lie down by the side
Of my darling, my darling, my life and my bride
   In her sepulchre there by the sea—
   In her tomb by the side of the sea.

ABRAHAM LINCOLN

(1809–1865)

My Childhood-Home I See Again

My childhood-home I see again,
   And gladden with the view;
And still as mem'ries crowd my brain,
   There's sadness in it too.

O memory! thou mid-way world
   'Twixt Earth and Paradise,
Where things decayed, and loved ones lost
   In dreamy shadows rise.

And freed from all that's gross or vile,
   Seem hallowed, pure, and bright,
Like scenes in some enchanted isle,
   All bathed in liquid light.

As distant mountains please the eye,
   When twilight chases day—
As bugle-tones, that, passing by,
   In distance die away—

As leaving some grand water-fall
   We ling'ring, list it's roar,
So memory will hallow all
   We've known, but know no more.

Now twenty years have passed away,
   Since here I bid farewell
To woods, and fields, and scenes of play
   And school-mates loved so well.

Where many were, how few remain
   Of old familiar things!

But seeing these to mind again
    The lost and absent brings.

The friends I left that parting day—
    How changed, as time has sped!
Young childhood grown, strong manhood grey,
    And half of all are dead.

I hear the lone survivors tell
    How nought from death could save,
Till every sound appears a knell,
    And every spot a grave.

I range the fields with pensive tread,
    And pace the hollow rooms;
And feel (companions of the dead)
    I'm living in the tombs.

And here's an object more of dread,
    Than ought the grave contains—
A human-form, with reason fled,
    While wretched life remains.

Poor Matthew! Once of genius bright,—
    A fortune-favored child—
Now locked for aye, in mental night,
    A haggard mad-man wild.

Poor Matthew! I have ne'er forgot
    When first with maddened will,
Yourself you maimed, your father fought,
    And mother strove to kill;

And terror spread, and neighbours ran,
    Your dang'rous strength to bind;
And soon a howling crazy man,
    Your limbs were fast confined.

How then you writhed and shrieked aloud,
  Your bones and sinnews bared;
And fiendish on the gaping crowd,
  With burning eye-balls glared.

And begged, and swore, and wept, and prayed,
  With maniac laughter joined—
How fearful are the signs displayed,
  By pangs that kill the mind!

And when at length, tho' drear and long,
  Time soothed your fiercer woes—
How plaintively your mournful song,
  Upon the still night rose.

I've heard it oft, as if I dreamed,
  Far-distant, sweet, and lone;
The funeral dirge it ever seemed
  Of reason dead and gone.

To drink it's strains, I've stole away,
  All silently and still,
Ere yet the rising god of day
  Had streaked the Eastern hill.

Air held his breath; the trees all still
  Seemed sorr'wing angels round.
Their swelling tears in dew-drops fell
  Upon the list'ning ground.

But this is past, and nought remains
  That raised you o'er the brute.
Your mad'ning shrieks and soothing strains
  Are like forever mute.

Now fare thee well: more thou the cause
  Than subject now of woe.
All mental pangs, but time's kind laws,
  Hast lost the power to know.

And now away to seek some scene
   Less painful than the last—
With less of horror mingled in
   The present and the past.

The very spot where grew the bread
   That formed my bones, I see.
How strange, old field, on thee to tread,
   And feel I'm part of thee!

OLIVER WENDELL HOLMES

(1809–1894)

Old Ironsides

Ay, tear her tattered ensign down!
    Long has it waved on high,
And many an eye has danced to see
    That banner in the sky;
Beneath it rung the battle shout,
    And burst the cannon's roar;—
The meteor of the ocean air
    Shall sweep the clouds no more!

Her deck, once red with heroes' blood
    Where knelt the vanquished foe,
When winds were hurrying o'er the flood
    And waves were white below,
No more shall feel the victor's tread,
    Or know the conquered knee;—
The harpies of the shore shall pluck
    The eagle of the sea!

O better that her shattered hulk
    Should sink beneath the wave;
Her thunders shook the mighty deep,
    And there should be her grave;
Nail to the mast her holy flag,
    Set every thread-bare sail,
And give her to the god of storms,—
    The lightning and the gale!

The Chambered Nautilus

This is the ship of pearl, which, poets feign,
    Sails the unshadowed main, —
    The venturous bark that flings
On the sweet summer wind its purpled wings
In gulfs enchanted, where the siren sings,
    And coral reefs lie bare,
Where the cold sea-maids rise to sun their streaming hair.

Its webs of living gauze no more unfurl;
    Wrecked is the ship of pearl!
    And every chambered cell,
Where its dim dreaming life was wont to dwell,
As the frail tenant shaped his growing shell,
    Before thee lies revealed, —
Its irised ceiling rent, its sunless crypt unsealed!

Year after year beheld the silent toil
    That spread his lustrous coil;
    Still, as the spiral grew,
He left the past year's dwelling for the new,
Stole with soft step its shining archway through,
    Built up its idle door,
Stretched in his last-found home, and knew the old no
       more.

Thanks for the heavenly message brought by thee,
    Child of the wandering sea,
    Cast from her lap forlorn!
From thy dead lips a clearer note is born
Than ever Triton blew from wreathèd horn!
    While on mine ear it rings,
Through the deep caves of thought I hear a voice that
       sings: —

Build thee more stately mansions, O my soul,
As the swift seasons roll!
Leave thy low-vaulted past!
Let each new temple, nobler than the last,
Shut thee from heaven with a dome more vast,
Till thou at length art free,
Leaving thine outgrown shell by life's unresting sea!

The Deacon's Masterpiece: or the Wonderful "One-Hoss-Shay"

A Logical Story

Have you heard of the wonderful one-hoss-shay,
That was built in such a logical way
It ran a hundred years to a day,
And then, of a sudden, it——ah, but stay,
I'll tell you what happened without delay,
Scaring the parson into fits,
Frightening people out of their wits,—
Have you ever heard of that, I say?

Seventeen hundred and fifty-five.
Georgius Secundus was then alive,—
Snuffy old drone from the German hive!
That was the year when Lisbon-town
Saw the earth open and gulp her down,
And Braddock's army was done so brown,
Left without a scalp to its crown.
It was on the terrible Earthquake-day
That the Deacon finished the one-hoss-shay.

Now in building of chaises, I tell you what,
There is always *somewhere* a weakest spot,—
In hub, tire, felloe, in spring or thill,
In panel, or crossbar, or floor, or sill,
In screw, bolt, thoroughbrace,—lurking still
Find it somewhere you must and will,—

Above or below, or within or without,—
And that's the reason, beyond a doubt,
A chaise *breaks down*, but doesn't *wear out*.

But the Deacon swore (as Deacons do,
With an "I dew vum," or an "I tell *yeou*,")
He would build one shay to beat the taown
'n' the keounty 'n' all the kentry raoun';
It should be so built that it *couldn'* break daown:
—"Fur," said the Deacon, " 't 's mighty plain
Thut the weakes' place mus' stan the strain;
'n' the way t' fix it, uz I maintain,
        Is only jest
T' make that place uz strong uz the rest."

So the Deacon inquired of the village folk
Where he could find the strongest oak,
That couldn't be split nor bent nor broke,—
That was for spokes and floor and sills;
He sent for lancewood to make the thills;
The crossbars were ash, from the straightest trees;
The panels of white-wood, that cuts like cheese,
But lasts like iron for things like these;
The hubs of logs from the "Settler's ellum,"—
Last of its timber,—they couldn't sell 'em,
Never an axe had seen their chips,
And the wedges flew from between their lips,
Their blunt ends frizzled like celery-tips;
Step and prop-iron, bolt and screw,
Spring, tire, axle, and linchpin too,
Steel of the finest, bright and blue;
Thoroughbrace bison-skin, thick and wide;
Boot, top, dasher, from tough old hide
Found in the pit when the tanner died.
That was the way he "put her through."—
"There!" said the Deacon, "naow she'll dew!"

Do! I tell you, I rather guess
She was a wonder, and nothing less!
Colts grew horses, beards turned gray,

Deacon and deaconess dropped away,
Children and grand-children—where were they?
But there stood the stout old one-hoss-shay
As fresh as on Lisbon-earthquake-day!

EIGHTEEN HUNDRED;—it came and found
The Deacon's Masterpiece strong and sound.
Eighteen hundred increased by ten;—
"Hahnsum kerridge" they called it then.
Eighteen hundred and twenty came;—
Running as usual; much the same.
Thirty and forty at last arrive,
And then come fifty, and FIFTY-FIVE.

Little of all we value here
Wakes on the morn of its hundredth year
Without both feeling and looking queer.
In fact, there's nothing that keeps its youth,
So far as I know, but a tree and truth.
(This is a moral that runs at large;
Take it.—You're welcome.—No extra charge.)

FIRST OF NOVEMBER,—the Earthquake-day.—
There are traces of age in the one-hoss-shay,
A general flavor of mild decay,
But nothing local, as one may say.
There couldn't be,—for the Deacon's art
Had made it so like in every part
That there wasn't a chance for one to start.
For the wheels were just as strong as the thills,
And the floor was just as strong as the sills,
And the panels just as strong as the floor,
And the whippletree neither less nor more,
And the back-crossbar as strong as the fore,
And spring and axle and hub *encore*.
And yet, *as a whole*, it is past a doubt
In another hour it will be *worn out!*

First of November, 'Fifty-five!
This morning the parson takes a drive.

Now, small boys, get out of the way!
Here comes the wonderful one-horse-shay,
Drawn by a rat-tailed, ewe-necked bay.
"Huddup!" said the parson. — Off went they.

The parson was working his Sunday's text, —
Had got to *fifthly*, and stopped perplexed
At what the — Moses — was coming next.
All at once the horse stood still,
Close by the meet'n'-house on the hill.
— First a shiver, and then a thrill,
Then something decidedly like a spill, —
And the parson was sitting upon a rock,
At half-past nine by the meet'n-house clock, —
Just the hour of the Earthquake shock!
— What do you think the parson found,
When he got up and stared around?
The poor old chaise in a heap or mound,
As if it had been to the mill and ground!
You see, of course, if you're not a dunce,
How it went to pieces all at once, —
All at once, and nothing first, —
Just as bubbles do when they burst.

End of the wonderful one-hoss-shay.
Logic is logic. That's all I say.

Nearing the Snow-Line

Slow toiling upward from the misty vale,
   I leave the bright enamelled zones below;
   No more for me their beauteous bloom shall glow,
Their lingering sweetness load the morning gale;
Few are the slender flowerets, scentless, pale,
   That on their ice-clad stems all trembling blow
   Along the margin of unmelting snow;
Yet with unsaddened voice thy verge I hail,
   White realm of peace above the flowering line;
Welcome thy frozen domes, thy rocky spires!
   O'er thee undimmed the moon-girt planets shine,
On thy majestic altars fade the fires
That filled the air with smoke of vain desires,
   And all the unclouded blue of heaven is thine!

THOMAS HOLLEY CHIVERS

(1809–1858)

Avalon

"I will open my dark saying upon the Harp."—DAVID.

*"All thy waves and billows are gone over me. I sink
in deep mire where there is no standing!"*—PSALMS.

*"There be tears of perfect moan
Wept for thee in Helicon."*—MILTON.

I

Death's pale cold orb has turned to an eclipse
  My Son of Love!
The worms are feeding on thy lily-lips,
  My milk-white Dove!
Pale purple tinges thy soft finger-tips!
While nectar thy pure soul in glory sips,
As Death's cold frost mine own forever nips!
    Where thou art lying
    Beside the beautiful undying
    In the Valley of the pausing of the Moon,
    Oh! AVALON! my son! my son!

II

Wake up, oh! AVALON! my son! my son!
  And come from Death!
Heave off the clod that lies so heavy on
  Thy breast beneath
In that cold grave, my more than Precious One!
And come to me! for I am here alone—
With none to comfort me!—my hopes are gone
    Where thou art lying
    Beside the beautiful undying
    In the Valley of the pausing of the Moon,
    Oh! AVALON! my son! my son!

III

Forever more must I, on this damp sod,
   Renew and keep
My Covenant of Sorrows with my God,
   And weep, weep, weep!
Writhing in pain beneath Death's iron rod!
Till I shall go to that DIVINE ABODE —
Treading the path that thy dear feet have trod —
     Where thou art lying
      Beside the beautiful undying
    In the Valley of the pausing of the Moon,
    Oh! AVALON! my son! my son!

IV

Oh! precious Saviour! gracious heavenly Lord!
   Refresh my soul!
Here, with the healings of thy heavenly Word,
   Make my heart whole!
My little Lambs are scattered now abroad
In Death's dark Valley, where they bleat unheard!
Dear Shepherd! give their Shepherd his reward
     Where they are lying
      Beside the beautiful undying
    In the Valley of the pausing of the Moon,
    With AVALON! my son! my son!

V

For thou didst tread with fire-ensandaled feet,
   Star-crowned, forgiven,
The burning diapason of the stars so sweet,
   To God in Heaven!
And, walking on the sapphire-paven street,
Didst take upon the highest Sill thy seat —
Waiting in glory there my soul to meet,
     When I am lying
      Beside the beautiful undying
    In the Valley of the pausing of the Moon,
    Oh! AVALON! my son! my son!

VI

Thou wert my Micro-Uranos below—
    My Little Heaven!
My Micro-Cosmos in this world of wo,
    From morn till even!
A living Lyre of God who charmed me so
With thy sweet songs, that I did seem to go
Out of this world where thou art shining now,
        But without lying
        Beside the beautiful undying
    In the Valley of the pausing of the Moon,
    Oh! AVALON! my son! my son!

VII

Thou wert my son of Melody alway,
    Oh! Child Divine!
Whose golden radiance filled the world with Day!
    For thou didst shine
A lustrous Diadem of Song for aye,
Whose Divertisments, through Heaven's Holyday,
    Now ravish Angel's ears—as well they may—
        While I am crying
        Beside the beautiful undying
    In the Valley of the pausing of the Moon,
    Oh! AVALON! my son! my son!

VIII

Thy soul did soar up to the Gates of God,
    Oh! Lark-like Child!
And through Heaven's Bowers of Bliss, by Angels trod,
    Poured Wood-notes wild!
In emulation of that Bird, which stood,
In solemn silence, listening to thy flood
Of golden Melody deluge the wood
        Where thou art lying
        Beside the beautiful undying
    In the Valley of the pausing of the Moon,
    Oh! AVALON! my son! my son!

IX

Throughout the Spring-time of Eternity,
  Oh! AVALON!
Paeans of thy selectest melody
  Pour forth, dear Son!
Clapping thy snow-white hands incessantly,
Amid Heaven's Bowers of Bliss in ecstasy—
The odor of thy song inviting me
    Where thou art lying
    Beside the beautiful undying
  In the Valley of the pausing of the Moon,
  Oh! AVALON! my son! my son!

X

The redolent quintessence of thy tongue,
  Oh! AVALON!
Embowered by Angels Heaven's sweet Bowers among—
  Many in one—
Is gathered from the choicest of the throng,
In an Æonian Hymn forever young,
Thou Philomelian Eclecticist of Song!
    While I am sighing
    Beside the beautiful undying
  In the Valley of the pausing of the Moon,
  For AVALON! my son! my son!

XI

Here lies dear Florence with her golden hair,
  And violet eyes;
Whom God, because she was for earth too fair,
  Took to the skies!
With whom my Zilly only could compare—
Or Eugene Percy, who was debonair,
And rivaled each in every thing most rare!
    These now are lying
    Beside the beautiful undying
  In the Valley of the pausing of the Moon,
  With AVALON! my son! my son!

XII

Her eyes were like two Violets bathed in dew
　　From morn till even—
The modest Myrtle's blossom-Angel blue,
　　And full of Heaven.
Up to the golden gates of God she flew,
To grow in glory as on earth she grew,
Heaven's own primeval joys again to view—
　　　While I am crying
　　　Beside the beautiful undying
　　In the Valley of the pausing of the Moon,
　　Oh! AVALON! my son! my son!

XIII

The Violet of her soul-suffused eyes
　　Was like that flower
Which blows its purple trumpet at the skies
　　For Dawn's first hour—
The Morning-glory at the first sunrise,
Nipt by Death's frost with all her glorious dyes!
For Florence rests where my dear Lily lies—
　　　Where thou art lying
　　　Beside the beautiful undying
　　In the Valley of the pausing of the Moon,
　　Oh! AVALON! my son! my son!

XIV

Four little Angels killed by one cold Death
　　To make God glad!
Four Cherubs gone to God, the best he hath—
　　And all I had!
Taken together, as if in His wrath,
While walking, singing, on Hope's flowery path—
Breathing out gladness at each odorous breath—
　　　Now they are lying
　　　Beside the beautiful undying
　　In the Valley of the pausing of the Moon,
　　Oh! AVALON! my son! my son!

XV

Thou wert like Taleisin, "full of eyes,"
  Bardling of Love!
My beautiful Divine Eumenides!
  My gentle Dove!
Thou silver Swan of Golden Elegies!
Whose Mendelsohnian Songs now fill the skies!
While I am weeping where my Lily lies!
    Where thou art lying
    Beside the beautiful undying
  In the Valley of the pausing of the Moon,
  Oh! AVALON! my son! my son!

XVI

Kindling the high-uplifted stars at even
  With thy sweet song,
The Angels, on the Sapphire Sills of Heaven,
  In rapturous throng,
Melted to milder meekness, with the Seven
Bright Lamps of God to glory given,
Leant down to hear thy voice roll up the leven,
    Where thou art lying
    Beside the beautiful undying
  In the valley of the pausing of the Moon,
  Oh! AVALON! my son! my son!

XVII

Can any thing that Christ has ever said,
  Make my heart whole?
Can less than bringing back the early dead,
  Restore my soul?
No! this alone can make my Heavenly bread—
Christ's Bread of Life brought down from Heaven, instead
Of this sad Song, on which my soul has fed,
    Where thou art lying
    Beside the beautiful undying
  In the Valley of the pausing of the Moon,
  Oh! AVALON! my son! my son!

XVIII

Have I not need to weep from Morn till Even,
    Far bitterer tears
Than cruel Earth, the unforgiven,
    Through his long years —
Inquisitorial Hell, or strictest Heaven,
Wrung from Christ's bleeding heart when riven?
Thus from one grief unto another driven,
        Where thou art lying
        Beside the beautiful undying
    In the Valley of the pausing of the Moon,
    Oh! AVALON! my son! my son!

XIX

Yes! I have need to weep, to groan, to cry,
    And never faint,
Till, battering down God's Golden Gates on high,
    With my complaint,
I soften his great heart to make reply,
By sending my dear son from Heaven on high —
Or causing me in this dark grave to lie,
        Where thou art lying
        Beside the beautiful undying
    In the Valley of the pausing of the Moon,
    Oh! AVALON! my son! my son!

XX

I see the BRIDEGROOM of the Heavenly Bride,
    In robes of light!
My little ONES now stand his form beside,
    In linen white!
Embowered by Angels, star-crowned, in their pride,
Singing Æonian songs in joyful tide —
Although much larger grown than when they died —
        While I am sighing
        Beside the beautiful undying
    In the Valley of the pausing of the Moon,
    Oh! AVALON! my son! my son!

Apollo

What are stars, but hieroglyphics of God's glory writ in
      lightning
   On the wide unfolded pages of the azure scroll above?
But the quenchless apotheoses of thoughts forever brightening
   In the mighty Mind immortal of the God, whose name is
      LOVE?
Diamond letters sculptured, rising, on the azure ether pages,
   That now sing to one another—unto one another shine—
God's eternal Scripture talking, through the midnight, to the
      Ages,
   Of the life that is immortal, of the life that is divine—
   Life that *cannot* be immortal, but the life that is divine.

Like some deep, impetuous river from the fountains everlasting,
   Down the serpentine soft valley of the vistas of all Time,
Over cataracts of adamant uplifted into mountains,
   Soared his soul to God in thunder on the wings of thought
      sublime,
With the rising golden glory of the sun in ministrations,
   Making oceans metropolitan of splendor for the dawn—
Piling pyramid on pyramid of music for the nations—
   Sings the Angel who sits shining everlasting in the sun,
   For the stars, which are the echoes of the shining of the
      sun.

Like the lightnings piled on lightnings, ever rising, never
      reaching,
   In one monument of glory towards the golden gates of
      God—
Voicing out themselves in thunder upon thunder in their
      preaching,
   Piled this Cyclop up his Epic where the Angels never trod.
Like the fountains everlasting that forever more are flowing
   From the throne within the centre of the City built on
      high,
With their genial irrigation life forever more bestowing—
   Flows his lucid, liquid river through the gardens of the sky,
   For the stars forever blooming in the gardens of the sky.

FANNY KEMBLE

(1809–1893)

To the Wissahiccon

My feet shall tread no more thy mossy side,
   When once they turn away, thou *Pleasant Water*,
Nor ever more, reflected in thy tide,
   Will shine the eyes of the White Island's daughter.
But often in my dreams, when I am gone
   Beyond the sea that parts thy home and mine,
   Upon thy banks the evening sun will shine,
And I shall hear thy low, still flowing on.
And when the burden of existence lies
   Upon my soul, darkly and heavily,
I'll clasp my hands over my weary eyes,
   Thou *Pleasant Water*, and thy clear waves see.
Bright be thy course for ever and for ever,
   Child of pure mountain springs, and mountain snow;
And as thou wanderest on to meet the river,
   Oh, still in light and music mayst thou flow!
I never shall come back to thee again,
When once my sail is shadowed on the main,
Nor ever shall I hear thy laughing voice
As on their rippling way thy waves rejoice,
Nor ever see the dark green cedar throw
Its gloomy shade o'er the clear depths below,
Never, from stony rifts of granite gray
Sparkling like diamond rocks in the sun's ray,
Shall I look down on thee, thou pleasant stream,
Beneath whose crystal folds the gold sands gleam;
Wherefore, farewell! but whensoe'er again
   The wintry spell melts from the earth and air;
And the young Spring comes dancing through thy glen,
   With fragrant, flowery breath, and sunny hair;
When through the snow the scarlet berries gleam,
Like jewels strewn upon thy banks, fair stream,
My spirit shall through many a summer's day
Return, among thy peaceful woods to stray.

MARGARET FULLER

(1810 – 1850)

Sistrum

Triune, shaping, restless power,
Life-flow from life's natal hour,
No music chords are in thy sound;
By some thou'rt but a rattle found;
Yet, without thy ceaseless motion,
To ice would turn their dead devotion.
Life-flow of my natal hour,
I will not weary of thy power,
Till in the changes of thy sound
A chord's three parts distinct are found.
I will faithful move with thee,
God-ordered, self-fed energy,
Nature in eternity.

Flaxman

We deemed the secret lost, the spirit gone,
Which spake in Greek simplicity of thought,
And in the forms of gods and heroes wrought
Eternal beauty from the sculptured stone, —
A higher charm than modern culture won
With all the wealth of metaphysic lore,
Gifted to analyze, dissect, explore.
A many-colored light flows from one sun;
Art, 'neath its beams, a motley thread has spun;
The prism modifies the perfect day;
But thou hast known such mediums to shun,
And cast once more on life a pure, white ray.
Absorbed in the creations of thy mind,
Forgetting daily self, my truest self I find.

EDMUND HAMILTON SEARS

(1810–1876)

"It came upon the midnight clear"

It came upon the midnight clear,
   That glorious song of old,
From angels bending near the earth
   To touch their harps of gold;
"Peace on the earth, good will to men
   From heaven's all-gracious King"—
The world in solemn stillness lay
   To hear the angels sing.

Still through the cloven skies they come
   With peaceful wings unfurled,
And still their heavenly music floats
   O'er all the weary world;
Above its sad and lowly plains
   They bend on hovering wing,
And ever o'er its Babel-sounds
   The blessed angels sing.

But with the woes of sin and strife
   The world has suffered long;
Beneath the angel-strain have rolled
   Two thousand years of wrong;
And man, at war with man, hears not
   The love-song which they bring;—
Oh hush the noise, ye men of strife,
   And hear the angels sing!

And ye, beneath life's crushing load,
   Whose forms are bending low,
Who toil along the climbing way
   With painful steps and slow,

Look now! for glad and golden hours
    Come swiftly on the wing;—
Oh, rest beside the weary road
    And hear the angels sing!

For lo! the days are hastening on
    By prophet bards foretold,
When with the ever circling years
    Comes round the age of gold;
When Peace shall over all the earth
    Its ancient splendors fling,
And the whole world give back the song
    Which now the angels sing.

CHRISTOPHER PEARSE CRANCH

(1813–1892)

Correspondences

All things in nature are beautiful types to the soul that can
    read them;
Nothing exists upon earth, but for unspeakable ends,
Every object that speaks to the senses was meant for the
    spirit;
Nature is but a scroll; God's handwriting thereon.
Ages ago when man was pure, ere the flood overwhelmed
    him,
While in the image of God every soul yet lived,
Every thing stood as a letter or word of a language familiar,
Telling of truths which now only the angels can read.
Lost to man was the key of those sacred hieroglyphics,
Stolen away by sin, till by heaven restored.
Now with infinite pains we here and there spell out a letter,
Here and there will the sense feebly shine through the dark.
When we perceive the light that breaks through the visible
    symbol,
What exultation is ours! *We* the discovery have made!
Yet is the meaning the same as when Adam lived sinless in
    Eden,
Only long hidden it slept, and now again is revealed.
Man unconsciously uses figures of speech every moment,
Little dreaming the cause why to such terms he is prone,
Little dreaming that every thing here has its own
    correspondence
Folded within its form, as in the body the soul.
Gleams of the mystery fall on us still, though much is
    forgotten,
And through our commonest speech, illumine the path of
    our thoughts.

Thus doth the lordly sun shine forth a type of the Godhead;
Wisdom and love the beams that stream on a darkened
      world.
Thus do the sparkling waters flow, giving joy to the desert,
And the fountain of life opens itself to the thirst.
Thus doth the word of God distil like the rain and the
      dew-drops;
Thus doth the warm wind breathe like to the Spirit of God;
And the green grass and the flowers are signs of the
      regeneration.

O thou Spirit of Truth, visit our minds once more,
Give us to read in letters of light the language celestial
Written all over the earth, written all over the sky—
Thus may we bring our hearts once more to know our
      Creator,
Seeing in all things around, types of the Infinite Mind.

Enosis

Thought is deeper than all speech,
    Feeling deeper than all thought;
Souls to souls can never teach
    What unto themselves was taught.

We are spirits clad in veils;
    Man by man was never seen;
All our deep communing fails
    To remove the shadowy screen.

Heart to heart was never known;
    Mind with mind did never meet;
We are columns left alone,
    Of a temple once complete.

Like the stars that gem the sky,
    Far apart, though seeming near,
In our light we scattered lie;
    All is thus but starlight here.

What is social company
    But a babbling summer stream?
What our wise philosophy
    But the glancing of a dream?

Only when the sun of love
    Melts the scattered stars of thought;
Only when we live above
    What the dim-eyed world hath taught;

Only when our souls are fed
    By the Fount which gave them birth,
And by inspiration led,
    Which they never drew from earth,

We like parted drops of rain
    Swelling till they meet and run,
Shall be all absorbed again,
    Melting, flowing into one.

The Cataract Isle

I wandered through the ancient wood
    That crowns the cataract isle.
I heard the roaring of the flood
    And saw its wild, fierce smile.

Through tall tree-tops the sunshine flecked
    The huge trunks and the ground,
And the pomp of fullest summer decked
    The island all around.

And winding paths led all along
    Where friends and lovers strayed,
And voices rose with laugh and song
    From sheltered nooks of shade.

Through opening forest vistas whirled
    The rapids' foamy flash,
As they boiled along and plunged and swirled,
    And neared the last long dash.

I crept to the island's outer verge,
    Where the grand, broad river fell, —
Fell sheer down mid foam and surge
    In a white and blinding hell.

The steady rainbow gayly shone
    Above the precipice,
And the deep low tone of a thunder groan
    Rolled up from the drear abyss.

And all the day sprang up the spray
    Where the broad white sheets were poured,
And fell around in showery play,
    Or upward curled and soared.

And all the night those sheets of white
    Gleamed through the spectral mist,
When o'er the isle the broad moonlight
    The wintry foam-flakes kissed.

Mirrored within my dreamy thought,
    I see it, feel it all, —
That island with sweet visions fraught,
    That awful waterfall.

With sunflecked trees, and birds and flowers,
    The Isle of Life is fair;
But one deep voice thrills through its hours,
    One spectral form is there, —

A power no mortal can resist,
    Rolling forever on, —
A floating cloud, a shadowy mist,
    Eternal undertone.

And through the sunny vistas gleam
    The fate, the solemn smile.
Life is Niagara's rushing stream;
    Its dreams — that peaceful isle!

In the Palais Royal Garden

In the Palais Royal Garden I stood listening to-day,
Just at sunset, in the crowd that flaunted up and down so gay
As the strains of "Casta Diva" rose and fell and died away.

Lonely in the crowd of French I stood and listened to the
    strain,
And the breath of happier hours came blowing from the past
    again;
But the music brought a pleasure that was near akin to pain.

Italy, dear Italy, came back, with all her orange flowers,
With her sapphire skies and ocean, with her shrines and
    crumbling towers,
And her dark-eyed women sitting under their vine-shaded
    bowers.

And the rich and brilliant concerts in my own far distant land,
Where the world-renownéd singers, circled by the orchestral
    band
Poured their music on the crowds like costly wine upon the
    sand.

All the aroma of the best and brightest hours of love and
    song
Mingled with the yearning music, floated to me o'er the
    throng.
But it died as died the sunset. Ah, it could not linger long!

Through the streets the carriages are rolling with a heavy jar,
Feebly o'er the staring gas-lamps glimmers here and there a
    star.
Night looks down through narrow spaces; men are near, the
    skies are far.

Far too are my friends, the cherished,—north and south and
    o'er the sea.
And to-night I pant for music and for life that cannot be,
For the foreign city's crowd is naught but solitude to me.

The Spirit of the Age

A wondrous light is filling the air,
And rimming the clouds of the old despair;
And hopeful eyes look up to see
Truth's mighty electricity,—
Auroral shimmerings swift and bright,
That wave and flash in the silent night,—
Magnetic billows travelling fast,
And flooding all the spaces vast
From dim horizon to farthest cope
Of heaven, in streams of gathering hope.
Silent they mount and spread apace,
And the watchers see old Europe's face
Lit with expression new and strange,—
The prophecy of coming change.

Meantime, while thousands, wrapt in dreams,
Sleep heedless of the electric gleams,
Or ply their wonted work and strife,
Or plot their pitiful games of life;
While the emperor bows in his formal halls,
And the clerk whirls on at the masking balls;
While the lawyer sits at his dreary files,
And the banker fingers his glittering piles,
And the priest kneels down at his lighted shrine,
And the fop flits by with his mistress fine,—
The diplomat works at his telegraph wires:
His back is turned to the heavenly fires.
Over him flows the magnetic tide,
And the candles are dimmed by the glow outside.
Mysterious forces overawe,
Absorb, suspend the usual law.
The needle stood northward an hour ago;
Now it veers like a weathercock to and fro.
The message he sends flies not as once;
The unwilling wires yield no response.
Those iron veins that pulsed but late
From a tyrant's will to a people's fate,
Flowing and ebbing with feverish strength,

Are seized by a Power whose breadth and length,
Whose height and depth, defy all gauge
Save the great spirit of the age.
The mute machine is moved by a law
That knows no accident or flaw,
And the iron thrills to a different chime
Than that which rang in the dead old time.
For Heaven is taking the matter in hand,
And baffling the tricks of the tyrant band.
The sky above and the earth beneath
Heave with a supermundane breath.
Half-truths, for centuries kept and prized,
By higher truths are polarized.
Like gamesters on a railroad train,
Careless of stoppage, sun or rain,
We juggle, plot, combine, arrange,
And are swept along by the rapid change.
And some who from their windows mark
The unwonted lights that flood the dark,
Little by little, in slow surprise
Lift into space their sleepy eyes;
Little by little are made aware
That a spirit of power is passing there,—
That a spirit is passing, strong and free,—
The soul of the nineteenth century.

An Old Cat's Confessions

I am a very old pussy,
    My name is Tabitha Jane;
I have had about fifty kittens,
    So I think that I mustn't complain.

Yet I've had my full share of cat's troubles:
    I was run over once by a cart;
And they drowned seventeen of my babies,
    Which came near breaking my heart.

A gentleman once singed my whiskers, —
    I shall never forgive him for that!
And once I was bit by a mad dog,
    And once was deceived by a rat.

I was tied by some boys in a meal-bag,
    And pelted and pounded with stones;
They thought I was mashed to a jelly,
    But it didn't break one of my bones.

For cats that have good constitutions
    Have eight more lives than a man;
Which proves we are better than humans
    To my mind, if anything can.

One night, as I wandered with Thomas, —
    We were singing a lovely duet, —
I was shot in the back by a bullet;
    When you stroke me, I feel it there yet.

A terrier once threatened my kittens;
    O, it gave me a terrible fright!
But I scratched him, and sent him off howling,
    And I think that I served him just right.

But I've failed to fulfill all my duties:
    I have purred half my life in a dream;
And I never devoured the canary,
    And I never lapped half enough cream.

But I've been a pretty good mouser,
    (What squirrels and birds I have caught!)
And have brought up my frolicsome kittens
    As a dutiful mother-cat ought.

Now I think I've a right, being aged,
    To take an old tabby's repose;
To have a good breakfast and dinner,
    And sit by the fire and doze.

I don't care much for the people
  Who are living with me in this house,
But I own that I love a good fire,
  And occasional herring and mouse.

Music

Read at the Annual Dinner of the Harvard Musical Association,
Boston, January 28, 1874.

When "Music, Heavenly Maid," was *very* young,
She did not sing as poets say she sung.
Unlike the mermaids of the fairy tales,
She paid but slight attention to her scales.
Besides, poor thing! she had no instruments
But such as rude barbaric art invents.
There were no Steinways then, no Chickerings,
No spinnets, harpsichords, or metal strings;
No hundred-handed orchestras, no schools
To corset her in contrapuntal rules.
Some rude half-octave of a shepherd's song,
Some childish strumming all the summer long
On sinews stretched across a tortoise-shell,
Such as they say Apollo loved so well;
Some squeaking flageolet or scrannel pipe,
Some lyre poetic of the banjo type,—
Such were the means she summoned to her aid,
Prized as divine; on these she sang or played.

Music was then an infant, while she saw
Her sister arts full grown. Greece stood in awe
Before the Phidian Jove. Apelles drew
And Zeuxis painted. Marble temples "grew
As grows the grass"; and never saw the sun
A statelier vision than the Parthenon.

But she, the Muse who in these latter days
Lifts us and floats us in the golden haze
Of melodies and harmonies divine,
And steeps our souls and senses in such wine

As never Ganymede nor Hebe poured
For gods, when quaffing at the Olympian board,—
She, Heavenly Maid, must ply her music thin,
And sit and thrum her tinkling mandolin,
Chant her rude staves, and only prophesy
Her far-off days of immortality.

E'en so poor Cinderella, when she cowered
Beside her hearth, and saw her sisters, dowered
With grace and wealth, go forth to accomplish all
Their haughty triumphs at the Prince's ball,
While she in russet gown sat mournfully
Singing her "Once a king there chanced to be,"
Yet knows her prince will come; her splendid days
Are all foreshadowed in her dreaming gaze.

Then, as the years and centuries rolled on,
Like Santa-Clauses they have come and gone,
Bringing all means of utterance to the Muse.
No penny-trumpets, such as children use,
No barbarous Indian drums, no twanging lutes,
No buzzing Jews-harps, no Pandean flutes,
Were stuffed into her stockings, though they hung
On Time's great chimney, as when she was young;
But every rare and costly instrument
That skill can fabricate or art invent,—
Pianos, organs, viols, horns, trombones,
Hautboys, and clarinets with reedy tones,
Boehm-flutes and cornets, bugles, harps, bassoons,
Huge double-basses, kettle-drum half-moons,
And every queer contrivance made for tunes.

Through these the master-spirits round her throng,
And Europe rings with instruments and song.
Through these she breathes her wondrous symphonies,
Enchanting airs, and choral litanies.
Through these she speaks the word that never dies,
The universal language of the skies.
Around her gather those who held their art
To be of life the dearest, noblest part.

Bach, Handel, Haydn, and Mozart are there;
Beethoven, chief of all. The southern air
Is ringing with Rossini's birdlike notes;
About the north more earnest music floats,
Where Weber, Schumann, Schubert, Mendelssohn,
And long processions of the lords of Tone
All come to attend her. Like a queen enthroned
She sits and rules the realms she long has owned,
And sways the willing sense, the aspiring soul,
Where thousands bow before her sweet control.

Ah! greater than all words of mine can say,
The heights, the depths, the glories, of that sway.
No mortal tongue can bring authentic speech
Of that enchanted world beyond its reach;
No tongue but hers, when, lifted on the waves
Of Tone and Harmony, beyond the graves
Of all we lose, we drift entranced away
Out of the discords of the common day;
And she, the immortal goddess, on her breast
Lulls us to visions of a sweet unrest,
Smiles at the tyrannies of time and space,
And folds us in a mother's fond embrace,
Till, sailing on upon that mystic sea,
We feel that Life is Immortality.

Bird Language

One day in the bluest of summer weather,
  Sketching under a whispering oak,
I heard five bobolinks laughing together
  Over some ornithological joke.

What the fun was I could n't discover.
  Language of birds is a riddle on earth.
What could they find in whiteweed and clover
  To split their sides with such musical mirth?

Was it some prank of the prodigal summer,
   Face in the cloud or voice in the breeze,
Querulous catbird, woodpecker drummer,
   Cawing of crows high over the trees?

Was it some chipmunk's chatter, or weasel
   Under the stone-wall stealthy and sly?
Or was the joke about me at my easel,
   Trying to catch the tints of the sky?

Still they flew tipsily, shaking all over,
   Bubbling with jollity, brimful of glee,
While I sat listening deep in the clover,
   Wondering what their jargon could be.

'T was but the voice of a morning the brightest
   That ever dawned over yon shadowy hills;
'T was but the song of all joy that is lightest,—
   Sunshine breaking in laughter and trills.

Vain to conjecture the words they are singing;
   Only by tones can we follow the tune
In the full heart of the summer fields ringing,
   Ringing the rhythmical gladness of June!

from *Seven Wonders of the World*

The Printing-Press

In boyhood's days we read with keen delight
How young Aladdin rubbed his lamp and raised
The towering Djin whose form his soul amazed,
Yet who was pledged to serve him day and night.
But Gutenberg evoked a giant sprite
Of vaster power, when Europe stood and gazed
To see him rub his types with ink. Then blazed
Across the lands a glorious shape of light,
Who stripped the cowl from priests, the crown from kings,
And hand in hand with Faith and Science wrought

To free the struggling spirit's limèd wings,
And guard the ancestral throne of sovereign Thought.
The world was dumb. Then first it found its tongue
And spake — and heaven and earth in answer rung.

The Locomotive

Whirling along its living freight, it came,
Hot, panting, fierce, yet docile to command —
The roaring monster, blazing through the land
Athwart the night, with crest of smoke and flame;
Like those weird bulls Medea learned to tame
By sorcery, yoked to plough the Colchian strand
In forced obedience under Jason's hand.
Yet modern skill outstripped this antique fame,
When o'er our plains and through the rocky bar
Of hills it pushed its ever-lengthening line
Of iron roads, with gain far more divine
Than when the daring Argonauts from far
Came for the golden fleece, which like a star
Hung clouded in the dragon-guarded shrine.

The Photograph

Phœbus Apollo, from Olympus driven,
Lived with Admetus, tending herds and flocks:
And strolling o'er the pastures and the rocks
He found his life much duller than in Heaven.
For he had left his bow, his songs, his lyre,
His divinations and his healing skill,
And as a serf obeyed his master's will.
One day a new thought waked an old desire.
He took to painting, with his colors seven,
The sheep, the cows, the faces of the swains,
All shapes and hues in forests and on plains.
These old sun-pictures all are lost, or given
Away among the gods. Man owns but half
The Sun-god's secret — in the Photograph.

CHARLES TIMOTHY BROOKS

(1813–1883)

Our Island Home

Though here no towering mountain-steep
 Leaps, forest-crowned, to meet the sky;
Nor prairie, with majestic sweep,
 Enchants the gazer's roaming eye,—

Yet ocean's glittering garden-bed,
 Summer and winter, cheers the sight:
Its rose, the sun, at noon flames red;
 The moon, its lily, blooms by night.

The white-winged ships, in fleet career,
 Like sea-birds o'er the ocean skim;
They rise, glide on, and disappear
 Behind the horizon's shadowy rim.

So sail the fleets of clouds; and so
 Stars rise, and climb the heavens, and set,
Like human thoughts, that come and go—
 Whence—whither—no man knoweth yet.

Far onward sweeps the billowy main;
 To meet it bends th' o'erarching sky:
Of God's vast being emblems twain;
 Deep unto deep gives glad reply.

These open, each, a broad highway;
 To endless realms the soul invite:
The trackless ocean-floor by day,
 The star-lit stairs of heaven by night.

Oh, enviable lot! to dwell
 Surrounded by the great-voiced sea,
Whose waves intone, with trumpet-swell,
 The hymn of Law and Liberty!

JONES VERY

(1813–1880)

The New Birth

'Tis a new life—thoughts move not as they did
With slow uncertain steps across my mind,
In thronging haste fast pressing on they bid
The portals open to the viewless wind;
That comes not, save when in the dust is laid
The crown of pride that gilds each mortal brow,
And from before man's vision melting fade
The heavens and earth—Their walls are falling now—
Fast crowding on each thought claims utterance strong,
Storm-lifted waves swift rushing to the shore
On from the sea they send their shouts along,
Back through the cave-worn rocks their thunders roar,
And I a child of God by Christ made free
Start from death's slumbers to eternity.

The Morning Watch

'Tis near the morning watch, the dim lamp burns
But scarcely shows how dark the slumbering street;
No sound of life the silent mart returns;
No friends from house to house their neighbors greet;
It is the sleep of death; a deeper sleep
Than e'er before on mortal eyelids fell;
No stars above the gloom their places keep;
No faithful watchmen of the morning tell;
Yet still they slumber on, though rising day
Hath through their windows poured the awakening light;
Or, turning in their sluggard trances, say—
"There yet are many hours to fill the night;"
They rise not yet; while on the bridegroom goes
'Till he the day's bright gates forever on them close!

The Garden

I saw the spot where our first parents dwelt;
And yet it wore to me no face of change,
For while amid its fields and groves I felt
As if I had not sinned, nor thought it strange;
My eye seemed but a part of every sight,
My ear heard music in each sound that rose,
Each sense forever found a new delight,
Such as the spirit's vision only knows;
Each act some new and ever-varying joy
Did by my Father's love for me prepare;
To dress the spot my ever fresh employ,
And in the glorious whole with Him to share;
No more without the flaming gate to stray,
No more for sin's dark stain the debt of death to pay.

The Song

When I would sing of crooked streams and fields,
On, on from me they stretch too far and wide,
And at their look my song all powerless yields,
And down the river bears me with its tide;
Amid the fields I am a child again,
The spots that then I loved I love the more,
My fingers drop the strangely-scrawling pen,
And I remember nought but nature's lore;
I plunge me in the river's cooling wave,
Or on the embroidered bank admiring lean,
Now some endangered insect life to save,
Now watch the pictured flowers and grasses green;
Forever playing where a boy I played,
By hill and grove, by field and stream delayed.

The Latter Rain

The latter rain, it falls in anxious haste
Upon the sun-dried fields and branches bare,
Loosening with searching drops the rigid waste
As if it would each root's lost strength repair;
But not a blade grows green as in the spring,
No swelling twig puts forth its thickening leaves;
The robins only mid the harvests sing
Pecking the grain that scatters from the sheaves;
The rain falls still—the fruit all ripened drops,
It pierces chestnut burr and walnut shell,
The furrowed fields disclose the yellow crops,
Each bursting pod of talents used can tell,
And all that once received the early rain
Declare to man it was not sent in vain.

The Dead

I see them crowd on crowd they walk the earth
Dry, leafless trees no Autumn wind laid bare;
And in their nakedness find cause for mirth,
And all unclad would winter's rudeness dare;
No sap doth through their clattering branches flow,
Whence springing leaves and blossoms bright appear;
Their hearts the living God have ceased to know,
Who gives the spring time to th'expectant year;
They mimic life, as if from him to steal
His glow of health to paint the livid cheek;
They borrow words for thoughts they cannot feel,
That with a seeming heart their tongue may speak;
And in their show of life more dead they live
Than those that to the earth with many tears they give.

Autumn Leaves

The leaves though thick are falling; one by one
Decayed they drop from off their parent tree;
Their work with autumn's latest day is done,
Thou see'st them borne upon its breezes free;
They lie strown here and there, their many dyes
That yesterday so caught thy passing eye;
Soiled by the rain each leaf neglected lies,
Upon the path where now thou hurriest by;
Yet think thee not their beauteous tints less fair,
Than when they hung so gaily o'er thy head;
But rather find thee eyes, and look thee there
Where now thy feet so heedless o'er them tread;
And thou shalt see where wasting now they lie,
The unseen hues of immortality.

The Cottage

The house my earthly parent left,
My heavenly Father e'er throws down;
For 'tis of air and sun bereft,
Nor stars its roof in beauty crown.

He gave it me, yet gave it not,
As one whose gifts are wise and good:
'Twas but a poor and clay-built cot,
And for a time the storms withstood;

But lengthening years, and frequent rain,
O'ercame its strength, it tottered, fell;
And left me homeless here again,
And where to go I could not tell.

But soon the light and open air,
Received me as a wandering child;
And I soon thought their house more fair,
And was from all my grief beguiled.

Mine was the grove, the pleasant field,
Where dwelt the flowers I daily trod;
And there beside them too I kneeled,
And called their friend, my Father, God.

The Wild Rose of Plymouth

Upon the Plymouth shore the wild rose blooms
As when the Pilgrims lived beside the bay
And scents the morning air with sweet perfumes,
Though new this hour more ancient far than they;
More ancient than the wild, yet friendly race,
That roved the land before the Pilgrims came;
And here for ages found a dwelling-place
Of whom our histories tell us but the name!
Though new this hour out from the Past it springs
Telling this summer morning of earth's prime;
And happy visions of the Future brings
That reach beyond, e'en to the verge of time;
Wreathing earth's children in one flowery chain
Of Love and Beauty ever to remain.

EPES SARGENT
(1813–1880)

The Planet Jupiter

Ever at night have I looked up for thee,
  O'er thy sidereal sisterhood supreme!
Ever at night have scanned the purple sea
  For the reflection of thy quivering beam!
When the white cloud thy diamond radiance screened,
  And the Bahama breeze began to wail,
How on the plunging bows for hours I've leaned,
  And watched the gradual lifting of thy veil!
Bright planet! lustrous effluence! thou ray
  From the Eternal Source of life and light!
Gleam on the track where Truth shall lead the way,
  And gild the inward as the outward night!
Shine but as now upon my dying eyes,
And Hope, from earth to thee, from thee to Heaven,
      shall rise!

The Sea-Breeze at Matanzas

After a night of languor without rest,—
  Striving to sleep, yet wishing morn might come,
By the pent, scorching atmosphere oppressed,
  Impatient of the vile mosquito's hum,—
With what reviving freshness from the sea,
  Its airy plumage glittering with the spray,
Comes the strong day-breeze, rushing joyously
  Into the bright arms of the encircling bay!
It tempers the keen ardor of the sun;
  The drooping frame with life renewed it fills;
It lashes the green waters as they run;
  It sways the graceful palm-tree on the hills;
It breathes of ocean solitudes, and caves,
  Luminous, vast, and cool, far down beneath the waves.

DANIEL DECATUR EMMETT

(1815–1904)

Dixie's Land

I wish I was in de land ob cotton,
Old times dar am not forgotten,
　　Look away! Look away! Look away! Dixie Land.
In Dixie Land whar I was born in,
Early on one frosty mornin,
　　Look away! Look away! Look away! Dixie Land.

　　　Den I wish I was in Dixie,
　　　　Hooray! Hooray!
　　　In Dixie Land, I'll took my stand,
　　　　To lib an die in Dixie,
　　Away, Away, Away down south in Dixie,
　　Away, Away, Away down south in Dixie.

Old Missus marry "Will-de-weaber,"
Willium was a gay deceaber;
　　Look away! Look away! Look away! Dixie Land.
But when he put his arm around 'er,
He smiled as fierce as a forty pounder.
　　Look away! Look away! Look away! Dixie Land.

　　Chorus.

His face was sharp as a butcher's cleaber,
But dat did not seem to greab 'er;
　　Look away! Look away! Look away! Dixie Land.
Old Missus acted de foolish part,
And died for a man dat broke her heart.
　　Look away! Look away! Look away! Dixie Land.

　　Chorus.

Now here's a health to the next old Missus,
An all de gals dat want to kiss us;
  Look away! Look away! Look away! Dixie Land.
But if you want to drive 'way sorrow,
Come and hear dis song to-morrow.
  Look away! Look away! Look away! Dixie Land.

  Chorus.

Dar's buck-wheat cakes an Ingen' batter,
Makes you fat or a little fatter;
  Look away! Look away! Look away! Dixie Land.
Den hoe it down an scratch your grabble,
To Dixie land I'm bound to trabble.
  Look away! Look away! Look away! Dixie Land.

  Chorus.

PHILIP PENDLETON COOKE

(1816–1850)

Florence Vane

I loved thee long and dearly,
    Florence Vane;
My life's bright dream, and early,
    Hath come again;
I renew, in my fond vision,
    My heart's dear pain,
My hope, and thy derision,
    Florence Vane.

The ruin lone and hoary,
    The ruin old,
Where thou didst hark my story,
    At even told,—
That spot—the hues Elysian
    Of sky and plain—
I treasure in my vision,
    Florence Vane.

Thou wast lovelier than the roses
    In their prime;
Thy voice excelled the closes
    Of sweetest rhyme;
Thy heart was as a river
    Without a main.
Would I had loved thee never,
    Florence Vane!

But, fairest, coldest wonder!
    Thy glorious clay
Lieth the green sod under—
    Alas the day!

And it boots not to remember
　　Thy disdain—
To quicken love's pale ember,
　　Florence Vane.

The lilies of the valley
　　By young graves weep,
The pansies love to dally
　　Where maidens sleep;
May their bloom, in beauty vying,
　　Never wane
Where thine earthly part is lying,
　　Florence Vane!

JOSIAH D. CANNING
(1816–1892)

The Indian Gone!

By night I saw the *Hunter's moon*
　Slow gliding in the placid sky;
Her lustre mocked the sun at noon —
　I asked myself the reason why?
And straightway came the sad reply:
　She shines as she was wont to do
To aid the Indian's aiming eye,
　When by her light he strung his bow,
　　　But where is he?

Beside the ancient flood I strayed,
　Where dark traditions mark the shore;
With wizzard vision I essayed
　Into the misty past to pore.
I heard a mournful voice deplore
　The perfidy that slew his race;
'T was in a dialect of yore,
　And of a long-departed race.
　　　It answered me!

I wrought with ardor at the plough
　One smoky Indian-summer day;
The dank locks swept my heated brow,
　I bade the panting oxen stay.
Beneath me in the furrow lay
　A relic of the chase, full low;
I brushed the crumbling soil away —
　The Indian fashioned it, I know,
　　　But where is he?

When pheasants drumming in the wood
　Allured me forth my aim to try,
Amid the forest lone I stood,

And the dead leaves went rustling by,
The breeze played in the branches high;
   Slow music filled my listening ear;
It was a wailing funeral cry,
   For Nature mourned her children dear.
      It answered me!

HENRY DAVID THOREAU

(1817–1862)

"They who prepare my evening meal below"

They who prepare my evening meal below
Carelessly hit the kettle as they go
With tongs or shovel,
And ringing round and round,
Out of this hovel
It makes an eastern temple by the sound.

At first I thought a cow bell right at hand
Mid birches sounded o'er the open land,
Where I plucked flowers
Many years ago,
Spending midsummer hours
With such secure delight they hardly seemed to flow.

"On fields oer which the reaper's hand has passd"

On fields oer which the reaper's hand has passd
Lit by the harvest moon and autumn sun,
My thoughts like stubble floating in the wind
And of such fineness as October airs,
There after harvest could I glean my life
A richer harvest reaping without toil,
And weaving gorgeous fancies at my will
In subtler webs than finest summer haze.

Fog

Dull water spirit—and Protean god
Descended cloud fast anchored to the earth
That drawest too much air for shallow coasts
Thou ocean branch that flowest to the sun
Incense of earth, perfumed with flowers—

302

Spirit of lakes and rivers— seas and rills
Come to revisit now thy native scenes
Night thoughts of earth—dream drapery
Dew cloth—and fairy napkin
Thou wind-blown meadow of the air

"Dong, sounds the brass in the east"

Dong, sounds the brass in the east,
As if to a funeral feast,
But I like that sound the best
Out of the fluttering west.

The steeple ringeth a knell,
But the fairies' silvery bell
Is the voice of that gentle folk,
Or else the horizon that spoke.

Its metal is not of brass,
But air, and water, and glass,
And under a cloud it is swung,
And by the wind it is rung.

When the steeple tolleth the noon,
It soundeth not so soon,
Yet it rings a far earlier hour,
And the sun has not reached its tower.

Rumors from an Æolian Harp

There is a vale which none hath seen,
Where foot of man has never been,
Such as here lives with toil and strife,
An anxious and a sinful life.

There every virtue has its birth,
Ere it descends upon the earth,
And thither every deed returns,
Which in the generous bosom burns.

There love is warm, and youth is young,
And poetry is yet unsung,
For Virtue still adventures there,
And freely breathes her native air.

And ever, if you hearken well,
You still may hear its vesper bell,
And tread of high-souled men go by,
Their thoughts conversing with the sky.

"My life has been the poem I would have writ"

My life has been the poem I would have writ,
But I could not both live and utter it.

"I am a parcel of vain strivings tied"

I am a parcel of vain strivings tied
    By a chance bond together,
  Dangling this way and that, their links
    Were made so loose and wide,
            Methinks,
        For milder weather.

A bunch of violets without their roots,
    And sorrel intermixed,
  Encircled by a wisp of straw
    Once coiled about their shoots,
            The law
        By which I'm fixed.

A nosegay which Time clutched from out
    Those fair Elysian fields,
  With weeds and broken stems, in haste,
    Doth make the rabble rout
            That waste
        The day he yields.

And here I bloom for a short hour unseen,
 Drinking my juices up,
 With no root in the land
  To keep my branches green,
   But stand
  In a bare cup.

Some tender buds were left upon my stem
 In mimicry of life,
 But ah! the children will not know,
  Till time has withered them,
   The woe
  With which they're rife.

But now I see I was not plucked for naught,
 And after in life's vase
 Of glass set while I might survive,
  But by a kind hand brought
   Alive
  To a strange place.

That stock thus thinned will soon redeem its hours,
 And by another year,
 Such as God knows, with freer air,
 More fruits and fairer flowers
  Will bear,
  While I droop here.

"Light-winged Smoke, Icarian bird"

Light-winged Smoke, Icarian bird,
Melting thy pinions in thy upward flight,
Lark without song, and messenger of dawn,
Circling above the hamlets as thy nest;
Or else, departing dream, and shadowy form
Of midnight vision, gathering up thy skirts;
By night star-veiling, and by day
Darkening the light and blotting out the sun;
Go thou my incense upward from this hearth,
And ask the gods to pardon this clear flame.

Music

Far from this atmosphere that music sounds
Piercing some azure chink in the dull clouds
Of sense that overarch my recent years,
And steal his freshness from the noonday sun.
Ah, I have wandered many ways and lost
The boyant step, the whole responsive life
That stood with joy to hear what seemed then
Its echo, its own harmony borne back
Upon its ear. This tells of better space,
Far far beyond the hills the woods the clouds
That bound my low and plodding valley life,
Far from my sin, remote from my distrust,
Where first my healthy morning life perchance
Trod lightly as on clouds, and not as yet
My weary and faint hearted noon had sunk
Upon the clod while the bright day went by.
　　Lately, I feared my life was empty, now
I know though a frail tenement that it still
Is worth repair, if yet its hollowness
Doth entertain so fine a guest within, and through
Its empty aisles there still doth ring
Though but the echo of so high a strain;
It shall be swept again and cleansed from sin
To be a thoroughfare for celestial airs;
Perchance the God who is proprietor
Will pity take on his poor tenant here
And countenance his efforts to improve
His property and make it worthy to revert,
At some late day Unto himself again.

CORNELIUS MATHEWS

(1817–1889)

from *Poems on Man in His Various Aspects Under the American Republic*

The Masses

When, wild and high, the uproar swells
  From crowds that gather at the set of day;
  When square and market roar in stormy play,
And fields of men, like lions, shake their fells
Of savage hair; when, quick and deep, call out the bells
    Through all the lower Heaven ringing,
      As if an earthquake's shock
      The city's base should rock,
    And set its troubled turrets singing:—

Remember, Men! on massy strength relying,
      There is a heart of right
      Not always open to the light,
Secret and still and force-defying.
In vast assemblies calm, let order rule,
  And, every shout a cadence owning,
  Make musical the vexed wind's moaning,
And be as little children at a singing-school.

But, when, thick as night, the sky is crusted o'er,
  Stifling life's pulse and making Heaven an idle dream,
Arise! and cry, up through the dark, to God's own throne:
  Your faces in a furnace glow,
  Your arms uplifted for the death-ward blow—
  Fiery and prompt as angry angels show:
Then draw the brand and fire the thunder-gun!
Be nothing said and all things done!
  Till every cobwebbed corner of the common-weal
  Is shaken free, and, creeping to its scabbard back the steel,
Let's shine again God's rightful sun!

WILLIAM ELLERY CHANNING

(1818–1901)

The Harbor

No more I seek, the prize is found,
  I furl my sails, my voyage is o'er;
The treacherous waves no longer sound
  But sing thy praise along the shore.

I steal from all I hoped of old,
  To throw more beauty round thy way;
The dross I part, and melt the gold,
  And stamp it with thy every-day.

I did not dream to welcome thee;
  Like all I have thou camest unknown,
An island in a misty sea,
  With stars, and flowers, and harvests strown.

A well is in the desert sand
  With purest water cold and clear,
Where overjoyed at rest I stand,
  And drink the sound I hoped to hear.

Hymn of the Earth

My highway is unfeatured air,
My consorts are the sleepless Stars,
And men, my giant arms upbear,
My arms unstained and free from scars.

I rest forever on my way,
Rolling around the happy Sun,
My children love the sunny day,
But noon and night to me are one.

My heart has pulses like their own,
I am their Mother, and my veins
Though built of the enduring stone,
Thrill as do theirs with godlike pains.

The forests and the mountains high,
The foaming ocean and the springs,
The plains,—O pleasant Company,
My voice through all your anthem rings.

Ye are so cheerful in your minds,
Content to smile, content to share,
My being in your Chorus finds
The echo of the spheral air.

No leaf may fall, no pebble roll,
No drop of water lose the road,
The issues of the general Soul
Are mirrored in its round abode.

WILLIAM WETMORE STORY

(1819–1895)

Cleopatra

[*Dedicated to J. L. M.*]

Here, Charmian, take my bracelets,
   They bar with a purple stain
My arms; turn over my pillows —
   They are hot where I have lain:
Open the lattice wider,
   A gauze o'er my bosom throw,
And let me inhale the odours
   That over the garden blow.

I dreamed I was with my Antony,
   And in his arms I lay;
Ah, me! the vision has vanished —
   The music has died away.
The flame and the perfume have perished —
   As this spiced aromatic pastille
That wound the blue smoke of its odour
   Is now but an ashy hill.

Scatter upon me rose-leaves,
   They cool me after my sleep,
And with sandal odours fan me
   Till into my veins they creep;
Reach down the lute, and play me
   A melancholy tune,
To rhyme with the dream that has vanished,
   And the slumbering afternoon.

There, drowsing in golden sunlight,
   Loiters the slow smooth Nile,
Through slender papyri, that cover
   The wary crocodile.

The lotus lolls on the water,
   And opens its heart of gold,
And over its broad leaf-pavement
   Never a ripple is rolled.
The twilight breeze is too lazy
   Those feathery palms to wave,
And yon little cloud is as motionless
   As a stone above a grave.

Ah, me! this lifeless nature
   Oppresses my heart and brain!
Oh! for a storm and thunder—
   For lightning and wild fierce rain!
Fling down that lute—I hate it!
   Take rather his buckler and sword,
And crash them and clash them together
   Till this sleeping world is stirred.

Hark! to my Indian beauty—
   My cockatoo, creamy white,
With roses under his feathers—
   That flashes across the light.
Look! listen! as backward and forward
   To his hoop of gold he clings,
How he trembles, with crest uplifted,
   And shrieks as he madly swings!
Oh, cockatoo, shriek for Antony!
   Cry, "Come, my love, come home!"
Shriek, "Antony! Antony! Antony!"
   Till he hears you even in Rome.

There—leave me, and take from my chamber
   That stupid little gazelle,
With its bright black eyes so meaningless,
   And its silly tinkling bell!
Take him,—my nerves he vexes—
   The thing without blood or brain,—
Or, by the body of Isis,
   I'll snap his thin neck in twain!

Leave me to gaze at the landscape
    Mistily stretching away,
Where the afternoon's opaline tremors
    O'er the mountains quivering play;
Till the fiercer splendour of sunset
    Pours from the west its fire,
And melted, as in a crucible,
    Their earthy forms expire;
And the bald blear skull of the desert
    With glowing mountains is crowned,
That burning like molten jewels
    Circle its temples round.

I will lie and dream of the past time,
    Æons of thought away,
And through the jungle of memory
    Loosen my fancy to play;
When, a smooth and velvety tiger,
    Ribbed with yellow and black,
Supple and cushion-footed
    I wandered, where never the track
Of a human creature had rustled
    The silence of mighty woods,
And, fierce in a tyrannous freedom,
    I knew but the law of my moods.
The elephant, trumpeting, started,
    When he heard my footstep near,
And the spotted giraffes fled wildly
    In a yellow cloud of fear.

I sucked in the noontide splendour,
    Quivering along the glade,
Or yawning, panting, and dreaming,
    Basked in the tamarisk shade,
Till I heard my wild mate roaring,
    As the shadows of night came on,
To brood in the trees' thick branches
    And the shadow of sleep was gone;
Then I roused, and roared in answer,

And unsheathed from my cushioned feet
My curving claws, and stretched me,
    And wandered my mate to greet.
We toyed in the amber moonlight,
    Upon the warm flat sand,
And struck at each other our massive arms—
    How powerful he was and grand!
His yellow eyes flashed fiercely
    As he crouched and gazed at me,
And his quivering tail, like a serpent,
    Twitched curving nervously.
Then like a storm he seized me,
    With a wild triumphant cry,
And we met, as two clouds in heaven
    When the thunders before them fly.
We grappled and struggled together,
    For his love like his rage was rude;
And his teeth in the swelling folds of my neck
    At times, in our play, drew blood.

Often another suitor—
    For I was flexile and fair—
Fought for me in the moonlight,
    While I lay couching there,
Till his blood was drained by the desert;
    And, ruffled with triumph and power,
He licked me and lay beside me
    To breathe him a vast half-hour.
Then down to the fountain we loitered,
    Where the antelopes came to drink;
Like a bolt we sprang upon them,
    Ere they had time to shrink.
We drank their blood and crushed them,
    And tore them limb from limb,
And the hungriest lion doubted
    Ere he disputed with him.
That was a life to live for!
    Not this weak human life,
With its frivolous bloodless passions,
    Its poor and petty strife!

Come to my arms, my hero,
   The shadows of twilight grow,
And the tiger's ancient fierceness
   In my veins begins to flow.
Come not cringing to sue me!
   Take me with triumph and power,
As a warrior storms a fortress!
   I will not shrink or cower.
Come, as you came in the desert,
   Ere we were women and men,
When the tiger passions were in us,
   And love as you loved me then!

JAMES RUSSELL LOWELL

(1819–1891)

from *A Fable for Critics*

"There comes Poe with his raven . . ."

There comes Poe with his raven, like Barnaby Rudge,
Three-fifths of him genius and two-fifths sheer fudge,
Who talks like a book of iambs and pentameters,
In a way to make people of common-sense damn metres,
Who has written some things quite the best of their kind,
But the heart somehow seems all squeezed out by the mind,
Who—but hey-day! What's this? Messieurs Mathews and
     Poe,
You mustn't fling mud-balls at Longfellow so,
Does it make a man worse that his character 's such
As to make his friends love him (as you think) too much?
Why, there is not a bard at this moment alive
More willing than he that his fellows should thrive;
While you are abusing him thus, even now
He would help either one of you out of a slough;
You may say that he's smooth and all that till you're hoarse,
But remember that elegance also is force;
After polishing granite as much as you will,
The heart keeps its tough old persistency still;
Deduct all you can that still keeps you at bay,—
Why, he'll live till men weary of Collins and Gray;
I'm not over-fond of Greek metres in English,
To me rhyme 's a gain, so it be not too jinglish,
And your modern hexameter verses are no more
Like Greek ones than sleek Mr. Pope is like Homer;
As the roar of the sea to the coo of a pigeon is,
So, compared to your moderns, sounds old Melesigenes;
I may be too partial, the reason, perhaps, o't is
That I've heard the old blind man recite his own rhapsodies,
And my ear with that music impregnate may be,
Like the poor exiled shell with the soul of the sea,

Or as one can't bear Strauss when his nature is cloven
To its deeps within deeps by the stroke of Beethoven;
But, set that aside, and 'tis truth that I speak,
Had Theocritus written in English, not Greek,
I believe that his exquisite sense would scarce change a line
In that rare, tender, virgin-like pastoral Evangeline.
That's not ancient nor modern, its place is apart
Where time has no sway, in the realm of pure Art,
'Tis a shrine of retreat from Earth's hubbub and strife
As quiet and chaste as the author's own life.

from *The Vision of Sir Launfal*

Prelude to Part the First

Earth gets its price for what Earth gives us;
    The beggar is taxed for a corner to die in,
The priest hath his fee who comes and shrives us,
    We bargain for the graves we lie in;
At the Devil's booth are all things sold,
Each ounce of dross costs its ounce of gold;
    For a cap and bells our lives we pay,
Bubbles we earn with a whole soul's tasking:
    'T is heaven alone that is given away,
'T is only God may be had for the asking;
There is no price set on the lavish summer,
And June may be had by the poorest comer.
And what is so rare as a day in June?
    Then, if ever, come perfect days;
Then Heaven tries the earth if it be in tune,
    And over it softly her warm ear lays:
Whether we look, or whether we listen,
We hear life murmur, or see it glisten;
Every clod feels a stir of might,
    An instinct within it that reaches and towers,
And, grasping blindly above it for light,
    Climbs to a soul in grass and flowers;
The flush of life may well be seen

Thrilling back over hills and valleys;
The cowslip startles in meadows green,
    The buttercup catches the sun in its chalice,
And there 's never a leaf or a blade too mean
    To be some happy creature's palace;
The little bird sits at his door in the sun,
    Atilt like a blossom among the leaves,
And lets his illumined being o'errun
    With the deluge of summer it receives;
His mate feels the eggs beneath her wings,
And the heart in her dumb breast flutters and sings;
He sings to the wide world, and she to her nest,—
In the nice ear of Nature which song is the best?

Now is the high-tide of the year,
    And whatever of life hath ebbed away
Comes flooding back, with a ripply cheer,
    Into every bare inlet and creek and bay;
Now the heart is so full that a drop overfills it,
We are happy now because God so wills it;
No matter how barren the past may have been,
'T is enough for us now that the leaves are green;
We sit in the warm shade and feel right well
How the sap creeps up and the blossoms swell;
We may shut our eyes, but we cannot help knowing
That skies are clear and grass is growing;
The breeze comes whispering in our ear,
That dandelions are blossoming near,
    That maize has sprouted, that streams are flowing,
That the river is bluer than the sky,
That the robin is plastering his house hard by;
And if the breeze kept the good news back,
For other couriers we should not lack;
    We could guess it all by yon heifer's lowing,—
And hark! how clear bold chanticleer,
Warmed with the new wine of the year,
    Tells all in his lusty crowing!

Joy comes, grief goes, we know not how;
Every thing is happy now,
    Every thing is upward striving;
'T is as easy now for the heart to be true
As for grass to be green or skies to be blue,—
    'T is the natural way of living:
Who knows whither the clouds have fled?
    In the unscarred heaven they leave no wake;
And the eyes forget the tears they have shed,
    The heart forgets its sorrow and ache;
The soul partakes the season's youth,
    And the sulphurous rifts of passion and woe
Lie deep 'neath a silence pure and smooth,
    Like burnt-out craters healed with snow.
What wonder if Sir Launfal now
Remembered the keeping of his vow?

lines 21 –95

Ode Recited at the Harvard Commemoration

July 21, 1865

I.

Weak-winged is song,
    Nor aims at that clear-ethered height
Whither the brave deed climbs for light:
    We seem to do them wrong,
Bringing our robin's-leaf to deck their hearse
Who in warm life-blood wrote their nobler verse,
Our trivial song to honor those who come
With ears attuned to strenuous trump and drum,
And shaped in squadron-strophes their desire,
Live battle-odes whose lines were steel and fire:
    Yet sometimes feathered words are strong,
A gracious memory to buoy up and save
From Lethe's dreamless ooze, the common grave
    Of the unventurous throng.

II.

To-day our Reverend Mother welcomes back
  Her wisest Scholars, those who understood
The deeper teaching of her mystic tome,
    And offered their fresh lives to make it good:
        No lore of Greece or Rome,
No science peddling with the names of things,
Or reading stars to find inglorious fates,
        Can lift our life with wings
Far from Death's idle gulf that for the many waits,
        And lengthen out our dates
With that clear fame whose memory sings
In manly hearts to come, and nerves them and dilates:
Nor such thy teaching, Mother of us all!
        Not such the trumpet-call
        Of thy diviner mood,
        That could thy sons entice
From happy homes and toils, the fruitful nest
Of those half-virtues which the world calls best,
        Into War's tumult rude;
        But rather far that stern device
The sponsors chose that round thy cradle stood
        In the dim, unventured wood,
        The VERITAS that lurks beneath
        The letter's unprolific sheath,
  Life of whate'er makes life worth living,
Seed-grain of high emprise, immortal food,
    One heavenly thing whereof earth hath the giving.

III.

Many loved Truth, and lavished life's best oil
  Amid the dust of books to find her,
Content at last, for guerdon of their toil,
  With the cast mantle she hath left behind her.
    Many in sad faith sought for her,
    Many with crossed hands sighed for her;
    But these, our brothers, fought for her,
    At life's dear peril wrought for her,
    So loved her that they died for her,

Tasting the raptured fleetness
Of her divine completeness:
    Their higher instinct knew
Those love her best who to themselves are true,
And what they dare to dream of dare to do;
    They followed her and found her
    Where all may hope to find,
Not in the ashes of the burnt-out mind,
But beautiful, with danger's sweetness round her;
    Where faith made whole with deed
    Breathes its awakening breath
    Into the lifeless creed,
    They saw her plumed and mailed,
    With sweet stern face unveiled,
And all-repaying eyes, look proud on them in death.

IV.

Our slender life runs rippling by, and glides
    Into the silent hollow of the past;
        What is there that abides
    To make the next age better for the last?
        Is earth too poor to give us
    Something to live for here that shall outlive us?
        Some more substantial boon
Than such as flows and ebbs with Fortune's fickle moon?
        The little that we see
        From doubt is never free;
        The little that we do
        Is but half-nobly true;
        With our laborious hiving
What men call treasure, and the gods call dross,
    Life seems a jest of Fate's contriving,
    Only secure in every one's conniving,
A long account of nothings paid with loss,
Where we poor puppets, jerked by unseen wires,
    After our little hour of strut and rave,
With all our pasteboard passions and desires,
Loves, hates, ambitions, and immortal fires,
    Are tossed pell-mell together in the grave.

But stay! no age was e'er degenerate,
Unless men held it at too cheap a rate,
For in our likeness still we shape our fate;
 Ah, there is something here
Unfathomed by the cynic's sneer,
Something that gives our feeble light
A high immunity from Night,
Something that leaps life's narrow bars
To claim its birthright with the hosts of heaven;
 A seed of sunshine that doth leaven
Our earthly dulness with the beams of stars,
  And glorify our clay
With light from fountains elder than the Day;
 A conscience more divine than we,
 A gladness fed with secret tears,
 A vexing, forward-reaching sense
Of some more noble permanence;
  A light across the sea,
Which haunts the soul and will not let it be,
Still glimmering from the heights of undegenerate years.

V.

  Whither leads the path
  To ampler fates that leads?
  Not down through flowery meads,
  To reap an aftermath
  Of youth's vainglorious weeds,
  But up the steep, amid the wrath
 And shock of deadly-hostile creeds,
  Where the world's best hope and stay
By battle's flashes gropes a desperate way,
And every turf the fierce foot clings-to bleeds.
  Peace hath her not ignoble wreath,
  Ere yet the sharp, decisive word
Light the black lips of cannon, and the sword
  Dreams in its easeful sheath;
But some day the live coal behind the thought,
  Whether from Baäl's stone obscene,
  Or from the shrine serene
  Of God's pure altar brought,

Bursts up in flame; the war of tongue and pen
Learns with what deadly purpose it was fraught,
And, helpless in the fiery passion caught,
Shakes all the pillared state with shock of men:
Some day the soft Ideal that we wooed
Confronts us fiercely, foe-beset, pursued,
And cries reproachful: "Was it, then, my praise,
And not myself was loved? Prove now thy truth;
I claim of thee the promise of thy youth;
Give me thy life, or cower in empty phrase,
The victim of thy genius, not its mate!"
    Life may be given in many ways,
    And loyalty to Truth be sealed
As bravely in the closet as the field,
        So bountiful is Fate;
        But then to stand beside her,
        When craven churls deride her,
To front a lie in arms and not to yield,
        This shows, methinks, God's plan
        And measure of a stalwart man,
        Limbed like the old heroic breeds,
        Who stands self-poised on manhood's solid earth,
    Not forced to frame excuses for his birth,
Fed from within with all the strength he needs.

                        VI.

Such was he, our Martyr-Chief,
        Whom late the Nation he had led,
        With ashes on her head,
Wept with the passion of an angry grief:
Forgive me, if from present things I turn
To speak what in my heart will beat and burn,
And hang my wreath on his world-honored urn.
        Nature, they say, doth dote,
        And cannot make a man
        Save on some worn-out plan,
        Repeating us by rote:
For him her Old World moulds aside she threw,
        And, choosing sweet clay from the breast

Of the unexhausted West,
With stuff untainted shaped a hero new,
Wise, steadfast in the strength of God, and true.
    How beautiful to see
Once more a shepherd of mankind indeed,
Who loved his charge, but never loved to lead;
One whose meek flock the people joyed to be,
    Not lured by any cheat of birth,
    But by his clear-grained human worth,
And brave old wisdom of sincerity!
    They knew that outward grace is dust;
    They could not choose but trust
In that sure-footed mind's unfaltering skill,
    And supple-tempered will
That bent like perfect steel to spring again and thrust.
    His was no lonely mountain-peak of mind,
    Thrusting to thin air o'er our cloudy bars,
    A sea-mark now, now lost in vapors blind;
    Broad prairie rather, genial, level-lined,
    Fruitful and friendly for all human kind,
Yet also nigh to Heaven and loved of loftiest stars.
    Nothing of Europe here,
Or, then, of Europe fronting mornward still,
    Ere any names of Serf and Peer
    Could Nature's equal scheme deface;
    Here was a type of the true elder race,
And one of Plutarch's men talked with us face to face.
    I praise him not; it were too late;
And some innative weakness there must be
In him who condescends to victory
Such as the Present gives, and cannot wait,
    Safe in himself as in a fate.
    So always firmly he:
    He knew to bide his time,
    And can his fame abide,
Still patient in his simple faith sublime,
    Till the wise years decide.
    Great captains, with their guns and drums,
    Disturb our judgment for the hour,
    But at last silence comes;

These all are gone, and, standing like a tower,
   Our children shall behold his fame,
     The kindly-earnest, brave, foreseeing man,
  Sagacious, patient, dreading praise, not blame,
   New birth of our new soil, the first American.

VII.

Long as man's hope insatiate can discern
   Or only guess some more inspiring goal
   Outside of Self, enduring as the pole,
Along whose course the flying axles burn
Of spirits bravely-pitched, earth's manlier brood;
   Long as below we cannot find
The meed that stills the inexorable mind;
So long this faith to some ideal Good,
   Under whatever mortal names it masks,
   Freedom, Law, Country, this ethereal mood
That thanks the Fates for their severer tasks,
   Feeling its challenged pulses leap,
   While others skulk in subterfuges cheap,
And, set in Danger's van, has all the boon it asks,
   Shall win man's praise and woman's love,
   Shall be a wisdom that we set above
All other skills and gifts to culture dear,
   A virtue round whose forehead we inwreathe
   Laurels that with a living passion breathe
When other crowns grow, while we twine them, sear.
   What brings us thronging these high rites to pay,
And seal these hours the noblest of our year,
   Save that our brothers found this better way?

VIII.

We sit here in the Promised Land
   That flows with Freedom's honey and milk;
   But 't was they won it, sword in hand,
Making the nettle danger soft for us as silk.
   We welcome back our bravest and our best;—
   Ah me! not all! some come not with the rest,
Who went forth brave and bright as any here!

I strive to mix some gladness with my strain,
   But the sad strings complain,
   And will not please the ear;
I sweep them for a pæan, but they wane
    Again and yet again
Into a dirge, and die away in pain.
In these brave ranks I only see the gaps,
Thinking of dear ones whom the dumb turf wraps,
Dark to the triumph which they died to gain:
   Fitlier may others greet the living,
   For me the past is unforgiving;
    I with uncovered head
    Salute the sacred dead,
Who went, and who return not. — Say not so!
'T is not the grapes of Canaan that repay,
But the high faith that failed not by the way;
Virtue treads paths that end not in the grave;
No ban of endless night exiles the brave;
    And to the saner mind
We rather seem the dead that stayed behind.
Blow, trumpets, all your exultations blow!
For never shall their aureoled presence lack:
I see them muster in a gleaming row,
With ever-youthful brows that nobler show;
We find in our dull road their shining track;
    In every nobler mood
We feel the orient of their spirit glow,
Part of our life's unalterable good,
Of all our saintlier aspiration;
    They come transfigured back,
Secure from change in their high-hearted ways,
Beautiful evermore, and with the rays
Of morn on their white Shields of Expectation!

IX.

   But is there hope to save
  Even this ethereal essence from the grave?
  What ever 'scaped Oblivion's subtle wrong
Save a few clarion names, or golden threads of song?

Before my musing eye
   The mighty ones of old sweep by,
Disvoicëd now and insubstantial things,
As noisy once as we; poor ghosts of kings,
Shadows of empire wholly gone to dust,
And many races, nameless long ago,
To darkness driven by that imperious gust
Of ever-rushing Time that here doth blow:
O visionary world, condition strange,
   Where naught abiding is but only Change,
Where the deep-bolted stars themselves still shift and range!
   Shall we to more continuance make pretence?
Renown builds tombs; a life-estate is Wit;
         And, bit by bit,
The cunning years steal all from us but woe;
   Leaves are we, whose decays no harvest sow.
         But, when we vanish hence,
Shall they lie forceless in the dark below,
Save to make green their little length of sods,
Or deepen pansies for a year or two,
Who now to us are shining-sweet as gods?
Was dying all they had the skill to do?
That were not fruitless: but the Soul resents
Such short-lived service, as if blind events
Ruled without her, or earth could so endure;
She claims a more divine investiture
Of longer tenure than Fame's airy rents;
Whate'er she touches doth her nature share;
Her inspiration haunts the ennobled air,
         Gives eyes to mountains blind,
Ears to the deaf earth, voices to the wind,
And her clear trump sings succor everywhere
By lonely bivouacs to the wakeful mind;
For soul inherits all that soul could dare:
         Yea, Manhood hath a wider span
And larger privilege of life than man.
The single deed, the private sacrifice,
So radiant now through proudly-hidden tears,
Is covered up erelong from mortal eyes
With thoughtless drift of the deciduous years;

But that high privilege that makes all men peers,
That leap of heart whereby a people rise
        Up to a noble anger's height,
And, flamed on by the Fates, not shrink, but grow more
        bright,
        That swift validity in noble veins,
        Of choosing danger and disdaining shame,
                Of being set on flame
        By the pure fire that flies all contact base,
But wraps its chosen with angelic might,
        These are imperishable gains,
    Sure as the sun, medicinal as light,
    These hold great futures in their lusty reins
And certify to earth a new imperial race.

X.

        Who now shall sneer?
    Who dare again to say we trace
    Our lines to a plebeian race?
        Roundhead and Cavalier!
Dumb are those names erewhile in battle loud;
Dream-footed as the shadow of a cloud,
        They flit across the ear:
That is best blood that hath most iron in 't
To edge resolve with, pouring without stint
        For what makes manhood dear.
        Tell us not of Plantagenets,
Hapsburgs, and Guelfs, whose thin bloods crawl
Down from some victor in a border-brawl!
        How poor their outworn coronets,
Matched with one leaf of that plain civic wreath
Our brave for honor's blazon shall bequeath,
    Through whose desert a rescued Nation sets
Her heel on treason, and the trumpet hears
Shout victory, tingling Europe's sullen ears
    With vain resentments and more vain regrets!

XI.

    Not in anger, not in pride,
    Pure from passion's mixture rude

Ever to base earth allied,
But with far-heard gratitude,
Still with heart and voice renewed,
To heroes living and dear martyrs dead,
The strain should close that consecrates our brave.
Lift the heart and lift the head!
Lofty be its mood and grave,
Not without a martial ring,
Not without a prouder tread
And a peal of exultation:
Little right has he to sing
Through whose heart in such an hour
Beats no march of conscious power,
Sweeps no tumult of elation!
'T is no Man we celebrate,
By his country's victories great,
A hero half, and half the whim of Fate,
But the pith and marrow of a Nation
Drawing force from all her men,
Highest, humblest, weakest, all,
For her time of need, and then
Pulsing it again through them,
Till the basest can no longer cower,
Feeling his soul spring up divinely tall,
Touched but in passing by her mantle-hem.
Come back, then, noble pride, for 't is her dower!
How could poet ever tower,
If his passions, hopes, and fears,
If his triumphs and his tears,
Kept not measure with his people?
Boom, cannon, boom to all the winds and waves!
Clash out, glad bells, from every rocking steeple!
Banners, adance with triumph, bend your staves!
And from every mountain-peak
Let beacon-fire to answering beacon speak,
Katahdin tell Monadnock, Whiteface he,
And so leap on in light from sea to sea,
Till the glad news be sent
Across a kindling continent,

Making earth feel more firm and air breathe braver:
"Be proud! for she is saved, and all have helped to save her!
    She that lifts up the manhood of the poor,
    She of the open soul and open door,
    With room about her hearth for all mankind!
    The fire is dreadful in her eyes no more;
    From her bold front the helm she doth unbind,
    Sends all her handmaid armies back to spin,
    And bids her navies, that so lately hurled
    Their crashing battle, hold their thunders in,
    Swimming like birds of calm along the unharmful shore.
    No challenge sends she to the elder world,
    That looked askance and hated; a light scorn
    Plays o'er her mouth, as round her mighty knees
    She calls her children back, and waits the morn
Of nobler day, enthroned between her subject seas."

XII.

Bow down, dear Land, for thou hast found release!
    Thy God, in these distempered days,
    Hath taught thee the sure wisdom of His ways,
And through thine enemies hath wrought thy peace!
    Bow down in prayer and praise!
No poorest in thy borders but may now
Lift to the juster skies a man's enfranchised brow
O Beautiful! my Country! ours once more!
Smoothing thy gold of war-dishevelled hair
O'er such sweet brows as never other wore,
    And letting thy set lips,
    Freed from wrath's pale eclipse,
The rosy edges of their smile lay bare,
What words divine of lover or of poet
Could tell our love and make thee know it,
Among the Nations bright beyond compare?
    What were our lives without thee?
    What all our lives to save thee?
    We reck not what we gave thee;
    We will not dare to doubt thee,
But ask whatever else, and we will dare!

JULIA WARD HOWE

(1819–1910)

My Last Dance

The shell of objects inwardly consumed
Will stand till some convulsive wind awakes;
Such sense hath Fire to waste the heart of things,
Nature such love to hold the form she makes.

Thus wasted joys will show their early bloom,
Yet crumble at the breath of a caress;
The golden fruitage hides the scathèd bough;
Snatch it, thou scatterest wide its emptiness.

For pleasure bidden, I went forth last night
To where, thick hung, the festal torches gleamed;
Here were the flowers, the music, as of old;
Almost the very olden time it seemed.

For one with cheek unfaded (though he brings
My buried brothers to me in his look)
Said, 'Will you dance?' At the accustomed words
I gave my hand, the old position took.

Sound, gladsome measure! at whose bidding once
I felt the flush of pleasure to my brow,
While my soul shook the burthen of the flesh,
And in its young pride said, 'Lie lightly, thou!'

Then, like a gallant swimmer, flinging high
My breast against the golden waves of sound,
I rode the madd'ning tumult of the dance,
Mocking fatigue, that never could be found.

Chide not—it was not vanity, nor sense,
(The brutish scorn such vaporous delight,)
But Nature, cadencing her joy of strength
To the harmonious limits of her right.

She gave her impulse to the dancing Hours,
To winds that weep, to stars that noiseless turn;
She marked the measure rapid hearts must keep,
Devised each pace that glancing feet should learn.

And sure, that prodigal o'erflow of life,
Unvowed as yet to family or state,
Sweet sounds, white garments, flowery coronals
Make holy in the pageant of our fate.

Sound, measure! but to stir my heart no more —
For, as I moved to join the dizzy race,
My youth fell from me; all its blooms were gone,
And others showed them, smiling, in my face.

Faintly I met the shock of circling forms
Linked each to other, Fashion's galley-slaves,
Dream-wondering, like an unaccustomed ghost
That starts, surprised, to stumble over graves.

For graves were 'neath my feet, whose placid masks
Smiled out upon my folly mournfully,
While all the host of the departed said,
'Tread lightly — thou art ashes, even as we.'

Battle-Hymn of the Republic

Mine eyes have seen the glory of the coming of the Lord:
He is trampling out the vintage where the grapes of wrath
    are stored;
He hath loosed the fateful lightning of his terrible swift
    sword:
        His truth is marching on.

I have seen Him in the watch-fires of a hundred circling
    camps;
They have builded Him an altar in the evening dews and
    damps;

I can read His righteous sentence by the dim and flaring
 lamps.
    His day is marching on.

I have read a fiery gospel, writ in burnished rows of steel:
"As ye deal with my contemners, so with you my grace shall
 deal;
Let the Hero, born of woman, crush the serpent with his
 heel,
    Since God is marching on."

He has sounded forth the trumpet that shall never call
 retreat;
He is sifting out the hearts of men before his judgment-
 seat:
Oh! be swift, my soul, to answer Him! be jubilant, my feet!
    Our God is marching on.

In the beauty of the lilies Christ was born across the sea,
With a glory in his bosom that transfigures you and me:
As he died to make men holy, let us die to make men free,
    While God is marching on.

JOSIAH GILBERT HOLLAND
(1819–1881)

from *The Marble Prophecy*

Laocöon! thou great embodiment
Of human life and human history!
Thou record of the past, thou prophecy
Of the sad future, thou majestic voice,
Pealing along the ages from old time!
Thou wail of agonized humanity!
There lives no thought in marble like to thee!
Thou hast no kindred in the Vatican,
But standest separate among the dreams
Of old mythologies—alone—alone!
The beautiful Apollo at thy side
Is but a marble dream, and dreams are all
The gods and goddesses and fauns and fates
That populate these wondrous halls; but thou,
Standing among them, liftest up thyself
In majesty of meaning, till they sink
Far from the sight, no more significant
Than the poor toys of children. For thou art
A voice from out the world's experience,
Speaking of all the generations past
To all the generations yet to come
Of the long struggle, the sublime despair,
The wild and weary agony of man!

Ay, Adam and his offspring, in the toils
Of the twin serpents Sin and Suffering,
Thou dost impersonate; and as I gaze
Upon the twining monsters that enfold
In unrelaxing, unrelenting coils,
Thy awful energies, and plant their fangs
Deep in thy quivering flesh, while still thy might
In fierce convulsion foils the fateful wrench
That would destroy thee, I am overwhelmed

With a strange sympathy of kindred pain,
And see through gathering tears the tragedy,
The curse and conflict of a ruined race!
Those Rhodian sculptors were gigantic men,
Whose inspirations came from other source
Than their religion, though they chose to speak
Through its familiar language,—men who saw,
And, seeing quite divinely, felt how weak
To cure the world's great woe were all the powers
Whose reign their age acknowledged. So they sat—
The immortal three—and pondered long and well
What one great work should speak the truth for them,—
What one great work should rise and testify
That they had found the topmost fact of life,
Above the reach of all philosophies
And all religions—every scheme of man
To placate or dethrone. That fact they found,
And moulded into form. The silly priest
Whose desecrations of the altar stirred
The vengeance of his God, and summoned forth
The wreathed gorgons of the slimy deep
To crush him and his children, was the word
By which they spoke to their own age and race,
That listened and applauded, knowing not
That high above the small significance
They apprehended, rose the grand intent
That mourned their doom and breathed a world's
            despair!

Be sure it was no fable that inspired
So grand an utterance. Perchance some leaf
From an old Hebrew record had conveyed
A knowledge of the genesis of man.
Perchance some fine conception rose in them
Of unity of nature and of race,
Springing from one beginning. Nay, perchance
Some vision flashed before their thoughtful eyes
Inspired by God, which showed the mighty man,
Who, unbegotten, had begot a race
That to his lot was linked through countless time

By living chains, from which in vain it strove
To wrest its tortured limbs and leap amain
To freedom and to rest! It matters not:
The double word—the fable and the fact,
The childish figment and the mighty truth,
Are blent in one. The first was for a day
And dying Rome; the last for later time
And all mankind.

        These sculptors spoke their word
And then they died; and Rome—imperial Rome—
The mistress of the world—debauched by blood
And foul with harlotries—fell prone at length
Among the trophies of her crimes and slept.
Down toppling one by one her helpless gods
Fell to the earth, and hid their shattered forms
Within the dust that bore them, and among
The ruined shrines and crumbling masonry
Of their old temples. Still this wondrous group,
From its long home upon the Esquiline,
Beheld the centuries of change, and stood,
Impersonating in its conscious stone
The unavailing struggle to crowd back
The closing folds of doom. It paused to hear
A strange New Name proclaimed among the streets,
And catch the dying shrieks of martyred men,
And see the light of hope and heroism
Kindling in many eyes; and then it fell;
And in the ashes of an empire swathed
Its aching sense, and hid its tortured forms.

The old life went, the new life came; and Rome
That slew the prophets built their sepulchres,
And filled her heathen temples with the shrines
Of Christian saints whom she had tossed to beasts,
Or crucified, or left to die in chains
Within her dungeons. Ay, the old life went
But came again. The primitive, true age—
The simple, earnest age—when Jesus Christ
The Crucified was only known and preached,

Struck hands with paganism and passed away.
Rome built new temples and installed new names;
Set up her graven images, and gave
To Pope and priests the keeping of her gods.
Again she grasped at power no longer hers
By right of Roman prowess, and stretched out
Her hand upon the consciences of men.
The godlike liberty with which the Christ
Had made his people free she stole from them,
And bound them slaves to new observances.
Her times, her days, her ceremonials
Imposed a burden grievous to be borne,
And millions groaned beneath it. Nay, she grew
The vengeful persecutor of the free
Who would not bear her yoke, and bathed her hands
In blood as sweet as ever burst from hearts
Torn from the bosoms of the early saints
Within her Coliseum. She assumed
To be the arbiter of destiny.

Those whom she bound or loosed upon the earth,
Were bound or loosed in heaven! In God's own place,
She sat as God—supreme, infallible!
She shut the door of knowledge to mankind,
And bound the Word Divine. She sucked the juice
Of all prosperities within her realms,
Until her gaudy temples blazed with gold,
And from a thousand altars flashed the fire
Of priceless gems. To win her countless wealth
She sold as merchandise the gift of God.
She took the burden which the cross had borne,
And bound it fast to scourged and writhing loins
In thriftless Penance, till her devotees
Fled from their kind to find the boon of peace,
And died in banishment. Beneath her sway,
The proud old Roman blood grew thin and mean
Till virtue was the name it gave to fear,
Till heroism and brigandage were one,
And neither slaves nor beggars knew their shame!

What marvel that a shadow fell, world-wide,
And brooded o'er the ages? Was it strange
That in those dim and drowsy centuries,
When the dumb earth had ceased to quake beneath
The sounding wheels of progress, and the life
That erst had flamed so high had sunk so low
In cold monastic glooms and forms as cold,
The buried gods should listen in their sleep
And dream of resurrection? Was it strange
That listening well they should at length awake,
And struggle from their pillows? Was it strange
That men whose vision grovelled should perceive
The dust in motion, and with rapture greet
Each ancient deity with loud acclaim,
As if he brought with him the good old days
Of manly art and poetry and power?
Nay, was it strange that as they raised themselves,
And cleaned their drowsy eyelids of the dust,
And took their godlike attitudes again,
The grand old forms should feel themselves at home —
Saving perhaps a painful sense that men
Had dwindled somewhat? Was it strange, at last,
That all these gods should be installed anew,
And share the palace with His Holiness,
And that the Pope and Christian Rome can show
No art that equals that which had its birth
In pagan inspiration? Ah, what shame!
That after two millenniums of Christ,
Rome calls to her the thirsty tribes of earth,
And smites the heathen marble with her rod,
And bids them drink the best she has to give!

And when the gods were on their feet again
It was thy time to rise, Laocöon!
Those Rhodian sculptors had foreseen it all.
Their word was true: thou hadst the right to live.

In the quick sunlight on the Esquiline,
Where thou didst sleep, De Fredis kept his vines;
And long above thee grew the grapes whose blood

Ran wild in Christian arteries, and fed
The fire of Christian revels. Ah what fruit
Sucked up the marrow of thy marble there!
What fierce, mad dreams were those that scared the souls
Of men who drank, nor guessed what ichor stung
Their crimson lips, and tingled in their veins!
Strange growths were those that sprang above thy sleep:
Vines that were serpents; huge and ugly trunks
That took the forms of human agony—
Contorted, gnarled and grim—and leaves that bore
The semblance of a thousand tortured hands,
And snaky tendrils that entwined themselves
Around all forms of life within their reach,
And crushed or blighted them!

                              At last the spade
Slid down to find the secret of the vines,
And touched thee with a thrill that startled Rome,
And swiftly called a shouting multitude
To witness thy unveiling.

                              Ah what joy
Greeted the rising from thy long repose!
And one, the mighty master of his time,
The king of Christian art, with strong, sad face
Looked on, and wondered with the giddy crowd,—
Looked on and learned (too late, alas! for him),
That his humanity and God's own truth
Were more than Christian Rome, and spoke in words
Of larger import. Humbled Angelo
Bowed to the masters of the early days,
Grasped their strong hands across the centuries,
And went his way despairing!

                              Thou, meantime,
Didst find thyself installed among the gods
Here in the Vatican; and thou, to-day,
Hast the same word for those who read thee well
As when thou wast created. Rome has failed:
Humanity is writhing in the toils

Of the old monsters as it writhed of old,
And there is neither help nor hope in her.
Her priests, her shrines, her rites, her mummeries,
Her pictures and her pageants, are as weak
To break the hold of Sin and Suffering
As those her reign displaced. Her iron hand
Shrivels the manhood it presumes to bless,
Drives to disgust or infidelity
The strong and free who dare to think and judge,
And wins a kiss from coward lips alone.
She does not preach the Gospel to the poor,
But takes it from their hands. The men who tread
The footsteps of the Master, and bow down
Alone to Him, she brands as heretics
Or hunts as fiends. She drives beyond her gates
The Christian worshippers of other climes,
And other folds and faiths, as if their brows
Were white with leprosy, and grants them there
With haughty scorn the privilege to kneel
In humble worship of the common Lord!

Is this the Christ, or look we still for Him?
Is the old problem solved, or lingers yet
The grand solution? Ay Laocöon!
Thy word is true, for Christian Rome has failed,
And I behold humanity in thee
As those who shaped thee saw it, when old Rome
In that far pagan evening fell asleep.

lines 145–392

THOMAS DUNN ENGLISH

(1819–1902)

Ben Bolt

Don't you remember sweet Alice, Ben Bolt—
   Sweet Alice whose hair was so brown,
Who wept with delight when you gave her a smile,
   And trembled with fear at your frown?
In the old church-yard in the valley, Ben Bolt,
   In a corner obscure and alone,
They have fitted a slab of the granite so grey,
   And Alice lies under the stone.

Under the hickory-tree, Ben Bolt,
   Which stood at the foot of the hill,
Together we've lain in the noonday shade,
   And listened to Appleton's mill.
The mill-wheel has fallen to pieces, Ben Bolt,
   The rafters have tumbled in,
And a quiet which crawls round the walls as you gaze
   Has followed the olden din.

Do you mind of the cabin of logs, Ben Bolt,
   At the edge of the pathless wood,
And the button-ball tree with its motley limbs,
   Which nigh by the door-step stood?
The cabin to ruin has gone, Ben Bolt,
   The tree you would seek for in vain;
And where once the lords of the forest waved
   Are grass and the golden grain.

And don't you remember the school, Ben Bolt,
   With the master so cruel and grim,
And the shaded nook in the running brook
   Where the children went to swim?

Grass grows on the master's grave, Ben Bolt,
  The spring of the brook is dry,
And of all the boys who were schoolmates then
  There are only you and I.

There is change in the things I loved, Ben Bolt,
  They have changed from the old to the new;
But I feel in the deeps of my spirit the truth,
  There never was change in you.
Twelvemonths twenty have past, Ben Bolt,
  Since first we were friends—yet I hail
Your presence a blessing, your friendship a truth,
  Ben Bolt of the salt-sea gale.

WALT WHITMAN

from *Leaves of Grass* (*1855*)

I celebrate myself,
And what I assume you shall assume,
For every atom belonging to me as good belongs to you.

I loafe and invite my soul,
I lean and loafe at my ease . . . . observing a spear of
    summer grass.

Houses and rooms are full of perfumes . . . . the shelves are
    crowded with perfumes,
I breathe the fragrance myself, and know it and like it,
The distillation would intoxicate me also, but I shall not let it.

The atmosphere is not a perfume . . . . it has no taste of the
    distillation . . . . it is odorless,
It is for my mouth forever . . . . I am in love with it,
I will go to the bank by the wood and become undisguised
    and naked,
I am mad for it to be in contact with me.

The smoke of my own breath,
Echos, ripples, and buzzed whispers . . . . loveroot,
    silkthread, crotch and vine,
My respiration and inspiration . . . . the beating of my heart
    . . . . the passing of blood and air through my lungs,
The sniff of green leaves and dry leaves, and of the shore and
    darkcolored sea-rocks, and of hay in the barn,
The sound of the belched words of my voice . . . . words
    loosed to the eddies of the wind,
A few light kisses . . . . a few embraces . . . . a reaching
    around of arms,
The play of shine and shade on the trees as the supple
    boughs wag,

The delight alone or in the rush of the streets, or along the
    fields and hillsides,
The feeling of health . . . . the full-noon trill . . . . the
    song of me rising from bed and meeting the sun.

Have you reckoned a thousand acres much? Have you
    reckoned the earth much?
Have you practiced so long to learn to read?
Have you felt so proud to get at the meaning of poems?

Stop this day and night with me and you shall possess the
    origin of all poems,
You shall possess the good of the earth and sun . . . . there
    are millions of suns left,
You shall no longer take things at second or third hand
    . . . . nor look through the eyes of the dead . . . . nor
    feed on the spectres in books,
You shall not look through my eyes either, nor take things
    from me,
You shall listen to all sides and filter them from yourself.

I have heard what the talkers were talking . . . . the talk of
    the beginning and the end,
But I do not talk of the beginning or the end.

There was never any more inception than there is now,
Nor any more youth or age than there is now;
And will never be any more perfection than there is now,
Nor any more heaven or hell than there is now.

Urge and urge and urge,
Always the procreant urge of the world.

Out of the dimness opposite equals advance . . . . Always
    substance and increase,
Always a knit of identity . . . . always distinction . . . .
    always a breed of life.

To elaborate is no avail . . . . Learned and unlearned feel
    that it is so.

Sure as the most certain sure . . . . plumb in the uprights,
     well entretied, braced in the beams,
Stout as a horse, affectionate, haughty, electrical,
I and this mystery here we stand.

Clear and sweet is my soul . . . . and clear and sweet is all
     that is not my soul.

Lack one lacks both . . . . and the unseen is proved by the
     seen,
Till that becomes unseen and receives proof in its turn.

Showing the best and dividing it from the worst, age vexes
     age,
Knowing the perfect fitness and equanimity of things, while
     they discuss I am silent, and go bathe and admire
     myself.

Welcome is every organ and attribute of me, and of any man
     hearty and clean,
Not an inch nor a particle of an inch is vile, and none shall
     be less familiar than the rest.

I am satisfied . . . . I see, dance, laugh, sing;
As God comes a loving bedfellow and sleeps at my side all
     night and close on the peep of the day,
And leaves for me baskets covered with white towels bulging
     the house with their plenty,
Shall I postpone my acceptation and realization and scream
     at my eyes,
That they turn from gazing after and down the road,
And forthwith cipher and show me to a cent,
Exactly the contents of one, and exactly the contents of two,
     and which is ahead?

Trippers and askers surround me,
People I meet . . . . . the effect upon me of my early life
     . . . . of the ward and city I live in . . . . of the nation,
The latest news . . . . discoveries, inventions, societies
     . . . . authors old and new,

My dinner, dress, associates, looks, business, compliments,
    dues,
The real or fancied indifference of some man or woman I
    love,
The sickness of one of my folks—or of myself . . . . or ill-
    doing . . . . or loss or lack of money . . . . or
    depressions or exaltations,
They come to me days and nights and go from me again,
But they are not the Me myself.

Apart from the pulling and hauling stands what I am,
Stands amused, complacent, compassionating, idle, unitary,
Looks down, is erect, bends an arm on an impalpable certain
    rest,
Looks with its sidecurved head curious what will come next,
Both in and out of the game, and watching and wondering
    at it.

Backward I see in my own days where I sweated through fog
    with linguists and contenders,
I have no mockings or arguments . . . . I witness and wait.

I believe in you my soul . . . . the other I am must not
    abase itself to you,
And you must not be abased to the other.

Loafe with me on the grass . . . . loose the stop from your
    throat,
Not words, not music or rhyme I want . . . . not custom or
    lecture, not even the best,
Only the lull I like, the hum of your valved voice.

I mind how we lay in June, such a transparent summer
    morning;
You settled your head athwart my hips and gently turned
    over upon me,
And parted the shirt from my bosom-bone, and plunged
    your tongue to my barestript heart,
And reached till you felt my beard, and reached till you held
    my feet.

Swiftly arose and spread around me the peace and joy and
    knowledge that pass all the art and argument of the
    earth;
And I know that the hand of God is the elderhand of my
    own,
And I know that the spirit of God is the eldest brother of my
    own,
And that all the men ever born are also my brothers . . . .
    and the women my sisters and lovers,
And that a kelson of the creation is love;
And limitless are leaves stiff or drooping in the fields,
And brown ants in the little wells beneath them,
And mossy scabs of the wormfence, and heaped stones, and
    elder and mullen and pokeweed.

A child said, What is the grass? fetching it to me with full
    hands;
How could I answer the child? . . . . I do not know what it
    is any more than he.

I guess it must be the flag of my disposition, out of hopeful
    green stuff woven.

Or I guess it is the handkerchief of the Lord,
A scented gift and remembrancer designedly dropped,
Bearing the owner's name someway in the corners, that we
    may see and remark, and say Whose?

Or I guess the grass is itself a child . . . . the produced
    babe of the vegetation.

Or I guess it is a uniform hieroglyphic,
And it means, Sprouting alike in broad zones and narrow
    zones,
Growing among black folks as among white,
Kanuck, Tuckahoe, Congressman, Cuff, I give them the
    same, I receive them the same.

And now it seems to me the beautiful uncut hair of
    graves.

Tenderly will I use you curling grass,
It may be you transpire from the breasts of young men,
It may be if I had known them I would have loved them;
It may be you are from old people and from women,
    and from offspring taken soon out of their mothers'
    laps,
And here you are the mothers' laps.

This grass is very dark to be from the white heads of old
    mothers,
Darker than the colorless beards of old men,
Dark to come from under the faint red roofs of mouths.

O I perceive after all so many uttering tongues!
And I perceive they do not come from the roofs of mouths
    for nothing.

I wish I could translate the hints about the dead young men
    and women,
And the hints about old men and mothers, and the offspring
    taken soon out of their laps.

What do you think has become of the young and old men?
And what do you think has become of the women and
    children?

They are alive and well somewhere;
The smallest sprout shows there is really no death,
And if ever there was it led forward life, and does not wait
    at the end to arrest it,
And ceased the moment life appeared.

All goes onward and outward . . . . and nothing collapses,
And to die is different from what any one supposed, and
    luckier.

Has any one supposed it lucky to be born?
I hasten to inform him or her it is just as lucky to die, and I
    know it.

I pass death with the dying, and birth with the new-washed
      babe . . . . and am not contained between my hat and
      boots,
And peruse manifold objects, no two alike, and every one
      good,
The earth good, and the stars good, and their adjuncts all
      good.

I am not an earth nor an adjunct of an earth,
I am the mate and companion of people, all just as immortal
      and fathomless as myself;
They do not know how immortal, but I know.

Every kind for itself and its own . . . . for me mine male
      and female,
For me all that have been boys and that love women,
For me the man that is proud and feels how it stings to be
      slighted,
For me the sweetheart and the old maid . . . . for me
      mothers and the mothers of mothers,
For me lips that have smiled, eyes that have shed tears,
For me children and the begetters of children.

Who need be afraid of the merge?
Undrape . . . . you are not guilty to me, nor stale nor
      discarded,
I see through the broadcloth and gingham whether
      or no,
And am around, tenacious, acquisitive, tireless . . . . and
      can never be shaken away.

The little one sleeps in its cradle,
I lift the gauze and look a long time, and silently brush away
      flies with my hand.

The youngster and the redfaced girl turn aside up the bushy
      hill,
I peeringly view them from the top.

The suicide sprawls on the bloody floor of the bedroom.
It is so . . . . I witnessed the corpse . . . . there the pistol
   had fallen.

The blab of the pave . . . . the tires of carts and sluff of
   bootsoles and talk of the promenaders,
The heavy omnibus, the driver with his interrogating thumb,
   the clank of the shod horses on the granite floor,
The carnival of sleighs, the clinking and shouted jokes and
   pelts of snowballs;
The hurrahs for popular favorites . . . . the fury of roused
   mobs,
The flap of the curtained litter—the sick man inside, borne
   to the hospital,
The meeting of enemies, the sudden oath, the blows and fall,
The excited crowd—the policeman with his star quickly
   working his passage to the centre of the crowd;
The impassive stones that receive and return so many echoes,
The souls moving along . . . . are they invisible while the
   least atom of the stones is visible?
What groans of overfed or half-starved who fall on the flags
   sunstruck or in fits,
What exclamations of women taken suddenly, who hurry
   home and give birth to babes,
What living and buried speech is always vibrating here . . . .
   what howls restrained by decorum,
Arrests of criminals, slights, adulterous offers made,
   acceptances, rejections with convex lips,
I mind them or the resonance of them . . . . I come again
   and again.

The big doors of the country-barn stand open and ready,
The dried grass of the harvest-time loads the slow-drawn
   wagon,
The clear light plays on the brown gray and green intertinged,
The armfuls are packed to the sagging mow:
I am there . . . . I help . . . . I came stretched atop of the
   load,
I felt its soft jolts . . . . one leg reclined on the other,

I jump from the crossbeams, and seize the clover and timothy,
And roll head over heels, and tangle my hair full of wisps.

Alone far in the wilds and mountains I hunt,
Wandering amazed at my own lightness and glee,
In the late afternoon choosing a safe spot to pass the night,
Kindling a fire and broiling the freshkilled game,
Soundly falling asleep on the gathered leaves, my dog and
    gun by my side.

The Yankee clipper is under her three skysails . . . . she cuts
    the sparkle and scud,
My eyes settle the land . . . . I bend at her prow or shout
    joyously from the deck.

The boatmen and clamdiggers arose early and stopped for me,
I tucked my trowser-ends in my boots and went and had a
    good time,
You should have been with us that day round the chowder-
    kettle.

I saw the marriage of the trapper in the open air in the far-
    west . . . . the bride was a red girl,
Her father and his friends sat near by crosslegged and
    dumbly smoking . . . . they had moccasins to their feet
    and large thick blankets hanging from their shoulders;
On a bank lounged the trapper . . . . he was dressed mostly
    in skins . . . . his luxuriant beard and curls protected
    his neck,
One hand rested on his rifle . . . . the other hand held
    firmly the wrist of the red girl,
She had long eyelashes . . . . her head was bare . . . . her
    coarse straight locks descended upon her voluptuous
    limbs and reached to her feet.

The runaway slave came to my house and stopped outside,
I heard his motions crackling the twigs of the woodpile,
Through the swung half-door of the kitchen I saw him
    limpsey and weak,

And went where he sat on a log, and led him in and assured
    him,
And brought water and filled a tub for his sweated body and
    bruised feet,
And gave him a room that entered from my own, and gave
    him some coarse clean clothes,
And remember perfectly well his revolving eyes and his
    awkwardness,
And remember putting plasters on the galls of his neck and
    ankles;
He staid with me a week before he was recuperated and
    passed north,
I had him sit next me at table . . . . my firelock leaned in
    the corner.

Twenty-eight young men bathe by the shore,
Twenty-eight young men, and all so friendly,
Twenty-eight years of womanly life, and all so lonesome.

She owns the fine house by the rise of the bank,
She hides handsome and richly drest aft the blinds of the
    window.

Which of the young men does she like the best?
Ah the homeliest of them is beautiful to her.

Where are you off to, lady? for I see you,
You splash in the water there, yet stay stock still in your room.

Dancing and laughing along the beach came the twenty-
    ninth bather,
The rest did not see her, but she saw them and loved them.

The beards of the young men glistened with wet, it ran from
    their long hair,
Little streams passed all over their bodies.

An unseen hand also passed over their bodies,
It descended tremblingly from their temples and ribs.

The young men float on their backs, their white bellies swell
　　　to the sun . . . . they do not ask who seizes fast to them,
They do not know who puffs and declines with pendant and
　　　bending arch,
They do not think whom they souse with spray.

The butcher—boy puts off his killing—clothes, or sharpens his
　　　knife at the stall in the market,
I loiter enjoying his repartee and his shuffle and breakdown.

Blacksmiths with grimed and hairy chests environ the anvil,
Each has his main—sledge . . . . they are all out . . . . there
　　　is a great heat in the fire.

From the cinder—strewed threshold I follow their movements,
The lithe sheer of their waists plays even with their massive
　　　arms,
Overhand the hammers roll—overhand so slow—overhand
　　　so sure,
They do not hasten, each man hits in his place.

The negro holds firmly the reins of his four horses . . . . the
　　　block swags underneath on its tied—over chain,
The negro that drives the huge dray of the stoneyard . . . .
　　　steady and tall he stands poised on one leg on the
　　　stringpiece,
His blue shirt exposes his ample neck and breast and loosens
　　　over his hipband,
His glance is calm and commanding . . . . he tosses the
　　　slouch of his hat away from his forehead,
The sun falls on his crispy hair and moustache . . . . falls on
　　　the black of his polish'd and perfect limbs.

I behold the picturesque giant and love him . . . . and I do
　　　not stop there,
I go with the team also.

In me the caresser of life wherever moving . . . . backward
　　　as well as forward slueing,
To niches aside and junior bending.

Oxen that rattle the yoke or halt in the shade, what is that
    you express in your eyes?
It seems to me more than all the print I have read in my life.

My tread scares the wood-drake and wood-duck on my
    distant and daylong ramble,
They rise together, they slowly circle around.
. . . . I believe in those winged purposes,
And acknowledge the red yellow and white playing within
    me,
And consider the green and violet and the tufted crown
    intentional;
And do not call the tortoise unworthy because she is not
    something else,
And the mockingbird in the swamp never studied the
    gamut, yet trills pretty well to me,
And the look of the bay mare shames silliness out of me.

The wild gander leads his flock through the cool night,
Ya-honk! he says, and sounds it down to me like an invitation;
The pert may suppose it meaningless, but I listen closer,
I find its purpose and place up there toward the November
    sky.

The sharphoofed moose of the north, the cat on the
    housesill, the chickadee, the prairie-dog,
The litter of the grunting sow as they tug at her teats,
The brood of the turkeyhen, and she with her halfspread
    wings,
I see in them and myself the same old law.

The press of my foot to the earth springs a hundred
    affections,
They scorn the best I can do to relate them.

I am enamoured of growing outdoors,
Of men that live among cattle or taste of the ocean or woods,
Of the builders and steerers of ships, of the wielders of axes
    and mauls, of the drivers of horses,
I can eat and sleep with them week in and week out.

What is commonest and cheapest and nearest and easiest
    is Me,
Me going in for my chances, spending for vast returns,
Adorning myself to bestow myself on the first that will
    take me,
Not asking the sky to come down to my goodwill,
Scattering it freely forever.

endless list?

The pure contralto sings in the organloft,
The carpenter dresses his plank . . . . the tongue of his
    foreplane whistles its wild ascending lisp,
The married and unmarried children ride home to their
    thanksgiving dinner,
The pilot seizes the king-pin, he heaves down with a strong
    arm,
The mate stands braced in the whaleboat, lance and harpoon
    are ready,
The duck-shooter walks by silent and cautious stretches,
The deacons are ordained with crossed hands at the altar,
The spinning-girl retreats and advances to the hum of the
    big wheel,
The farmer stops by the bars of a Sunday and looks at the
    oats and rye,
The lunatic is carried at last to the asylum a confirmed case,
He will never sleep any more as he did in the cot in his
    mother's bedroom;
The jour printer with gray head and gaunt jaws works at
    his case,
He turns his quid of tobacco, his eyes get blurred with the
    manuscript;
The malformed limbs are tied to the anatomist's table,
What is removed drops horribly in a pail;
The quadroon girl is sold at the stand . . . . the drunkard
    nods by the barroom stove,
The machinist rolls up his sleeves . . . . the policeman
    travels his beat . . . . the gate-keeper marks who pass,
The young fellow drives the express-wagon . . . . I love him
    though I do not know him;
The half-breed straps on his light boots to compete in
    the race,

The western turkey-shooting draws old and young . . . .
    some lean on their rifles, some sit on logs,
Out from the crowd steps the marksman and takes his
    position and levels his piece;
The groups of newly-come immigrants cover the wharf
    or levee,
The woollypates hoe in the sugarfield, the overseer views
    them from his saddle;
The bugle calls in the ballroom, the gentlemen run for their
    partners, the dancers bow to each other;
The youth lies awake in the cedar-roofed garret and harks to
    the musical rain,
The Wolverine sets traps on the creek that helps fill the
    Huron,
The reformer ascends the platform, he spouts with his
    mouth and nose,
The company returns from its excursion, the darkey brings
    up the rear and bears the well-riddled target,
The squaw wrapt in her yellow-hemmed cloth is offering
    moccasins and beadbags for sale,
The connoisseur peers along the exhibition-gallery with
    halfshut eyes bent sideways,
The deckhands make fast the steamboat, the plank is thrown
    for the shoregoing passengers,
The young sister holds out the skein, the elder sister
    winds it off in a ball and stops now and then for the
    knots,
The one-year wife is recovering and happy, a week ago she
    bore her first child,
The cleanhaired Yankee girl works with her sewing-machine
    or in the factory or mill,
The nine months' gone is in the parturition chamber, her
    faintness and pains are advancing;
The pavingman leans on his twohanded rammer — the
    reporter's lead flies swiftly over the notebook — the
    signpainter is lettering with red and gold,
The canal-boy trots on the towpath — the bookkeeper counts
    at his desk — the shoemaker waxes his thread,
The conductor beats time for the band and all the performers
    follow him,

The child is baptised—the convert is making the first
    professions,
The regatta is spread on the bay . . . . how the white sails
    sparkle!
The drover watches his drove, he sings out to them that
    would stray,
The pedlar sweats with his pack on his back—the purchaser
    higgles about the odd cent,
The camera and plate are prepared, the lady must sit for her
    daguerreotype,
The bride unrumples her white dress, the minutehand of the
    clock moves slowly,
The opium eater reclines with rigid head and just-opened lips,
The prostitute draggles her shawl, her bonnet bobs on her
    tipsy and pimpled neck,
The crowd laugh at her blackguard oaths, the men jeer and
    wink to each other,
(Miserable! I do not laugh at your oaths nor jeer you,)
The President holds a cabinet council, he is surrounded by
    the great secretaries,
On the piazza walk five friendly matrons with twined arms;
The crew of the fish-smack pack repeated layers of halibut in
    the hold,
The Missourian crosses the plains toting his wares and his
    cattle,
The fare-collector goes through the train—he gives notice
    by the jingling of loose change,
The floormen are laying the floor—the tinners are tinning
    the roof—the masons are calling for mortar,
In single file each shouldering his hod pass onward the
    laborers;
Seasons pursuing each other the indescribable crowd is
    gathered . . . . it is the Fourth of July . . . . what
    salutes of cannon and small arms!
Seasons pursuing each other the plougher ploughs and the
    mower mows and the wintergrain falls in the ground;
Off on the lakes the pikefisher watches and waits by the hole
    in the frozen surface,
The stumps stand thick round the clearing, the squatter
    strikes deep with his axe,

The flatboatmen make fast toward dusk near the cottonwood
    or pekantrees,
The coon-seekers go now through the regions of the Red
    river, or through those drained by the Tennessee, or
    through those of the Arkansas,
The torches shine in the dark that hangs on the
    Chattahoochee or Altamahaw;
Patriarchs sit at supper with sons and grandsons and great
    grandsons around them,
In walls of adobe, in canvass tents, rest hunters and trappers
    after their day's sport.
The city sleeps and the country sleeps,
The living sleep for their time . . . . the dead sleep
    for their time,
The old husband sleeps by his wife and the young husband
    sleeps by his wife;
And these one and all tend inward to me, and I tend
    outward to them,
And such as it is to be of these more or less I am.

I am of old and young, of the foolish as much as the wise,
Regardless of others, ever regardful of others,
Maternal as well as paternal, a child as well as a man,
Stuffed with the stuff that is coarse, and stuffed with the
    stuff that is fine,
One of the great nation, the nation of many nations—the
    smallest the same and the largest the same,
A southerner soon as a northerner, a planter nonchalant and
    hospitable,
A Yankee bound my own way . . . . ready for trade . . . .
    my joints the limberest joints on earth and the sternest
    joints on earth,
A Kentuckian walking the vale of the Elkhorn in my
    deerskin leggings,
A boatman over the lakes or bays or along coasts . . . . a
    Hoosier, a Badger, a Buckeye,
A Louisianian or Georgian, a poke-easy from sandhills and
    pines,
At home on Canadian snowshoes or up in the bush, or with
    fishermen off Newfoundland,

At home in the fleet of iceboats, sailing with the rest and
    tacking,
At home on the hills of Vermont or in the woods of Maine
    or the Texan ranch,
Comrade of Californians . . . . comrade of free
    northwesterners, loving their big proportions,
Comrade of raftsmen and coalmen — comrade of all who
    shake hands and welcome to drink and meat;
A learner with the simplest, a teacher of the thoughtfulest,
A novice beginning experient of myriads of seasons,
Of every hue and trade and rank, of every caste and religion,
Not merely of the New World but of Africa Europe or Asia
    . . . . a wandering savage,
A farmer, mechanic, or artist . . . . a gentleman, sailor,
    lover or quaker,
A prisoner, fancy-man, rowdy, lawyer, physician or priest.

I resist anything better than my own diversity,
And breathe the air and leave plenty after me,
And am not stuck up, and am in my place.

The moth and the fisheggs are in their place,
The suns I see and the suns I cannot see are in their place,
The palpable is in its place and the impalpable is in its
    place.

These are the thoughts of all men in all ages and lands, they
    are not original with me,
If they are not yours as much as mine they are nothing or
    next to nothing,
If they do not enclose everything they are next to nothing,
If they are not the riddle and the untying of the riddle they
    are nothing,
If they are not just as close as they are distant they are
    nothing.

This is the grass that grows wherever the land is and the
    water is,
This is the common air that bathes the globe.

This is the breath of laws and songs and behaviour,
This is the tasteless water of souls . . . . this is the true
    sustenance,
It is for the illiterate . . . . it is for the judges of the supreme
    court . . . . it is for the federal capitol and the state
    capitols,
It is for the admirable communes of literary men and
    composers and singers and lecturers and engineers and
    savans,
It is for the endless races of working people and farmers and
    seamen.

This is the trill of a thousand clear cornets and scream of the
    octave flute and strike of triangles.

I play not a march for victors only . . . . I play great marches
    for conquered and slain persons.

Have you heard that it was good to gain the day?
I also say it is good to fall . . . . battles are lost in the same
    spirit in which they are won.

I sound triumphal drums for the dead . . . . I fling through
    my embouchures the loudest and gayest music to them,
Vivas to those who have failed, and to those whose war-
    vessels sank in the sea, and those themselves who sank in
    the sea,
And to all generals that lost engagements, and all overcome
    heroes, and the numberless unknown heroes equal to
    the greatest heroes known.

This is the meal pleasantly set . . . . this is the meat and
    drink for natural hunger,
It is for the wicked just the same as the righteous I
    make appointments with all,
I will not have a single person slighted or left away,
The keptwoman and sponger and thief are hereby invited
    . . . . the heavy-lipped slave is invited . . . . the
    venerealee is invited,
There shall be no difference between them and the rest.

This is the press of a bashful hand . . . . this is the float and
    odor of hair,
This is the touch of my lips to yours . . . . this is the
    murmur of yearning,
This is the far-off depth and height reflecting my own
    face,
This is the thoughtful merge of myself and the outlet
    again.

Do you guess I have some intricate purpose?
Well I have . . . . for the April rain has, and the mica on the
    side of a rock has.

Do you take it I would astonish?
Does the daylight astonish? or the early redstart twittering
    through the woods?
Do I astonish more than they?

This hour I tell things in confidence,
I might not tell everybody but I will tell you.

Who goes there! hankering, gross, mystical, nude?
How is it I extract strength from the beef I eat?

What is a man anyhow? What am I? and what are you?
All I mark as my own you shall offset it with your own,
Else it were time lost listening to me.

I do not snivel that snivel the world over,
That months are vacuums and the ground but wallow
    and filth,
That life is a suck and a sell, and nothing remains at the end
    but threadbare crape and tears.

Whimpering and truckling fold with powders for invalids
    . . . . conformity goes to the fourth-removed,
I cock my hat as I please indoors or out.

Shall I pray? Shall I venerate and be ceremonious?

I have pried through the strata and analyzed to a hair,
And counselled with doctors and calculated close and found
    no sweeter fat than sticks to my own bones.

In all people I see myself, none more and not one a
    barleycorn less,
And the good or bad I say of myself I say of them.

And I know I am solid and sound,
To me the converging objects of the universe perpetually
    flow,
All are written to me, and I must get what the writing means.

And I know I am deathless,
I know this orbit of mine cannot be swept by a carpenter's
    compass,
I know I shall not pass like a child's carlacue cut with a burnt
    stick at night.

I know I am august,
I do not trouble my spirit to vindicate itself or be understood,
I see that the elementary laws never apologize,
I reckon I behave no prouder than the level I plant my house
    by after all.

I exist as I am, that is enough,
If no other in the world be aware I sit content,
And if each and all be aware I sit content.

One world is aware, and by far the largest to me, and that is
    myself,
And whether I come to my own today or in ten thousand or
    ten million years,
I can cheerfully take it now, or with equal cheerfulness I
    can wait.

My foothold is tenoned and mortised in granite,
I laugh at what you call dissolution,
And I know the amplitude of time.

I am the poet of the body,
And I am the poet of the soul.

The pleasures of heaven are with me, and the pains of hell
    are with me,
The first I graft and increase upon myself . . . . the latter I
    translate into a new tongue.

I am the poet of the woman the same as the man,
And I say it is as great to be a woman as to be a man,
And I say there is nothing greater than the mother of
    men.

I chant a new chant of dilation or pride,
We have had ducking and deprecating about enough,
I show that size is only developement.

Have you outstript the rest? Are you the President?
It is a trifle . . . . they will more than arrive there every
    one, and still pass on.

I am he that walks with the tender and growing night;
I call to the earth and sea half-held by the night.

Press close barebosomed night! Press close magnetic
    nourishing night!
Night of south winds! Night of the large few stars!
Still nodding night! Mad naked summer night!

Smile O voluptuous coolbreathed earth!
Earth of the slumbering and liquid trees!
Earth of departed sunset! Earth of the mountains misty-
    topt!
Earth of the vitreous pour of the full moon just tinged
    with blue!
Earth of shine and dark mottling the tide of the river!
Earth of the limpid gray of clouds brighter and clearer for
    my sake!
Far-swooping elbowed earth! Rich apple-blossomed earth!
Smile, for your lover comes!

Prodigal! you have given me love! . . . . therefore I to you
    give love!
O unspeakable passionate love!

Thruster holding me tight and that I hold tight!
We hurt each other as the bridegroom and the bride hurt
    each other.

You sea! I resign myself to you also . . . . I guess what
    you mean,
I behold from the beach your crooked inviting fingers,
I believe you refuse to go back without feeling of me;
We must have a turn together . . . . I undress . . . . hurry
    me out of sight of the land,
Cushion me soft . . . . rock me in billowy drowse,
Dash me with amorous wet . . . . I can repay you.

Sea of stretched ground-swells!
Sea breathing broad and convulsive breaths!
Sea of the brine of life! Sea of unshovelled and always-ready
    graves!
Howler and scooper of storms! Capricious and dainty sea!
I am integral with you . . . . I too am of one phase and of
    all phases.

Partaker of influx and efflux . . . . extoler of hate and
    conciliation,
Extoler of amies and those that sleep in each others' arms.

I am he attesting sympathy;
Shall I make my list of things in the house and skip the
    house that supports them?

I am the poet of commonsense and of the demonstrable and
    of immortality;
And am not the poet of goodness only . . . . I do not
    decline to be the poet of wickedness also.

Washes and razors for foofoos . . . . for me freckles and a
    bristling beard.

What blurt is it about virtue and about vice?
Evil propels me, and reform of evil propels me . . . . I stand
    indifferent,
My gait is no faultfinder's or rejecter's gait,
I moisten the roots of all that has grown.

Did you fear some scrofula out of the unflagging pregnancy?
Did you guess the celestial laws are yet to be worked over
    and rectified?

I step up to say that what we do is right and what we affirm
    is right . . . . and some is only the ore of right,
Witnesses of us . . . . one side a balance and the antipodal
    side a balance,
Soft doctrine as steady help as stable doctrine,
Thoughts and deeds of the present our rouse and early start.

This minute that comes to me over the past decillions,
There is no better than it and now.

What behaved well in the past or behaves well today is not
    such a wonder,
The wonder is always and always how there can be a mean
    man or an infidel.

Endless unfolding of words of ages!
And mine a word of the modern . . . . a word en masse.

A word of the faith that never balks,
One time as good as another time . . . . here or
    henceforward it is all the same to me.

A word of reality . . . . materialism first and last imbueing.

Hurrah for positive science! Long live exact demonstration!
Fetch stonecrop and mix it with cedar and branches of lilac;
This is the lexicographer or chemist . . . . this made a
    grammar of the old cartouches,
These mariners put the ship through dangerous unknown
    seas,

This is the geologist, and this works with the scalpel, and
     this is a mathematician.

Gentlemen I receive you, and attach and clasp hands with
     you,
The facts are useful and real . . . . they are not my dwelling
     . . . . I enter by them to an area of the dwelling.

I am less the reminder of property or qualities, and more the
     reminder of life,
And go on the square for my own sake and for others' sakes,
And make short account of neuters and geldings, and favor
     men and women fully equipped,
And beat the gong of revolt, and stop with fugitives and
     them that plot and conspire.

Walt Whitman, an American, one of the roughs, a kosmos,
Disorderly fleshy and sensual . . . . eating drinking and
     breeding,
No sentimentalist . . . . no stander above men and women or
     apart from them . . . . no more modest than immodest.

Unscrew the locks from the doors!
Unscrew the doors themselves from their jambs!

Whoever degrades another degrades me . . . . and whatever
     is done or said returns at last to me,
And whatever I do or say I also return.

Through me the afflatus surging and surging . . . . through
     me the current and index.

I speak the password primeval . . . . I give the sign of
     democracy;
By God! I will accept nothing which all cannot have their
     counterpart of on the same terms.

Through me many long dumb voices,
Voices of the interminable generations of slaves,
Voices of prostitutes and of deformed persons,

Voices of the diseased and despairing, and of thieves and
      dwarfs,
Voices of cycles of preparation and accretion,
And of the threads that connect the stars—and of wombs,
      and of the fatherstuff,
And of the rights of them the others are down upon,
Of the trivial and flat and foolish and despised,
Of fog in the air and beetles rolling balls of dung.

Through me forbidden voices,
Voices of sexes and lusts . . . . voices veiled, and I remove
      the veil,
Voices indecent by me clarified and transfigured.

I do not press my finger across my mouth,
I keep as delicate around the bowels as around the head and
      heart,
Copulation is no more rank to me than death is.

I believe in the flesh and the appetites,
Seeing hearing and feeling are miracles, and each part and
      tag of me is a miracle.

Divine am I inside and out, and I make holy whatever I
      touch or am touched from;
The scent of these arm-pits is aroma finer than prayer,
This head is more than churches or bibles or creeds.

If I worship any particular thing it shall be some of the
      spread of my body;
Translucent mould of me it shall be you,
Shaded ledges and rests, firm masculine coulter, it shall be you,
Whatever goes to the tilth of me it shall be you,
You my rich blood, your milky stream pale strippings of my
      life;
Breast that presses against other breasts it shall be you,
My brain it shall be your occult convolutions,
Root of washed sweet-flag, timorous pond-snipe, nest of
      guarded duplicate eggs, it shall be you,
Mixed tussled hay of head and beard and brawn it shall be you,

Trickling sap of maple, fibre of manly wheat, it shall be you;
Sun so generous it shall be you,
Vapors lighting and shading my face it shall be you,
You sweaty brooks and dews it shall be you,
Winds whose soft-tickling genitals rub against me it shall
    be you,
Broad muscular fields, branches of liveoak, loving lounger in
    my winding paths, it shall be you,
Hands I have taken, face I have kissed, mortal I have ever
    touched, it shall be you.

I dote on myself . . . . there is that lot of me, and all so
    luscious,
Each moment and whatever happens thrills me with joy.

I cannot tell how my ankles bend . . . . nor whence the
    cause of my faintest wish,
Nor the cause of the friendship I emit . . . . nor the cause
    of the friendship I take again.

To walk up my stoop is unaccountable . . . . I pause to
    consider if it really be,
That I eat and drink is spectacle enough for the great
    authors and schools,
A morning-glory at my window satisfies me more than the
    metaphysics of books.

To behold the daybreak!
The little light fades the immense and diaphanous shadows,
The air tastes good to my palate.

Hefts of the moving world at innocent gambols, silently
    rising, freshly exuding,
Scooting obliquely high and low.

Something I cannot see puts upward libidinous prongs,
Seas of bright juice suffuse heaven.

The earth by the sky staid with . . . . the daily close of their
    junction,

The heaved challenge from the east that moment over my
    head,
The mocking taunt, See then whether you shall be master!

Dazzling and tremendous how quick the sunrise would kill me,
If I could not now and always send sunrise out of me.

We also ascend dazzling and tremendous as the sun,
We found our own my soul in the calm and cool of the
    daybreak.

My voice goes after what my eyes cannot reach,
With the twirl of my tongue I encompass worlds and
    volumes of worlds.

Speech is the twin of my vision . . . . it is unequal to
    measure itself.

It provokes me forever,
It says sarcastically, Walt, you understand enough . . . . why
    don't you let it out then?

Come now I will not be tantalized . . . . you conceive too
    much of articulation.

Do you not know how the buds beneath are folded?
Waiting in gloom protected by frost,
The dirt receding before my prophetical screams,
I underlying causes to balance them at last,
My knowledge my live parts . . . . it keeping tally with the
    meaning of things,
Happiness . . . . which whoever hears me let him or her set
    out in search of this day.

My final merit I refuse you . . . . I refuse putting from me
    the best I am.

Encompass worlds but never try to encompass me,
I crowd your noisiest talk by looking toward you.

Writing and talk do not prove me,
I carry the plenum of proof and every thing else in my face,
With the hush of my lips I confound the topmost skeptic.

I think I will do nothing for a long time but listen,
And accrue what I hear into myself . . . . and let sounds
  contribute toward me.

I hear the bravuras of birds . . . . the bustle of growing
  wheat . . . . gossip of flames . . . . clack of sticks
  cooking my meals.

I hear the sound of the human voice . . . . a sound I love,
I hear all sounds as they are tuned to their uses . . . .
  sounds of the city and sounds out of the city . . . .
  sounds of the day and night;
Talkative young ones to those that like them . . . . the
  recitative of fish-pedlars and fruit-pedlars . . . . the
  loud laugh of workpeople at their meals,
The angry base of disjointed friendship . . . . the faint tones
  of the sick,
The judge with hands tight to the desk, his shaky lips
  pronouncing a death-sentence,
The heave'e'yo of stevedores unlading ships by the wharves
  . . . . the refrain of the anchor-lifters;
The ring of alarm-bells . . . . the cry of fire . . . . the whirr
  of swift-streaking engines and hose-carts with
  premonitory tinkles and colored lights,
The steam-whistle . . . . the solid roll of the train of
  approaching cars;
The slow-march played at night at the head of the association,
They go to guard some corpse . . . . the flag-tops are
  draped with black muslin.

I hear the violincello or man's heart's complaint,
And hear the keyed cornet or else the echo of sunset.

I hear the chorus . . . . it is a grand-opera . . . . this
  indeed is music!

A tenor large and fresh as the creation fills me,
The orbic flex of his mouth is pouring and filling me full.

I hear the trained soprano . . . . she convulses me like the
          climax of my love-grip;
The orchestra whirls me wider than Uranus flies,
It wrenches unnamable ardors from my breast,
It throbs me to gulps of the farthest down horror,
It sails me . . . . I dab with bare feet . . . . they are licked
          by the indolent waves,
I am exposed . . . . cut by bitter and poisoned hail,
Steeped amid honeyed morphine . . . . my windpipe
          squeezed in the fakes of death,
Let up again to feel the puzzle of puzzles,
And that we call Being.

To be in any form, what is that?
If nothing lay more developed the quahaug and its callous
          shell were enough.

Mine is no callous shell,
I have instant conductors all over me whether I pass or stop,
They seize every object and lead it harmlessly through me.

I merely stir, press, feel with my fingers, and am happy,
To touch my person to some one else's is about as much as I
          can stand.

Is this then a touch? . . . . quivering me to a new identity,
Flames and ether making a rush for my veins,
Treacherous tip of me reaching and crowding to help them,
My flesh and blood playing out lightning, to strike what is
          hardly different from myself,
On all sides prurient provokers stiffening my limbs,
Straining the udder of my heart for its withheld drip,
Behaving licentious toward me, taking no denial,
Depriving me of my best as for a purpose,
Unbuttoning my clothes and holding me by the bare waist,
Deluding my confusion with the calm of the sunlight and
          pasture fields,

Immodestly sliding the fellow-senses away,
They bribed to swap off with touch, and go and graze at the
    edges of me,
No consideration, no regard for my draining strength or my
    anger,
Fetching the rest of the herd around to enjoy them awhile,
Then all uniting to stand on a headland and worry me.

The sentries desert every other part of me,
They have left me helpless to a red marauder,
They all come to the headland to witness and assist against me.

I am given up by traitors;
I talk wildly . . . . I have lost my wits . . . . I and nobody
    else am the greatest traitor,
I went myself first to the headland . . . . my own hands
    carried me there.

You villain touch! what are you doing? . . . . my breath is
    tight in its throat;
Unclench your floodgates! you are too much for me.

Blind loving wrestling touch! Sheathed hooded sharptoothed
    touch!
Did it make you ache so leaving me?

Parting tracked by arriving . . . . perpetual payment of the
    perpetual loan,
Rich showering rain, and recompense richer afterward.

Sprouts take and accumulate . . . . stand by the curb
    prolific and vital,
Landscapes projected masculine full-sized and golden.

All truths wait in all things,
They neither hasten their own delivery nor resist it,
They do not need the obstetric forceps of the surgeon,
The insignificant is as big to me as any,
What is less or more than a touch?

Logic and sermons never convince,
The damp of the night drives deeper into my soul.

Only what proves itself to every man and woman is so,
Only what nobody denies is so.

A minute and a drop of me settle my brain;
I believe the soggy clods shall become lovers and lamps,
And a compend of compends is the meat of a man or
        woman,
And a summit and flower there is the feeling they have for
        each other,
And they are to branch boundlessly out of that lesson until
        it becomes omnific,
And until every one shall delight us, and we them.

I believe a leaf of grass is no less than the journeywork of
        the stars,
And the pismire is equally perfect, and a grain of sand, and
        the egg of the wren,
And the tree-toad is a chef-d'ouvre for the highest,
And the running blackberry would adorn the parlors of
        heaven,
And the narrowest hinge in my hand puts to scorn all
        machinery,
And the cow crunching with depressed head surpasses any
        statue,
And a mouse is miracle enough to stagger sextillions of
        infidels,
And I could come every afternoon of my life to look at the
        farmer's girl boiling her iron tea-kettle and baking
        shortcake.

I find I incorporate gneiss and coal and long-threaded moss
        and fruits and grains and esculent roots,
And am stucco'd with quadrupeds and birds all over,
And have distanced what is behind me for good reasons,
And call any thing close again when I desire it.

In vain the speeding or shyness,
In vain the plutonic rocks send their old heat against my
    approach,
In vain the mastadon retreats beneath its own powdered
    bones,
In vain objects stand leagues off and assume manifold shapes,
In vain the ocean settling in hollows and the great monsters
    lying low,
In vain the buzzard houses herself with the sky,
In vain the snake slides through the creepers and logs,
In vain the elk takes to the inner passes of the woods,
In vain the razorbilled auk sails far north to Labrador,
I follow quickly . . . . I ascend to the nest in the fissure of
    the cliff.

I think I could turn and live awhile with the animals . . . .
    they are so placid and self-contained,
I stand and look at them sometimes half the day long.

They do not sweat and whine about their condition,
They do not lie awake in the dark and weep for their sins,
They do not make me sick discussing their duty to God,
Not one is dissatisfied . . . . not one is demented with the
    mania of owning things,
Not one kneels to another nor to his kind that lived
    thousands of years ago,
Not one is respectable or industrious over the whole earth.

So they show their relations to me and I accept them;
They bring me tokens of myself . . . . they evince them
    plainly in their possession.

I do not know where they got those tokens,
I must have passed that way untold times ago and
    negligently dropt them,
Myself moving forward then and now and forever,
Gathering and showing more always and with velocity,
Infinite and omnigenous and the like of these among them;
Not too exclusive toward the reachers of my remembrancers,

Picking out here one that shall be my amie,
Choosing to go with him on brotherly terms.

A gigantic beauty of a stallion, fresh and responsive to my
    caresses,
Head high in the forehead and wide between the ears,
Limbs glossy and supple, tail dusting the ground,
Eyes well apart and full of sparkling wickedness . . . . ears
    finely cut and flexibly moving.

His nostrils dilate . . . . my heels embrace him . . . . his
    well built limbs tremble with pleasure . . . . we speed
    around and return.

I but use you a moment and then I resign you stallion . . . .
    and do not need your paces, and outgallop them,
And myself as I stand or sit pass faster than you.

Swift wind! Space! My Soul! Now I know it is true what I
    guessed at;
What I guessed when I loafed on the grass,
What I guessed while I lay alone in my bed . . . . and again
    as I walked the beach under the paling stars of the
    morning.

My ties and ballasts leave me . . . . I travel . . . . I sail
    . . . . my elbows rest in the sea-gaps,
I skirt the sierras . . . . my palms cover continents,
I am afoot with my vision.

By the city's quadrangular houses . . . . in log-huts, or
    camping with lumbermen,
Along the ruts of the turnpike . . . . along the dry gulch
    and rivulet bed,
Hoeing my onion-patch, and rows of carrots and parsnips
    . . . . crossing savannas . . . trailing in forests,
Prospecting . . . . gold-digging . . . . girdling the trees of
    a new purchase,
Scorched ankle-deep by the hot sand . . . . hauling my boat
    down the shallow river;

Where the panther walks to and fro on a limb overhead
    . . . . where the buck turns furiously at the hunter,
Where the rattlesnake suns his flabby length on a rock . . . .
    where the otter is feeding on fish,
Where the alligator in his tough pimples sleeps by the
    bayou,
Where the black bear is searching for roots or honey . . . .
    where the beaver pats the mud with his paddle-tail;
Over the growing sugar . . . . over the cottonplant . . . .
    over the rice in its low moist field;
Over the sharp-peaked farmhouse with its scalloped scum
    and slender shoots from the gutters;
Over the western persimmon . . . . over the longleaved
    corn and the delicate blueflowered flax;
Over the white and brown buckwheat, a hummer and a
    buzzer there with the rest,
Over the dusky green of the rye as it ripples and shades in
    the breeze;
Scaling mountains . . . . pulling myself cautiously up . . . .
    holding on by low scragged limbs,
Walking the path worn in the grass and beat through the
    leaves of the brush;
Where the quail is whistling betwixt the woods and the
    wheatlot,
Where the bat flies in the July eve . . . . where the great
    goldbug drops through the dark;
Where the flails keep time on the barn floor,
Where the brook puts out of the roots of the old tree and
    flows to the meadow,
Where cattle stand and shake away flies with the tremulous
    shuddering of their hides,
Where the cheese-cloth hangs in the kitchen, and andirons
    straddle the hearth-slab, and cobwebs fall in festoons
    from the rafters;
Where triphammers crash . . . . where the press is whirling
    its cylinders;
Wherever the human heart beats with terrible throes out of
    its ribs;
Where the pear-shaped balloon is floating aloft . . . .
    floating in it myself and looking composedly down;

the life-car is drawn on the slipnoose . . . . where
the heat hatches pale-green eggs in the dented sand,
Where the she-whale swims with her calves and never
    forsakes them,
Where the steamship trails hindways its long pennant
    of smoke,
Where the ground-shark's fin cuts like a black chip out of
    the water,
Where the half-burned brig is riding on unknown currents,
Where shells grow to her slimy deck, and the dead are
    corrupting below;
Where the striped and starred flag is borne at the head of
    the regiments;
Approaching Manhattan, up by the long-stretching island,
Under Niagara, the cataract falling like a veil over my
    countenance;
Upon a door-step . . . . upon the horse-block of hard wood
    outside,
Upon the race-course, or enjoying pic-nics or jigs or a good
    game of base-ball,
At he-festivals with blackguard jibes and ironical license and
    bull-dances and drinking and laughter,
At the cider-mill, tasting the sweet of the brown squash . . . .
    sucking the juice through a straw,
At apple-pealings, wanting kisses for all the red fruit I
    find,
At musters and beach-parties and friendly bees and huskings
    and house-raisings;
Where the mockingbird sounds his delicious gurgles, and
    cackles and screams and weeps,
Where the hay-rick stands in the barnyard, and the dry-stalks
    are scattered, and the brood cow waits in the hovel,
Where the bull advances to do his masculine work, and the
    stud to the mare, and the cock is treading the hen,
Where the heifers browse, and the geese nip their food with
    short jerks;
Where the sundown shadows lengthen over the limitless and
    lonesome prairie,
Where the herds of buffalo make a crawling spread of the
    square miles far and near;

Where the hummingbird shimmers . . . . where the neck of
    the longlived swan is curving and winding;

Where the laughing-gull scoots by the slappy shore and
    laughs her near-human laugh;

Where beehives range on a gray bench in the garden half-hid
    by the high weeds;

Where the band-necked partridges roost in a ring on the
    ground with their heads out;

Where burial coaches enter the arched gates of a cemetery;

Where winter wolves bark amid wastes of snow and icicled
    trees;

Where the yellow-crowned heron comes to the edge of the
    marsh at night and feeds upon small crabs;

Where the splash of swimmers and divers cools the warm
    noon;

Where the katydid works her chromatic reed on the walnut-
    tree over the well;

Through patches of citrons and cucumbers with silver-wired
    leaves,

Through the salt-lick or orange glade . . . . or under conical
    firs;

Through the gymnasium . . . . through the curtained
    saloon . . . . through the office or public hall;

Pleased with the native and pleased with the foreign . . . .
    pleased with the new and old,

Pleased with women, the homely as well as the handsome,

Pleased with the quakeress as she puts off her bonnet and
    talks melodiously,

Pleased with the primitive tunes of the choir of the
    whitewashed church,

Pleased with the earnest words of the sweating Methodist
    preacher, or any preacher . . . . looking seriously at the
    camp-meeting;

Looking in at the shop-windows in Broadway the whole
    forenoon . . . . pressing the flesh of my nose to the
    thick plate-glass,

Wandering the same afternoon with my face turned up to
    the clouds;

My right and left arms round the sides of two friends and I
    in the middle;

Coming home with the bearded and dark-cheeked bush-boy
   . . . . riding behind him at the drape of the day;
Far from the settlements studying the print of animals' feet,
   or the moccasin print;
By the cot in the hospital reaching lemonade to a feverish
   patient,
By the coffined corpse when all is still, examining with a
   candle;
Voyaging to every port to dicker and adventure;
Hurrying with the modern crowd, as eager and fickle as any,
Hot toward one I hate, ready in my madness to knife him;
Solitary at midnight in my back yard, my thoughts gone
   from me a long while,
Walking the old hills of Judea with the beautiful gentle god
   by my side;
Speeding through space . . . . speeding through heaven and
   the stars,
Speeding amid the seven satellites and the broad ring and
   the diameter of eighty thousand miles,
Speeding with tailed meteors . . . . throwing fire-balls like
   the rest,
Carrying the crescent child that carries its own full mother in
   its belly;
Storming enjoying planning loving cautioning,
Backing and filling, appearing and disappearing,
I tread day and night such roads.

I visit the orchards of God and look at the spheric product,
And look at quintillions ripened, and look at quintillions
   green.

I fly the flight of the fluid and swallowing soul,
My course runs below the soundings of plummets.

I help myself to material and immaterial,
No guard can shut me off, no law can prevent me.

I anchor my ship for a little while only,
My messengers continually cruise away or bring their returns
   to me.

I go hunting polar furs and the seal . . . . leaping chasms
     with a pike-pointed staff . . . . clinging to topples of
     brittle and blue.

I ascend to the foretruck . . . . I take my place late at night
     in the crow's nest . . . . we sail through the arctic sea
     . . . . it is plenty light enough,
Through the clear atmosphere I stretch around on the
     wonderful beauty,
The enormous masses of ice pass me and I pass them . . . .
     the scenery is plain in all directions,
The white-topped mountains point up in the distance . . . .
     I fling out my fancies toward them;
We are about approaching some great battlefield in which we
     are soon to be engaged,
We pass the colossal outposts of the encampments . . . .
     we pass with still feet and caution;
Or we are entering by the suburbs some vast and ruined city
     . . . . the blocks and fallen architecture more than all
     the living cities of the globe.

I am a free companion . . . . I bivouac by invading
     watchfires.

I turn the bridegroom out of bed and stay with the bride
     myself,
And tighten her all night to my thighs and lips.

My voice is the wife's voice, the screech by the rail of the
     stairs,
They fetch my man's body up dripping and drowned.

I understand the large hearts of heroes,
The courage of present times and all times;
How the skipper saw the crowded and rudderless wreck of the
     steamship, and death chasing it up and down the storm,
How he knuckled tight and gave not back one inch, and was
     faithful of days and faithful of nights,
And chalked in large letters on a board, Be of good cheer,
     We will not desert you;

saved the drifting company at last,
ow the lank loose-gowned women looked when boated
from the side of their prepared graves,
How the silent old-faced infants, and the lifted sick, and the
sharp-lipped unshaved men;
All this I swallow and it tastes good . . . . I like it well, and
it becomes mine,
I am the man . . . . I suffered . . . . I was there.

The disdain and calmness of martyrs,
The mother condemned for a witch and burnt with dry
wood, and her children gazing on;
The hounded slave that flags in the race and leans by the
fence, blowing and covered with sweat,
The twinges that sting like needles his legs and neck,
The murderous buckshot and the bullets,
All these I feel or am.

I am the hounded slave . . . . I wince at the bite of the dogs,
Hell and despair are upon me . . . . crack and again crack
the marksmen,
I clutch the rails of the fence . . . . my gore dribs thinned
with the ooze of my skin,
I fall on the weeds and stones,
The riders spur their unwilling horses and haul close,
They taunt my dizzy ears . . . . they beat me violently over
the head with their whip-stocks.

Agonies are one of my changes of garments;
I do not ask the wounded person how he feels I
myself become the wounded person,
My hurt turns livid upon me as I lean on a cane and observe.

I am the mashed fireman with breastbone broken . . . .
tumbling walls buried me in their debris,
Heat and smoke I inspired . . . . I heard the yelling shouts
of my comrades,
I heard the distant click of their picks and shovels;
They have cleared the beams away . . . . they tenderly lift
me forth.

I lie in the night air in my red shirt . . . . the pervading
     hush is for my sake,
Painless after all I lie, exhausted but not so unhappy,
White and beautiful are the faces around me . . . . the
     heads are bared of their fire-caps,
The kneeling crowd fades with the light of the torches.

Distant and dead resuscitate,
They show as the dial or move as the hands of me . . . .
     and I am the clock myself.

I am an old artillerist, and tell of some fort's bombardment
     . . . . and am there again.

Again the reveille of drummers . . . . again the attacking
     cannon and mortars and howitzers,
Again the attacked send their cannon responsive.

I take part . . . . I see and hear the whole,
The cries and curses and roar . . . . the plaudits for well
     aimed shots,
The ambulanza slowly passing and trailing its red drip,
Workmen searching after damages and to make indispensible
     repairs,
The fall of grenades through the rent roof . . . . the fan-
     shaped explosion,
The whizz of limbs heads stone wood and iron high in the air.

Again gurgles the mouth of my dying general . . . . he
     furiously waves with his hand,
He gasps through the clot . . . . Mind not me . . . . mind
     . . . . the entrenchments.

I tell not the fall of Alamo . . . . not one escaped to tell the
     fall of Alamo,
The hundred and fifty are dumb yet at Alamo.

Hear now the tale of a jetblack sunrise,
Hear of the murder in cold blood of four hundred and
     twelve young men.

Retreating they had formed in a hollow square with their
        baggage for breastworks,
Nine hundred lives out of the surrounding enemy's nine
        times their number was the price they took in advance,
Their colonel was wounded and their ammunition gone,
They treated for an honorable capitulation, received writing
        and seal, gave up their arms, and marched back
        prisoners of war.

They were the glory of the race of rangers,
Matchless with a horse, a rifle, a song, a supper or a
        courtship,
Large, turbulent, brave, handsome, generous, proud and
        affectionate,
Bearded, sunburnt, dressed in the free costume of hunters,
Not a single one over thirty years of age.

The second Sunday morning they were brought out in squads
        and massacred . . . . it was beautiful early summer,
The work commenced about five o'clock and was over by
        eight.

None obeyed the command to kneel,
Some made a mad and helpless rush . . . . some stood stark
        and straight,
A few fell at once, shot in the temple or heart . . . . the
        living and dead lay together,
The maimed and mangled dug in the dirt . . . . the new-
        comers saw them there;
Some half-killed attempted to crawl away,
These were dispatched with bayonets or battered with the
        blunts of muskets;
A youth not seventeen years old seized his assassin till two
        more came to release him,
The three were all torn, and covered with the boy's blood.

At eleven o'clock began the burning of the bodies;
And that is the tale of the murder of the four hundred and
        twelve young men,
And that was a jetblack sunrise.

Did you read in the seabooks of the oldfashioned frigate-
    fight?
Did you learn who won by the light of the moon and stars?

Our foe was no skulk in his ship, I tell you,
His was the English pluck, and there is no tougher or truer,
    and never was, and never will be;
Along the lowered eve he came, horribly raking us.

We closed with him . . . . the yards entangled . . . . the
    cannon touched,
My captain lashed fast with his own hands.

We had received some eighteen-pound shots under the water,
On our lower-gun-deck two large pieces had burst at the
    first fire, killing all around and blowing up overhead.

Ten o'clock at night, and the full moon shining and the leaks
    on the gain, and five feet of water reported,
The master-at-arms loosing the prisoners confined in the
    after-hold to give them a chance for themselves.

The transit to and from the magazine was now stopped by
    the sentinels,
They saw so many strange faces they did not know whom
    to trust.

Our frigate was afire . . . . the other asked if we demanded
    quarters? if our colors were struck and the fighting done?

I laughed content when I heard the voice of my little captain,
We have not struck, he composedly cried, We have just
    begun our part of the fighting.

Only three guns were in use,
One was directed by the captain himself against the enemy's
    mainmast,
Two well-served with grape and canister silenced his
    musketry and cleared his decks.

The tops alone seconded the fire of this little battery,
    especially the maintop,
They all held out bravely during the whole of the action.

Not a moment's cease,
The leaks gained fast on the pumps . . . . the fire eat
    toward the powder-magazine,
One of the pumps was shot away . . . . it was generally
    thought we were sinking.

Serene stood the little captain,
He was not hurried . . . . his voice was neither high nor low,
His eyes gave more light to us than our battle-lanterns.

Toward twelve at night, there in the beams of the moon they
    surrendered to us.

Stretched and still lay the midnight,
Two great hulls motionless on the breast of the darkness,
Our vessel riddled and slowly sinking . . . . preparations to
    pass to the one we had conquered,
The captain on the quarter deck coldly giving his orders
    through a countenance white as a sheet,
Near by the corpse of the child that served in the cabin,
The dead face of an old salt with long white hair and
    carefully curled whiskers,
The flames spite of all that could be done flickering aloft and
    below,
The husky voices of the two or three officers yet fit for duty,
Formless stacks of bodies and bodies by themselves . . . .
    dabs of flesh upon the masts and spars,
The cut of cordage and dangle of rigging . . . . the slight
    shock of the soothe of waves,
Black and impassive guns, and litter of powder-parcels, and
    the strong scent,
Delicate sniffs of the seabreeze . . . . smells of sedgy grass
    and fields by the shore . . . death-messages given in
    charge to survivors,
The hiss of the surgeon's knife and the gnawing teeth of his
    saw,

The wheeze, the cluck, the swash of falling blood . . . . the
    short wild scream, the long dull tapering groan,
These so . . . . . these irretrievable.

O Christ! My fit is mastering me!
What the rebel said gaily adjusting his throat to the rope-
    noose,
What the savage at the stump, his eye-sockets empty, his
    mouth spirting whoops and defiance,
What stills the traveler come to the vault at Mount Vernon,
What sobers the Brooklyn boy as he looks down the shores
    of the Wallabout and remembers the prison ships,
What burnt the gums of the redcoat at Saratoga when he
    surrendered his brigades,
These become mine and me every one, and they are but little,
I become as much more as I like.

I become any presence or truth of humanity here,
And see myself in prison shaped like another man,
And feel the dull unintermitted pain.

For me the keepers of convicts shoulder their carbines and
    keep watch,
It is I let out in the morning and barred at night.

Not a mutineer walks handcuffed to the jail, but I am
    handcuffed to him and walk by his side,
I am less the jolly one there, and more the silent one with
    sweat on my twitching lips.

Not a youngster is taken for larceny, but I go up too and
    am tried and sentenced.

Not a cholera patient lies at the last gasp, but I also lie at
    the last gasp,
My face is ash-colored, my sinews gnarl . . . . away from
    me people retreat.

Askers embody themselves in me, and I am embodied in them,
I project my hat and sit shamefaced and beg.

I rise extatic through all, and sweep with the true gravitation,
The whirling and whirling is elemental within me.

Somehow I have been stunned. Stand back!
Give me a little time beyond my cuffed head and slumbers
  and dreams and gaping,
I discover myself on a verge of the usual mistake.

That I could forget the mockers and insults!
That I could forget the trickling tears and the blows of the
  bludgeons and hammers!
That I could look with a separate look on my own
  crucifixion and bloody crowning!

I remember . . . . I resume the overstaid fraction,
The grave of rock multiplies what has been confided to it
  . . . . or to any graves,
The corpses rise . . . . the gashes heal . . . . the fastenings
  roll away.

I troop forth replenished with supreme power, one of an
  average unending procession,
We walk the roads of Ohio and Massachusetts and Virginia
  and Wisconsin and New York and New Orleans and
  Texas and Montreal and San Francisco and Charleston
  and Savannah and Mexico,
Inland and by the seacoast and boundary lines . . . . and we
  pass the boundary lines.

Our swift ordinances are on their way over the whole
  earth,
The blossoms we wear in our hats are the growth of two
  thousand years.

Eleves I salute you,
I see the approach of your numberless gangs . . . . I see
  you understand yourselves and me,
And know that they who have eyes are divine, and the blind
  and lame are equally divine,
And that my steps drag behind yours yet go before them,

And are aware how I am with you no more than I am with
    everybody.

The friendly and flowing savage . . . . Who is he?
Is he waiting for civilization or past it and mastering it?

Is he some southwesterner raised outdoors? Is he
    Canadian?
Is he from the Mississippi country? or from Iowa, Oregon
    or California? or from the mountains? or prairie life or
    bush-life? or from the sea?

Wherever he goes men and women accept and desire him,
They desire he should like them and touch them and speak
    to them and stay with them.

Behaviour lawless as snow-flakes . . . . words simple as
    grass . . . . uncombed head and laughter and naivete;
Slowstepping feet and the common features, and the
    common modes and emanations,
They descend in new forms from the tips of his fingers,
They are wafted with the odor of his body or breath . . . .
    they fly out of the glance of his eyes.

Flaunt of the sunshine I need not your bask . . . . lie
    over,
You light surfaces only . . . . I force the surfaces and the
    depths also.

Earth! you seem to look for something at my hands,
Say old topknot! what do you want?

Man or woman! I might tell how I like you, but cannot,
And might tell what it is in me and what it is in you, but
    cannot,
And might tell the pinings I have . . . . the pulse of my
    nights and days.

Behold I do not give lectures or a little charity,
What I give I give out of myself.

You there, impotent, loose in the knees, open your scarfed
    chops till I blow grit within you,
Spread your palms and lift the flaps of your pockets,
I am not to be denied . . . . I compel . . . . I have stores
    plenty and to spare,
And any thing I have I bestow.

I do not ask who you are . . . . that is not important to me,
You can do nothing and be nothing but what I will infold you.

To a drudge of the cottonfields or emptier of privies I lean
    . . . . on his right cheek I put the family kiss,
And in my soul I swear I never will deny him.

On women fit for conception I start bigger and nimbler babes,
This day I am jetting the stuff of far more arrogant republics.

To any one dying . . . . thither I speed and twist the knob
    of the door,
Turn the bedclothes toward the foot of the bed,
Let the physician and the priest go home.

I seize the descending man . . . . I raise him with resistless
    will.

O despairer, here is my neck,
By God! you shall not go down! Hang your whole weight
    upon me.

I dilate you with tremendous breath . . . . I buoy you up;
Every room of the house do I fill with an armed force . . . .
    lovers of me, bafflers of graves:
Sleep! I and they keep guard all night;
Not doubt, not decease shall dare to lay finger upon you,
I have embraced you, and henceforth possess you to myself,
And when you rise in the morning you will find what I tell
    you is so.

I am he bringing help for the sick as they pant on their backs,
And for strong upright men I bring yet more needed help.

I heard what was said of the universe,
Heard it and heard of several thousand years;
It is middling well as far as it goes . . . . but is that all?

Magnifying and applying come I,
Outbidding at the start the old cautious hucksters,
The most they offer for mankind and eternity less than a spirt
    of my own seminal wet,
Taking myself the exact dimensions of Jehovah and laying
    them away,
Lithographing Kronos and Zeus his son, and Hercules his
    grandson,
Buying drafts of Osiris and Isis and Belus and Brahma and
    Adonai,
In my portfolio placing Manito loose, and Allah on a leaf,
    and the crucifix engraved,
With Odin, and the hideous-faced Mexitli, and all idols and
    images,
Honestly taking them all for what they are worth, and not a
    cent more,
Admitting they were alive and did the work of their day,
Admitting they bore mites as for unfledged birds who have
    now to rise and fly and sing for themselves,
Accepting the rough deific sketches to fill out better in myself
    . . . . bestowing them freely on each man and woman I
    see,
Discovering as much or more in a framer framing a house,
Putting higher claims for him there with his rolled-up
    sleeves, driving the mallet and chisel;
Not objecting to special revelations . . . . considering a curl
    of smoke or a hair on the back of my hand as curious as
    any revelation;
Those ahold of fire-engines and hook-and-ladder ropes more
    to me than the gods of the antique wars,
Minding their voices peal through the crash of destruction,
Their brawny limbs passing safe over charred laths . . . .
    their white foreheads whole and unhurt out of the
    flames;
By the mechanic's wife with her babe at her nipple interceding
    for every person born;

Three scythes at harvest whizzing in a row from three lusty
    angels with shirts bagged out at their waists;
The snag-toothed hostler with red hair redeeming sins past
    and to come,
Selling all he possesses and traveling on foot to fee lawyers
    for his brother and sit by him while he is tried for
    forgery:
What was strewn in the amplest strewing the square rod
    about me, and not filling the square rod then;
The bull and the bug never worshipped half enough,
Dung and dirt more admirable than was dreamed,
The supernatural of no account . . . . myself waiting my
    time to be one of the supremes,
The day getting ready for me when I shall do as much good
    as the best, and be as prodigious,
Guessing when I am it will not tickle me much to receive
    puffs out of pulpit or print;
By my life-lumps! becoming already a creator!
Putting myself here and now to the ambushed womb of the
    shadows!

. . . . A call in the midst of the crowd,
My own voice, orotund sweeping and final.

Come my children,
Come my boys and girls, and my women and household and
    intimates,
Now the performer launches his nerve . . . . he has passed
    his prelude on the reeds within.

Easily written loosefingered chords! I feel the thrum of their
    climax and close.

My head evolves on my neck,
Music rolls, but not from the organ . . . . folks are around
    me, but they are no household of mine.

Ever the hard and unsunk ground,
Ever the eaters and drinkers . . . . ever the upward and
    downward sun . . . . ever the air and the ceaseless tides,

Ever myself and my neighbors, refreshing and wicked
        and real,
Ever the old inexplicable query . . . . ever that thorned
        thumb—that breath of itches and thirsts,
Ever the vexer's hoot! hoot! till we find where the sly one
        hides and bring him forth;
Ever love . . . . ever the sobbing liquid of life,
Ever the bandage under the chin . . . . ever the tressels
        of death.

Here and there with dimes on the eyes walking,
To feed the greed of the belly the brains liberally spooning,
Tickets buying or taking or selling, but in to the feast never
        once going;
Many sweating and ploughing and thrashing, and then the
        chaff for payment receiving,
A few idly owning, and they the wheat continually claiming.

This is the city . . . . and I am one of the citizens;
Whatever interests the rest interests me . . . . politics,
        churches, newspapers, schools,
Benevolent societies, improvements, banks, tariffs, steamships,
        factories, markets,
Stocks and stores and real estate and personal estate.

They who piddle and patter here in collars and tailed coats
        . . . . I am aware who they are . . . . and that they are
        not worms or fleas,
I acknowledge the duplicates of myself under all the scrape-
        lipped and pipe-legged concealments.

The weakest and shallowest is deathless with me,
What I do and say the same waits for them,
Every thought that flounders in me the same flounders in
        them.

I know perfectly well my own egotism,
And know my omniverous words, and cannot say any
        less,
And would fetch you whoever you are flush with myself.

My words are words of a questioning, and to indicate reality;
This printed and bound book . . . . but the printer and the
    printing-office boy?
The marriage estate and settlement . . . . but the body and
    mind of the bridegroom? also those of the bride?
The panorama of the sea . . . . but the sea itself?
The well-taken photographs . . . . but your wife or friend
    close and solid in your arms?
The fleet of ships of the line and all the modern
    improvements . . . . but the craft and pluck of the
    admiral?
The dishes and fare and furniture . . . . but the host and
    hostess, and the look out of their eyes?
The sky up there . . . . yet here or next door or across the
    way?
The saints and sages in history . . . . but you yourself?
Sermons and creeds and theology . . . . but the human
    brain, and what is called reason, and what is called love,
    and what is called life?

I do not despise you priests;
My faith is the greatest of faiths and the least of faiths,
Enclosing all worship ancient and modern, and all between
    ancient and modern,
Believing I shall come again upon the earth after five
    thousand years,
Waiting responses from oracles . . . . honoring the gods
    . . . . saluting the sun,
Making a fetish of the first rock or stump . . . . powowing
    with sticks in the circle of obis,
Helping the lama or brahmin as he trims the lamps of
    the idols,
Dancing yet through the streets in a phallic procession . . . .
    rapt and austere in the woods, a gymnosophist,
Drinking mead from the skull-cup . . . . to shasta and vedas
    admirant . . . . minding the koran,
Walking the teokallis, spotted with gore from the stone and
    knife—beating the serpent-skin drum;
Accepting the gospels, accepting him that was crucified,
    knowing assuredly that he is divine,

To the mass kneeling—to the puritan's prayer rising—sitting
    patiently in a pew,
Ranting and frothing in my insane crisis—waiting dead-like
    till my spirit arouses me;
Looking forth on pavement and land, and outside of
    pavement and land,
Belonging to the winders of the circuit of circuits.

One of that centripetal and centrifugal gang,
I turn and talk like a man leaving charges before a journey.

Down-hearted doubters, dull and excluded,
Frivolous sullen moping angry affected disheartened
    atheistical,
I know every one of you, and know the unspoken
    interrogatories,
By experience I know them.

How the flukes splash!
How they contort rapid as lightning, with spasms and spouts
    of blood!

Be at peace bloody flukes of doubters and sullen mopers,
I take my place among you as much as among any;
The past is the push of you and me and all precisely the same,
And the night is for you and me and all,
And what is yet untried and afterward is for you and me
    and all.

I do not know what is untried and afterward,
But I know it is sure and alive, and sufficient.

Each who passes is considered, and each who stops is
    considered, and not a single one can it fail.

It cannot fail the young man who died and was buried,
Nor the young woman who died and was put by his side,
Nor the little child that peeped in at the door and then drew
    back and was never seen again,
Nor the old man who has lived without purpose, and feels it
    with bitterness worse than gall,

Nor him in the poorhouse tubercled by rum and the bad
     disorder,
Nor the numberless slaughtered and wrecked . . . . nor the
     brutish koboo, called the ordure of humanity,
Nor the sacs merely floating with open mouths for food to
     slip in,
Nor any thing in the earth, or down in the oldest graves of
     the earth,
Nor any thing in the myriads of spheres, nor one of the
     myriads of myriads that inhabit them,
Nor the present, nor the least wisp that is known.

It is time to explain myself . . . . let us stand up.

What is known I strip away . . . . I launch all men and
     women forward with me into the unknown.

The clock indicates the moment . . . . but what does
     eternity indicate?

Eternity lies in bottomless reservoirs . . . . its buckets are
     rising forever and ever,
They pour and they pour and they exhale away.

We have thus far exhausted trillions of winters and summers;
There are trillions ahead, and trillions ahead of them.

Births have brought us richness and variety,
And other births will bring us richness and variety.

I do not call one greater and one smaller,
That which fills its period and place is equal to any.

Were mankind murderous or jealous upon you my brother
     or my sister?
I am sorry for you . . . . they are not murderous or jealous
     upon me;
All has been gentle with me . . . . . . I keep no account
     with lamentation;
What have I to do with lamentation?

I am an acme of things accomplished, and I an encloser of
    things to be.

My feet strike an apex of the apices of the stairs,
On every step bunches of ages, and larger bunches between
    the steps,
All below duly traveled—and still I mount and mount.

Rise after rise bow the phantoms behind me,
Afar down I see the huge first Nothing, the vapor from the
    nostrils of death,
I know I was even there . . . . I waited unseen and
    always,
And slept while God carried me through the lethargic
    mist,
And took my time . . . . and took no hurt from the fœtid
    carbon.

Long I was hugged close . . . . long and long.

Immense have been the preparations for me,
Faithful and friendly the arms that have helped me.

Cycles ferried my cradle, rowing and rowing like cheerful
    boatmen;
For room to me stars kept aside in their own rings,
They sent influences to look after what was to hold me.

Before I was born out of my mother generations guided me,
My embryo has never been torpid . . . . nothing could
    overlay it;
For it the nebula cohered to an orb . . . . the long slow
    strata piled to rest it on . . . . vast vegetables gave it
    sustenance,
Monstrous sauroids transported it in their mouths and
    deposited it with care.

All forces have been steadily employed to complete and
    delight me,
Now I stand on this spot with my soul.

Span of youth! Ever-pushed elasticity! Manhood balanced
and florid and full!

My lovers suffocate me!
Crowding my lips, and thick in the pores of my skin,
Jostling me through streets and public halls . . . . coming
naked to me at night,
Crying by day Ahoy from the rocks of the river . . . .
swinging and chirping over my head,
Calling my name from flowerbeds or vines or tangled
underbrush,
Or while I swim in the bath . . . . or drink from the
pump at the corner . . . . or the curtain is down at the
opera . . . . or I glimpse at a woman's face in the
railroad car;
Lighting on every moment of my life,
Bussing my body with soft and balsamic busses,
Noiselessly passing handfuls out of their hearts and giving
them to be mine.

Old age superbly rising! Ineffable grace of dying days!

Every condition promulges not only itself . . . . it promulges
what grows after and out of itself,
And the dark hush promulges as much as any.

I open my scuttle at night and see the far-sprinkled
systems,
And all I see, multiplied as high as I can cipher, edge but
the rim of the farther systems.

Wider and wider they spread, expanding and always
expanding,
Outward and outward and forever outward.

My sun has his sun, and round him obediently wheels,
He joins with his partners a group of superior circuit,
And greater sets follow, making specks of the greatest inside
them.

There is no stoppage, and never can be stoppage;
If I and you and the worlds and all beneath or upon their
    surfaces, and all the palpable life, were this moment
    reduced back to a pallid float, it would not avail in the
    long run,
We should surely bring up again where we now stand,
And as surely go as much farther, and then farther and farther.

A few quadrillions of eras, a few octillions of cubic leagues,
    do not hazard the span, or make it impatient,
They are but parts . . . . any thing is but a part.

See ever so far . . . . there is limitless space outside of that,
Count ever so much . . . . there is limitless time around that.

Our rendezvous is fitly appointed . . . . God will be there
    and wait till we come.

I know I have the best of time and space—and that I was
    never measured, and never will be measured.

I tramp a perpetual journey,
My signs are a rain-proof coat and good shoes and a staff
    cut from the woods;
No friend of mine takes his ease in my chair,
I have no chair, nor church nor philosophy;
I lead no man to a dinner-table or library or exchange,
But each man and each woman of you I lead upon a knoll,
My left hand hooks you round the waist,
My right hand points to landscapes of continents, and a
    plain public road.

Not I, not any one else can travel that road for you,
You must travel it for yourself.

It is not far . . . . it is within reach,
Perhaps you have been on it since you were born, and did
    not know,
Perhaps it is every where on water and on land.

Shoulder your duds, and I will mine, and let us hasten forth;
Wonderful cities and free nations we shall fetch as we go.

If you tire, give me both burdens, and rest the chuff of your
     hand on my hip,
And in due time you shall repay the same service to me;
For after we start we never lie by again.

This day before dawn I ascended a hill and looked at the
     crowded heaven,
And I said to my spirit, When we become the enfolders of
     those orbs and the pleasure and knowledge of every
     thing in them, shall we be filled and satisfied then?
And my spirit said No, we level that lift to pass and
     continue beyond.

You are also asking me questions, and I hear you;
I answer that I cannot answer . . . . you must find out for
     yourself.

Sit awhile wayfarer,
Here are biscuits to eat and here is milk to drink,
But as soon as you sleep and renew yourself in sweet clothes
     I will certainly kiss you with my goodbye kiss and open
     the gate for your egress hence.

Long enough have you dreamed contemptible dreams,
Now I wash the gum from your eyes,
You must habit yourself to the dazzle of the light and of
     every moment of your life

Long have you timidly waded, holding a plank by the shore,
Now I will you to be a bold swimmer,
To jump off in the midst of the sea, and rise again and nod
     to me and shout, and laughingly dash with your hair.

I am the teacher of athletes,
He that by me spreads a wider breast than my own proves
     the width of my own,
He most honors my style who learns under it to destroy the
     teacher.

The boy I love, the same becomes a man not through derived
     power but in his own right,
Wicked, rather than virtuous out of conformity or fear,
Fond of his sweetheart, relishing well his steak,
Unrequited love or a slight cutting him worse than a wound
     cuts,
First rate to ride, to fight, to hit the bull's eye, to sail a skiff,
     to sing a song or play on the banjo,
Preferring scars and faces pitted with smallpox over all
     latherers and those that keep out of the sun.

I teach straying from me, yet who can stray from me?
I follow you whoever you are from the present hour;
My words itch at your ears till you understand them.

I do not say these things for a dollar, or to fill up the time
     while I wait for a boat;
It is you talking just as much as myself . . . . I act as the
     tongue of you,
It was tied in your mouth . . . . in mine it begins to be
     loosened.

I swear I will never mention love or death inside a house,
And I swear I never will translate myself at all, only to him
     or her who privately stays with me in the open air.

If you would understand me go to the heights or water-shore,
The nearest gnat is an explanation and a drop or the motion
     of waves a key,
The maul the oar and the handsaw second my words.

No shuttered room or school can commune with me,
But roughs and little children better than they.

The young mechanic is closest to me . . . . he knows me
     pretty well,
The woodman that takes his axe and jug with him shall take
     me with him all day,
The farmboy ploughing in the field feels good at the sound
     of my voice,

In vessels that sail my words must sail . . . . I go with
 fishermen and seamen, and love them,
My face rubs to the hunter's face when he lies down alone in
 his blanket,
The driver thinking of me does not mind the jolt of his
 wagon,
The young mother and old mother shall comprehend me,
The girl and the wife rest the needle a moment and forget
 where they are,
They and all would resume what I have told them.

I have said that the soul is not more than the body,
And I have said that the body is not more than the soul,
And nothing, not God, is greater to one than one's-self is,
And whoever walks a furlong without sympathy walks to his
 own funeral, dressed in his shroud,
And I or you pocketless of a dime may purchase the pick of
 the earth,
And to glance with an eye or show a bean in its pod
 confounds the learning of all times,
And there is no trade or employment but the young man
 following it may become a hero,
And there is no object so soft but it makes a hub for the
 wheeled universe,
And any man or woman shall stand cool and supercilious
 before a million universes.

And I call to mankind, Be not curious about God,
For I who am curious about each am not curious about God,
No array of terms can say how much I am at peace about
 God and about death.

I hear and behold God in every object, yet I understand
 God not in the least,
Nor do I understand who there can be more wonderful than
 myself.

Why should I wish to see God better than this day?
I see something of God each hour of the twenty-four, and
 each moment then,

In the faces of men and women I see God, and in my own
 face in the glass;
I find letters from God dropped in the street, and every one
 is signed by God's name,
And I leave them where they are, for I know that others will
 punctually come forever and ever.

And as to you death, and you bitter hug of mortality . . . .
 it is idle to try to alarm me.

To his work without flinching the accoucheur comes,
I see the elderhand pressing receiving supporting,
I recline by the sills of the exquisite flexible doors . . . . and
 mark the outlet, and mark the relief and escape.

And as to you corpse I think you are good manure, but that
 does not offend me,
I smell the white roses sweetscented and growing,
I reach to the leafy lips . . . . I reach to the polished breasts
 of melons.

And as to you life, I reckon you are the leavings of many
 deaths,
No doubt I have died myself ten thousand times before.

I hear you whispering there O stars of heaven,
O suns . . . . O grass of graves . . . . O perpetual transfers
 and promotions . . . . if you do not say anything how
 can I say anything?

Of the turbid pool that lies in the autumn forest,
Of the moon that descends the steeps of the soughing
 twilight,
Toss, sparkles of day and dusk . . . . toss on the black stems
 that decay in the muck,
Toss to the moaning gibberish of the dry limbs.

I ascend from the moon . . . . I ascend from the night,
And perceive of the ghastly glitter the sunbeams
 reflected,

And debouch to the steady and central from the offspring
    great or small.

There is that in me . . . . I do not know what it is . . . .
    but I know it is in me.

Wrenched and sweaty . . . . calm and cool then my body
    becomes;
I sleep . . . . I sleep long.

I do not know it . . . . it is without name . . . . it is a word
    unsaid,
It is not in any dictionary or utterance or symbol.

Something it swings on more than the earth I swing on,
To it the creation is the friend whose embracing awakes me.

Perhaps I might tell more . . . . Outlines! I plead for my
    brothers and sisters.

Do you see O my brothers and sisters?
It is not chaos or death . . . . it is form and union and plan
    . . . . it is eternal life . . . . it is happiness.

The past and present wilt . . . . I have filled them and
    emptied them,
And proceed to fill my next fold of the future.

Listener up there! Here you . . . . what have you to confide
    to me?
Look in my face while I snuff the sidle of evening,
Talk honestly, for no one else hears you, and I stay only a
    minute longer.

Do I contradict myself?
Very well then . . . . I contradict myself;
I am large . . . . I contain multitudes.

I concentrate toward them that are nigh . . . . I wait on
    the door-slab.

Who has done his day's work and will soonest be through
    with his supper?
Who wishes to walk with me?

Will you speak before I am gone? Will you prove already too
    late?

The spotted hawk swoops by and accuses me . . . . he
    complains of my gab and my loitering.

I too am not a bit tamed . . . . I too am untranslatable,
I sound my barbaric yawp over the roofs of the world.

The last scud of day holds back for me,
It flings my likeness after the rest and true as any on the
    shadowed wilds,
It coaxes me to the vapor and the dusk.

I depart as air . . . . I shake my white locks at the runaway
    sun,
I effuse my flesh in eddies and drift it in lacy jags.

I bequeath myself to the dirt to grow from the grass I
    love,
If you want me again look for me under your bootsoles.

You will hardly know who I am or what I mean,
But I shall be good health to you nevertheless,
And filter and fibre your blood.

Failing to fetch me at first keep encouraged,
Missing me one place search another,
I stop some where waiting for you

———

I wander all night in my vision,
Stepping with light feet . . . . swiftly and noiselessly
    stepping and stopping,
Bending with open eyes over the shut eyes of sleepers;

Wandering and confused . . . . lost to myself . . . . ill-
     assorted . . . . contradictory,
Pausing and gazing and bending and stopping.

How solemn they look there, stretched and still;
How quiet they breathe, the little children in their cradles.

The wretched features of ennuyees, the white features of
     corpses, the livid faces of drunkards, the sick-gray faces
     of onanists,
The gashed bodies on battlefields, the insane in their strong-
     doored rooms, the sacred idiots,
The newborn emerging from gates and the dying emerging
     from gates,
The night pervades them and enfolds them.

The married couple sleep calmly in their bed, he with his
     palm on the hip of the wife, and she with her palm on
     the hip of the husband,
The sisters sleep lovingly side by side in their bed,
The men sleep lovingly side by side in theirs,
And the mother sleeps with her little child carefully wrapped.

The blind sleep, and the deaf and dumb sleep,
The prisoner sleeps well in the prison . . . . the runaway son
     sleeps,
The murderer that is to be hung next day . . . . how does he
     sleep?
And the murdered person . . . . how does he sleep?

The female that loves unrequited sleeps,
And the male that loves unrequited sleeps;
The head of the moneymaker that plotted all day sleeps,
And the enraged and treacherous dispositions sleep.

I stand with drooping eyes by the worstsuffering and
     restless,
I pass my hands soothingly to and fro a few inches from them;
The restless sink in their beds . . . . they fitfully sleep.

The earth recedes from me into the night,
I saw that it was beautiful . . . . and I see that what is not
    the earth is beautiful.

I go from bedside to bedside . . . . I sleep close with the
    other sleepers, each in turn;
I dream in my dream all the dreams of the other dreamers,
And I become the other dreamers.

I am a dance . . . . Play up there! the fit is whirling me fast.

I am the everlaughing . . . . it is new moon and twilight,
I see the hiding of douceurs . . . . I see nimble ghosts
    whichever way I look,
Cache and cache again deep in the ground and sea, and
    where it is neither ground or sea.

Well do they do their jobs, those journeymen divine,
Only from me can they hide nothing and would not if they
    could;
I reckon I am their boss, and they make me a pet besides,
And surround me, and lead me and run ahead when I walk,
And lift their cunning covers and signify me with stretched
    arms, and resume the way;
Onward we move, a gay gang of blackguards with
    mirthshouting music and wildflapping pennants of joy.

I am the actor and the actress . . . . the voter . . the
    politician,
The emigrant and the exile . . the criminal that stood in the
    box,
He who has been famous, and he who shall be famous after
    today,
The stammerer . . . . the wellformed person . . the wasted
    or feeble person.

I am she who adorned herself and folded her hair
    expectantly,
My truant lover has come and it is dark.

Double yourself and receive me darkness,
Receive me and my lover too . . . . he will not let me go
    without him.

I roll myself upon you as upon a bed . . . . I resign myself
    to the dusk.

He whom I call answers me and takes the place of my lover,
He rises with me silently from the bed.

Darkness you are gentler than my lover . . . . his flesh was
    sweaty and panting,
I feel the hot moisture yet that he left me.

My hands are spread forth . . I pass them in all directions,
I would sound up the shadowy shore to which you are
    journeying.

Be careful, darkness . . . . already, what was it touched me?
I thought my lover had gone . . . . else darkness and he
    are one,
I hear the heart-beat . . . . I follow . . I fade away.

O hotcheeked and blushing! O foolish hectic!
O for pity's sake, no one must see me now! . . . . my
    clothes were stolen while I was abed,
Now I am thrust forth, where shall I run?

Pier that I saw dimly last night when I looked from the
    windows,
Pier out from the main, let me catch myself with you and
    stay . . . . I will not chafe you;
I feel ashamed to go naked about the world,
And am curious to know where my feet stand . . . . and
    what is this flooding me, childhood or manhood . . . .
    and the hunger that crosses the bridge between.

The cloth laps a first sweet eating and drinking,
Laps life-swelling yolks . . . . laps ear of rose-corn, milky
    and just ripened:

The white teeth stay, and the boss-tooth advances in
    darkness,
And liquor is spilled on lips and bosoms by touching glasses,
    and the best liquor afterward.

I descend my western course . . . . my sinews are flaccid,
Perfume and youth course through me, and I am their wake.

It is my face yellow and wrinkled instead of the old
    woman's,
I sit low in a strawbottom chair and carefully darn my
    grandson's stockings.

It is I too . . . . the sleepless widow looking out on the
    winter midnight,
I see the sparkles of starshine on the icy and pallid earth.

A shroud I see—and I am the shroud . . . . I wrap a body
    and lie in the coffin;
It is dark here underground . . . . it is not evil or pain here
    . . . . it is blank here, for reasons.

It seems to me that everything in the light and air ought to
    be happy;
Whoever is not in his coffin and the dark grave, let him
    know he has enough.

I see a beautiful gigantic swimmer swimming naked through
    the eddies of the sea,
His brown hair lies close and even to his head . . . . he
    strikes out with courageous arms . . . . he urges
    himself with his legs.

I see his white body . . . . I see his undaunted eyes;
I hate the swift-running eddies that would dash him
    headforemost on the rocks.

What are you doing you ruffianly red-trickled waves?
Will you kill the courageous giant? Will you kill him in the
    prime of his middle age?

Steady and long he struggles;
He is baffled and banged and bruised . . . . he holds out
    while his strength holds out,
The slapping eddies are spotted with his blood . . . . they
    bear him away . . . . they roll him and swing him and
    turn him:
His beautiful body is borne in the circling eddies . . . . it is
    continually bruised on rocks,
Swiftly and out of sight is borne the brave corpse.

I turn but do not extricate myself;
Confused . . . . a pastreading . . . . another, but with
    darkness yet.

The beach is cut by the razory ice-wind . . . . the wreck-
    guns sound,
The tempest lulls and the moon comes floundering through
    the drifts.

I look where the ship helplessly heads end on . . . . I hear
    the burst as she strikes . . I hear the howls of dismay
    . . . . they grow fainter and fainter.

I cannot aid with my wringing fingers;
I can but rush to the surf and let it drench me and freeze
    upon me.

I search with the crowd . . . . not one of the company is
    washed to us alive;
In the morning I help pick up the dead and lay them in
    rows in a barn.

Now of the old war-days . . the defeat at Brooklyn;
Washington stands inside the lines . . he stands on the
    entrenched hills amid a crowd of officers,
His face is cold and damp . . . . he cannot repress the
    weeping drops . . . . he lifts the glass perpetually
    to his eyes . . . . the color is blanched from his
    cheeks,

He sees the slaughter of the southern braves confided to him
    by their parents.

The same at last and at last when peace is declared,
He stands in the room of the old tavern . . . . the
    wellbeloved soldiers all pass through,
The officers speechless and slow draw near in their turns,
The chief encircles their necks with his arm and kisses them
    on the cheek,
He kisses lightly the wet cheeks one after another . . . . he
    shakes hands and bids goodbye to the army.

Now I tell what my mother told me today as we sat at
    dinner together,
Of when she was a nearly grown girl living home with her
    parents on the old homestead.

A red squaw came one breakfasttime to the old
    homestead,
On her back she carried a bundle of rushes for
    rushbottoming chairs;
Her hair straight shiny coarse black and profuse
    halfenveloped her face,
Her step was free and elastic . . . . her voice sounded
    exquisitely as she spoke.

My mother looked in delight and amazement at the
    stranger,
She looked at the beauty of her tallborne face and full and
    pliant limbs,
The more she looked upon her she loved her,
Never before had she seen such wonderful beauty and
    purity;
She made her sit on a bench by the jamb of the fireplace . . . .
    she cooked food for her,
She had no work to give her but she gave her remembrance
    and fondness.

The red squaw staid all the forenoon, and toward the middle
    of the afternoon she went away;
O my mother was loth to have her go away,
All the week she thought of her . . . . she watched for her
    many a month,
She remembered her many a winter and many a summer,
But the red squaw never came nor was heard of there again.

Now Lucifer was not dead . . . . or if he was I am his
    sorrowful terrible heir;
I have been wronged . . . . I am oppressed . . . . I hate
    him that oppresses me,
I will either destroy him, or he shall release me.

Damn him! how he does defile me,
How he informs against my brother and sister and takes pay
    for their blood,
How he laughs when I look down the bend after the
    steamboat that carries away my woman.

Now the vast dusk bulk that is the whale's bulk . . . . it
    seems mine,
Warily, sportsman! though I lie so sleepy and sluggish, my
    tap is death.

A show of the summer softness . . . . a contact of something
    unseen . . . . an amour of the light and air;
I am jealous and overwhelmed with friendliness,
And will go gallivant with the light and the air myself,
And have an unseen something to be in contact with them
    also.

O love and summer! you are in the dreams and in me,
Autumn and winter are in the dreams . . . . the farmer goes
    with his thrift,
The droves and crops increase . . . . the barns are wellfilled.

Elements merge in the night . . . . ships make tacks in the
    dreams . . . . the sailor sails . . . . the exile returns
    home,

The fugitive returns unharmed . . . . the immigrant is back
    beyond months and years;
The poor Irishman lives in the simple house of his
    childhood, with the wellknown neighbors and faces,
They warmly welcome him . . . . he is barefoot again . . . .
    he forgets he is welloff;
The Dutchman voyages home, and the Scotchman and
    Welchman voyage home . . and the native of the
    Mediterranean voyages home;
To every port of England and France and Spain enter
    wellfilled ships;
The Swiss foots it toward his hills . . . . the Prussian goes
    his way, and the Hungarian his way, and the Pole goes
    his way,
The Swede returns, and the Dane and Norwegian return.

The homeward bound and the outward bound,
The beautiful lost swimmer, the ennuyee, the onanist, the
    female that loves unrequited, the moneymaker,
The actor and actress . . those through with their parts and
    those waiting to commence,
The affectionate boy, the husband and wife, the voter, the
    nominee that is chosen and the nominee that has
    failed,
The great already known, and the great anytime after to
    day,
The stammerer, the sick, the perfectformed, the homely,
The criminal that stood in the box, the judge that sat and
    sentenced him, the fluent lawyers, the jury, the
    audience,
The laugher and weeper, the dancer, the midnight widow,
    the red squaw,
The consumptive, the erysipalite, the idiot, he that is
    wronged,
The antipodes, and every one between this and them in the
    dark,
I swear they are averaged now . . . . one is no better than
    the other,
The night and sleep have likened them and restored them.

I swear they are all beautiful,
Every one that sleeps is beautiful . . . . every thing in the
    dim night is beautiful,
The wildest and bloodiest is over and all is peace.

Peace is always beautiful,
The myth of heaven indicates peace and night.

The myth of heaven indicates the soul;
The soul is always beautiful . . . . it appears more or it
    appears less . . . . it comes or lags behind,
It comes from its embowered garden and looks pleasantly on
    itself and encloses the world;
Perfect and clean the genitals previously jetting, and perfect
    and clean the womb cohering,
The head wellgrown and proportioned and plumb, and the
    bowels and joints proportioned and plumb.

The soul is always beautiful,
The universe is duly in order . . . . every thing is in its place,
What is arrived is in its place, and what waits is in its place;
The twisted skull waits . . . . the watery or rotten blood
    waits,
The child of the glutton or venerealee waits long, and the
    child of the drunkard waits long, and the drunkard
    himself waits long,
The sleepers that lived and died wait . . . . the far advanced
    are to go on in their turns, and the far behind are to go
    on in their turns,
The diverse shall be no less diverse, but they shall flow and
    unite . . . . they unite now.

The sleepers are very beautiful as they lie unclothed,
They flow hand in hand over the whole earth from east to
    west as they lie unclothed;
The Asiatic and African are hand in hand . . . . the European
    and American are hand in hand,
Learned and unlearned are hand in hand . . and male and
    female are hand in hand;

The bare arm of the girl crosses the bare breast of her lover
    . . . . they press close without lust . . . . his lips press
    her neck,
The father holds his grown or ungrown son in his arms with
    measureless love . . . . and the son holds the father in
    his arms with measureless love,
The white hair of the mother shines on the white wrist of
    the daughter,
The breath of the boy goes with the breath of the man . . . .
    friend is inarmed by friend,
The scholar kisses the teacher and the teacher kisses the
    scholar . . . . the wronged is made right,
The call of the slave is one with the master's call . . and the
    master salutes the slave,
The felon steps forth from the prison . . . . the insane
    becomes sane . . . . the suffering of sick persons is
    relieved,
The sweatings and fevers stop . . the throat that was
    unsound is sound . . the lungs of the consumptive are
    resumed . . the poor distressed head is free,
The joints of the rheumatic move as smoothly as ever, and
    smoother than ever,
Stiflings and passages open . . . . the paralysed become
    supple,
The swelled and convulsed and congested awake to themselves
    in condition,
They pass the invigoration of the night and the chemistry of
    the night and awake.

I too pass from the night;
I stay awhile away O night, but I return to you again and
    love you;
Why should I be afraid to trust myself to you?
I am not afraid . . . . I have been well brought forward
    by you;
I love the rich running day, but I do not desert her in whom
    I lay so long;
I know not how I came of you, and I know not where I go
    with you . . . . but I know I came well and shall go well.

I will stop only a time with the night . . . . and rise betimes.

I will duly pass the day O my mother and duly return to you;
Not you will yield forth the dawn again more surely than you
        will yield forth me again,
Not the womb yields the babe in its time more surely than I
        shall be yielded from you in my time.

———————————

The bodies of men and women engirth me, and I engirth
        them,
They will not let me off nor I them till I go with them and
        respond to them and love them.

Was it dreamed whether those who corrupted their own live
        bodies could conceal themselves?
And whether those who defiled the living were as bad as they
        who defiled the dead?

The expression of the body of man or woman balks account,
The male is perfect and that of the female is perfect.

The expression of a wellmade man appears not only in his face,
It is in his limbs and joints also . . . . it is curiously in the
        joints of his hips and wrists,
It is in his walk . . the carriage of his neck . . the flex of his
        waist and knees . . . . dress does not hide him,
The strong sweet supple quality he has strikes through the
        cotton and flannel;
To see him pass conveys as much as the best poem . .
        perhaps more,
You linger to see his back and the back of his neck and
        shoulderside.

The sprawl and fulness of babes . . . . the bosoms and heads
        of women . . . . the folds of their dress . . . . their
        style as we pass in the street . . . . the contour of their
        shape downwards;
The swimmer naked in the swimmingbath . . seen as he
        swims through the salt transparent greenshine, or lies
        on his back and rolls silently with the heave of the water;

Framers bare-armed framing a house . . hoisting the
    beams in their places . . or using the mallet and
    mortising-chisel,
The bending forward and backward of rowers in rowboats
    . . . . the horseman in his saddle;
Girls and mothers and housekeepers in all their exquisite
    offices,
The group of laborers seated at noontime with their open
    dinnerkettles, and their wives waiting,
The female soothing a child . . . . the farmer's daughter in
    the garden or cowyard,
The woodman rapidly swinging his axe in the woods . . . .
    the young fellow hoeing corn . . . . the sleighdriver
    guiding his six horses through the crowd,
The wrestle of wrestlers . . two apprentice-boys, quite
    grown, lusty, goodnatured, nativeborn, out on the
    vacant lot at sundown after work,
The coats vests and caps thrown down . . the embrace of
    love and resistance,
The upperhold and underhold — the hair rumpled over and
    blinding the eyes;
The march of firemen in their own costumes — the play of
    the masculine muscle through cleansetting trowsers and
    waistbands,
The slow return from the fire . . . . the pause when the
    bell strikes suddenly again — the listening on the alert,
The natural perfect and varied attitudes . . . . the bent head,
    the curved neck, the counting:
Suchlike I love . . . . I loosen myself and pass freely . . . .
    and am at the mother's breast with the little child,
And swim with the swimmer, and wrestle with wrestlers,
    and march in line with the firemen, and pause and listen
    and count.

I knew a man . . . . he was a common farmer . . . . he was
    the father of five sons . . . and in them were the fathers
    of sons . . . and in them were the fathers of sons.

This man was of wonderful vigor and calmness and beauty
    of person;

The shape of his head, the richness and breadth of his
        manners, the pale yellow and white of his hair and
        beard, the immeasurable meaning of his black eyes,
These I used to go and visit him to see . . . . He was wise
        also,
He was six feet tall . . . . he was over eighty years old . . . .
        his sons were massive clean bearded tanfaced and
     .   handsome,
They and his daughters loved him . . . all who saw him
        loved him . . . they did not love him by allowance . . .
        they loved him with personal love;
He drank water only . . . . the blood showed like scarlet
        through the clear brown skin of his face;
He was a frequent gunner and fisher . . . he sailed his boat
        himself . . . he had a fine one presented to him by a
        shipjoiner . . . . he had fowling-pieces, presented to
        him by men that loved him;
When he went with his five sons and many grandsons to
        hunt or fish you would pick him out as the most
        beautiful and vigorous of the gang,
You would wish long and long to be with him . . . . you
        would wish to sit by him in the boat that you and he
        might touch each other.

I have perceived that to be with those I like is enough,
To stop in company with the rest at evening is enough,
To be surrounded by beautiful curious breathing laughing
        flesh is enough,
To pass among them . . to touch any one . . . . to rest my
        arm ever so lightly round his or her neck for a moment
        . . . . what is this then?
I do not ask any more delight . . . . I swim in it as in a sea.

There is something in staying close to men and women and
        looking on them and in the contact and odor of them
        that pleases the soul well,
All things please the soul, but these please the soul well.

This is the female form,
A divine nimbus exhales from it from head to foot,

It attracts with fierce undeniable attraction,
I am drawn by its breath as if I were no more than a helpless
    vapor . . . . all falls aside but myself and it,
Books, art, religion, time . . the visible and solid earth . .
    the atmosphere and the fringed clouds . . what was
    expected of heaven or feared of hell are now consumed,
Mad filaments, ungovernable shoots play out of it . . the
    response likewise ungovernable,
Hair, bosom, hips, bend of legs, negligent falling hands—all
    diffused . . . . mine too diffused,
Ebb stung by the flow, and flow stung by the ebb . . . .
    loveflesh swelling and deliciously aching,
Limitless limpid jets of love hot and enormous . . . .
    quivering jelly of love . . . white-blow and delirious
    juice,
Bridegroom-night of love working surely and softly into the
    prostrate dawn,
Undulating into the willing and yielding day,
Lost in the cleave of the clasping and sweetfleshed day.

This is the nucleus . . . after the child is born of woman the
    man is born of woman,
This is the bath of birth . . . this is the merge of small and
    large and the outlet again.

Be not ashamed women . . your privilege encloses the rest . .
    it is the exit of the rest,
You are the gates of the body and you are the gates of the
    soul.

The female contains all qualities and tempers them . . . .
    she is in her place . . . . she moves with perfect balance,
She is all things duly veiled . . . . she is both passive and
    active . . . . she is to conceive daughters as well as sons
    and sons as well as daughters.

As I see my soul reflected in nature . . . . as I see through a
    mist one with inexpressible completeness and beauty
    . . . . see the bent head and arms folded over the breast
    . . . . the female I see,

I see the bearer of the great fruit which is immortality . . . .
    the good thereof is not tasted by roues, and never can be.

The male is not less the soul, nor more . . . . he too is in
    his place,
He too is all qualities . . . . he is action and power . . . .
    the flush of the known universe is in him,
Scorn becomes him well and appetite and defiance become
    him well,
The fiercest largest passions . . bliss that is utmost and
    sorrow that is utmost become him well . . . . pride is
    for him,
The fullspread pride of man is calming and excellent to the
    soul;
Knowledge becomes him . . . . he likes it always . . . . he
    brings everything to the test of himself,
Whatever the survey . . whatever the sea and the sail, he
    strikes soundings at last only here,
Where else does he strike soundings except here?

The man's body is sacred and the woman's body is sacred
    . . . . it is no matter who,
Is it a slave? Is it one of the dullfaced immigrants just landed
    on the wharf?

Each belongs here or anywhere just as much as the welloff
    . . . . just as much as you,
Each has his or her place in the procession.

All is a procession,
The universe is a procession with measured and beautiful
    motion.

Do you know so much that you call the slave or the dullface
    ignorant?
Do you suppose you have a right to a good sight . . . and
    he or she has no right to a sight?
Do you think matter has cohered together from its diffused
    float, and the soil is on the surface and water runs and
    vegetation sprouts for you . . and not for him and her?

A slave at auction!
I help the auctioneer . . . . the sloven does not half know
    his business.

Gentlemen look on this curious creature,
Whatever the bids of the bidders they cannot be high enough
    for him,
For him the globe lay preparing quintillions of years without
    one animal or plant,
For him the revolving cycles truly and steadily rolled.

In that head the allbaffling brain,
In it and below it the making of the attributes of heroes.

Examine these limbs, red black or white . . . . they are very
    cunning in tendon and nerve;
They shall be stript that you may see them.

Exquisite senses, lifelit eyes, pluck, volition,
Flakes of breastmuscle, pliant backbone and neck, flesh not
    flabby, goodsized arms and legs,
And wonders within there yet.

Within there runs his blood . . . . the same old blood . .
    the same red running blood;
There swells and jets his heart . . . . There all passions and
    desires . . all reachings and aspirations:
Do you think they are not there because they are not
    expressed in parlors and lecture-rooms?

This is not only one man . . . . he is the father of those
    who shall be fathers in their turns,
In him the start of populous states and rich republics,
Of him countless immortal lives with countless embodiments
    and enjoyments.

How do you know who shall come from the offspring of his
    offspring through the centuries?
Who might you find you have come from yourself if you
    could trace back through the centuries?

A woman at auction,
She too is not only herself . . . . she is the teeming mother
    of mothers,
She is the bearer of them that shall grow and be mates to the
    mothers.

Her daughters or their daughters' daughters . . who knows
    who shall mate with them?
Who knows through the centuries what heroes may come
    from them?

In them and of them natal love . . . . in them the divine
    mystery . . . . the same old beautiful mystery.

Have you ever loved a woman?
Your mother . . . . is she living? . . . . Have you been much
    with her? and has she been much with you?
Do you not see that these are exactly the same to all in all
    nations and times all over the earth?

If life and the soul are sacred the human body is sacred;
And the glory and sweet of a man is the token of manhood
    untainted,
And in man or woman a clean strong firmfibred body is
    beautiful as the most beautiful face.

Have you seen the fool that corrupted his own live body? or
    the fool that corrupted her own live body?
For they do not conceal themselves, and cannot conceal
    themselves.

Who degrades or defiles the living human body is cursed,
Who degrades or defiles the body of the dead is not more
    cursed.

———————

There was a child went forth every day,
And the first object he looked upon and received with
    wonder or pity or love or dread, that object he became,
And that object became part of him for the day or a certain
    part of the day . . . . or for many years or stretching
    cycles of years.

The early lilacs became part of this child,
And grass, and white and red morningglories, and white and
    red clover, and the song of the phœbe-bird,
And the March-born lambs, and the sow's pink-faint litter,
    and the mare's foal, and the cow's calf, and the noisy
    brood of the barnyard or by the mire of the pond-side
    . . and the fish suspending themselves so curiously
    below there . . and the beautiful curious liquid . . and
    the water-plants with their graceful flat heads . . all
    became part of him.

And the field-sprouts of April and May became part of him
    . . . . wintergrain sprouts, and those of the light
    yellow corn, and of the esculent roots of the garden,
And the appletrees covered with blossoms, and the fruit
    afterward . . . . and woodberries . . and the
    commonest weeds by the road;
And the old drunkard staggering home from the outhouse
    of the tavern whence he had lately risen,
And the schoolmistress that passed on her way to the school
    . . and the friendly boys that passed . . and the
    quarrelsome boys . . and the tidy and freshcheeked
    girls . . and the barefoot negro boy and girl,
And all the changes of city and country wherever he went.

His own parents . . he that had propelled the fatherstuff at
    night, and fathered him . . and she that conceived him
    in her womb and birthed him . . . . they gave this
    child more of themselves than that,
They gave him afterward every day . . . . they and of them
    became part of him.

The mother at home quietly placing the dishes on the
    suppertable,
The mother with mild words . . . . clean her cap and gown
    . . . . a wholesome odor falling off her person and
    clothes as she walks by:
The father, strong, selfsufficient, manly, mean, angered, unjust,
The blow, the quick loud word, the tight bargain, the crafty
    lure,
The family usages, the language, the company, the furniture
    . . . . the yearning and swelling heart,
Affection that will not be gainsayed . . . . The sense of
    what is real . . . . the thought if after all it should
    prove unreal,
The doubts of daytime and the doubts of nighttime . . .
    the curious whether and how,
Whether that which appears so is so . . . . Or is it all flashes
    and specks?
Men and women crowding fast in the streets . . if they are
    not flashes and specks what are they?
The streets themselves, and the facades of houses . . . .
    the goods in the windows,
Vehicles . . teams . . the tiered wharves, and the huge
    crossing at the ferries;
The village on the highland seen from afar at sunset . . . .
    the river between,
Shadows . . aureola and mist . . light falling on roofs and
    gables of white or brown, three miles off,
The schooner near by sleepily dropping down the tide . . the
    little boat slacktowed astern,
The hurrying tumbling waves and quickbroken crests and
    slapping;
The strata of colored clouds . . . . the long bar of
    maroontint away solitary by itself . . . . the spread of
    purity it lies motionless in,
The horizon's edge, the flying seacrow, the fragrance of
    saltmarsh and shoremud;
These became part of that child who went forth every day,
    and who now goes and will always go forth every day,
And these become of him or her that peruses them now.

from *Leaves of Grass* (*1860*)

Chants Democratic and Native American: 5

Respondez! Respondez!

Let every one answer! Let those who sleep be waked! Let
none evade—not you, any more than others!

(If it really be as is pretended, how much longer must we go
on with our affectations and sneaking?

Let me bring this to a close—I pronounce openly for a new
distribution of roles,)

Let that which stood in front go behind! and let that which
was behind advance to the front and speak!

Let murderers, thieves, bigots, fools, unclean persons, offer
new propositions!

Let the old propositions be postponed!

Let faces and theories be turned inside out! Let meanings be
freely criminal, as well as results!

Let there be no suggestion above the suggestion of
drudgery!

Let none be pointed toward his destination! (Say! do you
know your destination?)

Let trillions of men and women be mocked with bodies and
mocked with Souls!

Let the love that waits in them, wait! Let it die, or pass still-
born to other spheres!

Let the sympathy that waits in every man, wait! or let it also
pass, a dwarf, to other spheres!

Let contradictions prevail! Let one thing contradict another!
and let one line of my poems contradict another!

Let the people sprawl with yearning aimless hands! Let
their tongues be broken! Let their eyes be discouraged!
Let none descend into their hearts with the fresh
lusciousness of love!

Let the theory of America be management, caste,
comparison! (Say! what other theory would you?)

Let them that distrust birth and death lead the rest! (Say!
why shall they not lead you?)

Let the crust of hell be neared and trod on! Let the days be
     darker than the nights! Let slumber bring less slumber
     than waking-time brings!
Let the world never appear to him or her for whom it was all
     made!
Let the heart of the young man exile itself from the heart of
     the old man! and let the heart of the old man be exiled
     from that of the young man!
Let the sun and moon go! Let scenery take the applause of
     the audience! Let there be apathy under the stars!
Let freedom prove no man's inalienable right! Every one
     who can tyrannize, let him tyrannize to his
     satisfaction!
Let none but infidels be countenanced!
Let the eminence of meanness, treachery, sarcasm, hate,
     greed, indecency, impotence, lust, be taken for
     granted above all! Let writers, judges, governments,
     households, religions, philosophies, take such for
     granted above all!
Let the worst men beget children out of the worst women!
Let priests still play at immortality!
Let Death be inaugurated!
Let nothing remain upon the earth except the ashes of
     teachers, artists, moralists, lawyers, and learned and
     polite persons!
Let him who is without my poems be assassinated!
Let the cow, the horse, the camel, the garden-bee — Let the
     mud-fish, the lobster, the mussel, eel, the sting-ray, and
     the grunting pig-fish — Let these, and the like of these,
     be put on a perfect equality with man and woman!
Let churches accommodate serpents, vermin, and the corpses
     of those who have died of the most filthy of diseases!
Let marriage slip down among fools, and be for none but
     fools!
Let men among themselves talk and think obscenely of
     women! and let women among themselves talk and
     think obscenely of men!
Let every man doubt every woman! and let every woman
     trick every man!

Let us all, without missing one, be exposed in public, naked,
monthly, at the peril of our lives! Let our bodies be
freely handled and examined by whoever chooses!

Let nothing but copies, pictures, statues, reminiscences,
elegant works, be permitted to exist upon the earth!

Let the earth desert God, nor let there ever henceforth be
mentioned the name of God!

Let there be no God!

Let there be money, business, imports, exports, custom,
authority, precedents, pallor, dyspepsia, smut,
ignorance, unbelief!

Let judges and criminals be transposed! Let the prison-
keepers be put in prison! Let those that were prisoners
take the keys! (Say! why might they not just as well be
transposed?)

Let the slaves be masters! Let the masters become slaves!

Let the reformers descend from the stands where they are
forever bawling! Let an idiot or insane person appear
on each of the stands!

Let the Asiatic, the African, the European, the American
and the Australian, go armed against the murderous
stealthiness of each other! Let them sleep armed! Let
none believe in good-will!

Let there be no unfashionable wisdom! Let such be scorned
and derided off from the earth!

Let a floating cloud in the sky—Let a wave of the sea—Let
one glimpse of your eye-sight upon the landscape or
grass—Let growing mint, spinach, onions, tomatoes—
Let these be exhibited as shows at a great price for
admission!

Let all the men of These States stand aside for a few
smouchers! Let the few seize on what they choose!
Let the rest gawk, giggle, starve, obey!

Let shadows be furnished with genitals! Let substances be
deprived of their genitals!

Let there be wealthy and immense cities—but through
any of them, not a single poet, saviour, knower,
lover!

Let the infidels of These States laugh all faith away! If one
    man be found who has faith, let the rest set upon him!
    Let them affright faith! Let them destroy the power of
    breeding faith!
Let the she-harlots and the he-harlots be prudent! Let them
    dance on, while seeming lasts! (O seeming! seeming!
    seeming!)
Let the preachers recite creeds! Let them teach only what
    they have been taught!
Let the preachers of creeds never dare to go meditate
    candidly upon the hills, alone, by day or by night!
    (If one ever once dare, he is lost!)
Let insanity have charge of sanity!
Let books take the place of trees, animals, rivers,
    clouds!
Let the daubed portraits of heroes supersede heroes!
Let the manhood of man never take steps after itself! Let it
    take steps after eunuchs, and after consumptive and
    genteel persons!
Let the white person tread the black person under his heel!
    (Say! which is trodden under heel, after all?)
Let the reflections of the things of the world be studied
    in mirrors! Let the things themselves continue
    unstudied!
Let a man seek pleasure everywhere except in himself! Let a
    woman seek happiness everywhere except in herself!
    (Say! what real happiness have you had one single time
    through your whole life?)
Let the limited years of life do nothing for the limitless
    years of death! (Say! what do you suppose death will
    do, then?)

from *Leaves of Grass* (*1891–92*)

from *Children of Adam*

FROM PENT-UP ACHING RIVERS

From pent-up aching rivers,
From that of myself without which I were nothing,
From what I am determin'd to make illustrious, even if I
    stand sole among men,
From my own voice resonant, singing the phallus,
Singing the song of procreation,
Singing the need of superb children and therein superb
    grown people,
Singing the muscular urge and the blending,
Singing the bedfellow's song, (O resistless yearning!
O for any and each the body correlative attracting!
O for you whoever you are your correlative body! O it, more
    than all else, you delighting!)
From the hungry gnaw that eats me night and day,
From native moments, from bashful pains, singing them,
Seeking something yet unfound though I have diligently
    sought it many a long year,
Singing the true song of the soul fitful at random,
Renascent with grossest Nature or among animals,
Of that, of them and what goes with them my poems
    informing,
Of the smell of apples and lemons, of the pairing of birds,
Of the wet of woods, of the lapping of waves,
Of the mad pushes of waves upon the land, I them
    chanting,
The overture lightly sounding, the strain anticipating,
The welcome nearness, the sight of the perfect body,
The swimmer swimming naked in the bath, or motionless on
    his back lying and floating,
The female form approaching, I pensive, love-flesh tremulous
    aching,
The divine list for myself or you or for any one making,

The face, the limbs, the index from head to foot, and what it
    arouses,
The mystic deliria, the madness amorous, the utter
    abandonment,
(Hark close and still what I now whisper to you,
I love you, O you entirely possess me,
O that you and I escape from the rest and go utterly off, free
    and lawless,
Two hawks in the air, two fishes swimming in the sea not
    more lawless than we;)
The furious storm through me careering, I passionately
    trembling.
The oath of the inseparableness of two together, of the
    woman that loves me and whom I love more than my
    life, that oath swearing,
(O I willingly stake all for you,
O let me be lost if it must be so!
O you and I! what is it to us what the rest do or think?
What is all else to us? only that we enjoy each other and
    exhaust each other if it must be so;)
From the master, the pilot I yield the vessel to,
The general commanding me, commanding all, from him
    permission taking,
From time the programme hastening, (I have loiter'd too
    long as it is,)
From sex, from the warp and from the woof,
From privacy, from frequent repinings alone,
From plenty of persons near and yet the right person not
    near,
From the soft sliding of hands over me and thrusting of
    fingers through my hair and beard,
From the long sustain'd kiss upon the mouth or bosom,
From the close pressure that makes me or any man drunk,
    fainting with excess,
From what the divine husband knows, from the work of
    fatherhood,
From exultation, victory and relief, from the bedfellow's
    embrace in the night,
From the act-poems of eyes, hands, hips and bosoms,

From the cling of the trembling arm,
From the bending curve and the clinch,
From side by side the pliant coverlet off-throwing,
From the one so unwilling to have me leave, and me just as
    unwilling to leave,
(Yet a moment O tender waiter, and I return,)
From the hour of shining stars and dropping dews,
From the night a moment I emerging flitting out,
Celebrate you act divine and you children prepared for,
And you stalwart loins.

I HEARD YOU SOLEMN-SWEET PIPES
OF THE ORGAN

I heard you solemn-sweet pipes of the organ as last Sunday
    morn I pass'd the church,
Winds of autumn, as I walk'd the woods at dusk I heard your
    long-stretch'd sighs up above so mournful,
I heard the perfect Italian tenor singing at the opera, I heard
    the soprano in the midst of the quartet singing;
Heart of my love! you too I heard murmuring low through
    one of the wrists around my head,
Heard the pulse of you when all was still ringing little bells
    last night under my ear.

AS ADAM EARLY IN THE MORNING

As Adam early in the morning,
Walking forth from the bower refresh'd with sleep,
Behold me where I pass, hear my voice, approach,
Touch me, touch the palm of your hand to my body as I pass,
Be not afraid of my body.

from *Calamus*

I SAW IN LOUISIANA A LIVE-OAK GROWING

I saw in Louisiana a live-oak growing,
All alone stood it and the moss hung down from the branches,
Without any companion it grew there uttering joyous leaves
    of dark green,
And its look, rude, unbending, lusty, made me think of
    myself,
But I wonder'd how it could utter joyous leaves standing alone
    there without its friend near, for I knew I could not,
And I broke off a twig with a certain number of leaves upon
    it, and twined around it a little moss,
And brought it away, and I have placed it in sight in my room,
It is not needed to remind me as of my own dear friends,
(For I believe lately I think of little else than of them,)
Yet it remains to me a curious token, it makes me think of
    manly love;
For all that, and though the live-oak glistens there in
    Louisiana solitary in a wide flat space,
Uttering joyous leaves all its life without a friend a lover near,
I know very well I could not.

Crossing Brooklyn Ferry

I

Flood-tide below me! I see you face to face!
Clouds of the west—sun there half an hour high—I see you
    also face to face.

Crowds of men and women attired in the usual costumes,
    how curious you are to me!
On the ferry-boats the hundreds and hundreds that cross,
    returning home, are more curious to me than you
    suppose,

And you that shall cross from shore to shore years hence are
 more to me, and more in my meditations, than you
 might suppose.

2

The impalpable sustenance of me from all things at all hours
 of the day,
The simple, compact, well-join'd scheme, myself disintegrated,
 every one disintegrated yet part of the scheme,
The similitudes of the past and those of the future,
The glories strung like beads on my smallest sights and
 hearings, on the walk in the street and the passage over
 the river,
The current rushing so swiftly and swimming with me far
 away,
The others that are to follow me, the ties between me and
 them,
The certainty of others, the life, love, sight, hearing of others.

Others will enter the gates of the ferry and cross from shore
 to shore,
Others will watch the run of the flood-tide,
Others will see the shipping of Manhattan north and west,
 and the heights of Brooklyn to the south and east,
Others will see the islands large and small;
Fifty years hence, others will see them as they cross, the sun
 half an hour high,
A hundred years hence, or ever so many hundred years
 hence, others will see them,
Will enjoy the sunset, the pouring-in of the flood-tide, the
 falling-back to the sea of the ebb-tide.

3

It avails not, time nor place—distance avails not,
I am with you, you men and women of a generation, or ever
 so many generations hence,
Just as you feel when you look on the river and sky, so I felt,

Just as any of you is one of a living crowd, I was one of a
crowd,
Just as you are refresh'd by the gladness of the river and the
bright flow, I was refresh'd,
Just as you stand and lean on the rail, yet hurry with the swift
current, I stood yet was hurried,
Just as you look on the numberless masts of ships and the
thick-stemm'd pipes of steamboats, I look'd.

I too many and many a time cross'd the river of old,
Watched the Twelfth-month sea-gulls, saw them high in the
air floating with motionless wings, oscillating their
bodies,
Saw how the glistening yellow lit up parts of their bodies and
left the rest in strong shadow,
Saw the slow-wheeling circles and the gradual edging toward
the south,
Saw the reflection of the summer sky in the water,
Had my eyes dazzled by the shimmering track of beams,
Look'd at the fine centrifugal spokes of light round the shape
of my head in the sunlit water,
Look'd on the haze on the hills southward and south-
westward,
Look'd on the vapor as it flew in fleeces tinged with
violet,
Look'd toward the lower bay to notice the vessels arriving,
Saw their approach, saw aboard those that were near me,
Saw the white sails of schooners and sloops, saw the ships at
anchor,
The sailors at work in the rigging or out astride the spars,
The round masts, the swinging motion of the hulls, the
slender serpentine pennants,
The large and small steamers in motion, the pilots in their
pilot-houses,
The white wake left by the passage, the quick tremulous
whirl of the wheels,
The flags of all nations, the falling of them at sunset,
The scallop-edged waves in the twilight, the ladled cups, the
frolicsome crests and glistening,

The stretch afar growing dimmer and dimmer, the gray walls
    of the granite storehouses by the docks,
On the river the shadowy group, the big steam-tug closely
    flank'd on each side by the barges, the hay-boat, the
    belated lighter,
On the neighboring shore the fires from the foundry
    chimneys burning high and glaringly into the night,
Casting their flicker of black contrasted with wild red and
    yellow light over the tops of houses, and down into the
    clefts of streets.

4

These and all else were to me the same as they are to you,
I loved well those cities, loved well the stately and rapid river,
The men and women I saw were all near to me,
Others the same—others who look back on me because I
    look'd forward to them,
(The time will come, though I stop here to-day and to-night.)

5

What is it then between us?
What is the count of the scores or hundreds of years between
    us?

Whatever it is, it avails not—distance avails not, and place
    avails not,
I too lived, Brooklyn of ample hills was mine,
I too walk'd the streets of Manhattan island, and bathed in
    the waters around it,
I too felt the curious abrupt questionings stir within me,
In the day among crowds of people sometimes they came
    upon me,
In my walks home late at night or as I lay in my bed they
    came upon me,
I too had been struck from the float forever held in solution,
I too had receiv'd identity by my body,
That I was I knew was of my body, and what I should be I
    knew I should be of my body.

6

It is not upon you alone the dark patches fall,
The dark threw its patches down upon me also,
The best I had done seem'd to me blank and suspicious,
My great thoughts as I supposed them, were they not in
     reality meagre?
Nor is it you alone who know what it is to be evil,
I am he who knew what it was to be evil,
I too knotted the old knot of contrariety,
Blabb'd, blush'd, resented, lied, stole, grudg'd,
Had guile, anger, lust, hot wishes I dared not speak,
Was wayward, vain, greedy, shallow, sly, cowardly, malignant,
The wolf, the snake, the hog, not wanting in me,
The cheating look, the frivolous word, the adulterous wish,
     not wanting,
Refusals, hates, postponements, meanness, laziness, none of
     these wanting,
Was one with the rest, the days and haps of the rest,
Was call'd by my nighest name by clear loud voices of young
     men as they saw me approaching or passing,
Felt their arms on my neck as I stood, or the negligent
     leaning of their flesh against me as I sat,
Saw many I loved in the street or ferry-boat or public
     assembly, yet never told them a word,
Lived the same life with the rest, the same old laughing,
     gnawing, sleeping,
Play'd the part that still looks back on the actor or
     actress,
The same old role, the role that is what we make it, as great
     as we like,
Or as small as we like, or both great and small.

7

Closer yet I approach you,
What thought you have of me now, I had as much of you—I
     laid in my stores in advance,
I consider'd long and seriously of you before you were
     born.

Who was to know what should come home to me?
Who knows but I am enjoying this?
Who knows, for all the distance, but I am as good as looking
    at you now, for all you cannot see me?

8

Ah, what can ever be more stately and admirable to me than
    mast-hemm'd Manhattan?
River and sunset and scallop-edg'd waves of flood-tide?
The sea-gulls oscillating their bodies, the hay-boat in the
    twilight, and the belated lighter?
What gods can exceed these that clasp me by the hand, and
    with voices I love call me promptly and loudly by my
    nighest name as I approach?
What is more subtle than this which ties me to the woman or
    man that looks in my face?
Which fuses me into you now, and pours my meaning into
    you?

We understand then do we not?
What I promis'd without mentioning it, have you not
    accepted?
What the study could not teach—what the preaching could
    not accomplish is accomplish'd, is it not?

9

Flow on, river! flow with the flood-tide, and ebb with the
    ebb-tide!
Frolic on, crested and scallop-edg'd waves!
Gorgeous clouds of the sunset! drench with your splendor
    me, or the men and women generations after me!
Cross from shore to shore, countless crowds of passengers!
Stand up, tall masts of Mannahatta! stand up, beautiful hills
    of Brooklyn!
Throb, baffled and curious brain! throw out questions and
    answers!
Suspend here and everywhere, eternal float of solution!

Gaze, loving and thirsting eyes, in the house or street or
    public assembly!
Sound out, voices of young men! loudly and musically call
    me by my nighest name!
Live, old life! play the part that looks back on the actor or
    actress!
Play the old role, the role that is great or small according as
    one makes it!
Consider, you who peruse me, whether I may not in
    unknown ways be looking upon you;
Be firm, rail over the river, to support those who lean idly,
    yet haste with the hasting current;
Fly on, sea-birds! fly sideways, or wheel in large circles high
    in the air;
Receive the summer sky, you water, and faithfully hold it till
    all downcast eyes have time to take it from you!
Diverge, fine spokes of light, from the shape of my head, or
    any one's head, in the sunlit water!
Come on, ships from the lower bay! pass up or down, white-
    sail'd schooners, sloops, lighters!
Flaunt away, flags of all nations! be duly lower'd at sunset!
Burn high your fires, foundry chimneys! cast black shadows
    at nightfall! cast red and yellow light over the tops of the
    houses!
Appearances, now or henceforth, indicate what you are,
You necessary film, continue to envelop the soul,
About my body for me, and your body for you, be hung out
    divinest aromas,
Thrive, cities—bring your freight, bring your shows, ample
    and sufficient rivers,
Expand, being than which none else is perhaps more spiritual,
Keep your places, objects than which none else is more lasting.

You have waited, you always wait, you dumb, beautiful
    ministers,
We receive you with free sense at last, and are insatiate
    henceforward,
Not you any more shall be able to foil us, or withhold
    yourselves from us,

We use you, and do not cast you aside —we plant you
    permanently within us,
We fathom you not—we love you—there is perfection in
    you also,
You furnish your parts toward eternity,
Great or small, you furnish your parts toward the soul.

from *Sea-Drift*

OUT OF THE CRADLE ENDLESSLY ROCKING

Out of the cradle endlessly rocking,
Out of the mocking-bird's throat, the musical shuttle,
Out of the Ninth-month midnight,
Over the sterile sands and the fields beyond, where the child
    leaving his bed wander'd alone, bareheaded, barefoot,
Down from the shower'd halo,
Up from the mystic play of shadows twining and twisting as
    if they were alive,
Out from the patches of briers and blackberries,
From the memories of the bird that chanted to me,
From your memories sad brother, from the fitful risings and
    fallings I heard,
From under that yellow half-moon late-risen and swollen as if
    with tears,
From those beginning notes of yearning and love there in the
    mist,
From the thousand responses of my heart never to cease,
From the myriad thence-arous'd words,
From the word stronger and more delicious than any,
From such as now they start the scene revisiting,
As a flock, twittering, rising, or overhead passing,
Borne hither, ere all eludes me, hurriedly,
A man, yet by these tears a little boy again,
Throwing myself on the sand, confronting the waves,
I, chanter of pains and joys, uniter of here and hereafter,

Taking all hints to use them, but swiftly leaping beyond
     them,
A reminiscence sing.

Once Paumanok,
When the lilac-scent was in the air and Fifth-month grass was
     growing,
Up this seashore in some briers,
Two feather'd guests from Alabama, two together,
And their nest, and four light-green eggs spotted with brown,
And every day the he-bird to and fro near at hand,
And every day the she-bird crouch'd on her nest, silent, with
     bright eyes,
And every day I, a curious boy, never too close, never
     disturbing them,
Cautiously peering, absorbing, translating.

Shine! shine! shine!
Pour down your warmth, great sun!
While we bask, we two together.

Two together!
Winds blow south, or winds blow north,
Day come white, or night come black,
Home, or rivers and mountains from home,
Singing all time, minding no time,
While we two keep together.

Till of a sudden,
May-be kill'd, unknown to her mate,
One forenoon the she-bird crouch'd not on the nest,
Nor return'd that afternoon, nor the next,
Nor ever appear'd again.

And thenceforward all summer in the sound of the sea,
And at night under the full of the moon in calmer weather,
Over the hoarse surging of the sea,
Or flitting from brier to brier by day,
I saw, I heard at intervals the remaining one, the he-bird,
The solitary guest from Alabama.

Blow! blow! blow!
Blow up sea-winds along Paumanok's shore;
I wait and I wait till you blow my mate to me.

Yes, when the stars glisten'd,
All night long on the prong of a moss-scallop'd stake,
Down almost amid the slapping waves,
Sat the lone singer wonderful causing tears.

He call'd on his mate,
He pour'd forth the meanings which I of all men know.

Yes my brother I know,
The rest might not, but I have treasur'd every note,
For more than once dimly down to the beach gliding,
Silent, avoiding the moonbeams, blending myself with the
        shadows,
Recalling now the obscure shapes, the echoes, the sounds
        and sights after their sorts,
The white arms out in the breakers tirelessly tossing,
I, with bare feet, a child, the wind wafting my hair,
Listen'd long and long.

Listen'd to keep, to sing, now translating the notes,
Following you my brother.

Soothe! soothe! soothe!
Close on its wave soothes the wave behind,
And again another behind embracing and lapping, every one close,
But my love soothes not me, not me.

Low hangs the moon, it rose late,
It is lagging—O I think it is heavy with love, with love.

O madly the sea pushes upon the land,
With love, with love.

O night! do I not see my love fluttering out among the
        breakers?
What is that little black thing I see there in the white?

Loud! loud! loud!
Loud I call to you, my love!

High and clear I shoot my voice over the waves,
Surely you must know who is here, is here,
You must know who I am, my love.

Low-hanging moon!
What is that dusky spot in your brown yellow?
O it is the shape, the shape of my mate!
O moon do not keep her from me any longer.

Land! land! O land!
Whichever way I turn, O I think you could give me my mate
　　　back again if you only would,
For I am almost sure I see her dimly whichever way I look.

O rising stars!
Perhaps the one I want so much will rise, will rise with some of
　　　you.

O throat! O trembling throat!
Sound clearer through the atmosphere!
Pierce the woods, the earth,
Somewhere listening to catch you must be the one I want.

Shake out carols!
Solitary here, the night's carols!
Carols of lonesome love! death's carols!
Carols under that lagging, yellow, waning moon!
O under that moon where she droops almost down into the
　　　sea!
O reckless despairing carols.

But soft! sink low!
Soft! let me just murmur,
And do you wait a moment you husky-nois'd sea,
For somewhere I believe I heard my mate responding to me,

So faint, I must be still, be still to listen,
But not altogether still, for then she might not come immediately
to me.

Hither my love!
Here I am! here!
With this just-sustain'd note I announce myself to you,
This gentle call is for you my love, for you.

Do not be decoy'd elsewhere,
That is the whistle of the wind, it is not my voice,
That is the fluttering, the fluttering of the spray,
Those are the shadows of leaves.

O darkness! O in vain!
O I am very sick and sorrowful.

O brown halo in the sky near the moon, drooping upon the sea!
O troubled reflection in the sea!
O throat! O throbbing heart!
And I singing uselessly, uselessly all the night.

O past! O happy life! O songs of joy!
In the air, in the woods, over fields,
Loved! loved! loved! loved! loved!
But my mate no more, no more with me!
We two together no more.

The aria sinking,
All else continuing, the stars shining,
The winds blowing, the notes of the bird continuous echoing,
With angry moans the fierce old mother incessantly moaning,
On the sands of Paumanok's shore gray and rustling,
The yellow half-moon enlarged, sagging down, drooping, the
    face of the sea almost touching,
The boy ecstatic, with his bare feet the waves, with his hair
    the atmosphere dallying,
The love in the heart long pent, now loose, now at last
    tumultuously bursting,

The aria's meaning, the ears, the soul, swiftly depositing,
The strange tears down the cheeks coursing,
The colloquy there, the trio, each uttering,
The undertone, the savage old mother incessantly crying,
To the boy's soul's questions sullenly timing, some drown'd
    secret hissing,
To the outsetting bard.

Demon or bird! (said the boy's soul,)
Is it indeed toward your mate you sing? or is it really to
    me?
For I, that was a child, my tongue's use sleeping, now I have
    heard you,
Now in a moment I know what I am for, I awake,
And already a thousand singers, a thousand songs, clearer,
    louder and more sorrowful than yours,
A thousand warbling echoes have started to life within me,
    never to die.

O you singer solitary, singing by yourself, projecting me,
O solitary me listening, never more shall I cease perpetuating
    you,
Never more shall I escape, never more the reverberations,
Never more the cries of unsatisfied love be absent from me,
Never again leave me to be the peaceful child I was before
    what there in the night,
By the sea under the yellow and sagging moon,
The messenger there arous'd, the fire, the sweet hell within,
The unknown want, the destiny of me.

O give me the clew! (it lurks in the night here somewhere,)
O if I am to have so much, let me have more!

A word then, (for I will conquer it,)
The word final, superior to all,
Subtle, sent up—what is it?—I listen;
Are you whispering it, and have been all the time, you sea-
    waves?
Is that it from your liquid rims and wet sands?

Whereto answering, the sea,
Delaying not, hurrying not,
Whisper'd me through the night, and very plainly before
    daybreak,
Lisp'd to me the low and delicious word death,
And again death, death, death, death,
Hissing melodious, neither like the bird nor like my arous'd
    child's heart,
But edging near as privately for me rustling at my feet,
Creeping thence steadily up to my ears and laving me softly
    all over,
Death, death, death, death, death.

Which I do not forget,
But fuse the song of my dusky demon and brother,
That he sang to me in the moonlight on Paumanok's gray
    beach,
With the thousand responsive songs at random,
My own songs awaked from that hour,
And with them the key, the word up from the waves,
The word of the sweetest song and all songs,
That strong and delicious word which, creeping to my feet,
(Or like some old crone rocking the cradle, swathed in sweet
    garments, bending aside,)
The sea whisper'd me.

AS I EBB'D WITH THE OCEAN OF LIFE

I

As I ebb'd with the ocean of life,
As I wended the shores I know,
As I walk'd where the ripples continually wash you
    Paumanok,
Where they rustle up hoarse and sibilant,
Where the fierce old mother endlessly cries for her
    castaways,
I musing late in the autumn day, gazing off southward,

Held by this electric self out of the pride of which I utter
poems,
Was seiz'd by the spirit that trails in the lines underfoot,
The rim, the sediment that stands for all the water and all the
land of the globe.

Fascinated, my eyes reverting from the south, dropt, to
follow those slender windrows,
Chaff, straw, splinters of wood, weeds, and the sea-gluten,
Scum, scales from shining rocks, leaves of salt-lettuce, left by
the tide,
Miles walking, the sound of breaking waves the other side
of me,
Paumanok there and then as I thought the old thought of
likenesses,
These you presented to me you fish-shaped island,
As I wended the shores I know,
As I walk'd with that electric self seeking types.

2

As I wend to the shores I know not,
As I list to the dirge, the voices of men and women
wreck'd,
As I inhale the impalpable breezes that set in upon me,
As the ocean so mysterious rolls toward me closer and
closer,
I too but signify at the utmost a little wash'd-up drift,
A few sands and dead leaves to gather,
Gather, and merge myself as part of the sands and drift.

O baffled, balk'd, bent to the very earth,
Oppress'd with myself that I have dared to open my mouth,
Aware now that amid all that blab whose echoes recoil
upon me I have not once had the least idea who or
what I am,
But that before all my arrogant poems the real Me stands yet
untouch'd, untold, altogether unreach'd,
Withdrawn far, mocking me with mock-congratulatory signs
and bows,

With peals of distant ironical laughter at every word I have
        written,
Pointing in silence to these songs, and then to the sand
        beneath.

I perceive I have not really understood any thing, not a single
        object, and that no man ever can,
Nature here in sight of the sea taking advantage of me to dart
        upon me and sting me,
Because I have dared to open my mouth to sing at all.

3

You oceans both, I close with you,
We murmur alike reproachfully rolling sands and drift,
        knowing not why,
These little shreds indeed standing for you and me and all.

You friable shore with trails of debris,
You fish-shaped island, I take what is underfoot,
What is yours is mine my father.

I too Paumanok,
I too have bubbled up, floated the measureless float, and
        been wash'd on your shores,
I too am but a trail of drift and debris,
I too leave little wrecks upon you, you fish-shaped island.

I throw myself upon your breast my father,
I cling to you so that you cannot unloose me,
I hold you so firm till you answer me something.

Kiss me my father,
Touch me with your lips as I touch those I love,
Breathe to me while I hold you close the secret of the
        murmuring I envy.

4

Ebb, ocean of life, (the flow will return,)
Cease not your moaning you fierce old mother,

Endlessly cry for your castaways, but fear not, deny not me,
Rustle not up so hoarse and angry against my feet as I touch
you or gather from you.

I mean tenderly by you and all,
I gather for myself and for this phantom looking down
where we lead, and following me and mine.

Me and mine, loose windrows, little corpses,
Froth, snowy white, and bubbles,
(See, from my dead lips the ooze exuding at last,
See, the prismatic colors glistening and rolling,)
Tufts of straw, sands, fragments,
Buoy'd hither from many moods, one contradicting another,
From the storm, the long calm, the darkness, the swell,
Musing, pondering, a breath, a briny tear, a dab of liquid or
soil,
Up just as much out of fathomless workings fermented and
thrown,
A limp blossom or two, torn, just as much over waves
floating, drifted at random,
Just as much for us that sobbing dirge of Nature,
Just as much whence we come that blare of the cloudtrumpets,
We, capricious, brought hither we know not whence, spread
out before you,
You up there walking or sitting,
Whoever you are, we too lie in drifts at your feet.

from *Memories of President Lincoln*

WHEN LILACS LAST IN
THE DOORYARD BLOOM'D

I

When lilacs last in the dooryard bloom'd,
And the great star early droop'd in the western sky in the
night,
I mourn'd, and yet shall mourn with ever-returning spring.

Ever-returning spring, trinity sure to me you bring,
Lilac blooming perennial and drooping star in the west,
And thought of him I love.

2 *Star*

O powerful western fallen star!
O shades of night—O moody, tearful night!
O great star disappear'd—O the black murk that hides the
    star!
O cruel hands that hold me powerless—O helpless soul of
    me!
O harsh surrounding cloud that will not free my soul.

3 *Dooryard*

In the dooryard fronting an old farm-house near the white-
    wash'd palings,
Stands the lilac-bush tall-growing with heart-shaped leaves of
    rich green,
With many a pointed blossom rising delicate, with the
    perfume strong I love,
With every leaf a miracle—and from this bush in the
    dooryard,
With delicate-color'd blossoms and heart-shaped leaves of
    rich green,
A sprig with its flower I break.

4 *Bird*

In the swamp in secluded recesses,
A shy and hidden bird is warbling a song.

Solitary the thrush,
The hermit withdrawn to himself, avoiding the settlements,
Sings by himself a song.

Song of the bleeding throat,
Death's outlet song of life, (for well dear brother I know,
If thou wast not granted to sing thou would'st surely die.)

5 *coffin*

Over the breast of the spring, the land, amid cities,
Amid lanes and through old woods, where lately the violets
    peep'd from the ground, spotting the gray debris,
Amid the grass in the fields each side of the lanes, passing the
    endless grass,
Passing the yellow-spear'd wheat, every grain from its shroud
    in the dark-brown fields uprisen,
Passing the apple-tree blows of white and pink in the
    orchards,
Carrying a corpse to where it shall rest in the grave,
Night and day journeys a coffin.

6 *roads of states*

Coffin that passes through lanes and streets,
Through day and night with the great cloud darkening the
    land,
With the pomp of the inloop'd flags with the cities draped in
    black,
With the show of the States themselves as of crape-veil'd
    women standing,
With processions long and winding and the flambeaus of the
    night,
With the countless torches lit, with the silent sea of faces and
    the unbared heads,
With the waiting depot, the arriving coffin, and the sombre
    faces,
With dirges through the night, with the thousand voices
    rising strong and solemn,
With all the mournful voices of the dirges pour'd around the
    coffin,
The dim-lit churches and the shuddering organs—where
    amid these you journey,
With the tolling tolling bells' perpetual clang,
Here, coffin that slowly passes,
I give you my sprig of lilac.

7 *all deaths*

(Nor for you, for one alone,
Blossoms and branches green to coffins all I bring,
For fresh as the morning, thus would I chant a song for you
 O sane and sacred death.

All over bouquets of roses,
O death, I cover you over with roses and early lilies,
But mostly and now the lilac that blooms the first,
Copious I break, I break the sprigs from the bushes,
With loaded arms I come, pouring for you,
For you and the coffins all of you O death.)

8 *Star*

O western orb sailing the heaven,
Now I know what you must have meant as a month since I
 walk'd,
As I walk'd in silence the transparent shadowy night,
As I saw you had something to tell as you bent to me night
 after night,
As you droop'd from the sky low down as if to my side,
 (while the other stars all look'd on,)
As we wander'd together the solemn night, (for something I
 know not what kept me from sleep,)
As the night advanced, and I saw on the rim of the west how
 full you were of woe,
As I stood on the rising ground in the breeze in the cool
 transparent night,
As I watch'd where you pass'd and was lost in the
 netherward black of the night,
As my soul in its trouble dissatisfied sank, as where you
 sad orb,
Concluded, dropt in the night, and was gone.

9 *bird*

Sing on there in the swamp,
O singer bashful and tender, I hear your notes, I hear your
 call,

I hear, I come presently, I understand you,
But a moment I linger, for the lustrous star has detain'd me,
The star my departing comrade holds and detains me.

10

O how shall I warble myself for the dead one there I loved?
And how shall I deck my song for the large sweet soul that
    has gone?
And what shall my perfume be for the grave of him I love?

Sea-winds blown from east and west,
Blown from the Eastern sea and blown from the Western sea,
    till there on the prairies meeting,
These and with these and the breath of my chant,
I'll perfume the grave of him I love.

11

O what shall I hang on the chamber walls?
And what shall the pictures be that I hang on the walls,
To adorn the burial-house of him I love?

Pictures of growing spring and farms and homes,
With the Fourth-month eve at sundown, and the gray smoke
    lucid and bright,
With floods of the yellow gold of the gorgeous, indolent,
    sinking sun, burning, expanding the air,
With the fresh sweet herbage under foot, and the pale green
    leaves of the trees prolific,
In the distance the flowing glaze, the breast of the river, with
    a wind-dapple here and there,
With ranging hills on the banks, with many a line against the
    sky, and shadows,
And the city at hand with dwellings so dense, and stacks of
    chimneys,
And all the scenes of life and the workshops, and the
    workmen homeward returning.

12

Lo, body and soul—this land,
My own Manhattan with spires, and the sparkling and
    hurrying tides, and the ships,
The varied and ample land, the South and the North in the
    light, Ohio's shores and flashing Missouri,
And ever the far-spreading prairies cover'd with grass and corn.

Lo, the most excellent sun so calm and haughty,
The violet and purple morn with just-felt breezes,
The gentle soft-born measureless light,
The miracle spreading bathing all, the fulfill'd noon,
The coming eve delicious, the welcome night and the stars,
Over my cities shining all, enveloping man and land.

13

Sing on, sing on you gray-brown bird,
Sing from the swamps, the recesses, pour your chant from
    the bushes,
Limitless out of the dusk, out of the cedars and pines.

Sing on dearest brother, warble your reedy song,
Loud human song, with voice of uttermost woe.

O liquid and free and tender!
O wild and loose to my soul—O wondrous singer!
You only I hear—yet the star holds me, (but will soon depart,)
Yet the lilac with mastering odor holds me.

14

Now while I sat in the day and look'd forth,
In the close of the day with its light and the fields of spring,
    and the farmers preparing their crops,
In the large unconscious scenery of my land with its lakes and
    forests,
In the heavenly aerial beauty, (after the perturb'd winds and
    the storms,)

Under the arching heavens of the afternoon swift passing,
    and the voices of children and women,
The many-moving sea-tides, and I saw the ships how they
    sail'd,
And the summer approaching with richness, and the fields all
    busy with labor,
And the infinite separate houses, how they all went on, each
    with its meals and minutia of daily usages,
And the streets how their throbbings throbb'd, and the cities
    pent—lo, then and there,
Falling upon them all and among them all, enveloping me
    with the rest,
Appear'd the cloud, appear'd the long black trail,
And I knew death, its thought, and the sacred knowledge of
    death.

Then with the knowledge of death as walking one side of me,
And the thought of death close-walking the other side of me,
And I in the middle as with companions, and as holding the
    hands of companions,
I fled forth to the hiding receiving night that talks not,
Down to the shores of the water, the path by the swamp in
    the dimness,
To the solemn shadowy cedars and ghostly pines so still.

And the singer so shy to the rest receiv'd me,
The gray-brown bird I know receiv'd us comrades three,
And he sang the carol of death, and a verse for him I love.

From deep secluded recesses,
From the fragrant cedars and the ghostly pines so still,
Came the carol of the bird.

And the charm of the carol rapt me,
As I held as if by their hands my comrades in the night,
And the voice of my spirit tallied the song of the bird.

Come lovely and soothing death,
Undulate round the world, serenely arriving, arriving,
In the day, in the night, to all, to each,
Sooner or later delicate death.

Prais'd be the fathomless universe,
For life and joy, and for objects and knowledge curious,
And for love, sweet love — but praise! praise! praise!
For the sure-enwinding arms of cool-enfolding death.

Dark mother always gliding near with soft feet,
Have none chanted for thee a chant of fullest welcome?
Then I chant it for thee, I glorify thee above all,
I bring thee a song that when thou must indeed come, come
        unfalteringly.

Approach strong deliveress,
When it is so, when thou hast taken them I joyously sing the dead,
Lost in the loving floating ocean of thee,
Laved in the flood of thy bliss O death.

From me to thee glad serenades,
Dances for thee I propose saluting thee, adornments and
        feastings for thee,
And the sights of the open landscape and the high-spread sky are
        fitting,
And life and the fields, and the huge and thoughtful night.

The night in silence under many a star,
The ocean shore and the husky whispering wave whose voice I know,
And the soul turning to thee O vast and well-veil'd death,
And the body gratefully nestling close to thee.

Over the tree-tops I float thee a song,
Over the rising and sinking waves, over the myriad fields and
        the prairies wide,
Over the dense-pack'd cities all and the teeming wharves and
        ways,
I float this carol with joy, with joy to thee O death.

15

To the tally of my soul,
Loud and strong kept up the gray-brown bird,
With pure deliberate notes spreading filling the night.

Loud in the pines and cedars dim,
Clear in the freshness moist and the swamp-perfume,
And I with my comrades there in the night.

While my sight that was bound in my eyes unclosed,
As to long panoramas of visions.

And I saw askant the armies,
I saw as in noiseless dreams hundreds of battle-flags,
Borne through the smoke of the battles and pierc'd with
    missiles I saw them,
And carried hither and yon through the smoke, and torn and
    bloody,
And at last but a few shreds left on the staffs, (and all in
    silence,)
And the staffs all splinter'd and broken.

I saw battle-corpses, myriads of them,
And the white skeletons of young men, I saw them,
I saw the debris and debris of all the slain soldiers of the war,
But I saw they were not as was thought,
They themselves were fully at rest, they suffer'd not,
The living remain'd and suffer'd, the mother suffer'd,
And the wife and the child and the musing comrade suffer'd,
And the armies that remain'd suffer'd.

16

Passing the visions, passing the night,
Passing, unloosing the hold of my comrades' hands,
Passing the song of the hermit bird and the tallying song of
    my soul,
Victorious song, death's outlet song, yet varying ever-
    altering song,

As low and wailing, yet clear the notes, rising and falling,
    flooding the night,
Sadly sinking and fainting, as warning and warning, and yet
    again bursting with joy,
Covering the earth and filling the spread of the heaven,
As that powerful psalm in the night I heard from recesses,
Passing, I leave thee lilac with heart-shaped leaves,
I leave thee there in the door-yard, blooming, returning with
    spring.

I cease from my song for thee,
From my gaze on thee in the west, fronting the west,
    communing with thee,
O comrade lustrous with silver face in the night.

Yet each to keep and all, retrievements out of the night,
The song, the wondrous chant of the gray-brown bird,
And the tallying chant, the echo arous'd in my soul,
With the lustrous and drooping star with the countenance
    full of woe,
With the holders holding my hand nearing the call of the bird,
Comrades mine and I in the midst, and their memory ever to
    keep, for the dead I loved so well,
For the sweetest, wisest soul of all my days and lands—and
    this for his dear sake,
Lilac and star and bird twined with the chant of my soul,
There in the fragrant pines and the cedars dusk and dim.

from *Whispers of Heavenly Death*

A NOISELESS PATIENT SPIDER

A noiseless patient spider,
I mark'd where on a little promontory it stood isolated,
Mark'd how to explore the vacant vast surrounding,
It launch'd forth filament, filament, filament, out of itself,
Ever unreeling them, ever tirelessly speeding them.

And you O my soul where you stand,
Surrounded, detached, in measureless oceans of space,
Ceaselessly musing, venturing, throwing, seeking the spheres
    to connect them,
Till the bridge you will need be form'd, till the ductile
    anchor hold,
Till the gossamer thread you fling catch somewhere, O my
    soul.

HERMAN MELVILLE

(1819–1891)

Song from *Mardi*

Like the fish of the bright and twittering fin,
    Bright fish! diving deep as high soars the lark,
So, far, far, far, doth the maiden swim,
    Wild song, wild light, in still ocean's dark.

"The ribs and terrors in the whale"

The ribs and terrors in the whale,
    Arched over me a dismal gloom,
While all God's sun-lit waves rolled by,
    And left me deepening down to doom.

I saw the opening maw of hell,
    With endless pains and sorrows there;
Which none but they that feel can tell—
    Oh, I was plunging to despair.

In black distress, I called my God,
    When I could scarce believe him mine,
He bowed his ear to my complaints—
    No more the whale did me confine.

With speed he flew to my relief,
    As on a radiant dolphin borne;
Awful, yet bright, as lightning shone
    The face of my Deliverer God.

My song for ever shall record
    That terrible, that joyful hour;
I give the glory to my God,
    His all the mercy and the power.

The Portent

(1859)

Hanging from the beam,
  Slowly swaying (such the law),
Gaunt the shadow on your green,
  Shenandoah!
The cut is on the crown
(Lo, John Brown),
And the stabs shall heal no more.

Hidden in the cap
  Is the anguish none can draw;
So your future veils its face,
  Shenandoah!
But the streaming beard is shown
(Weird John Brown),
The meteor of the war.

Misgivings

(1860)

When ocean-clouds over inland hills
  Sweep storming in late autumn brown,
And horror the sodden valley fills,
  And the spire falls crashing in the town,
I muse upon my country's ills—
The tempest bursting from the waste of Time
On the world's fairest hope linked with man's foulest crime.

Nature's dark side is heeded now—
  (Ah! optimist-cheer disheartened flown)—
A child may read the moody brow
  Of yon black mountain lone.
With shouts the torrents down the gorges go,
  And storms are formed behind the storm we feel:
The hemlock shakes in the rafter, the oak in the driving keel.

The Conflict of Convictions

(1860–1)

On starry heights
 A bugle wails the long recall;
Derision stirs the deep abyss,
 Heaven's ominous silence over all.
Return, return, O eager Hope,
 And face man's latter fall.
Events, they make the dreamers quail;
Satan's old age is strong and hale,
A disciplined captain, gray in skill,
And Raphael a white enthusiast still;
Dashed aims, whereat Christ's martyrs pale,
Shall Mammon's slaves fulfill?

> *(Dismantle the fort,*
> *Cut down the fleet —*
> *Battle no more shall be!*
> *While the fields for fight in æons to come*
> *Congeal beneath the sea.)*

The terrors of truth and dart of death
 To faith alike are vain;
Though comets, gone a thousand years,
  Return again,
Patient she stands — she can no more —
And waits, nor heeds she waxes hoar.

> *(At a stony gate,*
> *A statue of stone,*
> *Weed overgrown —*
> *Long 'twill wait!)*

But God his former mind retains,
 Confirms his old decree;
The generations are inured to pains,

And strong Necessity
Surges, and heaps Time's strand with wrecks.
   The People spread like a weedy grass,
   The thing they will they bring to pass,
And prosper to the apoplex.
The rout it herds around the heart,
   The ghost is yielded in the gloom;
Kings wag their heads—Now save thyself
   Who wouldst rebuild the world in bloom.

> (*Tide-mark*
> *And top of the ages' strife,*
> *Verge where they called the world to come,*
> *The last advance of life*—
> *Ha ha, the rust on the Iron Dome!*)

Nay, but revere the hid event;
   In the cloud a sword is girded on,
I mark a twinkling in the tent
   Of Michael the warrior one.
Senior wisdom suits not now,
The light is on the youthful brow.

> (*Ay, in caves the miner see:*
> *His forehead bears a taper dim;*
> *Darkness so he feebly braves*
> *Which foldeth him!*)

But He who rules is old—is old:
Ah! faith is warm, but heaven with age is cold.

> (*Ho ho, ho ho,*
> *The cloistered doubt*
> *Of olden times*
> *Is blurted out!*)

The Ancient of Days forever is young,
  Forever the scheme of Nature thrives;
I know a wind in purpose strong—
   It spins *against* the way it drives.
What if the gulfs their slimed foundations bare?
So deep must the stones be hurled
Whereon the throes of ages rear
The final empire and the happier world.

> (*The poor old Past,*
> *The Future's slave,*
> *She drudged through pain and crime*
> *To bring about the blissful Prime,*
> *Then—perished.* There's *a grave!*)

  Power unanointed may come—
Dominion (unsought by the free)
  And the Iron Dome,
Stronger for stress and strain,
Fling her huge shadow athwart the main;
But the Founders' dream shall flee.
Age after age shall be
As age after age has been,
(From man's changeless heart their way they win);
And death be busy with all who strive—
Death, with silent negative.

> YEA AND NAY—
> EACH HATH HIS SAY;
> BUT GOD HE KEEPS THE MIDDLE WAY.
> NONE WAS BY
> WHEN HE SPREAD THE SKY;
> WISDOM IS VAIN, AND PROPHESY.

Shiloh

A Requiem

(APRIL, 1862)

Skimming lightly, wheeling still,
  The swallows fly low
Over the field in clouded days,
  The forest-field of Shiloh—
Over the field where April rain
Solaced the parched ones stretched in pain
Through the pause of night
That followed the Sunday fight
  Around the church of Shiloh—
The church so lone, the log-built one,
That echoed to many a parting groan
    And natural prayer
Of dying foemen mingled there—
Foemen at morn, but friends at eve—
  Fame or country least their care:
(What like a bullet can undeceive!)
  But now they lie low,
While over them the swallows skim,
  And all is hushed at Shiloh.

Malvern Hill

(JULY, 1862)

Ye elms that wave on Malvern Hill
  In prime of morn and May,
Recall ye how McClellan's men
    Here stood at bay?
While deep within yon forest dim
  Our rigid comrades lay—
Some with the cartridge in their mouth,
Others with fixed arms lifted South—
    Invoking so
The cypress glades? Ah wilds of woe!

The spires of Richmond, late beheld
   Through rifts in musket-haze,
Were closed from view in clouds of dust
      On leaf-walled ways,
Where streamed our wagons in caravan;
   And the Seven Nights and Days
Of march and fast, retreat and fight,
Pinched our grimed faces to ghastly plight—
      Does the elm wood
Recall the haggard beards of blood?

The battle-smoked flag, with stars eclipsed,
   We followed (it never fell!)—
In silence husbanded our strength—
      Received their yell;
Till on this slope we patient turned
   With cannon ordered well;
Reverse we proved was not defeat;
But ah, the sod what thousands meet!—
      Does Malvern Wood
Bethink itself, and muse and brood?

> *We elms of Malvern Hill*
>   *Remember every thing;*
> *But sap the twig will fill:*
> *Wag the world how it will,*
>   *Leaves must be green in Spring.*

The House-top

A Night Piece

(JULY, 1863)

No sleep. The sultriness pervades the air
And binds the brain—a dense oppression, such
As tawny tigers feel in matted shades,
Vexing their blood and making apt for ravage.
Beneath the stars the roofy desert spreads
Vacant as Libya. All is hushed near by.
Yet fitfully from far breaks a mixed surf

Of muffled sound, the Atheist roar of riot.
Yonder, where parching Sirius set in drought,
Balefully glares red Arson—there—and there.
The Town is taken by its rats—ship-rats
And rats of the wharves. All civil charms
And priestly spells which late held hearts in awe—
Fear-bound, subjected to a better sway
Than sway of self; these like a dream dissolve,
And man rebounds whole æons back in nature.
Hail to the low dull rumble, dull and dead,
And ponderous drag that shakes the wall.
Wise Draco comes, deep in the midnight roll
Of black artillery; he comes, though late;
In code corroborating Calvin's creed
And cynic tyrannies of honest kings;
He comes, nor parlies; and the Town, redeemed,
Gives thanks devout; nor, being thankful, heeds
The grimy slur on the Republic's faith implied,
Which holds that Man is naturally good,
And—more—is Nature's Roman, never to be scourged.

"The Coming Storm"

A Picture by S. R. Gifford, and owned by E. B.
Included in the N. A. Exhibition, April, 1865

All feeling hearts must feel for him
    Who felt this picture. Presage dim—
Dim inklings from the shadowy sphere
    Fixed him and fascinated here.

A demon-cloud like the mountain one
    Burst on a spirit as mild
As this urned lake, the home of shades.
    But Shakspeare's pensive child

Never the lines had lightly scanned,
    Steeped in fable, steeped in fate;
The Hamlet in his heart was 'ware,
    Such hearts can antedate.

No utter surprise can come to him
  Who reaches Shakspeare's core;
That which we seek and shun is there—
  Man's final lore.

"Formerly a Slave"

An idealized Portrait, by E. Vedder,
in the Spring Exhibition of the National Academy, 1865

The sufferance of her race is shown,
  And restrospect of life,
Which now too late deliverance dawns upon;
  Yet is she not at strife.

Her children's children they shall know
  The good withheld from her;
And so her reverie takes prophetic cheer—
  In spirit she sees the stir

Far down the depth of thousand years,
  And marks the revel shine;
Her dusky face is lit with sober light,
  Sibylline, yet benign.

America

I

Where the wings of a sunny Dome expand
I saw a Banner in gladsome air—
Starry, like Berenice's Hair—
Afloat in broadened bravery there;
With undulating long-drawn flow,
As rolled Brazilian billows go
Voluminously o'er the Line.
The Land reposed in peace below;
  The children in their glee
Were folded to the exulting heart
  Of young Maternity.

II

Later, and it streamed in fight
  When tempest mingled with the fray,
And over the spear-point of the shaft
  I saw the ambiguous lightning play.
Valor with Valor strove, and died:
Fierce was Despair, and cruel was Pride;
And the lorn Mother speechless stood,
Pale at the fury of her brood.

III

Yet later, and the silk did wind
    Her fair cold form;
Little availed the shining shroud,
  Though ruddy in hue, to cheer or warm.
A watcher looked upon her low, and said —
She sleeps, but sleeps, she is not dead.
  But in that sleep contortion showed
The terror of the vision there —
  A silent vision unavowed,
Revealing earth's foundation bare,
  And Gorgon in her hidden place.
It was a thing of fear to see
  So foul a dream upon so fair a face,
And the dreamer lying in that starry shroud.

IV

But from the trance she sudden broke —
  The trance, or death into promoted life;
At her feet a shivered yoke,
  And in her aspect turned to heaven
  No trace of passion or of strife —
A clear calm look. It spake of pain,
But such as purifies from stain —
Sharp pangs that never come again —
  And triumph repressed by knowledge meet,
Power dedicate, and hope grown wise,
  And youth matured for age's seat —

Law on her brow and empire in her eyes.
So she, with graver air and lifted flag;
While the shadow, chased by light,
Fled along the far-drawn height,
And left her on the crag.

from *Clarel: A Poem and Pilgrimage in the Holy Land*

The Hostel

In chamber low and scored by time,
Masonry old, late washed with lime—
Much like a tomb new-cut in stone;
Elbow on knee, and brow sustained
All motionless on sidelong hand,
A student sits, and broods alone.
The small deep casement sheds a ray
Which tells that in the Holy Town
It is the passing of the day—
The Vigil of Epiphany.
Beside him in the narrow cell
His luggage lies unpacked; thereon
The dust lies, and on him as well—
The dust of travel. But anon
His face he lifts—in feature fine,
Yet pale, and all but feminine
But for the eye and serious brow—
Then rises, paces to and fro,
And pauses, saying, "Other cheer
Than that anticipated here,
By me the learner, now I find.
Theology, art thou so blind?
What means this naturalistic knell
In lieu of Siloh's oracle
Which here should murmur? Snatched from grace,
And waylaid in the holy place!
Not thus it was but yesterday
Off Jaffa on the clear blue sea;

Nor thus, my heart, it was with thee
Landing amid the shouts and spray;
Nor thus when mounted, full equipped,
Out through the vaulted gate we slipped
Beyond the walls where gardens bright
With bloom and blossom cheered the sight.
　"The plain we crossed. In afternoon,
How like our early autumn bland—
So softly tempered for a boon—
The breath of Sharon's prairie land!
And was it, yes, her titled Rose,
That scarlet poppy oft at hand?
Then Ramleh gleamed, the sail-white town
At even. There I watched day close
From the fair tower, the suburb one:
Seaward and dazing set the sun:
Inland I turned me toward the wall
Of Ephraim, stretched in purple pall.
Romance of mountains! But in end
What change the near approach could lend.
　"The start this morning—gun and lance
Against the quarter-moon's low tide;
The thieves' huts where we hushed the ride;
Chill day-break in the lorn advance;
In stony strait the scorch of noon,
Thrown off by crags, reminding one
Of those hot paynims whose fierce hands
Flung showers of Afric's fiery sands
In face of that crusader-king,
Louis, to wither so his wing;
And, at the last, aloft for goal,
Like the ice-bastions round the Pole,
Thy blank, blank towers, Jerusalem!"

　　Again he droops, with brow on hand.
But, starting up, "Why, well I knew
Salem to be no Samarcand;
'Twas scarce surprise; and yet first view
Brings this eclipse. Needs be my soul,
Purged by the desert's subtle air

From bookish vapors, now is heir
To nature's influx of control;
Comes likewise now to consciousness
Of the true import of that press
Of inklings which in travel late
Through Latin lands, did vex my state,
And somehow seemed clandestine. Ah!
These under-formings in the mind,
Banked corals which ascend from far,
But little heed men that they wind
Unseen, unheard—till lo, the reef—
The reef and breaker, wreck and grief.
But here unlearning, how to me
Opes the expanse of time's vast sea!
Yes, I am young, but Asia old.
The books, the books not all have told.

   "And, for the rest, the facile chat
Of overweenings—what was that
The grave one said in Jaffa lane
Whom there I met, my countryman,
But new-returned from travel here;
Some word of mine provoked the strain;
His meaning now begins to clear:
Let me go over it again:—
   "Our New World's worldly wit so shrewd
Lacks the Semitic reverent mood,
Unworldly—hardly may confer
Fitness for just interpreter
Of Palestine. Forego the state
Of local minds inveterate,
Tied to one poor and casual form.
To avoid the deep saves not from storm.

   "Those things he said, and added more;
No clear authenticated lore
I deemed. But now, need now confess
My cultivated narrowness,
Though scarce indeed of sort he meant?
'Tis the uprooting of content!"

   So he, the student. 'Twas a mind,
Earnest by nature, long confined

Apart like Vesta in a grove
Collegiate, but let to rove
At last abroad among mankind,
And here in end confronted so
By the true genius, friend or foe,
And actual visage of a place
Before but dreamed of in the glow
Of fancy's spiritual grace.
  Further his meditations aim,
Reverting to his different frame
Bygone. And then: "Can faith remove
Her light, because of late no plea
I've lifted to her source above?"
Dropping thereat upon the knee,
His lips he parted; but the word
Against the utterance demurred
And failed him. With infirm intent
He sought the house-top. Set of sun:
His feet upon the yet warm stone,
He, Clarel, by the coping leant,
In silent gaze. The mountain town,
A walled and battlemented one,
With houseless suburbs front and rear,
And flanks built up from steeps severe,
Saddles and turrets the ascent—
Tower which rides the elephant.
Hence large the view. There where he stood,
Was Acra's upper neighborhood.
The circling hills he saw, with one
Excelling, ample in its crown,
Making the uplifted city low
By contrast—Olivet. The flow
Of eventide was at full brim;
Overlooked, the houses sloped from him—
Terraced or domed, unchimnied, gray,
All stone—a moor of roofs. No play
Of life; no smoke went up, no sound
Except low hum, and that half drowned.
  The inn abutted on the pool
Named Hezekiah's, a sunken court

Where silence and seclusion rule,
Hemmed round by walls of nature's sort,
Base to stone structures seeming one
E'en with the steeps they stand upon.

   As a three-decker's stern-lights peer
Down on the oily wake below,
Upon the sleek dark waters here
The inn's small lattices bestow
A rearward glance. And here and there
In flaws the languid evening air
Stirs the dull weeds adust, which trail
In festoons from the crag, and veil
The ancient fissures, overtopped
By the tall convent of the Copt,
Built like a light-house o'er the main.

   Blind arches showed in walls of wane,
Sealed windows, portals masoned fast,
And terraces where nothing passed
By parapets all dumb. No tarn
Among the Kaatskills, high above
Farm-house and stack, last lichened barn
And log-bridge rotting in remove—
More lonesome looks than this dead pool
In town where living creatures rule.

   Not here the spell might he undo;
The strangeness haunted him and grew.

   But twilight closes. He descends
And toward the inner court he wends.

Part I: Jerusalem, Canto 1

The Recluse

Ere yet they win that verge and line,
Reveal the stranger. Name him—Vine.
His home to tell—kin, tribe, estate—
Would naught avail. Alighting grow,
As on the tree the mistletoe,
All gifts unique. In seeds of fate

Borne on the winds these emigrate
And graft the stock.
                     Vine's manner shy
A clog, a hindrance might imply;
A lack of parlor-wont. But grace
Which is in substance deep and grain
May, peradventure, well pass by
The polish of veneer. No trace
Of passion's soil or lucre's stain,
Though life was now half ferried o'er.
If use he served not, but forbore —
Such indolence might still but pine
In dearth of rich incentive high:
Apollo slave in Mammon's mine?
Better Admetus' shepherd lie.

   A charm of subtle virtue shed
A personal influence coveted,
Whose source was difficult to tell
As ever was that perfumed spell
Of Paradise-flowers invisible
Which angels round Cecilia bred.
   A saint then do we here unfold?
Nay, the ripe flush, Venetian mould
Evinced no nature saintly fine,
But blood like swart Vesuvian wine.
What cooled the current? Under cheer
Of opulent softness, reigned austere
Control of self. Flesh, but scarce pride,
Was curbed: desire was mortified;
But less indeed by moral sway
Than doubt if happiness thro' clay
Be reachable. No sackclothed man;
Howbeit, in sort Carthusian
Tho' born a Sybarite. And yet
Not beauty might he all forget,
The beauty of the world, and charm:
He prized it tho' it scarce might warm.
   Like to the nunnery's denizen
His virgin soul communed with men
But thro' the wicket. Was it clear

This coyness bordered not on fear—
Fear or an apprehensive sense?
Not wholly seemed it diffidence
Recluse. Nor less did strangely wind
Ambiguous elfishness behind
All that: an Ariel unknown.
It seemed his very speech in tone
Betrayed disuse. Thronged streets astir
To Vine but ampler cloisters were.
Cloisters? No monk he was, allow;
But gleamed the richer for the shade
About him, as in sombre glade
Of Virgil's wood the Sibyl's Golden Bough.

Part I: Jerusalem, Canto 29

Via Crucis

Some leading thoroughfares of man
In wood-path, track, or trail began;
Though threading heart of proudest town,
They follow in controlling grade
A hint or dictate, nature's own,
By man, as by the brute, obeyed.

Within Jerusalem a lane,
Narrow, nor less an artery main
(Though little knoweth it of din),
In part suggests such origin.
The restoration or repair,
Successive through long ages there,
Of city upon city tumbled,
Might scarce divert that thoroughfare,
Whose hill abideth yet unhumbled
Above the valley-side it meets.
Pronounce its name, this natural street's:
The *Via Crucis*—even the way
Tradition claims to be the one
Trod on that Friday far away
By Him our pure exemplar shown.

'Tis Whitsun-tide. From paths without,
Through Stephen's gate—by many a vein
Convergent brought within this lane,
Ere sun-down shut the loiterer out—
As 'twere a frieze, behold the train!
Bowed water-carriers; Jews with staves;
Infirm gray monks; over-loaded slaves;
Turk soldiers—young, with home-sick eyes;
A Bey, bereaved through luxuries;
Strangers and exiles; Moslem dames
Long-veiled in monumental white,
Dumb from the mounds which memory claims;
A half-starved vagrant Edomite;
Sore-footed Arab girls, which toil
Depressed under heap of garden-spoil;
The patient ass with panniered urn;
Sour camels humped by heaven and man,
Whose languid necks through habit turn
For ease—for ease they hardly gain.
In varied forms of fate they wend—
Or man or animal, 'tis one:
Cross-bearers all, alike they tend
And follow, slowly follow on.

But, lagging after, who is he
Called early every hope to test,
And now, at close of rarer quest,
Finds so much more the heavier tree?
From slopes whence even Echo's gone,
Wending, he murmurs in low tone:
"They wire the world—far under sea
They talk; but never comes to me
A message from beneath the stone."

Dusked Olivet he leaves behind,
And, taking now a slender wynd,
Vanishes in the obscurer town.

Part IV: Bethlehem, Canto 34

The Tuft of Kelp

All dripping in tangles green,
　Cast up by a lonely sea,
If purer for that, O Weed,
　Bitterer, too, are ye?

The Maldive Shark

　About the Shark, phlegmatical one,
Pale sot of the Maldive sea,
The sleek little pilot-fish, azure and slim,
How alert in attendance be.
From his saw-pit of mouth, from his charnel of maw
They have nothing of harm to dread,
But liquidly glide on his ghastly flank
Or before his Gorgonian head;
Or lurk in the port of serrated teeth
In white triple tiers of glittering gates,
And there find a haven when peril's abroad,
An asylum in jaws of the Fates!

They are friends; and friendly they guide him to prey,
Yet never partake of the treat—
Eyes and brains to the dotard lethargic and dull,
Pale ravener of horrible meat.

The Berg

(*A Dream*)

I saw a Ship of martial build
(Her standards set, her brave apparel on)
Directed as by madness mere
Against a stolid Iceberg steer,
Nor budge it, though the infatuate Ship went down.
The impact made huge ice-cubes fall

Sullen, in tons that crashed the deck;
But that one avalanche was all—
No other movement save the foundering wreck.

Along the spurs of ridges pale
Not any slenderest shaft and frail,
A prism over glass-green gorges lone,
Toppled; nor lace of traceries fine,
Nor pendant drops in grot or mine
Were jarred, when the stunned Ship went down.

Nor sole the gulls in cloud that wheeled
Circling one snow-flanked peak afar,
But nearer fowl the floes that skimmed
And crystal beaches, felt no jar.
No thrill transmitted stirred the lock
Of jack-straw needle-ice at base;
Towers undermined by waves—the block
Atilt impending—kept their place.
Seals, dozing sleek on sliddery ledges
Slipt never, when by loftier edges,
Through very inertia overthrown,
The impetuous Ship in bafflement went down.

Hard Berg (methought) so cold, so vast,
With mortal damps self-overcast;
Exhaling still thy dankish breath—
Adrift dissolving, bound for death;
Though lumpish thou, a lumbering one—
A lumbering lubbard loitering slow,
Impingers rue thee and go down,
Sounding thy precipice below,
Nor stir the slimy slug that sprawls
Along thy dense stolidity of walls.

After the Pleasure Party

LINES TRACED
UNDER AN IMAGE OF
AMOR THREATENING

Fear me, virgin whosoever
Taking pride from love exempt,
Fear me, slighted. Never, never
Brave me, nor my fury tempt:
Downy wings, but wroth they beat
Tempest even in reason's seat.

Behind the house the upland falls
With many an odorous tree—
White marbles gleaming through green halls—
Terrace by terrace, down and down,
And meets the star-lit Mediterranean Sea.

'Tis Paradise. In such an hour
Some pangs that rend might take release.
Nor less perturbed who keeps this bower
Of balm, nor finds balsamic peace?
From whom the passionate words in vent
After long revery's discontent?

"Tired of the homeless deep,
Look how their flight yon hurrying billows urge
   Hitherward but to reap
Passive repulse from the iron-bound verge!
Insensate, can they never know
'Tis mad to wreck the impulsion so?

"An art of memory is, they tell:
But to forget! forget the glade
Wherein Fate sprung Love's ambuscade,
To flout pale years of cloistral life
And flush me in this sensuous strife.
'Tis Vesta struck with Sappho's smart.

No fable her delirious leap:
With more of cause in desperate heart,
Myself could take it—but to sleep!

"Now first I feel, what all may ween,
That soon or late, if faded e'en,
One's sex asserts itself. Desire,
The dear desire through love to sway,
Is like the Geysers that aspire—
Through cold obstruction win their fervid way.
But baffled here—to take disdain,
To feel rule's instinct, yet not reign;
To dote, to come to this drear shame—
Hence the winged blaze that sweeps my soul
Like prairie-fires that spurn control,
Where withering weeds incense the flame.

"And kept I long heaven's watch for this,
Contemning love, for this, even this?
O terrace chill in Northern air,
O reaching ranging tube I placed
Against yon skies, and fable chased
Till, fool, I hailed for sister there
Starred Cassiopea in Golden Chair.
In dream I throned me, nor I saw
In cell the idiot crowned with straw.

"And yet, ah yet, scarce ill I reigned,
Through self-illusion self-sustained,
When now—enlightened, undeceived—
What gain I, barrenly bereaved!
Than this can be yet lower decline—
Envy and spleen, can these be mine?

"The peasant-girl demure that trod
Beside our wheels that climbed the way,
And bore along a blossoming rod
That looked the sceptre of May-Day—
On her—to fire this petty hell,
His softened glance how moistly fell!

The cheat! on briers her buds were strung;
And wiles peeped forth from mien how meek.
The innocent bare-foot! young, so young!
To girls, strong man's a novice weak.
To tell such beads! And more remain,
Sad rosary of belittling pain.

"When after lunch and sallies gay
Like the Decameron folk we lay
In sylvan groups; and I——let be!
O, dreams he, can he dream that one
Because not roseate feels no sun?
The plain lone bramble thrills with Spring
As much as vines that grapes shall bring.

"Me now fair studies charm no more.
Shall great thoughts writ, or high themes sung
Damask wan cheeks—unlock his arm
About some radiant ninny flung?
How glad, with all my starry lore,
I'd buy the veriest wanton's rose
Would but my bee therein repose.

"Could I remake me! or set free
This sexless bound in sex, then plunge
Deeper than Sappho, in a lunge
Piercing Pan's paramount mystery!
For, Nature, in no shallow surge
Against thee either sex may urge,
Why hast thou made us but in halves—
Co-relatives? This makes us slaves.
If these co-relatives never meet
Self-hood itself seems incomplete.
And such the dicing of blind fate
Few matching halves here meet and mate.
What Cosmic jest or Anarch blunder
The human integral clove asunder
And shied the fractions through life's gate?

"Ye stars that long your votary knew
Rapt in her vigil, see me here!
Whither is gone the spell ye threw
When rose before me Cassiopea?
Usurped on by love's stronger reign—
But, lo, your very selves do wane:
Light breaks—truth breaks! Silvered no more,
But chilled by dawn that brings the gale
Shivers yon bramble above the vale,
And disillusion opens all the shore."

One knows not if Urania yet
The pleasure-party may forget;
Or whether she lived down the strain
Of turbulent heart and rebel brain;
For Amor so resents a slight,
And hers had been such haught disdain,
He long may wreak his boyish spite,
And boy-like, little reck the pain.

One knows not, no. But late in Rome
(For queens discrowned a congruous home)
Entering Albani's porch she stood
Fixed by an antique pagan stone
Colossal carved. No anchorite seer,
Not Thomas à Kempis, monk austere,
Religious more are in their tone;
Yet far, how far from Christian heart
That form august of heathen Art.
Swayed by its influence, long she stood,
Till surged emotion seething down,
She rallied and this mood she won:

"Languid in frame for me,
To-day by Mary's convent-shrine,
Touched by her picture's moving plea
In that poor nerveless hour of mine,
I mused—A wanderer still must grieve.
Half I resolved to kneel and believe,

Believe and submit, the veil take on.
But thee, arm'd Virgin! less benign,
Thee now I invoke, thou mightier one.
Helmeted woman—if such term
Befit thee, far from strife
Of that which makes the sexual feud
And clogs the aspirant life—
O self-reliant, strong and free,
Thou in whom power and peace unite,
Transcender! raise me up to thee,
Raise me and arm me!"

       Fond appeal.
For never passion peace shall bring,
Nor Art inanimate for long
Inspire. Nothing may help or heal
While Amor incensed remembers wrong.
Vindictive, not himself he'll spare;
For scope to give his vengeance play
Himself he'll blaspheme and betray.

 Then for Urania, virgins everywhere,
O pray! Example take too, and have care.

The Ravaged Villa

In shards the sylvan vases lie,
 Their links of dance undone,
And brambles wither by thy brim,
 Choked Fountain of the Sun!
The spider in the laurel spins,
 The weed exiles the flower:
And, flung to kiln, Apollo's bust
 Makes lime for Mammon's tower.

Art

In placid hours well-pleased we dream
Of many a brave unbodied scheme.
But form to lend, pulsed life create,
What unlike things must meet and mate:
A flame to melt—a wind to freeze;
Sad patience—joyous energies;
Humility—yet pride and scorn;
Instinct and study; love and hate;
Audacity—reverence. These must mate,
And fuse with Jacob's mystic heart,
To wrestle with the angel—Art.

Shelley's Vision

Wandering late by morning seas
When my heart with pain was low—
Hate the censor pelted me—
Deject I saw my shadow go.

In elf-caprice of bitter tone
I too would pelt the pelted one:
At my shadow I cast a stone.

When lo, upon that sun-lit ground
I saw the quivering phantom take
The likeness of Saint Stephen crowned:
Then did self-reverence awake.

In a Bye-Canal

A swoon of noon, a trance of tide,
The hushed siesta brooding wide
  Like calms far off Peru;
No floating wayfarer in sight,
Dumb noon, and haunted like the night
  When Jael the wiled one slew.

A languid impulse from the oar
Plied by my indolent gondolier
Tinkles against a palace hoar,
  And, hark, response I hear!
A lattice clicks; and, lo, I see,
Between the slats, mute summoning me,
What loveliest eyes of scintillation,
What basilisk glance of conjuration!

  Fronted I have, part taken the span
Of portents in nature and peril in man.
I have swum—I have been
'Twixt the whale's black flukes and the white shark's fin;
The enemy's desert have wandered in,
And there have turned, have turned and scanned,
Following me how noiselessly,
Envy and Slander, lepers hand in hand.
All this. But at the latticed eye—
"Hey! Gondolier, you sleep, my man;
Wake up!" And, shooting by, we ran;
The while I mused, This, surely, now,
Confutes the Naturalists, allow!
Sirens, true sirens verily be,
Sirens, waylayers in the sea.

Well, wooed by these same deadly misses,
  Is it shame to run?
No! flee them did divine Ulysses,
  Brave, wise, and Venus' son.

Pontoosuce

Crowning a bluff where gleams the lake below,
Some pillared pines in well-spaced order stand
And like an open temple show.
And here in best of seasons bland,
Autumnal noon-tide, I look out
From dusk arcades on sunshine all about.

Beyond the Lake, in upland cheer
Fields, pastoral fields, and barns appear,
They skirt the hills where lonely roads
Revealed in links through tiers of woods
Wind up to indistinct abodes
And faery-peopled neighborhoods;
While further fainter mountains keep
Hazed in romance impenetrably deep.

Look, corn in stacks, on many a farm,
And orchards ripe in languorous charm,
As dreamy Nature, feeling sure
Of all her genial labor done,
And the last mellow fruitage won,
Would idle out her term mature;
Reposing like a thing reclined
In kinship with man's meditative mind.

For me, within the brown arcade —
Rich life, methought; sweet here in shade
And pleasant abroad in air! — But, nay,
A counter thought intrusive played,
A thought as old as thought itself,
And who shall lay it on the shelf! —
I felt the beauty bless the day
In opulence of autumn's dower;
But evanescence will not stay!
A year ago was such an hour
As this, which but foreruns the blast
Shall sweep these live leaves to the dead leaves past.

All dies! —
     I stood in revery long.
Then, to forget death's ancient wrong,
I turned me in the brown arcade,
And there by chance in lateral glade
I saw low tawny mounds in lines
Relics of trunks of stately pines
Ranked erst in colonnades where, lo!
Erect succeeding pillars show!

All dies! and not alone
The aspiring trees and men and grass;
The poet's forms of beauty pass,
And noblest deeds they are undone.
Even truth itself decays, and lo,
From truth's sad ashes fraud and falsehood grow.
All dies!
The workman dies, and, after him, the work;
Like to these pines whose graves I trace,
Statue and statuary fall upon their face:
In very amaranths the worm doth lurk,
Even stars, Chaldæans say, have left their place.
Andes and Apalachee tell
Of havoc ere our Adam fell,
And present Nature as a moss doth show
On the ruins of the Nature of the æons of long ago.

But look — and hark!
     Adown the glade,
Where light and shadow sport at will,
Who cometh vocal, and arrayed
As in the first pale tints of morn —
So pure, rose-clear, and fresh and chill!
Some ground-pine sprigs her brow adorn,
The earthy rootlets tangled clinging.
Over tufts of moss which dead things made,
Under vital twigs which danced or swayed,
Along she floats, and lightly singing:

"Dies, all dies!
The grass it dies, but in vernal rain
Up it springs and it lives again;
Over and over, again and again
It lives, it dies and it lives again.
Who sighs that all dies?
Summer and winter, and pleasure and pain
And everything everywhere in God's reign,
They end, and anon they begin again:
Wane and wax, wax and wane:
Over and over and over amain
End, ever end, and begin again—
End, ever end, and forever and ever begin again!"
She ceased, and nearer slid, and hung

In dewy guise; then softlier sung:
"Since light and shade are equal set
And all revolves, nor more ye know;
Ah, why should tears the pale cheek fret
For aught that waneth here below.
Let go, let go!"

With that, her warm lips thrilled me through,
She kissed me, while her chaplet cold
Its rootlets brushed against my brow
With all their humid clinging mould.
She vanished, leaving fragrant breath
And warmth and chill of wedded life and death.

Billy in the Darbies

Good of the chaplain to enter Lone Bay
And down on his marrowbones here and pray
For the likes just o' me, Billy Budd.—But, look:
Through the port comes the moonshine astray!
It tips the guard's cutlass and silvers this nook;
But 'twill die in the dawning of Billy's last day.
A jewel-block they'll make of me tomorrow,
Pendant pearl from the yardarm-end
Like the eardrop I gave to Bristol Molly—
O, 'tis me, not the sentence they'll suspend.
Ay, ay, all is up; and I must up too,
Early in the morning, aloft from alow.
On an empty stomach now never it would do.
They'll give me a nibble—bit o' biscuit ere I go.
Sure, a messmate will reach me the last parting cup;
But, turning heads away from the hoist and the belay,
Heaven knows who will have the running of me up!
No pipe to those halyards.—But aren't it all sham?
A blur's in my eyes; it is dreaming that I am.
A hatchet to my hawser? All adrift to go?
The drum roll to grog, and Billy never know?
But Donald he has promised to stand by the plank;
So I'll shake a friendly hand ere I sink.
But—no! It is dead then I'll be, come to think.
I remember Taff the Welshman when he sank.
And his cheek it was like the bidding pink.
But me they'll lash in hammock, drop me deep.
Fathoms down, fathoms down, how I'll dream fast asleep.
I feel it stealing now. Sentry, are you there?
Just ease these darbies at the wrist,
And roll me over fair!
I am sleepy, and the oozy weeds about me twist.

HENRY HOWARD BROWNELL

(1820–1872)

The Battle Summers

Again the glory of the days!
   Once more the dreamy sunshine fills
   Noon after noon,—and all the hills
Lie soft and dim in autumn haze.

And lovely lie these meadows low
   In the slant sun—and quiet broods
   Above the splendor of the woods
All touched with autumn's tenderest glow.

The trees stand marshalled, clan by clan,
   A bannered army, far and near—
   (Mark how yon fiery maples rear
Their crimson colors in the van!)

Methinks, these ancient haunts among,
   A fuller life informs the fall—
   The crows in council sit and call,
The quail through stubble leads her young.

The woodcock whirrs by bush and brake,
   The partridge plies his cedar-search—
   (Old Andy says the trout and perch
Are larger now, in stream and lake.)

O'er the brown leaves, the forest floor,
   With nut and acorn scantly strewed,
   The small red people of the wood
Are out to seek their winter store.

To-day they gather, each and all,
   To take their last of autumn suns—
   E'en the gray squirrel lithely runs
Along the mossy pasture wall.

By marsh and brook, by copse and hill,
   To their old quiet haunts repair
   The feeble things of earth and air,
And feed and flutter at their will.

The feet that roved this woodland round,
   The hands that scared the timid race,
   Now mingle in a mightier chase,
Or mould on that great Hunting-Ground.

Strange calm and peace! — ah, who could deem,
   By this still glen, this lone hill-side,
   How three long summers, in their pride,
Have smiled above that awful Dream? —

Have ever woven a braver green,
   And ever arched a lovelier blue
   Yet nature, in her every hue,
Took color from the dread Unseen.

The haze of Indian Summer seemed
   Borne from far fields of sulphury breath —
   A subtile atmosphere of death
Was ever round us as we dreamed.

The horizon's dim heat-lightning played
   Like small-arms, still, through nights of drouth,
   And the low thunder of the south
Was dull and distant cannonade.

To us the glory or the gray
   Had still a stranger, stormier dye,
   Remembering how we watched the sky
Of many a waning battle day,

O'er many a field of loss or fame —
   How Shiloh's eve to ashes turned,
   And how Manassas' sunset burned
Incarnadine of blood and flame.

And how, in thunder, day by day,
   The hot sky hanging over all,
   Beneath that sullen, lurid pall,
The Week of Battles rolled away!

Give me my legions!—so, in grief,
   Like him of Rome, our Father cried—
   (A Nation's Flower lay down and died
In yon fell shade!)—ah, hapless chief—

Too late we learned thy star!—o'erta'en,
   (Of error or of fate o'erharsh,)
   Like Varus, in the fatal marsh
Where skill and valor all were vain!

All vain—Fair Oaks and Seven Pines!
   A deeper hue than dying Fall
   May lend, is yours!——yet over all
The mild Virginian autumn shines.

And still a Nation's Heart o'erhung
   The iron echoes pealed afar,
   Along a thousand leagues of war
The battle thunders tossed and flung.

Till, when our fortunes paled the most,
   And Hope had half forgot to wave
   Her banner o'er the wearied brave—
A morning saw the traitor host

Rolled back o'er red Potomac's wave,
   And the Great River burst his way!—
   And all on that dear Summer's Day
Day that our fathers died and gave.

Rest in thy calm, Eternal Right!
   For thee, though levin-scarred and torn,
   Through flame and death shall still be borne
The Red, the Azure, and the White.

We pass—we sink like summer's snow—
  Yet on the mighty Cause shall move,
  Though every field a Cannæ prove,
And every pass a Roncesvaux.

Though every summer burn anew
  A battle-summer—though each day
  We name a new Aceldama,
Or some dry Golgotha re-dew.

And thou, in lonely dream withdrawn!
  What dost thou, while in tempest dies
  The long drear Night, and all the skies
Are red with Freedom's fiery Dawn!

Behold, thy summer days are o'er—
  Yet dearer, lovelier these that fall
  Wrapped in red autumn's flag, than all
The green and glory gone before.

'Twas well to sing by stream and sod,
  And they there were that loved thy lays—
  But lo, where, 'neath yon battle-haze,
Thy brothers bare the breast for God!

Reck not of waning force nor breath—
  Some little aid may yet be thine,
  Some honor to the All-Divine,—
To-day, where, by yon River of Death,

His stars on Rosecrans look down—
  Or, on the morrow, by moat and wall,
  Once more when the Great Admiral
Thunders on traitor fleet and town.

O wearied heart! O darkening eye!
  (How long to hope and trust untrue!)
  What in the hurly can ye do?
Little, 'tis like—yet we can die.

ALICE CARY

(1820–1871)

Autumn

Shorter and shorter now the twilight clips
   The days, as through the sunset gates they crowd,
And Summer from her golden collar slips
   And strays through stubble-fields, and moans aloud,

Save when by fits the warmer air deceives,
   And, stealing hopeful to some sheltered bower,
She lies on pillows of the yellow leaves,
   And tries the old tunes over for an hour.

The wind, whose tender whisper in the May
   Set all the young blooms listening through th' grove,
Sits rustling in the faded boughs to-day
   And makes his cold and unsuccessful love.

The rose has taken off her tire of red —
   The mullein-stalk its yellow stars have lost,
And the proud meadow-pink hangs down her head
   Against earth's chilly bosom, witched with frost.

The robin, that was busy all the June,
   Before the sun had kissed the topmost bough,
Catching our hearts up in his golden tune,
   Has given place to the brown cricket now.

The very cock crows lonesomely at morn —
   Each flag and fern the shrinking stream divides —
Uneasy cattle low, and lambs forlorn
   Creep to their strawy sheds with nettled sides.

Shut up the door: who loves me must not look
   Upon the withered world, but haste to bring
His lighted candle, and his story-book,
   And live with me the poetry of Spring.

The West Country

Have you been in our wild west country? then
   You have often had to pass
Its cabins lying like birds' nests in
   The wild green prairie grass.

Have you seen the women forget their wheels
   As they sat at the door to spin—
Have you seen the darning fall away
   From their fingers worn and thin,

As they asked you news of the villages
   Where they were used to be,
Gay girls at work in the factories
   With their lovers gone to sea!

Ah, have you thought of the bravery
   That no loud praise provokes—
Of the tragedies acted in the lives
   Of poor, hard-working folks!

Of the little more, and the little more
   Of hardship which they press
Upon their own tired hands to make
   The toil for the children less:

And not in vain; for many a lad
   Born to rough work and ways,
Strips off his ragged coat, and makes
   Men clothe him with their praise.

JOHN HENRY HOPKINS, JR.

(1820–1891)

Three Kings of Orient

We Three Kings of Orient are,
Bearing gifts we traverse afar,
    Field and fountain,
    Moor, and mountain,
Following yonder Star.

    O Star of Wonder, Star of Night,
    Star with Royal Beauty bright,
    Westward leading,
    Still proceeding,
    Guide us to Thy perfect Light.

GASPARD.

Born a KING on Bethlehem plain,
GOLD I bring to crown Him again,
    King for ever,
    Ceasing never
Over us all to reign.

Chorus

MELCHIOR.

FRANKINCENSE to offer have I,
Incense owns a Deity nigh:
    Prayer and praising
    All men raising,
Worship Him GOD on High.

Chorus

BALTHAZAR.

MYRRH is mine; its bitter perfume
Breathes a life of gathering gloom;—
    Sorrowing, sighing,
    Bleeding, dying,
Sealed in the stone-cold tomb.

Chorus

Glorious now behold Him arise,
KING, and GOD, and SACRIFICE;
    Heav'n sings Hallelujah:
    Hallelujah the earth replies.

Chorus

FREDERICK GODDARD TUCKERMAN

(1821–1873)

from *Sonnets, First Series*

VII

Dank fens of cedar; hemlock-branches gray
With tress and trail of mosses wringing-wet;
Beds of the black pitch-pine in dead leaves set
Whose wasted red has wasted to white away;
Remnants of rain, and droppings of decay,—
Why hold ye so my heart, nor dimly let
Through your deep leaves the light of yesterday,
The faded glimmer of a sunshine set?
Is it that in your darkness, shut from strife,
The bread of tears becomes the bread of life?
Far from the roar of day, beneath your boughs
Fresh griefs beat tranquilly, and loves and vows
Grow green in your gray shadows, dearer far
Even than all lovely lights, and roses, are?

VIII

As when, down some broad River dropping, we,
Day after day, behold the assuming shores
Sink and grow dim, as the great Water-course
Pushes his banks apart and seeks the sea;
Benches of pines, high shelf and balcony,
To flats of willow and low sycamores
Subsiding, till, where'er the wave we see,
Himself is his horizon utterly:
So fades the portion of our early world.
Still on the ambit hangs the purple air;
Yet, while we lean to read the secret there,

The stream that by green shore-sides plashed and purled
Expands; the mountains melt to vapors rare,
And life alone circles out flat and bare.

X

An upper chamber in a darkened house,
Where, ere his footsteps reached ripe manhood's brink,
Terror and anguish were his cup to drink,—
I cannot rid the thought, nor hold it close;
But dimly dream upon that man alone;—
Now though the autumn clouds most softly pass;
The cricket chides beneath the doorstep stone,
And greener than the season grows the grass.
Nor can I drop my lids, nor shade my brows,
But there he stands beside the lifted sash;
And, with a swooning of the heart, I think
Where the black shingles slope to meet the boughs,
And—shattered on the roof like smallest snows—
The tiny petals of the mountain-ash.

XXII

The morning comes; not slow, with reddening gold,
But wildly driven, with windy shower, and sway
As though the wind would blow the dark away!
Voices of wail, of misery multifold,
Wake with the light, and its harsh glare obey;
And yet I walk betimes this day of spring,
Still my own private portion reckoning,
Not to compute, though every tear be told.
Oh, might I on the gale my sorrow fling!
But sweep, sweep on, wild blast! who bids thee stay?
Across the stormy headlands shriek and sing;
And, earlier than the daytime, bring the day
To pouring eyes, half-quenched with watery sight,
And breaking hearts that hate the morning light!

from *Sonnets, Second Series*

VII

His heart was in his garden; but his brain
Wandered at will among the fiery stars:
Bards, heroes, prophets, Homers, Hamilcars,
With many angels, stood, his eye to gain;
The devils, too, were his familiars.
And yet the cunning florist held his eyes
Close to the ground,—a tulip-bulb his prize,—
And talked of tan and bone-dust, cutworms, grubs,
As though all Nature held no higher strain;
Or, if he spoke of Art, he made the theme
Flow through box-borders, turf, and flower-tubs;
Or, like a garden-engine's, steered the stream,—
Now spouted rainbows to the silent skies;
Now kept it flat, and raked the walks and shrubs.

XVI

Under the mountain, as when first I knew
Its low dark roof, and chimney creeper-twined,
The red house stands; and yet my footsteps find
Vague in the walks, waste balm and feverfew.
But they are gone: no soft-eyed sisters trip
Across the porch or lintels; where, behind,
The mother sat,—sat knitting with pursed lip.
The house stands vacant in its green recess,
Absent of beauty as a broken heart;
The wild rain enters; and the sunset wind
Sighs in the chambers of their loveliness,
Or shakes the pane; and in the silent noons,
The glass falls from the window, part by part,
And ringeth faintly in the grassy stones.

from *Sonnets, Third Series*

V

How well do I recall that walk in state
Across the Common, by the paths we knew:
Myself in silver badge and riband blue,
My little sister with her book and slate;
The elm tree by the Pond, the fence of wood,
The burial place that at the corner stood
Where once we crossed, through the forbidden grate,
The stones that grudg'd us way, the graveside weed,
The ominous wind that turned us half about.
Smit by the flying drops, at what a speed
Across the paths, unblessed and unforgiven
We hurried homeward when the day was late
And heard, with awe that left no place for doubt,
God's anger mutter in the darkened heaven.

The Cricket

I

The humming bee purrs softly o'er his flower;
  From lawn and thicket
The dogday locust singeth in the sun
  From hour to hour:
Each has his bard, and thou, ere day be done,
  Shalt have no wrong.
So bright that murmur mid the insect crowd,
Muffled and lost in bottom-grass, or loud
  By pale and picket:
Shall I not take to help me in my song
  A little cooing cricket?

II

The afternoon is sleepy; let us lie
Beneath these branches whilst the burdened brook,
Muttering and moaning to himself, goes by;
And mark our minstrel's carol whilst we look
Toward the faint horizon swooning blue.
   Or in a garden bower,
Trellised and trammeled with deep drapery
   Of hanging green,
   Light glimmering through—
There let the dull hop be,
Let bloom, with poppy's dark refreshing flower:
Let the dead fragrance round our temples beat,
Stunning the sense to slumber, whilst between
The falling water and fluttering wind
   Mingle and meet,
   Murmur and mix,
No few faint pipings from the glades behind,
   Or alder-thicks:
But louder as the day declines,
From tingling tassel, blade, and sheath,
Rising from nets of river vines,
   Winrows and ricks,
   Above, beneath,
   At every breath,
At hand, around, illimitably
Rising and falling like the sea,
   Acres of cricks!

III

Dear to the child who hears thy rustling voice
Cease at his footstep, though he hears thee still,
Cease and resume with vibrance crisp and shrill,
Thou sittest in the sunshine to rejoice.
Night lover too; bringer of all things dark
And rest and silence; yet thou bringest to me
Always that burthen of the unresting Sea,
The moaning cliffs, the low rocks blackly stark;

These upland inland fields no more I view,
But the long flat seaside beach, the wild seamew,
  And the overturning wave!
Thou bringest too, dim accents from the grave
To him who walketh when the day is dim,
Dreaming of those who dream no more of him,
With edged remembrances of joy and pain;
And heyday looks and laughter come again:
Forms that in happy sunshine lie and leap,
With faces where but now a gap must be,
Renunciations, and partitions deep
And perfect tears, and crowning vacancy!
And to thy poet at the twilight's hush,
No chirping touch of lips with laugh and blush,
But wringing arms, hearts wild with love and woe,
Closed eyes, and kisses that would not let go!

IV

So wert thou loved in that old graceful time
  When Greece was fair,
While god and hero hearkened to thy chime;
  Softly astir
Where the long grasses fringed Caÿster's lip;
Long-drawn, with glimmering sails of swan and ship,
  And ship and swan;
  Or where
  Reedy Eurotas ran.
Did that low warble teach thy tender flute
  Xenaphyle?
Its breathings mild? say! did the grasshopper
Sit golden in thy purple hair
  O Psammathe?
  Or wert thou mute,
Grieving for Pan amid the alders there?
And by the water and along the hill
That thirsty tinkle in the herbage still,
Though the lost forest wailed to horns of Arcady?

V

Like the Enchanter old—
Who sought mid the dead water's weeds and scum
For evil growths beneath the moonbeam cold,
    Or mandrake or dorcynium;
And touched the leaf that opened both his ears,
So that articulate voices now he hears
In cry of beast, or bird, or insect's hum,—
Might I but find thy knowledge in thy song!
    That twittering tongue,
Ancient as light, returning like the years.
    So might I be,
Unwise to sing, thy true interpreter
Through denser stillness and in sounder dark,
Than ere thy notes have pierced to harrow me.
    So might I stir
    The world to hark
    To thee my lord and lawgiver,
    And cease my quest:
Content to bring thy wisdom to the world;
Content to gain at last some low applause,
    Now low, now lost
Like thine from mossy stone, amid the stems and straws,
    Or garden gravemound tricked and dressed—
    Powdered and pearled
    By stealing frost—
In dusky rainbow beauty of euphorbias!
For larger would be less indeed, and like
The ceaseless simmer in the summer grass
To him who toileth in the windy field,
    Or where the sunbeams strike,
Naught in innumerable numerousness.
    So might I much possess,
    So much must yield;
But failing this, the dell and grassy dike,
The water and the waste shall still be dear,
And all the pleasant plots and places

Where thou hast sung, and I have hung
　To ignorantly hear.
Then Cricket, sing thy song! or answer mine!
Thine whispers blame, but mine has naught but praises.
It matters not. Behold! the autumn goes,
　The shadow grows,
The moments take hold of eternity;
Even while we stop to wrangle or repine
　Our lives are gone—
Like thinnest mist,
Like yon escaping color in the tree;
Rejoice! rejoice! whilst yet the hours exist—
Rejoice or mourn, and let the world swing on
Unmoved by cricket song of thee or me.

MARIA WHITE LOWELL

(1821–1853)

Rouen

Place de la Pucelle

Here blooms the legend fed with time and chance,
Fresh as the morning, though in centuries old;
The whitest lily in the shield of France,
       With heart of virgin gold.

Along this square she moved, sweet Joan of Arc,
With face more pallid than a day-lit star,
Half seen, half doubted, while before her dark
       Stretched the array of war.

Swift furled the battle-smoke of lying breath
From off her path, as if a wind had blown,
And showed no faithless king, but righteous death
       On the low, wooden throne.

He would reward her; she who meekly wore
Alike her gilded mail and peasant gown,
Meekly received one earthly honor more,—
       The formless, fiery crown.

A white dove trembled up the heated air,
And in the opening zenith found its goal;
Soft as a downward feather fell a prayer
       For each repentant soul.

JAMES MONROE WHITFIELD

(1822–1871)

America

America, it is to thee,
Thou boasted land of liberty,—
It is to thee I raise my song,
Thou land of blood, and crime, and wrong.
It is to thee, my native land,
From whence has issued many a band
To tear the black man from his soil,
And force him here to delve and toil;
Chained on your blood-bemoistened sod,
Cringing beneath a tyrant's rod,
Stripped of those rights which Nature's God
   Bequeathed to all the human race,
Bound to a petty tyrant's nod,
   Because he wears a paler face.
Was it for this, that freedom's fires
Were kindled by your patriot sires?
Was it for this, they shed their blood,
On hill and plain, on field and flood?
Was it for this, that wealth and life
Were staked upon that desperate strife,
Which drenched this land for seven long years
With blood of men, and women's tears?
When black and white fought side by side,
   Upon the well-contested field,—
Turned back the fierce opposing tide,
   And made the proud invader yield—
When, wounded, side by side they lay,
   And heard with joy the proud hurrah
From their victorious comrades say
   That they had waged successful war,
The thought ne'er entered in their brains
That they endured those toils and pains,
To forge fresh fetters, heavier chains

For their own children, in whose veins
Should flow that patriotic blood,
So freely shed on field and flood.
Oh no; they fought, as they believed,
    For the inherent rights of man;
But mark, how they have been deceived
    By slavery's accursed plan.
They never thought, when thus they shed
    Their heart's best blood, in freedom's cause,
That their own sons would live in dread,
    Under unjust, oppressive laws:
That those who quietly enjoyed
    The rights for which they fought and fell,
Could be the framers of a code,
    That would disgrace the fiends of hell!
Could they have looked, with prophet's ken,
    Down to the present evil time,
    Seen free-born men, uncharged with crime,
Consigned unto a slaver's pen,—
Or thrust into a prison cell,
With thieves and murderers to dwell—
While that same flag whose stripes and stars
Had been their guide through freedom's wars
As proudly waved above the pen
Of dealers in the souls of men!
Or could the shades of all the dead,
    Who fell beneath that starry flag,
Visit the scenes where they once bled,
    On hill and plain, on vale and crag,
By peaceful brook, or ocean's strand,
    By inland lake, or dark green wood,
Where'er the soil of this wide land
    Was moistened by their patriot blood,—
And then survey the country o'er,
    From north to south, from east to west,
And hear the agonizing cry
Ascending up to God on high,
From western wilds to ocean's shore,
    The fervent prayer of the oppressed;
The cry of helpless infancy

Torn from the parent's fond caress
By some base tool of tyranny,
  And doomed to woe and wretchedness;
The indignant wail of fiery youth,
  Its noble aspirations crushed,
Its generous zeal, its love of truth,
  Trampled by tyrants in the dust;
The aerial piles which fancy reared,
  And hopes too bright to be enjoyed,
Have passed and left his young heart seared,
  And all its dreams of bliss destroyed.
The shriek of virgin purity,
  Doomed to some libertine's embrace,
Should rouse the strongest sympathy
  Of each one of the human race;
And weak old age, oppressed with care,
  As he reviews the scene of strife,
Puts up to God a fervent prayer,
  To close his dark and troubled life.
The cry of fathers, mothers, wives,
  Severed from all their hearts hold dear,
And doomed to spend their wretched lives
  In gloom, and doubt, and hate, and fear:
And manhood, too, with soul of fire,
And arm of strength, and smothered ire,
Stands pondering with brow of gloom,
Upon his dark unhappy doom,
Whether to plunge in battle's strife,
And buy his freedom with his life,
And with stout heart and weapon strong,
Pay back the tyrant wrong for wrong,
Or wait the promised time of God,
  When his Almighty ire shall wake,
And smite the oppressor in his wrath,
And hurl red ruin in his path,
And with the terrors of his rod,
  Cause adamantine hearts to quake.
Here Christian writhes in bondage still,
  Beneath his brother Christian's rod,
And pastors trample down at will,

The image of the living God.
While prayers go up in lofty strains,
   And pealing hymns ascend to heaven,
The captive, toiling in his chains,
   With tortured limbs and bosom riven,
Raises his fettered hand on high,
   And in the accents of despair,
To him who rules both earth and sky,
   Puts up a sad, a fervent prayer,
To free him from the awful blast
   Of slavery's bitter galling shame —
Although his portion should be cast
   With demons in eternal flame!
Almighty God! 'tis this they call
   The land of liberty and law;
Part of its sons in baser thrall
   Than Babylon or Egypt saw —
Worse scenes of rapine, lust and shame,
   Than Babylonian ever knew,
Are perpetrated in the name
   Of God, the holy, just, and true;
And darker doom than Egypt felt,
May yet repay this nation's guilt.
Almighty God! thy aid impart,
And fire anew each faltering heart,
And strengthen every patriot's hand,
Who aims to save our native land.
We do not come before thy throne,
   With carnal weapons drenched in gore,
Although our blood has freely flown,
   In adding to the tyrant's store.
Father! before thy throne we come,
   Not in the panoply of war,
With pealing trump, and rolling drum,
   And cannon booming loud and far;
Striving in blood to wash out blood,
   Through wrong to seek redress for wrong;
For while thou 'rt holy, just and good,
   The battle is not to the strong;
But in the sacred name of peace,

Of justice, virtue, love and truth,
We pray, and never mean to cease,
    Till weak old age and fiery youth
In freedom's cause their voices raise,
And burst the bonds of every slave;
Till, north and south, and east and west,
The wrongs we bear shall be redressed.

THOMAS BUCHANAN READ

(1822–1872)

Sheridan's Ride

Up from the South at break of day,
Bringing to Winchester fresh dismay,
  The affrighted air with a shudder bore,
  Like a herald in haste, to the chieftain's door,
  The terrible grumble, and rumble, and roar,
  Telling the battle was on once more,
And Sheridan twenty miles away.

And wider still those billows of war,
Thundered along the horizon's bar;
And louder yet into Winchester rolled
The roar of that red sea uncontrolled,
Making the blood of the listener cold,
As he thought of the stake in that fiery fray,
And Sheridan twenty miles away.

But there is a road from Winchester town,
A good broad highway leading down;
And there, through the flush of the morning light,
A steed as black as the steeds of night,
Was seen to pass, as with eagle flight,
As if he knew the terrible need;
He stretched away with his utmost speed;
Hills rose and fell; but his heart was gay,
With Sheridan fifteen miles away.

Still sprung from those swift hoofs, thundering South,
The dust, like smoke from the cannon's mouth;
Or the trail of a comet, sweeping faster and faster,
Foreboding to traitors the doom of disaster.
The heart of the steed, and the heart of the master
Were beating like prisoners assaulting their walls,
Impatient to be where the battle-field calls;

Every nerve of the charger was strained to full play,
With Sheridan only ten miles away.

Under his spurning feet the road
Like an arrowy Alpine river flowed,
And the landscape sped away behind
Like an ocean flying before the wind,
And the steed, like a bark fed with furnace ire,
Swept on, with his wild eye full of fire.
But lo! he is nearing his heart's desire;
He is snuffing the smoke of the roaring fray,
With Sheridan only five miles away.

The first that the general saw were the groups
Of stragglers, and then the retreating troops,
What was done? what to do? a glance told him both,
Then striking his spurs, with a terrible oath,
He dashed down the line, 'mid a storm of huzzas,
And the wave of retreat checked its course there, because
The sight of the master compelled it to pause.
With foam and with dust, the black charger was gray;
By the flash of his eye, and the red nostril's play,
He seemed to the whole great army to say,
"I have brought you Sheridan all the way
From Winchester, down to save the day!"

Hurrah! hurrah for Sheridan!
Hurrah! hurrah for horse and man!
And when their statues are placed on high,
Under the dome of the Union sky,
The American soldiers' Temple of Fame;
There with the glorious general's name,
Be it said, in letters both bold and bright,
    "Here is the steed that saved the day,
By carrying Sheridan into the fight,
    From Winchester, twenty miles away!"

GEORGE HENRY BOKER

(1823–1890)

from *Sonnets: A Sequence on Profane Love*

The leaden eyelids of wan twilight close
Upon the sun; and now the misty dew
Trails its wet skirts across the glades, and through
The tangled grasses of the meadow goes,
Shaking a drop in every open rose,
In every lily's cup; Yon dreary yew
Alone looks darker for the tears that strew
Its dusky leaves, and deeper shadow throws,
And closer gathers; as if it would sit
As one who, mourning, wraps his mantle tight,
And huddles nearer to the dismal sight
Of some lost love; so yonder tree seems knit
Fast to the grave beneath; my heart takes flight,
To that lone yew, and cowers under it.

———————

As stands a statue on its pedestal,
Amidst the storms of civil mutiny,
With an unchanged and high serenity,
Though Caesar's self be toppled to his fall;
So stands my faith in thee amidst the brawl
Within my heart—the woeful tragedy
Of passions that conspire for mastery
Above the power that holds their rage in thrall.
Image of comfort! Lustrous as the star
That crests the morning, and as virgin pure,
All is not lost if thou wilt but endure!
If through the dust and turmoil of this war,
I may behold thee, stately and secure,
Brooding on things unearthly and afar.

———————

My darling's features, painted by the light;
As in the convex of a mirror, see
Her face diminished so fantastically
It scarcely hints her lovely self aright.
Away, poor mockery! My outraged sight
Turns from the fraud you perpetrate on me;
This is no transcript, but a forgery,
As far from semblance as is black from white.
Breathe, smile, blush, kiss me! Murmur in my ear
The things we know—we only! and give heed
To this deep sigh and this descending tear,
Ere from my senses you can win the meed
Of faith, to make your doubtful title clear,
And so convince me you are she indeed.

"Oh! craven, craven! while my brothers fall"

Oh! craven, craven! while my brothers fall,
  Like grass before the mower, in the fight,
  I, easy vassal to my own delight,
  Am bound with flowers, a far too willing thrall.
Day after day along the streets I crawl,
  Shamed in my manhood, reddening at the sight
  Of every soldier who upholds the right
  With no more motive than his country's call.
I love thee more than honor; ay, above
  That simple duty, conscience-plain and clear
  To dullest minds, whose summons all men hear.
Yet as I blush and loiter, who should move
  In the grand marches, I cannot but fear
  That thou wilt scorn me for my very love.

JAMES MATHEWES LEGARÉ

(1823–1859)

To a Lily

Go bow thy head in gentle spite,
Thou lily white.
For she who spies thee waving here,
With thee in beauty can compare
As day with night.

Soft are thy leaves and white: Her arms
Boast whiter charms.
Thy stem prone bent with loveliness
Of maiden grace possesseth less:
Therein she charms.

Thou in thy lake dost see
Thyself: So she
Beholds her image in her eyes
Reflected. Thus did Venus rise
From out the sea.

Inconsolate, bloom not again
Thou rival vain
Of her whose charms have thine outdone:
Whose purity might spot the sun,
And make thy leaf a stain.

GEORGE BOYER VASHON

(1824–1878)

from *Vincent Ogé*

There is, at times, an evening sky—
   The twilight's gift—of sombre hue,
All checkered wild and gorgeously
   With streaks of crimson, gold and blue;—
A sky that strikes the soul with awe,
   And, though not brilliant as the sheen,
Which in the east at morn we saw,
   Is far more glorious, I ween;—
So glorious that, when night hath come
And shrouded it in deepest gloom,
We turn aside with inward pain
And pray to see that sky again.
Such sight is like the struggle made
When freedom bids unbare the blade,
And calls from every mountain-glen—
   From every hill—from every plain,
Her chosen ones to stand like men,
   And cleanse their souls from every stain
Which wretches, steeped in crime and blood,
Have cast upon the form of God.
Though peace like morning's golden hue,
   With blooming groves and waving fields,
Is mildly pleasing to the view,
   And all the blessings that it yields
Are fondly welcomed by the breast
   Which finds delight in passion's rest,
That breast with joy foregoes them all,
While listening to Freedom's call.
Though red the carnage,—though the strife
Be filled with groans of parting life,—
Though battle's dark, ensanguined skies
Give echo but to agonies—
   To shrieks of wild despairing,—

We willingly repress a sigh —
Nay, gaze with rapture in our eye,
Whilst "FREEDOM!" is the rally-cry
   That calls to deeds of daring.

    *   *   *   *   *   *   *   *

The waves dash brightly on thy shore,
   Fair island of the southern seas!
As bright in joy as when of yore
   They gladly hailed the Genoese, —
That daring soul who gave to Spain
A world — last trophy of her reign!
Basking in beauty, thou dost seem
A vision in a poet's dream!
Thou look'st as though thou claim'st not birth
With sea and sky and other earth,
That smile around thee but to show
Thy beauty in a brighter glow, —
That are unto thee as the foil
   Artistic hands have featly set
Around Golconda's radiant spoil,
   To grace some lofty coronet, —
A foil which serves to make the gem
The glory of that diadem!

    *   *   *   *   *   *   *   *

If Eden claimed a favored haunt,
   Most hallowed of that blessed ground,
Where tempting fiend with guileful taunt
   A resting-place would ne'er have found, —
As shadowing it well might seek
   The loveliest home in that fair isle,
Which in its radiance seemed to speak
   As to the charmed doth Beauty's smile,
That whispers of a thousand things
For which words find no picturings.
Like to the gifted Greek who strove
   To paint a crowning work of art,
And form his ideal Queen of Love,
   By choosing from each grace a part,
Blending them in one beauteous whole,
To charm the eye, transfix the soul,

And hold it in enraptured fires,
Such as a dream of heaven inspires,—
So seem the glad waves to have sought
   From every place its richest treasure,
And borne it to that lovely spot,
   To found thereon a home of pleasure;—
A home where balmy airs might float
   Through spicy bower and orange grove;
Where bright-winged birds might turn the note
   Which tells of pure and constant love;
Where earthquake stay its demon force,
And hurricane its wrathful course;
Where nymph and fairy find a home,
And foot of spoiler never come.

   *   *   *   *   *   *   *   *

And Ogé stands mid this array
   Of matchless beauty, but his brow
Is brightened not by pleasure's play;
   He stands unmoved—nay, saddened now,
As doth the lorn and mateless bird
That constant mourns, whilst all unheard,
The breezes freighted with the strains
Of other songsters sweep the plain,—
That ne'er breathes forth a joyous note,
Though odors on the zephyrs float—
The tribute of a thousand bowers,
Rich in their store of fragrant flowers.
Yet Ogé's was a mind that joyed
   With nature in her every mood,
Whether in sunshine unalloyed
   With darkness, or in tempest rude
And, by the dashing waterfall,
   Or by the gently flowing river,
Or listening to the thunder's call,
   He'd joy away his life forever.
But ah! life is a changeful thing,
   And pleasures swiftly pass away,
And we may turn, with shuddering,
   From what we sighed for yesterday.
The guest, at banquet-table spread

With choicest viands, shakes with dread,
Nor heeds the goblet bright and fair,
Nor tastes the dainties rich and rare,
Nor bids his eye with pleasure trace
The wreathed flowers that deck the place,
If he but knows there is a draught
Among the cordials, that, if quaffed,
Will send swift poison through his veins.
　So Ogé seems; nor does his eye
With pleasure view the flowery plains,
　The bounding sea, the spangled sky,
As, in the short and soft twilight,
　The stars peep brightly forth in heaven,
And hasten to the realms of night,
　As handmaids of the Even.

lines 1 –125

CHARLES GODFREY LELAND

(1824–1903)

Ballad

By Hans Breitmann

Der noble Ritter Hugo
  Von Schwillensaufenstein,
Rode out mit shpeer and helmet,
  Und he coom to de panks of de Rhine.

Und oop dere rose a meer-maid,
  Vot hadn't got nodings on,
Und she say, "Oh, Ritter Hugo,
  Vhere you goes mit yourself alone?"

And he says, "I rides in de creenwood,
  Mit helmet und mit shpeer,
Till I cooms into em Gasthaus,
  Und dere I trinks some beer."

Und den outsphoke de maiden
  Vot hadn't got nodings on:
"I tont dink mooch of beoplesh
  Dat goes mit demselfs alone.

"You'd petter coom down in de wasser,
  Vhere dere's heaps of dings to see,
Und hafe a shplendid tinner
  Und drafel along mit me.

"Dere you sees de fisch a schwimmin',
  Und you catches dem efery one:"—
So sang dis wasser maiden
  Vot hadn't got nodings on.

"Dere ish drunks all full mit money
    In ships dat vent down of old;
Und you helpsh yourself, by dunder!
    To shimmerin' crowns of gold.

"Shoost look at dese shpoons und vatches!
    Shoost see dese diamant rings!
Coom down and fill your bockets,
    Und I'll giss you like efery dings.

"Vot you vantsh mit your schnapps und lager?
    Coom down into der Rhine!
Der ish pottles der Kaiser Charlemagne
    Vonce filled mit gold-red wine!"

Dat fetched him—he shtood all shpell pound;
    She pooled his coat-tails down,
She drawed him oonder der wasser,
    De maiden mit nodings on.

Breitmann in Paris

"Recessit in Franciam."

*"Et affectu pectoris,
    Et toto gestu corporis,
    Et scholares maxime,
    Qui festa colunt optime."*
—CARMINA BURANA, 13TH CENTURY.

Der teufel 's los in Bal Mabille,
    Dere 's hell-fire in de air,
De fiddlers can't blay noding else
    Boot Orphée aux Enfers:
Vot makes de beoples howl mit shoy?
    Da capo—bravo!—bis!!
It 's a Deutscher aus Amerikà:
    Hans Breitmann in Paris.

Dere's silber toughts vot might hafe peen,
  Dere's golden deeds vot *must*:
Der Hans ish come to Frankenland
  On one eternal bust.
Der same old rowdy Argonaut
  Vot hoont de same oldt vleece,
A hafin all de foon dere ish—
  Der Breitmann in Paris.

Mit a gal on eider shoulder
  A holdin py his beard,
He tantz de Cancan, sacrament!
  Dill all das Volk vas skeered.
Like a roarin hippopotamos,
  Mit a kangarunic shoomp,
Dey feared he'd smash de Catacombs,
  Each dime der Breitmann bump.

De pretty liddle cocodettes
  Lofe efery dings ish new,
"D'ou vient il donc ce grand M'sieu?
  O sacré nom de Dieu!"
In fain dey kicks deir veet on high,
  And sky like vlyin geese,
Dey can not kick de hat afay
  From Breitmann in Paris.

O vhere vas id der Breitmann life?
  Oopon de Rond Point gay,
Vot shdreet lie shoost pehind his house?
  La rue de Rabelais.
Aroundt de corner Harper's shtands
  Vhere Yankee drinks dey mill,
Vhile shdraight ahet, agross de shdreet,
  Dere lies de Bal Mabille.

Id's all along de Elysées,
  Id's oop de Boulevarce,
He's sampled all de weinshops,
  Und he's vinked at efery garçe.

Dou schveet plack-silken Gabrielle,
  O let me learn from dee,
If 'tis in lofe—or absinthe drunks,
  Dat dis wild ghost may pe?

Und dou may'st kneel in Notre Dame,
  Und veep avay dy sin,
Vhile I go vight at Barriere balls,
  Oontil mine poots cave in;
Boot if ve pray, or if ve sin—
  Vhile nodings ish refuse,
'Tis all de same in Paris here,
  So long ash *l'on s'amuse.*

O life, mein dear, at pest or vorst,
  Ish boot a vancy ball,
Its cratest shoy a vild *gallop*,
  Vhere madness goferns all.
Und should dey toorn ids gas-light off,
  Und nefer leafe a shbark,
Sdill I'd find my vay to Heafen—or—
  Dy lips, lofe, in de dark.

O crown your het mit roses, lofe!
  O keep a liddel sprung!
Oonendless wisdom ish but dis:
  To go it vhile you're yung!
Und Age vas nefer coom to him,
  To him Spring plooms afresh,
Who finds a livin' spirit in
  Der Teufel und der Flesh.

PHOEBE CARY

(1824–1871)

"The Day Is Done"

The day is done, and darkness
  From the wing of night is loosed,
As a feather is wafted downward
  From a chicken going to roost.

I see the lights of the baker
  Gleam through the rain and mist,
And a feeling of sadness comes o'er me,
  That I cannot well resist.

A feeling of sadness and *longing*,
  That is not like being sick,
And resembles sorrow only
  As a brick-bat resembles a brick.

Come, get for me some supper,—
  A good and regular meal,
That shall soothe this restless feeling,
  And banish the pain I feel.

Not from the pastry baker's,
  Not from the shops for cake,
I would n't give a farthing
  For all that they can make.

For, like the soup at dinner,
  Such things would but suggest
Some dishes more substantial,
  And to-night I want the best.

Go to some honest butcher,
  Whose beef is fresh and nice
As any they have in the city,
  And get a liberal slice.

Such things through days of labor,
   And nights devoid of ease,
For sad and desperate feelings
   Are wonderful remedies.

They have an astonishing power
   To aid and reinforce,
And come like the "Finally, brethren,"
   That follows a long discourse.

Then get me a tender sirloin
   From off the bench or hook,
And lend to its sterling goodness
   The science of the cook.

And the night shall be filled with comfort,
   And the cares with which it begun
Shall fold up their blankets like Indians,
   And silently cut and run.

Jacob

He dwelt among "apartments let,"
   About five stories high;
A man I thought that none would get,
   And very few would try.

A boulder, by a larger stone
   Half hidden in the mud,
Fair as a man when only one
   Is in the neighborhood.

He lived unknown, and few could tell
   When Jacob was not free;
But he has got a wife,—and O!
   The difference to me!

"When Lovely Woman"

When lovely woman wants a favor,
    And finds, too late, that man wont bend,
What earthly circumstance can save her
    From disappointment in the end?

The only way to bring him over,
    The last experiment to try,
Whether a husband or a lover,
    If he have feeling, is, to cry!

Advice Gratis to Certain Women

By a Woman

O, my strong-minded sisters, aspiring to vote,
And to row with your brothers, all in the same boat,
When you come out to speak to the public your mind,
Leave your tricks, and your airs, and your graces behind!

For instance, when you by the world would be seen
As reporter, or editor (first-class, I mean),
I think—just to come to the point in one line—
What you write will be finer, if 'tis not too fine.

Pray, don't let the thread of your subject be strung
With "golden," and "shimmer," "sweet," "filter," and
    "flung;"
Nor compel, by your style, all your readers to guess
You've been looking up words Webster marks *obs.*

And another thing: whatever else you may say,
Do keep personalities out of the way;
Don't try every sentence to make people see
What a dear, charming creature the writer must be!

Leave out affectations and pretty appeals;
Don't "drag yourself in by the neck and the heels,"
Your dear little boots, and your gloves; and take heed,
Nor pull your curls over men's eyes while they read.

Don't mistake me; I mean that the public's not home,
You must do as the Romans do, when you're in Rome;
I would have you be womanly, while you are wise;
'Tis the weak and the womanish tricks I despise.

On the other hand: don't write and dress in such styles
As astonish the natives, and frighten the isles;
Do look, on the platform, so folks in the show
Needn't ask, "Which are lions, and which tigers?" you
        know!

'Tis a good thing to write, and to rule in the state,
But to be a true, womanly woman is great:
And if ever you come to be that, 'twill be when
You can cease to be babies, nor try to be men!

BAYARD TAYLOR

(1825–1878)

from *The Echo Club*

Night the Second:
All or Nothing

Whoso answers my questions
  Knoweth more than me;
Hunger is but knowledge
  In a less degree:
Prophet, priest, and poet
  Oft prevaricate,
And the surest sentence
  Hath the greatest weight.

When upon my gaiters
  Drops the morning dew,
Somewhat of Life's riddle
  Soaks my spirit through.
I am buskined by the goddess
  Of Monadnock's crest,
And my wings extended
  Touch the East and West.

Or ever coal was hardened
  In the cells of earth,
Or flowed the founts of Bourbon,
  Lo! I had my birth.
I am crowned coeval
  With the Saurian eggs,
And my fancy firmly
  Stands on its own legs.

Wouldst thou know the secret
  Of the barberry-bush,
Catch the slippery whistle

Of the moulting thrush,
Dance upon the mushrooms,
Dive beneath the sea,
Or anything else remarkable,
Thou must follow me!

Night the Eighth:
Camerados

Everywhere, everywhere, following me;
Taking me by the buttonhole, pulling off my boots, hustling
    me with the elbows;
Sitting down with me to clams and the chowder-kettle;
Plunging naked at my side into the sleek, irascible surges;
Soothing me with the strain that I neither permit nor
    prohibit;
Flocking this way and that, reverent, eager, orotund,
    irrepressible;
Denser than sycamore leaves when the north-winds are
    scouring Paumanok;
What can I do to restrain them? Nothing, verily nothing.
Everywhere, everywhere, crying aloud for me;
Crying, I hear; and I satisfy them out of my nature;
And he that comes at the end of the feast shall find
    something over.
Whatever they want I give; though it be something else,
    they shall have it.
Drunkard, leper, Tammanyite, small-pox and cholera patient,
    shoddy, and codfish millionnaire,
And the beautiful young men, and the beautiful young
    women, all the same,
Crowding, hundreds of thousands, cosmical multitudes,
Buss me and hang on my hips and lean up to my shoulders,
Everywhere listening to my yawp and glad whenever they
    hear it;
Everywhere saying, say it, Walt, we believe it:
Everywhere, everywhere.

FRANCES ELLEN WATKINS HARPER

(1825–1911)

Bible Defence of Slavery

Take sackcloth of the darkest dye,
  And shroud the pulpits round!
Servants of Him that cannot lie,
  Sit mourning on the ground.

Let holy horror blanch each cheek,
  Pale every brow with fears;
And rocks and stones, if ye could speak,
  Ye well might melt to tears!

Let sorrow breathe in every tone,
  In every strain ye raise;
Insult not God's majestic throne
  With th' mockery of praise.

A "reverend" man, whose light should be
  The guide of age and youth,
Brings to the shrine of Slavery
  The sacrifice of truth!

For the direst wrong by man imposed,
  Since Sodom's fearful cry,
The word of life has been unclos'd,
  To give your God the lie.

Oh! when ye pray for heathen lands,
  And plead for their dark shores,
Remember Slavery's cruel hands
  Make heathens at your doors!

The Slave Auction

The sale began—young girls were there,
  Defenceless in their wretchedness,
Whose stifled sobs of deep despair
  Revealed their anguish and distress.

And mothers stood, with streaming eyes,
  And saw their dearest children sold;
Unheeded rose their bitter cries,
  While tyrants barter'd them for gold.

And woman, with her love and truth—
  For these in sable forms may dwell—
Gaz'd on the husband of her youth,
  With anguish none may paint or tell.

And men, whose sole crime was their hue,
  The impress of their Maker's hand,
And frail and shrinking children too,
  Were gathered in that mournful band.

Ye who have laid your lov'd to rest,
  And wept above their lifeless clay,
Know not the anguish of that breast,
  Whose lov'd are rudely torn away.

Ye may not know how desolate
  Are bosoms rudely forced to part,
And how a dull and heavy weight
  Will press the life-drops from the heart.

STEPHEN FOSTER

(1826–1864)

Old Folks at Home

Way down upon de Swanee ribber,
Far, far away,
Dere's wha my heart is turning ebber,
Dere's wha de old folks stay.
All up and down de whole creation,
Sadly I roam,
Still longing for de old plantation,
And for de old folks at home.

> *All de world am sad and dreary,*
> *Ebry where I roam,*
> *Oh! darkeys how my heart grows weary,*
> *Far from de old folks at home.*

All round de little farm I wandered
When I was young,
Den many happy days I squandered,
Many de songs I sung.
When I was playing wid my brudder
Happy was I—.
Oh! take me to my kind old mudder,
Dere let me live and die.

Chorus

One little hut among de bushes,
One dat I love,
Still sadly to my mem'ry rushes,
No matter where I rove
When will I see de bees a humming
All round de comb?
When will I hear de banjo tumming
Down in my good old home?

Chorus

My Old Kentucky Home, Good-Night!

The sun shines bright in the old Kentucky home,
'Tis summer, the darkies are gay,
The corn top's ripe and the meadow's in the bloom
While the birds make music all the day.
The young folks roll on the little cabin floor,
All merry, all happy and bright:
By'n by Hard Times comes a knocking at the door,
Then my old Kentucky Home, good night!

Weep no more, my lady, oh! weep no more to-day!
We will sing one song
For the old Kentucky Home,
For the old Kentucky Home, far away.

They hunt no more for the possum and the coon
On the meadow, the hill and the shore,
They sing no more by the glimmer of the moon,
On the bench by the old cabin door.
The day goes by like a shadow o'er the heart,
With sorrow where all was delight:
The time has come when the darkies have to part,
Then my old Kentucky Home, good-night!

Chorus

The head must bow and the back will have to bend,
Wherever the darkey may go:
A few more days, and the trouble all will end
In the field where the sugar-canes grow.
A few more days for to tote the weary load,
No matter 'twill never be light,
A few more days till we totter on the road,
Then my old Kentucky Home, good-night!

Chorus

ROBERT LOWRY

(1826–1899)

Beautiful River

*"And he showed me a pure River of Water of Life, clear as crystal,
proceeding out of the Throne of God and of the Lamb."*

—Rev. xxii. 1.

Shall we gather at the river
  Where bright angel feet have trod;
With its crystal tide forever
  Flowing by the throne of God?

Yes, we'll gather at the river,
  The beautiful, the beautiful river —
Gather with the saints at the river
That flows by the throne of God.

On the margin of the river,
  Washing up its silver spray,
We will walk and worship ever,
  All the happy, golden day.

Chorus

On the bosom of the river,
  Where the Saviour-king we own,
We shall meet, and sorrow never
  'Neath the glory of the throne.

Chorus

Ere we reach the shining river,
  Lay we every burden down;
Grace our spirits will deliver,
  And provide a robe and crown.

Chorus

At the smiling of the river,
  Rippling with the Saviour's face,
Saints, whom death will never sever,
  Lift their songs of saving grace.

Chorus

Soon we'll reach the shining river,
  Soon our pilgrimage will cease,
Soon our happy hearts will quiver
  With the melody of peace.

Chorus

ROSE TERRY COOKE

(1827–1892)

Blue-Beard's Closet

Fasten the chamber!
Hide the red key;
Cover the portal,
That eyes may not see.
Get thee to market,
To wedding and prayer;
Labor or revel,
The chamber is there!

In comes a stranger—
"Thy pictures how fine,
Titian or Guido,
Whose is the sign?"
Looks he behind them?
Ah! have a care!
"Here is a finer."
The chamber is there!

Fair spreads the banquet,
Rich the array;
See the bright torches
Mimicking day;
When harp and viol
Thrill the soft air,
Comes a light whisper:
The chamber is there!

Marble and painting,
Jasper and gold,
Purple from Tyrus,
Fold upon fold,
Blossoms and jewels,

Thy palace prepare:
Pale grows the monarch;
The chamber is there!

Once it was open
As shore to the sea;
White were the turrets,
Goodly to see;
All through the casements
Flowed the sweet air;
Now it is darkness;
The chamber is there!

Silence and horror
Brood on the walls;
Through every crevice
A little voice calls:
"Quicken, mad footsteps,
On pavement and stair;
Look not behind thee,
The chamber is there!"

Out of the gateway,
Through the wide world,
Into the tempest
Beaten and hurled,
Vain is thy wandering,
Sure thy despair,
Flying or staying,
The chamber is there!

Arachne

I watch her in the corner there,
As, restless, bold, and unafraid,
She slips and floats along the air
Till all her subtile house is made.

Her home, her bed, her daily food
All from that hidden store she draws;
She fashions it and knows it good,
By instinct's strong and sacred laws.

No tenuous threads to weave her nest,
She seeks and gathers there or here;
But spins it from her faithful breast,
Renewing still, till leaves are sere.

Then, worn with toil, and tired of life,
In vain her shining traps are set.
Her frost hath hushed the insect strife
And gilded flies her charm forget.

But swinging in the snares she spun,
She sways to every wintry wind:
Her joy, her toil, her errand done,
Her corse the sport of storms unkind.

Poor sister of the spinster clan!
I too from out my store within
My daily life and living plan,
My home, my rest, my pleasure spin.

I know thy heart when heartless hands
Sweep all that hard-earned web away:
Destroy its pearled and glittering bands,
And leave thee homeless by the way.

I know thy peace when all is done.
Each anchored thread, each tiny knot,
Soft shining in the autumn sun;
A sheltered, silent, tranquil lot.

I know what thou hast never known,
—Sad presage to a soul allowed;—
That not for life I spin, alone.
But day by day I spin my shroud.

FRANCIS MILES FINCH

(1827–1907)

The Blue and the Gray

"The women of Columbus, Mississippi, animated by nobler sentiments than are many of their sisters, have shown themselves impartial in their offerings made to the memory of the dead. They strewed flowers alike on the graves of the Confederate and of the National soldiers."

—New York Tribune.

By the flow of the inland river,
   Whence the fleets of iron have fled,
Where the blades of the grave-grass quiver,
   Asleep are the ranks of the dead;—
     Under the sod and the dew,
      Waiting the judgment day;—
     Under the one, the Blue;
      Under the other, the Gray.

These in the robings of glory,
   Those in the gloom of defeat,
All with the battle-blood gory,
   In the dusk of eternity meet;—
     Under the sod and the dew,
      Waiting the judgment day;—
     Under the laurel, the Blue;
      Under the willow, the Gray.

From the silence of sorrowful hours
   The desolate mourners go,
Lovingly laden with flowers
   Alike for the friend and the foe;—
     Under the sod and the dew,
      Waiting the judgment day;—
     Under the roses, the Blue;
      Under the lilies, the Gray.

So with an equal splendor
   The morning sun-rays fall,
With a touch, impartially tender,
   On the blossoms blooming for all;
      Under the sod and the dew,
         Waiting the judgment day;—
         Broidered with gold, the Blue;
            Mellowed with gold, the Gray.

So, when the Summer calleth,
   On forest and field of grain
With an equal murmur falleth
   The cooling drip of the rain;—
      Under the sod and the dew,
         Waiting the judgment day;—
         Wet with the rain, the Blue;
            Wet with the rain, the Gray.

Sadly, but not with upbraiding,
   The generous deed was done;
In the storm of the years that are fading,
   No braver battle was won;—
      Under the sod and the dew,
         Waiting the judgment day;—
         Under the blossoms, the Blue,
            Under the garlands, the Gray.

No more shall the war-cry sever,
   Or the winding rivers be red;
They banish our anger forever
   When they laurel the graves of our dead!
      Under the sod and the dew,
         Waiting the judgment day;—
         Love and tears for the Blue,
            Tears and love for the Gray.

JOHN ROLLIN RIDGE

(1827–1867)

Mount Shasta

Behold the dread Mt. Shasta, where it stands
Imperial midst the lesser heights, and, like
Some mighty unimpassioned mind, companionless
And cold. The storms of Heaven may beat in wrath
Against it, but it stands in unpolluted
Grandeur still; and from the rolling mists upheaves
Its tower of pride e'en purer than before.
The wintry showers and white-winged tempests leave
Their frozen tributes on its brow, and it
Doth make of them an everlasting crown.
Thus doth it, day by day and age by age,
Defy each stroke of time: still rising highest
Into Heaven!
Aspiring to the eagle's cloudless height,
No human foot has stained its snowy side;
No human breath has dimmed the icy mirror which
It holds unto the moon and stars and sov'reign sun.
We may not grow familiar with the secrets
Of its hoary top, whereon the Genius
Of that mountain builds his glorious throne!
Far lifted in the boundless blue, he doth
Encircle, with his gaze supreme, the broad
Dominions of the West, which lie beneath
His feet, in pictures of sublime repose
No artist ever drew. He sees the tall
Gigantic hills arise in silentness
And peace, and in the long review of distance
Range themselves in order grand. He sees the sunlight
Play upon the golden streams which through the valleys
Glide. He hears the music of the great and solemn sea,
And overlooks the huge old western wall
To view the birth-place of undying Melody!

Itself all light, save when some loftiest cloud
Doth for a while embrace its cold forbidding
Form, that monarch mountain casts its mighty
Shadow down upon the crownless peaks below,
That, like inferior minds to some great
Spirit, stand in strong contrasted littleness!
All through the long and Summery months of our
Most tranquil year, it points its icy shaft
On high, to catch the dazzling beams that fall
In showers of splendor round that crystal cone,
And roll in floods of far magnificence
Away from that lone, vast Reflector in
The dome of Heaven.
Still watchful of the fertile
Vale and undulating plains below, the grass
Grows greener in its shade, and sweeter bloom
The flowers. Strong purifier! From its snowy
Side the breezes cool are wafted to the "peaceful
Homes of men," who shelter at its feet, and love
To gaze upon its honored form, aye standing
There the guarantee of health and happiness.
Well might it win communities so blest
To loftier feelings and to nobler thoughts—
The great material symbol of eternal
Things! And well I ween, in after years, how
In the middle of his furrowed track the plowman
In some sultry hour will pause, and wiping
From his brow the dusty sweat, with reverence
Gaze upon that hoary peak. The herdsman
Oft will rein his charger in the plain, and drink
Into his inmost soul the calm sublimity;
And little children, playing on the green, shall
Cease their sport, and, turning to that mountain
Old, shall of their mother ask: "Who made it?"
And she shall answer,— "GOD!"

And well this Golden State shall thrive, if like
Its own Mt. Shasta, Sovereign Law shall lift
Itself in purer atmosphere—so high
That human feeling, human passion at its base

Shall lie subdued; e'en pity's tears shall on
Its summit freeze; to warm it e'en the sunlight
Of deep sympathy shall fail:
Its pure administration shall be like
The snow immaculate upon that mountain's brow!

A Cherokee Love Song

Oh come with me by moonlight, love,
    And let us seek the river's shore;
My light canoe awaits thee, love,
    The sweetest burden e'er it bore!

The soft, low winds are whispering there
    Of human beauty, human love,
And with approving faces, too,
    The stars are shining from above.

Come place thy small white hand in mine,
    My boat is 'neath those willow trees,
And with my practised arm, the oar
    Will ask no favor from the breeze.

Now, now we're on the waters, love,
    Alone upon the murmuring tide—
Alone! but why should we regret,
    If there were none on earth beside?

What matters it, if all were gone?
    Thy bird-like voice could yet beguile,
And earth were heaven's substitute,
    If thou were left to make it smile!

Oh, mark how soft the dipping oar,
    That silent cleaves the yielding blue—
Oh list, the low, sweet melody
    Of waves that beat our vessel too!

Oh, look to heaven, how pure it seems,
    No cloud to dim, no blot, no stain,
And say — if we refuse to love,
    Ought we to hope or smile again?

That island green, with roses gemmed,
    Let's seek it, love — how sweet a spot?
Then let the hours of night speed on,
    We live to love — it matters not!

JOHN TOWNSEND TROWBRIDGE

(1827–1916)

Circumstance

Stalking before the lords of life, one came,
　A Titan shape! But often he will crawl,
　Their most subservient, helpful, humble thrall;
Swift as the light, or sluggish, laggard, lame;
Stony-eyed archer, launching without aim
　Arrows and lightnings, heedless how they fall,—
　Blind Circumstance, that makes or baffles all,
Happiness, length of days, power, riches, fame.
Could we but take each wingèd chance aright!
　A timely word let fall, a wind-blown germ,
　　May crown our glebe with many a golden sheaf;
A thought may touch and edge our life with light,
　Fill all its sphere, as yonder crescent worm
　　Brightens upon the old moon's dusky leaf.

The Old Lobsterman

Cape Arundel, Kennebunkport, Maine

Just back from a beach of sand and shells,
　And shingle the tides leave oozy and dank,
Summer and winter the old man dwells
　In his low brown house on the river bank.
Tempest and sea-fog sweep the hoar
And wrinkled sand-drifts round his door,
Where often I see him sit, as gray
And weather-beaten and lonely as they.

Coarse grasses wave on the arid swells
　In the wind; and two bright poplar-trees
Seem hung all over with silver bells
　That tinkle and twinkle in sun and breeze.

544

All else is desolate sand and stone:
And here the old lobsterman lives alone:
Nor other companionship has he
But to sit in his house and gaze at the sea.

A furlong or more away to the south,
    On the bar beyond the huge sea-walls
That keep the channel and guard its mouth,
    The high, curved billow whitens and falls;
And the racing tides through the granite gate,
On their wild errands that will not wait,
Forever, unresting, to and fro,
Course with impetuous ebb and flow.

They bury the barnacled ledge, and make
    Into every inlet and crooked creek,
And flood the flats with a shining lake,
    Which the proud ship plows with foam at her beak:
The ships go up to yonder town,
Or over the sea their hulls sink down,
And many a pleasure pinnace rides
On the restless backs of the rushing tides.

I try to fathom the gazer's dreams,
    But little I gain from his gruff replies;
Far off, far off the spirit seems,
    As he looks at me with those strange gray eyes;
Never a hail from the shipwrecked heart!
Mysterious oceans seem to part
The desolate man from all his kind—
The Selkirk of his lonely mind.

He has growls for me when I bring him back
    My unused bait—his way to thank;
And a good shrill curse for the fishing-smack
    That jams his dory against the bank;
But never a word of love to give
For love,—ah! how can he bear to live?
I marvel, and make my own heart ache
With thinking how his must sometimes break.

Solace he finds in the sea, no doubt.
  To catch the ebb he is up and away.
I see him silently pushing out
  On the broad bright gleam at break of day;
And watch his lessening dory toss
On the purple crests as he pulls across,
Round reefs where silvery surges leap,
And meets the dawn on the rosy deep.

His soul, is it open to sea and sky?
  His spirit, alive to sound and sight?
What wondrous tints on the water lie —
  Wild, wavering, liquid realm of light!
Between two glories looms the shape
Of the wood-crested, cool green cape,
Sloping all round to foam-laced ledge,
And cavern and cove, at the bright sea's edge.

He makes for the floats that mark the spots,
  And rises and falls on the sweeping swells,
Ships oars, and pulls his lobster-pots,
  And tumbles the tangled claws and shells
In the leaky bottom; and bails his skiff;
While the slow waves thunder along the cliff,
And foam far away where sun and mist
Edge all the region with amethyst.

I watch him, and fancy how, a boy,
  Round these same reefs, in the rising sun,
He rowed and rocked, and shouted for joy,
  As over the boat-side one by one
He lifted and launched his lobster-traps,
And reckoned his gains, and dreamed, perhaps,
Of a future as glorious, vast and bright
As the ocean, unrolled in the morning light.

He quitted his skiff for a merchant-ship;
  Was sailor-boy, mate, — gained skill and command;
And brought home once from a fortunate trip
  A wife he had found in a foreign land:

So the story is told: then settled down
With the nabobs of his native town,—
Jolly old skippers, bluff and hale,
Who owned the bottoms they used to sail.

Does he sometimes now, in his loneliness,
    Live over again that happy time,
Beguile his poverty and distress
    With pictures of his prosperous prime?
Does ever, at dusk, a fond young bride
Start forth and sit by the old man's side;
Children frolic, and friends look in;
With all the blessings that might have been?

Yet might not be! The same sad day
    Saw wife and babe to the churchyard borne;
And he sailed away, he sailed away,—
    For that is the sailor's way to mourn.
And ever, 't is said, as he sailed and sailed,
Heart grew reckless and fortune failed,
Till old age drifted him back to shore,
To his hut and his lobster-pots once more.

The house is empty, the board is bare;
    His dish he scours, his jacket he mends;
And now 't is the dory that needs repair;
    He fishes; his lobster-traps he tends;
And, rowing at nightfall many a mile,
Brings floodwood home to his winter pile;
Then his fire 's to kindle, and supper to cook;
The storm his music, his thoughts his book.

He sleeps, he wakes; and this is his life.
    Nor kindred nor friend in all the earth;
Nor laughter of child, nor gossip of wife;
    Not even a cat to his silent hearth!
Only the sand-hills, wrinkled and hoar,
Bask in the sunset, round his door,
Where now I can see him sit, as gray
And weather-beaten and lonely as they.

HENRY TIMROD

(1828–1867)

Dreams

Who first said "false as dreams?" Not one who saw
  Into the wild and wondrous world they sway;
No thinker who hath read their mystic law;
  No Poet who hath weaved them in his lay.

Else had he known that through the human breast
  Cross and recross a thousand fleeting gleams,
That, passed unnoticed in the day's unrest,
  Come out at night, like stars, in shining dreams;

That minds too busy or to dull to mark
  The dim suggestions of the noisier hours,
By dreams in the deep silence of the dark,
  Are roused at midnight with their folded powers.

Like that old fount beneath Dodona's oaks,
  That, dry and voiceless in the garish noon,
When the calm night arose with modest looks,
  Caught with full wave the sparkle of the moon.

If, now and then, a ghastly shape glide in,
  And fright us with its horrid gloom or glee,
It is the ghost of some forgotten sin
  We failed to exorcise on bended knee.

And that sweet face which only yesternight
  Came to thy solace, dreamer (did'st thou read
The blessing in its eyes of tearful light?)
  Was but the spirit of some gentle deed.

Each has its lesson; for our dreams in sooth,
  Come they in shape of demons, gods, or elves,
Are allegories with deep hearts of truth
  That tell us solemn secrets of ourselves.

Ethnogenesis

*Written during the meeting of the first Southern Congress,
at Montgomery, February, 1861.*

I.

Hath not the morning dawned with added light?
And will not evening call another star
Out of the infinite regions of the night,
To mark this day in Heaven? At last, we are
A nation among nations; and the world
Shall soon behold in many a distant port
      Another Flag unfurled!
Now, come what may, whose favor need we court?
And, under God, whose thunder need we fear?
      Thank Him who placed us here
Beneath so kind a sky—the very sun
Takes part with us; and on our errands run
All breezes of the ocean; dew and rain
Do noiseless battle for us; and the Year,
And all the gentle daughters in her train,
March in our ranks, and in our service wield
      Long spears of golden grain!
A yellow blossom as her fairy shield,
June flings her azure banner to the wind,
  While in the order of their birth
Her sisters pass, and many an ample field
Grows white beneath their steps, till now, behold
      Its endless sheets unfold
THE SNOW OF SOUTHERN SUMMERS! Let the earth
Rejoice! beneath those fleeces soft and warm
      Our happy land shall sleep
      In a repose as deep
  As if we lay intrenched behind
Whole leagues of Russian ice and Arctic storm!

II.

And what if, mad with wrongs themselves have wrought,
  In their own treachery caught,
  By their own fears made bold,
  And leagued with him of old,
Who long since in the limits of the North
Set up his evil throne, and warred with God—
What if, both mad and blinded in their rage,
Our foes should fling us down their mortal gage,
And with a hostile step profane our sod!
We shall not shrink, my brothers, but go forth
To meet them, marshalled by the Lord of Hosts,
And overshadowed by the mighty ghosts
Of Moultrie and of Eutaw—who shall foil
Auxiliars such as these? Nor these alone,
  But every stock and stone
  Shall help us: but the very soil,
And all the generous wealth it gives to toil,
And all for which we love our noble land,
Shall fight beside, and through us, sea and strand,
  The heart of woman, and her hand,
Tree, fruit, and flower, and every influence,
  Gentle, or grave, or grand;
  The winds in our defence
Shall seem to blow; to us the hills shall lend
  Their firmness and their calm;
And in our stiffened sinews we shall blend
  The strength of pine and palm!

III.

Nor would we shun the battle-ground,
  Though weak as we are strong;
Call up the clashing elements around,
  And test the right and wrong!
On one side, creeds that dare to teach
What Christ and Paul refrained to preach;
Codes built upon a broken pledge,
And Charity that whets a poniard's edge;
Fair schemes that leave the neighboring poor

To starve and shiver at the schemer's door,
While in the world's most liberal ranks enrolled,
He turns some vast philanthropy to gold;
Religion, taking every mortal form
But that a pure and Christian faith makes warm,
Where not to vile fanatic passion urged,
Or not in vague philosophies submerged,
Repulsive with all Pharisaic leaven,
And making laws to stay the laws of Heaven!
And on the other, scorn of sordid gain,
Unblemished honor, truth without a stain,
Faith, justice, reverence, charitable wealth,
And, for the poor and humble, laws which give,
Not the mean right to buy the right to live,
     But life, and home, and health!
To doubt the end were want of trust in God,
     Who, if he has decreed
  That we must pass a redder sea
Than that which rang to Miriam's holy glee,
     Will surely raise at need
     A Moses with his rod!

IV.

But let our fears—if fears we have—be still,
And turn us to the future! Could we climb
Some mighty Alp, and view the coming time,
We should indeed behold a sight to fill
     Our eyes with happy tears!
Not for the glories which a hundred years
Shall bring us; not for lands from sea to sea,
And wealth, and power, and peace, though these shall be;
But for the distant peoples we shall bless,
And the hushed murmurs of a world's distress:
For, to give labor to the poor,
     The whole sad planet o'er,
And save from want and crime the humblest door,
Is one among the many ends for which
     God makes us great and rich!
The hour perchance is not yet wholly ripe

When all shall own it, but the type
Whereby we shall be known in every land
Is that vast gulf which laves our Southern strand,
And through the cold, untempered ocean pours
Its genial streams, that far off Arctic shores
May sometimes catch upon the softened breeze
Strange tropic warmth and hints of summer seas.

The Cotton Boll

While I recline
At ease beneath
This immemorial pine,
Small sphere!
(By dusky fingers brought this morning here
And shown with boastful smiles),
I turn thy cloven sheath,
Through which the soft white fibres peer,
That, with their gossamer bands,
Unite, like love, the sea-divided lands,
And slowly, thread by thread,
Draw forth the folded strands,
Than which the trembling line,
By whose frail help yon startled spider fled
Down the tall spear-grass from his swinging bed,
Is scarce more fine;
And as the tangled skein
Unravels in my hands,
Betwixt me and the noonday light,
A veil seems lifted, and for miles and miles
The landscape broadens on my sight,
As, in the little boll, there lurked a spell
Like that which, in the ocean shell,
With mystic sound,
Breaks down the narrow walls that hem us round,
And turns some city lane
Into the restless main,
With all his capes and isles!

Yonder bird
Which floats, as if at rest,
In those blue tracts above the thunder, where
No vapors cloud the stainless air,
And never sound is heard,
Unless at such rare time
When, from the City of the Blest,
Rings down some golden chime,
Sees not from his high place
So vast a cirque of summer space
As widens round me in one mighty field,
Which, rimmed by seas and sands,
Doth hail its earliest daylight in the beams
Of gray Atlantic dawns;
And, broad as realms made up of many lands,
Is lost afar
Behind the crimson hills and purple lawns
Of sunset, among plains which roll their streams
Against the Evening Star!
And lo!
To the remotest point of sight,
Although I gaze upon no waste of snow,
The endless field is white;
And the whole landscape glows,
For many a shining league away,
With such accumulated light
As Polar lands would flash beneath a tropic day!
Nor lack there (for the vision grows,
And the small charm within my hands—
More potent even than the fabled one,
Which oped whatever golden mystery
Lay hid in fairy wood or magic vale,
The curious ointment of the Arabian tale—
Beyond all mortal sense
Doth stretch my sight's horizon, and I see
Beneath its simple influence,
As if, with Uriel's crown,
I stood in some great temple of the Sun,
And looked, as Uriel, down)!
Nor lack there pastures rich and fields all green

With all the common gifts of God,
For temperate airs and torrid sheen
Weave Edens of the sod;
Through lands which look one sea of billowy gold
Broad rivers wind their devious ways;
A hundred isles in their embraces fold
A hundred luminous bays;
And through yon purple haze
Vast mountains lift their plumed peaks cloud-crowned;
And, save where up their sides the ploughman creeps,
An unhewn forest girds them grandly round,
In whose dark shades a future navy sleeps!
Ye Stars, which though unseen, yet with me gaze
Upon this loveliest fragment of the earth!
Thou Sun, that kindlest all thy gentlest rays
Above it, as to light a favorite hearth!
Ye Clouds, that in your temples in the West
See nothing brighter than its humblest flowers!
And, you, ye Winds, that on the ocean's breast
Are kissed to coolness ere ye reach its bowers!
Bear witness with me in my song of praise,
And tell the world that, since the world began,
No fairer land hath fired a poet's lays,
Or given a home to man!

But these are charms already widely blown!
His be the meed whose pencil's trace
Hath touched our very swamps with grace,
And round whose tuneful way
All Southern laurels bloom;
The Poet of "The Woodlands," unto whom
Alike are known
The flute's low breathing and the trumpet's tone,
And the soft west-wind's sighs;
But who shall utter all the debt,
O, Land! wherein all powers are met
That bind a people's heart,
The world doth owe thee at this day,
And which it never can repay,
Yet scarcely deigns to own!

Where sleeps the poet who shall fitly sing
The source wherefrom doth spring
That mighty commerce which, confined
To the mean channels of no selfish mart,
Goes out to every shore
Of this broad earth, and throngs the sea with ships
That bear no thunders; hushes hungry lips
In alien lands;
Joins with a delicate web remotest strands;
And gladdening rich and poor,
Doth gild Parisian domes,
Or feed the cottage-smoke of English homes,
And only bounds its blessings by mankind!
In offices like these, thy mission lies,
My Country! and it shall not end
As long as rain shall fall and Heaven bend
In blue above thee; though thy foes be hard
And cruel as their weapons, it shall guard
Thy hearth-stones as a bulwark; make thee great
In white and bloodless state;
And, haply, as the years increase —
Still working through its humbler reach
With that large wisdom which the ages teach —

Revive the half-dead dream of universal peace!
As men who labor in that mine
Of Cornwall, hollowed out beneath the bed
Of ocean, when a storm rolls overhead,
Hear the dull booming of the world of brine
Above them, and a mighty muffled roar
Of winds and waters, yet toil calmly on,
And split the rock, and pile the massive ore,
Or carve a niche, or shape the arched roof;
So I, as calmly, weave my woof
Of song, chanting the days to come,
Unsilenced, though the quiet summer air
Stirs with the bruit of battles, and each dawn
Wakes from its starry silence to the hum
Of many gathering armies. Still,
In that we sometimes hear,

Upon the Northern winds the voice of woe
Not wholly drowned in triumph, though I know
The end must crown us, and a few brief years
Dry all our tears,
I may not sing too gladly. To Thy will
Resigned, O Lord! we cannot all forget
That there is much even Victory must regret.
And, therefore, not too long
From the great burthen of our country's wrong
Delay our just release!
And, if it may be, save
These sacred fields of peace
From stain of patriot or of hostile blood!
Oh, help us Lord! to roll the crimson flood
Back on its course, and, while our banners wing
Northward, strike with us! till the Goth shall cling
To his own blasted altar-stones, and crave
Mercy; and we shall grant it, and dictate
The lenient future of his fate
There, where some rotting ships and crumbling quays
Shall one day mark the Port which ruled the Western seas.

PAUL HAMILTON HAYNE

(1830–1886)

October

The passionate Summer's dead! the sky's a-glow,
  With roseate flushes of matured desire,
The winds at eve are musical and low,
  As sweeping chords of a lamenting lyre,
  Far up among the pillared clouds of fire,
Whose pomp of strange procession upward rolls,
With gorgeous blazonry of pictured folds,
  To celebrate the Summer's past renown;
  Ah, me! how regally the Heavens look down,
O'ershadowing beautiful autumnal woods,
  And harvest fields with hoarded increase brown,
And deep-toned majesty of golden floods,
  That raise their solemn dirges to the sky,
  To swell the purple pomp that floateth by.

On the Occurrence of a Spell of Arctic Weather in May, 1858

We thought that Winter with his hungry pack
Of hounding Winds had closed his dreary chase,—
For virgin Spring, with arch, triumphant face,
Lightly descending, had strewed o'er his track
Gay flowers that hid the stormy season's wrack.
Vain thought! for, wheeling on his northward path,
And girt by all his hungry Blasts, in wrath
The shrill-voiced Huntsman hurries swiftly back,—
The frightened vernal Zephyrs shrink and die
Through the chilled forest,—the rare blooms expire,—
And Spring herself, too terror-struck to fly,
Seized by the ravening Winds with fury dire,
Dies 'mid the scarlet flowers that round her lie,
Like waning flames of some rich funeral fire!

HELEN HUNT JACKSON

(1830—1885)

My Lighthouses

At westward window of a palace gray,
Which its own secret still so safely keeps
That no man now its builder's name can say,
I lie and idly sun myself to-day,
Dreaming awake far more than one who sleeps,
Serenely glad, although my gladness weeps.

I look across the harbor's misty blue,
And find and lose that magic shifting line
Where sky one shade less blue meets sea, and through
The air I catch one flush as if it knew
Some secret of that meeting, which no sign
Can show to eyes so far and dim as mine.

More ships than I can count build mast by mast
Gay lattice-work with waving green and red
Across my window-panes. The voyage past,
They crowd to anchorage so glad, so fast,
Gliding like ghosts, with noiseless breath and tread,
Mooring like ghosts, with noiseless iron and lead.

"O ships and patient men who fare by sea,"
I stretch my hands and vainly questioning cry,
"Sailed ye from west? How many nights could ye
Tell by the lights just where my dear and free
And lovely land lay sleeping? Passed ye by
Some danger safe, because her fires were nigh?"

Ah me! my selfish yearning thoughts forget
How darkness but a hand's-breadth from the coast
With danger in an evil league is set!
Ah! helpless ships and men more helpless yet,
Who trust the land-lights' short and empty boast;
The lights ye bear aloft and prayers avail ye most.

But I—ah, patient men who fare by sea,
Ye would but smile to hear this empty speech,—
I have such beacon-lights to burn for me,
In that dear west so lovely, new, and free,
That evil league by day, by night, can teach
No spell whose harm my little bark can reach.

No towers of stone uphold those beacon-lights;
No distance hides them, and no storm can shake;
In valleys they light up the darkest nights,
They outshine sunny days on sunny heights;
They blaze from every house where sleep or wake
My own who love me for my own poor sake.

Each thought they think of me lights road of flame
Across the seas; no travel on it tires
My heart. I go if they but speak my name;
From Heaven I should come and go the same,
And find this glow forestalling my desires.
My darlings, do you hear me? Trim the fires!

Crossed Threads

The silken threads by viewless spinners spun,
Which float so idly on the summer air,
And help to make each summer morning fair,
Shining like silver in the summer sun,
Are caught by wayward breezes, one by one,
And blown to east and west and fastened there,
Weaving on all the roads their sudden snare.
No sign which road doth safest, freest run,
The wingèd insects know, that soar so gay
To meet their death upon each summer day.
How dare we any human deed arraign;
Attempt to reckon any moment's cost;
Or any pathway trust as safe and plain
Because we see not where the threads have crossed?

September

The golden-rod is yellow;
　The corn is turning brown;
The trees in apple orchards
　With fruit are bending down.

The gentian's bluest fringes
　Are curling in the sun;
In dusty pods the milkweed
　Its hidden silk has spun.

The sedges flaunt their harvest,
　In every meadow nook;
And asters by the brook-side
　Make asters in the brook.

From dewy lanes at morning
　The grapes' sweet odors rise;
At noon the roads all flutter
　With yellow butterflies.

By all these lovely tokens
　September days are here,
With summer's best of weather,
　And autumn's best of cheer.

But none of all this beauty
　Which floods the earth and air
Is unto me the secret
　Which makes September fair.

'T is a thing which I remember;
　To name it thrills me yet:
One day of one September
　I never can forget.

EMILY DICKINSON

(1830–1886)

Success is counted sweetest
By those who ne'er succeed.
To comprehend a nectar
Requires sorest need.

Not one of all the purple Host
Who took the Flag today
Can tell the definition
So clear of Victory

As he defeated—dying—
On whose forbidden ear
The distant strains of triumph
Burst agonized and clear!

———

Our lives are Swiss—
So still—so Cool—
Till some odd afternoon
The Alps neglect their Curtains
And we look farther on!

Italy stands the other side!
While like a guard between—
The solemn Alps—
The siren Alps
Forever intervene!

———

Bring me the sunset in a cup,
Reckon the morning's flagons up
And say how many Dew,
Tell me how far the morning leaps—
Tell me what time the weaver sleeps
Who spun the breadths of blue!

Write me how many notes there be
In the new Robin's ecstasy
Among astonished boughs—
How many trips the Tortoise makes—
How many cups the Bee partakes,
The Debauchee of Dews!

Also, who laid the Rainbow's piers,
Also, who leads the docile spheres
By withes of supple blue?
Whose fingers string the stalactite—
Who counts the wampum of the night
To see that none is due?

Who built this little Alban House
And shut the windows down so close
My spirit cannot see?
Who'll let me out some gala day
With implements to fly away,
Passing Pomposity?

———————

A *Wounded* Deer—leaps highest—
I've heard the Hunter tell—
'Tis but the Ecstasy of *death*—
And then the Brake is still!

The *Smitten* Rock that gushes!
The *trampled* Steel that springs!
A Cheek is always redder
Just where the Hectic stings!

Mirth is the Mail of Anguish—
In which it Cautious Arm,
Lest anybody spy the blood
And "you're hurt" exclaim!

"Faith" is a fine invention
    When Gentlemen can *see*—
But *Microscopes* are prudent
    In an Emergency.

I taste a liquor never brewed—
From Tankards scooped in Pearl—
Not all the Vats upon the Rhine
Yield such an Alcohol!

Inebriate of Air—am I—
And Debauchee of Dew—
Reeling—thro endless summer days—
From inns of Molten Blue—

When "Landlords" turn the drunken Bee
Out of the Foxglove's door—
When Butterflies—renounce their "drams"—
I shall but drink the more!

Till Seraphs swing their snowy Hats—
And Saints—to windows run—
To see the little Tippler
Leaning against the—Sun—

Safe in their Alabaster Chambers—
Untouched by Morning—
And untouched by Noon—
Lie the meek members of the Resurrection—
Rafter of Satin—and Roof of Stone!

Grand go the Years—in the Crescent—above them—
Worlds scoop their Arcs—
And Firmaments—row—
Diadems—drop—and Doges—surrender—
Soundless as dots—on a Disc of Snow—

———————

Wild Nights—Wild Nights!
Were I with thee
Wild Nights should be
Our luxury!

Futile—the Winds—
To a Heart in port—
Done with the Compass—
Done with the Chart!

Rowing in Eden—
Ah, the Sea!
Might I but moor—Tonight—
In Thee!

———————

"Hope" is the thing with feathers—
That perches in the soul—
And sings the tune without the words—
And never stops—at all—

And sweetest—in the Gale—is heard—
And sore must be the storm—
That could abash the little Bird
That kept so many warm—

I've heard it in the chillest land—
And on the strangest Sea—
Yet, never, in Extremity,
It asked a crumb—of Me.

There's a certain Slant of light,
Winter Afternoons—
That oppresses, like the Heft
Of Cathedral Tunes—

Heavenly Hurt, it gives us—
We can find no scar,
But internal difference,
Where the Meanings, are—

None may teach it—Any—
'Tis the Seal Despair—
An imperial affliction
Sent us of the Air—

When it comes, the Landscape listens—
Shadows—hold their breath—
When it goes, 'tis like the Distance
On the look of Death—

A single Screw of Flesh
Is all that pins the Soul
That stands for Deity, to Mine,
Upon my side the Veil—

Once witnessed of the Gauze—
Its name is put away
As far from mine, as if no plight
Had printed yesterday,

In tender—solemn Alphabet,
My eyes just turned to see,
When it was smuggled by my sight
Into Eternity—

More Hands—to hold—These are but Two—
One more new-mailed Nerve
Just granted, for the Peril's sake—
Some striding—Giant—Love—

So greater than the Gods can show,
They slink before the Clay,
That not for all their Heaven can boast
Will let its Keepsake—go

I felt a Funeral, in my Brain,
And Mourners to and fro
Kept treading—treading—till it seemed
That Sense was breaking through—

And when they all were seated,
A Service, like a Drum—
Kept beating—beating—till I thought
My Mind was going numb—

And then I heard them lift a Box
And creak across my Soul
With those same Boots of Lead, again,
Then Space—began to toll,

As all the Heavens were a Bell,
And Being, but an Ear,
And I, and Silence, some strange Race
Wrecked, solitary, here —

And then a Plank in Reason, broke,
And I dropped down, and down —
And hit a World, at every plunge,
And Finished knowing — then —

A Clock stopped —
Not the Mantel's —
Geneva's farthest skill
Can't put the puppet bowing —
That just now dangled still —

An awe came on the Trinket!
The Figures hunched, with pain —
Then quivered out of Decimals —
Into Degreeless Noon —

It will not stir for Doctors —
This Pendulum of snow —
This Shopman importunes it —
While cool — concernless No —

Nods from the Gilded pointers —
Nods from the Seconds slim —
Decades of Arrogance between
The Dial life —
And Him —

I'm Nobody! Who are you?
Are you—Nobody—Too?
Then there's a pair of us!
Don't tell! they'd advertise—you know!

How dreary—to be—Somebody!
How public—like a Frog—
To tell one's name—the livelong June—
To an admiring Bog!

———

I reason, Earth is short—
And Anguish—absolute—
And many hurt,
But, what of that?

I reason, we could die—
The best Vitality
Cannot excel Decay,
But, what of that?

I reason, that in Heaven—
Somehow, it will be even—
Some new Equation, given—
But, what of that?

———

The Soul selects her own Society—
Then—shuts the Door—
To her divine Majority—
Present no more—

Unmoved—she notes the Chariots—pausing—
At her low Gate—
Unmoved—an Emperor be kneeling
Upon her Mat—

I've known her—from an ample nation—
Choose One—
Then—close the Valves of her attention—
Like Stone—

———————

The Soul's Superior instants
Occur to Her—alone—
When friend—and Earth's occasion
Have infinite withdrawn—

Or She—Herself—ascended
To too remote a Height
For lower Recognition
Than Her Omnipotent—

This Mortal Abolition
Is seldom—but as fair
As Apparition—subject
To Autocratic Air—

Eternity's disclosure
To favorites—a few—
Of the Colossal substance
Of Immortality

———————

I cannot dance upon my Toes—
No Man instructed me—
But oftentimes, among my mind,
A Glee possesseth me,

That had I Ballet knowledge—
Would put itself abroad
In Pirouette to blanch a Troupe—
Or lay a Prima, mad,

And though I had no Gown of Gauze—
No Ringlet, to my Hair,
Nor hopped to Audiences—like Birds,
One Claw upon the Air,

Nor tossed my shape in Eider Balls,
Nor rolled on wheels of snow
Till I was out of sight, in sound,
The House encore me so—

Nor any know I know the Art
I mention—easy—Here—
Nor any Placard boast me—
It's full as Opera—

A Bird came down the Walk—
He did not know I saw—
He bit an Angleworm in halves
And ate the fellow, raw,

And then he drank a Dew
From a convenient Grass—
And then hopped sidewise to the Wall
To let a Beetle pass—

He glanced with rapid eyes
That hurried all around—
They looked like frightened Beads, I thought—
He stirred his Velvet Head

Like one in danger, Cautious,
I offered him a Crumb
And he unrolled his feathers
And rowed him softer home—

Than Oars divide the Ocean,
Too silver for a seam—
Or Butterflies, off Banks of Noon
Leap, plashless as they swim.

I know that He exists.
Somewhere— in Silence—
He has hid his rare life
From our gross eyes.

'Tis an instant's play.
'Tis a fond Ambush—
Just to make Bliss
Earn her own surprise!

But—should the play
Prove piercing earnest—
Should the glee—glaze—
In Death's—stiff—stare—

Would not the fun
Look too expensive!
Would not the jest--
Have crawled too far!

After great pain, a formal feeling comes—
The Nerves sit ceremonious, like Tombs—
The stiff Heart questions was it He, that bore,
And Yesterday, or Centuries before?

The Feet, mechanical, go round—
Of Ground, or Air, or Ought—
A Wooden way
Regardless grown,
A Quartz contentment, like a stone—

This is the Hour of Lead—
Remembered, if outlived,
As Freezing persons, recollect the Snow—
First—Chill—then Stupor—then the letting go—

I dreaded that first Robin, so,
But He is mastered, now,
I'm some accustomed to Him grown,
He hurts a little, though—

I thought if I could only live
Till that first Shout got by—
Not all Pianos in the Woods
Had power to mangle me—

I dared not meet the Daffodils—
For fear their Yellow Gown
Would pierce me with a fashion
So foreign to my own—

I wished the Grass would hurry—
So—when 'twas time to see—
He'd be too tall, the tallest one
Could stretch—to look at me—

I could not bear the Bees should come,
I wished they'd stay away
In those dim countries where they go,
What word had they, for me?

They're here, though; not a creature failed—
No Blossom stayed away
In gentle deference to me—
The Queen of Calvary—

Each one salutes me, as he goes,
And I, my childish Plumes,
Lift, in bereaved acknowledgment
Of their unthinking Drums—

A precious—mouldering pleasure—'tis—
To meet an Antique Book—
In just the Dress his Century wore—
A privilege—I think—

His venerable Hand to take—
And warming in our own—
A passage back—or two—to make—
To Times when he—was young—

His quaint opinions—to inspect—
His thought to ascertain
On Themes concern our mutual mind—
The Literature of Man—

What interested Scholars—most—
What Competitions ran—
When Plato—was a Certainty—
And Sophocles—a Man—

When Sappho—was a living Girl—
And Beatrice wore
The Gown that Dante—deified—
Facts Centuries before

He traverses—familiar—
As One should come to Town—
And tell you all your Dreams—were true—
He lived—where Dreams were born—

His presence is Enchantment—
You beg him not to go—
Old Volumes shake their Vellum Heads
And tantalize—just so—

A Visitor in Marl—
Who influences Flowers—
Till they are orderly as Busts—
And Elegant—as Glass—

Who visits in the Night—
And just before the Sun—
Concludes his glistening interview—
Caresses—and is gone—

But whom his fingers touched—
And where his feet have run—
And whatsoever Mouth he kissed—
Is as it had not been—

———————

The Wind—tapped like a tired Man—
And like a Host—"Come in"
I boldly answered—entered then
My Residence within

A Rapid—footless Guest—
To offer whom a Chair
Were as impossible as hand
A Sofa to the Air—

No Bone had He to bind Him—
His Speech was like the Push
Of numerous Humming Birds at once
From a superior Bush—

His Countenance—a Billow—
His Fingers, as He passed
Let go a music—as of tunes
Blown tremulous in Glass—

He visited—still flitting—
Then like a timid Man
Again, He tapped—'twas flurriedly—
And I became alone—

This is my letter to the World
That never wrote to Me—
The simple News that Nature told—
With tender Majesty

Her Message is committed
To Hands I cannot see—
For love of Her—Sweet—countrymen—
Judge tenderly—of Me

I died for Beauty—but was scarce
Adjusted in the Tomb
When One who died for Truth, was lain
In an adjoining Room—

He questioned softly "Why I failed"?
"For Beauty", I replied—
"And I—for Truth—Themself are One—
We Brethren, are", He said—

And so, as Kinsmen, met a Night—
We talked between the Rooms—
Until the Moss had reached our lips—
And covered up—our names—

I heard a Fly buzz—when I died—
The Stillness in the Room
Was like the Stillness in the Air—
Between the Heaves of Storm—

The Eyes around—had wrung them dry—
And Breaths were gathering firm
For that last Onset—when the King
Be witnessed—in the Room—

I willed my Keepsakes—Signed away
What portion of me be
Assignable—and then it was
There interposed a Fly—

With Blue—uncertain stumbling Buzz—
Between the light—and me—
And then the Windows failed—and then
I could not see to see—

It was not Death, for I stood up,
And all the Dead, lie down—
It was not Night, for all the Bells
Put out their Tongues, for Noon.

It was not Frost, for on my Flesh
I felt Siroccos—crawl—
Nor Fire—for just my Marble feet
Could keep a Chancel, cool—

And yet, it tasted, like them all,
The Figures I have seen
Set orderly, for Burial,
Reminded me, of mine—

As if my life were shaven,
And fitted to a frame,
And could not breathe without a key,
And 'twas like Midnight, some—

When everything that ticked—has stopped—
And Space stares all around—
Or Grisly frosts—first Autumn morns,
Repeal the Beating Ground—

But, most, like Chaos—Stopless—cool—
Without a Chance, or Spar—
Or even a Report of Land—
To justify—Despair.

———————

I started Early—Took my Dog—
And visited the Sea—
The Mermaids in the Basement
Came out to look at me—

And Frigates—in the Upper Floor
Extended Hempen Hands—
Presuming Me to be a Mouse—
Aground—upon the Sands—

But no Man moved Me—till the Tide
Went past my simple Shoe—
And past my Apron—and my Belt
And past my Bodice—too—

And made as He would eat me up—
As wholly as a Dew
Upon a Dandelion's Sleeve—
And then—I started—too—

And He — He followed — close behind —
I felt His Silver Heel
Upon my Ankle — Then my Shoes
Would overflow with Pearl —

Until We met the Solid Town —
No One He seemed to know —
And bowing — with a Mighty look —
At me — The Sea withdrew —

———————— *Train*

I like to see it lap the Miles —
And lick the Valleys up —
And stop to feed itself at Tanks —
And then — prodigious step

Around a Pile of Mountains —
And supercilious peer
In Shanties — by the sides of Roads —
And then a Quarry pare

To fit its Ribs
And crawl between
Complaining all the while
In horrid — hooting stanza —
Then chase itself down Hill —

And neigh like Boanerges —
Then — punctual as a Star
Stop — docile and omnipotent
At its own stable door —

————————

What care the Dead, for Chanticleer —
What care the Dead for Day?
'Tis late your Sunrise vex their face —
And Purple Ribaldry — of Morning

Pour as blank on them
As on the Tier of Wall
The Mason builded, yesterday,
And equally as cool—

What care the Dead for Summer?
The Solstice had no Sun
Could waste the Snow before their Gate—
And knew One Bird a Tune—

Could thrill their Mortised Ear
Of all the Birds that be—
This One—beloved of Mankind
Henceforward cherished be—

What care the Dead for Winter?
Themselves as easy freeze—
June Noon—as January Night—
As soon the South—her Breeze

Of Sycamore—or Cinnamon--
Deposit in a Stone
And put a Stone to keep it Warm—
Give Spices—unto Men—

———————

Our journey had advanced—
Our feet were almost come
To that odd Fork in Being's Road—
Eternity—by Term—

Our pace took sudden awe—
Our feet—reluctant—led—
Before—were Cities—but Between—
The Forest of the Dead—

Retreat—was out of Hope—
Behind—a Sealed Route—
Eternity's White Flag—Before—
And God—at every Gate—

The Tint I cannot take—is best—
The Color too remote
That I could show it in Bazaar—
A Guinea at a sight—

The fine—impalpable Array—
That swaggers on the eye
Like Cleopatra's Company—
Repeated—in the sky—

The Moments of Dominion
That happen on the Soul
And leave it with a Discontent
Too exquisite—to tell—

The eager look—on Landscapes—
As if they just repressed
Some Secret—that was pushing
Like Chariots—in the Vest—

The Pleading of the Summer—
That other Prank—of Snow—
That Cushions Mystery with Tulle,
For fear the Squirrels—know.

Their Graspless manners—mock us—
Until the Cheated Eye
Shuts arrogantly—in the Grave—
Another way—to see—

The Brain— is wider than the Sky—
For—put them side by side—
The one the other will contain
With ease—and You—beside—

The Brain is deeper than the sea—
For—hold them—Blue to Blue—
The one the other will absorb—
As Sponges—Buckets—do—

The Brain is just the weight of God—
For—Heft them—Pound for Pound—
And they will differ—if they do—
As Syllable from Sound—

————————

I cannot live with You—
It would be Life—
And Life is over there—
Behind the Shelf

The Sexton keeps the Key to—
Putting up
Our Life—His Porcelain—
Like a Cup—

Discarded of the Housewife—
Quaint—or Broke—
A newer Sevres pleases—
Old Ones crack—

I could not die—with You—
For One must wait
To shut the Other's Gaze down—
You—could not—

And I—Could I stand by
And see You—freeze—
Without my Right of Frost—
Death's privilege?

Nor could I rise—with You—
Because Your Face
Would put out Jesus'—
That New Grace

Glow plain—and foreign
On my homesick Eye—
Except that You than He
Shone closer by—

They'd judge Us—How—
For You—served Heaven—You know,
Or sought to—
I could not—

Because You saturated Sight—
And I had no more Eyes
For sordid excellence
As Paradise

And were You lost, I would be—
Though My Name
Rang loudest
On the Heavenly fame—

And were You—saved—
And I—condemned to be
Where You were not—
That self—were Hell to Me—

So We must meet apart—
You there—I—here—
With just the Door ajar
That Oceans are—and Prayer—
And that White Sustenance—
Despair—

I dwell in Possibility—
A fairer House than Prose—
More numerous of Windows—
Superior—for Doors—

Of Chambers as the Cedars—
Impregnable of Eye—
And for an Everlasting Roof
The Gambrels of the Sky—

Of Visitors—the fairest—
For Occupation—This—
The spreading wide my narrow Hands
To gather Paradise—

Essential Oils—are wrung—
The Attar from the Rose
Be not expressed by Suns—alone—
It is the gift of Screws—

The General Rose—decay—
But this—in Lady's Drawer
Make Summer—When the Lady lie
In Ceaseless Rosemary—

They say that "Time assuages"—
Time never did assuage—
An actual suffering strengthens
As Sinews do, with age—

Time is a Test of Trouble—
But not a Remedy—
If such it prove, it prove too
There was no Malady—

———

The Sun kept setting—setting—still
No Hue of Afternoon—
Upon the Village I perceived—
From House to House 'twas Noon—

The Dusk kept dropping—dropping—still
No Dew upon the Grass—
But only on my Forehead stopped—
And wandered in my Face—

My Feet kept drowsing—drowsing—still
My fingers were awake—
Yet why so little sound—Myself
Unto my Seeming—make?

How well I knew the Light before—
I could see it now—
'Tis Dying—I am doing—but
I'm not afraid to know—

———

Because I could not stop for Death—
He kindly stopped for me—
The Carriage held but just Ourselves—
And Immortality.

We slowly drove—He knew no haste
And I had put away
My labor and my leisure too,
For His Civility—

We passed the School, where Children strove
At Recess—in the Ring—
We passed the Fields of Gazing Grain—
We passed the Setting Sun—

Or rather—He passed Us—
The Dews drew quivering and chill—
For only Gossamer, my Gown—
My Tippet—only Tulle—

We paused before a House that seemed
A Swelling of the Ground—
The Roof was scarcely visible—
The Cornice—in the Ground—

Since then—'tis Centuries— and yet
Feels shorter than the Day
I first surmised the Horses' Heads
Were toward Eternity—

My Life had stood— a Loaded Gun—
In Corners—till a Day
The Owner passed—identified—
And carried Me away—

And now We roam in Sovereign Woods—
And now We hunt the Doe—
And every time I speak for Him—
The Mountains straight reply—

And do I smile, such cordial light
Upon the Valley glow—
It is as a Vesuvian face
Had let its pleasure through—

And when at Night—Our good Day done—
I guard My Master's Head—
'Tis better than the Eider-Duck's
Deep Pillow—to have shared—

To foe of His—I'm deadly foe—
None stir the second time—
On whom I lay a Yellow Eye—
Or an emphatic Thumb—

Though I than He—may longer live
He longer must—than I—
For I have but the power to kill,
Without—the power to die—

———

On a Columnar Self—
How ample to rely
In Tumult—or Extremity—
How good the Certainty

That Lever cannot pry—
And Wedge cannot divide
Conviction—That Granitic Base—
Though None be on our Side—

Suffice Us—for a Crowd—
Ourself—and Rectitude—
And that Assembly—not far off
From furthest Spirit—God—

———

A Light exists in Spring
Not present on the Year
At any other period—
When March is scarcely here

A Color stands abroad
On Solitary Fields
That Science cannot overtake
But Human Nature feels.

It waits upon the Lawn,
It shows the furthest Tree
Upon the furthest Slope you know
It almost speaks to you.

Then as Horizons step
Or Noons report away
Without the Formula of sound
It passes and we stay—

A quality of loss
Affecting our Content
As Trade had suddenly encroached
Upon a Sacrament.

———————

The Only News I know
Is Bulletins all Day
From Immortality.

The Only Shows I see—
Tomorrow and Today—
Perchance Eternity—

The Only One I meet
Is God—The Only Street—
Existence—This traversed

If Other News there be—
Or Admirabler Show—
I'll tell it You—

———————

Split the Lark—and you'll find the Music—
Bulb after Bulb, in Silver rolled—
Scantily dealt to the Summer Morning
Saved for your Ear when Lutes be old.

Loose the Flood—you shall find it patent—
Gush after Gush, reserved for you—
Scarlet Experiment! Sceptic Thomas!
Now, do you doubt that your Bird was true?

———————

There is a Zone whose even Years
No Solstice interrupt—
Whose Sun constructs perpetual Noon
Whose perfect Seasons wait—

Whose Summer set in Summer, till
The Centuries of June
And Centuries of August cease
And Consciousness—is Noon.

———————

Further in Summer than the Birds
Pathetic from the Grass
A minor Nation celebrates
Its unobtrusive Mass.

No Ordinance be seen
So gradual the Grace
A pensive Custom it becomes
Enlarging Loneliness.

Antiquest felt at Noon
When August burning low
Arise this spectral Canticle
Repose to typify

Remit as yet no Grace
No Furrow on the Glow
Yet a Druidic Difference
Enhances Nature now

———————

At Half past Three, a single Bird
Unto a silent Sky
Propounded but a single term
Of cautious melody.

At Half past Four, Experiment
Had subjugated test
And lo, Her silver Principle
Supplanted all the rest.

At Half past Seven, Element
Nor Implement, be seen—
And Place was where the Presence was
Circumference between.

———————

Tell all the Truth but tell it slant—
Success in Circuit lies
Too bright for our infirm Delight
The Truth's superb surprise
As Lightning to the Children eased
With explanation kind
The Truth must dazzle gradually
Or every man be blind—

Great Streets of silence led away
To Neighborhoods of Pause—
Here was no Notice—no Dissent
No Universe—no Laws—

By Clocks, 'twas Morning, and for Night
The Bells at Distance called—
But Epoch had no basis here
For Period exhaled.

My Triumph lasted till the Drums
Had left the Dead alone
And then I dropped my Victory
And chastened stole along
To where the finished Faces
Conclusion turned on me .
And then I hated Glory
And wished myself were They.

What is to be is best descried
When it has also been—
Could Prospect taste of Retrospect
The tyrannies of Men
Were Tenderer—diviner
The Transitive toward.
A Bayonet's contrition
Is nothing to the Dead.

There is no Frigate like a Book
To take us Lands away
Nor any Coursers like a Page
Of prancing Poetry —
This Traverse may the poorest take
Without oppress of Toll —
How frugal is the Chariot
That bears the Human soul.

A Route of Evanescence
With a revolving Wheel —
A Resonance of Emerald —
A Rush of Cochineal —
And every Blossom on the Bush
Adjusts its tumbled Head —
The mail from Tunis, probably,
An easy Morning's Ride —

One of the ones that Midas touched
Who failed to touch us all
Was that confiding Prodigal
The reeling Oriole —

So drunk he disavows it
With badinage divine —
So dazzling we mistake him
For an alighting Mine —

A Pleader—a Dissembler—
An Epicure—a Thief—
Betimes an Oratorio—
An Ecstasy in chief—

The Jesuit of Orchards
He cheats as he enchants
Of an entire Attar
For his decamping wants—

The splendor of a Burmah
The Meteor of Birds,
Departing like a Pageant
Of Ballads and of Bards—

I never thought that Jason sought
For any Golden Fleece
But then I am a rural man
With thoughts that make for Peace—

But if there were a Jason,
Tradition bear with me
Behold his lost Aggrandizement
Upon the Apple Tree—

———————

The Moon upon her fluent Route
Defiant of a Road—
The Star's Etruscan Argument
Substantiate a God—

If Aims impel these Astral Ones
The ones allowed to know
Know that which makes them as forgot
As Dawn forgets them—now—

———————

As imperceptibly as Grief
The Summer lapsed away—
Too imperceptible at last
To seem like Perfidy—
A Quietness distilled
As Twilight long begun,
Or Nature spending with herself
Sequestered Afternoon—
The Dusk drew earlier in—
The Morning foreign shone—
A courteous, yet harrowing Grace,
As Guest, that would be gone—
And thus, without a Wing
Or service of a Keel
Our Summer made her light escape
Into the Beautiful.

———

The Clock strikes one that just struck two—
Some schism in the Sum—
A Vagabond for Genesis
Has wrecked the Pendulum—

———

There came a Wind like a Bugle—
It quivered through the Grass
And a Green Chill upon the Heat
So ominous did pass
We barred the Windows and the Doors
As from an Emerald Ghost—
The Doom's electric Moccasin
That very instant passed—
On a strange Mob of panting Trees
And Fences fled away

And Rivers where the Houses ran
Those looked that lived—that Day—
The Bell within the steeple wild
The flying tidings told—
How much can come
And much can go,
And yet abide the World!

In Winter in my Room
I came upon a Worm—
Pink, lank and warm—
But as he was a worm
And worms presume
Not quite with him at home—
Secured him by a string
To something neighboring
And went along.

A Trifle afterward
A thing occurred
I'd not believe it if I heard
But state with creeping blood—
A snake with mottles rare
Surveyed my chamber floor
In feature as the worm before
But ringed with power—
The very string with which
I tied him—too
When he was mean and new
That string was there—

I shrank—"How fair you are"!
Propitiation's claw—
"Afraid," he hissed
"Of me"?
"No cordiality"—
He fathomed me—

Then to a Rhythm *Slim*
Secreted in his Form
As Patterns swim
Projected him.

That time I flew
Both eyes his way
Lest he pursue
Nor ever ceased to run
Till in a distant Town
Towns on from mine
I set me down
This was a dream.

————————
is the Pit = Hell

A Pit—but Heaven over it—
And Heaven beside, and Heaven abroad,
And yet a Pit—
With Heaven over it.

To stir would be to slip—
To look would be to drop—
To dream—to sap the Prop
That holds my chances up.
Ah! Pit! With Heaven over it!

The depth is all my thought—
I dare not ask my feet—
'Twould start us where we sit
So straight you'd scarce suspect
It was a Pit—with fathoms under it—
Its Circuit just the same.
Seed—summer—tomb—
Whose Doom to whom?

————————

By a departing light
We see acuter, quite,
Than by a wick that stays.
There's something in the flight
That clarifies the sight
And decks the rays.

———————

I took one Draught of Life—
I'll tell you what I paid—
Precisely an existence—
The market price, they said.

They weighed me, Dust by Dust—
They balanced Film with Film,
Then handed me my Being's worth—
A single Dram of Heaven!

———————

My life closed twice before its close—
It yet remains to see
If Immortality unveil
A third event to me

So huge, so hopeless to conceive
As these that twice befell.
Parting is all we know of heaven,
And all we need of hell.

———————

That it will never come again
Is what makes life so sweet.
Believing what we don't believe
Does not exhilarate.

That if it be, it be at best
An ablative estate —
This instigates an appetite
Precisely opposite.

———

This docile one inter
While we who dare to live
Arraign the sunny brevity
That sparkled to the Grave

On her departing span
No wilderness remain
As dauntless in the House of Death
As if it were her own —

———

'Twas here my summer paused
What ripeness after then
To other scene or other soul
My sentence had begun.

To winter to remove
With winter to abide
Go manacle your icicle
Against your Tropic Bride.

———

Experiment escorts us last—
His pungent company
Will not allow an Axiom
An Opportunity

———

Too happy Time dissolves itself
And leaves no remnant by—
'Tis Anguish not a Feather hath
Or too much weight to fly—

———

The earth has many keys.
Where melody is not
Is the unknown peninsula.
Beauty is nature's fact.

But witness for her land,
And witness for her sea,
The cricket is her utmost
Of elegy to me.

BENJAMIN PAUL BLOOD

(1832–1919)

Late

"Ye cannot enter now."

And shall it ever be again—the joy
That greeted the fond bard when books were few,
And title-pages opened into Heaven?
How swelled the isles of Greece when Homer sung!
How soared the tulip night with loftier bloom,
And poured serener dreams o'er Maro's lay!
E'en thou, sad Harold, of the lonesome string,
Shall lyrist thrill the world again as thou,
The young, the beautiful?—beautiful and broken,
As for the bread of Life! (May the white hands
Of seraphs win thee to the Fatherhouse,
And soothe the sobbing locks, so heavy—heavy
From these Judean hills!)

      Oh, where was Fame
In that red morning when I was, like thee,
Soft-eyed and open-necked to the wild wind—
In love with mine own motions, ere my steps
Forgot the barefoot feel of the clay world?
My days lay open to the universe,
And all night long the clang of their musical gates
Retold the echoes of Apollo's harp,
And Mars his gory shield!—I wooed in vain.
Above my weedy and untitled moors
The mantle of a blooded Moon swept on,
With old regalia strange to me. . . . 'Twas well.
I lacked the builder's skill, the delver's faith;
I lacked the nether compass—maybe more
I lacked the central fire, the reckless poise
Of the born-drunken and the autocrat,
That breathe the courage of the soul's farewells.

But manhood came, nor yet her trumpet spoke—
And Disillusion mocked the arts of Art . . .
I saw the One of all things—branching trees
That fork the bird-nests, as the branching rivers
That fork the nests of men—and saw, beyond,
The field transcend the One, where tangent spirits
Would leave to slaves all spheric harmonies—
Till knowledge fells the last man as the first.

How long Redemption waits!—For they are gone—
The rosebloom of my youth, the tireless limbs,
The velvet-pointed lips that beauty wooed
With long, mute kisses in the hooded night,
Or on the spongy mead when sodden June
Gushed milk in the rank-sprouting grass, and blood
Hot, fitful, fateful, through the yearning arms,
And to the throbbing heart.—Could I forget!
Throw off this sorry wisdom, and inch deep
Besmear my wrinkles—young by torchlight yet!
Then leap to the arena!—who should know
The smiling athlete had a grewsome cheek,
Until the lamps were lowering?—Late, oh, late!
The westering pathos glooms the fervent hours.
Again my gray gull lifts against the nightfall,
And takes the damp leagues with a shoreless eye.

ELIZABETH AKERS ALLEN

(1832–1911)

Rock Me to Sleep

Backward, turn backward, O Time, in your flight,
Make me a child again just for to-night!
Mother, come back from the echoless shore,
Take me again to your heart as of yore;
Kiss from my forehead the furrows of care,
Smooth the few silver threads out of my hair;
Over my slumbers your loving watch keep;—
Rock me to sleep, mother,—rock me to sleep!

Backward, flow backward, O tide of the years!
I am so weary of toil and of tears,—
Toil without recompense, tears all in vain,—
Take them, and give me my childhood again!
I have grown weary of dust and decay,—
Weary of flinging my soul-wealth away;
Weary of sowing for others to reap;—
Rock me to sleep, mother,—rock me to sleep!

Tired of the hollow, the base, the untrue,
Mother, O mother, my heart calls for you!
Many a summer the grass has grown green,
Blossomed and faded, our faces between:
Yet, with strong yearning and passionate pain,
Long I to-night for your presence again.
Come from the silence so long and so deep;—
Rock me to sleep, mother,—rock me to sleep!

Over my heart, in the days that are flown,
No love like mother-love ever has shone;
No other worship abides and endures,—
Faithful, unselfish, and patient like yours:
None like a mother can charm away pain

From the sick soul and the world-weary brain.
Slumber's soft calms o'er my heavy lids creep;—
Rock me to sleep, mother,—rock me to sleep!

Come, let your brown hair, just lighted with gold,
Fall on your shoulders again as of old;
Let it drop over my forehead to-night,
Shading my faint eyes away from the light;
For with its sunny-edged shadows once more
Haply will throng the sweet visions of yore;
Lovingly, softly, its bright billows sweep;—
Rock me to sleep, mother,—rock me to sleep!

Mother, dear mother, the years have been long
Since I last listened your lullaby song:
Sing, then, and unto my soul it shall seem
Womanhood's years have been only a dream.
Clasped to your heart in a loving embrace,
With your light lashes just sweeping my face,
Never hereafter to wake or to weep;—
Rock me to sleep, mother,—rock me to sleep!

HENRY CLAY WORK

(1832–1884)

Marching Through Georgia

Bring the good old bugle, boys! we'll sing another song—
Sing it with a spirit that will start the world along—
Sing it as we used to sing it, fifty thousand strong,
While we were marching through Georgia.

> *"Hurrah! Hurrah! we bring the Jubilee!*
> *Hurrah! Hurrah! the flag that makes you free!"*
> *So we sang the chorus from Atlanta to the sea,*
> *While we were marching through Georgia.*

How the darkeys shouted when they heard the joyful
    sound!
How the turkeys gobbled which our commissary found!
How the sweet potatoes even started from the ground,
While we were marching through Georgia.

Chorus

Yes, and there were Union men who wept with joyful tears,
When they saw the honor'd flag they had not seen for years;
Hardly could they be restrained from breaking forth in
    cheers,
While we were marching through Georgia.

Chorus

"Sherman's dashing Yankee boys will never reach the coast!"
So the saucy rebels said, and 'twas a handsome boast,
Had they not forgot, alas! to reckon with the host,
While we were marching through Georgia.

Chorus

So we made a thoroughfare for Freedom and her train,
Sixty miles in latitude—three hundred to the main;
Treason fled before us, for resistance was in vain,
While we were marching through Georgia.

Chorus

EDMUND CLARENCE STEDMAN

(1833–1908)

Prelude to *An American Anthology*

I saw the constellated matin choir
Then when they sang together in the dawn,—
The morning stars of this first rounded day
Hesperian, hundred-houred, that ending leaves
Youth's fillet still upon the New World's brow;
Then when they sang together,—sang for joy
Of mount and wood and cataract, and stretch
Of keen-aired vasty reaches happy-homed,—
I heard the stately hymning, saw their light
Resolve in flame that evil long inwrought
With what was else the goodliest demain
Of freedom warded by the ancient sea;
So sang they, rose they, to meridian,
And westering down the firmament led on
Cluster and train of younger celebrants
That beaconed as they might, by adverse skies
Shrouded, but stayed not nor discomfited,—
Of whom how many, and how dear, alas,
The voices stilled mid-orbit, stars eclipsed
Long ere the hour of setting; yet in turn
Others oncoming shine, nor fail to chant
New anthems, yet not alien, for the time
Goes not out darkling nor of music mute
To the next age,—that quickened now awaits
Their heralding, their more impassioned song.

JOHN JAMES PIATT

(1835–1917)

To the Statue on the Capitol

Looking Eastward at Dawn

What sunken splendor in the Eastern skies
   Seest thou, O Watcher, from thy lifted place? —
Thine old Atlantic dream is in thine eyes,
   But the new Western morning on thy face.

Beholdest thou, in reäpparent light,
   Thy lost Republics? They were visions, fled.
Their ghosts in ruin'd cities walk by night—
   It is no resurrection of their dead.

But look, behind thee, where in sunshine lie
   Thy boundless fields of harvest in the West,
Whose savage garments from thy shoulders fly,
   Whose eagle clings in sunrise to thy crest!

My Shadow's Stature

Whene'er, in morning airs, I walk abroad,
Breasting upon the hills the buoyant wind,
Up from the vale my shadow climbs behind,
An earth-born giant climbing toward his god;
Against the sun, on heights before untrod,
I stand: faint glorified, but undefined,
Far down the slope in misty meadows blind,
I see my ghostly follower slowly plod.
"O stature of my shade," I muse and sigh,
"How great art thou, how small am I the while!"
Then the vague giant blandly answers, "True,
But though thou art small thy head is in the sky,
Crown'd with the sun and all the Heaven's smile—
My head is in the shade and valley too."

Taking the Night-Train

A tremulous word, a lingering hand, the burning
   Of restless passion smoldering—so we part;
Ah, slowly from the dark the world is turning
   When midnight stars shine in a heavy heart.

The streets are lighted, and the myriad faces
   Move through the gaslight, and the homesick feet
Pass by me, homeless; sweet and close embraces
   Charm many a threshold—laughs and kisses sweet.

From great hotels the stranger throng is streaming,
   The hurrying wheels in many a street are loud;
Within the depot, in the gaslight gleaming,
   A glare of faces, stands the waiting crowd.

The whistle screams; the wheels are rumbling slowly,
   The path before us glides into the light:
Behind, the city sinks in silence wholly;
   The panting engine leaps into the night.

I seem to see each street a mystery growing,
   In mist of dreamland—vague, forgotten air:
Does no sweet soul, awakened, feel me going?
   Loves no dear heart, in dreams, to keep me there?

AUGUSTA COOPER BRISTOL

(1835–1910)

Night

I stood and watched the still, mysterious Night,
Steal from her shadowy caverns in the East,
To work her deep enchantments on the world.
Her black veil floated down the silent glens,
While her dark sandalled feet, with noiseless tread,
Moved to a secret harmony. Along
The brows of the majestic hills, she strung
Her glorious diamonds so stealthily,
It never marred their dreams; and in the deep,
Cool thickets of the wood, where scarce the Day
Could reach the dim retreat, her dusky hand
Pinned on the breast of the exhaling flower,
A glittering gem; while all the tangled ferns
And forest lace-work, as she moved along,
Grew moist and shining.

     Who would e'er have guessed,
The queenly Night would deign to stoop and love
A little flower! And yet, with all her stealth,
I saw her press her damp and cooling lip
Upon the feverish bosom of a Rose;
At which a watchful bird poured sudden forth
A love-sick song, of sweet and saddest strain.

Upon the ivied rocks, and rugged crags
On which the ocean billows break, she hung
Her sombre mantle; and the gray old sea
That had been high in tumult all the day,
Became so mesmerized beneath her wiles,
He seemed a mere reflection of herself.
The billows sank into a dimpled sleep;
Only the little tide-waves glided up
To kiss the blackness of the airy robe
That floated o'er them.

Long I stood and watched
The mystic, spell-like influence of Night;
Till o'er the eastern hills, came up the first
Faint glories of the crown that Phœbus wears.
And soon, the Earth, surprised to see the work
That Night had wrought, began to glow and blush,
Like maidens, conscious of the glance of Love.
While she,—the dark Enchantress,—like to one
Who decorates her bower with all things fair,
Wherewith to please her lover, but yet flees
At his approaching step,—at the first gleam
That lit the zenith from the Day-god's eye,
Fled timid o'er the distant western hills.

ADAH ISAACS MENKEN

(1835?–1868)

Judith

"*Repent, or I will come unto thee quickly, and will
fight thee with the sword of my mouth.*"
—REVELATION ii. 16.

I.

Ashkelon is not cut off with the remnant of a valley.
Baldness dwells not upon Gaza.
The field of the valley is mine, and it is clothed in verdure.
The steepness of Baal-perazim is mine;
And the Philistines spread themselves in the valley of
Rephaim.
They shall yet be delivered into my hands.
For the God of Battles has gone before me!
The sword of the mouth shall smite them to dust.
I have slept in the darkness—
But the seventh angel woke me, and giving me a sword of
flame, points to the blood-ribbed cloud, that lifts his reeking
head above the mountain.
Thus am I the prophet.
I see the dawn that heralds to my waiting soul the advent
of power.
      Power that will unseal the thunders!
      Power that will give voice to graves!
         Graves of the living;
         Graves of the dying;
         Graves of the sinning;
         Graves of the loving;
         Graves of despairing;
And oh! graves of the deserted!
These shall speak, each as their voices shall be loosed.
And the day is dawning.

II.

Stand back, ye Philistines!
Practice what ye preach to me;
I heed ye not, for I know ye all.

Ye are living burning lies, and profanation to the garments
which with stately steps ye sweep your marble palaces.

Your palaces of Sin, around which the damning evidence
of guilt hangs like a reeking vapor.

Stand back!

I would pass up the golden road of the world.

A place in the ranks awaits me.

I know that ye are hedged on the borders of my path.

Lie and tremble, for ye well know that I hold with iron
grasp the battle axe.

Creep back to your dark tents in the valley.

Slouch back to your haunts of crime.

Ye do not know me, neither do ye see me.

But the sword of the mouth is unsealed, and ye coil
yourselves in slime and bitterness at my feet.

I mix your jeweled heads, and your gleaming eyes, and
your hissing tongues with the dust.

My garments shall bear no mark of ye.

When I shall return this sword to the angel, your foul
blood will not stain its edge.

It will glimmer with the light of truth, and the strong arm
shall rest.

III.

Stand back!

I am no Magdalene waiting to kiss the hem of your
garment.

It is mid-day.

See ye not what is written on my forehead?

I am Judith!

I wait for the head of my Holofernes!

Ere the last tremble of the conscious death-agony shall
have shuddered, I will show it to ye with the long black hair
clinging to the glazed eyes, and the great mouth opened in
search of voice, and the strong throat all hot and reeking

with blood, that will thrill me with wild unspeakable joy as it courses down my bare body and dabbles my cold feet!

My sensuous soul will quake with the burden of so much bliss.

Oh, what wild passionate kisses will I draw up from that bleeding mouth!

I will strangle this pallid throat of mine on the sweet blood!

I will revel in my passion.

At midnight I will feast on it in the darkness.

For it was that which thrilled its crimson tides of reckless passion through the blue veins of my life, and made them leap up in the wild sweetness of Love and agony of Revenge!

I am starving for this feast.

Oh forget not that I am Judith!

And I know where sleeps Holofernes.

MARK TWAIN
(1835–1910)

Ode to Stephen Dowling Bots, Dec'd.

And did young Stephen sicken,
  And did young Stephen die?
And did the sad hearts thicken,
  And did the mourners cry?

No; such was not the fate of
  Young Stephen Dowling Bots;
Though sad hearts round him thickened,
  'Twas not from sickness' shots.

No whooping-cough did rack his frame,
  Nor measles drear, with spots;
Not these impaired the sacred name
  Of Stephen Dowling Bots.

Despised love struck not with woe
  That head of curly knots,
Nor stomach troubles laid him low,
  Young Stephen Dowling Bots.

O no. Then list with tearful eye,
  Whilst I his fate do tell.
His soul did from this cold world fly,
  By falling down a well.

They got him out and emptied him;
  Alas it was too late;
His spirit was gone for to sport aloft
  In the realms of the good and great.

PHILLIPS BROOKS
(1835–1893)

O Little Town of Bethlehem

O little town of Bethlehem!
  How still we see thee lie,
Above thy deep and dreamless sleep,
  The silent stars go by;
Yet in thy dark streets shineth
  The Everlasting light;
The hopes and fears of all the years,
  Are met in thee tonight.

For Christ is born of Mary,
  And gathered all above,
While mortals sleep the angels keep
  Their watch of wondering love.
O morning stars together
  Proclaim the holy birth!
And praises sing to God the King,
  And peace to men on earth.

How silently, how silently,
  The wondrous gift is given;
So God imparts to human hearts
  The blessings of his heaven.
No ear may hear his coming,
  But in this world of sin,
Where meek souls will receive him still,
  The dear Christ enters in.

O holy child of Bethlehem!
  Descend to us, we pray,
Cast out our sin and enter in,
  Be born in us to-day.
We hear the Christmas angels,
  The great glad tidings tell,
O, come to us, abide with us,
  Our Lord Emmanuel!

BRET HARTE
(1836–1902)

Plain Language from Truthful James

Table Mountain, 1870

Which I wish to remark,—
    And my language is plain,—
That for ways that are dark
    And for tricks that are vain,
The heathen Chinee is peculiar.
    Which the same I would rise to explain.

Ah Sin was his name;
    And I shall not deny
In regard to the same
    What that name might imply,
But his smile it was pensive and childlike,
    As I frequent remarked to Bill Nye.

It was August the third;
    And quite soft was the skies;
Which it might be inferred
    That Ah Sin was likewise;
Yet he played it that day upon William
    And me in a way I despise.

Which we had a small game,
    And Ah Sin took a hand:
It was Euchre. The same
    He did not understand;
But he smiled as he sat by the table,
    With the smile that was childlike and bland.

Yet the cards they were stocked
    In a way that I grieve,
And my feelings were shocked

At the state of Nye's sleeve:
Which was stuffed full of aces and bowers,
    And the same with intent to deceive.

But the hands that were played
    By that heathen Chinee,
And the points that he made,
    Were quite frightful to see,—
Till at last he put down a right bower,
    Which the same Nye had dealt unto me.

Then I looked up at Nye,
    And he gazed upon me;
And he rose with a sigh,
    And said, "Can this be?
We are ruined by Chinese cheap labor,"—
    And he went for that heathen Chinee.

In the scene that ensued
    I did not take a hand,
But the floor it was strewed
    Like the leaves on the strand
With the cards that Ah Sin had been hiding,
    In the game "he did not understand."

In his sleeves, which were long,
    He had twenty-four jacks,—
Which was coming it strong,
    Yet I state but the facts;
And we found on his nails, which were taper,
    What is frequent in tapers,—that's wax.

Which is why I remark,
    And my language is plain,
That for ways that are dark,
    And for tricks that are vain,
The heathen Chinee is peculiar,—
    Which the same I am free to maintain.

What the Bullet Sang

O joy of creation
      To be!
O rapture to fly
      And be free!
Be the battle lost or won,
  Though its smoke shall hide the sun,
I shall find my love—The one
      Born for me!

I shall know him where he stands,
      All alone,
With the power in his hands
      Not o'erthrown;
I shall know him by his face,
  By his god-like front and grace;
I shall hold him for a space,
      All my own!

It is he—O my love!
      So bold!
It is I—All thy love
      Foretold!
It is I. O love what bliss!
  Dost thou answer to my kiss?
Oh! sweetheart, what is this!
      Lieth there so cold!

Chicago

(October 10, 1871.)

Blackened and bleeding, helpless, panting, prone,
On the charred fragments of her shattered throne
Lies she who stood but yesterday alone.

Queen of the West! by some enchanter taught
To lift the glory of Aladdin's court,
Then lose the spell that all that wonder wrought.

Like her own prairies by some chance seed sown,
Like her own prairies in one brief day grown,
Like her own prairies in one fierce night mown.

She lifts her voice, and in her pleading call
We hear the cry of Macedon to Paul—
The cry for help that makes her kin to all.

But haply with wan fingers may she feel
The silver cup hid in the proffered meal—
The gifts her kinship and our loves reveal.

SARAH MORGAN PIATT

(1836–1919)

Giving Back the Flower

So, because you chose to follow me into the subtle sadness
of night,
  And to stand in the half-set moon with the weird fall-light
on your glimmering hair,
Till your presence hid all of the earth and all of the sky from
my sight,
  And to give me a little scarlet bud, that was dying of
frost, to wear,

Say, must you taunt me forever, forever? You looked at my
hand and you knew
  That I was the slave of the Ring, while you were as free as
the wind is free.
When I saw your corpse in your coffin, I flung back your
flower to you;
  It was all of yours that I ever had; you must keep it,
and—keep from me.

Ah? so God is your witness. Has God, then, no world to
look after but ours?
  May He not have been searching for that wild star, with
the trailing plumage, that flew
Far over a part of our darkness while we were there by the
freezing flowers,
  Or else brightening some planet's luminous rings, instead
of thinking of you?

Or, if He was near us at all, do you think that He would sit
listening there
  Because you sang "Hear me, Norma," to a woman in
jewels and lace,
While, so close to us, down in another street, in the wet,
unlighted air,

There were children crying for bread and fire, and
    mothers who questioned His grace?

Or perhaps He had gone to the ghastly field where the fight
    had been that day,
  To number the bloody stabs that were there, to look at
    and judge the dead;
Or else to the place full of fever and moans where the
    wretched wounded lay;
  At least I do not believe that He cares to remember a
    word that you said.

So take back your flower, I tell you—of its sweetness I now
    have no need;
  Yes, take back your flower down into the stillness and
    mystery to keep;
When you wake I will take it, and God, then, perhaps will
    witness indeed,
  But go, now, and tell Death he must watch you, and not
    let you walk in your sleep.

WILLIAM DEAN HOWELLS

(1837–1920)

The Empty House

The wet trees hung above the walks
  Purple with damps and earthish stains,
  And strewn by moody, absent rains
With rose-leaves from the wild-grown stalks.

Unmown, in heavy, tangled swaths,
  The ripe June-grass is wanton blown;
  Snails slime the untrodden threshold-stone;
Along the sills hang drowsy moths.

Down the blank visage of the wall,
  Where many a wavering trace appears,
  Like a forgotten trace of tears,
From swollen eaves the slow drops crawl.

Where everything was wide before,
  The curious wind, that comes and goes,
  Finds all the latticed windows close,
Secret and close the bolted door.

And with the shrewd and curious wind,
  That in the archéd doorway cries,
  And at the bolted portal tries,
And harks and listens at the blind,—

Forever lurks my thought about,
  And in the ghostly middle-night
  Finds all the hidden windows bright,
And sees the guests go in and out,

And lingers till the pallid dawn,
   And feels the mystery deeper there
   In silent, gust-swept chambers, bare,
With all the midnight revel gone;

But wanders through the lonesome rooms,
   Where harsh the astonished cricket calls,
   And, from the hollows of the walls
Vanishing, start unshapen glooms;

And lingers yet, and cannot come
   Out of the drear and desolate place,
   So full of ruin's solemn grace,
And haunted with the ghost of home.

In Earliest Spring

Tossing his mane of snows in wildest eddies and tangles,
   Lion-like, March cometh in, hoarse, with tempestuous
      breath,
Through all the moaning chimneys, and thwart all the
      hollows and angles
   Round the shuddering house, threating of winter and
      death.

But in my heart I feel the life of the wood and the meadow
   Thrilling the pulses that own kindred with fibres
      that lift
Bud and blade to the sunward, within the inscrutable
      shadow,
   Deep in the oak's chill core, under the gathering drift.

Nay, to earth's life in mine some prescience, or dream, or
      desire
   (How shall I name it aright?) comes for a moment and
      goes,—
Rapture of life ineffable, perfect,—as if in the brier,
   Leafless there by my door, trembled a sense of the rose.

November

Impression

A weft of leafless spray
Woven fine against the gray
Of the autumnal day,
And blurred along those ghostly garden tops
Clusters of berries crimson as the drops
That my heart bleeds when I remember
How often, in how many a far November,
Of childhood and my children's childhood I was glad,
With the wild rapture of the Fall,
Of all the beauty, and of all
The ruin, now so intolerably sad.

FORCEYTHE WILLSON

(1837–1867)

In State

I.

O Keeper of the Sacred Key,
And the Great Seal of Destiny,
Whose eye is the blue canopy,
Look down upon the warring world, and tell us what the
     end will be.

"Lo, through the wintry atmosphere,
On the white bosom of the sphere,
A cluster of five lakes appear;
And all the land looks like a couch, or warrior's shield, or
     sheeted bier.

"And on that vast and hollow field,
With both lips closed and both eyes sealed,
A mighty Figure is revealed,—
Stretched at full length, and stiff and stark, as in the hollow
     of a shield.

"The winds have tied the drifted snow
Around the face and chin; and lo,
The sceptred Giants come and go,
And shake their shadowy crowns and say: "We always feared
     it would be so!"

"She came of an heroic race:
A giant's strength, a maiden's grace,
Like two in one seem to embrace,
And match, and blend, and thorough-blend, in her colossal
     form and face.

"Where can her dazzling falchion be?
One hand is fallen in the sea;
The Gulf-Stream drifts it far and free;
And in that hand her shining brand gleams from the depths
      resplendently.

"And by the other, in its rest,
The starry banner of the West
Is clasped forever to her breast;
And of her silver helmet, lo, a soaring eagle is the crest.

"And on her brow, a softened light,
As of a star concealed from sight
By some thin veil of fleecy white,—
Or of the rising moon behind the rainy vapors of the night.

"The Sisterhood that was so sweet,
The Starry System sphered complete,
Which the mazed Orient used to greet,
The Four and Thirty fallen Stars glimmer and glitter at her
      feet.

"And over her,—and over all,
For panoply and coronal,—
The mighty Immemorial,
And everlasting Canopy and starry Arch and Shield of All."

II.

"Three cold, bright moons have marched and wheeled;
And the white cerement that revealed
A Figure stretched upon a Shield,
Is turned to verdure; and the Land is now one mighty
      Battle-Field.

"And lo, the children which she bred,
And more than all else cherishéd,
To make them true in heart and head,
Stand face to face, as mortal foes, with their swords crossed
      above the dead.

"Each hath a mighty stroke and stride:
One true—the more that he is tried;
The other dark and evil-eyed;—
And by the hand of one of them, his own dear mother
    surely died!

"A stealthy step—a gleam of hell,—
It is the simple truth to tell,—
The Son stabbed and the Mother fell:
And so she lies, all mute and pale, and pure and
    irreproachable!

"And then the battle-trumpet blew;
And the true brother sprang and drew
His blade to smite the traitor through;
And so they clashed above the bier, and the Night sweated
    bloody dew.

"And all their children, far and wide,
That are so greatly multiplied,
Rise up in frensy and divide;
And choosing, each whom he will serve, unsheathe the
    sword and take their side.

"And in the low sun's bloodshot rays,
Portentous of the coming days,
The Two great Oceans blush and blaze,
With the emergent continent between them, wrapt in
    crimson haze.

"Now whichsoever stand or fall,
As God is great and man is small,
The Truth shall triumph over all,—
Forever and forevermore, the Truth shall triumph over
    all!"

III.

"I see the champion sword-strokes flash;
I see them fall and hear them clash;
I hear the murderous engines crash;
I see a brother stoop to loose a foeman-brother's bloody
      sash.

"I see the torn and mangled corse,
The dead and dying heaped in scores,
The headless rider by his horse,
The wounded captive bayoneted through and through
      without remorse.

"I hear the dying sufferer cry,
With his crushed face turned to the sky,
I see him crawl in agony
To the foul pool, and bow his head into its bloody slime and
      die.

"I see the assassin crouch and fire,
I see his victim fall—expire;
I see the murderer creeping nigher
To strip the dead: He turns the head: The face! The son
      beholds his sire!

"I hear the curses and the thanks;
I see the mad charge on the flanks,
The rents—the gaps—the broken ranks,—
The vanquished squadrons driven headlong down the river's
      bridgeless banks.

"I see the death-gripe on the plain,
The grappling monsters on the main,
The tens of thousands that are slain,
And all the speechless suffering and agony of heart and
      brain.

"I see the dark and bloody spots,
The crowded rooms and crowded cots,
The bleaching bones, the battle-blots,—
And writ on many a nameless grave, a legend of forget-me-
      nots.

"I see the gorgéd prison-den,
The dead line and the pent-up pen,
The thousands quartered in the fen,
The living-deaths of skin and bone that were the goodly
      shapes of men.

"And still the bloody Dew must fall!
And His great Darkness with the Pall
Of His dread Judgment cover all,
Till the Dead Nation rise Transformed by Truth to triumph
      over all!"

"AND LAST—AND LAST I SEE—THE DEED."

Thus saith the Keeper of the Key,
And the Great Seal of Destiny,
Whose Eye is the blue canopy,
And leaves the Pall of His great Darkness over all the Land
      and Sea.

JOAQUIN MILLER

(1837–1913)

In Père La Chaise

I.

An avenue of tombs! I stand before
The tomb of Abelard and Eloise.
A long, a dark bent line of cypress trees
Leads past and on to other shrines; but o'er
This tomb the boughs hang darkest and most dense,
Like leaning mourners clad in black. The sense
Of awe oppresses you. This solitude
Means more than common sorrow. Down the wood
Still lovers pass, then pause, then turn again,
And weep like silent, unobtrusive rain.

II.

'Tis but a simple, antique tomb that kneels
As one that weeps above the broken clay.
'Tis stained with storms, 'tis eaten well away,
Nor half the old-new story now reveals
Of heart that held beyond the tomb to heart.
But oh, it tells of love! And that true page
Is more in this cold, hard, commercial age,
When love is calmly counted some lost art,
Than all man's mighty monuments of war
Or archives vast of art and science arc.

III.

Here poets pause and dream a listless hour;
Here silly pilgrims stoop and kiss the clay;
Here sweetest maidens leave a cross or flower,
While vandals bear the tomb in bits away.
The ancient stone is scarred with name and scrawl
Of many tender fools. But over all,

And high above all other scrawls, is writ
One simple thing, most touching and most fit.
Some pitying soul has tiptoed high above,
And with a nail has scrawled but this: "O Love!"

IV.

O Love! . . . I turn; I climb the hill of tombs,
Where sleeps the "bravest of the brave," below,
His bed of scarlet blooms in zone of snow—
No cross nor sign, save this red bed of blooms,
I see grand tombs to France's lesser dead,—
Colossal steeds, white pyramids, still red
At base with blood, still torn with shot and shell,
To testify that here the Commune fell:
And yet I turn once more from all of these,
And stand before the tomb of Eloise.

At Our Golden Gate

At our gate he groaneth, groaneth,
Chafes as chained, and chafes all day;
As leashed greyhound moaneth, moaneth,
When the master keeps away.
Men have seen him steal in lowly,
Lick the island's feet and face,
Lift a cold wet nose up slowly,
Then turn empty to his place:
Empty, idle, hungered, waiting
For some hero, dauntless-souled,
Glory-loving, pleasure-hating,
Minted in God's ancient mold.

What ship yonder stealing, stealing,
Pirate-like, as if ashamed?
Black men, brown men, red, revealing—
Not one white man to be named!
What flag yonder, proud, defiant,
Topmast, saucy, and sea blown?

Tall ships lordly and reliant—
All flags yonder save our own!
Surged atop yon half-world water
Once a tuneful tall ship ran;
Ran the storm king, too, and caught her,
Caught and laughed as laughs a man:

Laughed and held her, and so holden,
Holden high, foam-crest and free
As famed harper, hoar and olden,
Held his great harp on his knee.
Then his fingers wildly flinging
Through chords, ropes—such symphony
As if some wild Wagner singing—
Some wild Wagner of the sea!
Sang he of such poor cowed weaklings,
Cowed, weak landsmen such as we.
While ten thousand storied sea kings
Foam-white, storm-blown, sat the sea.

Oh, for England's old sea thunder!
Oh, for England's bold sea men,
When we banged her over, under
And she banged us back again!
Better old time strife and stresses,
Cloud top't towers, walls, distrust;
Better wars than lazinesses,
Better loot than wine and lust!
Give us seas? Why, we have oceans!
Give us manhood, sea men, men!
Give us deeds, loves, hates, emotions!
Else give back these seas again.

Columbus

Behind him lay the gray Azores,
  Behind the Gates of Hercules;
Before him not the ghost of shores,
  Before him only shoreless seas.

The good mate said: "Now must we pray,
    For lo! the very stars are gone.
Brave Adm'r'l, speak; what shall I say?"
    "Why, say: 'Sail on! sail on! and on!'"

"My men grow mutinous day by day;
    My men grow ghastly wan and weak."
The stout mate thought of home; a spray
    Of salt wave washed his swarthy cheek.
"What shall I say, brave Adm'r'l, say,
    If we sight naught but seas at dawn?"
"Why, you shall say at break of day:
    'Sail on! sail on! sail on! and on!'"

They sailed and sailed, as winds might blow,
    Until at last the blanched mate said:
"Why, now not even God would know
    Should I and all my men fall dead.
These very winds forget their way,
    For God from these dread seas is gone.
Now speak, brave Adm'r'l; speak and say——"
    He said: "Sail on! sail on! and on!"

They sailed. They sailed. Then spake the mate:
    "This mad sea shows its teeth to-night.
He curls his lip, he lies in wait,
    With lifted teeth, as if to bite!
Brave Adm'r'l, say but one good word;
    What shall we do when hope is gone?"
The words leapt as a leaping sword:
    "Sail on! sail on! sail on! and on!"

Then, pale and worn, he kept his deck,
    And peered through darkness. Ah, that night
Of all dark nights! And then a speck—
    A light! A light! A light! A light!
It grew, a starlit flag unfurled!
    It grew to be Time's burst of dawn.
He gained a world; he gave that world
    Its grandest lesson: "On! sail on!"

ABRAM JOSEPH RYAN
(1838–1886)

Lines

*Respectfully Inscribed to the Ladies' Memorial Association
of Fredericksburg, Va.*

Gather the sacred dust
  Of the warriors tried and true,
Who bore the Flag of our nation's trust,
And fell in a cause as great as just,
  And died for me and you.

Wherever the brave have died
  They should not rest apart;
Living they struggled side by side—
Why should the hand of Death divide
  A single heart from heart?

Gather them, each and all,
  From the Private to the Chief;
Came they from cabin or lordly hall,
Over their dust let the fresh tears fall
  Of a nation's holy grief.

No matter whence they came—
  Dear is their lifeless clay—
Whether unknown or known to fame,
Their cause and country were the same—
  They died—and wore the Gray.

Gather the corpses strown
  O'er many a battle plain—
From many a grave that lies so lone,
Without a name and without a stone—
  Gather the Southern slain.

And the dead shall meet the dead,
    While the living o'er them weep;
For the men whom Lee and Stonewall led,
And the hearts that once together bled,
    Should now together sleep.

WILLIAM REED HUNTINGTON
(1838 – 1909)

The Cold Meteorite

While through our air thy kindling course was run
   A momentary glory filled the night;
   The envious stars shone fainter, for thy light
Garnered the wealth of all their fires in one.
Ah, short-lived splendor! journey ill-begun!
   Half-buried in the Earth that broke thy flight,
   No longer in thy broidered raiment dight,
Here liest thou dishonored, cold, undone.
"Nay, critic mine, far better 't is to die
   "The death that flashes gladness, than alone,
"In frigid dignity, to live on high;
   "Better in burning sacrifice be thrown
"Against the world to perish, than the sky
   "To circle endlessly a barren stone."

Lowlands

As one who goes from holding converse sweet
   In cloistered walls with great ones of the past,
   And steps, enwrapt in visions high and vast,
To meet his fellows in the noisy street;
So we, descending from the mountain's height,
   Feel strange discordance in the world below.
   Is this the calm that there enchanted so?
It cannot be that we beheld aright.
But courage! not for ever on the mount;
   Far oftener in the valley must we move;
   The things that lie about us learn to love,
And for the work allotted us account;
   Content if, now and then, we track above
The tumbling waters to their placid fount.

JOHN HAY
(1838–1905)

Jim Bludso,
Of the Prairie Belle

Wall, no! I can't tell whar he lives,
   Becase he don't live, you see;
Leastways, he 's got out of the habit
   Of livin' like you and me.
Whar have you been for the last three year
   That you have n't heard folks tell
How Jimmy Bludso passed in his checks
   The night of the Prairie Belle?

He were n't no saint,—them engineers
   Is all pretty much alike,—
One wife in Natchez-under-the-Hill
   And another one here, in Pike;
A keerless man in his talk was Jim,
   And an awkward hand in a row,
But he never flunked, and he never lied,—
   I reckon he never knowed how.

And this was all the religion he had,—
   To treat his engine well;
Never be passed on the river
   To mind the pilot 's bell;
And if ever the Prairie Belle took fire,—
   A thousand times he swore,
He 'd hold her nozzle agin the bank
   Till the last soul got ashore.

All boats has their day on the Mississip,
   And her day come at last,—
The Movastar was a better boat,
   But the Belle she *would n't* be passed.

And so she come tearin' along that night--
    The oldest craft on the line—
With a nigger squat on her safety-valve,
    And her furnace crammed, rosin and pine.

The fire bust out as she clared the bar,
    And burnt a hole in the night,
And quick as a flash she turned, and made
    For that willer-bank on the right.
There was runnin' and cursin', but Jim yelled out,
    Over all the infernal roar,
"I'll hold her nozzle agin the bank
    Till the last galoot's ashore."

Through the hot, black breath of the burnin' boat
    Jim Bludso's voice was heard,
And they all had trust in his cussedness,
    And knowed he would keep his word.
And, sure's you're born, they all got off
    Afore the smokestacks fell,—
And Bludso's ghost went up alone
    In the smoke of the Prairie Belle.

He were n't no saint,—but at jedgment
    I'd run my chance with Jim,
'Longside of some pious gentlemen
    That would n't shook hands with him.
He seen his duty, a dead-sure thing,—
    And went for it thar and then;
And Christ ain't a going to be too hard
    On a man that died for men.

HENRY ADAMS

(1838–1918)

Buddha and Brahma

To John Hay

The Buddha, known to men by many names—
Siddartha, Sakya Muni, Blessed One,—
Sat in the forest, as had been his wont
These many years since he attained perfection;
In silent thought, abstraction, purity,
His eyes fixed on the Lotus in his hand,
He meditated on the perfect Life,
While his disciples, sitting round him, waited
His words of teaching, every syllable
More and more precious as the Master gently
Warned them how near was come his day of parting.
In silence, as the Master gave example,
They meditated on the Path and Law,
Till one, Malunka, looking up and speaking,
Said to the Buddha: "O Omniscient One,
Teach us, if such be in the Perfect Way,
Whether the World exists eternally."

The Buddha made no answer, and in silence
All the disciples bent their contemplation
On the perfection of the Eight-fold Way,
Until Malunka spoke again: "O Master,
What answer shall we offer to the Brahman
Who asks us if our Master holds the World
To be, or not, Eternal?"
                    Still the Buddha sat
As though he heard not, contemplating
The pure white Lotus in his sacred hand,
Till a third time Malunka questioned him:
"Lord of the World, we know not what we ask;
We fear to teach what thou hast not made pure."

Then gently, still in silence, lost in thought,
The Buddha raised the Lotus in his hand,
His eyes bent downward, fixed upon the flower.
No more! A moment so he held it only,
Then his hand sank into its former rest.

Long the disciples pondered on the lesson.
Much they discussed its mystery and meaning,
Each finding something he could make his own,
Some hope or danger in the Noble Way,
Some guide or warning to the Perfect Life.
Among them sat the last of the disciples,
Listening and pondering, silently and still;
And when the scholars found no certain meaning
In Buddha's answer to Malunka's prayer,
The young man pondered: I will seek my father,
The wisest man of all men in the world,
And he with one word will reveal this secret,
And make me in an instant reach the light
Which these in many years have not attained
Though guided by the Buddha and the Law.

So the boy sought his father—an old man
Famous for human wisdom, subtle counsel,
Boldness in action, recklessness in war—
Gautama's friend, the Rajah of Mogadha.
No follower of Buddha, but a Brahman,
Devoted first to Vishnu, then to caste,
He made no sign of anger or remonstrance
When his son left him at Siddartha's bidding
To take the vows of poverty and prayer—
If Vishnu willed it, let his will be done!

The Rajah sat at evening in his palace,
Deep in the solitude of his own thought,
When silently the young man entering
Crouched at a distance, waiting till his father
Should give some sign of favor. Then he spoke:
"Father, you are wise! I come to ask you
A secret meaning none of us can read;

For, when Malunka three times asked the Master
Whether the world was or was not eternal,
Siddartha for a moment lifted up
The Lotus, and kept silence."

The Rajah pondered long, with darkened features,
As though in doubt increasing. Then he said:
"Reflect, my son! The Master had not meant
This last and deepest lesson to be learned
From any but himself—by any means
But silent thought, abstraction, purity,
The living spirit of his Eight-fold Way,
The jewels of his Lotus. Least of all
Had he, whose first and easiest lesson taught
The nothingness of caste, intended you
To seek out me, a Warrior, Kshatriya,
Knowing no duties but to caste and sword,
To teach the Buddha and unveil his shrine.
My teaching is not his; mine not his way;
You quit your Master when you question me."

Silent they sat, and long. Then slowly spoke
The younger: "Father, you are wise.
I must have Wisdom." "Not so, my son.
Old men are often fools, but young men always.
Your duty is to act; leave thought to us."
The younger sat in patience, eyes cast down,
Voice low and gentle as the Master taught;
But still repeated the same prayer: "You are wise;
I must have wisdom. Life for me is thought,
But, were it action, how, in youth or age,
Can man act wisely, leaving thought aside?"

The Rajah made no answer, but almost
His mouth seemed curving to a sudden smile
That hardened to a frown; and then he spoke:
"If Vishnu wills it, let his will be done!
The child sees jewels on his father's sword,
And cries until he gets it for a plaything.
He cannot use it but to wound himself;

Its perfect workmanship wakes no delight;
Its jewels are for him but common glass;
The sword means nothing that the child can know;
But when at last the child has grown to man,
Has learned the beauty of the weapon's art,
And proved its purpose on the necks of men,
Still must he tell himself, as I tell you:
Use it, but ask no questions! *Think not! Strike!*
This counsel you reject, for you want wisdom.
So be it! Yet I swear to you in truth
That all my wisdom lies in these three words.

"You ask Gautama's meaning, for you know
That since his birth, his thoughts and acts alike
Have been to me a mirror, clearer far
Than to himself, for no man sees himself.
With the solemnity of youth, you ask
Of me, on whom the charm of childhood still
Works greater miracles than magicians know,
To tell, as though it were a juggler's trick
The secret meaning which himself but now
Could tell you only by a mystic sign,
The symbol of a symbol—so far-thought,
So vague and vast and intricate its scope.
And I, whom you compel to speak for him,
Must give his thought through mine, for his
Passes your powers—yours and all your school.

"Your Master, Sakya Muni, Gautama,
Is, like myself and you, a Kshatriya,
And in our youths we both, like you, rebelled
Against the priesthood and their laws of caste.
We sought new paths, desperate to find escape
Out of the jungle that the priests had made.
Gautama found a path. You follow it.
I found none, and I stay here, in the jungle,
Content to tolerate what I cannot mend.
I blame not him or you, but would you know
Gautama's meaning, you must fathom mine.
He failed to cope with life; renounced its cares;

Fled to the forest, and attained the End,
Reaching the End by sacrificing life.
You know both End and Path. You, too, attain.
I could not. Ten years older, I;
Already trained to rule, to fight, to scheme,
To strive for objects that I dared not tell,
Not for myself alone, but for us all;
Had I thrown down my sword, and fled my throne,
Not all the hermits, priests, and saints of Ind,
Buddhist or Brahman, could have saved our heads
From rolling in the dirt; for Rajahs know
A quicker than the Eight-fold Noble Way
To help their scholars to attain the End.
Renounce I could not, and could not reform.
How could I battle with the Brahman priests,
Or free the people from the yoke of caste,
When, with the utmost aid that priests could give,
And willing service from each caste in turn,
I saved but barely both my throne and them.

"So came it that our paths were separate,
And his led up to so supreme a height
That from its summit he can now look down
And see where still the jungle stifles me.
Yet was our starting-point the same, and though
We now seem worlds apart—hold fast to this!—
The Starting-point must be the End-point too!
You know the Veda, and need not be taught
The first and last idea of all true knowledge:
One single spirit from which all things spring;
One thought containing all thoughts possible;
Not merely those that we, in our thin reason,
Hold to be true, but all their opposites;
For Brahma is Beginning, Middle, End,
Matter and Mind, Time, Space, Form, Life and Death.
The Universal has no limit. Thought
Travelling in constant circles, round and round,
Must ever pass through endless contradictions,
Returning on itself at last, till lost
In silence.

"This is the Veda, as you know,
The alphabet of all philosophy,
For he who cannot or who dares not grasp
And follow this necessity of Brahma,
Is but a fool and weakling; and must perish
Among the follies of his own reflection.

"Your Master, you, and I, and all wise men,
Have one sole purpose which we never lose:
Through different paths we each seek to attain,
Sooner or later, as our paths allow,
A perfect union with the single Spirit.
Gautama's way is best, but all are good.
He breaks a path at once to what he seeks.
By silence and absorption he unites
His soul with the great soul from which it started.
But we, who cannot fly the world, must seek
To live two separate lives; one, in the world
Which we must ever seem to treat as real;
The other in ourselves, behind a veil
Not to be raised without disturbing both.

"The Rajah is an instrument of Brahma,
No more, no less, than sunshine, lightning, rain;
And when he meets resistance in his path,
And when his sword falls on a victim's neck,
It strikes as strikes the lightning—as it must;
Rending its way through darkness to the point
It needs must seek, by no choice of its own.
Thus in the life of Ruler, Warrior, Master,
The wise man knows his wisdom has no place,
And when most wise, we act by rule and law,
Talk to conceal our thought, and think
Only within the range of daily need,
Ruling our subjects while ourselves rebel,
Death always on our lips and in our act.

"This is the jungle in which we must stay,
According to the teachings of the Master,
Never can we attain the Perfect Life.

Yet in this world of selfishness and striving
The wise man lives as deeply sunk in silence,
As conscious of the Perfect Life he covets,
As any recluse in his forest shadows,
As any Yogi in his mystic trances.
We need no Noble Way to teach us Freedom
Amid the clamor of a world of slaves.
We need no Lotus to love purity
Where life is else corruption.

"So read Siddartha's secret! He has taught
A certain pathway to attain the End;
And best and simplest yet devised by man,
Yet still so hard that every energy
Must be devoted to its sacred law.
Then, when Malunka turns to ask for knowledge,
Would seek what lies beyond the Path he teaches,
What distant horizon transcends his own,
He bids you look in silence on the Lotus.
For you, he means no more. For me, this meaning
Points back and forward to that common goal
From which all paths diverge; to which,
All paths must tend—Brahma, the only Truth!

"Gautama tells me my way too is good;
Life, Time, Space, Thought, the World, the Universe
End where they first begin, in one sole Thought
Of Purity in Silence."

JAMES RYDER RANDALL
(1839–1908)

Maryland

The despot's heel is on thy shore,
    Maryland!
His torch is at thy temple door,
    Maryland!
Avenge the patriotic gore
That flecked the streets of Baltimore,
And be the battle-queen of yore,
    Maryland! My Maryland!

Hark to a wand'ring son's appeal,
    Maryland!
My mother State! to thee I kneel,
    Maryland!
For life and death, for woe and weal,
Thy peerless chivalry reveal,
And gird thy beauteous limbs with steel,
    Maryland! My Maryland!

Thou wilt not cower in the dust,
    Maryland!
Thy beaming sword shall never rust,
    Maryland!
Remember Carroll's sacred trust,
Remember Howard's warlike thrust—
And all thy slumberers with the just,
    Maryland! My Maryland!

Come! 'tis the red dawn of the day,
    Maryland!
Come! with thy panoplied array,
    Maryland!
With Ringgold's spirit for the fray,

With Watson's blood at Monterey,
With fearless Lowe and dashing May,
        Maryland! My Maryland!

Come! for thy shield is bright and strong,
        Maryland!
Come! for thy dalliance does thee wrong,
        Maryland!
Come! to thine own heroic throng,
That stalks with Liberty along,
And give a new *Key* to thy song,
        Maryland! My Maryland!

Dear Mother! burst the tyrant's chain,
        Maryland!
Virginia should not call in vain,
        Maryland!
She meets her sisters on the plain—
"Sic semper," 'tis the proud refrain,
That baffles minions back amain,
        Maryland!
Arise, in majesty again,
        Maryland! My Maryland!

I see the blush upon thy cheek,
        Maryland!
But thou wast ever bravely meek,
        Maryland!
But lo! there surges forth a shriek
From hill to hill, from creek to creek—
Potomac calls to Chesapeake,
        Maryland! My Maryland!

Thou wilt not yield the Vandal toll,
        Maryland!
Thou wilt not crook to his control,
        Maryland!
Better the fire upon thee roll,

Better the blade, the shot, the bowl,
Than crucifixion of the soul,
  Maryland! My Maryland!

I hear the distant thunder-hum,
  Maryland!
The Old Line's bugle, fife and drum,
  Maryland!
She is not dead, nor deaf, nor dumb—
Huzza! she spurns the Northern scum!
She breathes—she burns! she'll come! she'll come!
  Maryland! My Maryland!

CONSTANCE FENIMORE WOOLSON

(1840–1894)

The Florida Beach

Our drift-wood fire burns drowsily,
  The fog hangs low afar,
A thousand sea-birds fearlessly
  Hover above the bar;
Our boat is drawn far up the strand,
  Beyond the tide's long reach;
Like a fringe to the dark green winter land,
  Shines the silvery Florida beach.

Behind, the broad pine barrens lie
  Without a path or trail,
Before, the ocean meets the sky
  Without a rock or sail.
We call across to Africa,
  As a poet called to Spain:
A murmur of "Antony! Antony!"
  The waves bring back in refrain.

Far to the south the beach shines on,
  Dotted with giant shells;
Coral sprays from the white reef won,
  Radiate spiny cells;
Glass-like creatures that ride the waves,
  With azure sail and oar,
And wide-mouthed things from the deep sea caves
  That melt away on the shore.

Wild ducks gaze as we pass along:
  They have not learned to fear;
The mocking-bird keeps on his song
  In the low palmetto near;

The sluggish stream from the everglade
  Shows the alligator's track,
And the sea is broken in light and shade
  With the heave of the dolphin's back.

The Spanish light-house stands in haze:
  The keeper trims his light;
No sail he sees through the long, long days,
  No sail through the still, still night;
But ships that pass far out at sea,
  Along the warm Gulf Stream,
From Cuba and tropic Carribee,
  Keep watch for his distant gleam.

Alone, alone we wander on,
  In the southern winter day.
Through the dreamy veil the fog has spun
  The world seems far away;
The tide comes in—the birds fly low,
  As if to catch our speech.
Ah, Destiny! Why must we ever go
  Away from the Florida beach?

EDWARD ROWLAND SILL

(1841–1887)

Opportunity

This I beheld, or dreamed it in a dream:—
There spread a cloud of dust along a plain;
And underneath the cloud, or in it, raged
A furious battle, and men yelled, and swords
Shocked upon swords and shields. A prince's banner
Wavered, then staggered backward, hemmed by foes.
A craven hung along the battle's edge,
And thought, "Had I a sword of keener steel—
That blue blade that the king's son bears,—but this
Blunt thing—!" he snapt and flung it from his hand,
And lowering crept away and left the field.
Then came the king's son, wounded, sore bestead,
And weaponless, and saw the broken sword,
Hilt-buried in the dry and trodden sand,
And ran and snatched it, and with battle-shout
Lifted afresh he hewed his enemy down,
And saved a great cause that heroic day.

California Winter

This is not winter: where is the crisp air,
And snow upon the roof, and frozen ponds,
And the star-fire that tips the icicle?

Here blooms the late rose, pale and odorless;
And the vague fragrance in the garden walks
Is but a doubtful dream of mignonette.
In some smooth spot, under a sleeping oak
That has not dreamed of such a thing as spring,
The ground has stolen a kiss from the cool sun
And thrilled a little, and the tender grass

Has sprung untimely, for these great bright days,
Staring upon it, will not let it live.
The sky is blue, and 't is a goodly time,
And the round, barren hillsides tempt the feet;
But 't is not winter: such as seems to man
What June is to the roses, sending floods
Of life and color through the tingling veins.

It is a land without a fireside. Far
Is the old home, where, even this very night,
Roars the great chimney with its glorious fire,
And old friends look into each other's eyes
Quietly, for each knows the other's trust.

Heaven is not far away such winter nights:
The big white stars are sparkling in the east,
And glitter in the gaze of solemn eyes;
For many things have faded with the flowers,
And many things their resurrection wait;
Earth like a sepulchre is sealed with frost,
And Morn and Even beside the silent door
Sit watching, and their soft and folded wings
Are white with feathery snow.

Yet even here
We are not quite forgotten by the Hours,
Could human eyes but see the beautiful
Save through the glamour of a memory.
Soon comes the strong south wind, and shouts aloud
Its jubilant anthem. Soon the singing rain
Comes from warm seas, and in its skyey tent
Enwraps the drowsy world. And when, some night,
Its flowing folds invisibly withdraw,
Lo! the new life in all created things.
The azure mountains and the ocean gates
Against the lovely sky stand clean and clear
As a new purpose in the wiser soul.

CHARLES EDWARD CARRYL

(1841–1920)

A Nautical Ballad

A capital ship for an ocean trip
   Was "The Walloping Window-blind;"
No gale that blew dismayed her crew
   Or troubled the captain's mind.
The man at the wheel was taught to feel
   Contempt for the wildest blow,
And it often appeared, when the weather had cleared,
   That he'd been in his bunk below.

The boatswain's mate was very sedate,
   Yet fond of amusement, too;
And he played hop-scotch with the starboard watch,
   While the captain tickled the crew.
And the gunner we had was apparently mad,
   For he sat on the after-rail,
And fired salutes with the captain's boots,
   In the teeth of the booming gale.

The captain sat in a commodore's hat,
   And dined, in a royal way,
On toasted pigs and pickles and figs
   And gummery bread, each day.
But the cook was Dutch, and behaved as such;
   For the food that he gave the crew
Was a number of tons of hot-cross buns,
   Chopped up with sugar and glue.

And we all felt ill as mariners will,
   On a diet that's cheap and rude;
And we shivered and shook as we dipped the cook
   In a tub of his gluesome food.
Then nautical pride we laid aside,

And we cast the vessel ashore
On the Gulliby Isles, where the Poohpooh smiles,
And the Anagazanders roar.

Composed of sand was that favored land,
And trimmed with cinnamon straws;
And pink and blue was the pleasing hue
Of the Tickletoeteaser's claws.
And we sat on the edge of a sandy ledge
And shot at the whistling bee;
And the Binnacle-bats wore water-proof hats
As they danced in the sounding sea.

On rubagub bark, from dawn to dark,
We fed, till we all had grown
Uncommonly shrunk,—when a Chinese junk
Came by from the torriby zone.
She was stubby and square, but we didn't much care,
And we cheerily put to sea;
And we left the crew of the junk to chew
The bark of the rubagub tree.

SIDNEY LANIER

(1842–1881)

from *Hymns of the Marshes*

Marsh Song—At Sunset

Over the monstrous shambling sea,
   Over the Caliban sea,
Bright Ariel-cloud, thou lingerest:
Oh wait, oh wait, in the warm red West,—
   Thy Prospero I'll be.

Over the humped and fishy sea,
   Over the Caliban sea,
O cloud in the West, like a thought in the heart
Of pardon, loose thy wing and start,
   And do a grace for me.

Over the huge and huddling sea,
   Over the Caliban sea,
Bring hither my brother Antonio,—Man,—
My injurer: night breaks the ban;
   Brother, I pardon thee.

The Marshes of Glynn

Glooms of the live-oaks, beautiful-braided and woven
With intricate shades of the vines that myriad-cloven
   Clamber the forks of the multiform boughs,—
     Emerald twilights,—
     Virginal shy lights,
Wrought of the leaves to allure to the whisper of vows,
When lovers pace timidly down through the green
        colonnades
   Of the dim sweet woods, of the dear dark woods,
    Of the heavenly woods and glades,

That run to the radiant marginal sand-beach within
    The wide sea-marshes of Glynn;—

  Beautiful glooms, soft dusks in the noon-day fire,—
  Wildwood privacies, closets of lone desire,
Chamber from chamber parted with wavering arras of
      leaves,—
Cells for the passionate pleasure of prayer to the soul that
      grieves,
  Pure with a sense of the passing of saints through the
      wood,
  Cool for the dutiful weighing of ill with good;—

O braided dusks of the oak and woven shades of the vine,
While the riotous noon-day sun of the June-day long did
      shine,
Ye held me fast in your heart and I held you fast in mine;
  But now when the noon is no more, and riot is rest,
  And the sun is a-wait at the ponderous gate of the West,
    And the slant yellow beam down the wood-aisle doth
      seem
    Like a lane into heaven that leads from a dream,—
Ay, now, when my soul all day hath drunken the soul of the
      oak,
And my heart is at ease from men, and the wearisome sound
      of the stroke
  Of the scythe of time and the trowel of trade is low,
  And belief overmasters doubt, and I know that I know,
  And my spirit is grown to a lordly great compass within,
  That the length and the breadth and the sweep of the
      marshes of Glynn
  Will work me no fear like the fear they have wrought me
      of yore
    When length was fatigue, and when breadth was but
      bitterness sore,
    And when terror and shrinking and dreary unnamable
      pain
    Drew over me out of the merciless miles of the plain,—
    Oh, now, unafraid, I am fain to face
      The vast sweet visage of space.

To the edge of the wood I am drawn, I am drawn,
Where the gray beach glimmering runs, as a belt of the
    dawn,
    For a mete and a mark
    To the forest-dark: —
        So:
    Affable live-oak, leaning low, —
    Thus — with your favor — soft, with a reverent hand,
    (Not lightly touching your person, Lord of the land!)
    Bending your beauty aside, with a step I stand
        On the firm-packed sand,
            Free
    By a world of marsh that borders a world of sea.
Sinuous southward and sinuous northward the
                shimmering band
Of the sand-beach fastens the fringe of the marsh to the
                folds of the land.
Inward and outward to northward and southward the beach-
                lines linger and curl
As a silver-wrought garment that clings to and follows the
                firm sweet limbs of a girl.
    Vanishing, swerving, evermore curving again into sight,
    Softly the sand-beach wavers away to a dim gray looping
                of light.
    And what if behind me to westward the wall of the woods
                stands high?
    The world lies east: how ample, the marsh and the sea and
                the sky!
    A league and a league of marsh-grass, waist-high, broad in
                the blade,
    Green, and all of a height, and unflecked with a light or a
                shade,
        Stretch leisurely off, in a pleasant plain,
        To the terminal blue of the main.

    Oh, what is abroad in the marsh and the terminal sea?
        Somehow my soul seems suddenly free
    From the weighing of fate and the sad discussion of sin,
    By the length and the breadth and the sweep of the
                marshes of Glynn.

Ye marshes, how candid and simple and nothing-
        withholding and free
Ye publish yourselves to the sky and offer yourselves to the
        sea!
Tolerant plains, that suffer the sea and the rains and the sun,
Ye spread and span like the catholic man who hath mightily
        won
  God out of knowledge and good out of infinite pain
  And sight out of blindness and purity out of a stain.

As the marsh-hen secretly builds on the watery sod,
Behold I will build me a nest on the greatness of God:
I will fly in the greatness of God as the marsh-hen flies
In the freedom that fills all the space 'twixt the marsh and
        the skies:
By so many roots as the marsh-grass sends in the sod
I will heartily lay me a-hold on the greatness of God:
Oh, like to the greatness of God is the greatness within
The range of the marshes, the liberal marshes of Glynn.

And the sea lends large, as the marsh: lo, out of his plenty
        the sea
Pours fast: full soon the time of the flood-tide must be:
  Look how the grace of the sea doth go
About and about through the intricate channels that flow
     Here and there,
     Everywhere,
Till his waters have flooded the uttermost creeks and the
       low-lying lanes,
  And the marsh is meshed with a million veins,
  That like as with rosy and silvery essences flow
    In the rose-and-silver evening glow.
     Farewell, my lord Sun!
The creeks overflow: a thousand rivulets run
'Twixt the roots of the sod; the blades of the marsh-grass
       stir;
Passeth a hurrying sound of wings that westward whirr;
Passeth, and all is still; and the currents cease to run;
    And the sea and the marsh are one.

How still the plains of the waters be!
The tide is in his ecstasy.
The tide is at his highest height:
    And it is night.

And now from the Vast of the Lord will the waters of
        sleep
    Roll in on the souls of men,
    But who will reveal to our waking ken
    The forms that swim and the shapes that creep
        Under the waters of sleep?
And I would I could know what swimmeth below when the
        tide comes in
On the length and the breadth of the marvellous marshes of
        Glynn.

Song of the Chattahoochee

    Out of the hills of Habersham,
    Down the valleys of Hall,
I hurry amain to reach the plain,
Run the rapid and leap the fall,
Split at the rock and together again,
Accept my bed, or narrow or wide,
And flee from folly on every side
With a lover's pain to attain the plain
    Far from the hills of Habersham,
    Far from the valleys of Hall.

    All down the hills of Habersham,
    All through the valleys of Hall,
The rushes cried *Abide, abide,*
The willful waterweeds held me thrall,
The laving laurel turned my tide,
The ferns and the fondling grass said *Stay,*
The dewberry dipped for to work delay,
And the little reeds sighed *Abide, abide,*
    Here in the hills of Habersham,
    Here in the valleys of Hall.

High o'er the hills of Habersham,
    Veiling the valleys of Hall,
The hickory told me manifold
Fair tales of shade, the poplar tall
Wrought me her shadowy self to hold,
The chestnut, the oak, the walnut, the pine,
Overleaning, with flickering meaning and sign,
Said, *Pass not, so cold, these manifold*
    Deep shades of the hills of Habersham,
    These glades in the valleys of Hall.

And oft in the hills of Habersham,
    And oft in the valleys of Hall,
The white quartz shone, and the smooth brook-stone
Did bar me of passage with friendly brawl,
And many a luminous jewel lone
—Crystals clear or a-cloud with mist,
Ruby, garnet and amethyst—
Made lures with the lights of streaming stone
    In the clefts of the hills of Habersham,
    In the beds of the valleys of Hall.

But oh, not the hills of Habersham,
    And oh, not the valleys of Hall
Avail: I am fain for to water the plain.
Downward the voices of Duty call—
Downward, to toil and be mixed with the main,
The dry fields burn, and the mills are to turn,
And a myriad flowers mortally yearn,
And the lordly main from beyond the plain
    Calls o'er the hills of Habersham,
    Calls through the valleys of Hall.

From the Flats

What heartache—ne'er a hill!
Inexorable, vapid, vague, and chill
The drear sand-levels drain my spirit low.
With one poor word they tell me all they know;

Whereat their stupid tongues, to tease my pain,
Do drawl it o'er again and o'er again.
They hurt my heart with griefs I cannot name:
     Always the same, the same.

     Nature hath no surprise,
No ambuscade of beauty 'gainst mine eyes
From brake or lurking dell or deep defile;
No humors, frolic forms—this mile, that mile;
No rich reserves or happy-valley hopes
Beyond the bends of roads, the distant slopes.
Her fancy fails, her wild is all run tame:
     Ever the same, the same.

     Oh, might I through these tears
But glimpse some hill my Georgia high uprears,
Where white the quartz and pink the pebble shine,
The hickory heavenward strives, the muscadine
Swings o'er the slope, the oak's far-falling shade
Darkens the dogwood in the bottom glade,
And down the hollow from a ferny nook
     Bright leaps a living brook!

The Mocking Bird

Superb and sole, upon a plumèd spray
     That o'er the general leafage boldly grew,
     He summ'd the woods in song; or typic drew
The watch of hungry hawks, the lone dismay
Of languid doves when long their lovers stray,
     And all birds' passion-plays that sprinkle dew
     At morn in brake or bosky avenue.
Whate'er birds did or dreamed, this bird could say.
Then down he shot, bounced airily along
The sward, twitched-in a grasshopper, made song
     Midflight, perched, primped, and to his art again.
     Sweet Science, this large riddle read me plain:
          How may the death of that dull insect be
          The life of yon trim Shakspere on the tree?

from *Street Cries*

To Richard Wagner

I saw a sky of stars that rolled in grime.
　　All glory twinkled through some sweat of fight.
From each tall chimney of the roaring time
　　That shot his fire far up the sooty night
Mixt fuels—Labor's Right and Labor's Crime—
　　Sent upward throb on throb of scarlet light
Till huge hot blushes in the heavens blent
With golden hues of Trade's high firmament.

Fierce burned the furnaces; yet all seemed well.
　　Hope dreamed rich music in the rattling mills.
"Ye foundries, ye shall cast my church a bell,"
　　Loud cried the Future from the farthest hills:
"Ye groaning forces, crack me every shell
　　Of customs, old constraints, and narrow ills:
Thou, lithe Invention, wake and pry and guess,
Till thy deft mind invents me Happiness."

And I beheld high scaffoldings of creeds
　　Crumbling from round Religion's perfect Fane:
And a vast noise of rights, wrongs, powers, needs,
　　--Cries of new Faiths that called "This Way is plain,"
—Grindings of upper against lower greeds—
　　—Fond sighs for old things, shouts for new,--did reign
Below that stream of golden fire that broke,
Mottled with red, above the seas of smoke.

Hark! Gay fanfares from horns of old Romance
　　Strike through the clouds of clamor: who be these
That, paired in rich processional, advance
　　From darkness o'er the murk mad factories
Into yon flaming road, and sink, strange Ministrants!
　　Sheer down to earth, with many minstrelsies
And motions fine, and mix about the scene
And fill the Time with forms of ancient mien?

Bright ladies and brave knights of Fatherland;
 Sad mariners, no harbor e'er may hold;
A swan soft floating tow'rds a tragic strand;
 Dim ghosts, of earth, air, water, fire, steel, gold,
Wind, grief, and love; a lewd and lurking band
 Of Powers—dark Conspiracy, Cunning cold,
Gray Sorcery; magic cloaks and rings and rods;
Valkyries, heroes, Rhinemaids, giants, gods!

   * * * * *

O Wagner, westward bring thy heavenly art.
 No trifler thou: Siegfried and Wotan be
Names for big ballads of the modern heart.
 Thine ears hear deeper than thine eyes can see.
Voice of the monstrous mill, the shouting mart,
 Not less of airy cloud and wave and tree,
Thou, thou, if even to thyself unknown,
Hast power to say the Time in terms of tone.

The Raven Days

I.

Our hearths are gone out, and our hearts are broken,
  And but the ghosts of homes to us remain,
And ghostly eyes and hollow sighs give token
  From friend to friend of an unspoken pain.

II.

O, Raven Days, dark Raven Days of sorrow,
  Bring to us, in your whetted ivory beaks,
Some sign out of the far land of To-morrow,
  Some strip of sea-green dawn, some orange streaks.

III.

Ye float in dusky files, forever croaking—
  Ye chill our manhood with your dreary shade.
Pale, in the dark, not even God invoking,
  We lie in chains, too weak to be afraid.

IV.

O, Raven Days, dark Raven Days of sorrow,
  Will ever any warm light come again?
Will ever the lit mountains of To-morrow
  Begin to gleam across the mournful plain?

AMBROSE BIERCE
(1842–1914?)

Alone

In contact, lo! the flint and steel,
By spark and flame, the thought reveal
That he the metal, she the stone,
Had cherished secretly alone.

Elegy

The cur foretells the knell of parting day;
  The loafing herd winds slowly o'er the lea;
The wise man homeward plods; I only stay
  To fiddle-faddle in a minor key.

Lead

Hail, holy Lead!—of human feuds the great
  And universal arbiter; endowed
  With penetration to pierce any cloud
Fogging the field of controversial hate,
And with a swift, inevitable, straight,
  Searching precision find the unavowed
  But vital point. Thy judgment, when allowed
By the chirurgeon, settles the debate.
O useful metal!—were it not for thee
  We'd grapple one another's ears alway:
But when we hear thee buzzing like a bee
  We, like old Muhlenberg, "care not to stay."
And when the quick have run away like pullets
Jack Satan smelts the dead to make new bullets.

The Passing Show

I.

I know not if it was a dream. I viewed
A city where the restless multitude,
   Between the eastern and the western deep
Had reared gigantic fabrics, strong and rude.

Colossal palaces crowned every height;
Towers from valleys climbed into the light;
   O'er dwellings at their feet, great golden domes
Hung in the blue, barbarically bright.

But now, new-glimmering to-east, the day
Touched the black masses with a grace of gray,
   Dim spires of temples to the nation's God
Studding high spaces of the wide survey.

Well did the roofs their solemn secret keep
Of life and death stayed by the truce of sleep,
   Yet whispered of an hour when sleepers wake,
The fool to hope afresh, the wise to weep.

The gardens greened upon the builded hills
Above the tethered thunders of the mills
   With sleeping wheels unstirred to service yet
By the tamed torrents and the quickened rills.

A hewn acclivity, reprieved a space,
Looked on the builder's blocks about his base
   And bared his wounded breast in sign to say:
"Strike! 't is my destiny to lodge your race.

" 'T was but a breath ago the mammoth browsed
   Upon my slopes, and in my caves I housed
      Your shaggy fathers in their nakedness,
While on their foeman's offal they caroused."

Ships from afar afforested the bay,
Within their huge and chambered bodies lay
   The wealth of continents; and merrily sailed
The hardy argosies to far Cathay.

Beside the city of the living spread—
Strange fellowship!—the city of the dead;
   And much I wondered what its humble folk,
To see how bravely they were housed, had said.

Noting how firm their habitations stood,
Broad-based and free of perishable wood—
   How deep in granite and how high in brass
The names were wrought of eminent and good,

I said: "When gold or power is their aim,
The smile of beauty or the wage of shame,
   Men dwell in cities; to this place they fare
When they would conquer an abiding fame."

From the red East the sun—a solemn rite—
Crowned with a flame the cross upon a height
   Above the dead; and then with all his strength
Struck the great city all aroar with light!

II.

I know not if it was a dream. I came
Unto a land where something seemed the same
   That I had known as 't were but yesterday,
But what it was I could not rightly name.

It was a strange and melancholy land,
Silent and desolate. On either hand
   Lay waters of a sea that seemed as dead,
And dead above it seemed the hills to stand.

Grayed all with age, those lonely hills —ah me,
How worn and weary they appeared to be!
  Between their feet long dusty fissures clove
The plain in aimless windings to the sea.

One hill there was which, parted from the rest,
Stood where the eastern water curved a-west.
  Silent and passionless it stood. I thought
I saw a scar upon its giant breast.

The sun with sullen and portentous gleam
Hung like a menace on the sea's extreme;
  Nor the dead waters, nor the far, bleak bars
Of cloud were conscious of his failing beam.

It was a dismal and a dreadful sight,
That desert in its cold, uncanny light;
  No soul but I alone to mark the fear
And imminence of everlasting night!

All presages and prophecies of doom
Glimmered and babbled in the ghastly gloom,
  And in the midst of that accursèd scene
A wolf sat howling on a broken tomb.

To the Bartholdi Statue

O Liberty, God-gifted—
    Young and immortal maid—
In your high hand uplifted,
    The torch declares your trade.

Its crimson menace, flaming
    Upon the sea and shore,
Is, trumpet-like, proclaiming
    That Law shall be no more.

Austere incendiary,
    We're blinking in the light;
Where is your customary
    Grenade of dynamite?

Where are your staves and switches
    For men of gentle birth?
Your mask and dirk for riches?
    Your chains for wit and worth?

Perhaps, you've brought the halters
    You used in the old days,
When round religion's altars
    You stabled Cromwell's bays?

Behind you, unsuspected,
    Have you the axe, fair wench,
Wherewith you once collected
    A poll-tax from the French?

America salutes you—
    Preparing to disgorge.
Take everything that suits you,
    And marry Henry George.

RICHARD WATSON GILDER

(1844–1909)

The Sonnet

(*In Answer to a Question.*)

What is a sonnet? 'T is the pearly shell
  That murmurs of the far-off murmuring sea;
  A precious jewel carved most curiously;
  It is a little picture painted well.
What is a sonnet? 'T is the tear that fell
  From a great poet's hidden ecstasy;
  A two-edged sword, a star, a song—ah me!
  Sometimes a heavy-tolling funeral bell.
This was the flame that shook with Dante's breath;
  The solemn organ whereon Milton played,
  And the clear glass where Shakespeare's shadow falls:
A sea this is—beware who ventureth!
  For like a fjord the narrow floor is laid
  Deep as mid-ocean to the sheer mountain walls.

On the Bay

This watery vague how vast! This misty globe,
Seen from this center where the ferry plies,—
It plies, but seems to poise in middle air,—
Soft gray below gray heavens, and in the west
A rose-gray memory of the sunken sun;
And, where gray water touches grayer sky,
A band of darker gray pricked out with lights,—
A diamond-twinkling circlet bounding all;
And where the statue looms, a quenchless star;
And where the lighthouse, a red, pulsing flame;
While the great bridge its starry diadem
Shows through the gray, itself in grayness lost!

GEORGE WASHINGTON CABLE

(1844–1925)

Creole Slave Songs

Belle Layotte

> *I done been 'roun' to evvy spot*
> *Don't foun' nair match fo' sweet Layotte.*

I done hunt all dis settle*ment*
All de way 'roun' fum Pierre Soniat';
Never see yalla gal w'at kin
'Gin to lay 'longside sweet Layotte.

> *I done been, etc.*

I yeh dey talk 'bout 'Loïse gal—
Loïse, w'at b'long to Pierre Soniat';
I see her, but she can't biggin
Stan' up 'longside my sweet Layotte.

> *I done been, etc.*

I been meet up wid John Bayou,
Say to him, "John Bayou, my son,
Yalla gal nevva meet yo' view
Got a face lak dat chahmin' one!"

> *I done been, etc.*

"The English muskets went bim! bim!"

The English muskets went bim! bim!
Kentucky rifles went zim! zim!
I said to myself, save your skin!
I scampered along the water's edge;
When I got back it was day-break.
Mistress flew into a passion;
She had me whipped at the 'four stakes,'
Because I didn't stay with master;
But the 'four stakes' for me is better than
A musket shot from an Englishman.

The Dirge of St. Malo

Alas! young men, come, make lament
For poor St. Malo in distress!
They chased, they hunted him with dogs,
They fired at him with a gun,

.   .   .   .   .

They hauled him from the cypress swamp.
His arms they tied behind his back,
They tied his hands in front of him;
They tied him to a horse's tail,
They dragged him up into the town.
Before those grand Cabildo men
They charged that he had made a plot
To cut the throats of all the whites.
They asked him who his comrades were;
Poor St. Malo said not a word!
The judge his sentence read to him,
And then they raised the gallows-tree.
They drew the horse—the cart moved off—
And left St. Malo hanging there.
The sun was up an hour high
When on the Levee he was hung;
They left his body swinging there,
For carrion crows to feed upon.

JOHN BANISTER TABB
(1845–1909)

Evolution

Out of the dusk a shadow,
   Then, a spark;
Out of the cloud a silence,
   Then, a lark;
Out of the heart a rapture,
   Then, a pain;
Out of the dead, cold ashes,
   Life again.

Milton

So fair thy vision that the night
Abided with thee, lest the light,
A flaming sword before thine eyes,
Had shut thee out from Paradise.

Whisper

Close cleaving unto Silence, into sound
   She ventures as a timorous child from land,
Still glancing, at each wary step, around,
   Lest suddenly she lose her sister's hand.

The Shadow

O Shadow, in thy fleeting form I see
The friend of fortune that once clung to me.
In flattering light, thy constancy is shown;
In darkness, thou wilt leave me all alone.

A Winter Twilight

Blood-shotten through the bleak gigantic trees
    The sunset, o'er a wilderness of snow,
    Startles the wolfish winds that wilder grow
As hunger mocks their howling miseries.
In every skulking shadow Fancy sees
    The menace of an undiscovered foe—
    A sullen footstep, treacherous and slow,
That comes, or into deeper darkness flees.

Nor Day nor Night, in Time's eternal round
    Whereof the tides are telling, e'er hath passed
This Isthmus-hour—this dim, mysterious land
    That sets their lives asunder—where up-cast
Their earliest and their latest waves resound,
    As each, alternate, nears or leaves the strand.

Echo

    O famished Prodigal, in vain—
    Thy portion spent—thou seek'st again
        Thy father's door;
    His all with latest sigh bequeathed
    To thee the wanderer—he breathed,
        Alas! no more.

The Mid-Day Moon

    Behold, whatever wind prevail,
    Slow westering, a phantom sail—
    The lonely soul of Yesterday—
    Unpiloted, pursues her way.

EMMA LAZARUS

(1849–1887)

Echoes

Late-born and woman-souled I dare not hope,
The freshness of the elder lays, the might
Of manly, modern passion shall alight
Upon my Muse's lips, nor may I cope
(Who veiled and screened by womanhood must grope)
With the world's strong-armed warriors and recite
The dangers, wounds, and triumphs of the fight;
Twanging the full-stringed lyre through all its scope.
But if thou ever in some lake-floored cave
O'erbrowed by rocks, a wild voice wooed and heard,
Answering at once from heaven and earth and wave,
Lending elf-music to thy harshest word,
Misprize thou not these echoes that belong
To one in love with solitude and song.

The New Colossus

Not like the brazen giant of Greek fame,
With conquering limbs astride from land to land;
Here at our sea-washed, sunset gates shall stand
A mighty woman with a torch, whose flame
Is the imprisoned lightning, and her name
Mother of Exiles. From her beacon-hand
Glows world-wide welcome; her mild eyes command
The air-bridged harbor that twin cities frame.
"Keep, ancient lands, your storied pomp!" cries she
With silent lips. "Give me your tired, your poor,
Your huddled masses yearning to breathe free,
The wretched refuse of your teeming shore.
Send these, the homeless, tempest-tost to me,
I lift my lamp beside the golden door!"

Venus of the Louvre

Down the long hall she glistens like a star,
The foam-born mother of Love, transfixed to stone,
Yet none the less immortal, breathing on.
Time's brutal hand hath maimed but could not mar.
When first the enthralled enchantress from afar
Dazzled mine eyes, I saw not her alone,
Serenely poised on her world-worshipped throne,
As when she guided once her dove-drawn car,—
But at her feet a pale, death-stricken Jew,
Her life adorer, sobbed farewell to love.
Here *Heine* wept! Here still he weeps anew,
Nor ever shall his shadow lift or move,
While mourns one ardent heart, one poet-brain,
For vanished Hellas and Hebraic pain.

Long Island Sound

I see it as it looked one afternoon
In August,—by a fresh soft breeze o'erblown.
The swiftness of the tide, the light thereon,
A far-off sail, white as a crescent moon.
The shining waters with pale currents strewn,
The quiet fishing-smacks, the Eastern cove,
The semi-circle of its dark, green grove.
The luminous grasses, and the merry sun
In the grave sky; the sparkle far and wide,
Laughter of unseen children, cheerful chirp
Of crickets, and low lisp of rippling tide,
Light summer clouds fantastical as sleep
Changing unnoted while I gazed thereon.
All these fair sounds and sights I made my own.

In Exile

"Since that day till now our life is one unbroken paradise.
We live a true brotherly life. Every evening after supper we
take a seat under the mighty oak and sing our songs."
—Extract from a letter of a Russian refugee in Texas.

Twilight is here, soft breezes bow the grass,
   Day's sounds of various toil break slowly off,
The yoke-freed oxen low, the patient ass
   Dips his dry nostril in the cool, deep trough.
Up from the prairie the tanned herdsmen pass
   With frothy pails, guiding with voices rough
Their udder-lightened kine. Fresh smells of earth,
The rich, black furrows of the glebe send forth.

After the Southern day of heavy toil,
   How good to lie, with limbs relaxed, brows bare
To evening's fan, and watch the smoke-wreaths coil
   Up from one's pipe-stem through the rayless air.
So deem these unused tillers of the soil,
   Who stretched beneath the shadowing oak-tree, stare
Peacefully on the star-unfolding skies,
And name their life unbroken paradise.

The hounded stag that has escaped the pack,
   And pants at ease within a thick-leaved dell;
The unimprisoned bird that finds the track
   Through sun-bathed space, to where his fellows
      dwell;
The martyr, granted respite from the rack,
   The death-doomed victim pardoned from his cell,—
Such only know the joy these exiles gain,—
Life's sharpest rapture is surcease of pain.

Strange faces theirs, wherethrough the Orient sun
   Gleams from the eyes and glows athwart the skin.
Grave lines of studious thought and purpose run
   From curl-crowned forehead to dark-bearded chin.
And over all the seal is stamped thereon

Of anguish branded by a world of sin,
In fire and blood through ages on their name,
Their seal of glory and the Gentiles' shame.

Freedom to love the law that Moses brought,
To sing the songs of David, and to think
The thoughts Gabirol to Spinoza taught,
Freedom to dig the common earth, to drink
The universal air—for this they sought
Refuge o'er wave and continent, to link
Egypt with Texas in their mystic chain,
And truth's perpetual lamp forbid to wane.

Hark! through the quiet evening air, their song
Floats forth with wild sweet rhythm and glad refrain.
They sing the conquest of the spirit strong,
The soul that wrests the victory from pain;
The noble joys of manhood that belong
To comrades and to brothers. In their strain
Rustle of palms and Eastern streams one hears,
And the broad prairie melts in mist of tears.

1492

Thou two-faced year, Mother of Change and Fate,
Didst weep when Spain cast forth with flaming sword,
The children of the prophets of the Lord,
Prince, priest, and people, spurned by zealot hate.
Hounded from sea to sea, from state to state,
The West refused them, and the East abhorred.
No anchorage the known world could afford,
Close-locked was every port, barred every gate.

Then smiling, thou unveil'dst, O two-faced year,
A virgin world where doors of sunset part,
Saying, "Ho, all who weary, enter here!
There falls each ancient barrier that the art
Of race or creed or rank devised, to rear
Grim bulwarked hatred between heart and heart!"

SARAH ORNE JEWETT

(1849–1909)

At Home from Church

The lilacs lift in generous bloom
   Their plumes of dear old-fashioned flowers;
Their fragrance fills the still old house
   Where left alone I count the hours.

High in the apple-trees the bees
   Are humming, busy in the sun,—
An idle robin cries for rain
   But once or twice and then is done.

The Sunday-morning quiet holds
   In heavy slumber all the street,
While from the church, just out of sight
   Behind the elms, comes slow and sweet

The organ's drone, the voices faint
   That sing the quaint long-meter hymn—
I somehow feel as if shut out
   From some mysterious temple, dim

And beautiful with blue and red
   And golden lights from windows high,
Where angels in the shadows stand
   And earth seems very near the sky.

The day-dream fades—and so I try
   Again to catch the tune that brings
No thought of temple nor of priest,
   But only of a voice that sings.

A Caged Bird

High at the window in her cage
  The old canary flits and sings,
Nor sees across the curtain pass
  The shadow of a swallow's wings.

A poor deceit and copy, this,
  Of larger lives that mark their span,
Unreckoning of wider worlds
  Or gifts that Heaven keeps for man.

She gathers piteous bits and shreds,
  This solitary, mateless thing,
To patient build again the nest
  So rudely scattered spring by spring;

And sings her brief, unlistened songs,
  Her dreams of bird life wild and free,
Yet never beats her prison bars
  At sound of song from bush or tree.

But in my busiest hours I pause,
  Held by a sense of urgent speech,
Bewildered by that spark-like soul,
  Able my very soul to reach.

She will be heard; she chirps me loud,
  When I forget those gravest cares,
Her small provision to supply,
  Clear water or her seedsman's wares.

She begs me now for that chief joy
  The round great world is made to grow,—
Her wisp of greenness. Hear her chide,
  Because my answering thought is slow!

What can my life seem like to her?
　　A dull, unpunctual service mine;
Stupid before her eager call,
　　Her flitting steps, her insight fine.

To open wide thy prison door,
　　Poor friend, would give thee to thy foes;
And yet a plaintive note I hear,
　　As if to tell how slowly goes

The time of thy long prisoning.
　　Bird! does some promise keep thee sane?
Will there be better days for thee?
　　Will thy soul too know life again?

Ah, none of us have more than this:
　　If one true friend green leaves can reach
From out some fairer, wider place,
　　And understand our wistful speech!

JAMES WHITCOMB RILEY

(1849–1916)

When the Frost Is on the Punkin

When the frost is on the punkin and the fodder's in the
      shock,
And you hear the kyouck and gobble of the struttin' turkey-
      cock,
And the clackin' of the guineys, and the cluckin' of the hens,
And the rooster's hallylooer as he tiptoes on the fence;
O, it's then's the times a feller is a-feelin' at his best,
With the risin' sun to greet him from a night of peaceful
      rest,
As he leaves the house, bareheaded, and goes out to feed
      the stock,
When the frost is on the punkin and the fodder's in the
      shock.

They's something kindo' harty-like about the atmusfere
When the heat of summer's over and the coolin' fall is
      here—
Of course we miss the flowers, and the blossums on the
      trees,
And the mumble of the hummin'-birds and buzzin' of the
      bees;
But the air's so appetizin'; and the landscape through the
      haze
Of a crisp and sunny morning of the airly autumn days
Is a pictur' that no painter has the colorin' to mock—
When the frost is on the punkin and the fodder's in the
      shock.

The husky, rusty russel of the tossels of the corn,
And the raspin' of the tangled leaves, as golden as the morn;
The stubble in the furries—kindo' lonesome-like, but still
A-preachin' sermons to us of the barns they growed to fill;
The strawstack in the medder, and the reaper in the shed;

The hosses in theyr stalls below—the clover overhead!—
O, it sets my hart a-clickin' like the tickin' of a clock,
When the frost is on the punkin and the fodder's in the
        shock!

Then your apples all is gethered, and the ones a feller keeps
Is poured around the celler-floor in red and yeller heaps;
And your cider-makin' 's over, and your wimmern-folks is
        through
With their mince and apple-butter, and theyr souse and
        saussage, too! . . .
I don't know how to tell it—but ef sich a thing could be
As the Angels wantin' boardin', and they'd call around on
        me—
I'd want to 'commodate 'em—all the whole-indurin'
        flock—
When the frost is on the punkin and the fodder's in the
        shock!

Little Orphant Annie

Little Orphant Annie's come to our house to stay
An' wash the cups and saucers up, and brush the crumbs
        away,
An' shoo the chickens off the porch, an' dust the hearth, an'
        sweep,
An' make the fire, an' bake the bread, an' earn her board-
        an'-keep;
An' all us other children, when the supper things is done,
We set around the kitchen fire an' has the mostest fun
A-list'nin' to the witch tales 'at Annie tells about,
An' the gobble-uns 'at gits you
                Ef you
            Don't
            Watch
                Out!

Onc't they was a little boy wouldn't say his pray'rs—
An' when he went to bed 'at night, away up stairs,
His mammy heerd him holler, an' his daddy heerd him
    bawl,
An' when they turn't the kivvers down, he wasn't there at
    all!
An' they seeked him in the rafter-room, an' cubby-hole, an'
    press,
An' seeked him up the chimbly-flue, an' ever 'wheres, I
    guess,
But all they ever found was thist his pants an' round-
    about!—
An' the gobble-uns 'll git you
            Ef you
                Don't
                    Watch
                        Out!

An' one time a little girl 'ud allus laugh an' grin,
An' make fun of ever' one an' all her blood-an'-kin,
An' onc't when they was "company," an' ole folks was
    there,
She mocked 'em an' shocked 'em, an' said she didn't care!
An' thist as she kicked her heels, an' turn't to run an' hide,
They was two great big Black Things a-standin' by her side,
An' they snatched her through the ceilin' 'fore she know'd
    what she's about!
An' the gobble-uns 'll git you
            Ef you
                Don't
                    Watch
                        Out!

An' little Orphant Annie says, when the blaze is blue,
An' the lampwick sputters, an' the wind goes woo-oo!
An' you hear the crickets quit, an' the moon is gray
An' the lightnin'-bugs in dew is all squenched away,—

You better mind yer parents, and yer teachers fond and dear,
An' churish them 'at loves you, an' dry the orphant's tear,
An' he'p the pore an' needy ones 'at clusters all about,
Er the gobble-uns 'll git you
    Ef you
      Don't
        Watch
         Out!

EUGENE FIELD

(1850 – 1895)

Dutch Lullaby

Wynken, Blynken, and Nod one night
   Sailed off in a wooden shoe,—
Sailed on a river of misty light
   Into a sea of dew.
"Where are you going, and what do you wish?"
   The old moon asked the three.
"We have come to fish for the herring-fish
   That live in this beautiful sea;
   Nets of silver and gold have we,"
       Said Wynken,
       Blynken,
       And Nod.

The old moon laughed and sung a song,
   As they rocked in the wooden shoe;
And the wind that sped them all night long
   Ruffled the waves of dew;
The little stars were the herring-fish
   That lived in the beautiful sea.
"Now cast your nets wherever you wish,
   But never afeard are we!"
   So cried the stars to the fishermen three,
       Wynken,
       Blynken,
       And Nod.

All night long their nets they threw
   For the fish in the twinkling foam,
Then down from the sky came the wooden shoe,
   Bringing the fishermen home;
'T was all so pretty a sail, it seemed
   As if it could not be;

And some folk thought 't was a dream they'd dreamed
   Of sailing that beautiful sea;
But I shall name you the fishermen three:
            Wynken,
            Blynken,
            And Nod.

Wynken and Blynken are two little eyes,
   And Nod is a little head,
And the wooden shoe that sailed the skies
   Is a wee one's trundle-bed;
So shut your eyes while Mother sings
   Of wonderful sights that be,
And you shall see the beautiful things
   As you rock on the misty sea
   Where the old shoe rocked the fishermen three,—
            Wynken,
            Blynken,
            And Nod.

ELLA WHEELER WILCOX

(1850–1919)

The Engine

Into the gloom of the deep, dark night,
  With panting breath and a startled scream;
Swift as a bird in sudden flight
  Darts this creature of steel and steam.

Awful dangers are lurking nigh,
  Rocks and chasms are near the track,
But straight by the light of its great white eye
  It speeds through the shadows, dense and black.

Terrible thoughts and fierce desires
  Trouble its mad heart many an hour,
Where burn and smoulder the hidden fires,
  Coupled ever with might and power.

It hates, as a wild horse hates the rein,
  The narrow track by vale and hill;
And shrieks with a cry of startled pain,
  And longs to follow its own wild will.

Nothing New

Oh, what am I but an engine, shod
  With muscle and flesh, by the hand of God,
Speeding on through the dense, dark night,
  Guided alone by the soul's white light.

Often and often my mad heart tires,
  And hates its way with a bitter hate,
And longs to follow its own desires,
  And leave the end in the hands of fate.

O, mighty engine of steel and steam;
   O, human engine of blood and bone,
Follow the white light's certain beam—
   There lies safety, and there alone.

The narrow track of fearless truth,
   Lit by the soul's great eye of light,
O passionate heart of restless youth,
   Alone will carry you through the night.

ROSE HARTWICK THORPE
(1850–1939)

Curfew Must Not Ring To-Night

England's sun was slowly setting o'er the hill-tops far away,
Filling all the land with beauty at the close of one sad day;
And its last rays kissed the forehead of a man and maiden
      fair,—
He with steps so slow and weary, she with sunny, floating
      hair:
He with bowed head, sad and thoughtful; she with lips so
      cold and white,
Struggled to keep back the murmur, "Curfew must not ring
      to-night!"

"Sexton," Bessie's white lips faltered, pointing to the prison
      old,
With its walls so tall and gloomy,—moss-grown walls dark,
      damp, and cold,—
"I've a lover in that prison, doomed this very night to die
At the ringing of the curfew, and no earthly help is nigh.
Cromwell will not come till sunset"; and her lips grew
      strangely white
As she spoke in husky whispers, "Curfew must not ring
      to-night!"

"Bessie," calmly spoke the sexton (every word pierced her
      young heart
Like a gleaming death-winged arrow, like a deadly
      poisoned dart),
"Long, long years I've rung the curfew from that gloomy,
      shadowed tower;
Every evening, just at sunset, it has tolled the twilight hour.
I have done my duty ever, tried to do it just and right;
Now I'm old I will not miss it: Curfew bell must ring
      to-night!"

Wild her eyes and pale her features, stern and white her
    thoughtful brow,
And within her heart's deep centre Bessie made a solemn
    vow.
She had listened while the judges read, without a tear or
    sigh,
"At the ringing of the curfew Basil Underwood *must die*."
And her breath came fast and faster, and her eyes grew
    large and bright;
One low murmur, faintly spoken, "Curfew *must not* ring
    to-night!"

She with quick step bounded forward, sprang within the
    old church door,
Left the old man coming, slowly, paths he'd trod so oft
    before.
Not one moment paused the maiden, but, with cheek and
    brow aglow,
Staggered up the gloomy tower where the bell swung to
    and fro;
As she climbed the slimy ladder, on which fell no ray of
    light,
Upward still, her pale lips saying, "Curfew *shall not* ring
    to-night!"

She has reached the topmost ladder; o'er her hangs the
    great, dark bell;
Awful is the gloom beneath her, like the pathway down to
    hell.
See, the ponderous tongue is swinging! 't is the hour of
    curfew now!
And the sight has chilled her bosom, stopped her breath
    and paled her brow.
Shall she let it ring? No, never! Her eyes flash with sudden
    light,
As she springs and grasps it firmly: "Curfew *shall not* ring
    to-night!"

Out she swung, far out; the city seemed a speck of light
    below,
There 'twixt heaven and earth suspended, as the bell swung
    to and fro.
And the sexton at the bell-rope, old and deaf, heard not the
    bell;
Sadly thought that twilight curfew rang young Basil's
    funeral knell.
Still the maiden, clinging firmly, quivering lip and fair face
    white,
Stilled her frightened heart's wild beating: *"Curfew shall not
    ring to-night!"*

It was o'er!—the bell ceased swaying, and the maiden
    stepped once more
Firmly on the damp old ladder, where, for hundred years
    before,
Human foot had not been planted. The brave deed that she
    had done
Should be told long ages after. As the rays of setting sun
Light the sky with golden beauty, aged sires, with heads of
    white,
Tell the children why the curfew did not ring that one sad
    night.

O'er the distant hills comes Cromwell. Bessie sees him, and
    her brow,
Lately white with sickening horror, has no anxious traces
    now.
At his feet she tells her story, shows her hands, all bruised
    and torn;
And her sweet young face, still haggard with the anguish it
    had worn,
Touched his heart with sudden pity, lit his eyes with misty
    light.
"Go! your lover lives," cried Cromwell. "Curfew shall not
    ring to-night!"

Wide they flung the massive portals, led the prisoner forth
    to die,
All his bright young life before him, 'neath the darkening
    English sky.
Bessie came, with flying footsteps, eyes aglow with
    lovelight sweet,
Kneeling on the turf beside him, laid his pardon at his feet.
In his brave, strong arms he clasped her, kissed the face
    upturned and white,
Whispered, "Darling, you have saved me! curfew will not
    ring to-night."

ALBERY ALLSON WHITMAN

(1851–1901)

from *Twasinta's Seminoles*

or Rape of Florida

Have I not seen the hills of Candahar
Clothed in the fury of a thunder storm,
When Majesty rolled in His cloud-dark car—
Wreathed His dread brow with lightning's livid form,
And with a deluge robed His threat'ning arm!
Not seen, when night fled His terrific feet,
The great deep rose to utter forth alarm,
The hills in dreadful hurry rushed to meet,
And rocking mountains started from their darkened seat!

In happy childhood I have even loved
To sport the wild, and in the front and face
Of dreadest Nature, watch the storm unmoved,
That tore the oak tree from its ancient place
And took the hilltops in its dark embrace;
And then I've loved the pleasing after-view—
The quiet valleys spanned with light and grace—
The watery field, replete with life anew,
And sunset robing earth in love's sublimest hue.

Thus, when afar the wide Bahamas shone,—
In lucent stillness gleamed the sunset sea —
When day's last rim sank like a molten zone,
Emblaz'ning in Omnific heraldry
The far-off crag and latest mountain tree;
Thus, on a stand dividing worlds I've stood,
Till, touched by the dark wand of mystery,
I felt the brow of night, and earth imbued
With dread emotions of a great eternal Good.

Upon the shells by Carribea's wave
I've heard the anthems of the mighty sea;
Heard there the dark pines that their voices gave,
And heard a stream denote its minstrelsy —
How sweet, *all* lonely, was it there to be!
The stars were bright, the moon was up and clear;
But, when I thought of those who once were free,
And came at wonted times to worship there;
The sea's deep voice grew sad and claimed of me a tear!

Oh! sing it in the light of freedom's morn,
Tho' tyrant wars have made the earth a grave;
The good, the great, and true, are, if so, born,
And so with slaves, *chains do not make the slave!*
If high-souled birth be what the mother gave, —
If manly birth, and manly to the core, —
Whate'er the test, the man will he behave!
Crush him to earth and crush him o'er and o'er,
A man he'll rise at last and meet you as before.

Part I, stanzas 15–19

The Lute of Afric's Tribe

When Israel sate by Babel's stream and wept,
The heathen said, "Sing one of Zion's songs;"
But tuneless lay the lyre of those who slept
Where Sharon bloomed and Oreb vigil kept;
For holy song to holy ears belongs.

So, when her iron clutch the Slave power reached,
And sable generations captive held;
When Wrong the gospel of endurance preached;
The lute of Afric's tribe, tho' oft beseeched,
In all its wild, sweet warblings never swelled.

And yet when Freedom's lispings o'er it stole,
Soft as the breath of undefiled morn,
A wand'ring accent from its strings would stroll —
Thus was our Simpson, man of song and soul,
And stalwart energies, to bless us born.

When all our nation's sky was overcast
With rayless clouds of deepening misery,
His soaring vision mounted thro' the blast,
And from behind its gloom approaching fast,
Beheld the glorious Sun of Liberty.

He sang exultant: "Let her banner wave!"
And cheering senates, fired by his zeal,
Helped snatch their country from rebellion's grave
Looked through brave tears upon the injured slave,
And raised the battle-arm to break his gyves of steel.

But hushed the bard, his harp no longer sings
The woes and longings of a shackled mind;
For death's cold fingers swept its trembling strings,
And shut the bosom of its murmurings
Forever on the hearing of mankind.

The bird that dips his flight in noonday sun,
May fall, and spread his plumage on the plain;
But when immortal mind its work hath done
On earth, in heaven a nobler work 's begun,
And it can never downward turn again.

Of him, whose harp then, lies by death unstrung—
A harp that long his lowly brethren cheered,
May 'nt we now say, that, sainted choirs among,
An everlasting theme inspires his tongue,
Where slaves ne'er groan, and death is never feared?

Yes, he is harping on the "Sea of glass,"
Where saints begin, and angels join the strain;
While Spheres in one profound, eternal bass,
Sing thro' their orbs, illumined as they pass,
And constellations catch the long refrain.

EDWIN MARKHAM
(1852–1940)

The Man with the Hoe

Written after seeing Millet's World-Famous Painting

God made man in His own image,
in the image of God made He him. —GENESIS.

Bowed by the weight of centuries he leans
Upon his hoe and gazes on the ground,
The emptiness of ages in his face,
And on his back the burden of the world.
Who made him dead to rapture and despair,
A thing that grieves not and that never hopes,
Stolid and stunned, a brother to the ox?
Who loosened and let down this brutal jaw?
Whose was the hand that slanted back this brow?
Whose breath blew out the light within this brain?

Is this the Thing the Lord God made and gave
To have dominion over sea and land;
To trace the stars and search the heavens for power;
To feel the passion of Eternity?
Is this the Dream He dreamed who shaped the suns
And pillared the blue firmament with light?
Down all the stretch of Hell to its last gulf
There is no shape more terrible than this—
More tongued with censure of the world's blind greed—
More filled with signs and portents for the soul—
More fraught with menace to the universe.

What gulfs between him and the seraphim!
Slave of the wheel of labor, what to him
Are Plato and the swing of Pleiades?
What the long reaches of the peaks of song,
The rift of dawn, the reddening of the rose?

Through this dread shape the suffering ages look;
Time's tragedy is in that aching stoop;
Through this dread shape humanity betrayed,
Plundered, profaned and disinherited,
Cries protest to the Judges of the World,
A protest that is also prophecy.

O masters, lords and rulers in all lands,
Is this the handiwork you give to God,
This monstrous thing distorted and soul-quenched?
How will you ever straighten up this shape;
Touch it again with immortality;
Give back the upward looking and the light;
Rebuild in it the music and the dream;
Make right the immemorial infamies,
Perfidious wrongs, immedicable woes?

O masters, lords and rulers in all lands,
How will the Future reckon with this Man?
How answer his brute question in that hour
When whirlwinds of rebellion shake the world?
How will it be with kingdoms and with kings—
With those who shaped him to the thing he is—
When this dumb Terror shall reply to God,
After the silence of the centuries?

ERNEST FENOLLOSA

(1853–1908)

from *East and West*

from *The Separated East*

O sweet dead artist and seer, O tender prophetic priest,
Draw me aside the curtain that veils the heart of your East.

O wing of the Empress of mountains,
Brood white o'er a world of surprises;
And soar to thy Sun as she rises
From the mazarine arch of her fountains.
For thine islands she dropped in the reeds
As a girdle of emerald beads,
And her rainbow promise of genius spanned
As a bridge for the gods to their chosen land.
And her last pure poet shall sing
Like a farewell note
From a nightingale's throat
Of her peace, through thy roseate window of Spring.

I saw him last in the solemn grove
Where the orange temples of Kásǔga shine,
Feeding the timorous deer that rove
Through her tall, dark, purple pillars of pine,
And marking the pattern of leaves
Which the golden mesh of the willow weaves
On the olive bed of her moss-grown eaves.
And I cried to my painter-sage,
"O spirit lone of a bygone age,
Smiling mid ruin and change,
With faith in the beautiful soul of things,
I would gaze on the jewels thy vision brings
From the calm interior depths of its range.
For I 've flown from my West
Like a desolate bird from a broken nest

698

To learn thy secret of joy and rest.
Quaff from thy fancy's chalice,
And build me anew the fairy palace
With arches gilded and ceiling pearled
Where dwells the soul of thine Asian world."

Then I thought that his smile grew finer,
As if touched with an insight diviner;
Dear Hogai, my master,
Perched on a wild wistaria stem.
And I marked the light on his mantle's hem
Of a halo pure as a purple aster.
And the cold green blades of a bamboo spear
Pierced to his hand through the atmosphere,
Like the note of a silver bell to the ear.
And his voice came soft as the hymn
Which the snow-clad virgins in cloister dim
Were chanting, with rhythmical sway of limb.
"The past is the seed in the heart of a rose
Whose petalled present shall fade as it blows.
The past is the seed in the soul of man,
The infinite Now of the spirit's span.
For flesh is a flower
That blooms for an hour;
And the soul is the seed
Which determines the breed,
The past in the present
For monarch or peasant.
Eye to eye
'T is ourselves we spy;
For doom or grace
One manifold face;
Life's triumphs and errors
In self-resurrections,
Like endless reflections
From parallel mirrors.

"Now I speed on a charger of wind
To the snow-capped castles of Ind.
Mid statues of Buddha the meek,

Link between Mongol and Greek,
Kanishka haughty and lone
Here lolled on his sculptured throne,
The great Vasubandhu to mark,
Lion-faced patriarch.
Now moss like a pall
Shrouds the ruined wall;
Afar in the desert the tigers call.
One pilgrim alone
From its sandy bed
Is lifting a beautiful Buddha's head.
'O take me, loved of the dragon throne,
Back to thy pious imperial prince;
For ages and ages since
'T was I who carved that form
From the limestone warm.
I 'll show thee where germinate in the soil
A thousand truncated gods for thy spoil.
Gather these Bodhisats,
And battle-scarred features of grim Arhats,
And arrogant alabaster kings
With eyes of jacinth
Dethroned from their plinth,
And the masterful heads of Scythian knights
Scowling in mortal fights
With misshapen elemental things.
And hurry thy laden ship
On a heaven-blessed homeward trip;—
So shall the Northern and Eastern plains
Clap their hands at thy gains.
For the light of unborn states
From these things radiates;
Blood for solution
Of crystal worlds Confucian;
Stars for the final Asian man
Rising in far Japan.
I 'll paint on the wall
Of thy Tartar capital
Blue gods unmoved in everlasting flame,
Vast planetary coils without a name,

Invigorating thrills
From unseen wills.
And spurred by these I shall cast
Black bronze in an infinite mould,
As high as a pine
And as fine
As the patient jeweller carves his gold;
Impersonal types which shall last
As the noblest ideals of the Past.'

lines 1–116

Fuji at Sunrise

Startling the cool gray depths of morning air
   She throws aside her counterpane of clouds,
   And stands half folded in her silken shrouds
With calm white breast and snowy shoulder bare.
High o'er her head a flush all pink and rare
   Thrills her with foregleam of an unknown bliss,
   A virgin pure who waits the bridal kiss,
Faint with expectant joy she fears to share.
Lo, now he comes, the dazzling prince of day!
   Flings his full glory o'er her radiant breast;
   Enfolds her to the rapture of his rest,
Transfigured in the throbbing of his ray.
O fly, my soul, where love's warm transports are;
And seek eternal bliss in yon pink kindling star!

JAMES A. BLAND

(1854–1911)

Oh, Dem Golden Slippers!

Oh, my golden slippers am laid away,
Kase I don't 'spect to wear 'em till my weddin' day,
And my long-tail'd coat, dat I loved so well,
I will wear up in de chariot in de morn;
And my long, white robe dat I bought last June,
I'm gwine to git changed kase it fits too soon,
And de ole grey hoss dat I used to drive,
I will hitch him to de chariot in de morn.

> *Oh, dem golden slippers! Oh, dem golden slippers!*
> *Golden slippers I'm gwine to wear, becase dey look so neat;*
> *Oh, dem golden slippers! Oh, dem golden slippers!*
> *Golden slippers Ise gwine to wear, to walk de golden street.*

Oh, my ole banjo hangs on de wall,
Kase it aint been tuned since way last fall,
But de darks all say we will hab a good time,
When we ride up in de chariot in de morn;
Dar 's ole Brudder Ben and Sister Luce,
Dey will telegraph de news to Uncle Bacco Juice,
What a great camp-meetin' der will be dat day,
When we ride up in de chariot in de morn.

Chorus.

So, it 's good bye, children, I will have to go
Whar de rain don't fall or de wind don't blow,
And yer ulster coats, why, yer will not need,
When yer ride up in de chariot in de morn;
But yer golden slippers must be nice and clean,
And yer age must be just sweet sixteen,
And yer white kid gloves yer will have to wear,
When yer ride up in de chariot in de morn.

Chorus.

LIZETTE WOODWORTH REESE

(1856–1935)

Love, Weeping, Laid This Song

On a Copy of the Iliad Found with the Mummy of a Young Girl

Lo! an old song, yellow with centuries!
   She, she who with her young dust kept it sweet;
   She, in some green court on a carvëd seat,
Read it at dusk fair-paged upon her knees;
And, looking up, saw there, beyond the trees,
   Tall Helen through the darkling shadows fleet;
   And heard, out in the fading river-street,
The roar of battle like the roar of seas.
Love, weeping, laid this song when she was dead
   In that sealed chamber, strange with nard and musk.
      Outliving Egypt, see it here at last.
We touch its leaves: back rush the seasons sped;
   For us, as once for her, in that old dusk,
      Troy trembles like a reed before the blast!

One Night

One lily scented all the dark. It grew
Down the drenched walk a spike of ghostly white.
Fine, sweet, sad noises thrilled the tender night,
From insects couched on blades that dripped with dew.
The road beyond, cleaving the great fields through,
Echoed no footstep; like a streak of light,
The gaunt and blossoming elder gleamed in sight.
The boughs began to quake, and warm winds blew,
And whirled a myriad petals down the air.
An instant, peaked and black the old house stood;
The next, its gables showed a tremulous gray,
Then deepening gold; the next, the world lay bare!
The moon slipped out the leash of the tall wood,
And through the heavenly meadows fled away.

April in Town

Straight from the east the wind blows sharp with rain,
  That just now drove its wild ranks down the street,
  And westward rushed into the sunset sweet.
Spouts brawl, boughs drip and cease and drip again,
Bricks gleam; keen saffron glows each window-pane,
  And every pool beneath the passing feet.
  Innumerable odors fine and fleet
Are blown this way from blossoming lawn and lane.
Wet roofs show black against a tender sky;
  The almond bushes in the lean-fenced square,
    Beaten to the walks, show all their draggled white.
A troop of laborers comes slowly by;
  One bears a daffodil, and seems to bear
    A new-lit candle through the fading light.

A Lyric on the Lyric

This road our blithe-heart elders knew,
  And down it trooped together;
They plucked their reeds from out the dew,
  And piped the morning weather.

Shepherd or gallant, cloak or smock,
  They lead where we do follow;
Hear Colin there among his flock
  To Phyllis in the hollow!

Corinna goes a-Maying yet;
  Phillida's laugh is ringing;
And see Castara, violet
  Of early English singing.

But were these lovers never sad,
  Did not some heart go breaking?
Were youth and cowslips to be had
  Just for the simple taking?

Oh, Sorrow, too, has gone this way,
   And Loss as well as Leisure;
Yet Sorrow lasted for a day,
   And Loss through scarce a measure.

And here Beau Waller stayed to snatch,
   Just at Oblivion's portal,
A single rose that none can match —
   And after grew immortal.

No rain can strip it of its red;
   No gust pelt out its savor;
Though Celia died and he is dead,
   This is the rose he gave her.

What riverside shall grow once more
   The reed bared of dull teaching?
And who shall bring unto our door
   Music instead of preaching?

Yet here forget the evil days;
   Let go the Now and After;
Our blithe-heart elders trooped these ways,
   And filled them full of Laughter!

KATHARINE LEE BATES
(1859–1929)

America the Beautiful

O beautiful for spacious skies,
  For amber waves of grain,
For purple mountain majesties
  Above the fruited plain!
    America! America!
  God shed His grace on thee
And crown thy good with brotherhood
  From sea to shining sea!

O beautiful for pilgrim feet,
  Whose stern, impassioned stress
A thoroughfare for freedom beat
  Across the wilderness!
    America! America!
  God mend thine every flaw,
Confirm thy soul in self-control,
  Thy liberty in law!

O beautiful for heroes proved
  In liberating strife,
Who more than self their country loved,
  And mercy more than life!
    America! America!
  May God thy gold refine,
Till all success be nobleness,
  And every gain divine!

O beautiful for patriot dream
  That sees beyond the years
Thine alabaster cities gleam
  Undimmed by human tears!
    America! America!
  God shed His grace on thee
And crown thy good with brotherhood
  From sea to shining sea!

CLINTON SCOLLARD

(1860—1932)

A Bit of Marble

This bit of polished marble—this—
  Was found where Athens proudly rears
Its temple-crowned Acropolis
  So hoar with years.

In antique time some sculptor's hand,
  Deft-turning, carved it fine and small,
A part of base, or column grand,
  Or capital.

Pentelicus' white heart it knew
  Before the chisel fashioned it;
Long ere so fair of form it grew,
  And delicate.

Regarding it, I mind me so
  A song should be, with ardor wrought,—
Cut in the firm Pentelic snow
  Of lofty thought.

HAMLIN GARLAND

(1860-1940)

Indian Summer

At last there came
The sudden fall of frost, when Time
Dreaming through russet September days
Suddenly awoke, and lifting his head, strode
Swiftly forward—made one vast desolating sweep
Of his scythe, then, rapt with the glory
That burned under his feet, fell dreaming again.
And the clouds soared and the crickets sang
In the brief heat of noon; the corn,
So green, grew sere and dry—
 And in the mist the ploughman's team
 Moved silently, as if in dream—
And it was Indian summer on the plain.

On the Mississippi

Through wild and tangled forests
 The broad, unhasting river flows—
 Spotted with rain-drops, gray with night;
  Upon its curving breast there goes
A lonely steamboat's larboard light,
  A blood-red star against the shadowy oaks;
Noiseless as a ghost, through greenish gleam
Of fire-flies, before the boat's wild scream—
  A heron flaps away
  Like silence taking flight.

HARRIET MONROE

To W. S. M.

With a copy of Shelley.

Behold, I send thee to the heights of song,
My brother! Let thine eyes awake as clear
As morning dew, within whose glowing sphere
Is mirrored half a world; and listen long,
Till in thine ears, famished to keenness, throng
The bugles of the soul—till far and near
Silence grows populous, and wind and mere
Are phantom-choked with voices. Then be strong—
Then halt not till thou seest the beacons flare
Souls mad for truth have lit from peak to peak.
Haste on to breathe the intoxicating air—
Wine to the brave and poison to the weak—
Far in the blue where angels' feet have trod,
Where earth is one with heaven, and man with God.

LOUISE IMOGEN GUINEY
(1861–1920)

At a Symphony

Oh, I would have these tongues oracular
Dip into silence, tease no more, let be!
They madden, like some choral of the free
Gusty and sweet against a prison-bar.
To earth the boast that her gold empires are,
The menace of delicious death to me,
Great Undesign, strong as by God's decree,
Piercing the heart with beauty from afar!
Music too winning to the sense forlorn!
Of what angelic lineage was she born,
Bred in what rapture?—These her sires and friends:
Censure, Denial, Gloom, and Hunger's throe.
Praised be the Spirit that thro' thee, Schubert! so
Wrests evil unto wholly heavenly ends.

Fog

Like bodiless water passing in a sigh,
Thro' palsied streets the fatal shadows flow,
And in their sharp disastrous undertow
Suck in the morning sun, and all the sky.
The towery vista sinks upon the eye,
As if it heard the Hebrew bugles blow,
Black and dissolved; nor could the founders know
How what was built so bright should daily die.

Thy mood with man's is broken and blent in,
City of Stains! and ache of thought doth drown
The primitive light in which thy life began;
Great as thy dole is, smirchèd with his sin,
Greater and elder yet the love of man
Full in thy look, tho' the dark visor's down.

Strikers in Hyde Park

A woof reversed the fatal shuttles weave,
How slow! but never once they slip the thread.
Hither, upon the Georgian idlers' tread,
Up spacious ways the lindens interleave,
Clouding the royal air since yester-eve,
Come men bereft of time and scant of bread,
Loud, who were dumb, immortal, who were dead,
Thro' the cowed world their kingdom to retrieve.

What ails thee, England? Altar, mart, and grange
Dream of the knife by night; not so, not so
The clear Republic waits the general throe,
Along her noonday mountains' open range.
God be with both! for one is young to know
The other's rote of evil and of change.

In the Reading-Room of the British Museum

Praised be the moon of books! that doth above
A world of men, the fallen Past behold,
And fill the spaces else so void and cold
To make a very heaven again thereof;
As when the sun is set behind a grove,
And faintly unto nether ether rolled,
All night his whiter image and his mould
Grows beautiful with looking on her love.

Thou therefore, moon of so divine a ray,
Lend to our steps both fortitude and light!
Feebly along a venerable way
They climb the infinite, or perish quite;
Nothing are days and deeds to such as they,
While in this liberal house thy face is bright.

EDITH WHARTON

(1862–1937)

Chartres

I

Immense, august, like some Titanic bloom,
  The mighty choir unfolds its lithic core,
Petalled with panes of azure, gules and or,
  Splendidly lambent in the Gothic gloom,
And stamened with keen flamelets that illume
  The pale high-altar. On the prayer-worn floor,
By worshippers innumerous thronged of yore,
  A few brown crones, familiars of the tomb,
The stranded driftwood of Faith's ebbing sea—
  For these alone the finials fret the skies,
The topmost bosses shake their blossoms free,
  While from the triple portals, with grave eyes,
Tranquil, and fixed upon eternity,
  The cloud of witnesses still testifies.

II

The crimson panes like blood-drops stigmatise
  The western floor. The aisles are mute and cold.
A rigid fetich in her robe of gold,
  The Virgin of the Pillar, with blank eyes,
Enthroned beneath her votive canopies,
  Gathers a meagre remnant to her fold.
The rest is solitude; the church, grown old,
  Stands stark and grey beneath the burning skies.
Well-nigh again its mighty framework grows
  To be a part of nature's self, withdrawn
From hot humanity's impatient woes;
  The floor is ridged like some rude mountain lawn,
And in the east one giant window shows
  The roseate coldness of an Alp at dawn.

Two Backgrounds

I

La Vierge au Donateur

Here by the ample river's argent sweep,
Bosomed in tilth and vintage to her walls,
A tower-crowned Cybele in armoured sleep
The city lies, fat plenty in her halls,
With calm parochial spires that hold in fee
The friendly gables clustered at their base,
And, equipoised o'er tower and market-place,
The Gothic minster's winged immensity;
And in that narrow burgh, with equal mood,
Two placid hearts, to all life's good resigned,
Might, from the altar to the lych-gate, find
Long years of peace and dreamless plenitude.

II

Mona Lisa

Yon strange blue city crowns a scarpèd steep
No mortal foot hath bloodlessly essayed;
Dreams and illusions beacon from its keep,
But at the gate an Angel bares his blade;
And tales are told of those who thought to gain
At dawn its ramparts; but when evening fell
Far off they saw each fading pinnacle
Lit with wild lightnings from the heaven of pain;
Yet there two souls, whom life's perversities
Had mocked with want in plenty, tears in mirth,
Might meet in dreams, ungarmented of earth,
And drain Joy's awful chalice to the lees.

An Autumn Sunset

I

Leaguered in fire
The wild black promontories of the coast extend
Their savage silhouettes;
The sun in universal carnage sets,
And, halting higher,
The motionless storm-clouds mass their sullen threats,
Like an advancing mob in sword-points penned,
That, balked, yet stands at bay.
Mid-zenith hangs the fascinated day
In wind-lustrated hollows crystalline,
A wan Valkyrie whose wide pinions shine
Across the ensanguined ruins of the fray,
And in her hand swings high o'erhead,
Above the waste of war,
The silver torch-light of the evening star
Wherewith to search the faces of the dead.

II

Lagooned in gold,
Seem not those jetty promontories rather
The outposts of some ancient land forlorn,
Uncomforted of morn,
Where old oblivions gather,
The melancholy unconsoling fold
Of all things that go utterly to death
And mix no more, no more
With life's perpetually awakening breath?
Shall Time not ferry me to such a shore,
Over such sailless seas,
To walk with hope's slain importunities
In miserable marriage? Nay, shall not
All things be there forgot,
Save the sea's golden barrier and the black
Close-crouching promontories?
Dead to all shames, forgotten of all glories,

Shall I not wander there, a shadow's shade,
A spectre self-destroyed,
So purged of all remembrance and sucked back
Into the primal void,
That should we on that shore phantasmal meet
I should not know the coming of your feet?

JOHN JAY CHAPMAN

(1862–1933)

Bismarck

At midnight, Death dismissed the chancellor
But left the soul of Bismarck on his face.
Titanic, in the peace and power of bronze,
With three red roses loosely in his grasp,
Lies the Constructor. His machinery
Revolving in the wheels of destiny
Rolls onward over him. Alive, inspired,
Vast, intricate, complete, unthinkable,
Nice as a watch and strong as dynamite,
An empire and a whirlwind, on it moves,
While he that set it rolling lies so still.

Unity! Out of chaos, petty courts,
Princelings and potentates—thrift, jealousy,
Weakness, distemper, cowardice, distrust
To build a nation: the material—
The fibres to be twisted: human strands.
One race, one tongue, one instinct. Unify
By banking prejudice and, gaining power,
Attract by vanity, compel by fear.
Arm to the teeth: your friends will love you more,
And we have much to do for Germany.
Organized hatred, that is unity.

Prussia's a unit; Denmark's enmity
Is so much gain, and gives us all the North.
Next: humble Austria, a rapid stroke
That leaves us laurels and a policy.
Now for some chance, some—any fluke or crime
By which a war with France can be brought on:
And, God be glorified, the thing is done.
Organized hatred. That foundation reaches
The very bottom rock of Germany

And out of it the structure rises up
Bristling with arms.

"But you forget the soul,
"The universal shout, the Kaiser's name,
"Fatherland, anthems, the heroic dead,
"The discipline, the courage, the control,
"The glory and the passion and the flame—"
Are calculated by the captain's eye
Are used, subdued, like electricity
Turned on or off, are set to making roads,
Or building monuments, or writing verse,
Twitched by the inspired whim of tyranny
To make that tyranny perpetual
And kill what intellect it cannot use.

The age is just beginning, yet we see
The fruits of hatred ripen hourly
And Germany's in bondage—muzzled press—
The private mind suppressed, while shade on shade
Is darkening o'er the intellectual sky.
And world-forgotten, outworn crimes and cries
With dungeon tongue accost the citizen
And send him trembling to his family.

Organized hatred. Educated men
Live in habitual scorn of intellect,
Hate France, hate England, hate America.
Talk corporals, talk until Napoleon
(—Who never could subdue the mind of France)
Seems like some harmless passing episode,
Unable to reveal to modern man
What tyranny could compass. Years of this
Will leave a Germany devoid of fire,
Unlettered, unrebellious, impotent,
Nursing the name of German unity
And doing pilgrimage to Bismarck's shrine,
Bismarck the god, who having but one thought,
Wrote it out largely over Germany
But could not stay to read it. Those who can,

Who reap the crop he sowed may count the grains
And every seed a scourge. For on the heart
One or a million, each envenomed throb
Relentlessly records an injury,
While the encrusted nation loses health,
And like a chemical experiment
The crucible gives back its quantities.

The thing this man employed so cleverly
Was poison then, and poison in the end,
And Germany is writhing in its grip.
For Bismarck, Caesar's broker, bought the men.
They paid their liberties and got revenge—
The ancient bargain. But upon a scale
A scope, a consequence, a stretch of time
That made a camp of Europe, and set back
The cultured continent for centuries.
The fear of fire-arms has dwarfed the French
To gibbering lunatics; and Zola's friends
Are all that France can show for common-sense.
Italy's bankrupt, Russia barbarous
Kept so by isolation, and the force,
The only force that can improve the world,
Enlightened public thought in private men,
Is minimized in Europe, till The Powers
Stand over Crete to watch a butchery
And diplomats decide the fate of men.

Bismarck, how much of all lies in thy head
Thought cannot fathom. But, gigantic wreck,
Thou wast the Instrument. And thy huge limbs
Cover nine kingdoms as thou lie'st asleep.

GEORGE SANTAYANA

(1863–1952)

Sonnet III

O world, thou choosest not the better part!
It is not wisdom to be only wise,
And on the inward vision close the eyes,
But it is wisdom to believe the heart.
Columbus found a world, and had no chart,
Save one that faith deciphered in the skies;
To trust the soul's invincible surmise
Was all his science and his only art.
Our knowledge is a torch of smoky pine
That lights the pathway but one step ahead
Across a void of mystery and dread.
Bid, then, the tender light of faith to shine
By which alone the mortal heart is led
Unto the thinking of the thought divine.

On a Piece of Tapestry

Hold high the woof, dear friends, that we may see
The cunning mixture of its colours rare.
Nothing in nature purposely is fair,—
Her beauties in their freedom disagree;
But here all vivid dyes that garish be,
To that tint mellowed which the sense will bear,
Glow, and not wound the eye that, resting there,
Lingers to feed its gentle ecstasy.
Crimson and purple and all hues of wine,
Saffron and russet, brown and sober green
Are rich the shadowy depths of blue between;
While silver threads with golden intertwine,
To catch the glimmer of a fickle sheen,—
All the long labour of some captive queen.

Cape Cod

The low sandy beach and the thin scrub pine,
The wide reach of bay and the long sky line,—
    O, I am far from home!

The salt, salt smell of the thick sea air,
And the smooth round stones that the ebbtides wear,—
    When will the good ship come?

The wretched stumps all charred and burned,
And the deep soft rut where the cartwheel turned,—
    Why is the world so old?

The lapping wave, and the broad gray sky
Where the cawing crows and the slow gulls fly,—
    Where are the dead untold?

The thin, slant willows by the flooded bog,
The huge stranded hulk and the floating log,—
    Sorrow with life began!

And among the dark pines, and along the flat shore,
O the wind, and the wind, for evermore!
    What will become of man?

On an Unfinished Statue

By Michael Angelo in the Bargello,
Called an Apollo or a David

What beauteous form beneath a marble veil
    Awaited in this block the Master's hand?
Could not the magic of his art avail
    To unseal that beauty's tomb and bid it stand?

Alas! the torpid and unwilling mass
    Misknew the sweetness of the mind's control,
And the quick shifting of the winds, alas!
    Denied a body to that flickering soul.

Fair homeless spirit, harbinger of bliss,
    It wooed dead matter that they both might live,
But dreamful earth still slumbered through the kiss
    And missed the blessing heaven stooped to give,

As when Endymion, locked in dullard sleep,
    Endured the gaze of Dian, till she turned
Stung with immortal wrath and doomed to weep
    Her maiden passion ignorantly spurned.

How should the vision stay to guide the hand,
    How should the holy thought and ardour stay,
When the false deeps of all the soul are sand
    And the loose rivets of the spirit clay?

What chisel shaking in the pulse of lust
    Shall find the perfect line, immortal, pure?
What fancy blown by every random gust
    Shall mount the breathless heavens and endure?

Vain was the trance through which a thrill of joy
    Passed for the nonce, when a vague hand, unled,
Half shaped the image of this lovely boy
    And caught the angel's garment as he fled.

Leave, leave, distracted hand, the baffling stone,
    And on that clay, thy fickle heart, begin.
Mould first some steadfast virtue of thine own
    Out of the sodden substance of thy sin.

They who wrought wonders by the Nile of old,
    Bequeathing their immortal part to us,
Cast their own spirit first into the mould
    And were themselves the rock they fashioned thus.

Ever their docile and unwearied eye
    Traced the same ancient pageant to the grave,
And awe made rich their spirit's husbandry
    With the perpetual refluence of its wave,

Till 'twixt the desert and the constant Nile
  Sphinx, pyramid, and awful temple grew,
And the vast gods, self-knowing, learned to smile
  Beneath the sky's unalterable blue.

Long, long ere first the rapt Arcadian swain
  Heard Pan's wild music pulsing through the grove,
His people's shepherds held paternal reign
  Beneath the large benignity of Jove.

Long mused the Delphic sibyl in her cave
  Ere mid his laurels she beheld the god,
And Beauty rose a virgin from the wave
  In lands the foot of Heracles had trod.

Athena reared her consecrated wall,
  Poseidon laid its rocky basement sure,
When Theseus had the monstrous race in thrall
  And made the worship of his people pure.

Long had the stripling stood in silence, veiled,
  Hearing the heroes' legend o'er and o'er,
Long in the keen palaestra striven, nor quailed
  To tame the body to the task it bore,

Ere soul and body, shaped by patient art,
  Walked linkèd with the gods, like friend with friend,
And reason, mirrored in the sage's heart,
  Beheld her purpose and confessed her end.

Mould, then, thyself and let the marble be.
  Look not to frailty for immortal themes,
Nor mock the travail of mortality
  With barren husks and harvesting of dreams.

STUART MERRILL

(1863–1915)

Ballade of the Chinese Lover

Down the waves of the Yang-tse-Kiang,
  In a gilded barge with saffron sails,
I wooed my Li to the brazen clang
  Of kettledrums, and the weary wails
  Of flutes, whilst under her spangled veils
She would sway her willowy waist, and sing
  Sweet songs that made me dream of the dales
Of Han-Yang, Woo-hoo and far Tchin-Ting.

Past the porcelain towers of Keou-Kang,
  And its peach blooms, loud with nightingales,
We drifted fast, as the dim gongs rang,
  Toward the horizon's purple pales.
  Hark! our hoarse pilot once more hails
The anchored junks, as they swerve and swing,
  Laden with silk and balsam bales
From Han-Yang, Woo-hoo and far Tchin-Ting.

Of nights, when the hour had come to hang
  Our paper lamps to their bamboo rails,
And afar we heard the silvery twang
  Of lutes from the tea fleet's moonlit trails,
  Then, oh my Li of the jasper nails,
As on the shore swooned the winds of spring,
  I lay at thy feet and told thee tales,
Of Han-Yang, Woo-hoo and far Tchin-Ting.

ENVOY.

  Loved Princess, ere my fantasy fails,
Farewell, and I'll make thy praises ring
  O'er the Flowery Kingdom's fields and swales,
From Han-Yang, Woo-hoo to far Tchin-Ting.

Ballade of the Outcasts

The Voice of the Men.

We are the Vagabonds that sleep
  In ditches by the midnight ways
Where wolves beneath the gibbets leap:
  Our hands against black Fate we raise
  In lifelong turmoil of affrays,
Until we die, in some dark den,
  The death of dogs that hunger slays:
For we are hated of all men.

The Voice of the Women.

We are the Courtesans that creep
  Beyond the town's lamp-litten haze,
Toward the bridges of the deep:
  We watch the dawn with sinful gaze,
  And dreaming of the golden days
When Jesus hallowed Magdalen,
  We seek death in the river's maze:
For we are hated of all men.

The Voice of the Children.

We are the Innocents that weep,
  While our bones rot with foul decays,
For all the woes that we must reap:
  No mother sings us lulling lays,
  No father o'er our slumber prays,
But forth we fare from den to den
  To filch the death bread of the strays:
For we are hated by all men.

The Envoy of the Outcasts.

  Beware, O Kings whom Mammon sways,
Lest morrows nearer than ye ken
  With our red flags of battle blaze!
For we are hated of all men.

ERNEST LAWRENCE THAYER

(1863–1940)

Casey at the Bat

A Ballad of the Republic, Sung in the Year 1888

The outlook wasn't brilliant for the Mudville nine that day;
The score stood four to two with but one inning more to
    play.
And then when Cooney died at first, and Barrows did the
    same,
A sickly silence fell upon the patrons of the game.

A straggling few got up to go in deep despair. The rest
Clung to that hope which springs eternal in the human
    breast;
They thought if only Casey could but get a whack at that—
We'd put up even money now with Casey at the bat.

But Flynn preceded Casey, as did also Jimmy Blake,
And the former was a lulu and the latter was a cake;
So upon that stricken multitude grim melancholy sat,
For there seemed but little chance of Casey's getting to the
    bat.

But Flynn let drive a single, to the wonderment of all,
And Blake, the much despis-ed, tore the cover off the ball;
And when the dust had lifted, and the men saw what had
    occurred,
There was Jimmy safe at second and Flynn a-hugging third.

Then from 5,000 throats and more there rose a lusty yell;
It rumbled through the valley, it rattled in the dell;
It knocked upon the mountain and recoiled upon the flat,
For Casey, mighty Casey, was advancing to the bat.

There was ease in Casey's manner as he stepped into his
    place;
There was pride in Casey's bearing and a smile on Casey's
    face.
And when, responding to the cheers, he lightly doffed his
    hat,
No stranger in the crowd could doubt 'twas Casey at the
    bat.

Ten thousand eyes were on him as he rubbed his hands
    with dirt;
Five thousand tongues applauded when he wiped them on
    his shirt.
Then while the writhing pitcher ground the ball into his
    hip,
Defiance gleamed in Casey's eye, a sneer curled Casey's lip.

And now the leather-covered sphere came hurtling through
    the air,
And Casey stood a-watching it in haughty grandeur there.
Close by the sturdy batsman the ball unheeded sped—
"That ain't my style," said Casey. "Strike one," the umpire
    said.

From the benches, black with people, there went up a
    muffled roar,
Like the beating of the storm-waves on a stern and distant
    shore.
"Kill him! Kill the umpire!" shouted some one on the stand;
  And it's likely they'd have killed him had not Casey raised
    his hand.

With a smile of Christian charity great Casey's visage
    shone;
He stilled the rising tumult; he bade the game go on;
He signaled to the pitcher, and once more the spheroid
    flew;
But Casey still ignored it, and the umpire said, "Strike
    two."

"Fraud!" cried the maddened thousands, and echo answered
  fraud;
But one scornful look from Casey and the audience was
  awed.
They saw his face grow stern and cold, they saw his
  muscles strain,
And they knew that Casey wouldn't let that ball go by
  again.

The sneer is gone from Casey's lip, his teeth are clinched in
  hate;
He pounds with cruel violence his bat upon the plate.
And now the pitcher holds the ball, and now he lets it go,
And now the air is shattered by the force of Casey's blow.

————

Oh, somewhere in this favored land the sun is shining
  bright;
The band is playing somewhere, and somewhere hearts are
  light,
And somewhere men are laughing, and somewhere children
  shout;
But there is no joy in Mudville — mighty Casey has struck
  out.

RICHARD HOVEY

(1864–1900)

Evening on the Potomac

The fervid breath of our flushed Southern May
Is sweet upon the city's throat and lips,
As a lover's whose tired arm slips
Listlessly over the shoulder of a queen.

Far away
The river melts in the unseen.
Oh, beautiful Girl-City, how she dips
Her feet in the stream
With a touch that is half a kiss and half a dream!
Her face is very fair,
With flowers for smiles and sunlight in her hair.

My westland flower-town, how serene she is!
Here on this hill from which I look at her,
All is still as if a worshipper
Left at some shrine his offering.

Soft winds kiss
My cheek with a slow lingering.
A luring whisper where the laurels stir
Wiles my heart back to woodland-ward again.

But lo,
Across the sky the sunset couriers run,
And I remain
To watch the imperial pageant of the Sun
Mock me, an impotent Cortez here below,
With splendors of its vaster Mexico.

O Eldorado of the templed clouds!
O golden city of the western sky!

Not like the Spaniard would I storm thy gates;
Not like the babe stretch chubby hands and cry
To have thee for a toy; but far from crowds,
Like my Faun brother in the ferny glen,
Peer from the wood's edge while thy glory waits,
And in the darkening thickets plunge again.

The Mocking-Bird

Hear! hear! hear!
Listen! the word
Of the mocking-bird!
Hear! hear! hear!
I will make all clear;
I will let you know
Where the footfalls go
That through the thicket and over the hill
Allure, allure.
How the bird-voice cleaves
Through the weft of leaves
With a leap and a thrill
Like the flash of a weaver's shuttle, swift and sudden and
          sure!

And lo, he is gone—even while I turn
The wisdom of his runes to learn.
He knows the mystery of the wood,
The secret of the solitude;
But he will not tell, he will not tell,
For all he promises so well.

Accident in Art

What painter has not with a careless smutch
Accomplished his despair?—one touch revealing
All he had put of life, thought, vigor, feeling,
Into the canvas that without that touch
Showed of his love and labor just so much
Raw pigment, scarce a scrap of soul concealing!
What poet has not found his spirit kneeling
A-sudden at the sound of such or such
Strange verses staring from his manuscript,
Written he knows not how, but which will sound
Like trumpets down the years? So Accident
Itself unmasks the likeness of Intent,
And ever in blind Chance's darkest crypt
The shrine-lamp of God's purposing is found.

MADISON CAWEIN

(1865–1914)

Rome

Above the Circus of the World she sat,
Beautiful and base, a harlot crowned with pride:
Fierce nations, upon whom she sneered and spat,—
Shrieked at her feet and for her pastime died.

On Reading the Life of Haroun Er Reshid

Down all the lanterned Bagdad of our youth
He steals, with golden justice for the poor:
Within his palace—you shall know the truth—
A blood-smeared headsman hides behind each door.

Echo

Dweller in hollow places, hills and rocks,
Daughter of Silence and old Solitude,
Tip-toe she stands within her cave or wood,
Her only life the noises that she mocks.

Mnemosyne

In classic beauty, cold, immaculate,
  A voiceful sculpture, stern and still she stands,
Upon her brow deep-chiselled love and hate,
  That sorrow o'er dead roses in her hands.

Caverns

Written of Colossal Cave, Kentucky

Aisles and abysses; leagues no man explores,
    Of rock that labyrinths and night that drips;
    Where everlasting silence broods, with lips
Of adamant, o'er earthquake-builded floors.
Where forms, such as the Demon-World adores,
    Laborious water carves; whence echo slips
    Wild-tongued o'er pools where petrifaction strips
Her breasts of crystal from which crystal pours.—
Here where primordial fear, the Gorgon, sits
    Staring all life to stone in ghastly mirth,
    I seem to tread, with awe no tongue can tell,—
Beneath vast domes, by torrent-tortured pits,
    'Mid wrecks terrific of the ruined Earth,—
    An ancient causeway of forgotten Hell.

Dead Cities

Out of it all but this remains:—
I was with one who crossed wide chains
Of the Cordilleras, whose peaks
Lock in the wilds of Yucatan,
Chiapas and Honduras. Weeks—
And then a city that no man
Had ever seen; so dim and old,
No chronicle has ever told
The history of men who piled
Its temples and huge teocallis
Among mimosa-blooming valleys;
Or how its altars were defiled
With human blood; whose idols there
With eyes of stone still stand and stare.

So old the moon can only know
How old, since ancient forests grow
On mighty wall and pyramid.

Huge ceïbas, whose trunks were scarred
With ages, and dense yuccas, hid
Fanes 'mid the cacti, scarlet-starred.
I looked upon its paven ways,
And saw it in its kingliest days;
When from the lordly palace one,
A victim, walked with prince and priest,
Who turned brown faces toward the east
In worship of the rising sun:
At night ten hundred temples' spires
On gold burnt everlasting fires.

Uxmal? Palenque? or Copan?
I know not. Only how no man
Had ever seen; and still my soul
Believes it vaster than the three.
Volcanic rock walled in the whole,
Lost in the woods as in some sea.
I only read its hieroglyphs,
Perused its monster monoliths
Of death, gigantic heads; and read
The pictured codex of its fate,
The perished Toltec; while in hate
Mad monkeys cursed me, as if dead
Priests of its past had taken form
To guard its ruined shrines from harm.

GELETT BURGESS

(1866–1951)

The Purple Cow

I never saw a PURPLE COW,
I never HOPE to see one;
But I can tell you, anyhow,
I'd rather SEE than BE one!

The Purple Cow: Suite

Ah, yes, I wrote the "Purple Cow"—
I'm Sorry, now, I wrote it;
But I can tell you Anyhow
I'll Kill you if you Quote it!

WILLIAM VAUGHN MOODY

(1869–1910)

An Ode in Time of Hesitation

(*After seeing at Boston the statue of Robert Gould Shaw,
killed while storming Fort Wagner, July 18, 1863, at the head of
the first enlisted negro regiment, the 54th Massachusetts.*)

I

Before the solemn bronze Saint Gaudens made
To thrill the heedless passer's heart with awe,
And set here in the city's talk and trade
To the good memory of Robert Shaw,
This bright March morn I stand,
And hear the distant spring come up the land;
Knowing that what I hear is not unheard
Of this boy soldier and his negro band,
For all their gaze is fixed so stern ahead,
For all the fatal rhythm of their tread.
The land they died to save from death and shame
Trembles and waits, hearing the spring's great name,
And by her pangs these resolute ghosts are stirred.

II

Through street and mall the tides of people go
Heedless; the trees upon the Common show
No hint of green; but to my listening heart
The still earth doth impart
Assurance of her jubilant emprise,
And it is clear to my long-searching eyes
That love at last has might upon the skies.
The ice is runneled on the little pond;
A telltale patter drips from off the trees;
The air is touched with southland spiceries,
As if but yesterday it tossed the frond
Of pendent mosses where the live-oaks grow
Beyond Virginia and the Carolines,

Or had its will among the fruits and vines
Of aromatic isles asleep beyond
Florida and the Gulf of Mexico.

III

Soon shall the Cape Ann children shout in glee,
Spying the arbutus, spring's dear recluse;
Hill lads at dawn shall hearken the wild goose
Go honking northward over Tennessee;
West from Oswego to Sault Sainte-Marie,
And on to where the Pictured Rocks are hung,
And yonder where, gigantic, willful, young,
Chicago sitteth at the northwest gates,
With restless violent hands and casual tongue
Moulding her mighty fates,
The Lakes shall robe them in ethereal sheen;
And like a larger sea, the vital green
Of springing wheat shall vastly be outflung
Over Dakota and the prairie states.
By desert people immemorial
On Arizonan mesas shall be done
Dim rites unto the thunder and the sun;
Nor shall the primal gods lack sacrifice
More splendid, when the white Sierras call
Unto the Rockies straightway to arise
And dance before the unveiled ark of the year,
Sounding their windy cedars as for shawms,
Unrolling rivers clear
For flutter of broad phylacteries;
While Shasta signals to Alaskan seas
That watch old sluggish glaciers downward creep
To fling their icebergs thundering from the steep,
And Mariposa through the purple calms
Gazes at far Hawaii crowned with palms
Where East and West are met,—
A rich seal on the ocean's bosom set
To say that East and West are twain,
With different loss and gain:
The Lord hath sundered them; let them be sundered yet.

IV

Alas! what sounds are these that come
Sullenly over the Pacific seas,—
Sounds of ignoble battle, striking dumb
The season's half-awakened ecstasies?
Must I be humble, then,
Now when my heart hath need of pride?
Wild love falls on me from these sculptured men;
By loving much the land for which they died
I would be justified.
My spirit was away on pinions wide
To soothe in praise of her its passionate mood
And ease it of its ache of gratitude.
Too sorely heavy is the debt they lay
On me and the companions of my day.
I would remember now
My country's goodliness, make sweet her name.
Alas! what shade art thou
Of sorrow or of blame
Liftest the lyric leafage from her brow,
And pointest a slow finger at her shame?

V

Lies! lies! It cannot be! The wars we wage
Are noble, and our battles still are won
By justice for us, ere we lift the gage.
We have not sold our loftiest heritage.
The proud republic hath not stooped to cheat
And scramble in the market-place of war;
Her forehead weareth yet its solemn star.
Here is her witness: this, her perfect son,
This delicate and proud New England soul
Who leads despisèd men, with just-unshackled feet,
Up the large ways where death and glory meet,
To show all peoples that our shame is done,
That once more we are clean and spirit-whole.

VI

Crouched in the sea fog on the moaning sand
All night he lay, speaking some simple word
From hour to hour to the slow minds that heard,
Holding each poor life gently in his hand
And breathing on the base rejected clay
Till each dark face shone mystical and grand
Against the breaking day;
And lo, the shard the potter cast away
Was grown a fiery chalice crystal-fine
Fulfilled of the divine
Great wine of battle wrath by God's ring-finger stirred.
Then upward, where the shadowy bastion loomed
Huge on the mountain in the wet sea light,
Whence now, and now, infernal flowerage bloomed,
Bloomed, burst, and scattered down its deadly seed,—
They swept, and died like freemen on the height,
Like freemen, and like men of noble breed;
And when the battle fell away at night
By hasty and contemptuous hands were thrust
Obscurely in a common grave with him
The fair-haired keeper of their love and trust.
Now limb doth mingle with dissolvèd limb
In nature's busy old democracy
To flush the mountain laurel when she blows
Sweet by the southern sea,
And heart with crumbled heart climbs in the rose:—
The untaught hearts with the high heart that knew
This mountain fortress for no earthly hold
Of temporal quarrel, but the bastion old
Of spiritual wrong,
Built by an unjust nation sheer and strong,
Expugnable but by a nation's rue
And bowing down before that equal shrine
By all men held divine,
Whereof his band and he were the most holy sign.

VII

O bitter, bitter shade!
Wilt thou not put the scorn
And instant tragic question from thine eyes?
Do thy dark brows yet crave
That swift and angry stave—
Unmeet for this desirous morn—
That I have striven, striven to evade?
Gazing on him, must I not deem they err
Whose careless lips in street and shop aver
As common tidings, deeds to make his cheek
Flush from the bronze, and his dead throat to speak?
Surely some elder singer would arise,
Whose harp hath leave to threaten and to mourn
Above this people when they go astray.
Is Whitman, the strong spirit, overworn?
Has Whittier put his yearning wrath away?
I will not and I dare not yet believe!
Though furtively the sunlight seems to grieve,
And the spring-laden breeze
Out of the gladdening west is sinister
With sounds of nameless battle overseas;
Though when we turn and question in suspense
If these things be indeed after these ways,
And what things are to follow after these,
Our fluent men of place and consequence
Fumble and fill their mouths with hollow phrase,
Or for the end-all of deep arguments
Intone their dull commercial liturgies—
I dare not yet believe! My ears are shut!
I will not hear the thin satiric praise
And muffled laughter of our enemies,
Bidding us never sheathe our valiant sword
Till we have changed our birthright for a gourd
Of wild pulse stolen from a barbarian's hut;
Showing how wise it is to cast away
The symbols of our spiritual sway,
That so our hands with better ease
May wield the driver's whip and grasp the jailer's keys.

VIII

Was it for this our fathers kept the law?
This crown shall crown their struggle and their ruth?
Are we the eagle nation Milton saw
Mewing its mighty youth,
Soon to possess the mountain winds of truth,
And be a swift familiar of the sun
Where aye before God's face his trumpets run?
Or have we but the talons and the maw,
And for the abject likeness of our heart
Shall some less lordly bird be set apart? —
Some gross-billed wader where the swamps are fat?
Some gorger in the sun? Some prowler with the bat?

IX

Ah no!
We have not fallen so.
We are our fathers' sons: let those who lead us know!
'T was only yesterday sick Cuba's cry
Came up the tropic wind, "Now help us, for we die!"
Then Alabama heard,
And rising, pale, to Maine and Idaho
Shouted a burning word.
Proud state with proud impassioned state conferred,
And at the lifting of a hand sprang forth,
East, west, and south, and north,
Beautiful armies. Oh, by the sweet blood and young
Shed on the awful hill slope at San Juan,
By the unforgotten names of eager boys
Who might have tasted girls' love and been stung
With the old mystic joys
And starry griefs, now the spring nights come on,
But that the heart of youth is generous, —
We charge you, ye who lead us,
Breathe on their chivalry no hint of stain!
Turn not their new-world victories to gain!
One least leaf plucked for chaffer from the bays
Of their dear praise,
One jot of their pure conquest put to hire,

The implacable republic will require;
With clamor, in the glare and gaze of noon,
Or subtly, coming as a thief at night,
But surely, very surely, slow or soon
That insult deep we deeply will require.
Tempt not our weakness, our cupidity!
For save we let the island men go free,
Those baffled and dislaureled ghosts
Will curse us from the lamentable coasts
Where walk the frustrate dead.
The cup of trembling shall be drainèd quite,
Eaten the sour bread of astonishment,
With ashes of the hearth shall be made white
Our hair, and wailing shall be in the tent;
Then on your guiltier head
Shall our intolerable self-disdain
Wreak suddenly its anger and its pain;
For manifest in that disastrous light
We shall discern the right
And do it, tardily.—O ye who lead,
Take heed!
Blindness we may forgive, but baseness we will smite.

Harmonics

This string upon my harp was best beloved:
I thought I knew its secrets through and through;
Till an old man, whose young eyes lightened blue
'Neath his white hair, bent over me and moved
His fingers up and down, and broke the wire
To such a laddered music, rung on rung,
As from the patriarch's pillow skyward sprung
Crowded with wide-flung wings and feet of fire.

O vibrant heart! so metely tuned and strung
That any untaught hand can draw from thee
One clear gold note that makes the tired years young—
What of the time when Love had whispered me
Where slept thy nodes, and my hand pausefully
Gave to the dim harmonics voice and tongue?

EDWIN ARLINGTON ROBINSON
(1869–1935)

The Torrent

I found a torrent falling in a glen
Where the sun's light shone silvered and leaf-split;
The boom, the foam, and the mad flash of it
All made a magic symphony; but when
I thought upon the coming of hard men
To cut those patriarchal trees away,
And turn to gold the silver of that spray,
I shuddered. Yet a gladness now and then
Did wake me to myself till I was glad
In earnest, and was welcoming the time
For screaming saws to sound above the chime
Of idle waters, and for me to know
The jealous visionings that I had had
Were steps to the great place where trees and torrents go.

Boston

My northern pines are good enough for me,
But there 's a town my memory uprears—
A town that always like a friend appears,
And always in the sunrise by the sea.
And over it, somehow, there seems to be
A downward flash of something new and fierce,
That ever strives to clear, but never clears
The dimness of a charmed antiquity.

I know my Boston is a counterfeit,—
A frameless imitation, all bereft
Of living nearness, noise, and common speech;
But I am glad for every glimpse of it,—
And there it is, plain as a name that 's left
In letters by warm hands I cannot reach.

The Children of the Night

For those that never know the light,
　　The darkness is a sullen thing;
And they, the Children of the Night,
　　Seem lost in Fortune's winnowing.

But some are strong and some are weak,—
　　And there's the story. House and home
Are shut from countless hearts that seek
　　World-refuge that will never come.

And if there be no other life,
　　And if there be no other chance
To weigh their sorrow and their strife
　　Than in the scales of circumstance,

'T were better, ere the sun go down
　　Upon the first day we embark,
In life's imbittered sea to drown,
　　Than sail forever in the dark.

But if there be a soul on earth
　　So blinded with its own misuse
Of man's revealed, incessant worth,
　　Or worn with anguish, that it views

No light but for a mortal eye,
　　No rest but of a mortal sleep,
No God but in a prophet's lie,
　　No faith for "honest doubt" to keep;

If there be nothing, good or bad,
　　But chaos for a soul to trust,—
God counts it for a soul gone mad,
　　And if God be God, He is just.

And if God be God, He is Love;
    And though the Dawn be still so dim,
It shows us we have played enough
    With creeds that make a fiend of Him.

There is one creed, and only one,
    That glorifies God's excellence;
So cherish, that His will be done,
    The common creed of common sense.

It is the crimson, not the gray,
    That charms the twilight of all time;
It is the promise of the day
    That makes the starry sky sublime;

It is the faith within the fear
    That holds us to the life we curse;—
So let us in ourselves revere
    The Self which is the Universe!

Let us, the Children of the Night,
    Put off the cloak that hides the scar!
Let us be Children of the Light,
    And tell the ages what we are!

John Evereldown

"Where are you going to-night, to-night,—
    Where are you going, John Evereldown?
There's never the sign of a star in sight,
    Nor a lamp that's nearer than Tilbury Town.
Why do you stare as a dead man might?
Where are you pointing away from the light?
And where are you going to-night, to-night,—
    Where are you going, John Evereldown?"

"Right through the forest, where none can see,
    There's where I'm going, to Tilbury Town.
The men are asleep,—or awake, may be,—

But the women are calling John Evereldown.
Ever and ever they call for me,
And while they call can a man be free?
So right through the forest, where none can see,
    There's where I'm going, to Tilbury Town."

"But why are you going so late, so late,—
    Why are you going, John Evereldown?
Though the road be smooth and the path be straight,
    There are two long leagues to Tilbury Town.
Come in by the fire, old man, and wait!
Why do you chatter out there by the gate?
And why are you going so late, so late,—
    Why are you going, John Evereldown?"

"I follow the women wherever they call,—
    That's why I'm going to Tilbury Town.
God knows if I pray to be done with it all,
    But God is no friend to John Evereldown.
So the clouds may come and the rain may fall,
The shadows may creep and the dead men crawl,—
But I follow the women wherever they call,
    And that's why I'm going to Tilbury Town."

Luke Havergal

Go to the western gate, Luke Havergal,—
There where the vines cling crimson on the wall,—
And in the twilight wait for what will come.
The wind will moan, the leaves will whisper some—
Whisper of her, and strike you as they fall;
But go, and if you trust her she will call.
Go to the western gate, Luke Havergal—
Luke Havergal.

No, there is not a dawn in eastern skies
To rift the fiery night that's in your eyes;
But there, where western glooms are gathering,
The dark will end the dark, if anything:

God slays Himself with every leaf that flies,
And hell is more than half of paradise.
No, there is not a dawn in eastern skies—
In eastern skies.

Out of a grave I come to tell you this,—
Out of a grave I come to quench the kiss
That flames upon your forehead with a glow
That blinds you to the way that you must go.
Yes, there is yet one way to where she is,—
Bitter, but one that faith can never miss.
Out of a grave I come to tell you this—
To tell you this.

There is the western gate, Luke Havergal,
There are the crimson leaves upon the wall.
Go,—for the winds are tearing them away,—
Nor think to riddle the dead words they say,
Nor any more to feel them as they fall;
But go! and if you trust her she will call.
There is the western gate, Luke Havergal—
Luke Havergal.

Ballade of Broken Flutes

(To A. T. SCHUMANN.)

In dreams I crossed a barren land,
    A land of ruin, far away;
Around me hung on every hand
    A deathful stillness of decay;
    And silent, as in bleak dismay
That song should thus forsaken be,
    On that forgotten ground there lay
The broken flutes of Arcady.

The forest that was all so grand
    When pipes and tabors had their sway
Stood leafless now, a ghostly band

Of skeletons in cold array.
    A lonely surge of ancient spray
Told of an unforgetful sea,
    But iron blows had hushed for aye
The broken flutes of Arcady.

No more by summer breezes fanned,
    The place was desolate and gray;
But still my dream was to command
    New life into that shrunken clay.
    I tried it. Yes, you scan to-day,
With uncommiserating glee,
    The songs of one who strove to play
The broken flutes of Arcady.

ENVOY

So, Rock, I join the common fray,
    To fight where Mammon may decree;
And leave, to crumble as they may,
    The broken flutes of Arcady.

The House on the Hill

They are all gone away,
    The House is shut and still,
There is nothing more to say.

Through broken walls and gray
    The winds blow bleak and shrill:
They are all gone away.

Nor is there one to-day
    To speak them good or ill:
There is nothing more to say.

Why is it then we stray
    Around that sunken sill?
They are all gone away,

And our poor fancy-play
   For them is wasted skill:
There is nothing more to say.

There is ruin and decay
   In the House on the Hill:
They are all gone away,
There is nothing more to say.

Richard Cory

Whenever Richard Cory went down town,
We people on the pavement looked at him:
He was a gentleman from sole to crown,
Clean favored, and imperially slim.

And he was always quietly arrayed,
And he was always human when he talked;
But still he fluttered pulses when he said,
"Good-morning," and he glittered when he walked.

And he was rich,—yes, richer than a king,—
And admirably schooled in every grace:
In fine, we thought that he was everything
To make us wish that we were in his place.

So on we worked, and waited for the light,
And went without the meat, and cursed the bread;
And Richard Cory, one calm summer night,
Went home and put a bullet through his head.

The Pity of the Leaves

Vengeful across the cold November moors,
Loud with ancestral shame there came the bleak
Sad wind that shrieked, and answered with a shriek,
Reverberant through lonely corridors.
The old man heard it; and he heard, perforce,
Words out of lips that were no more to speak—
Words of the past that shook the old man's cheek
Like dead, remembered footsteps on old floors.

And then there were the leaves that plagued him so!
The brown, thin leaves that on the stones outside
Skipped with a freezing whisper. Now and then
They stopped, and stayed there—just to let him know
How dead they were; but if the old man cried,
They fluttered off like withered souls of men.

Reuben Bright

Because he was a butcher and thereby
Did earn an honest living (and did right),
I would not have you think that Reuben Bright
Was any more a brute than you or I;
For when they told him that his wife must die,
He stared at them, and shook with grief and fright,
And cried like a great baby half that night,
And made the women cry to see him cry.

And after she was dead, and he had paid
The singers and the sexton and the rest,
He packed a lot of things that she had made
Most mournfully away in an old chest
Of hers, and put some chopped-up cedar boughs
In with them, and tore down the slaughter-house.

"The master and the slave go hand in hand"

The master and the slave go hand in hand,
Though touch be lost. The poet is a slave,
And there be kings do sorrowfully crave
The joyance that a scullion may command.
But, ah, the sonnet-slave must understand
The mission of his bondage, or the grave
May clasp his bones, or ever he shall save
The perfect word that is the poet's wand!

The sonnet is a crown, whereof the rhymes
Are for Thought's purest gold the jewel-stones;
But shapes and echoes that are never done
Will haunt the workshop, as regret sometimes
Will bring with human yearning to sad thrones
The crash of battles that are never won.

George Crabbe

Give him the darkest inch your shelf allows,
Hide him in lonely garrets, if you will,—
But his hard, human pulse is throbbing still
With the sure strength that fearless truth endows:—

In spite of all fine science disavows,
Of his plain excellence and stubborn skill
There yet remains what fashion cannot kill,
Though years have thinned the laurel from his brows.

Whether or not we read him, we can feel
From time to time the vigor of his name
Against us like a finger for the shame
And emptiness of what our souls reveal
In books that are as altars where we kneel
To consecrate the flicker, not the flame.

STEPHEN CRANE

(1871–1900)

from *The Black Riders and Other Lines*

I

Black riders came from the sea.
There was clang and clang of spear and shield,
And clash and clash of hoof and heel,
Wild shouts and the wave of hair
In the rush upon the wind:
Thus the ride of sin.

III

In the desert
I saw a creature, naked, bestial,
Who, squatting upon the ground,
Held his heart in his hands,
And ate of it.
I said, "Is it good, friend?"
"It is bitter—bitter," he answered;
"But I like it
"Because it is bitter,
"And because it is my heart."

XXIV

I saw a man pursuing the horizon;
Round and round they sped.
I was disturbed at this;
I accosted the man.
"It is futile," I said,
"You can never——"

"You lie," he cried,
And ran on.

XXVI

There was set before me a mighty hill,
And long days I climbed
Through regions of snow.
When I had before me the summit-view,
It seemed that my labor
Had been to see gardens
Lying at impossible distances.

XXVII

A youth in apparel that glittered
Went to walk in a grim forest.
There he met an assassin
Attired all in garb of old days;
He, scowling through the thickets,
And dagger poised quivering,
Rushed upon the youth.
"Sir," said this latter,
"I am enchanted, believe me,
"To die, thus,
"In this medieval fashion,
"According to the best legends;
"Ah, what joy!"
Then took he the wound, smiling,
And died, content.

LVI

A man feared that he might find an assassin;
Another that he might find a victim.
One was more wise than the other.

LXVII

God lay dead in Heaven;
Angels sang the hymn of the end;
Purple winds went moaning,
Their wings drip-dripping
With blood
That fell upon the earth.
It, groaning thing,
Turned black and sank.
Then from the far caverns
Of dead sins
Came monsters, livid with desire.
They fought,
Wrangled over the world,
A morsel.
But of all sadness this was sad,—
A woman's arms tried to shield
The head of a sleeping man
From the jaws of the final beast.

from *War Is Kind*

Do not weep, maiden, for war is kind.
Because your lover threw wild hands toward the sky
And the affrighted steed ran on alone,
Do not weep.
War is kind.

> Hoarse, booming drums of the regiment
> Little souls who thirst for fight,
> These men were born to drill and die
> The unexplained glory flies above them
> Great is the battle-god, great, and his kingdom——
> A field where a thousand corpses lie.

Do not weep, babe, for war is kind.
Because your father tumbled in the yellow trenches,
Raged at his breast, gulped and died,
Do not weep.
War is kind.

    Swift, blazing flag of the regiment
    Eagle with crest of red and gold,
    These men were born to drill and die
    Point for them the virtue of slaughter
    Make plain to them the excellence of killing
    And a field where a thousand corpses lie.

Mother whose heart hung humble as a button
On the bright splendid shroud of your son,
Do not weep.
War is kind.

    The wayfarer
    Perceiving the pathway to truth
    Was struck with astonishment.
    It was thickly grown with weeds.
"Ha," he said,
"I see that none has passed here
"In a long time."
    Later he saw that each weed
    Was a singular knife.
"Well," he mumbled at last,
"Doubtless there are other roads."

    A man said to the universe:
"Sir, I exist!"
"However," replied the universe,
"The fact has not created in me
"A sense of obligation."

"Little birds of the night"

Little birds of the night
Aye, they have much to tell
Perching there in rows
Blinking at me with their serious eyes
Recounting of flowers they have seen and loved
Of meadows and groves of the distance
And pale sands at the foot of the sea
And breezes that fly in the leaves.
They are vast in experience
These little birds that come in the night

"There is a grey thing that lives in the tree-tops"

There is a grey thing that lives in the tree-tops
None know the horror of its sight
Save those who meet death in the wilderness
But one is enabled to see
To see branches move at its passing
To hear at times the wail of black laughter
And to come often upon mystic places
Places where the thing has just been.

PAUL LAURENCE DUNBAR
(1872–1906)

Accountability

Folks aint got no right to censuah uthah folks about dcy
    habits;
Him dat giv de squir'ls de bushtails made de bobtails fu' de
    rabbits.
Him dat built de grea' big mountains hollered out de little
    valleys,
Him dat made de streets an' driveways wasn't shamed to
    make de alleys.

We is all constructed diff'rent, d'ain't no two of us de same;
We can't he'p ouah likes an' dislikes, ef we'se bad we ain't to
    blame.
Ef we'se good, we needn't show off, case you bet it ain't
    ouah doin'
We gits into su'ttain channels dat we jes caint he'p pu'suin'.

But we all fits into places dat no othah ones cud fill
An' we does the things we has to, big er little, good er ill.
John cain't tek de place o' Henry, Su an' Sally ain't alike;
Bass ain't nuthin' like a suckah, chub ain't nuthin' like a
    pike.

When you come to think about it, how it's all planned out
    it's splendid.
Nuthin's done er evah happens, 'dout hit's somefin' dat's
    intended;
Don't keer whut you does, you has to, an' hit sholy beats de
    dickens,—
Viney go put on de kittle, I got one o' mastah's chickens.

Song of Summer

Dis is gospel weathah sho'—
   Hills is sawt o' hazy.
Meddahs level ez a flo'
   Callin' to de lazy.
Sky all white wif streaks o' blue,
   Sunshine softly gleamin',
D'ain't no wuk hit 's right to do,
   Nothin' 's right but dreamin'.

Dreamin' by de rivah side
   Wif de watahs glist'nin',
Feelin' good an' satisfied
   Ez you lay a-list'nin'
To the little nakid boys
   Splashin' in de watah,
Hollerin' fu' to spress deir joys
   Jes' lak youngsters ought to.

Squir'l a-tippin' on his toes,
   So 's to hide an' view you;
Whole flocks o' camp-meetin' crows
   Shoutin' hallelujah.
Peckahwood erpon de tree
   Tappin' lak a hammah;
Jaybird chattin' wif a bee,
   Tryin' to teach him grammah.

Breeze is blowin' wif perfume,
   Jes' enough to tease you;
Hollyhocks is all in bloom,
   Smellin' fu' to please you.
Go 'way, folks, an' let me 'lone,
   Times is gettin' dearah—
Summah 's settin' on de th'one,
   An' I'm a-layin' neah huh!

We Wear the Mask

We wear the mask that grins and lies,
It hides our cheeks and shades our eyes —
This debt we pay to human guile;
With torn and bleeding hearts we smile
And mouth with myriad subtleties,

Why should the world be over-wise,
In counting all our tears and sighs?
Nay, let them only see us, while
          We wear the mask.

We smile, but oh great Christ, our cries
To Thee from tortured souls arise.
We sing, but oh the clay is vile
Beneath our feet, and long the mile,
But let the world dream otherwise,
          We wear the mask!

Compensation

Because I had loved so deeply,
    Because I had loved so long,
God in His great compassion
    Gave me the gift of song.

Because I have loved so vainly,
    And sung with such faltering breath,
The Master in infinite mercy
    Offers the boon of Death.

When Malindy Sings

G'way an' quit dat noise, Miss Lucy —
    Put dat music book away;
What's de use to keep on tryin'?
    Ef you practise twell you 're gray,

You cain't sta't no notes a-flyin'
　　Lak de ones dat rants and rings
F'om de kitchen to de big woods
　　When Malindy sings.

You ain't got de nachel o'gans
　　Fu' to make de soun' come right,
You ain't got de tu'ns an' twistin's
　　Fu' to make it sweet an' light.
Tell you one thing now, Miss Lucy,
　　An' I 'm tellin' you fu' true,
When hit comes to raal right singin',
　　'T ain't no easy thing to do.

Easy 'nough fu' folks to hollah,
　　Lookin' at de lines an' dots,
When dey ain't no one kin sence it,
　　An' de chune comes in, in spots;
But fu' real melojous music,
　　Dat jes' strikes yo' hea't and clings,
Jes' you stan' an' listen wif me
　　When Malindy sings.

Ain't you nevah hyeahd Malindy?
　　Blessed soul, tek up de cross!
Look hyeah, ain't you jokin', honey?
　　Well, you don't know whut you los'.
Y' ought to hyeah dat gal a-wa'blin',
　　Robins, la'ks, an' all dem things,
Heish dey moufs an' hides dey faces
　　When Malindy sings.

Fiddlin' man jes' stop his fiddlin',
　　Lay his fiddle on de she'f;
Mockin'-bird quit tryin' to whistle,
　　'Cause he jes' so shamed hisse'f.
Folks a-playin' on de banjo
　　Draps dey fingahs on de strings—
Bless yo' soul—fu'gits to move 'em,
　　When Malindy sings.

She jes' spreads huh mouf and hollahs,
  "Come to Jesus," twell you hyeah
Sinnahs' tremblin' steps and voices,
  Timid-lak a-drawin' neah;
Den she tu'ns to "Rock of Ages,"
  Simply to de cross she clings,
An' you fin' yo' teahs a-drappin'
  When Malindy sings.

Who dat says dat humble praises
  Wif de Master nevah counts?
Heish yo' mouf, I hyeah dat music,
  Ez hit rises up an' mounts—
Floatin' by de hills an' valleys,
  Way above dis buryin' sod,
Ez hit makes its way in glory
  To de very gates of God!

Oh, hit 's sweetah dan de music
  Of an edicated band;
An' hit 's dearah dan de battle's
  Song o' triumph in de lan'.
It seems holier dan evenin'
  When de solemn chu'ch bell rings,
Ez I sit an' ca'mly listen
  While Malindy sings.

Towsah, stop dat ba'kin', hyeah me!
  Mandy, mek dat chile keep still;
Don't you hyeah de echoes callin'
  F'om de valley to de hill?
Let me listen, I can hyeah it,
  Th'oo de bresh of angel's wings,
Sof' an' sweet, "Swing Low, Sweet Chariot,"
  Ez Malindy sings.

Signs of the Times

Air a-gittin' cool an' coolah,
  Frost a-comin' in de night,
Hicka' nuts an' wa'nuts fallin',
  Possum keepin' out o' sight.
Tu'key struttin' in de ba'nya'd,
  Nary step so proud ez his;
Keep on struttin', Mistah Tu'key,
  Yo' do' know whut time it is.

Cidah press commence a-squeakin'
  Eatin' apples sto'ed away,
Chillun swa'min' 'roun' lak ho'nets,
  Huntin' aigs ermung de hay.
Mistah Tu'key keep on gobblin'
  At de geese a-flyin' souf,
Oomph! dat bird do' know whut 's comin';
  Ef he did he 'd shet his mouf.

Pumpkin gittin' good an' yallah
  Mek me open up my eyes;
Seems lak it 's a-lookin' at me
  Jes' a-la'in' dah sayin' "Pies."
Tu'key gobbler gwine 'roun' blowin',
  Gwine 'roun' gibbin' sass an' slack;
Keep on talkin', Mistah Tu'key,
  You ain't seed no almanac.

Fa'mer walkin' th'oo de ba'nya'd
  Seein' how things is comin' on,
Sees ef all de fowls is fatt'nin'—
  Good times comin' sho 's you bo'n,
Hyeahs dat tu'key gobbler braggin',
  Den his face break in a smile—
Nebbah min', you sassy rascal,
  He 's gwine nab you atter while.

Choppin' suet in de kitchen,
   Stonin' raisins in de hall,
Beef a-cookin' fu' de mince meat,
   Spices groun'—I smell 'em all.
Look hyeah, Tu'key, stop dat gobblin',
   You ain' luned de sense ob feah,
You ol' fool, yo' naik 's in dangah,
   Do' you know Thanksgibbin 's hyeah?

ALEXANDER L. POSEY

(1873–1908)

Song of the Oktahutchee

Far, far, far are my silver waters drawn;
　The hills embrace me, loth to let me go;
The maidens think me fair to look upon,
　And trees lean over, glad to hear me flow.
Thro' field and valley, green because of me,
I wander, wander to the distant sea.

Thro' lonely places and thro' crowded ways,
　Thro' noise of strife and thro' the solitude,
And on thro' cloudy days and sunny days,
　I journey till I meet, in sisterhood,
The broad Canadian, red with the sunset,
Now calm, now raging in a mighty fret!

On either hand, in a grand colonnade,
　The cottonwoods rise in the azure sky,
And purple mountains cast a purple shade
　As I, now grave, now laughing, pass them by;
The birds of air dip bright wings in my tide,
In sunny reaches where I noiseless glide.

O'er sandy reaches with rocks and mussel-shells,
　Blue over spacious beds of amber sand,
By hanging cliffs, by glens where echo dwells—
　Elusive spirit of the shadow-land—
Forever blest and blessing do I go,
A-wid'ning in the morning's roseate glow.

Tho' I sing my song in a minor key,
　Broad lands and fair attest the good I do;
Tho' I carry no white sails to the sea,
　Towns nestle in the vales I wander thro';
And quails are whistling in the waving grain,
And herds are scattered o'er the verdant plain.

Midsummer

I see the millet combing gold
   From summer sun,
In hussar caps, all day;
   And brown quails run
Far down the dusty way,
   Fly up and whistle from the wold;

Sweet delusions on the mountains,
   Of hounds in chase,
     Beguiling every care
   Of life apace,
     Though only fevered air
That trembles, and dies in mounting.

Autumn

In the dreamy silence
Of the afternoon, a
Cloth of gold is woven
Over wood and prairie;
And the jaybird, newly
Fallen from the heaven,
Scatters cordial greetings,
And the air is filled with
Scarlet leaves, that, dropping,
Rise again, as ever,
With a useless sigh for
Rest—and it is Autumn.

GEORGE CABOT LODGE

(1873–1909)

Tuckanuck, I

I am content to live the patient day:
    The wind sea-laden loiters to the land
    And on the glittering gold of naked sand
    The eternity of blue sea pales to spray.
In such a world we have no need to pray;
    The holy voices of the sea and air
    Are sacramental, like a mighty prayer
    In which the earth has dreamed its tears away.
We row across the waters' fluent gold
    And age seems blessèd, for the world is old.
    Softly we take from Nature's open palm
The dower of the sunset and the sky,
    And dream an Eastern dream, starred by the cry
    Of sea-birds homing through the mighty calm.

Fall

Nay, be content—our door that opens wide
    On whitened fields this autumn dawn, all furred
    With silver imagery, the sudden bird
That soothes the crystal air, the windless tide
Of light across the world from roof to floor—
    Thy heart can ask no more.
The fringed horizon of the pines
    Is delicate with frore,
And holds our world within its shadow shore,
Our world where beauty fresh with dewy wines
    Sits naked at our door.
Thine eyes in mine! The vineyard's dusky bloom,
    The garnered grain, are gifts of autumn's mirth;
And now, while softly through the forest gloom

The warm awakening of the good wet earth
Suspires through the dawn, we need not fear
  The ceaseless pageantry of death and birth,
The swallow's passing with the changing year.
  Our souls could say, "Perfection was and is;
    Death comes like slumber,"—if to-morrow's sun
Should find us fallen with the summer's rose.
This moment stolen from the centuries,
This foretaste of the soul's oblivion
We hold and cherish, and because of this
Are life and death made perfect, and thy woes
Turn lyric through the glory we have won.
The morning flower that drew its petals close
And slept the cold night through is now unfurled
To catch the breathless moment; big and sane
Our autumn day forsakes the gates of rose,
And like a lion shakes its golden mane
  And leaps upon the world.

On an Æolian Harp

Lure of the night's dædalian sea-born breath,
  Wild as the heart's uncomprehended dole,
  Strange as the grieving of a mighty soul
  Touched with the lyric woe of life and death.
Phraser of world-wide monotones that toll
  Like far enormous bells from sky to sky,
  Voice of the vaster solitudes that lie
  With life's solution past the mind's control.
The golden eyes of long-forgotten days,
  The dolorous memory of simple things,
  Sadden thy lapsing chords:—the present pays
The past's arrears of sorrow, and they seem
  To wake a sense, among thy weeping strings,
  Of other lives, like some unceasing dream.

Lower New York

I

Before Dawn

Time has no spectacle more stern and strange;
    Life has no sleep so dense as that which lies
    On walls and windows, blank as sightless eyes,
    On court and prison, warehouse and exchange.
Earth has no silence such as fills the range
    Of streets left bare beneath the haughty skies:—
    Of unremembered human miseries
    Churned without purpose in the trough of change.
For here where day by day the tide-race rolls
    Of sordid greed and passions mean and blind,
    Here is a vast necropolis of souls!
And life, that waits as with suspended breath,
    Weary and still, here seems more dead than death,
    Aimless and empty as an idiot's mind.

II

At Dawn

Here is the dawn a hopeless thing to see:
    Sordid and pale as is the face of one
    Who sinks exhausted in oblivion
    After a night of deep debauchery.
Here, as the light reveals relentlessly
    All that the soul has lost and greed has won,
    Scarce we believe that somewhere now the sun
    Dawns overseas in stainless majesty.
Yet the day comes!—ghastly and harsh and thin
    Down the cold street; and now, from far away,
    We hear a vast and sullen rumor run,
As of the tides of ocean turning in . . .
    And know, for yet another human day,
    The world's dull, dreadful labor is begun!

TRUMBULL STICKNEY

(1874–1904)

In Ampezzo

Only once more and not again—the larches
Shake to the wind their echo, "Not again,"—
We see, below the sky that over-arches
Heavy and blue, the plain

Between Tofana lying and Cristallo
In meadowy earths above the ringing stream:
Whence interchangeably desire may follow,
Hesitant as in dream,

At sunset, south, by lilac promontories
Under green skies to Italy, or forth
By calms of morning beyond Lavinores
Tyrolward and to north:

As now, this last of latter days, when over
The brownish field by peasants are undone
Some widths of grass, some plots of mountain clover
Under the autumn sun,

With honey-warm perfume that risen lingers
In mazes of low heat, or takes the air,
Passing delicious as a woman's fingers
Passing amid the hair;

When scythes are swishing and the mower's muscle
Spans a repeated crescent to and fro,
Or in dry stalks of corn the sickles rustle,
Tangle, detach and go,

Far thro' the wide blue day and greening meadow
Whose blots of amber beaded are with sheaves,
Whereover pallidly a cloud-shadow
Deadens the earth and leaves:

Whilst high around and near, their heads of iron
Sunken in sky whose azure overlights
Ravine and edges, stand the gray and maron
Desolate Dolomites,—

And older than decay from the small summit
Unfolds a stream of pebbly wreckage down
Under the suns of midday, like some comet
Struck into gravel stone.

Faintly across this gold and amethystine
September, images of summer fade;
And gentle dreams now freshen on the pristine
Viols, awhile unplayed,

Of many a place where lovingly we wander,
More dearly held that quickly we forsake,—
A pine by sullen coasts, an oleander
Reddening on the lake.

And there, each year with more familiar motion,
From many a bird and windy forestries,
Or along shaking fringes of the ocean
Vapours of music rise.

From many easts the morning gives her splendour;
The shadows fill with colours we forget;
Remembered tints at evening grow tender,
Tarnished with violet.

Let us away! soon sheets of winter metal
On this discoloured mountain-land will close,
While elsewhere Spring-time weaves a crimson petal,
Builds and perfumes a rose.

Away! for here the mountain sinks in gravel.
Let us forget the unhappy site with change,
And go, if only happiness be travel
After the new and strange:—

Unless 't were better to be very single,
To follow some diviner monotone,
And in all beauties, where ourselves commingle,
Love but a love, but one,

Across this shadowy minute of our living,
What time our hearts so magically sing,
To meditate our fever, simply giving
All in a little thing?

Just as here, past yon dumb and melancholy
Sameness of ruin, while the mountains ail,
Summer and sunset-coloured autumn slowly
Dissipate down the vale;

And all these lines along the sky that measure,
Sorapis and the rocks of Mezzodì
Crumble by foamy miles into the azure
Mediterranean sea:

Whereas to-day at sunrise, under brambles,
A league above the moss and dying pines
I picked this little—in my hand that trembles—
Parcel of columbines.

Mnemosyne

It's autumn in the country I remember.

How warm a wind blew here about the ways!
And shadows on the hillside lay to slumber
During the long sun-sweetened summer-days.

It's cold abroad the country I remember.

The swallows veering skimmed the golden grain
At midday with a wing aslant and limber;
And yellow cattle browsed upon the plain.

It's empty down the country I remember.

I had a sister lovely in my sight:
Her hair was dark, her eyes were very sombre;
We sang together in the woods at night.

It's lonely in the country I remember.

The babble of our children fills my ears,
And on our hearth I stare the perished ember
To flames that show all starry thro' my tears.

It's dark about the country I remember.

There are the mountains where I lived. The path
Is slushed with cattle-tracks and fallen timber,
The stumps are twisted by the tempests' wrath.

But that I knew these places are my own,
I'd ask how came such wretchedness to cumber
The earth, and I to people it alone.

It rains across the country I remember.

Eride, V

Now in the palace gardens warm with age,
On lawn and flower-bed this afternoon
The thin November-coloured foliage
Just as last year unfastens lilting down,

And round the terrace in gray attitude
The very statues are becoming sere
With long presentiment of solitude.
Most of the life that I have lived is here,

Here by the path and autumn's earthy grass
And chestnuts standing down the breadths of sky:
Indeed I know not how it came to pass,
The life I lived here so unhappily.

Yet blessing over all! I do not care
What wormwood I have ate to cups of gall;
I care not what despairs are buried there
Under the ground, no, I care not at all.

Nay, if the heart have beaten, let it break!
I have not loved and lived but only this
Betwixt my birth and grave. Dear Spirit, take
The gratitude that pains, so deep it is.

When Spring shall be again, and at your door
You stand to feel the mellower evening wind,
Remember if you will my heart is pure,
Perfectly pure and altogether kind;

That not an aftercry of all our strife
Troubles the love I give you and the faith:
Say to yourself that at the ends of life
My arms are open to you, life and death.—

How much it aches to linger in these things!
I thought the perfect end of love was peace
Over the long-forgiven sufferings.
But something else, I know not what it is,

The words that came so nearly and then not,
The vanity, the error of the whole,
The strong cross-purpose, oh, I know not what
Cries dreadfully in the distracted soul.

The evening fills the garden, hardly red;
And autumn goes away, like one alone.
Would I were with the leaves that thread by thread
Soften to soil, I would that I were one.

On Some Shells Found Inland

These are my murmur-laden shells that keep
A fresh voice tho' the years be very gray.
The wave that washed their lips and tuned their lay
Is gone, gone with the faded ocean sweep,
The royal tide, gray ebb and sunken neap
And purple midday,—gone! To this hot clay
Must sing my shells, where yet the primal day,
Its roar and rhythm and splendour will not sleep.
What hand shall join them to their proper sea
If all be gone? Shall they forever feel
Glories undone and worlds that cannot be?—
'Twere mercy to stamp out this agèd wrong,
Dash them to earth and crunch them with the heel
And make a dust of their seraphic song.

"Be still. The Hanging Gardens were a dream"

Be still. The Hanging Gardens were a dream
That over Persian roses flew to kiss
The curlèd lashes of Semiramis.
Troy never was, nor green Skamander stream.
Provence and Troubadour are merest lies.
The glorious hair of Venice was a beam
Made within Titian's eye. The sunsets seem,
The world is very old and nothing is.
Be still. Thou foolish thing, thou canst not wake,
Nor thy tears wedge thy soldered lids apart,
But patter in the darkness of thy heart.
Thy brain is plagued. Thou art a frighted owl
Blind with the light of life thou'ldst not forsake,
And Error loves and nourishes thy soul.

Lakeward

'Twill soon be sunrise. Down the valley waiting
Far over slope and mountain-height the firs
Undulate dull and furry under the beating
     Heaven of autumn stars.

To westward yet the summits hang in slumber
Like frozen smoke; there, growing wheel on wheel,
As 'twere an upward wind of rose and amber
     Goes up the sky of steel;

And indistinguishable thro' the valley
An endless murmur freshens as of bees,—
The stream that gathering torrents frantically
     Churns away thro' the trees.—

Mountains, farewell! Into your crystal winter
To linger on unworlded and alone
And feel the glaciers of your bosom enter
     One and another my own,

And on the snow that falling edges nearer
To lose my very shade,—'t were well, 't were done
Had I not in me the soul of a wayfarer!
     No, let me wander down

The road that, as the boulders higher and higher
Go narrower each to each and hold the gloom,
Follows like me the waters' loud desire
     Of a sun-sweetened home.

And as I pass, methinks once more the Titan
From in the bosom of the humid rocks,
Where yet his aged eyes grow vague and whiten
     Weary and wet his locks,

Gazes away upon this brightened weather
As asking it in reason and in rhyme
How long shall mountain iron and ice together
        Hold against summer-time.

Long, surely! long, perhaps! but not for ever.
Now here across the buried road and field,
Torn from the dizzy flanks up there that quiver,
        Down to the plain and spilled

In sand and wreckage lies the avalanche's
Dead mass under the sun, and not a sound!—
The morning grows and from the rich pine-branches
        Shadows make blue the ground.

To wander south! Already here the grasses
Feather and glint across the sunny air.
It's warmer. Up the road a peasant passes
        Brown-skinned and dark of hair.

Some of an autumn glamour on the highway
Softens the dust, and yonder I have seen
Catching the sunlight something in the byway
        Else than an evergreen,

And weeds along the ditch are parching.—Sudden
Once more from either side the ranges draw
Near each to each; beneath struggle and madden
        Down in the foamy flaw

The waters, and, a span across, the boulders
Stand to the burning heaven upright and cold.
Then drawing lengthily along their shoulders
        Vapours of white and gold

Blow from the lowland upward; all the gloaming
Quivers with violet; here in the wedge
The tunnelled road goes narrow and outcoming
        Stealthily on the edge

Lies free. The outlines have a gentle meaning.
Willows and clematis, foliage and grain!
And the last mountain falls in terraces to the greening
     Infinite autumn plain.

O further southward, down the brooks and valley, on
And past the lazy farms and orchards, on!
It smells of hay, and thro' the long Italian
     Flowerful afternoon

Sodden with sunlight, green and gold, the country
Suspends her fruit and stretches ripe and still
Between the clumsy fig and silver plane-tree
     Circled, from hill to hill

And down the vale along the running river:
The vale, the river and the hills, that take
The perfect south and here at last for ever
     Merge into thee, O Lake! —

Sunset-enamoured in the autumnal hours!
When large and westering his heavy rays
Fall from the vineyards and the garden-flowers
     Hazily o'er thy face,

And colouring thy bosom with a lover's
Warm and quick lips and hesitating hand,
He murmurs to thee while the twilight hovers
     Lilac about the strand,

Thou, mid the grape-hung terraces low-levelled,
Lookest into the green and crimson sky
With swimming eyes and auburn hair dishevelled,
     Radiant in ecstasy. —

'Tis evening. In the open blueness stretches
A feathery lawn of light from moon to shore,
And a boat-load of labourers homeward plashes,
     Singing "Amor, Amor."

At Sainte-Marguerite

The gray tide flows and flounders in the rocks
Along the crannies up the swollen sand.
Far out the reefs lie naked—dunes and blocks
Low in the watery wind. A shaft of land
Going to sea thins out the western strand.

It rains, and all along and always gulls
Career sea-screaming in and weather-glossed.
It blows here, pushing round the cliff; in lulls
Within the humid stone a motion lost
Ekes out the flurried heart-beat of the coast.

It blows and rains a pale and whirling mist
This summer morning. I that hither came—
Was it to pluck this savage from the schist,
This crazy yellowish bloom without a name,
With leathern blade and tortured wiry frame?

Why here alone, away, the forehead pricked
With dripping salt and fingers damp with brine,
Before the offal and the derelict
And where the hungry sea-wolves howl and whine
Live human hours? now that the columbine

Stands somewhere shaded near the fields that fall
Great starry sheaves of the delighted year,
And globing rosy on the garden wall
The peach and apricot and soon the pear
Drip in the teasing hand their sugared tear.

Inland a little way the summer lies.
Inland a little and but yesterday
I saw the weary teams, I heard the cries
Of sicklemen across the fallen hay,
And buried in the sunburned stacks I lay

Tasting the straws and tossing, laughing soft
Into the sky's great eyes of gold and blue
And nodding to the breezy leaves aloft
Over the harvest's mellow residue.
But sudden then —then strangely dark it grew.

How good it is, before the dreary flow
Of cloud and water, here to lie alone
And in this desolation to let go
Down the ravine one with another, down
Across the surf to linger or to drown

The loves that none can give and none receive,
The fearful asking and the small retort,
The life to dream of and the dream to live!
Very much more is nothing than a part,
Nothing at all and darkness in the heart.

I would my manhood now were like the sea.—
Thou at high-tide, when compassing the land
Thou find'st the issue short, questioningly
A moment poised, thy floods then down the strand
Sink without rancour, sink without command,

Sink of themselves in peace without despair,
And turn as still the calm horizon turns,
Till they repose little by little nowhere
And the long light unfathomable burns
Clear from the zenith stars to the sea-ferns.

Thou art thy Priest, thy Victim and thy God.
Thy life is bulwarked with a thread of foam,
And of the sky, the mountains and the sod
Thou askest nothing, evermore at home
In thy own self's perennial masterdom.

from *Sonnets from Greece*

Sunium

These are the strings of the Ægean lyre
Across the sky and sea in glory hung:
Columns of white thro' which the wind has flung
The clouds and stars, and drawn the rain and fire.
Their flutings now to fill the notes' desire
Are strained and dubious, yet in music young
They cast their full-blown answer far along
To where in sea the island hills expire.
How bravely from the quarry's earthen gloom
In snow they rose amid the blue to stand
Melodious and alone on Sunium!
They shall not wither back into the land.
The sun that harps them with his golden hand
Doth slowly with his hand of gold consume.

Mt. Lykaion

Alone on Lykaion since man hath been
Stand on the height two columns, where at rest
Two eagles hewn of gold sit looking East
Forever; and the sun goes up between.
Far down around the mountain's oval green
An order keeps the falling stones abreast.
Below within the chaos last and least
A river like a curl of light is seen.
Beyond the river lies the even sea,
Beyond the sea another ghost of sky,—
O God, support the sickness of my eye
Lest the far space and long antiquity
Suck out my heart, and on this awful ground
The great wind kill my little shell with sound.

Near Helikon

By such an all-embalming summer day
As sweetens now among the mountain pines
Down to the cornland yonder and the vines,
To where the sky and sea are mixed in gray,
How do all things together take their way
Harmonious to the harvest, bringing wines
And bread and light and whatsoe'er combines
In the large wreath to make it round and gay.
To me my troubled life doth now appear
Like scarce distinguishable summits hung
Around the blue horizon: places where
Not even a traveller purposeth to steer,—
Whereof a migrant bird in passing sung,
And the girl closed her window not to hear.

Eleusis

Here for a thousand years processional
Winding around the Eleusinian bay,
The world with drooping eyes has made her way
By stair and portal to the sombre Hall.
As then the litanies antiphonal
Obscurely through the pillars sang away,
It dawned, and in the shaft of sudden day
Demeter smiling gave her bread to all.
They drew as waves out of a twilight main,
Long genuflecting multitudes, to feed
With God upon the sacramental grain.
And lo, the temple veil was rent in twain;
But thro' the rift their choirs in silver train
Still passing out rehearsed the human creed.

Six O'Clock

Now burst above the city's cold twilight
The piercing whistles and the tower-clocks:
For day is done. Along the frozen docks
The workmen set their ragged shirts aright.
Thro' factory doors a stream of dingy light
Follows the scrimmage as it quickly flocks
To hut and home among the snow's gray blocks.—
I love you, human labourers. Good-night!
Good-night to all the blackened arms that ache!
Good-night to every sick and sweated brow,
To the poor girl that strength and love forsake,
To the poor boy who can no more! I vow
The victim soon shall shudder at the stake
And fall in blood: we bring him even now.

from *Dramatic Fragments*

V

Sir, say no more.
Within me 't is as if
The green and climbing eyesight of a cat
Crawled near my mind's poor birds.

IX

I hear a river thro' the valley wander
Whose water runs, the song alone remaining.
A rainbow stands and summer passes under.

AMERICAN INDIAN POETRY

The Song of the Lenape Warriors Going Against the Enemy

(*Delaware*)

O poor me!
Who am going out to fight the enemy,
And know not whether I shall return again,
To enjoy the embraces of my children
And my wife.
O poor creature!
Whose life is not in his own hands,
Who has no power over his own body,
But tries to do his duty
For the welfare of his nation.
O! thou Great Spirit above!
Take pity on my children
And on my wife!
Prevent their mourning on my account!
Grant that I may be successful in this attempt—
That I may slay my enemy,
And bring home the trophies of war
To my dear family and friends,
That we may rejoice together.
O! take pity on me!
Give me strength and courage to meet my enemy,
Suffer me to return again to my children,
To my wife
And to my relations!
Take pity on me and preserve my life
And I will make to thee a sacrifice.

John Heckewelder, *An Account of the History, Manners, and Customs of the Indian Nations Who Once Inhabited Pennsylvania and the Neighbouring States,* 1819.

Song for Medicine Hunting —
Rarely for the Metai

(*Ojibwa*)

 I wished to be born, I was born, and after I was
born I made all spirits.

 I created the spirits.

 He sat down Na-na-bush; his fire burns forever.

 Notwithstanding you speak evil of me, from above
are my friends, my friends.

 I can use many kinds of wood to make a bear
unable to walk.

 Of you I think, that you use the We-nis-ze-bug-
gone, I think this of you.

 That which I take is blood, that which I take.

 Now I have something to eat.

 I cover my head, sitting down to sleep, ye spirits.

 I fill my kettle for the spirit.

Long ago, in the old time, since I laid myself down,
ye are spirits.

 I open you for a bear, I open you.

 That is a Spirit which comes both from above and
below.

 I am he that giveth success, because all spirits help
me.

 The feather, the feather; it is the thing, the feather.

 Who is a spirit? He that walketh with the serpent,
walking on the ground; he is a spirit.

 Now they will eat something, my women; now I tell
them they will eat.

 This yellow ochre, I will try it.

 Now I wish to try my bird; sometimes I used to try,
and sometimes it used to be something.

 I can kill any animal, because the loud-speaking
thunder helps me; I can kill any animal.

 I take a bear, his heart I take.

A rattle snake makes a noise on the poles of my
           lodge; he makes a noise.

 To a Shawnee, the four sticks used in this song
           belonged. When struck together they were
           heard all over the country.

 I come up from below; I come down from above; I
           see the spirit; I see beavers.

 I can make an east wind come and pass over the
           ground.

 Thus have I sat down, and the earth above and
           below has listened to me sitting here.

 I make to crawl, a bear, I make to crawl.

*A Narrative of the Captivity and Adventures of John Tanner
During Thirty Years Residence Among the Indians in the
Interior of North America,* Edwin S. James, editor, 1830.

The Loon Upon the Lake

(*Ojibwa*)

I looked across the water,
   I bent o'er it and listened,
I thought it was my lover,
   My true lover's paddle glistened.
Joyous thus his light canoe would the silver ripples wake.—
But no!—it is the loon alone—the loon upon the lake.
Ah me! it is the loon alone—the loon upon the lake.

   I see the fallen maple
      Where he stood, his red scarf waving,
   Though waters nearly bury
      Boughs they then were newly laving.
I hear his last farewell, as it echoed from the brake.—
But no, it is the loon alone—the loon upon the lake,
Ah me! it is the loon alone—the loon upon the lake.

> Charles Fenno Hoffman, in Henry Rowe Schoolcraft,
> *Oneóta, or Characteristics of the Red Race of America,* 1845.

Chant to the Fire-Fly

(*Ojibwa*)

Fire-fly, fire-fly, light me to bed.
Come, come, little insect of light,
You are my candle, and light me to go.

> Henry Rowe Schoolcraft, *Information Respecting
> the History, Condition, and Prospects of
> the Indian Tribes of the United States,* vol. 5, 1855.

Songs and Chants

(*Southern Paiute*)

The Home of the River

The edge of the sky
Is the home of the river

Song of the Mountain Sheep

My curved horns
Like a necklace stand

(*Untitled*)

As feathers are drifted
So is the foam in the Colorado
Where the creeks run in

My Love

In yonder distant glen
Perchance she's cutting reeds

A Morning Walk

Over the land over the land
I walked at morn
Singing and trembling with cold

Winter Song

The feathers of the reed
Are lying on the ground
And the quails are perched on the pines

The Tobacco Plant

The tobacco plant is standing
Where the babbling water runs
On the side of the mountain

Our Song

Our song will enter
That distant land
That gleaming land
That gleaming land
And roll the lake in waves

Music

Over the land at night
Slowly the music floats

The Traveller's Rest

In the red valley I sleep
On my way to a far distant land

The Trout

In the blue water
The trout wags its tail

The Spirit

The spirit
Is swaying and singing

The Storm Creek

Along the land
A-down the gulch
The mountain stream
The feathery mountain stream

The Pines

The lofty pines
The tops of the lofty pines
The lofty pines
Are swaying with the winds

The Desert

The land is hungry
The ants are starving

The Storm Crown

It rains on the mountains
It rains on the mountains
A white crown encircles the mountain

The Blue Bird

At the foot of the cliff
On the face of the cliff
The blue bird sings

The Kai-nu-shuk

Through the cleft of the rock
In the land far away
The water was dashed from the mountain

The Mountain Peak

On the peak of the mountain
The eagle is dancing,
The tempest is roaring

The Storm

The sky will fall
The red water eddies

Cave Lake Song

The twilight has a home
And the black fish has a home

The Rattlesnake

In the stony land
Near by a rock
With head erect you crawled along

A Dream

Upon the Un-kar-tu-wan-an
I quiver, I quiver
Suspended from the mountain

Don D. Fowler and Catherine S. Fowler, eds.,
*Anthropology of the Numa: John Wesley Powell's
Manuscripts on the Numic Peoples of
Western North America, 1868–1880,* 1971.

from *Sacred Songs of the Konkau*

Red Cloud's Song
(Heard by the mother of Oan-koi'-tu-peh)

I am the Red Cloud.
My father formed me out of the sky.
I sing among the mountain flowers.
I sing among the flowering chamize of the mountains.
I sing in the mountains like the *wēk'-wēk*.
I sing among the rocks like the *wēk'-wēk*.
In the morning I cry in the mountains.
In the morning I walk the path.
I cry to the morning stars.

The Acorn Song

The acorns come down from heaven.
I plant the short acorns in the valley.
I plant the long acorns in the valley.
I sprout, I, the black-oak acorn, sprout, I sprout.

Ki-u-nad'-dis-si's Song

I am the only one, the only one left.
An old man, I carry the gambling-board; an old man, I sing
      the gambling song.
The roots I eat of the valley.
The pepper-ball is round.
The water trickles, trickles.
The water-leaves grow along the river bank.
I rub the hands, I wiggle the tail.
I am a doctor, I am a doctor.

Stephen Powers, "Tribes of California,"
Contributions to North American Ethnology, 1877.

Hunter's Song

(*Hitchiti*)

Somewhere the deer lies on the ground, I think; I walk
    about.
    Awake, arise, stand up!
It is raising up its head, I believe; I walk about.
    Awake, arise, stand up!
It attempts to rise, I believe; I walk about.
    Awake, arise, stand up!
Slowly it raises its body, I think; I walk about.
    Awake, arise, stand up!
It has now risen on its feet, I presume; I walk about.
    Awake, arise, stand up!

Albert S. Gatschet, *A Migration
Legend of the Creek Indians*, 1884.

The Song of the Stars

(*Passamaquoddy*)

We are the stars which sing,
We sing with our light;
We are the birds of fire,
We fly over the sky.
Our light is a voice;
We make a road for spirits,
For the spirits to pass over.
Among us are three hunters
Who chase a bear;
There never was a time
When they were not hunting.
We look down on the mountains.
This is the Song of the Stars.

Charles Godfrey Leland, *The Algonquin Legends of
New England; or, Myths and Folk Lore of the Micmac,
Passamaquoddy, and Penobscot Tribes*, 1884.

from *The Walam Olum, or Red Score,*
of the Lenâpé

(*Delaware*)

I.

 At first, in that place, at all times, above the earth,

 On the earth, was an extended fog, and there the
great Manito was.

 At first, forever, lost in space, everywhere, the great
Manito was.

 He made the extended land and sky.

 He made the sun, the moon, the stars.

 He made them all to move evenly.

 Then the wind blew violently, and it cleared, and
the water flowed off far and strong.

 And groups of islands grew newly, and there
remained.

Anew spoke the great Manito, a manito to manitos,

 To beings, mortals, souls and all,

And ever after he was a manito to men, and their
grandfather.

 He gave the first mother, the mother of beings.

 He gave the fish, he gave the turtles, he gave the
beasts, he gave the birds.

 But an evil Manito made evil beings only, monsters,

 He made the flies, he made the gnats.

 All beings were then friendly.

 Truly the manitos were active and kindly

 To those very first men, and to those first mothers;
fetched them wives,

 And fetched them food, when first they desired it.

 All had cheerful knowledge, all had leisure, all
thought in gladness.

 But very secretly an evil being, a mighty magician,
came on earth,

 And with him brought badness, quarreling,
unhappiness,

Brought bad weather, brought sickness, brought death.

 All this took place of old on the earth, beyond the great tide-water, at the first.

II.

 Long ago there was a mighty snake, and beings evil to men.

 This mighty snake hated those who were there and greatly disquieted those whom he hated.

 They both did harm, they both injured each other, both were not in peace.

 Driven from their homes they fought with this murderer.

 The mighty snake firmly resolved to harm the men.

 He brought three persons, he brought a monster, he brought a rushing water.

Between the hills the water rushed and rushed, dashing through and through, destroying much.

Nanabush, the Strong White One, grandfather of beings, grandfather of men, was on the Turtle Island.

There he was walking and creating, as he passed by and created the turtle.

 Beings and men all go forth, they walk in the floods and shallow waters, down stream thither to the Turtle Island.

 There were many monster fishes, which ate some of them.

 The Manito daughter, coming, helped with her canoe, helped all, as they came and came.

 And also Nanabush, Nanabush, the grandfather of all, the grandfather of beings, the grandfather of men, the grandfather of the turtle.

 The men then were together on the turtle, like to turtles.

 Frightened on the turtle, they prayed on the turtle that what was spoiled should be restored.

 The water ran off, the earth dried, the lakes were at rest, all was silent, and the mighty snake departed.

III.

After the rushing waters had subsided the Lenape of the turtle were close together, in hollow houses, living together there.

It freezes where they abode, it snows where they abode, it storms where they abode, it is cold where they abode.

 At this northern place they speak favorably of mild, cool lands, with many deer and buffaloes.

 As they journeyed, some being strong, some rich, they separated into house-builders and hunters;

 The strongest, the most united, the purest, were the hunters.

 The hunters showed themselves at the north, at the east, at the south, at the west.

 In that ancient country, in that northern country, in that turtle country, the best of the Lenape were the Turtle men.

 All the cabin fires of that land were disquieted, and all said to their priest, "Let us go."

 To the Snake land to the east they went forth, going away, earnestly grieving.

 Split asunder, weak, trembling, their land burned, they went, torn and broken, to the Snake Island.

Those from the north being free, without care, went forth from the land of snow, in different directions.

The fathers of the Bald Eagle and the White Wolf remain along the sea, rich in fish and muscles.

Floating up the streams in their canoes, our fathers were rich, they were in the light, when they were at those islands.

Head Beaver and Big Bird said,
"Let us go to Snake Island," they said.

All say they will go along to destroy all the land.

Those of the north agreed,
Those of the east agreed.
Over the water, the frozen sea,
They went to enjoy it.

On the wonderful, slippery water,
On the stone-hard water all went,
On the great Tidal Sea, the muscle-bearing sea.

Ten thousand at night,
All in one night,
To the Snake Island, to the east, at night,
They walk and walk, all of them.

The men from the north, the east, the south,
The Eagle clan, the Beaver clan, the Wolf clan,
The best men, the rich men, the head men,
Those with wives, those with daughters, those with
    dogs,

They all come, they tarry at the land of the spruce
    pines;
Those from the west come with hesitation,
Esteeming highly their old home at the Turtle land.

Daniel Garrison Brinton, *The Lenâpé and*
Their Legends; with the Complete Text
and Symbols of the Walam Olum, 1885.

from *The Mountain Chant*

(*Navajo*)

Twelfth Song of the Thunder

The voice that beautifies the land!
The voice above,
The voice of the thunder
Within the dark cloud
Again and again it sounds,
The voice that beautifies the land.

The voice that beautifies the land!
The voice below,
The voice of the grasshopper
Among the plants
Again and again it sounds,
The voice that beautifies the land.

Sixth Song of the Holy Young Men

There's a god on each side.
Now the Holy Young Man
Is the god on top of the black mountain,
With his black notched stick,
The implement of his dance, his magic wand.

There's a god on each side.
Now the Holy Young Woman
Is the god on top of the blue mountain,
With her blue notched stick,
The implement of her dance, her magic wand.

> Washington Matthews, "The Mountain Chant:
> A Navajo Ceremony," *Fifth Annual Report
> of the Bureau of Ethnology,* 1887.

Chinook Songs

Whose sweetheart is very drunk?
My sweetheart is very drunk!
You do not like me,
You do not like me,
You do not like me!
I know you.

———

I cry always.
Far away is my country now.

———

Because my relations are dead,
When the steamboat leaves, I cry.

———

Good-bye, barkeeper! I am going now to-day.
Come! give me a full cocktail.

———

Ya, always I long
For my husband in California.

———

Very unhappy I was
With my wife,
In Victoria.
Nobody
Said good-day to us
In Victoria.

———

Good-bye, oh my dear Charlie!
When you take a wife,
Don't forget me.

———

What is Billy doing now?
He is going to the beerhouse.
The American says: Get out of the way!
He goes and cries aloud.

———

Kittie Apples is very unhappy
This winter.
Who will take her away?
The steamboat Hope.

———

I am very glad
When the steamboat comes here.
I think I shall cry
When the steamboat leaves.

———

A white man is now your husband, Mary.
Ha, cast me off thus!
I do not care now.
Ya aya aya.

———

Aya, aya!
I have seen
Sitka your country.
Never mind, if I die
Now soon.

———

I don't care
If you desert me.
Many pretty boys are in the town.
Soon I shall take another one.
That is not hard for me!

Franz Boas, "Chinook Songs,"
Journal of American Folk-Lore, 1888.

Pawnee War-Song

Let us see, is this real,
Let us see, is this real,
Let us see, is this real,
Let us see, is this real,
This life I am living?
Ye gods, who dwell everywhere,
Let us see, is this real,
This life I am living?

Daniel Garrison Brinton, *Essays of an Americanist*, 1890.

The Thanksgivings

(*Iroquois*)

We who are here present thank the Great Spirit that we are
    here to praise Him.

We thank Him that He has created men and women, and
    ordered that these beings shall always be living to
    multiply the earth.

We thank Him for making the earth and giving these beings
    its products to live on.

We thank Him for the water that comes out of the earth and
    runs for our lands.

We thank Him for all the animals on the earth.

We thank Him for certain timbers that grow and have fluids
    coming from them for us all.

We thank Him for the branches of the trees that grow
    shadows for our shelter.

We thank Him for the beings that come from the west, the
    thunder and lightning that water the earth.

We thank Him for the light which we call our oldest
    brother, the sun that works for our good.

We thank Him for all the fruits that grow on the trees and
    vines.

We thank Him for his goodness in making the forests, and
    thank all its trees.

We thank Him for the darkness that gives us rest, and for
    the kind Being of the darkness that gives us light, the
    moon.

We thank Him for the bright spots in the skies that give us
    signs, the stars.

We give Him thanks for our supporters, who have charge of
    our harvests.

We give thanks that the voice of the Great Spirit can still be
    heard through the words of Ga-ne-o-di-o.

We thank the Great Spirit that we have the privilege of this
    pleasant occasion.

We give thanks for the persons who can sing the Great
      Spirit's music, and hope they will be privileged to
      continue in his faith.
We thank the Great Spirit for all the persons who perform
      the ceremonies on this occasion.

Harriet Maxwell Converse, Journal of American Folk-Lore, 1891.

from *The Hardening of the World, and the First Settlement of Men*

(*Zuni*)

That the earth be made safer for men, and more stable,
Let us shelter the land where our children be resting,
Yea! the depths and the valleys beyond shall be sheltered
By the shade of our cloud-shield! Let us lay to its circle
Our firebolts of thunder, aimed to all the four regions,
Then smite with our arrows of lightning from under.
Lo! the earth shall heave upward and downward with
      thunder!
Lo! fire shall belch outward and burn the world over,
And floods of hot water shall seethe swift before it!
Lo! smoke of earth-stenches shall blacken the daylight
And deaden the senses of them else escaping
And lessen the number of fierce preying monsters!
That earth be made safer for men, and more stable.

Frank Hamilton Cushing, "Outlines of Zuñi
Creation Myths," <i>Thirteenth Annual Report
of the Bureau of American Ethnology,</i> 1896.</div>

from *The Generation of the Seeds,*
or the Origin of Corn

(*Zuni*)

Lo! ye children of men and the Mother,
Ye Brothers of Seed,
Elder, younger,
Behold the *seed plants of all seeds!*
The grass-seeds ye planted, in secret,
Were seen of the stars and the regions,
Are shown in the forms of these tassels!
The plumes that ye planted beside them
Were felt in the far away spaces,
Are shown in the forms of their leaf-blades!
But the seed that ye see growing from them,
Is the gift of my seven bright maidens,
The stars of the house of my children!
Look well, that ye cherish their persons,
Nor change ye the gift of their being,—
As fertile of flesh for all men
To the bearing of children for men,—
Lest ye lose them, to seek them in vain!
Be ye brothers ye people, and people;
Be ye happy ye Priests of the Corn!
Lo! the seed of all seed-plants is born!

> Frank Hamilton Cushing, "Outlines of Zuñi
> Creation Myths," *Thirteenth Annual Report
> of the Bureau of American Ethnology,* 1896.

Ghost-Dance Songs of the Paiute

The snow lies there —*ro' răni'* !
The snow lies there —*ro' răni'* !
The snow lies there —*ro' răni'* !
The snow lies there —*ro' răni'* !
The Milky Way lies there,
The Milky Way lies there.

———

A slender antelope, a slender antelope,
A slender antelope, a slender antelope,
He is wallowing upon the ground,
He is wallowing upon the ground,
He is wallowing upon the ground,
He is wallowing upon the ground.

———

The black rock, the black rock,
The black rock, the black rock,
The rock is broken, the rock is broken,
The rock is broken, the rock is broken.

———

The wind stirs the willows,
The wind stirs the willows,
The wind stirs the willows,
The wind stirs the grasses,
The wind stirs the grasses,
The wind stirs the grasses.

———

Fog! Fog!
Lightning! Lightning!
Whirlwind! Whirlwind!

———

The whirlwind! The whirlwind!
The whirlwind! The whirlwind!
The snowy earth comes gliding, the snowy earth comes
    gliding;
The snowy earth comes gliding, the snowy earth comes
    gliding.

———

There is dust from the whirlwind,
There is dust from the whirlwind,
There is dust from the whirlwind.
The whirlwind on the mountain,
The whirlwind on the mountain,
The whirlwind on the mountain.

The rocks are ringing,
The rocks are ringing,
The rocks are ringing.
They are ringing in the mountains,
They are ringing in the mountains,
They are ringing in the mountains.

The cottonwoods are growing tall,
The cottonwoods are growing tall,
The cottonwoods are growing tall.
They are growing tall and verdant,
They are growing tall and verdant,
They are growing tall and verdant.

> James Mooney, "The Ghost-Dance Religion and
> the Sioux Outbreak of 1890," *Fourteenth Annual
> Report of the Bureau of American Ethnology*, 1896.

Songs of the Kwakiutl Indians

Love Song

Like pain of fire runs down my body my love to you, my
    dear!
Like pain runs down my body my love to you, my dear!
Just as sickness is my love to you, my dear.
Just as a boil pains me my love to you, my dear.
Just as fire burns me my love to you, my dear.
I am thinking of what you said to me.
I am thinking of the love you bear me.
I am afraid of your love, my dear.

O pain! o pain!
Oh, where is my true love going, my dear?
Oh, they say she will be taken away far from here. She will
    leave me, my true love, my dear.
My body feels numb on account of what I said, my true
    love, my dear.
Good bye, my true love, my dear.

Warsong of the Kwakiutl

I am the thunder of my tribe.
I am the seamonster of my tribe.
I am the earthquake of my tribe.
When I start to fly the thunder resounds through the world.
When I am maddened, the voice of the seabear resounds
    through the world.

Franz Boas, "Songs of the Kwakiutl Indians,"
Internationales Archiv für Ethnographie, 1896.

The Mocking-Bird's Song

(Tigua)

Rain, people, rain!
The rain is all around us.
It is going to come pouring down,
And the summer will be fair to see,
The mocking-bird has said so.

Alice C. Fletcher, *Indian Story and
Song from North America*, 1900.

The Wizard's Chant

(Passamaquoddy)

I sit and beat the wizard's magic drum;
And by its mystic sound I call the beasts.
From mountain lair and forest nook they throng;
E'en mighty storms obey the dreadful sound.

I sit and beat the wizard's magic drum;
The storm and thunder answer when it calls.
Aplasemwesit, mighty whirlwind, stops
To hearken to the mystic sound I make.

I sit and beat the wizard's magic drum;
And Chibela'kwe, night-air spirit, flies
To hearken to the mystic sound I make;
And old Wu'cho'sen, storm-bird of the North,
Rests his great pinions, causing calm to reign,
To hearken to the mystic sound I make.

I sit and beat the wizard's magic drum;
And Lumpeguin, who dwells beneath the wave,
Arises to the surface struck with awe,
To hearken to the mystic sound I make.
E'en Atwuskniges, armed with axe of stone,
Will cease his endless chopping, and be still
To hearken to the mystic sound I make.

I sit and beat the wizard's magic drum;
And Appodumken, with his long, red hair,
Ariseth from the depths, and draweth near
To hearken to the mystic sound I make.

The lightning, thunder, storm and forest sprite,
The whirlwind, gale, and spirit of the deep,
The Chibela'kwe, loathly night-air ghost,
All come together, and with reverent mien
Will hearken to the mystic sound I make.

Charles Godfrey Leland and John Dyneley Prince,
Kulóskap the Master and Other Algonkin Poems, 1902.

from *The Night Chant*

(*Navajo*)

Prayer of First Dancers

In Tse'gíhi,
In the house made of the dawn,
In the house made of the evening twilight,
In the house made of the dark cloud,
In the house made of the he-rain,
In the house made of the dark mist,
In the house made of the she-rain,
In the house made of pollen,
In the house made of grasshoppers,
Where the dark mist curtains the doorway,
The path to which is on the rainbow,
Where the zigzag lightning stands high on top,
Where the he-rain stands high on top,
Oh, male divinity!
With your moccasins of dark cloud, come to us.
With your leggings of dark cloud, come to us.
With your shirt of dark cloud, come to us.
With your head-dress of dark cloud, come to us.
With your mind enveloped in dark cloud, come to us.
With the dark thunder above you, come to us soaring.
With the shapen cloud at your feet, come to us soaring.
With the far darkness made of the dark cloud over your
      head, come to us soaring.
With the far darkness made of the he-rain over your head,
      come to us soaring.
With the far darkness made of the dark mist over your head,
      come to us soaring.
With the far darkness made of the she-rain over your head,
      come to us soaring.
With the zigzag lightning flung out on high over your head,
      come to us soaring.
With the rainbow hanging high over your head, come to us
      soaring.

With the far darkness made of the dark cloud on the ends of
     your wings, come to us soaring.
With the far darkness made of the he-rain on the ends of
     your wings, come to us soaring.
With the far darkness made of the dark mist on the ends of
     your wings, come to us soaring.
With the far darkness made of the she-rain on the ends of
     your wings, come to us soaring.
With the zigzag lightning flung out on high on the ends of
     your wings, come to us soaring.
With the rainbow hanging high on the ends of your wings,
     come to us soaring.
With the near darkness made of the dark cloud, of the
     he-rain, of the dark mist and of the she-rain, come
     to us.
With the darkness on the earth, come to us.
With these I wish the foam floating on the flowing water
     over the roots of the great corn.
I have made your sacrifice.
I have prepared a smoke for you.
My feet restore for me.
My limbs restore for me.
My body restore for me.
My mind restore for me.
My voice restore for me.
To-day, take out your spell for me.
To-day, take away your spell for me.
Away from me you have taken it.
Far off from me it is taken.
Far off you have done it.
Happily I recover.
Happily my interior becomes cool.
Happily my eyes regain their power.
Happily my head becomes cool.
Happily my limbs regain their power.
Happily I hear again.
Happily for me the spell is taken off.
Happily I walk.
Impervious to pain, I walk.
Feeling light within, I walk.

With lively feelings, I walk.
Happily abundant dark clouds I desire.
Happily abundant dark mists I desire.
Happily abundant passing showers I desire.
Happily an abundance of vegetation I desire.
Happily an abundance of pollen I desire.
Happily abundant dew I desire.
Happily may fair white corn, to the ends of the earth, come
    with you.
Happily may fair yellow corn, to the ends of the earth, come
    with you.
Happily may fair blue corn, to the ends of the earth, come
    with you.
Happily may fair corn of all kinds, to the ends of the earth,
    come with you.
Happily may fair plants of all kinds, to the ends of the earth,
    come with you.
Happily may fair goods of all kinds, to the ends of the earth,
    come with you.
Happily may fair jewels of all kinds, to the ends of the earth,
    come with you.
With these before you, happily may they come with you.
With these behind you, happily may they come with you.
With these below you, happily may they come with you.
With these above you, happily may they come with you.
With these all around you, happily may they come with you.
Thus happily you accomplish your tasks.
Happily the old men will regard you.
Happily the old women will regard you.
Happily the young men will regard you.
Happily the young women will regard you.
Happily the boys will regard you.
Happily the girls will regard you.
Happily the children will regard you.
Happily the chiefs will regard you.
Happily, as they scatter in different directions, they will
    regard you.
Happily, as they approach their homes, they will regard you.
Happily may their roads home be on the trail of pollen.
Happily may they all get back.

In beauty I walk.
With beauty before me, I walk.
With beauty behind me, I walk.
With beauty below me, I walk.
With beauty above me, I walk.
With beauty all around me, I walk.
It is finished again in beauty,
It is finished in beauty,
It is finished in beauty,
It is finished in beauty.

Washington Matthews, "The Night Chant,
a Navaho Ceremony," *Memoirs of the
American Museum of Natural History*, 1902.

from *The Hako*

(*Pawnee*)

from *Mother Corn Assumes Leadership*

I

Mother with the life-giving power now comes,
Stepping out of far distant days she comes,
Days wherein to our fathers gave she food;
As to them, so now unto us she gives,
Thus she will to our children faithful be.
Mother with the life-giving power now comes!

II

Mother with the life-giving power is here.
Stepping out of far distant days she comes.
Now she forward moves, leading as we walk
Toward the future, where blessings she will give,
Gifts for which we have prayed granting to us.
Mother with the life-giving power is here!

Song to the Trees and Streams

I

Dark against the sky yonder distant line
Lies before us. Trees we see, long the line of trees,
Bending, swaying in the breeze.

II

Bright with flashing light yonder distant line
Runs before us, swiftly runs, swift the river runs,
Winding, flowing o'er the land.

III

Hark! Oh hark! A sound, yonder distant sound
Comes to greet us, singing comes, soft the river's song,
Rippling gently 'neath the trees.

Song of the Promise of the Buffalo

I

Clouds of dust arise, rolling up from earth,
Spreading onward; herds are there.
Speeding on before,
Going straight where we must journey.

II

What are those we see moving in the dust?
This way coming from the herd;
Buffalo and calf!
Food they promise for the Children.

Alice C. Fletcher, "The Hako: A Pawnee
Ceremony," *Twenty-second Annual Report
of the Bureau of American Ethnology*, 1904.

from *History Myth of the Coming of the A'shiwi as Narrated by ᵗKiäklo*

(*Zuni*)

Following their road of exit, they stooped over and came
      out.
They walked this way.
They came to the gaming-stick spring.
They came to the gaming-ring spring.
They came to the Ne'wekwe baton spring.
They came to the spring with prayer plume standing.
They came to the cat-tail place.
They came to the moss spring.
They came to the muddy spring.
They came to the sun-ray spring.
They came to the spring by many aspens.
They came to shell place.
They came to dragon-fly place.
They came to flower place.
They came to the place of trees with drooping limbs.
They came to fish spring.
They came to young-squash spring.
They came to listening spring.

*   *   *

We come this way. We come to a large lake; here we get up
      and move on. We come to a valley with watercress in
      the middle; here we get up and move on.
We come to the stealing place; here we get up and move on.
We come to houses built in mesa walls; here we get up and
      move on.
We come to the last of a row of springs; here we get up and
      move on.
We come to the middle of a row of springs; here we get up
      and move on.
We come again to the middle of a row of springs; here we
      get up and move on.

We come to the house of Ko'loowisi; here we get up and
    move on.
We come to watercress place; here we get up and move on.
We come to a small spring; here we get up and move on.
We come to a spring in a hollow place in a mound, hidden
        by tall bending grasses; here we get up and move on.
We come to ashes spring; here we get up and move on.
We come to high-grass spring; here we get up and move on.
We come to rainbow spring; here we get up and move on.
We come to place of the Sha'läko; here we get up and move
    on.
We come to the place with many springs; here we get up
    and move on.
We come to moss place; here we get up and move on.
We come to stone-lodged-in-a-cleft place; here we get up
    and move on.
We come to stone-picture place; here we get up and move
    on.
We come to poison-oak place; here we get up and move on.
We come to a spring in a mesa wall; here we get up and
    move on.
We come to rush place; here we get up and move on.
We come to a place of bad-smelling water; here we get up
    and move on.
We come to the place of sack of meal hanging; here we get
        up and move on.
We come to the blue-jay spring; here we get up and move
    on.
We come to Corn mountain; here we get up and move on.
We come to the spring at the base of the mesa; here we get
        up and move on.
We come to the ant-entering place; here we get up and
    move on.
We come to vulva spring; here we get up and move on.
We come to a spring high in the mountain; here we get up
    and move on.
We come to Apache spring; here we get up and move on.
We come to coyote spring; here we get up and move on.

We come to salt place; here we get up and move on.
We come to a place with fumes like burning sulphur; here
    we get up and move on.
We come to ant place; here we get up and move on.
We come to the Middle place.

Matilda Coxe Stevenson, "The Zuñi Indians: Their
Mythology, Esoteric Fraternities, and Ceremonies,"
*Twenty-third Annual Report of the
Bureau of American Ethnology,* 1904.

FOLK SONGS AND SPIRITUALS

The Cowboy's Lament

As I walked out in the streets of Laredo,
As I walked out in Laredo one day,
I spied a poor cowboy wrapped up in white linen,
Wrapped up in white linen as cold as the clay.

"Oh, beat the drum slowly and play the fife lowly,
Play the Dead March as you carry me along;
Take me to the green valley, there lay the sod o'er me,
For I'm a young cowboy and I know I've done wrong.

"I see by your outfit that you are a cowboy,"
These words he did say as I boldly stepped by.
"Come sit down beside me and hear my sad story;
I was shot in the breast and I know I must die.

"Let sixteen gamblers come handle my coffin,
Let sixteen cowboys come sing me a song.
Take me to the graveyard and lay the sod o'er me,
For I'm a poor cowboy and I know I've done wrong.

"My friends and relations, they live in the Nation,
They know not where their boy has gone.
He first came to Texas and hired to a ranchman,
Oh, I'm a young cowboy and I know I've done wrong.

"Go write a letter to my gray-haired mother,
And carry the same to my sister so dear;
But not a word of this shall you mention
When a crowd gathers round you my story to hear.

"Then beat your drum lowly and play your fife slowly,
Beat the Dead March as you carry me along;
We all love our cowboys so young and so handsome,
We all love our cowboys although they've done wrong.

"There is another more dear than a sister,
    She'll bitterly weep when she hears I am gone.
    There is another who will win her affections,
    For I'm a young cowboy and they say I've done wrong.

"Go gather around you a crowd of young cowboys,
    And tell them the story of this my sad fate;
    Tell one and the other before they go further
    To stop their wild roving before 'tis too late.

"Oh muffle your drums, then play your fifes merrily;
    Play the Dead March as you go along.
    And fire your guns right over my coffin;
    There goes an unfortunate boy to his home.

"It was once in the saddle I used to go dashing,
    It was once in the saddle I used to go gay;
    First to the dram-house, then to the card-house,
    Got shot in the breast, I am dying to-day.

"Got six jolly cowboys to carry my coffin;
    Get six pretty maidens to bear up my pall.
    Put bunches of roses all over my coffin,
    Put roses to deaden the clods as they fall.

"Then swing your rope slowly and rattle your spurs lowly,
    And give a wild whoop as you carry me along;
    And in the grave throw me and roll the sod o'er me,
    For I'm a young cowboy and I know I've done wrong.

"Go bring me a cup, a cup of cold water,
    To cool my parched lips," the cowboy said;
    Before I turned, the spirit had left him
    And gone to its Giver,—the cowboy was dead.

We beat the drum slowly and played the fife lowly,
    And bitterly wept as we bore him along;
    For we all loved our comrade, so brave, young, and
            handsome,
    We all loved our comrade although he'd done wrong.

Deep River

Deep river,
My home is over Jordan,
Deep river,
Lord, I want to cross over into camp ground,
Lord, I want to cross over into camp ground,
Lord, I want to cross over into camp ground,
Lord, I want to cross over into camp ground.

Oh, don't you want to go to that Gospel feast,
That promis'd land where all is peace?

I'll go into heaven, and take my seat,
Cast my crown at Jesus' feet.

Oh, when I get to heav'n, I'll walk all about,
There's nobody there for to turn me out.

Dere's No Hidin' Place Down Dere

Dere's no hidin' place down dere,
Dere's no hidin' place down dere,
Oh I went to de rock to hide my face,
De rock cried out, "No hidin' place,"
Dere's no hidin' place down dere.

Oh de rock cried, "I'm burnin' too,"
Oh de rock cried, "I'm burnin' too,"
Oh de rock cried out I'm burnin' too,
I want a go to hebben as well as you,
Dere's no hidin' place down dere.

Oh de sinner man he gambled an' fell,
Oh de sinner man he gambled, an' fell,
Oh de sinner man gambled, he gambled an' fell;
He wanted to go to hebben, but he had to go to hell
Dere's no hidin' place down dere.

Down in the Valley

Down in the valley, valley so low,
Hang your head over, hear the wind blow.
　　Hear the wind blow, love, hear the wind blow,
　　Hang your head over, hear the wind blow.

If you don't love me, love whom you please,
But throw your arms round me, give my heart ease.
　　Give my heart ease, dear, give my heart ease.
　　Throw your arms round me, give my heart ease.

Down in the valley, walking between,
Telling our story, here's what it sings:
　　Here's what it sings, dear, here's what it sings,
　　Telling our story, here's what it sings:

Roses of sunshine, vi'lets of dew,
Angels in heaven knows I love you,
　　Knows I love you, dear, knows I love you,
　　Angels in heaven knows I love you.

Build me a castle forty feet high,
So I can see her as she goes by,
　　As she goes by, dear, as she goes by,
　　So I can see her as she goes by.

Bird in a cage, love, bird in a cage,
Dying for freedom, ever a slave;
　　Ever a slave, dear, ever a slave,
　　Dying for freedom, ever a slave.

Write me a letter, send it by mail,
And back it in care of the Birmingham jail.
　　Birmingham jail, love, Birmingham jail,
　　And back it in care of the Birmingham jail.

Ev'ry Time I Feel the Spirit

Ev'ry time I feel the Spirit
Moving in my heart I will pray.

Upon the mountain my Lord spoke,
Out His mouth came fire and smoke.

All around me looks so shine,
Ask my Lord if all was mine.

Jordan river is chilly and cold,
Chills the body but not the soul.

Ezekiel Saw de Wheel

Ezekiel saw de wheel,
'Way up in de middle ob de air,
Ezekiel saw de wheel,
'Way in de middle ob de air;
An' de little wheel run by faith,
An' de big wheel run by de grace ob God,
'Tis a wheel in a wheel,
'Way in de middle ob de air.

Some go to church fo' to sing an' shout,
'Way in de middle ob de air;
Befo' six months dey are all turned out,
'Way in de middle ob de air.

Let me tell you what a hypocrit 'll do,
'Way in de middle ob de air;
He'll talk 'bout me an' he'll talk 'bout yo',
'Way in de middle ob de air.

One o' dese days, 'bout twelve o'clock,
'Way in de middle ob de air;
Dis ole worl' gwine reel an' rock,
'Way in de middle ob de air.

Frankie and Albert

Frankie was a good woman,
Ev'rybody knows,
She spent a hundred dollars
For to buy her man some clothes.
  He was her man,
  But he done her wrong.

Frankie went a-walkin'
Did not go for fun,
Underneath her little red petticoat
She had Albert's forty-one.
  Gonna kill her man
  For doin' her wrong.

Frankie went to the barroom
Ordered her a glass of beer,
Says to the bartender,
"Has my lovin' man been here?
  He's my man,
  But he's doin' me wrong."

"I will not tell you no story,
I will not tell you no lie,—
Albert left here about an hour ago
With a gal named Alice Fly.
  He's your man,
  But he's doin' you wrong."

Frankie went by the house,
She did not give no 'larm,
She looked in through the window glass
And saw Albert in the woman's arms.
  He was her man, Lawd,
  Doin' her wrong.

When Albert, he saw Frankie,
For the backdoor, he did scoot,
Frankie drew that forty-four,
Went —*rooty-toot-toot-toot-toot!*
    She shot her man,
    For doin' her wrong.

First time she shot him, he staggered,
Next time she shot him, he fell,
Third time she shot him, O Lawdy,
There was a new man's face in hell.
    She killed her man,
    For doin' her wrong.

When Frankie, she shot Albert,
He fell all in a knot,
Cryin', "O Mrs. Johnson,
See where your son is shot.
    She's killed your son,
    The only one.

"O turn me over doctor,
Turn me over slow,
I got a bullet in my lef' han' side,
Great God, is hurtin' me so.
    I was her man,
    But I done her wrong."

Frankie went to Mrs. Johnson,
Fell down on her knees,
Cryin' "O Mrs. Johnson,
Will you forgive me please?
    I kilt your son,
    The onlies' one."

"I will forgive you Frankie,
I will forgive you not,
You shot my lovin' Albert,
The only support I'm got.
    Kilt my son,
    The only one."

Poor boy, poor boy,
Poor boy, poor boy.
Done gone, done gone,
Done gone, done gone.

Frankie went to the graveyard,
Fell down on her knees,—
"Speak one word, Albert,
And give my heart some ease.
    You was my man,
    But you done me wrong."

A rubber tir'ed buggy,
A decorated hack
Took po' Albert to the graveyard
But it didn't bring him back.
    He was her man,
    But he done her wrong.

Poor boy, poor boy,
Poor boy, poor boy.
Done gone, done gone,
Done gone, done gone.

Frankie looked down Main street,
Far as she could see,
All she could hear was a two string bow,
Playin' *Nearer My God to Thee,*
    All over town,
    Po' Albert's dead.

Frankie said to the sheriff,
"What do you think it'll be?"
The sheriff said, "It looks jest like
Murder in the first degree,
    He was your man,
    But you shot him down."

It was not murder in the first degree,
Nor murder in the third,
A woman simply dropped her man,
Like a hunter dropped a bird.
    She shot her man,
    For doin' her wrong.

Last time I saw Frankie
She was sittin' in the 'lectric chair,
Waitin' for to go and meet her God
With the sweat drippin' outa her hair.
    He was her man
    But he done her wrong.

        Poor gal, poor gal,
        Poor gal, poor gal.
        Done gone, done gone,
        Done gone, done gone.

Free at Last

        Free at last, free at last;
        I thank God I'm free at last;
        Free at last, free at last,
        I thank God I'm free at last,
        O free at last.

'Way down yonder in the grave-yard walk,
I thank God I'm free at last,
Me and my Jesus goin' to meet and talk,
I thank God I'm free at last,
O free at last.

On-a my knees when the light pass'd by,
I thank God I'm free at last,
Tho't my soul would rise and fly,
I thank God I'm free at last,
O free at last.

Some of these mornings, bright and fair,
I thank God I'm free at last,
Goin' meet King Jesus in the air,
I thank God I'm free at last,
O free at last.

Got a Home in That Rock

I've got a home in a-that Rock,
Don't you see? Don't you see?
I've got a home in a-that Rock,
Don't you see? Don't you see?
Between the earth and sky,
Thought I heard my Saviour cry,
I've got a home in a-that Rock,
Don't you see?

Poor old Laz'rus, poor as I,
Don't you see? Don't you see?
Poor old Laz'rus, poor as I,
Don't you see? Don't you see?
Poor old Laz'rus, poor as I
When he died had a home on high.
He had a home in a-that Rock,
Don't you see?

Rich man, Dives, lived so well,
Don't you see? Don't you see?
Rich man, Dives, lived so well,

Don't you see? Don't you see?
Rich man, Dives, lived so well,
When he died he found a home in hell,
Had no home in that Rock,
Don't you see?

God gave Noah the Rainbow sign,
Don't you see? Don't you see?
God gave Noah the Rainbow sign,
Don't you see? Don't you see?
God gave Noah the Rainbow sign,
No more water but fire next time,
Better get a home in that Rock,
Don't you see?

He Never Said a Mumblin' Word

O they took my blessed Lawd,
Blessed Lawd, Blessed Lawd,
O they took my blessed Lawd,
An' He never said a mumblin' word,
Not a word, not a word, not a word.

O they lead Him to Pilate's bar,
Pilate's bar, Pilate's bar,
O they lead Him to Pilate's bar,
An' He never said a mumblin' word,
Not a word, not a word, not a word.

O they bound Him with a purple cord,
Purple cord, purple cord,
O they bound Him with a purple cord,
An' He never said a mumblin' word,
Not a word, not a word, not a word.

O they plaited Him a crown o' thorn,
Crown o' thorn, crown o' thorn,
O they plaited Him a crown o' thorn,
An' He never said a mumblin' word,
Not a word, not a word, not a word.

O they put it on His head,
On His head, on His head,
O they put it on His head,
An' He never said a mumblin' word,
Not a word, not a word, not a word.

An' the blood come streamin' down,
Streamin' down, streamin' down,
O the blood come streamin' down,
An' He never said a mumblin' word,
Not a word, not a word, not a word.

An' they judged Him all night long,
All night long, all night long,
Yes they judged Him all night long,
An' He never said a mumblin' word,
Not a word, not a word, not a word.

An' they whipped Him up the hill,
Up the hill, up the hill,
O they whipped Him up the hill,
An' He never said a mumblin' word,
Not a word, not a word, not a word.

Then they nailed Him to the cross,
To the cross, to the cross,
Yes they nailed Him to the cross,
An' He never said a mumblin' word,
Not a word, not a word, not a word.

An' the blood come tricklin' down,
Tricklin' down, tricklin' down,
O the blood come tricklin' down,
An' He never said a mumblin' word,
Not a word, not a word, not a word.

An' the stars refused to shine,
'Fused to shine, 'fused to shine,
Yes the stars refused to shine,
An' He never said a mumblin' word,
Not a word, not a word, not a word.

O wasn't that a pity an' a shame,
Pity an' a shame, pity an' a shame?
O wasn't that a pity an' a shame?
An' He never said a mumblin' word,
Not a word, not a word, not a word.

A Home on the Range

Oh, give me a home where the buffalo roam,
Where the deer and the antelope play,
Where seldom is heard a discouraging word
And the skies are not cloudy all day.

Home, home on the range,
Where the deer and the antelope play;
Where seldom is heard a discouraging word
And the skies are not cloudy all day.

Where the air is so pure, the zephyrs so free,
The breezes so balmy and light,
That I would not exchange my home on the range
For all of the cities so bright.

The red man was pressed from this part of the West,
He's likely no more to return
To the banks of Red River where seldom if ever
Their flickering camp-fires burn.

How often at night when the heavens are bright
With the light of the glittering stars,
Have I stood here amazed and asked as I gazed
If their glory exceeds that of ours.

Oh, I love these wild flowers in this dear land of ours,
The curlew I love to hear scream,
And I love the white rocks and the antelope flocks
That graze on the mountain-tops green.

Oh, give me a land where the bright diamond sand
Flows leisurely down to the stream;
Where the graceful white swan goes gliding along
Like a maid in a heavenly dream.

Then I would not exchange my home on the range,
Where the deer and the antelope play;
Where seldom is heard a discouraging word
And the skies are not cloudy all day.

> *Home, home on the range,*
> *Where the deer and the antelope play;*
> *Where seldom is heard a discouraging word*
> *And the skies are not cloudy all day.*

I Know Moon-Rise

I know moon-rise, I know star-rise,
  Lay dis body down.
I walk in de moonlight, I walk in de starlight,
  To lay dis body down.
I 'll walk in de graveyard, I 'll walk through de
      graveyard,
  To lay dis body down.
I 'll lie in de grave and stretch out my arms;
  Lay dis body down.
I go to de judgment in de evenin' of de day,
  When I lay dis body down;
And my soul and your soul will meet in de day
  When I lay dis body down.

Jesse James

Jesse James was a lad that killed many a man,
He robbed the Danville train;
But that dirty little coward that shot Mr. Howard,
Has laid Jesse James in his grave.
It was little Robert Ford, that dirty little coward;
I wonder how does he feel;
For he ate of Jesse's bread and slept in Jesse's bed,
Then laid Jesse James in his grave.

Poor Jesse had a wife, to mourn for his life,
Children they were brave;
But that dirty little coward, that shot Mr. Howard
Has laid Jesse James in his grave.

It was with his brother Frank, he robbed the Gallatin bank,
And carried the money from the town;
It was at this very place they had a little chase,
For they shot Capt. Sheets to the ground.
They went to a crossing not very far from there,
And there they did the same,
With the agent on his knees he delivered up the keys
To the outlaws Frank and Jesse James.

It was on a Wednesday night, the moon was shining bright,
They robbed the Danville train;
The people they did say for many miles away,
It was robbed by Frank and Jesse James.
It was on Saturday night, the moon was shining bright,
Talking with his family brave,
Robert Ford came along like a thief in the night,
And he laid Jesse James in his grave.

The people held their breath when they heard of Jesse's
          death,
And wondered however he came to die.
It was one of the gang called little Robert Ford,
He shot Jesse James on the sly.
This song was made by Billy LaShade,

As soon as the news did arrive;
He said there's no man with the law in his hand
Can take Jesse James alive.

Jim Crack Corn

or the Blue Tail Fly

When I was young I us'd to wait
On Massa and hand him de plate;
Pass down de bottle when he git dry,
And bresh away de blue tail fly.

Jim crack corn I don't care,
Jim crack corn I don't care,
Jim crack corn I don't care,
Ole Massa gone away.

Den arter dinner massa sleep,
He bid dis niggar vigil keep;
An' when he gwine to shut his eye,
He tell me watch de blue tail fly.

An' when he ride in de arternoon,
I foller wid a hickory broom;
De poney being berry shy,
When bitten by de blue tail fly.

One day he rode aroun' de farm,
De flies so numerous dey did swarm;
One chance to bite 'im on the thigh,
De debble take dat blue tail fly.

De poney run, he jump an' pitch,
An' tumble massa in de ditch;
He died, an' de jury wonder'd why
De virdic was de blue tail fly.

Dey laid 'im under a 'simmon tree,
His epitaph am dar to see:
'Beneath dis stone I'm forced to lie,
All by de means ob de blue tail fly.

Ole massa gone, now let 'im rest,
Dey say all tings am for de best;
I nebber forget till de day I die,
Ole massa an' dat blue tail fly.

John Brown's Body

John Brown's body lies a-mould'ring in the grave,
John Brown's body lies a-mould'ring in the grave,
John Brown's body lies a-mould'ring in the grave,
His soul is marching on.

Glory, glory, hallelujah!
Glory, glory, hallelujah!
Glory, glory, hallelujah!
His soul is marching on!

The stars of heaven are looking kindly down,
On the grave of old John Brown.

He's gone to be a soldier in the army of the Lord,
His soul is marching on.

John Brown died that the slave might be free,
But his soul goes marching on.

He captured Harper's Ferry with his nineteen men so true,
And he frightened old Virginia till she trembled through
and through;
They hung him for a traitor, themselves the traitor crew,
But his soul goes marching on.

John Brown's knapsack is strapped to his back,
His soul is marching on.

His pet lambs will meet on the way,
    And they'll go marching on.

They will hang Jeff Davis on a sour apple tree,
    As they go marching on.

Now has come the glorious jubilee,
    When all mankind are free.

John Henry

John Henry was a little baby,
Sittin' on his mamy's knee,
Said, "The Big Bend tunnel on the C. & O. road
Gonna be the death of me,
Lawd, Lawd, gonna be the death of me."

John Henry was a little baby,
Sittin' on his daddy's knee,
Point his finger at a little piece of steel,
"That's gonna be the death of me,
Lawd, Lawd, that's gonna be the death of me."

John Henry had a little woman
And her name was Mary Magdelene,
She would go to the tunnel and sing for John
Jes' to hear John Henry's hammer ring,
Lawd, Lawd, jes' to hear John Henry's hammer ring.

John Henry had a little woman
And her name was Polly Anne,
John Henry took sick and he had to go to bed,
Polly Anne drove steel like a man,
Lawd, Lawd, Polly Anne drove steel like a man.

Cap'n says to John Henry,
"Gonna bring me a steam drill 'round,

Gonna take that steam drill out on the job,
Gonna whop that steel on down,
Lawd, Lawd, gonna whop that steel on down."

John Henry told his cap'n,
Said, "A man ain't nothin' but a man,
And befo' I'd let that steam drill beat me down
I'd die with this hammer in my hand,
Lawd, Lawd, I'd die with the hammer in my hand."

Sun were hot and burnin',
Weren't no breeze atall,
Sweat ran down like water down a hill,
That day John let his hammer fall,
Lawd, Lawd, that day John let his hammer fall.

White man told John Henry,
"Nigger, damn yo' soul,
You may beat dis steam and drill of mine,—
When the rocks in the mountains turn to gold,
Lawd, Lawd, when the rocks in the mountains turn to
          gold."

John Henry said to his shaker,
"Shaker, why don't you sing?
I'm throwin' twelve pounds from my hips on down,
Jes' lissen to the cold steel ring,
Lawd, Lawd, jes' lissen to the cold steel ring."

O, the cap'n told John Henry,
"I b'lieve this mountain's sinkin' in."
John Henry said to his cap'n, O my!
"It's my hammer just a-hossin' in the wind,
Lawd, Lawd, it's my hammer just a-hossin' in the wind."

John Henry told his shaker,
"Shaker, you better pray,
For, if I miss this six-foot steel,
Tomorrow be yo' buryin' day,
Lawd, Lawd, tomorrow be yo' buryin' day."

John Henry told his captain,
"Looky yonder what I see—
Yo' drill's done broke an' yo' hole's done choke,
An' you can't drive steel like me,
Lawd, Lawd, an' you can't drive steel like me."

John Henry was hammerin' on the mountain,
An' his hammer was strikin' fire,
He drove so hard till he broke his pore heart,
An' he lied down his hammer an' he died,
Lawd, Lawd, an' he lied down his hammer an' he died.

They took John Henry to the graveyard
An' they buried him in the sand
An' ev'ry locomotive come roarin' by,
Says, "There lays a steel drivin' man,
Lawd, Lawd, says, "There lays a steel drivin' man."

John Henry had a little woman,
An' the dress she wore was blue,
She went walkin' down the track and she never looked back,
Said, "John Henry, I've been true to you,
Lawd, Lawd, John Henry, I've been true to you."

"Now who's gonna shoe your little feetses?
An' who's gonna glove your hands?
An' who's gonna kiss yo' red, rosy lips?
An' who's gonna be your man,
Lawd, Lawd, who's gonna be your man?"

"O my mama's gonna shoe my little feetses,
An' my papa's gonna gloves my little hands,
And my sister's gonna kiss my red, rosy lips,
An' I don' need no man,
Lawd, Lawd, an' I don' need no man."

Joshua Fit de Battle ob Jerico

Joshua fit de battle ob Jerico,
Jerico, Jerico,
Joshua fit de battle ob Jerico,
An' de walls come tumblin' down.

You may talk about yo' king ob Gideon,
You may talk about yo' man ob Saul,
Dere's none like good ole Joshua
At de battle ob Jerico.

Up to de walls ob Jerico,
He marched with spear in han'
"Go blow dem ram horns" Joshua cried,
"Kase de battle am in my han'."

Den de lam 'ram sheep horns begin to blow,
Trumpets begin to soun',
Joshua commanded the chillen to shout,
An' de walls come tumblin' down.

Dat mornin' Joshua fit de battle ob Jerico,
Jerico, Jerico,
Joshua fit de battle ob Jerico,
An' de walls come tumblin' down.

Let My People Go

A Song of the "Contrabands"

When Israel was in Egypt's land,
   O let my people go!
Oppressed so hard they could not stand,
   O let my people go!

O go down, Moses
Away down to Egypt's land,
And tell King Pharaoh,
To let my people go!

Thus saith the Lord, bold Moses said,
   O let my people go!
If not, I'll smite your first born dead,
   O let my people go!

No more shall they in bondage toil,
   O let my people go!
Let them come out with Egypt's spoil,
   O let my people go!

Then Israel out of Egypt came,
   O let my people go!
And left the proud oppressive land,
   O let my people go!

O 'twas a dark and dismal night,
   O let my people go!
When Moses led the Israelites,
   O let my people go!

'Twas good old Moses, and Aaron, too,
   O let my people go!
'Twas they that led the armies through,
   O let my people go!

The Lord told Moses what to do,
   O let my people go!
To lead the children of Israel through,
   O let my people go!

O come along Moses, you'll not get lost,
   O let my people go!
Stretch out your rod and come across,
   O let my people go!

As Israel stood by the water side,
  O let my people go!
At the command of God it did divide,
  O let my people go!

When they had reached the other shore,
  O let my people go!
They sang a song of triumph o'er,
  O let my people go!

Pharaoh said he would go across,
  O let my people go!
But Pharaoh and his host were lost,
  O let my people go!

O Moses, the cloud shall cleave the way,
  O let my people go!
A fire by night, a shade by day,
  O let my people go!

You'll not get lost in the wilderness,
  O let my people go!
With a lighted candle in your breast,
  O let my people go!

Jordan shall stand up like a wall,
  O let my people go!
And the walls of Jericho shall fall,
  O let my people go!

Your foe shall not before you stand,
  O let my people go!
And you'll possess fair Canaan's land,
  O let my people go!

'Twas just about in harvest time,
  O let my people go!
When Joshua led his host Divine,
  O let my people go!

O let us all from bondage flee,
   O let my people go!
And let us all in Christ be free,
   O let my people go!

We need not always weep and mourn,
   O let my people go!
And wear these Slavery chains forlorn,
   O let my people go!

This world's a wilderness of woe,
   O let my people go!
O let us on to Canaan go,
   O let my people go!

What a beautiful morning that will be!
   O let my people go!
When time breaks up in eternity,
   O let my people go!

Lonesome Valley

You got to walk that lonesome valley,
You got to go there by yourself,
Ain't nobody here can go there for you,
You got to go there by yourself.

If you cannot preach like Peter,
If you cannot pray like Paul,
You can tell the love of Jesus,
You can say he died for all.

Your mother's got to walk that lonesome valley,
She's got to go there by herself,
Ain't nobody else can go there for her,
She's got to go there by herself.

Your father's got to walk that lonesome valley,
He's got to go there by himself,
Ain't nobody else can go there for him,
He's got to go there by himself.

Your brother's got to walk that lonesome valley,
He's got to go there by himself,
Ain't nobody else can go there for him,
He's got to go there by himself.

Michael Row the Boat Ashore

Michael row de boat ashore,
Hallelujah!

Michael boat a gospel boat,
Hallelujah!

I wonder where my mudder deh,
Hallelujah!

See my mudder on de rock gwine home,
Hallelujah!

On de rock gwine home in Jesus' name,
Hallelujah!

Michael boat a music boat,
Hallelujah!

Gabriel blow de trumpet horn,
Hallelujah!

O you mind your boastin' talk,
Hallelujah!

Boastin' talk will sink your soul,
Hallelujah!

Brudder, lend a helpin' hand,
Hallelujah!

Sister, help for trim dat boat,
Hallelujah!

Jordan stream is wide and deep,
Hallelujah!

Jesus stand on t' oder side,
Hallelujah!

I wonder if my maussa deh,
Hallelujah!

My fader gone to unknown land,
Hallelujah!

O de Lord he plant his garden deh,
Hallelujah!

He raise de fruit for you to eat,
Hallelujah!

He dat eat shall neber die,
Hallelujah!

When de riber overflow,
Hallelujah!

O poor sinner, how you land?
Hallelujah!

Riber run and darkness comin',
Hallelujah!

Sinner row to save your soul,
Hallelujah!

My Lord, What a Morning

My Lord, what a morning,
My Lord, what a morning,
My Lord, what a morning,
When de stars begin to fall.

You'll hear de trumpet sound,
  To wake de nations underground,
Look in my God's right hand,
  When de stars begin to fall.
You'll hear de sinner moan,
  To wake de nations underground,
Look in my God's right hand,
  When de stars begin to fall.

You'll hear de Christians shout,
  To wake de nations underground,
Look in my God's right hand,
  When de stars begin to fall.
You'll hear de angels sing,
  To wake de nations underground,
Look in my God's right hand,
  When de stars begin to fall.

You'll see my Jesus come,
  To wake de nations underground,
Look in my God's right hand,
  When de stars begin to fall.
His chariot wheels roll round,
  To wake de nations underground,
Look in my God's right hand,
  When de stars begin to fall.

Oh My Darling Clementine

In a cabin, in a canon,
An excavation for a mine;
Dwelt a miner, a Forty-niner,
And his daughter Clementine.

> *Oh my darling, oh my darling,*
> *Oh my darling Clementine,*
> *You are lost and gone forever,*
> *Drefful sorry, Clementine.*

She drove her ducklets, to the river,
Ev'ry morning just at nine;
She stubb'd her toe against a sliver,
And fell into the foaming brine.

I saw her lips above the water,
Blowing bubbles soft and fine;
Alas for me, I was no swimmer,
And so I lost my Clementine.

One More River

O, Jordan bank was a great old bank!
  Dere ain't but one more river to cross.
We have some valiant soldier here,
  Dere ain't but one more river to cross.
O, Jordan stream will never run dry,
  Dere ain't but one more river to cross.
Dere 's a hill on my leff, and he catch on my right,
  Dere ain't but one more river to cross.

Red River Valley

From this valley they say you are going,
We will miss your bright eyes and sweet smile,
For they say you are taking the sunshine
That brightens our pathway awhile.

Come and sit by my side if you love me,
Do not hasten to bid me adieu,
But remember the Red River Valley
And the girl that has loved you so true.

For a long time I have been waiting
For those dear words you never would say,
But at last all my fond hopes have vanished,
For they say you are going away.

Won't you think of the valley you're leaving?
Oh how lonely, how sad it will be.
Oh think of the fond heart you're breaking,
And the grief you are causing me to see?

From this valley they say you are going;
When you go, may your darling go too?
Would you leave her behind unprotected
When she loves no other but you?

I have promised you, darling, that never
Will a word from my lips cause you pain;
And my life,—it will be yours forever
If you only will love me again.

Must the past with its joys be blighted
By the future of sorrow and pain,
And the vows that was spoken be slighted?
Don't you think you can love me again?

As you go to your home by the ocean,
May you never forget those sweet hours,
That we spent in Red River Valley,
And the love we exchanged 'mid the flowers.

There never could be such a longing
In the heart of a pure maiden's breast,
That dwells in the heart you are breaking
As I wait in my home in the West.

And the dark maiden's prayer for her lover
To the Spirit that rules over the world;
May his pathway be ever in sunshine,
Is the prayer of the Red River girl.

Shenandoah

Missouri, she's a mighty river.
   Away, you rolling river.
The redskins' camp lies on its borders
   Ah ha I'm bound away, 'cross the wide Missouri.

The white man loved the Indian maiden,
   Away, you rolling river.
With notions his canoe was laden.
   Ah ha I'm bound away, 'cross the wide Missouri.

"O, Shenandoah, I love your daughter,"
   Away, you rolling river.
"I'll take her 'cross yon rolling water."
   Ah ha I'm bound away, 'cross the wide Missouri.

The chief disdained the trader's dollars;
   Away, you rolling river.
"My daughter never you shall follow."
   Ah ha I'm bound away, 'cross the wide Missouri.

At last there came a Yankee skipper,
   Away, you rolling river.
He winked his eye, and he tipped his flipper.
   Ah ha I'm bound away, 'cross the wide Missouri.

He sold the chief that fire-water,
    Away, you rolling river.
And 'cross the river he stole his daughter.
    Ah ha I'm bound away, 'cross the wide Missouri.

"O, Shenandoah, I long to hear you,"
    Away, you rolling river.
"Across that wide and rolling river."
    Ah ha I'm bound away, 'cross the wide Missouri.

Simple Gifts

'Tis the gift to be simple, 'tis the gift to be free,
'Tis the gift to come down where we ought to be,
And when we find ourselves in the place just right,
'Twill be in the valley of love and delight.
When true simplicity is gain'd,
To bow and to bend we shan't be asham'd,
To turn, turn will be our delight
'Till by turning, turning we come round right.

Steal Away

    Steal away, steal away, steal away to Jesus!
    Steal away, steal away home,
    I hain't got long to stay here.

My Lord calls me,
    He calls me by the thunder;
The trumpet sounds it in my soul:
    I hain't got long to stay here.

Green trees are bending,
    Poor sinners stand trembling;
The trumpet sounds it in my soul:
    I hain't got long to stay here.

My Lord calls me,
 He calls me by the lightning;
The trumpet sounds it in my soul:
 I hain't got long to stay here.

Tombstones are bursting,
 Poor sinners stand trembling;
The trumpet sounds it in my soul:
 I hain't got long to stay here.

Swing Low, Sweet Chariot

Swing low, sweet chariot,
Coming for to carry me home,
Swing low, sweet chariot,
Coming for to carry me home.

I looked over Jordan, and what did I see,
Coming for to carry me home?
A band of angels coming after me,
Coming for to carry me home.

If you get there before I do,
Coming for to carry me home,
Tell all my friends I'm coming too,
Coming for to carry me home.

The brightest day that ever I saw,
Coming for to carry me home,
When Jesus wash'd my sins away,
Coming for to carry me home.

I'm sometimes up and sometimes down,
Coming for to carry me home,
But still my soul feels heavenly bound,
Coming for to carry me home.

What Yo' Gwine t' Do
When de Lamp Burn Down?

Oh, po' sinner,
Now is yo' time
Oh, po' sinner
What yo' gwine to do when de lamp burn down?

Oh, de lamp burn down an' yo' cannot see;
  What yo' gwine t' do when de lamp burn down?
Oh, de lamp burn down an' yo' cannot see;
  What yo' gwine t' do when de lamp burn down?

Ezekiel saw dat wheel o' time;
  What yo' gwine t' do when de lamp burn down?
An' ev'ry spoke was of human kind;
  What yo' gwine t' do when de lamp burn down?

God made man an' He made him out o' clay,
  What yo' gwine t' do when de lamp burn down?
An' put him on de earth, but not to stay;
  What yo' gwine t' do when de lamp burn down?

Dey cast ole Daniel in de lion's den;
  What yo' gwine t' do when de lamp burn down?
An' Jesus locked de lion's jaw;
  What yo' gwine t' do when de lamp burn down?

Ole Satan's mad an' I am glad;
  What yo' gwine t' do when de lamp burn down?
He miss one soul he thought he had,
  What yo' gwine t' do when de lamp burn down?

Ole Satan's a liar an' a conjurer too;
  What yo' gwine t' do when de lamp burn down?
If yo' don't mind, he slip in on yo'
  What yo' gwine t' do when de lamp burn down?

Whoopee Ti Yi Yo, Git Along Little Dogies

As I walked out one morning for pleasure,
I spied a cow-puncher all riding alone;
His hat was throwed back and his spurs was a jingling,
As he approached me a-singin' this song,

> *Whoopee ti yi yo, git along little dogies,*
> *It's your misfortune, and none of my own.*
> *Whoopee ti yi yo, git along little dogies,*
> *For you know Wyoming will be your new home.*

Early in the spring we round up the dogies,
Mark and brand and bob off their tails;
Round up our horses, load up the chuck-wagon,
Then throw the dogies upon the trail.

It's whooping and yelling and driving the dogies;
Oh how I wish you would go on;
It's whooping and punching and go on little dogies,
For you know Wyoming will be your new home.

Some boys goes up the trail for pleasure,
But that's where you get it most awfully wrong;
For you haven't any idea the trouble they give us
While we go driving them all along.

When the night comes on and we hold them on the
        bedground,
These little dogies that roll on so slow;
Roll up the herd and cut out the strays,
And roll the little dogies that never rolled before.

Your mother she was raised way down in Texas,
Where the jimson weed and sand-burrs grow;
Now we'll fill you up on prickly pear and cholla
Till you are ready for the trail to Idaho.

Oh, you'll be soup for Uncle Sam's Injuns;
"It's beef, heap beef," I hear them cry.
Git along, git along, git along little dogies,
You're going to be beef steers by and by.

Working on the Railway

In eighteen hundred and forty-one
I put my corduroy breeches on,
I put my corduroy breeches on,
To work upon the railway.

For-o-my-or-o-my-or-o-my-ay,
For-o-my-or-o-my-or-o-my-ay,
For-o-my-or-o-my-or-o-my-ay,
To work upon the railway.

In eighteen hundred and forty-two
I left the old world for the new,
The emigrationists put me through,
To work upon the railway.

In eighteen hundred and forty-three,
'Twas first I met sweet Biddy McGee,
And an iligant wife she's been to me
While working on the railway.

In eighteen hundred and forty-four,
It left me where I was before;
Bad cess to luck that brought me o'er
To work upon the railway.

In eighteen hundred and forty-five,
Dan O'Connell was then alive,
And Teddy McGuinness to my surprise
Was working on the railway.

In eighteen hundred and forty-six,
I got meself in the divils' own fix
For callin' some gents a parcel o' micks,
As works upon the railway.

In eighteen hundred and forty-seven,
Sweet Biddy McGee has gone to heaven,
If she left one child she left eleven
To work upon the railway.

In eighteen hundred and forty-eight,
I learned to take my whiskey straight.
'Tis a beautiful drink and can't be bate
For working on the railway.

In eighteen hundred and fifty-two,
My earthly career is almost through,
And there's nothing on earth that I can do
But work upon the railway.

In eighteen hundred and fifty-three,
The imps and the divil they took me
To work upon the machinery
In the Sub-terranean Railway.

BIOGRAPHICAL NOTES

NOTE ON THE TEXTS

NOTES

INDEXES

Biographical Notes

HENRY ADAMS (February 16, 1838–March 27, 1918) b. Boston, Massachusetts. Third son of Abigail Brooks and Charles Francis Adams; grandson of John Quincy Adams, at whose home he was a frequent summer visitor; great-grandson of John Adams. Graduated Harvard 1858; studied law in Berlin and Dresden until 1860; traveled in Austria and Italy, publishing Italian travel letters in *Boston Daily Courier*. After father's reelection to Congress in 1860, accompanied him to Washington to serve as his secretary; Washington correspondent for *Boston Daily Advertiser*. Father appointed minister to Great Britain in 1861; served as his secretary until 1868. As London correspondent of *New York Times* (1861–62), reported British reaction to Civil War; traveled on Continent with mother and other family members; published scholarly articles. Returned to Washington in 1868 to work as journalist and to lobby for reform; attacked spoils system and campaigned for free trade and establishment of civil service. Appointed assistant professor of history at Harvard (1870–77); assumed editorship of *North American Review* (1870–76). On travels in Far West formed friendship with Clarence King of United States Geological Survey. Married Marion (Clover) Hooper in June 1872; they made wedding journey to England, the Continent, and Egypt. Published biography *The Life of Albert Gallatin* (1879). Formed friendships with Senator James D. Cameron, his wife Elizabeth, and John Hay. With Hay, his wife Clara, and Clarence King, the Adamses formed salon "The Five of Hearts." Traveled in Europe to research detailed history of Jefferson and Madison administrations. *Democracy*, fictional attack on Washington corruption, published anonymously in 1880, followed by biography *John Randolph* (1882) and another novel, *Esther* (1884). Wife committed suicide in December 1885. The following spring made four-month tour of Japan with artist John La Farge; met Ernest Fenollosa. *History of the United States during the Administrations of Thomas Jefferson and James Madison* published 1889–91. Traveled (1890–91) with La Farge in South Pacific, meeting Robert Louis Stevenson in Samoa; made other journeys to Cuba and Mexico. Lived mostly in Europe between 1897 and 1900, and afterwards spent part of most years in Europe. *Mont Saint Michel and Chartres* (1904) and *The Education of Henry Adams* (1907) published in private editions; *The Life of George Cabot Lodge* appeared 1911. Trade edition of *Mont Saint Michel and Chartres* enjoyed wide success. Died in Washington. *The Education of Henry Adams* awarded Pulitzer Prize posthumously the following year.

JOHN QUINCY ADAMS (July 11, 1767–February 21, 1848) b. Braintree, Massachusetts. Eldest son of Abigail Smith and John Adams. In 1778 accompanied his father on diplomatic mission to France and attended school in Paris until their return to America the following year. Served (1781–82) as private secretary to Francis Dana, minister to Russia; subsequently rejoined father in the Netherlands, traveling with him to England after signing of the

Treaty of Paris in September 1783. Returned to America and graduated Harvard College 1787. Began law practice in 1790 in Newburyport. Contributed articles to Benjamin Russell's *Columbian Centinel*, including reply to Thomas Paine's *The Rights of Man*. Appointed by George Washington as minister to the Netherlands. In 1797 married Louisa Johnson; they had a daughter and three sons (including Charles Francis Adams, diplomat and father of Henry Adams). Appointed minister to Prussia following his father's election as president; travels resulted in *Letters on Silesia* (1804) and translation of Christoph Wieland's heroic poem *Oberon*. Elected to the Senate in 1803; resigned in 1808 after being repudiated by fellow Massachusetts Federalists for supporting Jefferson's Embargo Act of 1807. Named Professor of Rhetoric and Belles-Lettres at Harvard in 1806; *Lectures on Rhetoric and Oratory* published 1810. Resumed diplomatic career in 1809 when James Madison appointed him minister to Russia; declined appointment to Supreme Court. As leader of American peace commissioners, helped negotiate Treaty of Ghent (1814) ending the War of 1812. Appointed minister to England in 1815. Served as secretary of state under James Monroe, 1817–25; supported Andrew Jackson's invasion of Florida; negotiated Spain's cession of Florida, abandonment of Spanish claims in the Pacific Northwest, and Anglo-American agreement on the Canadian boundary; played major role in formulating the Monroe Doctrine. In 1824 presidential election, ran second to Andrew Jackson in the electoral vote; when none of the four candidates received an electoral majority, Adams was elected president by the House of Representatives with the support of Henry Clay (whom Adams then appointed secretary of state). Presidency (1825–29) was clouded by bitter party conflict among Jacksonians, Democratic Republicans, and Adams-Clay National Republicans, and he was defeated decisively by Jackson in presidential election of 1828. Elected to Congress in 1830 as independent candidate and served until his death. As congressman, actively opposed extension of slavery and annexation of Texas; led long, ultimately successful fight (1836–44) to overturn "gag rule" preventing congressional debate of antislavery petitions. In 1841 successfully defended African mutineers of the slave ship *Amistad* before the Supreme Court. Published narrative poem *Dermot MacMorrogh; or, the Conquest of Ireland* (1832), and verse collection *Poems of Religion and Society* (1848). Suffered a stroke during a session of Congress and died in the Capitol two days later; last words said to have been, "This is the end of earth—I am content." Diary (1794–1846) published posthumously in twelve volumes as *Memoirs* (1874–77).

A. BRONSON ALCOTT (November 29, 1799–March 4, 1888) b. at Spindle Hill near Wolcott, Connecticut. Son of Anna Bronson (daughter of Connecticut sea captain) and Joseph Chatfield Alcox (farmer of Puritan ancestry); given name Amos Bronson Alcox. Raised on family farm; received little formal education. Employed in clock factory and worked as itinerant peddler (1818–23) in Virginia and the Carolinas after efforts to establish teaching career in Virginia failed. Became schoolteacher in Bristol, Wolcott, and Cheshire, Connecticut. In 1830, married Abigail May, sister of well-known

Unitarian clergyman, and they moved to Germantown, Pennsylvania, where Alcott opened a school; they had four daughters, Anna, Louisa May, Elizabeth, and Abby. Studied writings of Swiss educator Johann Pestalozzi. Founded the Masonic Temple School in Boston in 1834; developed conversational method aimed at discovering innate ethical ideas. Views on education (centered on "self-realization" and "personalism") attracted attention in the United States and Europe. Introduced organized play, gymnastics, the honor system, and children's libraries; minimized corporal punishment and sought to create recreational atmosphere for learning. In 1835 his assistant Elizabeth Peabody detailed Alcott's educational methods in anonymously published journal, *Record of a School, Exemplifying the General Principles of Spiritual Culture*. Alcott published *The Doctrine and Discipline of Human Culture* in 1836; in *Conversations with Children on the Gospels* (1836–37) gave detailed examples of his teaching practices. Margaret Fuller taught at school, 1836–37. Alcott and the school came under attack for unorthodox religious ideas, discussion of human physiology with students, and for admitting a black student; the school lost a majority of its pupils and Alcott went deeply into debt; school closed in 1839. In 1840 moved to Concord, Massachusetts; made failed attempt to support family by farming; "Orphic Sayings" published in *The Dial*. Intimate friend of Ralph Waldo Emerson, Henry David Thoreau, and William Ellery Channing; regarded as a leader among the Transcendentalists. (Emerson later remarked, "As pure intellect I have never seen his equal"; Thoreau called him "the sanest man I ever knew.") Went to England (with funds supplied by Emerson) in 1842 to meet English admirers who had founded a school called "Alcott House"; met and eventually quarreled with Thomas Carlyle. Returned home with three English disciples and tried unsuccessfully (1843–45) to establish a utopian community incorporating vegetarian principles, the "Consociate Family," at Fruitlands, a farm near Harvard, Massachusetts. After the experiment failed in 1845, the family relied on earnings of Abigail and Louisa for support. Eventually eked out a living on the lyceum circuit with lectures and discussions (called "conversations") which, after 1853, he delivered in Cincinnati, Cleveland, Chicago, St. Louis, and other Western cities. Daughter Elizabeth died of scarlet fever in 1858. In 1859 became superintendent of the Concord schools. The success of Louisa's novel *Little Women* in 1868–69 brought the family financial security. Wife Abigail died in 1877; daughter Abigail May died in Paris in 1879. Alcott's conversations and lectures at home were later formalized into Concord Summer School of Philosophy and Literature, which held first sessions in 1879 and continued until Alcott's death. In later years published *Tablets* (1868), *Concord Days* (1872), *Table Talk* (1877), *New Connecticut, An Autobiographical Poem* (1881), and *Sonnets and Canzonets* (1882). Maintained voluminous correspondence on topics including abolition, vegetarianism, women's rights, philosophy, and health with Mary Baker Eddy, Oliver Wendell Holmes, Julia Ward Howe, Henry James, Sr., James Russell Lowell, Elizabeth Cady Stanton, Walt Whitman, and others. In 1882 suffered a stroke from which he never fully recovered; subsequently cared for by surviving daughters; Louisa died two days after him.

ELIZABETH AKERS ALLEN   (October 9, 1832–August 7, 1911)   b. Elizabeth Chase in Strong, Maine. Daughter of Mercy Fenno Barton and Thomas Chase (a lawyer). Mother died when she was a child, and she was sent to live with relatives in Farmington, Maine. Began to write at age 15 under pen name "Florence Percy." In 1851 married Marshall Taylor, son of Presbyterian minister; marriage soon ended in divorce after Taylor left her and their daughter and moved to California. Moved to Portland, Maine, and became assistant editor of *Portland Transcript*; published collection of poems, *Forest Buds* (1855). Contributed to *Atlantic Monthly* from 1858. Traveled in Europe, 1859–60, sending letters to the *Transcript* and *Boston Evening Gazette*. The poem "Rock Me to Sleep" appeared in *Saturday Evening Post* in 1860; was set to music by Ernest Leslie and became enormously popular, but controversy over authorship (with Alexander M. W. Ball and others claiming to have written it) ensued. Married sculptor Benjamin Paul Akers, whom she had met in Rome, in 1860; he was already seriously ill with tuberculosis and died the following year after the couple had moved to Philadelphia; their daughter died in infancy. Akers resumed editorial position in Portland. In 1863 took a clerkship in Washington, D.C., where she also worked in hospitals with wounded soldiers. In 1865 married E. M. Allen, a lumber merchant. In 1866 a second collection of poetry published, including "Rock Me to Sleep"; her authorship of the poem was finally vindicated in *The New York Times* in 1867. Lived with her husband in Richmond, Virginia, 1866–73; returned to Maine to become literary editor of Portland *Daily Advertiser*. In 1882 moved with her husband to Tuckahoe, New York. Published many volumes of verse, including *Queen Catherine's Rose* (1885), *The Silver Bridge* (1886), *The High-Top Sweeting* (1891), *The Ballad of the Bronx* (1901), and *The Sunset Song* (1902).

WASHINGTON ALLSTON   (November 5, 1779–July 9, 1843)   b. on family plantation in Waccamaw Neck, South Carolina. Son of Rachel Moore (of Huguenot descent) and Captain William Allston (who served under Francis Marion in the Revolutionary War). Father died suddenly in 1781, upon returning home from battle of Cowpens (rumored to have been poisoned by a servant). After early schooling in Charleston and mother's remarriage (to Dr. Henry C. Flagg, chief of General Greene's medical staff), sent for further education in 1787 to Newport, Rhode Island; remained there for nine years, studying at private boarding school of Robert Rogers; formed friendship with fellow students William Ellery Channing (uncle of the poet of the same name) and Edmund Dana (brother of Richard Henry Dana). Developed interest in painting while at Newport, and was influenced by local portrait painter Samuel King and miniaturist Edward Greene Malbone. Attended Harvard, 1796–1800. Became engaged to Ann Channing, sister of William Ellery Channing. Upon graduation, sold his interest in the family property to finance art study abroad, and sailed for England with Malbone; studied from 1801 to November 1803 at Royal Academy in London under Benjamin West and Henry Fuseli. Traveled to Paris with artist John Vanderlyn; painted first major works, "The Rising of a Thunderstorm at Sea" and "The Deluge."

From Paris went to Italy by way of Switzerland; remained in Rome 1804–08, establishing artistic reputation (known in local art circles as "the American Titian"); became acquainted with artists Antonio Canova and Gottlieb Schick and formed close friendships with Washington Irving and Samuel Taylor Coleridge. Returned to America in 1808 to marry Ann Channing; settled in Boston, where he wrote most of the poems later collected in *The Sylphs of the Seasons*. In 1810 read a long poem (possibly the title work of that collection) before Phi Beta Kappa Society of Harvard. Returned to England in 1811, accompanied by wife Ann and friend and pupil Samuel F. B. Morse (later joined by painter Charles R. Leslie). Became close friend of John Howard Payne. Painted series of religious pictures, including "Dead Man Revived by Touching the Bones of the Prophet Elisha" and "Saint Peter in Prison." In 1813 *The Sylphs of the Seasons* published, receiving high praise from Coleridge; that summer suffered severe and prolonged illness that permanently affected his health; taken to Bristol for treatment. In 1814 met painters John Martin and William Collins; exhibited paintings at Bristol during summer. Wife Ann died in February 1815. Confirmed as Anglican and devoted himself intensively to religion. Completed paintings "Uriel in the Sun" and "Jacob's Ladder." Returned to America in 1818 (unanimously elected to Royal Academy after departure from England); opened studio in Boston. Contributed essays to Richard Henry Dana's magazine *The Idle Man*. Exhibited paintings at Boston Athenaeum in 1827. Worked on large painting "Belshazzar's Feast," begun in England; admirers raised thousands of dollars to encourage its completion, but in 25 years of work Allston did not finish it. In later paintings moved away from large-scale narrative to concentrate on landscapes and portraits. Married late wife's cousin, Martha Dana, sister of Edmund and Richard Henry Dana, in 1830; settled in Cambridgeport, Massachusetts. At urging of friends, mounted successful exhibit of 45 paintings in Boston in 1839; interviewed in connection with exhibit by Margaret Fuller, who published an admiring essay on his work in *The Dial*. In 1841 published *Monaldi, a Tale*, Gothic romance set in Italy among painters, written two decades earlier. *Lectures on Art, and Poems*, edited by Dana, appeared posthumously in 1850.

JOEL BARLOW (March 24, 1754–December 24, 1812) b. Redding, Connecticut. Son of Esther Hull and Samuel Barlow. In 1776, while an undergraduate at Yale College, volunteered for temporary military service in the Revolutionary Army. At Yale, tutored by Timothy Dwight; friends included Noah Webster and Oliver Wolcott; graduated 1778 (first important poem "The Prospect of Peace" read at commencement). Taught school briefly in New Haven, then returned to Yale for graduate work. Employed as usher at Timothy Dwight's school in Northampton in 1779; during that time outlined epic poem about Columbus. Served in the Revolution as chaplain in the 3rd Massachusetts brigade, 1780–83. Married Ruth Baldwin in 1781; they settled in Hartford the following year. Formed business partnership (1784–85) with Elisha Babcock, selling and publishing books (including Barlow's revision of Isaac Watts' version of the Psalms) and co-editing *The American Mercury*. In

1786 admitted to the bar. Associated with so-called "Connecticut Wits," group of poets with Federalist and Calvinist leanings including Timothy Dwight, John Trumbull, David Humphreys, and Lemuel Hopkins; with them collaborated on mock-heroic verse series *The Anarchiad* (published 1786–87 in *The New Haven Gazette* and *The Connecticut Magazine*). Columbus epic published in 1787 as *The Vision of Columbus*; advance subscribers to the edition included George Washington, Benjamin Franklin, Thomas Paine, Alexander Hamilton, and the Marquis de Lafayette. In 1788 traveled to France as agent of the Ohio Company, selling Ohio River Valley real estate. In Paris, formed lifelong friendship with Thomas Jefferson, socialized with the Marquis de Lafayette, and witnessed scenes of French Revolution. By 1791, land venture had collapsed amid accusations of fraud and threats against Barlow. Resided in London, 1791–92; associates there included Thomas Paine, Mary Wollstonecraft, William Godwin, and Joseph Priestley. In 1792 published writings defending French Revolution including *Advice to the Privileged Orders*, *A Letter to the National Convention of France, on the Defects in the Constitution of 1791*, and verse satire *The Conspiracy of Kings*. Found enthusiastic reception for his ideas in France; in February 1793 made honorary French citizen; defeated in Savoy as Girondist candidate for deputy to the National Convention. In early 1793 wrote mock epic *The Hasty Pudding* (published 1796), which was widely reprinted. Many French friends and associates killed during Reign of Terror. Entrusted by Thomas Paine with manuscript of the first part of *The Age of Reason* following his arrest in Paris in December 1793 (Barlow arranged book's publication the following year). Enriched himself as middle man involved in shipping goods in and out of France. Visited Hamburg, 1794–95, where he studied German language and literature; met German poet Friedrich Gottlieb Klopstock. Returning to Paris, established friendship with James Monroe. In 1795 appointed U.S. consul at Algiers; over 21-month period negotiated release of American prisoners held by Dey of Algiers. Returned to Paris in 1797; in 1798, letter bluntly criticizing Adams administration's policy toward France published in American newspapers; Barlow widely attacked as seditious and atheistic by critics including old friend Noah Webster; Barlow clarified his position in *Letters from Paris* (1799). Became close friend of inventor Robert Fulton, who lived with the Barlows in their Paris home over a period of seven years; Barlow and Fulton collaborated on uncompleted scientific poem *The Canal*. Returned to America after 17-year European stay in 1804. Settled near Washington in mansion Kalorama, which became meeting place for leading political and intellectual figures. Proposed national research institution in *Prospectus of a National Institution* (1805). Lived in Philadelphia for over a year to supervise publication of extensively revised version of his epic, now titled *The Columbiad* and dedicated to Fulton; the book was published in an elaborate and expensive edition in 1807. In 1811 appointed by President Madison to negotiate trade agreement with Napoleon. After delays by French government, arranged meeting with French foreign minister Petry in Vilna (now Vilnius, Lithuania); over two-month period journeyed from Paris to Vilna, passing through region devastated by war; during two-week stay in Vilna wrote "Advice to a Raven in Russia." In the meantime Napoleon had suffered military catastrophe in Russia, and the French army was in full retreat. Barlow left Vilna for Warsaw and was caught up in the retreat during his journey. Contracted lung inflammation; died a few days after leaving Warsaw in Zarnowiec, a village near Cracow.

KATHARINE LEE BATES (August 12, 1859–March 28, 1929) b. Falmouth, Massachusetts. Youngest of five children of Cornelia Frances Lee and William Bates, a Congregational minister who died a month after her birth. Family moved to Grantville (now Wellesley), Massachusetts, where Bates attended local schools. Graduated Wellesley College in 1880. Taught high school in Natick, Massachusetts, and at girls' preparatory schools near Wellesley. In 1885 returned to Wellesley as English instructor and remained there 40 years, becoming the guiding force of Wellesley's English department. In 1893 published *The English Religious Drama* and was invited to lecture on the subject at Colorado College; en route, visited World's Columbian Exhibition in Chicago; at Colorado College, met Hamlin Garland and Woodrow Wilson. Early in her stay, after an outing to Pike's Peak in a prairie wagon, wrote "America the Beautiful." Poem published in *The Congregationalist* on July 4, 1895; set to melody based on "Materna" by Samuel Augustus Ward; revised versions appeared in 1904 and 1911. Verse collections included *The College Beautiful* (1887), *America the Beautiful* (1911), *The Retinue* (1918), *Yellow Clover* (1922), *The Pilgrim Ship* (1926), and *America the Dream* (1930). Also published fictional works *Rose and Thorn* (1888) and *Hermit Island* (1891); other prose including critical survey *American Literature* (1898) and travel books *Spanish Highways and By-Ways* (1900) and *From Gretna Green to Land's End* (1907); and poetry and plays for children including *Sunshine and Other Verses for Children* (1890), *Fairy Gold* (1916), and *Little Robin Stay-Behind* (1923).

AMBROSE BIERCE (June 24, 1842–1914?) b. Ambrose Gwinnett Bierce on farm near Horse Cave Creek, Ohio. Son of Laura Sherwood and Marcus Aurelius Bierce; one of many children of poor but well-read farm family; received limited education at home and at high school in Warsaw, Indiana. Attended Kentucky Military Institute, 1859–60. Enlisted in 9th Indiana Infantry in 1861; fought at Shiloh, Murfreesboro, Chattanooga, and Franklin; wounded at Kenesaw Mountain. After the war, served for a time as custodian of captured and abandoned property in Selma, Alabama. Accompanied General W. B. Hazen on tour of northwestern army posts. Joined brother Albert in San Francisco, working with him at the U.S. sub-treasury. Contributed journalism to *The Californian*, *The Golden Era*, *Overland Monthly*, and *San Francisco News Letter and California Advertiser* (of which he became editor in 1868). Married Mary Ellen (Mollie) Day in 1871; they had two sons and one daughter. Lived in England (where his associates included W. S. Gilbert) and in France, 1872–75. Worked on editorial staff of *Fun*; wrote two issues of *The Lantern* (a periodical subsidized by exiled Empress Eugénie);

contributed to *Figaro* and *Hood's Comic Annual*. Collected mordantly humor-
ous sketches in three volumes, *The Fiend's Delight* (1873), *Nuggets and Dust
Panned Out in California* (1873), and *Cobwebs from an Empty Skull* (1874),
all published under pseudonym "Dod Grile." Returning to San Francisco
in 1875, wrote for *The Argonaut*. In 1880 worked as general agent for Black
Hills Placer Mining Company in Dakota Territory. Edited *The Wasp*, 1881–
86. From 1887, columnist and editor for William Randolph Hearst's *Exam-
iner*. Literary associates at this time included George Sterling and Herman
Scheffauer. A volume of short stories, *Tales of Soldiers and Civilians*,
was printed in 1891 (but not published until 1892, simultaneously with the
English edition, *In the Midst of Life*), followed by *The Monk and the
Hangman's Daughter* (1892), a medieval story adapted from translation by
G. A. Danziger of German work by Richard Voss, *Black Beetles in Amber*
(1892), a collection of satirical verse, and *Can Such Things Be?* (1893), a vol-
ume of supernatural tales. In January 1896 sent to Washington by Hearst to
head lobby opposing congressional approval of Collis Huntington's Funding
Bill for Central and Southern Pacific railroads. Bill defeated, largely through
Bierce's efforts. Began writing for Hearst's *New York Journal*. In November
1896 returned to San Francisco. Moved permanently to Washington in 1899.
On payroll of *New York Journal*, but his material also appeared in *New York
American* and *San Francisco Examiner*. Son Leigh died of pneumonia in
1901. In 1906 began writing for *Cosmopolitan*, which took over his salary in
1906. Later books included *Fantastic Fables* (1899); *Shapes of Clay* (1903), a
poetry collection; *The Cynic's Word Book*, a sardonic lexicon interspersed with
pseudonymous poems (later retitled *The Devil's Dictionary*); *The Shadow on
the Dial* (1909); and *Write It Right* (1909), a manual of style. *Collected Works*
published in 12 volumes (1909–12). Divorced from his wife in 1905. After
settling his affairs, disappeared into Mexico in 1913, writing to a friend: "If
you hear of my being stood up against a Mexican stone wall and shot to rags
please know that I think it a pretty good way to depart this life."

JAMES A. BLAND   (October 22, 1854–May 5, 1911)   b. Flushing, New York;
lived in Philadelphia during childhood. His mother was a free black from
Wilmington, Delaware; his father, Allen Bland, also free-born, was the first
black examiner in the U.S. Patent Office in Washington, D.C. Learned to
play banjo and, by age 14, worked as musician in local clubs and hotels,
performing popular songs of the day; within a year, began to compose his
own songs. Graduated high school in Washington; studied briefly at Howard
University, but soon neglected college work to study musical composition
privately. Became acquainted with future U.S. Marine Band leader John
Philip Sousa, who later used some of Bland's melodies in his band arrange-
ments. Met minstrel celebrity George Primrose at Ford's Theatre in 1874,
performing for him newly written song "Carry Me Back to Old Virginny";
Primrose premiered the song with his minstrel show in Baltimore. In 1878
joined the Georgia Minstrels, first successful all-black minstrel group
(founded as Callender's Original and Georgia Minstrels in 1865). Performed

"Carry Me Back to Old Virginny" with the troupe; other successful songs included "Oh, Dem Golden Slippers" (of which 100,000 copies were sold by 1880), "In the Evening by the Moonlight," "In the Morning by the Bright Light," and "De Golden Wedding"; said to have written as many as 600 songs during his career. Troupe evolved into large-scale show, the Minstrel Carnival of Genuine Colored Minstrels; played Niblo's Garden in New York City in 1879; toured England in 1881. Bland remained in Europe as successful solo performer until 1901, occasionally returning to the U.S.; known as "The Idol of the Music Halls"; gave command performance before Queen Victoria and the Prince of Wales. In 1910 returned destitute to Washington, D.C.; found a job in the law office of an old friend, William Silence; wrote musical *The Sporting Girl*, but realized only $250 on words and music. Moved to Philadelphia where he made unsuccessful effort to renew career as stage performer; died of tuberculosis.

BENJAMIN PAUL BLOOD (November 21, 1832 – January 15, 1919) b. Amsterdam, New York, where he was a lifelong resident. Son of Mary Stanton and John Blood; descended on mother's side from *Mayflower* pilgrim John Howland, on father's from 18th-century Irish immigrant. Attended Amsterdam Academy and Union College; inherited family farm. Married twice, to Mary E. Sayles (who died in 1893) and Harriet A. Lefferts. Early writings included *The Philosophy of Justice Between God and Man* (1851), an unorthodox Christian treatise; *The Bride of the Iconoclast* (1854), a narrative poem in Spenserian stanzas, written before age 21; *Optimism, the Lesson of the Ages* (1860), an essay in theological speculation; *Napoleon I: A Historical Lecture* (1863); and *The Colonnades* (1868), a philosophical epic in blank verse. After being administered nitrous oxide in a dentist's office, underwent mystical experience; repeated the experience at frequent intervals, expounding philosophical conclusions from it in *The Anaesthetic Revelation and the Gist of Philosophy* (1874). Sent book to a number of American and European writers, leading to correspondence with William James and Alfred Tennyson. (James later commented on *The Anaesthetic Revelation*: "It fascinated me so 'weirdly' that I am conscious of its having been one of the stepping-stones of my thinking ever since," and went on to publish in 1910 "A Pluralistic Mystic," an article praising Blood.) In 1886 the *Journal of Speculative Philosophy* published some of his writings as "Philosophical Reveries," and eight poems appeared in *Scribner's Magazine* between 1892 and 1904; most of his other works were privately printed and distributed. Other writings included *The Flaw in Supremacy: A Sketch of the Nature, Process and Status of Philosophy, as Inferring the Miracle of Nature, the Contingency of History, the Equation of Reason and Unreason, &c., &c.* (1893), and the posthumously published *Pluriverse* (1920), in which he criticized his earlier monism in favor of a pluralistic philosophy. His uncollected poems were gathered in *Heirlooms: A Book of Poems* (1924).

FRANZ BOAS (July 9, 1858 – December 21, 1942) b. Minden, Westphalian Prussia. Educated at universities of Heidelberg, Bonn, and Kiel; trained as physicist and geographer. Member of German expedition to Arctic, 1883–84; exposure to Eskimo life in Baffinland shifted his interests to ethnology. Traveled to Pacific Northwest in 1886 where he made first studies of Kwakiutl and other tribes; settled in U.S. as editor of *Science*. Joined faculty of Clark University in Worcester, Massachusetts, in 1888; supervised exhibit of physical anthropology for Chicago Columbian Exposition of 1893. In 1896 became first professor of anthropology at Columbia University, creating influential department of which he remained head until his retirement in 1936; students included Ruth Benedict, Ruth Bunzel, Zora Neale Hurston, Alfred Kroeber, Robert Lowie, Margaret Mead, Edward Sapir, and John R. Swanton. Served as curator of anthropology at American Museum of Natural History, 1901–05. Systematic research methods and opposition to 19th-century theories of race transformed fields of anthropology and linguistics; continued field work on Northwest coast until 1931. In final years, active in opposing Nazi theories of race. His many publications included *The Central Eskimo* (1888), *The Social Organization and the Secret Societies of the Kwakiutl Indians* (1897), *The Mythology of the Bella Coola Indians* (1898), *The Kwakiutl of Vancouver Island* (1909), *The Mind of Primitive Man* (1911), *Tsimshian Mythology* (1916), *Ethnology of the Kwakiutl* (1921), *Primitive Art* (1927), *Anthropology and Modern Life* (1928), *The Religion of the Kwakiutl Indians* (1930), and *Race, Language and Culture* (1940). Edited *Handbook of American Indian Languages* (1911).

MANOAH BODMAN (January 28, 1765–January 1, 1850) b. Sunderland, Massachusetts. First of seven children born to Esther Field and Joseph Bodman; sometimes known as Noah Bodman. In 1779 the family moved to Williamsburg, Massachusetts (where Joseph Bodman's brothers William and Samuel had settled), and became prominent in local business and politics. In his youth, by his own account, Bodman "participated in divine grace" during Calvinist religious revival that swept Williamsburg. Following brother's death at age 19 in 1790, experienced troubling visions he attributed to Satan. In 1799 married Theodosia Green; she died during the first year of their marriage; they had no children, and Bodman never remarried. Practiced law. Following wife's death, experienced another and more intense series of diabolical apparitions and religious visions. Delivered confessional speeches in Williamsburg and other neighboring towns. Published *An Oration on Death* (1817), an account of his religious experiences interspersed with occasional poems; other publications included *Washington's Birth Day, An Oration* (1814) and *Oration on the Birth of Our Savior* (1826).

GEORGE HENRY BOKER (October 6, 1823–January 2, 1890) b. Philadelphia, Pennsylvania, son of Charles Boker, wealthy banker. Attended College of New Jersey (now Princeton), graduating in 1842. Relative and boyhood companion Charles Godfrey Leland described Boker in his youth as "quite familiar, in a refined and gentlemanly way, with all the dissipations of Philadelphia and New York." In 1844 married Julia Mandeville Riggs, with whom, after a brief European tour, he settled in Philadelphia; they had one son, George. Abandoned study of law to pursue career as verse dramatist and lyric poet. In 1848 published first poetry collection, *A Lesson of Life*, and completed *Calaynos*, a blank verse tragedy set in medieval Spain; successful London production in 1849 led to American premiere in 1851. Other plays included *Anne Boleyn* (1850, unproduced); *The Betrothal* (1850), romance of medieval Italy; *The World a Mask* (1851), social satire set in England; *The Widow's Marriage*, unproduced blank verse comedy; *Leonor de Guzman* (1853), heroic tragedy; and his greatest success, the verse play *Francesca da Rimini* (1855), which continued to be revived into the 20th century. Stopped writing for theater after failure of *The Bankrupt* in 1855. In 1856 collected chief writings in *Plays and Poems*. Father's death the following year embroiled him in legal and financial difficulties; forced to defend father's reputation from lingering charges of financial malfeasance in his conduct at the Girard Bank. Around this time, wrote (but withheld from publication) *The Book of the Dead*, a volume of poetry inspired by his ultimately successful struggle to vindicate his father's name. During Civil War, patriotic activities included founding Union League of Philadelphia (of which he was secretary, 1861–71). Wrote much poetry inspired by the conflict, gathered in *Poems of the War* (1864); another volume of poetry, *Königsmark, The Legend of the Hounds, and Other Poems* appeared 1869. In postwar period literary associates included Leland, Richard Henry Stoddard, William Gilmore Simms, and Paul Hamilton Hayne. Appointed by Ulysses S. Grant as minister to Turkey, 1871–75; helped restore diplomatic relations with Ottoman government. On trip to Egypt with Leland in 1872, met Ralph Waldo Emerson at Misraim. In 1875 named minister to Russia; served with distinction until recalled by Hayes administration in 1878. Returned to Philadelphia, where he received many honors; devoted himself to improvement of city's park system. Encouraged by successful revival of *Francesca da Rimini* in 1882 to resume literary career, wrote unproduced dramatic adaptation of *The Last Days of Pompeii* (entitled in successive versions *Nydia* and *Glaucus*), and published *The Book of the Dead* (1882) and *Sonnets* (1886).

DANIEL GARRISON BRINTON (May 13, 1837–July 31, 1899) b. Thornbury, Pennsylvania. Son of Ann Garrison and Lewis Brinton. Graduated Yale College in 1858. First published work, *Notes on the Floridian Peninsula, its Literary History, Indian Tribes, and Antiquities*, appeared in 1859. Received medical degree from Jefferson Medical College, Philadephia, 1860; spent a year in further study at Heidelberg and Paris. Practiced medicine in West Chester, Pennsylvania. In 1862 became surgeon in Union Army; served at battles of Chancellorsville and Gettysburg; suffered sunstroke in 1863 and was restricted to work at army hospital in Quincy, Illinois. After leaving the army in 1865 married Sarah Tillson; resumed medical practice in West Chester. Moved to Philadelphia in 1867 to work on staff of *The Medical and Surgical Reporter*, of which he became editor in 1874. Professor of ethnology and archaeology at Academy of Natural Sciences in Philadelphia, 1884–86; in 1886 professor of American linguistics and archaeology at University of Pennsylvania. Retired from medicine in 1887 to devote himself to research. In the eight volumes of his *Library of Aboriginal American Literature* (1882–90) was first to undertake systematic publication of translations of American Indian texts. Anthropological studies included *The Myths of the New World* (1868), *American Hero-Myths* (1882), *Aboriginal American Authors and Their Productions* (1883), *The Lenâpé and Their Legends* (1884), *A Lenâpé-English Dictionary* (1888, with A. S. Anthony), *Essays of an Americanist* (1890), *The American Race* (1891), and *Religions of Primitive Peoples* (1897). Also published many briefer linguistic and archaeological papers; literary studies of Robert Browning, Alfred Tennyson, and Walt Whitman; and poetry including the verse drama *Maria Candelaria* (1897). President of American Folk-Lore Society (1890) and American Association for the Advancement of Science (1894).

AUGUSTA COOPER BRISTOL (April 17, 1835–May 9, 1910) b. Croydon, New Hampshire; educated at Kimball Union Academy. In 1850 became a teacher. Married Louis Bristol in 1866. Published three volumes of poetry: *Poems* (1868), *The Web of Life* (1895), and *A Spray of Cosmos* (1904). Known primarily as lecturer and writer on social and philosophical issues; published a number of lectures in pamphlet form, including *The Relation of the Maternal Function to the Woman's Intellect* (1876), *The Philosophy of Art* (1878), *Science and Its Relations to Human Character* (1878), and *The Present Phase of Woman's Advancement* (1880); these and other lectures posthumously collected in *The Present Phase of Women's Advancement and Other Addresses* (1916). Went to France in 1880 to study Equitable Association of Labor and Capital at Guise; later that year attended International Convention of Freethinkers in Brussels. Elected state lecturer by Patrons of Husbandry (a vehicle for the National Grange movement, an organization of farmers and agricultural workers) in New Jersey; after 1884, traveled in this capacity throughout the country. Died in Vineland, New Jersey.

CHARLES TIMOTHY BROOKS (June 20, 1813–June 4, 1883) b. Salem, Massachusetts. Son of Mary King Mason and Timothy Brooks. Heard Emerson preach at South Church, Boston, in 1831. Graduated Harvard College (where he studied German literature with refugee scholar Charles Follen) in 1832; classmates included Charles Sumner and Oliver Wendell Holmes; graduated Harvard Divinity School (where classmates included Theodore Parker and Christopher Pearse Cranch) in 1835. Officiated in several New England churches, including brief terms at Nahant, Massachusetts, Bangor and Augusta, Maine, and Windsor, Vermont; ordained (by the elder William Ellery Channing) pastor of Unitarian Congregational Church in Newport, Rhode Island, 1837; served at the church until 1870, when failing eyesight forced his retirement. Married Harriet Lyman Hazard, daughter of Rhode Island legislator, in 1837; they had two sons and two daughters. Published translations from German, including Schiller's *William Tell* (1837) and *Homage of the Arts* (1847); anthologies *Songs and Ballads* (1842), to which Henry Wadsworth

Longfellow and others also contributed, and *German Lyrics* (1853); and Goethe's *Faust* (1856) in the original meters. Established friendship with Ralph Waldo Emerson. Original writings included two volumes of poetry, *Aquidneck and Other Commemorative Pieces* (1848) and *Songs of Field and Flood* (1853); *The Old Stone Mill Controversy* (1851), an archaeological essay on the Newport site alleged to have been built by Norsemen; a volume of sermons, *The Simplicity of Christ's Teachings* (1859); and *William Ellery Channing, A Centennial Memory* (1880). Traveled on several occasions for his health, including trips to India (1853–54) and Europe (1865–66). *Poems, Original and Translated* published posthumously in 1885 with a memoir of Brooks by Charles W. Wendt.

MARIA GOWEN BROOKS (1794?–November 11, 1845) b. Medford, Massachusetts, of Welsh ancestry. Daughter of Eleanor Cutter and William Gowen (a goldsmith); given name Abigail Gowen but legally changed it to Mary at the time of her marriage; "Maria" was her own adopted usage. Influenced by reading, at age nine, of Robert Southey's poem *Madoc*. Her father died bankrupt when she was 14. John Brooks, her guardian (previously married to her sister Lucretia), arranged for completion of her education and in 1810 married her; they had two sons, Horace (later a brigadier general in the U.S. Army) and Edgar. Husband, a Boston merchant, suffered heavy financial losses during War of 1812; thereafter they lived in Portland, Maine, in reduced circumstances. In 1820 Brooks published poetry collection *Judith, Esther and Other Poems* "by a Lover of the Fine Arts." Husband died in 1823 and she moved with sons and stepsons to an uncle's coffee plantation in Matanzas, Cuba, where she built a small house and began *Zophiël, or the Bride of Seven*, epic poem concerning the love of a fallen angel for a mortal, based on episode in apocryphal Book of Tobit. In 1825 published first canto of *Zophiël*; began correspondence with Robert Southey, who called her "the most impassioned and most imaginative of all poetesses," and compared her favorably to Sappho. In 1829 inherited her uncle's Cuban property, and with income now secure, traveled with son Horace to Hanover, New Hampshire, where he attended Dartmouth college while she pursued studies in the college library; son Edgar remained in Cuba with stepbrothers, overseeing plantation. In 1830, with brother Hammond Gowen, traveled to Paris, where she met Washington Irving and the Marquis de Lafayette (whose recommendation helped son Horace gain entrance to West Point); in spring of 1831 visited Southey's English estate, Keswick, remaining for a number of weeks. Returned to U.S. in late spring 1831 and moved to West Point, where Horace was now a cadet; continued to write and publish in periodicals. Southey edited and published *Zophiël* in 1833 under pseudonym "Maria del Occidente"; poem praised by Charles Lamb and John Quincy Adams; American edition of *Zophiël* appeared in 1834, but sold few copies. Devastated by deaths of son Edgar (1838) and a stepson (1839), returned to Cuba to erect a small monument; dedicated *Ode to the Departed* (1843) to their memory. Rufus Griswold, in *Poets and Poetry of America* (1842), called her the foremost American woman poet. Autobiographical prose romance *Idomen, or the Vale of Yamuri* (said to be based on unhappy love affair with a Canadian army officer) serialized in Boston *Saturday Evening Gazette* in 1838; published privately in book form in 1843, while Brooks was living with Horace, stationed at Governor's Island, New York City. Late in life, returned to Cuban estate, where she died of tropical fever.

PHILLIPS BROOKS (December 13, 1835–January 23, 1893)   b. Boston, Massachusetts. Son of Mary Phillips and William Gray Brooks; ancestors on mother's side included founders of Phillips Exeter Academy, Phillips Andover Academy, and Andover Theological Seminary; father was a Boston businessman. Early education at Boston Latin School. Graduated Harvard 1855; studied theology at seminary in Alexandria, Virginia; ordained Episcopal priest in 1859; became rector of Church of the Advent in Philadelphia in 1859, then of Church of the Holy Trinity in Philadelphia in 1862. Drew attention for eloquence of prayer delivered at Harvard Commemoration for Civil War dead in 1865. Wrote "O Little Town of Bethlehem" for his Sunday school; first performed publicly Christmas 1868. In 1869 became rector of Trinity Church in Boston. Invited to preach at Westminister Abbey and before Queen Victoria at Windsor in 1880, the first American so honored. Elected bishop in 1891. Publications included *Lectures on Preaching* (1877), *Sermons* (1878), *The Influence of Jesus* (1879), *Baptism and Confirmation* (1880), *The Candle of the Lord* (1881), and *The Light of the World* (1890), *Essays and Addresses* (1892), and the posthumous volumes *New Starts in Life* (1896) and *The Law of Growth* (1902).

HENRY HOWARD BROWNELL (February 6, 1820–October 31, 1872) b. Providence, Rhode Island. Son of Lucia de Wolf and Dr. Pardon Brownell; nephew of Episcopalian bishop Thomas Church Brownell. Graduated Washington College (now Trinity) in Hartford, Connecticut, 1841; taught briefly in Mobile, Alabama, before returning to Hartford to study law; admitted to bar 1844. Turned to writing career, publishing *Poems* (1847), *The People's Book of Ancient History* (1851), *The Discoverers, Pioneers and Settlers of North and South America* (1853), and *Ephemerson* (1855). In 1862 wrote poem based on Admiral Farragut's "General Orders" to his fleet in the attack on New Orleans; published in various newspapers, poem came to attention of Farragut, who corresponded with Brownell and (supposedly in response to Brownell's expressed desire to witness a naval battle) offered him position as acting ensign on flagship *Hartford*. Wrote descriptive poems about a number of naval engagements that he witnessed, including battle of Mobile Bay. War poems, published as *Lyrics of a Day, or Newspaper Poems*, earned admiration of Oliver Wendell Holmes, who called Brownell "Our Battle Laureate." Accompanied Farragut as secretary on cruises to European ports, 1865–68. Final volume of poetry, *War Lyrics and Other Poems*, appeared in 1866.

WILLIAM CULLEN BRYANT (November 3, 1794–June 12, 1878)   b. Cummington, Massachusetts. Son of Sarah Snell and Dr. Peter Bryant. Began writing poems at early age, and published poems in *New Hampshire Gazette* in 1807; anti-Jeffersonian satire, *The Embargo . . . By a Youth of Thirteen*, published in Boston with father's help in 1808. After private tutoring, entered Williams College in 1810, but withdrew after a year without degree. At age 20 wrote, but made no attempt to publish, "To a Waterfowl" and "Thanatopsis." Studied law and was admitted to bar in 1815; began law practice in Great Barrington, Massachusetts. Gained immediate recognition as poet after publication of "Thanatopsis" in *North American Review* in 1817; contributed articles to the *Review*, including survey of American poetic achievement and essay on prosody. In 1820 elected town clerk of Great Barrington and appointed justice of the peace of Berkshire County. In 1821, married Frances Fairchild, whom he had met five years earlier; they had two daughters, Fanny and Julia. Read "The Ages" at Harvard as Phi Beta Kappa poem; published first verse collection, *Poems* (1822); became close friend of Richard Henry Dana and contributed poems to his short-lived magazine *The Idle Man*. Gave up law in 1825 to pursue literary career in New York; became co-editor with Henry Anderson of *New York Review and Athenaeum Magazine*; as member (later president) of Bread and Cheese Club, associated with James Fenimore Cooper, Fitz-Greene Halleck, Gulian Verplanck, Robert Sands, Samuel F. B. Morse, Asher B. Durand, and Thomas Cole. Lent support to artists, encouraging formation of National Academy of Design (1826). With Sands and Verplanck, published *The Talisman*, first of annual series of gift books, in 1827. Became editor-in-chief of the New York *Evening Post* in 1829, remaining in that position until his death. Most of his best known poems were already written by the time the *Poems* of 1832 appeared (in the same year, a London edition with the same title was published, edited by Washington Irving, who took the liberty of altering some lines to avoid offending British political sensitivities). In 1832 visited Washington, D.C., where he met President Jackson and various cabinet members; moved to Hoboken, New Jersey; traveled to Illinois and toured the prairie, visiting ancient Indian mounds along Illinois River. Toured Canada and northern New England in 1833, and the following year sailed to Europe in 1834 with wife and daughters for two-year visit, traveling in France, Italy, Austria, and Germany; spent much time in Heidelberg with Henry Wadsworth Longfellow in the winter of 1835–36. Arranged publication of Richard Henry Dana Jr.'s *Two Years Before the Mast* (1840). During late 1830s and 1840s shared vacations, visits, and walking tours with William Gilmore Simms, Thomas Cole, Samuel Tilden, and Richard Henry Dana; entertained Charles Dickens in New York in 1842; crusaded for international copyright protection and against the death penalty; was a proponent of homeopathic medicine; served three terms as president of American Art Union. Published *The Fountain and Other Poems* (1842) and *The White Footed Deer and Other Poems* (1844). Built residence Springbank in Roslyn, New York, where he resided from 1844. In 1845 traveled in England, Scotland, Ireland, France, Belgium, Holland, Germany, Bohemia, Austria, Italy, and Switzerland, and over the next two years traveled widely in the United States. In 1848 delivered funeral oration for Thomas Cole; the following year Asher B. Durand presented him with the painting "Kindred Spirits," a portrait of

Bryant and Cole in the Catskills. Left Democratic party in 1848 to support Free Soil candidates. In 1849 visited Georgia, South Carolina, and Cuba; later in the year traveled to England and the Continent, recounting the voyage in *Letters of a Traveller* (1850). In 1851 presided at dinner in honor of Hungarian revolutionary Louis Kossuth. In 1852 eulogized Cooper, who had died in September of the previous year; served reluctantly as intermediary in discussions preceding divorce trial of actor Edwin Forrest; visited Europe, Egypt, and the Holy Land. Two-volume edition of the collected poems published in 1854. In 1856 supported Republican John Charles Frémont for president. In 1857–58, traveled in Spain, France, Italy (where he spent time with Nathaniel Hawthorne, Walter Savage Landor, and Robert and Elizabeth Barrett Browning), and England. Became a Unitarian. In February 1860, introduced Abraham Lincoln at Cooper Union. In April, eulogized Washington Irving, who had died the year before. In 1861 advised Lincoln on cabinet appointments; conferred with him a year later in Washington. Elected president of New York Medical College (1862) and president of American Free-Trade League (1863). In 1864, on 70th birthday, honored by "Bryant Festival" at New York's Century Club, with speakers including Bayard Taylor, Oliver Wendell Holmes, George Henry Boker, and Julia Ward Howe. In 1865 wrote poems on death of Lincoln and abolition of slavery. Wife Frances died in July 1866. Sailed in October for Europe, visiting Spain and Italy (where he spent time with Giuseppe Garibaldi, whom he had met years earlier in New York). In 1869 delivered addresses in commemoration of Fitz-Greene Halleck and upon founding of Metropolitan Museum of Art. Published translations of Homer's *Iliad* (1870) and *Odyssey* (1871–72). In 1872 traveled in the Bahamas, Cuba, and Mexico (where he received honors from President Juárez). Prepared final edition of poems in 1876. In final years maintained busy schedule of dinners and addresses; last public address was an oration at unveiling of Mazzini statue in Central Park; died from injuries received in a fall following the ceremony.

GELETT BURGESS (January 30, 1866–September 18, 1951) b. Boston, Massachusetts. Son of Caroline Brooks and Thomas Harvey Burgess; given name Frank Gelett Burgess. Graduated Massachusetts Institute of Technology with engineering degree in 1887. Worked for three years as draftsman for Southern Pacific Railroad; in 1890 became instructor in topographical drawing at University of California at Berkeley. In 1894 named editor of San Francisco society magazine *Wave*; associated with literary group known as Les Jeunes; close friend of Frank Norris. Edited literary magazine *The Lark* (1895–97), where he published humorous drawings and celebrated four-line poem "The Purple Cow." Moved in 1897 to New York City; married actress Estelle Loomis in 1914. Lived in Paris during World War I. Published *The Heart Line* (1907), a novel of San Francisco, but was best known for long series of comic writings and drawings including *Goops and How to Be Them* (1900); *Are You a Bromide? Or, The Sulphitic Theory* (1907); *Blue Goops and Red* (1909); *Burgess Unabridged: A New Dictionary of Words You Have Always Needed* (1914), which coined among other neologisms the word "blurb"; *The Goop Encyclopaedia* (1915); *Why Men Hate Women* (1927); *Look Eleven Years Younger* (1937); *Ladies in Boxes* (1942); and *New Goops: How to Know Them* (1951). Died in Carmel, California.

GEORGE WASHINGTON CABLE (October 12, 1844–January 31, 1925) b. New Orleans, Louisiana. Son of Rebecca Boardman (a New Englander) and George W. Cable (a businessman from an old Virginia slaveholding family). Schooling ended at age 14 due to father's death; thereafter worked to support family. Family left New Orleans in 1863 during Union occupation. Joined 4th Mississippi Cavalry and saw much fighting; was wounded twice. Pursued intense course of self-education, teaching himself French, Latin, and mathematics. At war's end worked briefly as surveyor; contracted malaria and was ill for two years. Married Louise S. Bartlett in 1869; they had seven children. In 1870 began to write columns, articles, and poems for *New Orleans Picayune*; left paper the following year after a quarrel with management. Worked as bookkeeper for firm of cotton factors; eventually resumed writing for *Picayune*, under different management. Contributed fiction, in part based on research in New Orleans city archives, to *Scribner's Monthly*; stories collected in *Old Creole Days* (1879). Devoted himself full-time to writing; literary reputation furthered by historical novel *The Grandissimes* (1880). Historical study *The Creoles of Louisiana* (1884) and political essays (in defense of freedmen's rights, election reform, prison reform, and other causes) collected in *The Silent South* (1885) met with much local opposition; left New Orleans in 1885 and settled in Northampton, Massachusetts. Gave lectures and readings nationwide; toured with Mark Twain 1884–85; published translations of Creole slave songs in *The Century* in 1886. Continued to address political issues in *The Negro Question* (1888) and *The Southern Struggle for Pure Government* (1890). Later fiction included *Dr. Sevier* (1885), *Bonaventure* (1888), *Strange True Stories of Louisiana* (1889), *Strong Hearts* (1899), *Bylow Hill* (1902), *Posson Jone and Père Raphaël* (1909), *Gideon's Band* (1914), *The Flower of the Chapdelaines* (1918), and *Lovers of Louisiana* (1918). First wife, Louise, died in 1904; married Eva C. Stevenson in 1906; after her death in 1923, married Hanna Cowing. Died in St. Petersburg, Florida.

JOSIAH D. CANNING (1816–March 25, 1892) b. Gill, Massachusetts. Son of the Rev. Josiah W. Canning. Informal education in the classics at home. While still in his teens, built his own printing press and taught himself to print; published local newspaper, *The Village Post*. For the next five years, attempted to establish himself as printer, first in Detroit, where his brother Ebenezer was associate editor of the *Detroit Courier*; then in Wheeling, Virginia (now West Virginia), where his brother Edward lived, and finally in the newly established territory of Wisconsin. In 1838 returned to Gill; a farmer most of his life, he also worked over the years as postmaster, town clerk, and treasurer. Published poetry in *The Knickerbocker*, whose editor Louis Gaylord Clarke dubbed him "the Peasant Bard" (a phrase which Canning adopted as pseudonym for several of his books), and in local newspapers and magazines. Published works included *Poems* (1838); *Thanksgiving Eve* (1847); *The Harp and Plow* (1852); *The Shad Fishers*, a self-published pamphlet (1854); and *Connecticut River Reeds* (1892), poems issued posthumously as commemorative volume.

CHARLES EDWARD CARRYL (December 30, 1841–July 3, 1920) b. New York City. Son of Nathan Taylor Carryl. Early education in New York City and at Irving Institute, Tarrytown. Career as officer and director in railroad corporation flourished during the 1860s. Married Mary Wetmore in 1869; they had two children, Constance and Guy (who later became known as writer of fiction, verse, and journalism). In 1874, became member of New York Stock Exchange, retaining seat until 1908; published *The Stock Exchange Primer* in 1882. In his forties began writing juvenile fantasies interspersed with verse in the manner of Lewis Carroll, of which the first was the highly successful *Davy and the Goblin* (1885). Later publications included children's story *The Admiral's Caravan* (1892); *The River Syndicate*, sole attempt at adult fiction (1899); and *Charades by an Idle Man* (1911).

ALICE CARY (April 26, 1820–February 12, 1871) b. Miami Valley, Ohio, near Cincinnati. Daughter of Elizabeth Jessup and Robert Cary (an early settler of Cincinnati). Raised on family farm, the fourth of nine children; received limited education at home. Mother died of tuberculosis in 1835; father remarried two years later; unhappy relationship with stepmother. In 1838, published first poem in Cincinnati newspaper, and continued to make unpaid contributions to periodicals for next decade; began to attract attention with sketches published under pseudonym "Patty Lee" in *The National Era*. Represented (along with her sister Phoebe) in Rufus Griswold's *Female Poets of America* (1848); Edgar Allan Poe praised her contribution "Pictures of Memory" as "the noblest in the book"; visited in Cincinnati by Horace Greeley. *Poems of Alice and Phoebe Cary* published in 1850. Later that year, made a trip to New England and met John Greenleaf Whittier, who had repeatedly invited them (he later commemorated the visit in his poem "The Singer"). Moved to New York in the autumn of 1850; joined the following year by Phoebe and their younger sister Elmina; Alice and Phoebe supported themselves by literary work. Alice published fiction and verse in many periodicals including *Harper's*, *Putnam's*, and *Atlantic Monthly*. Enjoyed success with sketches based on home life in Ohio, collected in *Clovernook* (1852–53) and *Clovernook Children* (1854); other prose works included *Hagar: A Story of Today* (1852), *Married, Not Mated* (1856), *Pictures of Country Life* (1859), and *The Bishop's Son* (1867). A second verse collection, *Lyra and Other Poems* (1852), was followed by *Poems* (1855), *Ballads, Lyrics and Hymns* (1866), and *The Lover's Diary* (1868). In 1856 the Cary sisters bought a house on 20th Street, and their Sunday evening receptions became a highlight of literary and artistic circles, frequented by such figures as Horace Greeley, Bayard Taylor, John Greenleaf Whittier, Thomas Bailey Aldrich, George Ripley, Elizabeth

Cady Stanton, and P. T. Barnum. In addition to literary work, was first president of women's club Sorosis; active in many social causes, including abolition and women's rights; with Phoebe, briefly assisted Susan B. Anthony in editing suffrage paper *The Revolution*. Died after many years as an invalid during which she was cared for by Phoebe. *The Last Poems of Alice and Phoebe Cary*, edited by Mary Clemmer Ames, appeared in 1873.

PHOEBE CARY (September 4, 1824–July 31, 1871) b. Miami Valley, Ohio. Younger sister of Alice Cary; educated at home, as was her sister. Contributed to 1850 collection *Poems of Alice and Phoebe Cary*. After moving New York in 1851 to join Alice, assumed most domestic responsibilities and took care of Alice, who was often in ill health; with Alice, presided over renowned weekly salon; close friendship with P. T. Barnum. Published two volumes of poems independently of her sister, *Poems and Parodies* (1854) and *Poems of Faith, Hope and Love* (1869). With Alice, briefly assisted Susan B. Anthony in editing suffrage paper *The Revolution*. Assisted C. F. Deems in editing *Hymns for All Christians* in 1869. Celebrated as wit; also known for religious verse. Published tribute to Alice, "Light," after the latter's death in early 1871; died five months after her sister. Her late work was collected in *The Last Poems of Alice and Phoebe Cary* (1873), edited by Mary Clemmer Ames.

MADISON CAWEIN (March 23, 1865–December 8, 1914) b. Louisville, Kentucky. Full name Madison Julius Cawein; father William Cawein, a German of Huguenot ancestry who arrived in America in the 1840s, was a herbalist and maker of patent medicines; mother Christiana Stelsly, whose parents were German immigrants, was a spiritualist who believed herself endowed with mediumistic gifts. Apart from three years in New Albany, Indiana, as an adolescent, lived all his life in Louisville. Following graduation in 1886 from local high school, worked for six years as cashier in local pool hall, which was also center for legal off-track betting. At 22 published first collection of poetry, *Blooms of the Berry* (1887). Book was reviewed favorably by William Dean Howells in *Harper's Monthly*; Cawein dedicated second volume, *The Triumph of Music* (1888), to Howells. Supporting himself through real estate and stock market speculation, published 36 volumes of poetry, including *Ascolon of Gaul* (1889), *Lyrics and Idyls* (1890), *Days and Dreams* (1891), *Red Leaves and Roses* (1893), *The Garden of Dreams* (1896), *Idyllic Monologues* (1898), *Weeds by the Wall* (1901), *A Voice on the Wind* (1902), *Vale of Tempe* (1905), *The Message of the Lilies* (1913), and *Minions of the Moon* (1913). Much of his poetry made use of detailed knowledge of Kentucky natural history. Maintained literary friendships with Edwin Arlington Robinson, Henry van Dyke, and James Whitcomb Riley; received belated recognition when Edmund Gosse prepared British collection of his work, *Kentucky Poems*, in 1902. In 1903 married Gertrude Foster McKelvey; they had one son, Preston. Suffered heavy financial losses in San Francisco earthquake in 1906. Five-volume illustrated edition of his work, *The Poems of Madison Cawein*, appeared in 1907. Died as a result of apoplectic attack in which he fell and hit his head on bathtub railing.

WILLIAM ELLERY CHANNING (November 29, 1818–December 23, 1901) b. Boston, Massachusetts. Son of Barbara Perkins and Dr. Walter Channing (distinguished surgeon and Harvard professor); nephew of the Unitarian clergyman of the same name. Following his mother's death in 1823, raised in household of great-aunt Mrs. Bennett Forbes (born Margaret Perkins) in Milton, Massachusetts. Early education at Round Hill School (Northampton), the Boston Latin School, and Hubbard's Academy in Brookline. Entered Harvard College in 1834, but left after only a few months to devote himself to poetry. Began publishing poems, essays, and sketches in 1835 in the Boston *Mercantile Journal* and *New England Magazine*. Continued studies on his own; family distressed that he had not secured a vocation. In 1839 purchased a farm in McHenry County, Illinois, and relocated there, returning home for occasional visits. Emerson reviewed his verses favorably in *The Dial* in 1840; the two men met in December while Channing was visiting from Illinois. In 1841, sold Illinois farm and moved to Cincinnati where he worked as tutor and journalist, and read desultorily for law; met Ellen Fuller (sister of Margaret Fuller), whom he married in September 1841 against the wishes of his family; the couple had two daughters and three sons. Returned to Massachusetts in 1842, living for a short time in Cambridge before settling with Ellen in Concord. During 1844–45, worked in New York on editorial staff of Horace Greeley's *New-York Tribune*; traveled briefly to Italy from March to July of 1846; published book based on 16-day stay in Rome, *Conversations in Rome between an Artist, a Catholic, and a Critic* (1847). Marriage troubled by Channing's neglect of family responsibilities; Ellen left him in 1853, returned in 1855, and died in 1856. Children reared by relatives as Channing lived alone in Concord, virtually cut off from family. Edited *New Bedford Mercury*, 1856–58. Continued friendship with Emerson; other friends included Nathaniel Hawthorne, Margaret Fuller, Bronson Alcott, James Russell Lowell, and especially Henry David Thoreau, whom he accompanied on trips to Cape Cod, Maine, and Canada, and on frequent excursions around Concord. (Wrote first biography of Thoreau, *Thoreau, The Poet-Naturalist*, 1873; edited a number of Thoreau's works in collaboration with Thoreau's sister Sophia.) Last years spent in the home of his friend Franklin B. Sanborn. Published verse collections *Poems* (1843), *Poems, Second Series* (1847), and *The Woodman* (1849), and book-length poems *Near Home* (1858), *The Wanderer* (1871), *Eliot* (1885), and *John Brown and the Heroes of Harper's Ferry* (1886).

JOHN JAY CHAPMAN (March 2, 1862–November 4, 1933) b. New York, New York. Son of Eleanor Jay and Henry Grafton Chapman. Graduated Harvard 1885; attended Harvard Law School. In 1887 deliberately burned left hand (necessitating amputation) as self-punishment for having beaten another young man in fit of misguided jealousy after he had shown attention to Minna Timmins of Boston. Married Minna in 1889, and settled in New York; she died in 1897, shortly after birth of their third son. Involved in political opposition to Tammany Hall as member of City Reform Club, founded by Theodore Roosevelt. Published first book, *Emerson and Other Essays*, in 1898, followed by political writings collected in *Causes and Consequences* (1898) and *Practical Agitation* (1900). Broke with Theodore Roosevelt when Roosevelt repudiated Independent candidacy in favor of Republican nomination for New York governorship. Ended law practice in 1898. In April 1898 married second wife, Elizabeth Chanler of New York; son Chanler born 1900; shortly thereafter Chapman suffered serious mental breakdown and spent years recuperating, chiefly at Chanler family estate in Barrytown, New York, where he lived much of the time after 1905. In 1912 held public prayer meeting in Coatesville, Pennsylvania, on first anniversary of the lynching of a black man there. Wrote literary criticism, essays, and translations, as well as plays and poems. Friend of Owen Wister. Later publications included *Four Plays for Children* (1908), plays *The Maid's Forgiveness* (1908), *A Sausage from Bologna* (1909), and *Benedict Arnold, A Play for a Greek Theatre* (1911), *Learning and Other Essays* (1911), *Neptune's Isle* (1912), *William Lloyd Garrison* (1913), poetry collection *Homeric Scenes* (1914), *Memories and Milestones* (1915), *Deutschland über Alles* (1915), *Notes on Religion* (1915), *Greek Genius and Other Essays* (1915), *Songs and Poems* (1919), *A Glance Toward Shakespeare* (1922), and *Letters and Religion* (1924). Son Victor, a pilot in the Lafayette Escadrille, was the first American aviator to die in World War I. In later years adopted conservative positions, including militant opposition to Roman Catholic influence in American life and politics.

LYDIA MARIA CHILD (February 11, 1802 – October 20, 1880) b. Medford, Massachusetts. Daughter of Susannah Rand and Convers Francis (a baker); sister of prominent Unitarian minister Convers Francis. After mother's death in 1814, sent to live with older sister in Norridgewock, Maine. Moved to Boston in 1821 to rejoin brother Convers; met Emerson, then a student at Harvard; developed interest in Swedenborgianism, joining Boston Society of the New Jerusalem in 1822. *Hobomok* (1824), novel about Indians in 17th-century New England, established reputation as writer; she became acquainted with literary figures including George Ticknor, William Ellery Channing, and Nathaniel P. Willis. A second novel, *The Rebels, or Boston Before the Revolution* (1825), was less well received. Edited first American children's magazine, *The Juvenile Miscellany* (1826–29); during same period ran private school in Watertown, Massachusetts; made acquaintance of Margaret Fuller. Married David Lee Child, lawyer and newspaper editor, in 1828; they had no children. Wrote financially successful household manual *The Frugal Housewife* (1829). Husband's financial difficulties resulted in his being briefly jailed for debt in 1830. Along with her husband, became increasingly involved in abolitionist movement, and published series of controversial anti-slavery works: *An Appeal in Favor of That Class of Americans Called Africans* (1833), *The Oasis* (1834), and *An Anti-Slavery Catechism* (1836). In the same period published two-volume *History of the Condition of Women in Various Ages and Nations* (1835) and *Philothea* (1836), philosophical novel set in ancient Athens. Moved to New York to edit *The National Anti-Slavery Standard* (1841–44), boarding with family of abolitionist Isaac T. Hopper; newspaper articles collected in successful *Letters from New York* (1843); resigned from *Standard* following disagreements with other abolitionists. Remaining in New York, enjoyed renewed friendship with Margaret Fuller. In 1850 reunited with husband (who had undergone continual financial problems, and whom she had seen only sporadically since coming to New York) and returned with him to Massachusetts. After many years of work, published three-volume history *The Progress of Religious Ideas Through Successive Ages* in 1855. In October 1859, following John Brown's raid on Harpers Ferry, offered to help nurse Brown in prison; resulting controversy summarized in *Correspondence Between Lydia Maria Child, Governor Wise, and Mrs. Mason* (1860). Edited and wrote introduction for fugitive slave Harriet Jacobs' *Incidents in the Life of a Slave Girl* (1860); also published *The Duty of Disobedience to the Fugitive Slave Act* (1860) and *The Right Way, the Safe Way* (1860), pamphlet urging freeing of slaves. In 1865 published *Looking Toward Sunset*, anthology of prose and poetry for the elderly, and *The Freedmen's Book*, collection of educational readings intended for emancipated slaves. Closely involved in politics of Reconstruction under Johnson and Grant administrations. *A Romance of the Republic* (1867) gave fictional account of mulatto life in New Orleans. Husband David died in 1874. Final book, religious anthology *Aspirations of the World*, published 1878.

THOMAS HOLLEY CHIVERS (October 18, 1809–December 18, 1858) b. on cotton plantation near Washington, Georgia; son of a Miss Digby and wealthy landholder and slave-owner Colonel Robert Chivers. Married cousin Frances Chivers in 1827; deserted by wife within first year of marriage while she was pregnant with daughter Frances, whom he never met; series of lawsuits followed on both sides, including unsuccessful suit by Chivers for divorce. Graduated from Transylvania University in Kentucky with medical degree in 1830; soon gave up medicine to pursue literary career. While recuperating from illness, reported having vision of fountain of water and angels playing harps. Unhappy marital experience provided basis for first book of poetry, *The Path of Sorrow, or the Lament of Youth* (1832), published, like all of Chivers' books, at his own expense. In 1831–34 traveled in Mississippi Valley, Cherokee Nation, Cincinnati, St. Louis, New York, and Philadelphia; published *Conrad and Eudora* (1834), drama based on so-called "Kentucky tragedy," the Sharpe-Beauchamp murder of 1826; volume also contained 29 poems. Returned to Georgia, 1835–36. Married Harriette Hunt, 18-year-old jeweler's daughter from Springfield, Massachusetts, in New York in 1837 (divorce from first wife, Frances, not final until 1842, but marriage legal under Georgia law); with second wife had five children. The couple lived in New York City and Middletown, Connecticut, until 1842. Next poetic collection, *Nacoochee; or The Beautiful Star* (1837), contained preface formulating his view of poetry: "Poetry is that crystal river of the soul which runs through all the avenues of life, and after purifying the affections of the heart, empties itself into the Sea of God." Began long-term correspondence with Edgar Allan Poe beginning in 1840; Poe published several of Chivers' poems in *Graham's Magazine*. Returned to Georgia in 1842; daughter Allegra Florence died in

October of that year, a tragedy commemorated in the elegies of *The Lost Pleiad* (1845). While visiting New York in 1845 to arrange for the book's publication, met Poe on several occasions. In 1848 three of his other children died in rapid succession. Became increasingly interested in mystical experience and Swedenborgianism; published prose treatise *Search After Truth; or, A New Revelation of the Psycho-Physiological Nature of Man* (1848); contributed poetry and visionary prose to *The Univercoelum* (1848–49), periodical devoted to ideas of mesmerist Andrew Jackson Davis (known as "the Poughkeepsie seer"). After Poe's death in 1849, worked on a never-completed biography of Poe (first published 1952). Literary correspondent to *The Georgia Citizen*, 1850–54. Later volumes (some of whose contents were written decades earlier) were poetic collections *Eonchs of Ruby, A Gift of Love* (1851); *Memoralia; or, Phials of Amber Full of the Tears of Love* (1853) and *Virginalia; or, Songs of My Summer Nights* (1853), the long poem *Atlanta: or The True Blessed Island of Poesy, A Paul Epic—In Three Lustra* (1853), the play *The Sons of Usna: a TragiApotheosis* (1854, published 1858), and a patriotic poem, *Birth-Day Song of Liberty* (1856). In 1853 published articles in *The Waverley Magazine* charging Poe with having plagiarized his work; heated tone of articles led to protracted controversy and attacks on Chivers by other writers. Spent much time in New York and Connecticut in later years. Returned to Georgia three years before his death, and moved from Washington to Decatur, where he died.

THOMAS COLE (February 1, 1801–February 11, 1848) b. Bolton-le-Moor, Lancashire, England, seventh of eight children of Mary and James Cole, unsuccessful woolen manufacturer. Attended school in Chester. From around 1815 worked in Liverpool as engraver's assistant; became engraver of designs for calico. Immigrated with family to America in 1819. Worked as wood engraver in Philadelphia, where father opened dry goods shop. Traveled in St. Eustatius in West Indies, then rejoined family in Steubenville, Ohio, where he assisted father in manufacturing wallpaper. After unsuccessful attempts to support himself as itinerant portraitist, stayed with family briefly at new home in Pittsburgh; returned to Philadelphia in 1823 for two years of study at Philadelphia Academy of Fine Arts. Wrote poetry and fiction, some published in *Saturday Evening Post*. Rejoined family in New York City in 1825, painting in their house on Greenwich Street. Made sketching trips to Weehawken, the Palisades, the Highlands, and elsewhere in Hudson River Valley. Met and received encouragement from artists John Trumbull, William Dunlap, and Asher B. Durand; rapidly achieved celebrity for paintings of American landscapes. Spent winters painting and exhibiting in New York City, his summers traveling and sketching in the Hudson Valley and elsewhere. As member of Bread and Cheese Club, associated with William Cullen Bryant, Samuel F. B. Morse, Asher B. Durand, James Fenimore Cooper; contributed art to Bryant's periodical *The Talisman*. Traveled in Europe, 1829–32; in England, visited poet Samuel Rogers and painters Thomas Lawrence, J. M. W. Turner, John Constable, and John Martin; paintings exhibited at Royal Academy and British Institution. Toured France and Italy; in Rome used Claude Lorrain's old studio and associated with Samuel F. B. Morse and Horatio Greenough. Between 1833 and 1836 painted allegorical series "The Course of Empire," praised as his masterpiece by Cooper and others. Married Maria Bartow in November 1836; settled in Catskill, New York. In 1840 completed four-part allegory "The Voyage of Life" and "The Architect's Dream," fanciful combination of Egyptian, Greek, Roman, Moorish, and Gothic styles. In 1841 traveled again to Europe, returning to Catskill the following year. Accepted Frederick Edwin Church as student in 1844. Died in Catskill of lung inflammation while working on uncompleted allegorical series "The Cross and the World."

HARRIET MAXWELL CONVERSE (1836–November 18, 1903) b. Elmira, New York. Daughter of Marie Purdy and Thomas Maxwell, a New York assemblyman and congressman. In 1861, after death of first husband, married Frank Buchanan Converse, inventor and musician. After five years of travel in Asia, Africa, and Europe, took up residence in New York. Published collection of poetry, *Sheaves* (1882); contributed regularly to periodicals in America and Great Britain. Beginning in early 1880s, devoted herself to study of Indians of New York; in 1885 adopted into Snipe Clan on Cattaraugus Reservation in western New York. Helped defeat legislation unfavorable to the Iroquois in 1891, and was made legal member of Iroquois Nation. Collected artifacts for New York State Museum, the Peabody, and American Museum of Natural History. *Myths and Legends of the New York State Iroquois* published posthumously in 1908.

PHILIP PENDLETON COOKE (October 26, 1816–January 20, 1850) b. Martinsburg, Virginia (now West Virginia). Son of Maria Pendleton and John Rogers Cooke (a prominent lawyer); brother of novelist John Esten Cooke and cousin of novelist John Pendleton Kennedy. As undergraduate at Princeton, began writing poems that were published in *The Knickerbocker* in 1833. Graduated 1834 and returned to family estate Glengary; studied law with father; admitted to bar before age 21. Contributed poetry and critical essays on English poets to *Southern Literary Messenger*, 1835–36. In 1837 married Willianne Burwell; they had five children. Father lost fortune in financial panic of 1837; Glengary burned two years later. Practiced law in Martinsburg. Best-known poem "Florence Vane" published (under editorial auspices of Edgar Allan Poe) in *Burton's Gentleman's Magazine* in 1840. Work praised by Poe (in *The Broadway Journal*) as "exquisitely graceful and delicate"; included in new edition of Rufus Griswold's *Poets and Poetry of America*. Wife inherited 1,000-acre estate ("Vineyard") near Winchester in 1845. Only published volume of poetry, *Froissart Ballads and Other Poems*, appeared 1847. In last years devoted himself mostly to prose tales published in *Southern Literary Messenger*, including "John Carper, the Hunter of Lost River," "The Two Country Houses," "The Gregories of Hackwood," and "The Crime of Andrew Blair," and only novel *The Chevalier Merlin* (left unfinished at his death). Favorite pursuit apart from writing was hunting. Died of pneumonia contracted on a hunting trip.

ROSE TERRY COOKE (February 17, 1827–July 18, 1892) b. West Hartford, Connecticut. Elder of two daughters of Anne Hurlbut and Henry Wadsworth Terry. At age six, moved with family into the Wadsworth mansion, owned by paternal grandmother, in Hartford. Educated Hartford Female Seminary, graduating 1843; officially joined Congregational Church. Taught briefly in Hartford and then for four years at a Presbyterian church school in Burlington, New Jersey, where she also worked as governess for the minister's family. In 1848, received inheritance from a great uncle, which enabled her to devote herself to writing poetry and fiction, and to establish a home in Hartford. In 1852, began publishing poems in the *New-York Tribune*, where Charles A. Dana was editor. Beginning in 1855—though earlier stories may have appeared pseudonymously—Cooke published short stories in various periodicals, including *Harper's*, *Putnam's*, *The Galaxy*, and *Atlantic Monthly*, whose inaugural issue in November 1857 carried her story "Sally Parson's Duty." In the late 1850s, after her sister Alice fell ill, reared her two children. *Poems*, first verse collection, published 1861. In April 1873 married Rollin H. Cooke, a widower (with two children) 16 years younger than her. Moved to Winsted, Connecticut, where she continued to write and where husband worked in a bank. Writing helped support the family, which suffered financial setbacks as result of husband's and father-in-law's business failures. Close friend of Harriet Prescott Spofford and James T. and Annie Fields; work admired by William Dean Howells. Wrote two adult novels, *Happy Dodd* (1878) and *Steadfast* (1889), and one novel for children, *No* (1886). Many of her stories collected in *Somebody's Neighbors* (1881), *Root-Bound and Other Sketches* (1885), *The Sphinx's Children and Other People's* (1886), and *Huckleberries Gathered from New England Hills* (1891). Invited to read her poetry at Smith College commencement exercises in 1881; *Poems*, an expanded collection, published 1888. Family moved again in 1887 to Pittsfield, Massachusetts. Cooke died after suffering several serious bouts of influenza.

CHRISTOPHER PEARSE CRANCH (March 8, 1813–January 20, 1892) b. Arlington, Virginia (then part of District of Columbia). Son of Anna Greenleaf and William Cranch (a federal judge and Supreme Court reporter); aunt, Rebecca Greenleaf, was married to Noah Webster; grandmother, Mary Smith, was sister of Abigail Adams. Received early training as draftsman. Graduated from Columbian College (now George Washington University) in 1831 and from Harvard Divinity School in 1835 (classmates included Charles Timothy Brooks and Theodore Parker). As an itinerant Unitarian minister preached in Andover, Bangor, and Portland, Maine, and in Boston, Richmond, St. Louis (home of cousin William Greenleaf Eliot, grandfather of T. S. Eliot), Cincinnati, Peoria, Louisville, and elsewhere. While preaching in Louisville, 1837–38, assisted James Freeman Clarke in editing *The Western Messenger*, Unitarian journal associated with the Transcendentalists, to which

oetry and articles. In Boston in 1840, met Emerson (who
of his poems in *The Dial*) and became frequent visitor at
inity Brook Farm. Married a cousin, Elizabeth de Windt
ughter of John Adams), in 1843; they had two daughters and a
dicated to Emerson, published in 1844. Moved to New York to
begin care.. is landscape painter. Traveled with his wife and author George
William Curtis to Italy in 1846; remained there for three years, studying art
and spending time with Robert and Elizabeth Barrett Browning, Margaret
Fuller, William Wetmore Story, and others. After four years in New York,
family moved in 1853 to Paris, where Cranch painted and cultivated many
acquaintances, including friendship with James Russell Lowell; exhibited
paintings in Paris. Returned to the U.S. in 1863, following death of son
George in Civil War. Elected to National Academy of Design in 1864, and
contributed to its exhibitions for a number of years. After period of residence
on Staten Island settled in 1873 in Cambridge, Massachusetts. In 1880, made
last trip to Europe; met Frank Duveneck, who painted his portrait. Later
verse collected in *Satan: A Libretto* (1874), *The Bird and the Bell* (1875), and
Ariel and Caliban (1887); also published children's books *The Last of the Hug-
germuggers* (1856) and *Kobboltozo* (1857), and a blank verse translation of *The
Aeneid* (1842).

STEPHEN CRANE (November 1, 1871 – June 5, 1900) b. Newark, New Jer-
sey. Youngest of 14 children of Mary Helen Peck and the Rev. Jonathan Town-
ley Crane (who died in 1880). Early education at Hudson River Institute,
Claverack, New York. In 1890–91, studied at Lafayette College and Syracuse
University; left school to become a writer, working first as journalist; met
Hamlin Garland. Mother died 1891; Crane established base in New York City.
Wrote articles, poems, stories, and the novella *Maggie: A Girl of the Streets*
(privately printed 1893), which won the admiration of Garland, who drew it to
the attention of William Dean Howells. *The Red Badge of Courage* appeared in
abridged form as a syndicated newspaper serial in 1894; revised extensively by
Crane before book publication in October 1895; became a bestseller and es-
tablished his reputation as a writer. Published revised version of *Maggie*
(1896), novels *George's Mother* (1896) and *The Third Violet* (1897); collection
of stories, *The Little Regiment and Other Episodes of the American Civil War*
(1896); poetry collected in *The Black Riders and Other Lines* (1895) and *War
Is Kind* (1899). As syndicated newswriter, traveled to Mexico and the Ameri-
can West in 1895. In 1896, traveled by way of Florida to cover Cuban Revolu-
tion; met Cora Howorth Steward, proprietor of Hotel de Dream in
Jacksonville. Shipwrecked in January 1897 off Florida coast (incident became
basis for story "The Open Boat"). Traveled to Greece (where he was joined
by Cora) to cover Greek-Turkish War; he and Cora traveled to England as
husband and wife in 1897; friends in England included Joseph Conrad, Henry
James, Ford Madox Ford, Harold Frederic, and H. G. Wells. Went to Cuba
in 1898 to cover Spanish-American War. In 1899 Crane and Cora returned to
England where they rented ancient manor house Brede Place in Sussex. Con-

tinued to publish articles, stories, and poems despite ill health; last publications included *The Open Boat and Other Tales of Adventure* (1898), *Active Service* (1899), *The Monster and Other Stories* (1899), and *Whilomville Stories* (1900). Died of tuberculosis at sanatorium in the Black Forest, Germany.

FRANK HAMILTON CUSHING (July 22, 1857–April 10, 1900) b. North East, Pennsylvania. Son of Sarah Ann Harding and Thomas Cushing, a doctor. When he was three, family moved to Barre Center, New York. Studied natural science briefly at Cornell University. Hired in 1875 as a research assistant by the Smithsonian, and conducted several archaeological digs; presented papers before Anthropological Society of Washington. Oversaw ethnological exhibit at Centennial Exposition of 1876. In 1879, appointed to Bureau of Ethnology by John Wesley Powell. Spent five years studying the Zuni in New Mexico; admitted to Bow Priesthood and given Zuni name Tenatsali (Medicine Flower). Explored archaeological sites in Salt River Valley, Arizona, and Key Marco, Florida. Publications included "My Adventures in Zuñi" (1882–83), *Zuñi Fetiches* (1883), *A Study of Pueblo Pottery* (1886), *Outlines of Zuñi Creation Myths* (1896), *Exploration of Ancient Key Dwellers' Remains of the Gulf Coast of Florida* (1896), and the posthumously published *Zuñi Folk Tales* (1901) and *Zuñi Breadstuff* (1920).

RICHARD HENRY DANA (November 15, 1787–February 2, 1879) b. Cambridge, Massachusetts. Son of Elizabeth Ellery (daughter of William Ellery, signer of Declaration of Independence, and a descendant of Anne Bradstreet) and Francis Dana (diplomat and jurist); close relationship with maternal grandfather William Ellery. Educated in Newport, Rhode Island, before entering Harvard in 1804; expelled in 1807 for participation in dining hall riot (known as "Rotten Cabbage Rebellion"). Under pressure of family financial difficulties decided to enter legal profession; from 1809 studied law in offices of cousin Francis Dana Channing; admitted to bar 1812, and began practice in Sutton, Massachusetts (he abandoned his largely unsuccessful legal career in 1819). In 1813 moved to Cambridgeport and married schoolteacher Ruth Charlotte Smith; they had four children (including Richard Jr., author of *Two Years Before the Mast*). From 1818 served as assistant editor of *North America Review* under his cousin Edward Tyrrel Channing; contributed literary criticism, including reviews of Washington Allston, William Hazlitt, and Washington Irving. Left staff of *Review* when, following Channing's resignation, he was passed over for editorship in favor of Edward Everett in 1819. In 1821, founded short-lived literary magazine *The Idle Man* in New York, with contributors including Washington Allston (college friend of Dana's brother Edmund) and close friend William Cullen Bryant. His wife and infant daughter died in 1822, and he discontinued publication of *The Idle Man*; last issue contained story "Paul Felton," criticized for its morbid tone. Converted to Congregationalism in 1826 under influence of Lyman Beecher, and became involved in controversy between Congregationalists and Unitarians in Cambridge. Sister Martha married Washington Allston in 1830. Poems, essays, and fiction appeared in Bryant's *New York Review* and other periodicals; published *The Buccaneer and Other Poems* (1827) and *Poems and Prose Writings* (1833). From 1835 taught classes for women on English literature; lectured on Shakespeare in Providence in 1838. Confirmed as Episcopalian in 1843, and the following year was a founder and senior warden of the Church of the Advent (first American church to embrace the Anglo-Catholic movement). After lecture series in 1849 and 1850 and publication of second edition of *Poems and Prose Writings* (1850), spent later life in retirement in Boston, Cambridge, and Cape Ann.

EMILY DICKINSON (December 10, 1830–May 15, 1886) b. Emily Elizabeth Dickinson in Amherst, Massachusetts. Second of three children of Emily Norcross and Edward Dickinson (prominent lawyer who later served as state senator and national congressman); paternal grandfather Samuel Fowler Dickinson was a founder of Amherst College; siblings were older brother William Austin and younger sister Lavinia. Educated at Amherst Academy, 1840–46. In 1844 spent a month in Boston with mother's sister Lavinia to recover from ill health and depression following death of friend Sophia Holland. Attended Mount Holyoke Female Seminary in South Hadley, Massachusetts, 1847–48. Returned to family home, the Homestead, and lived there permanently, rarely leaving except for trips to Washington (where her father was serving a term in Congress) and Philadelphia in 1855 and in 1864–65 to Boston and Cambridge (where she spent seven months undergoing treatment for eye problems). Resisted the influence of local religious revivals in which other family members and friends (including Lavinia, Austin, and Austin's future wife Susan Gilbert) became involved. Cultivated intense intellectual friendships with several men including Benjamin F. Newton (a law clerk in her father's office) and the Rev. Charles Wadsworth (with whom she appears to have had close personal relationship). Composed over 1,700 brief lyrics, most intensively in the years 1859–65; only a few were published, primarily in the *Springfield Daily Republican*, during her lifetime (most without her consent and in heavily edited form). In 1858 she began binding her poems into what her editor Mabel Loomis Todd later termed "fascicles": homemade booklets made from folded stationery paper stitched together with thread. In April 1862, initiated literary correspondence with Thomas Wentworth Higginson, whom she knew only through his work in *Atlantic Monthly* (first letter began: "Are you too deeply occupied to say if my Verse is alive?"). They continued to write to each other for more than 20 years; he discouraged her from publishing her work; she received several visits from Higginson in the 1870s. Small circle of friends to whom she occasionally showed poems included Samuel Bowles, Josiah Gilbert Holland and his wife Elizabeth (with whom she had a long correspondence), and Helen Hunt Jackson. Close relationship with Judge Otis Lord, with whom she corresponded extensively. Brother Austin married Susan Gilbert in 1856, and they settled in the house next door to the Homestead, the Evergreens. Father died in 1874, and mother's health declined. In later years rarely left house. Fell ill in June 1884, and never fully recovered; Helen Hunt Jackson asked to be made her literary executor, but died before Dickinson, in 1885. After her death, sister Lavinia found 40 fascicles of poems, along with many unstitched and loose pages, and with Mabel Loomis Todd, Higginson helped prepare *Poems by Emily Dickinson* (1890) and *Poems: Second Series* (1891); *Poems: Third Series*, edited by Todd, appeared in 1896.

SAMUEL HENRY DICKSON (September 20, 1798–March 31, 1872) b. Charleston, South Carolina. Son of Mary Neilson and Samuel Dickson (a schoolmaster), Presbyterians who had emigrated from Belfast, Ireland, before American Revolution. Graduated Yale College 1814. Studied medicine with Dr. Philip Gendron Prioleau; practiced during yellow fever epidemic of 1817; received medical degree from University of Pennsylvania in 1819. Practiced in Charleston, primarily among yellow fever patients. Lectured on physiology; participated in founding of medical college in Charleston, of which he was made professor of medicine. Resigned after disagreement with college; in 1833 founded Medical College of South Carolina. Achieved minor literary celebrity for poem "I Sigh for the Land of the Cypress and Pine," written in 1830. Close friend of William Gilmore Simms, who dedicated *The Yemassee* (1835) to him. First wife, Elizabeth Brownlee Robertson, died in 1832; two years later married her sister Jane Robertson, who died in 1842; in 1845 married Marie Seabrook DePre. *Poems* appeared in privately printed edition in 1844; reviewed in *Southern Literary Messenger*. Pamphlet *Essays on Slavery* (1845) defended institution and asserted racial inferiority of blacks. In 1847 became professor of practice of medicine at New York University; after three years returned to former professorship in Charleston. Was among group of writers associated with Russell's Bookstore in Charleston during 1850s. Returned in 1858 to Philadelphia, assuming professorship at Jefferson Medical College, and remained at post until shortly before his death. Wrote and lectured prolifically on medicine and other topics, including early contributions to anthropometry (comparison of body measurements). Medical works included *Manual of Pathology and Practice* (1839), *Essays on Pathology and Therapeutics* (1845), *Essays on Life, Sleep, Pain, Intellection, and Hygiene* (1852), *Elements of Medicine* (1855) and *Studies in Pathology and Therapeutics* (1867).

JOSEPH RODMAN DRAKE (August 7, 1795–September 21, 1820) b. New York City. Fourth child and only son of Hannah Lawrence (of Flushing, Long Island) and Jonathan Drake (a dry goods merchant). Shortly after Drake's birth, father suffered financial ruin after investing in fraudulent "Yazoo" land companies, leaving family impoverished; he died in 1797. In 1809, mother married widower Robert Muir Welman, a merchant, and moved with him (and two of her daughters) to New Orleans. Drake remained in New York with sister Caroline under guardianship of relatives in Hunts Point in the Bronx; took position as clerk in mercantile house of Norris L. Martin. In 1813 began studying medicine, supported by great-uncle Colonel Joseph Drake; established friendship with James Ellsworth De Kay, physician and naturalist, who introduced him to poet Fitz-Greene Halleck; Drake and Halleck became close friends and literary associates (the two were described after Drake's death as "the Damon and Pythias of American letters"). In 1816 awarded medical degree from Queens College in New Brunswick, New Jersey (later Rutgers College); began private practice in New York. Later the same year married Sarah Eckford, daughter of prosperous Scottish-born shipbuilder and naval architect Henry Eckford; father-in-law enjoyed literary company, and his house in Love Lane (present-day West 24th St.) served as gathering place for Drake, Halleck, De Kay, and others. In 1816 Drake's poem "The Culprit Fay" (fairy fantasy set along the Hudson near West Point) was, according to Halleck, "written, begun and finished, in three days." In 1818 traveled with wife to Europe, visiting Great Britain, France, and Holland. After return to New York in fall of 1818, initiated "The Croakers," series of pseudonymous satirical poems dealing with political, social, and theatrical life of New York City; Halleck joined him as collaborator; the poems appeared throughout spring and summer in New York *Evening Post*, and were collected in a volume late in 1819. During same year, opened drugstore in partnership with William Langstaff. Began to suffer symptoms of tuberculosis, and in an effort to regain health visited sisters in New Orleans, March–April 1820. Died on September 21 at his New York home. (On deathbed, said to have asked De Kay to burn unpublished poems. In 1821 Halleck published elegy "On the Death of Joseph Rodman Drake" in a New York literary magazine. *The Culprit Fay and Other Poems*, edited by daughter Janet Halleck Drake, was published in 1835.)

PAUL LAURENCE DUNBAR (June 27, 1872–February 9, 1906) b. Dayton, Ohio. Only child of former Kentucky slaves Matilda Murphy and Joshua Dunbar. Father had escaped to Canada before Civil War, in which he served with Massachusetts 55th Regiment; mother had two sons from a previous marriage. Parents separated shortly after Dunbar's birth and divorced in 1876; he remained with mother, a laundry worker, who taught him to read and encouraged his literary efforts. Educated at Dayton's public schools; graduated in 1891 from Central High School, where he was editor of the school paper, class poet, and only black member of his class. Wrote poetry from early age; first published poem appeared in *Dayton Herald* in 1888; while still in high school founded short-lived newspaper *The Dayton Tattler*, printed by classmate and future aviator Orville Wright. Worked as elevator operator in Dayton while continuing to publish poems and stories in local newspapers. In 1892 invited by former teacher Helen Truesdale to address Western Association of Writers; asked to become member. After newspaper accounts of his poetry, received letter of encouragement from James Whitcomb Riley. Published chapbook *Oak and Ivy* (1893) at his own expense; book sold well enough to reimburse printing costs. Found work as page at Dayton courthouse; received encouragement from white patrons James Newton Matthews, Charles A. Thatcher, and Henry A. Tobey; gave paid public readings of his work. Employed by Frederick Douglass in 1893 as clerk at Haiti Building of World's Columbian Exposition in Chicago; in Chicago met wide circle of black writers and activists including Angelina Grimké, Ida B. Wells, James Campbell, and composer Will Marion Cook. Work began to appear in *The Century*, *The New York Times*, and other leading publications. Second book, *Majors and Minors* (1895), praised in *Harper's* by William Dean Howells, who called Dunbar "the only man of pure African blood and of American civilization to feel the negro life aesthetically and express it lyrically." Howells' review made Dunbar suddenly famous. Signed with Pond Lecture Bureau and through Pond's efforts secured contract with Dodd, Mead for next collection, *Lyrics of Lowly Life* (1896), which sold well. Went to England in February 1897 on reading tour; major reading in London set up by American ambassador John Hay. Returned to U.S. after six months and in 1897 moved to Washington, D.C., to assume post as reading room clerk at Library of Congress. In March 1898 married poet and teacher Alice Ruth Moore, with whom he had corresponded for a number of years. Published short story collection *Folks from Dixie* (1898) and first novel, *The Uncalled* (1898). Literary success made it possible for him to resign job at library; gave numerous readings; also contributed lyrics and librettos to musical comedies. Had busy social life in Washington; involved in fundraising for Hampton Institute; appeared in Boston with W.E.B. DuBois and Booker T. Washington at benefit for Tuskegee Institute. Received honorary degree from Atlanta University in 1899. On reading tour to promote *Lyrics of the Hearthside* (1899), contracted pneumonia; diagnosed with tuberculosis; health problems compounded by heavy drinking. Settled briefly in Harmon, Colorado, to recuperate. Continued to give public readings and produced further novels (*The Love of Landry*, 1900, *The Fanatics*, 1901, and *The Sport of the Gods*, 1902), story collections *The Strength of Gideon and Other Stories*, 1900, *In Old Plantation Days*, 1903, and *The Heart of Happy Hollow*, 1904), and volumes of verse (*Lyrics of Love and Laughter*, 1903, and *Lyrics of Sunshine and Shadow*, 1905). In 1900 stayed with James Weldon Johnson in Jacksonville, Florida, while recovering from physical breakdown. Separated from wife in 1902; after leaving Washington spent time in New York and Chicago before returning in 1903 to spend final years in Dayton, living with his mother in a house that he had built for her.

RALPH WALDO EMERSON (May 25, 1803–April 27, 1882) b. Boston, Massachusetts, fourth of eight children of Ruth Haskins and William Emerson (minister of First Church of Boston). Father died when he was eight; raised by mother and by father's sister, Mary Moody Emerson, whose strong religious views influenced him. Early education at Boston Public Latin School where, at age eight, he began writing verses. The youngest member of the class of 1821, Emerson worked his way through Harvard as an orderly, a waiter, and a tutor; won prizes for oratory and essays. Began keeping a journal in 1820. After graduating, became teacher at a school for young women in Boston operated by his brother. Studied briefly at Harvard Divinity School in 1825; forced to interrupt courses because of eye trouble. In 1826 began career as minister; suffering from lung ailment, traveled to South Carolina and Florida for health. Ordained pastor of Second Church of Boston in March, 1829; later that year, married Ellen Tucker, who was already ill with tuberculosis; she died in 1831, aged 19. A year later, when research persuaded him that the sacrament of communion was not in fact divinely authorized, gave up position as minister and sailed for Europe; traveled in Italy, France, England, and Scotland; met Walter Savage Landor, John Stuart Mill, Samuel Taylor Coleridge, William Wordsworth, and Thomas Carlyle. Returned to Boston and resumed itinerant preaching; began long correspondence with Carlyle. In 1834 settled in Concord, Massachusetts; a year later married Lydia Jackson. What would eventually be called the Transcendental Club began to form around Emerson; members included Margaret Fuller, Bronson Alcott, and Orestes Brownson. Published first significant work in 1836, the long essay *Nature*; it was followed by two influential orations, "The American Scholar" (delivered at Harvard in 1837 before the Phi Beta Kappa Society), and the July 1838 address to the Harvard Divinity School, which created a scandal due to the unorthodoxy of its religious views. Became closely associated with Henry David Thoreau, sharing his walks and employing him in his house; befriended the poets Jones Very and William Ellery Channing, both of whose work he helped to publish. Virtually gave up preaching in favor of lecturing by 1838; collaborated with Margaret Fuller on *The Dial* (1840–44), succeeding her as editor in July 1842; regularly contributed to the journal. Published *Essays* in 1841 (later retitled *Essays: First Series*), and *Essays: Second Series* in 1844. Continued to lecture extensively. *Poems* published 1846. Launched public attacks on Mexican War and slavery; became involved with abolitionist movement. Returning to Europe in 1847, made contact with wide range of writers and thinkers (including Charles Dickens, George Eliot, Alexis de Tocqueville, Alfred Tennyson, and Harriet Martineau), having become internationally known through essays. Published further collections of essays and public addresses—*Nature; Addresses, and Lectures* (1849), *Representative Men* (1850), *English Traits* (1856), *The Conduct of Life* (1860)—while lecturing throughout Northeast, as well as in the western states and Canada; continued agitation against slavery. Responded enthusiastically to first editon of Whitman's *Leaves of Grass* (1855), but attempted to persuade poet to tone down sexual imagery prominent in poems added to subsequent editions. Spoke at meetings held to benefit John Brown's family after the latter's execution for his part in the Harpers Ferry raid. After Civil War, continued to lecture energetically; published verse collection *May-Day and Other Pieces* (1867), and *Society and Solitude* (1870). In 1872 health began to fail; traveled to Europe once more before returning to Concord and settling into a quieter routine as his memory gradually weakened. *Selected Poems* published in 1876. Died of pneumonia in Concord.

DANIEL DECATUR EMMETT   (October 29, 1815– June 28, 1904)   b. Clinton, Ohio. Son of Sarah Zerick and Abraham Emmett (a blacksmith). Worked from early age in father's blacksmith shop; received little schooling. Taught himself music. Apprenticed to printer, and in his teens worked for *Huron*

Reflector in Norwalk, Ohio, and *Western Aurora* in Mount Vernon, Ohio. Moved to Cincinnati around 1834 to work as printer; enlisted for three year stint in army, falsifying his age; stationed at Newport Barracks in Kentucky; played drums and fife; later relocated to Jefferson Barracks near St. Louis. Discharged from army in 1835 because of discovery that he had misrepresented his age. Traveled with various circus troupes in the late 1830s. From around 1841 associated with Frank Brower in minstrel shows; with Brower, organized the Virginia Minstrels, musical quartet that made debut at Bowery Amphitheatre in New York in February 1843. The Minstrels were immensely successful in New York and other American cities (although British tour proved disappointment); they introduced many songs of which words or music were attributed to Emmett, including "My Old Aunt Sally," "The Blue-Tail Fly," "Old Dan Tucker," "Walk Along, John," "De Boatman's Dance," and "Jordan Is a Hard Road to Travel." Emmett performed widely as actor and musician with various ensembles. Around 1852 married Catherine Rives. In 1858 joined the Bryant Minstrels, for whom in 1859 he composed "Dixie's Land" ("Dixie"); played in 1861 at inauguration of Jefferson Davis, song was adopted as unofficial anthem of Confederacy. Emmett songs performed with Bryant Minstrels included "The Road to Richmond" and "Here We Are, or Cross Ober Jordan"; toured with them sporadically until 1866. Settled in Chicago in 1867; managed a saloon there, 1872–74; continued to perform, primarily as fiddler, until the late 1870s. Wife Catherine died in 1875; married Mary Louise Bird in 1879. Money raised for him in public benefits in 1880 and 1882; toured with Leavitt's Gigantean Minstrels, 1881–82. In 1888 retired to Mount Vernon, Ohio, where he lived in relative poverty, assisted by stipend from Actors' Fund of America. Made final tour in the South, 1895–96.

THOMAS DUNN ENGLISH (June 29, 1819–April 1, 1902) b. in Philadelphia, Pennsylvania. Son of Robert English. Family were Irish Quakers, their original name Angelos. Educated at Wilson's Academy in Philadelphia and the Friends' Academy in Burlington, New Jersey; in 1839 graduated with degree in medicine from University of Pennsylvania; thesis was defense of phrenology. Subsequently studied law; called to bar in 1842. Began literary career early, contributing frequently to *Burton's Gentleman's Magazine* (one of whose editors at the time was Edgar Allan Poe). Formed friendship with Poe, which later turned to bitter enmity. Best-known work, the poem "Ben Bolt," first appeared in the *New-York Mirror* in September 1843. Settled in New York in 1844; briefly edited political paper, *Aurora*, that supported John Tyler; awarded with position as customs weigher in New York; founded short-lived magazine *The Aristidean* (1845). In New York, quarrel with Edgar Allan Poe in 1845 led to fistfight; subsequently caricatured Poe as mad poet Marmaduke Hammerhead in anonymous novella *1844* (1846) serialized in the *New-York Mirror*; other attacks on Poe by English in the *Mirror* led to Poe's successful libel suit against the paper. Became editor of short-lived humor magazine *John Donkey* (1848), which failed because of libel suits resulting from English's frequent attacks on contemporaries. Married Annie Maxwell Meade in 1849; they had four children. Practiced law and medicine in Lawnsville, Virginia (1852–56); served as town's mayor. After a year's residence in New York, established medical practice in 1856 near Newark, New Jersey. Served in New Jersey legislature, 1863–64, as a "Copperhead" Democrat. Another magazine, *The Old Guard* (1870), also failed. In 1878 worked on staff of Newark *Sunday Call*. Served as Democratic congressman, 1891–95. Published three novels under his own name—*Walter Woolfe* (1844), *Ambrose Fecit* (1867), and *Jacob Schuyler's Millions* (1870)—and others under pseudonyms. Wrote many plays including *The Mormons: or, Life at Salt Lake* (1858). Poetry collected in *Poems* (1855), *American Ballads* (1880), *Boy's Book of Battle Lyrics* (1885), and *Select Poems of Dr. Thomas Dunn English* (1894).

ERNEST FENOLLOSA (February 18, 1853–September 21, 1908) b. Salem, Massachusetts. His father, Manuel Francisco Ciriaco Fenollosa, a Spanish musician who arrived in the United States in 1838 and eventually settled in Salem, Massachusetts; taught piano and married one of his pupils, Mary Silsbee, daughter of prominent mercantile family. Fenollosa attended Harvard and studied work of Hegel and Herbert Spencer with enthusiasm. Graduated first in class of 1874, and was class poet; awarded fellowship enabling him to continue studies at Cambridge University in England, where he specialized in philosophy and, briefly, divinity. Shifted studies to art in 1877, attending newly founded school at Boston Museum of Fine Arts. Married Lizzie Goodhue Millett in June 1878; they had a son and a daughter. Under arrangement made by Edward Sylvester Morse, went to Japan in 1878, remaining there for 12 years, for the first eight of which he taught political economy, philosophy, and logic at Imperial University in Tokyo. In close association with Japanese artist Kano Hogai, encouraged preservation and cultivation of traditional Japanese art practices imperiled by Westernization. With Morse and wealthy Bostonian collector William Sturgis Bigelow, traveled throughout the country examining pottery, sculpture, and paintings; with Bigelow's patronage amassed collection of East Asian art (ultimately sold to Boston Museum of Fine Arts). Befriended Percival Lowell, who arrived in Japan in 1883, and Henry Adams and John La Farge, who arrived in 1886. In 1886, on behalf of Japanese government, traveled in Europe and America with Okakura Kakuzō (later author of *The Book of Tea*) surveying Western methods of art education. Became manager of Tokyo Fine Arts Academy and Imperial Museum when they opened in 1888. Under tutelage of Sakurai Keitoku Ajari of Homyōin Temple in Kyoto, converted to Tendai sect of Buddhism. Emperor awarded him Fourth and Third Class Orders of the Rising Sun and Third Class Order of the Sacred Mirror. Fenollosa returned to America in 1890 to become curator of Oriental department of Boston Museum of Fine Arts. In 1891 met painter and printmaker Arthur Dow and introduced him to Asian art, working with him to develop methods of teaching Asian artistic principles to Western students. In 1892 read poem "East and West" to Phi Beta Kappa Society at Harvard; only published volume of poetry, *East and*

West: The Discovery of America and Other Poems, appeared 1893. Represented Japan at World's Columbian Exposition in Chicago in 1893; curated major exhibition of Japanese prints at Boston Museum of Fine Arts in 1894. Divorced wife Lizzie in 1895 and shortly thereafter married Mary McNeill, scandalizing Boston society; relocated briefly to New York before returning by way of Europe to Japan, where Mary converted to Tendai Buddhism. Study of Japanese woodblock art, *The Masters of Ukioye*, published 1896. Resumed teaching career in 1897 as professor of English literature at Imperial Normal School of Tokyo. During second Japanese sojourn, made extensive notes on Chinese poetry and Japanese Noh drama. Placed in financial difficulties by lawsuit with first wife over property settlement. Returned to U.S. in 1900; wrote on Oriental religion, art, and literature, and lectured widely. Helped Charles L. Freer develop Japanese art collection now housed in Freer Gallery of Art, Washington, D.C. Died following a stroke while on a visit to London. Working from her husband's "rough pencil draft" (written in three months in 1906), Mary Fenollosa edited two-volume *Epochs of Chinese and Japanese Art* (1911), and appointed Ezra Pound as executor of Fenollosa's notes and unpublished translations, which Pound edited and amplified in *Cathay* (1915), *Certain Noble Plays of Japan* (1916), '*Noh*'; *or, Accomplishment, a Study of the Classical Stage of Japan* (1916), and *The Chinese Written Character as a Medium for Poetry* (1936).

EUGENE FIELD (September 2, 1850–November 4, 1895) b. St. Louis, Missouri. Father, Roswell Field, a native of Vermont, served as legal counsel for Dred Scott; mother, Frances Reed, died when Field was six years old. Field and brother Roswell Jr. (later a journalist and author who sometimes collaborated with his brother) cared for by cousin Mary Field French in Amherst, Massachusetts. Attended private school in Massachusetts and (briefly) Williams College, Knox College, and the University of Missouri (where he won a prize for oratory in 1872); did not obtain degree. Father died in 1869; in 1872, having received an $8,000 advance on inheritance from father's estate, went to Europe with friend Edgar Comstock; spent much of his inheritance there. Returning the following year, married Edgar Comstock's 16-year-old sister Julia Sutherland Comstock, of St. Joseph, Missouri; they had eight children. Devoted himself to newspaper work, serving as editor on *St. Joseph Gazette*, *St. Louis Journal*, *Kansas City Times*, and *Denver Tribune*. Joined Chicago *Morning News* (later *Record*) in 1883; remained there for rest of life, contributing daily column "Sharps and Flats," which often featured his own verse. Well-known for pranks and practical jokes, some literary, such as attributing his own poems to celebrated public figures. Spent 14 months in Europe, 1889–90, for health reasons, while continuing to write his column. In later years devoted himself to book-collecting (left unfinished a prose work entitled *The Love Affairs of a Bibliomaniac*) and, with his brother, to translations of Horace's poetry, collected in *Echoes from the Sabine Farm* (1892). Poetry (some written in a variety of dialects, and much of it originally published in newspapers) collected in *A Little Book of Western Verse*

(1889), *Second Book of Verse* (1892), and *With Trumpet and Drum* (1892). Other publications, many of them collections of newspaper sketches, included *The Tribune Primer* (1882), *A Little Book of Profitable Tales* (1890), and *The Holy Cross and Other Tales* (1893). Died in his sleep of heart failure. A ten-volume collected edition of his work was published posthumously in 1896.

FRANCIS MILES FINCH (June 9, 1827–July 31, 1907) b. Ithaca, New York. Son of Tryphena Farling and Miles Finch, a merchant. Educated Ithaca Academy; graduated Yale 1849. At Yale edited *Yale Literary Magazine* and was class poet; continued to write poetry at intervals for rest of life. Admitted to bar in Ithaca and began practicing law with success. In 1853 married Elizabeth Brooke of Philadelphia. Poem "The Blue and the Gray" first published in *Atlantic Monthly* in 1867; widely reprinted, it earned him celebrity as poet. Served as district tax collector during Grant's first administration. In 1880 appointed to fill vacancy as associate judge of New York Court of Appeals, and then elected to 14-year term, serving until retirement from bench in 1895. Close friend of Ezra Cornell; active as trustee in founding of Cornell University; served as lecturer in law, dean, and ultimately professor of legal history. In 1899 became president of New York State Bar Association. Of his literary career, he commented: "My whole life as a lawyer has been a battle against literary longings. I have kept the most earnest part of my nature in chains. I fear I have done it so long as to make full liberty dangerous to me." Late in life edited collected poems, published posthumously as *The Blue and the Gray and Other Verses* (1909).

ALICE CUNNINGHAM FLETCHER (March 15, 1838–April 6, 1923) b. Havana, Cuba, where her parents were temporarily residing. Attended New York private schools. Traveled in Europe as a young woman; lectured for temperance, anti-tobacco, and women's rights movements, as well as on anthropological topics. Met Frederic W. Putnam and Lewis Henry Morgan. In 1879, met Suzette (Bright Eyes) and Francis La Flesche (whom she eventually adopted as her son) of Omaha tribe; visited Omaha reservation in 1881. Drafted petition in support of land allotment to individual Indian landowners; campaign led to passage of Omaha Act of 1882, which served as prototype for broader Dawes Severalty Act of 1887. Oversaw allotment of small farming plots among Omaha (1883–84), Winnebago (1887–89), and Nez Percé (1890–93). Officially joined Peabody Museum as assistant in 1886; first woman with paid academic appointment at Harvard. In 1891 received fellowship to work as collector and scholar. Produced important early studies of American Indian music and religious ceremonies, especially among the Omaha, Pawnee, and Dakota Sioux; publications included *Indian Ceremonies* (1884), *A Study of Omaha Indian Music* (1893), *Indian Story and Song from North America* (1900), *The Hako: A Pawnee Ceremony* (1904), *The Omaha Tribe* (1911, with Francis La Flesche), and *Indian Games and Dances with Native Songs* (1915). In 1903 served as president of American Anthropo-

logical Society of Washington, and in 1905 as president of American Folk-
Lore Society. Died at her home in Washington.

STEPHEN FOSTER (July 4, 1826–January 13, 1864) b. Stephen Collins Fos-
ter in Pittsburgh, Pennsylvania. Ninth of ten children of Eliza Clayland Tom-
linson and merchant William Barclay Foster. Educated Allegheny Academy
(Allegheny, Pennsylvania), and Athens Academy (Tioga Point, Pennsylvania).
Briefly attended Jefferson College (Canonsburg, Pennsylvania) in July 1841;
education continued in Pittsburgh by tutors. Began to compose at an early
age; published first song, "Open Thy Lattice, Love" in 1844. Family, object-
ing to musical career, sent him to Cincinnati in 1846 to work as bookkeeper
for brother Dunning Foster. A number of his songs were published in *Songs
of the Sable Harmonists* (1848) and *Foster's Ethiopian Melodies* (1849). In 1850,
success of his songs (including "Louisiana Belle," "O Susannah," "Uncle
Ned," and "Away Down South") led him to return home to Pittsburgh and
devote himself exclusively to music. Later that year, married Jane Denny Mc-
Dowell of Pittsburgh; daughter Marion born April 1851. Songs popularized by
Christy's Minstrels, Campbell Minstrels, and New Orleans Serenaders; in 1851
sold exclusive pre-publication performance rights to E. P. Christy, inaugurat-
ing profitable business arrangement for both parties. During 1850s, produced
series of popular songs including "De Camptown Races" (1850), "Ring De
Banjo" (1851), "The Old Folks at Home" (1851), "Massa's in de Cold
Ground" (1852), "My Old Kentucky Home" (1853), "Old Dog Tray" (1853),
"Jeanie with the Light Brown Hair" (1854), and "Come Where My Love
Lies Dreaming" (1855). Thereafter productivity and popularity fell off; final
minstrel hit was "Old Black Joe" (1860). Foster moved to New York with
family in 1860; marital troubles led, by 1862, to a separation, with Jane and
Marion living in Lewistown, Pennsylvania. Foster composed prolifically, but
without recapturing former success; drank heavily and was reduced to pov-
erty. Lived his last days in a Bowery hotel; died in Bellevue Hospital from
wounds received when he fell in his hotel room, lacerating neck and face.

PHILIP FRENEAU (January 2, 1752–December 19, 1832) b. New York City.
Son of Agnes Watson and Pierre Fresneau. Of French Huguenot descent;
grandfather André Fresneau established as wine importer in New York
around 1709. Educated at College of New Jersey (now Princeton); classmates
included James Madison and Hugh Henry Brackenridge; wrote satirical anti-
Tory verses. With Brackenridge collaborated on *Father Bombo's Pilgrimage*
(1770), sometimes called earliest example of American prose fiction, and *A
Poem on the Rising Glory of America* (1772). Following graduation in 1771, em-
ployed briefly as teacher on Long Island and in Maryland. Pastoral poem *The
American Village* (1772) followed by patriotic and satirical verse including
American Liberty (1775), *A Voyage to Boston* (1775), *General Gage's Soliloquy*
(1775), and *General Gage's Confession* (1775). Secretary to planter in Santa Cruz
(now St. Croix) in West Indies, 1776–78. During Revolutionary War served
intermittently as member of the Monmouth (N.J.) Militia, and in 1779 sailed

as commander of privateering brig *Rebecca*; as militiaman, assisted in capture of British brig *Brittania* off New Jersey coast in December 1779. As third mate on privateer *Aurora*, captured by the British in May 1780; brutal treatment during six weeks as prisoner of war on prison ship *Scorpion* and hospital ship *Hunter* in New York harbor recounted in poem *The British Prison-Ship* (1781). Following release and recuperation at Mount Pleasant (family plantation near Middletown Point, New Jersey), moved to Philadelphia to work on the staff of Francis Bailey's *Freeman's Journal*, to which he contributed poetry and polemical prose; employed as clerk in Philadelphia post office, 1782–84. Worked sporadically as master of trading ships along the Atlantic coast, 1784–89. First major verse collection, *The Poems of Philip Freneau*, published in 1786, followed by *Journey from Philadelphia to New York* (1787) and *Miscellaneous Works* (1788). In 1790 married Eleanor Forman, with whom he had four daughters. Settled in New York; edited *Daily Advertiser*, 1790–91; following removal of federal government to Philadelphia, hired by Jefferson as translating clerk in State Department, 1791–93; in 1791 began publishing the *National Gazette*, launching virulent attacks on Alexander Hamilton; fervently supported French Revolution and controversial French envoy Edmond Charles Genêt. Washington, annoyed by Freneau's radicalism, suggested to Jefferson that his appointment be revoked; Jefferson responded, "I will not do it. . . . His paper has saved our constitution which was galloping fast into monarchy." Upon Jefferson's retirement from the State Department, Freneau resigned his government clerical job. Worked as printer and bookseller in New Jersey; edited *Jersey Chronicle* (1795–96), in which he published satirical essays featuring "Tomo Cheeki, the Creek Indian in Philadelphia." In New York, edited Antifederalist newspaper *The Time-Piece*, 1797–98. Poetry collected in *The Village Merchant* (1794), *Poems Written Between the Years 1768 and 1794* (1795), and two-volume *Poems Written and Published During the American Revolutionary War* (1809); satirical journalism published under pseudonym "Robert Slender" collected in *Letters on Various Interesting and Important Subjects* (1799). After 1798 retired from journalism; in later years lived mostly at Mount Pleasant; served as ship's captain, 1802–04 and 1809. During War of 1812 wrote topical patriotic poems, some published in *A Collection of Poems on American Affairs* (1815). Many of his manuscript poems were destroyed in a fire at Mount Pleasant in 1818. Increasingly impoverished in later years; much of property sold to creditors. Died when caught in a blizzard while walking home.

MARGARET FULLER (May 23, 1810–July 19, 1850) b. Cambridge, Massachusetts. Daughter of Margaret Crane (former schoolteacher) and Timothy Fuller (lawyer, state senator, and congressman); given name Sarah Margaret Fuller. Rigorously educated at home by father, by tutors, with Dr. John Park in Boston, and at boarding school conducted by Susan Prescott in Groton, Massachusetts (1823–24); by age 15 she was proficient in Latin, Greek, French, and Italian. Made intensive study of German literature; close friend of James Freeman Clarke. Family settled in Groton when father took up farming in 1833. Following father's death in 1835, taught for several months at Bronson Alcott's Temple School in Boston; left due to Alcott's inability to pay her. Became teacher at Hiram Fuller's Greene-Street School in Providence, Rhode Island (1836–38); formed friendship with Sarah Helen Whitman. Moved to Boston area, where she taught privately; contributed essays to Clarke's *Western Messenger*; published translation of Eckermann's *Conversations with Goethe* (1839). Conducted successful women's education program of "conversations" focusing on philosophy, education, and women's rights, 1839–44. Close friend of Ralph Waldo Emerson; became editor of *The Dial*, 1840–42, frequently contributing essays and poems. Friends and intellectual associates in Boston and Cambridge included George Ripley, Theodore Parker, Caroline Sturgis, William Henry Channing, and many others. Greatly impressed by meeting with English writer Harriet Martineau in 1835; occasionally visited Brook Farm community beginning in 1841. Sister Ellen married poet William Ellery Channing in 1841. In the summer of 1843 traveled in Illinois and Wisconsin; her account of the journey, *A Summer on the Lakes* (1844), led to invitation from Horace Greeley to serve as literary critic for *New-York Tribune*. During vacation in Hudson Valley with close friend Caroline Sturgis, wrote *Woman in the Nineteenth Century* (published 1845). Moved to New York in 1844; lived for a time in Greeley household; literary associates in New York included Lydia Maria Child, Anne Lynch, Christopher Pearse Cranch, Cornelius Mathews, William Gilmore Simms, and Evert Duyckinck. Criticism collected in *Papers on Literature and Art* (1846). Sailed to Europe in the summer of 1846; wrote for *Tribune* as foreign correspondent (articles reprinted in *At Home and Abroad* in 1856). In England met Thomas Carlyle, William Wordsworth, Thomas De Quincey, and Italian revolutionary leader Giuseppe Mazzini; in France, George Sand, Pierre de Beranger, and Polish poet Adam Mickiewicz. In Italy, associated with Robert and Elizabeth Barrett Browning and artists William Wetmore Story, Hiram Powers, and Horatio Greenough; renewed friendship with Christopher Pearse Cranch. Met the Marchese Angelo Ossoli, impoverished Roman aristocrat and republican, whose son she bore in September 1848 (exact date of marriage to Ossoli, or if they married, is unknown). Became involved in Italian revolution of 1848–49, and celebrated it in articles for *Tribune*; cared for wounded during siege of Rome by French and Austrian forces; fled with Ossoli to mountain village of Rieti after defeat of Roman republic in June 1849; soon relocated to Florence. In 1850 sailed with Ossoli and young child to America, carrying manuscript of her history of the failed revolution. Ship wrecked off Fire Island; Fuller perished with family and many others aboard. Letters, journals, and poems collected posthumously in *The Memoirs of Margaret Fuller Ossoli* (1852); complete works published in 1869 under Greeley's direction.

HAMLIN GARLAND (September 14, 1860–March 4, 1940) b. Hannibal Hamlin Garland, on farm near New Salem, Wisconsin. Son of Isabelle McClintock and Richard H. Garland. Worked with father on succession of family farms in Wisconsin, Iowa, and Dakota Territory. Graduated Cedar Valley Seminary (Osage, Iowa) 1881. Worked as itinerant carpenter and handyman; taught school briefly in Illinois, 1882–83. Homesteaded in Dakotas, 1883–84; earned enough to move to Boston, where he engaged in intensive studies at Boston Public Library; also taught at Boston School of Oratory (1884–91) and wrote book reviews for Boston papers. Introduced himself to William Dean Howells, who became close friend. Trips back home to Iowa and Dakota Territory in the late 1880s led to *Main-Travelled Roads* (1891), collection of realistic stories drawing on midwestern experiences (writing defended publicly by Howells: "If anyone is still at a loss to account for that uprising of the farmers in the West, let him read *Main-Travelled Roads*"). Met the young Stephen Crane and gave him literary encouragement. Became ardent partisan of single-tax economic theories of Henry George (with whom he formed close friendship) and campaigned for Populist party in election of 1892. Four novels published in 1892—*Jason Edwards, A Member of the Third House, A Spoil of Office,* and *A Little Norsk*—followed by poetry collection *Prairie Songs* (1893) and another volume of Middle Border stories, *Prairie Folks* (1893). Moved to Chicago in 1893; associates there included realist novelist Henry Blake Fuller (who later satirized Garland in short story "The Downfall of Abner Joyce") and sculptor Lorado Taft. Active in many causes and movements: organized Central Art Association; campaigned for women's rights, conservation, and fair treatment for American Indians; pursued interest in spiritualism. Published *Crumbling Idols: Twelve Essays on Art* (1894), novel *Rose of Dutcher's Coolly* (1895), biography *Ulysses S. Grant* (1898), and *The Trail of the Goldseekers* (1899), an account of travels in Canada and Alaska. Married Zuline Taft (sister of Lorado Taft) in 1899; they had two daughters. Made first trip to England in 1899 and cultivated many literary acquaintances there. Realism of early fiction replaced by more romantic tone in series of popular novels including *The Spirit of Sweetwater* (1898), *The Captain of the Gray-Horse Troop* (1902), *The Light of the Star* (1904), and *The Forester's Daughter* (1914); treated spiritualist themes in novels *The Tyranny of the Dark* (1905), *The Shadow World* (1908), and *Victor Ollnee's Discipline* (1911). Moved to New York City in 1916. Consulted by friend Theodore Roosevelt on federal policy toward American Indians; stories on Indian themes collected in *The Book of the American Indian* (1923). In later years wrote series of volumes of autobiography and family history, of which the most successful were *A Son of the Middle Border* (1917) and *A Daughter of the Middle Border* (1922), for which he won the Pulitzer Prize. *Roadside Meetings* (1930) initiated series of literary memoirs based on diaries. Moved in 1930 to Los Angeles, California. Later poems collected in *Iowa, O Iowa!* (1935); occult studies summarized in *Forty Years of Psychic Research* (1940) and *The Mystery of the Buried Crosses* (1939).

ALBERT SAMUEL GATSCHET (October 3, 1832–March 16, 1907) b. Saint Beatenberg, Switzerland. Son of Mary Ziegler and minister Karl Albert Gatschet. Educated at schools of Neuchâtel and Bern; entered University of

Bern 1852; completed linguistic and theological studies at University of Berlin, where he specialized in Greek language and doctrinal criticism. Wrote for literary and scientific journals in Bern for several years before immigrating to New York in 1868, where he worked as writer and teacher. Interest in American Indian languages originated in 1872, when he was asked to compare vocabularies collected from a geographical survey of the Southwest. Hired in 1877 by John Wesley Powell as philologist for Rocky Mountain Geological Survey; did field work among various tribes in California and Oregon, including the Klamath and Modoc. Member of the Bureau of Ethnology from its organization in 1879 to his retirement in 1905; studied scores of languages of southeastern U.S. and Gulf of Mexico; on visits to the Catawba in South Carolina, and the Biloxi and Tunica of Louisiana and Mississippi, uncovered linguistic relation between these and the Sioux. In addition to vast archival collection, published work included *A Migration Legend of the Creek Indians* (two volumes, 1884 and 1888), and *The Klamath Indians of Southwestern Oregon* (1890). Did much work with Indian delegates and students in Washington. Married at age 70 in 1892. Poor health forced abandonment of final project, a comparative study of Algonquian languages; retired from Bureau in 1905. Died in Washington, D.C.

RICHARD WATSON GILDER (February 8, 1844–November 18, 1909) b. Bordentown, New Jersey. Son of Jane Nutt and William Henry Gilder, Methodist minister who conducted Belle Vue Female Seminary in Bordentown. In Gilder's early years, family moved often, as father served as teacher or minister in Flushing, New York, in Redding and Fair Haven, Connecticut, and in Yonkers, New York. They returned to Bordentown at outbreak of Civil War, during which Gilder joined 1st Philadelphia Artillery, a company formed to defend Harrisburg, but did not see much active service; formed friendship with Charles Godfrey Leland. After father's death in 1864, worked as railroad paymaster and later as reporter for *Newark Daily Advertiser*; with R. Newton Crane founded *Newark Morning Register* in 1868. In 1869 became editor of *Hours at Home*, and upon its merger into *Scribner's Monthly* in 1870 became assistant editor of *Scribner's Monthly* under Josiah G. Holland. Helen Hunt (later Helen Hunt Jackson) introduced him to Helena de Kay (granddaughter of poet Joseph Rodman Drake), whom he married in 1874; they had five children. Gilder's love poems to Helena (originally published in *Scribner's*) were collected in *The New Day* (1875). The Gilders' Manhattan homes (off Union Square and Washington Square), and their Massachusetts summer homes on Buzzards Bay and in the Berkshires, became important centers of cultural life; guests included Henry James, John La Farge, Augustus Saint-Gaudens, Stanford White, Helena Modjeska, Joseph Jefferson, Walt Whitman, Rudyard Kipling, Edmund Clarence Stedman, Thomas Bailey Aldrich, Mark Twain, and Grover Cleveland (who became a close friend). Involved in foundation of Society of American Artists (1877) and Authors' Club (1882). In 1879 the Gilders traveled in Europe for a year; in France, Gilder formed links with Provençal poets including Frédéric Mistral; in England renewed friendship with George MacDonald whom he had met earlier in the U.S. Following the resignation in 1881 of Holland (who died later the same year), Gilder assumed full editorship of the magazine, now renamed *The Century*, while he was editor, contributors included Henry James, Mark Twain, William Dean Howells, George Washington Cable, John Hay and Hamlin Garland. Campaigned for civil service reform; participated in founding of Anti-Spoils League in 1893. Became increasingly involved in New York civic affairs; as chairman of state commission investigating tenement buildings, exposed unsafe conditions in tenements owned by Corporation of Trinity Church; campaigned against Tammany Hall corruption. Traveled in Europe and the Holy Land, 1894–95. Published 16 volumes of verse, including *The Poet and His Master* (1878), *The Celestial Passion* (1887), *The Great Remembrance and Other Poems* (1893), *In Palestine and Other Poems* (1898), *In the Heights* (1905), *A Book of Music* (1906), *The Fire Divine* (1907), and *Poems* (1908). Also published books about Abraham Lincoln and Grover Cleveland. In later years awarded honorary degrees by Yale, Princeton, Harvard, and several other institutions.

LOUISE IMOGEN GUINEY (January 7, 1861–November 2, 1920) b. Boston, Massachusetts. Daughter of Janet Margaret Doyle and Patrick Robert Guiney, a Civil War brigadier general who later practiced law. Raised as Roman Catholic. Father died in 1877. Graduated in 1879 from Elmhurst Academy at Convent of Sacred Heart in Providence, Rhode Island; moved with her mother to Auburndale, Massachusetts. First poetry collection, *Songs at the Start*, published 1884, followed by essays in *Goose-Quill Papers* (1885); work praised by Oliver Wendell Holmes and Richard Watson Gilder. Second collection, *The White Sail and Other Poems*, appeared in 1887. Wrote children's stories collected in *Brownies and Bogles* (1888). With mother, made long visit to England, 1889–91. *The Crust of Society*, adaptation of *Le Demi-Monde* by Aléxandre Dumas fils, produced in Boston and New York in 1892. *A Roadside Harp* (1893) was considered by Guiney and her contemporaries to be her most important collection of poems; essays on English literature collected in *A Little English Gallery* (1894), followed by story collection *Lovers' Saint Ruth's and Three Other Tales* (1895) and privately printed *Nine Sonnets Written at Oxford* (1895). Contributed poems to close friend Alice Brown's study of Robert Louis Stevenson, 1895. Postmistress of Auburndale, 1894–97; endured opposition and boycotts from residents hostile to Roman Catholicism. Made walking tour of England and Wales in the summer of 1895 (forming friendship with English poet Lionel Johnson). Associated with Fred Holland Day and Herbert Copeland in publication of fine editions, under whose Copeland and Day imprint a number of her works appeared. Magazine articles collected in *Patrins* (1897); edited *James Clarence Mangan: His Selected Poems* (1897). English edition of selected poems published as *England and Yesterday: A Book of Short Poems* (1898); *The Martyrs' Idyl and Shorter Poems* (1899) consisted largely of revisions of earlier work. In 1899 took job as cataloguer at Boston Public Library. Traveled again to England with her aunt in 1901, settling in Oxford. Prepared editions of various English literary works by authors including Henry Vaughan, Katherine Philips, and Thomas Stanley; published *Robert Emmet* (1904), biography of Irish nationalist, and *Blessed Edmund Campion* (1908), study of Elizabethan Catholic martyr. Wrote little poetry in later years; *Happy Ending* (1909, enlarged 1927) was her final selection of the poems she wished to preserve. Edited *Some Poems of Lionel Johnson, Newly Selected* (1912). Devoted much scholarly work to projected edition of Henry Vaughan and anthology of English Catholic poetry (neither project was completed by her, although the anthology eventually appeared, co-edited by Geoffrey Bliss, as *Recusant Poets* in 1938). Returned to Boston in 1909 to care for her mother, who died the following spring, after which Guiney returned permanently to England. Later years marked by poverty, deafness, and increasing ill health.

FITZ-GREENE HALLECK (July 8, 1790–November 19, 1867) b. Guilford, Connecticut. Son of Mary Eliot (farmer's daughter descended from missionary John Eliot) and Israel Halleck (associated with Tory cause during Revolution). Educated locally. Went to New York in 1811 to work for banking house of Jacob Barker, where he was employed for the next 18 years. Gained early reputation as wit and scholar. Co-author (with close friend Joseph Rodman Drake) of "The Croakers," series of local satires that appeared in New York *Evening Post* in 1819. Anonymously published *Fanny* (1819), satirical poem about New York society. Traveled in Europe in 1822. From 1825 contributed poetry frequently to William Cullen Bryant's *New York Review* and other publications; "Marco Bozzaris" achieved wide popularity as poem for recitation. Wrote little verse after publication of *Alnwick Castle, with Other Poems* (1827), but remained active in New York literary circles, maintaining friendships with William Cullen Bryant, James Kirke Paulding, James Fenimore Cooper, and others. Worked as confidential clerk in counting house of John Jacob Astor beginning in 1832. Edited *The Works of Byron in Prose and Verse* (1833) and *Selections from the British Poets* (1840); in 1837 elected vice-president of Authors' Club of New York, of which Washington Irving was president. *The Works of Fitz-Greene Halleck* (1847) went through three editions during his lifetime. Bryant called Halleck "the favorite poet of the city of New York, where his name is cherished with a peculiar fondness and enthusiasm." John Jacob Astor died in 1848, leaving Halleck an annuity and naming him trustee of the Astor Library; retired to Guilford.

FRANCES ELLEN WATKINS HARPER (September 24, 1825–February 22, 1911) b. Baltimore, Maryland. Parents were free blacks; given name Frances Ellen Watkins; she was orphaned at early age. Attended school run by uncle, the Rev. William Watkins (a frequent contributor to *The Liberator*). Found work in a bookshop in Baltimore. Published collection of poetry, *Forest Leaves* (1845), of which no copies are known to be extant. In 1850 took position teaching sewing at Union Seminary, near Columbus, Ohio, a school for free blacks founded by the African Methodist Episcopal Church. Two years later left for Little York, Pennsylvania, where she obtained another teaching position. Met black abolitionist William Grant Still, who became close friend; in 1854 moved to Philadelphia and became active in anti-slavery movement, working under Still's direction for Underground Railroad. *Poems on Miscellaneous Subjects* (1854), published with a preface by William Lloyd Garrison, enjoyed wide circulation and went through several editions. Lectured widely, 1854–60, initially for Maine Antislavery Society, and then throughout New England, in Canada, and in western states. Her poems, stories, lectures, and speeches published regularly in abolitionist press. Married widower Fenton Harper (who had three children) in 1860 and settled in Columbus, Ohio; they had a daughter, Mary. After husband's death in 1864, resumed career as lecturer and organizer; toured South frequently in late 1860s and early 1870s. Published two volumes of narrative poetry, *Moses: A Story of the Nile* (1869; expanded 1889; later incorporated in *Idylls of the Bible*, 1901) and *Sketches of Southern Life* (1872), as well as the verse collection *Poems* (1871). In 1871 settled permanently in Philadelphia. Founder and assistant superintendent of a YMCA Sabbath School from 1872. Active in many political and social organizations in later years, including American Association of Education of Colored Youth (of which she became director in 1894), Women's Christian Temperance Union, American Woman Suffrage Association, and American Equal Rights Association; associates included Frederick Douglass, Ida Wells Barnett, Harriet Tubman, Susan B. Anthony, and Elizabeth Cady Stanton. Novel *Iola Leroy, or Shadows Uplifted* published in 1892; later poetry collected in *Atlanta Offering* (1895). Addressed World Congress of Representative Women in 1893 at World's Columbian Exposition in Chicago. In 1896 helped found National Association of Colored Women, of which she became vice-president the following year.

BRET HARTE (August 25, 1836–May 5, 1902) b. Francis Brett Harte in Albany, New York. Son of Elizabeth Rebecca Ostrander and Henry Harte; paternal grandfather, Bernard Hart, was prominent Jewish merchant of New York. Father was a teacher and lecturer whose lack of success led to family's frequently moving. During Harte's childhood, family lived in six different northeastern cities, settling, after father's death in 1845, in New York City, where Harte attended school until age 13. Left school and worked as lawyer's assistant and in counting-house, becoming self-supporting by age 15. In 1853, mother moved to California and married Andrew Williams, who became mayor of Oakland; with his younger sister Margaret, Harte joined her there the following year. For several years drifted in northern California, working at various minor jobs including druggist's assistant, tutor, and stage coach guard. Moved in 1858 to Union (now Arcata), on Humboldt Bay, where he received training as printer on local newspaper, *The Northern Californian*; soon began contributing articles and poems. Local response to his editorial protest in *Northern Californian* against "indiscriminate massacre" of 60 Wiyot Indians on Gunther's Island in February 1860 forced him to leave Arcata. Moved to San Francisco; worked as typesetter for *The Golden Era* and contributed many items to paper including column "Town and Table Talk" and first major short story, "The Work on Red Mountain." Cultivated personal connections with San Francisco society, notably with Jessie Frémont (wife of General John C. Frémont) and minister Thomas Starr King; obtained job as clerk in surveyor-general's office. Married Anna Griswold of New York in 1862; they had four children (born between 1865 and 1875). The following year switched to job in new U.S. Mint, where he worked for six years. Edited local poetry anthology *Outcroppings* (1866); published collections of prose sketches, *The Lost Galleon and Other Tales* (1867) and *Condensed Novels and Other Papers* (1867). Appointed editor of *Overland Monthly* in 1868, attracting national attention with his short stories "The Luck of Roaring Camp" (1868) and "The Outcasts of Poker Flat" (1869). Publication in 1870 of humorous poem "Plain Language from Truthful James" and collection *The Luck of Roaring Camp and Other Sketches* made him world-famous (although Harte described poem as "the worst I ever wrote"). Friends in San Francisco included Mark Twain, Charles Warren Stoddard, Ambrose Bierce, Ina Coolbrith, and Adah Isaacs Menken. Declined offers of employment as professor of literature at the University of California and as editor of Chicago *Lakeside Monthly*. Relocated to the East in 1871; spent a week in Boston with William Dean Howells; settled (after intervals in New York City and Newport, Rhode Island) in Morristown, New Jersey. Lived increasingly separately from wife and children. Given lucrative exclusive contract with *Atlantic Monthly*, but contributions found little favor. Continued to publish fiction, including *Mrs. Skaggs's Husbands* (1873), *Tales of the Argonauts* (1875), *Gabriel Conroy* (1876), and *The Story of a Mine* (1877); wrote plays *Two Men of Sandy Bar* (1876) and, in collaboration with Mark Twain, *Ah Sin* (1877), but these enjoyed slight success; verse collected in *East and West Poems* (1871), *Poetical Works* (1872), *Echoes of the Foot-Hills* (1872), and other volumes. Fell into debt; lectured widely beginning in the early 1870s; unsuccessfully tried to launch magazine in Washington, D.C. Accepted appointment by Rutherford B. Hayes to American consulate in Krefeld, Prussia, and went to Germany alone in July 1878; while officially serving there, spent much time in London. In London acquaintances included Henry James, George Du Maurier, Thomas Hardy; formed close friendship with Arthur and Marguerite Van de Velde, with whom he frequently stayed. Appointed in 1880 to U.S. consulate in Glasgow; dismissed in 1885 for inattention to duty. Settled permanently in London, living with the Van de Veldes; wrote prolifically, supporting himself entirely by writing after loss of consular job. Later publications included *Flip and Other Stories* (1882), *On the Frontier* (1884), *By Shore and Sedge* (1885), *Maruja* (1885), *The Queen of the Pirate Isle* (1886), *The Heritage of Dedlow Marsh and Other Tales* (1889), *In a Hollow of the Hills* (1895), *Tales of Trail and Town* (1898), and many other works. Wife Anna came to England (where their son Frank had settled five years earlier) in 1898; they saw each other occasionally but never again lived together.

NATHANIEL HAWTHORNE (July 4, 1804–May 19, 1864) b. Salem, Massachusetts. Son of Elizabeth Clarke Manning and Nathaniel Hawthorne (a sea captain). Father died in Dutch Guiana 1808; mother became recluse. Graduated 1825 from Bowdoin College; classmate of Henry Wadsworth Longfellow and close friend of Franklin Pierce. Returned to Salem and devoted himself to writing. *Fanshawe* (1828), first novel, published anonymously. Published stories in *The Token* under editorship of S. G. Goodrich, collected in *Twice-Told Tales* (1837). Edited *American Magazine of Useful and Entertaining Knowledge*, compiled *Peter Parley's Universal History* (1837), and wrote a number of children's books. Worked 1839–40 at Boston custom house; lost patronage job after Whig victory. Associated for six or seven months in 1841 with utopian community Brook Farm in West Roxbury, Massachusetts. Married Sophia Peabody in 1842; they had two daughters and a son. Moved to Concord, where he became acquainted with Transcendentalist circle including Ralph Waldo Emerson, Henry David Thoreau, and Bronson Alcott. Second volume of *Twice-Told Tales* (1842) followed by *Mosses from an Old Manse* (1846). Returned to Salem in 1846 as Surveyor of Port of Salem and served for three years. In 1850 published *The Scarlet Letter*. Moved to Lenox, Massachusetts; formed friendship with Herman Melville, who had reviewed his work enthusiastically. Published *The House of the Seven Gables* (1851), *The Snow-Image and Other Twice-Told Tales* (1851), *The Blithedale Romance* (1852), inspired by experiences at Brook Farm, and two books of stories for children, *A Wonder Book* (1852) and *Tanglewood Tales* (1853). In 1852 wrote campaign biography for Franklin Pierce; following Pierce's election as president, appointed U.S. consul in Liverpool. After holding position for four years (1853–57), lived in Italy (1858–59) and England (1859–60) before returning to Concord. Final novel, *The Marble Faun*, published in 1860. Published essays on England, *Our Old Home* (1863). In later years kept voluminous notebooks that were published posthumously, along with fragments of several unfinished novels.

JOHN HAY (October 8, 1838–July 1, 1905) b. Salem, Indiana. One of six children of Helen Leonard and Dr. Charles Hay, a country doctor; family settled eventually in Spunky Point (now Warsaw), Illinois. Studied at a private school in Pittsfield, Illinois, and at a college in Springfield, Illinois. Graduated Brown University 1858, and returned to Springfield to study law in uncle Milton Hay's law office; made acquaintance of Abraham Lincoln, whose office was next door. Campaigned for Lincoln in 1860 and traveled to Washington in 1861 as his assistant private secretary; remained close to Lincoln through Civil War years, keeping a detailed diary. Served as military aide from 1864 under Generals Hunter and Gillmore, attaining rank of colonel. Following war, appointed first secretary to American legation in Paris, 1865–67; during this period devoted himself to writing occasional verse and prose. After brief return to America, went abroad again to serve successively as chargé d'affaires in Vienna (1867–68) and legation secretary in Madrid (1868–70). Returned to America intending career in journalism; became editorial writer for *New-York Tribune* under Horace Greeley; published popular dialect ballads "Little Breeches" and "Jim Bludso" in the *Tribune*. Volume of Spanish reminiscences, *Castilian Days* (1871), followed by collection of dialect poems, *Pike County Ballads and Other Pieces* (1871). Married Clara Louise Stone of Cleveland, Ohio, in February 1874; they had two daughters and a son. Abandoned journalism and settled in Cleveland as business partner of wealthy father-in-law Amasa Stone. Served as Assistant Secretary of State under Rutherford B. Hayes, 1879–81. In Washington began close friendship with Henry Adams; they built adjoining houses and formed nexus of intellectual group including Clarence King and Henry Cabot Lodge. Returned to *New-York Tribune* as temporary editor-in-chief, 1881–82. Political novel *The Bread-Winners*, an attack on labor unions, published anonymously in 1884. In collaboration with John Nicolay (friend from Springfield who was another of Lincoln's secretaries) worked on *Abraham Lincoln: A History*, serialized over a four-year period in *The Century*, and published in ten volumes in 1890. *Poems* (1890) contained little new work. During 1890s spent much time traveling in Europe. Was close adviser of William McKinley, who appointed him ambassador to Great Britain in 1897. Involved in diplomatic maneuvering relating to Spanish-American War and annexation of Philippines, which he enthusiastically supported. In 1898, despite ill health, appointed Secretary of State by McKinley; instrumental in promulgating Open Door policy in China. Retained post during administrations of Theodore Roosevelt, but was less active in determining policy. Among first seven members elected to American Academy of Arts and Letters in 1904. *Addresses* collected posthumously in 1906; *Complete Poetical Works* published 1916.

PAUL HAMILTON HAYNE (January 1, 1830–July 6, 1886) b. Charleston, South Carolina, of distinguished family; son of Emily McElhenny and naval lieutenant Paul Hamilton Hayne; descendant of Revolutionary War hero Colonel Isaac Hayne. Father died of yellow fever at sea when Hayne was not yet two; raised by mother and by uncle Robert Young Hayne, governor of South Carolina and previously a U.S. senator. At Christopher Cotes' Classical School in Charleston, formed enduring friendship with Henry Timrod. First poem published in *Charleston Courier* in 1845; continued to contribute verse to magazines including *Southern Literary Messenger*, *Southern Literary Gazette*, and *Graham's Magazine*. Graduated College of Charleston in 1850. Studied law with prominent attorney James L. Petigru; admitted to bar 1852. Married Mary Middleton Michel in 1852 (their son William was born in 1856). Worked as assistant editor and then editor of *Southern Literary Gazette*, 1852–54. A member, with William Gilmore Simms, of group of Southern writers who gathered at John Russell's bookstore in Charleston; edited *Russell's Magazine*, 1857–60. First collections of verse—*Poems* (1855), *Sonnets and Other Poems* (1857), and *Avolio: A Legend of the Island of Cos* (1860)—won praise from Holmes, Bryant, and Longfellow. Served as aide-de-camp to South Carolina governor Francis Pickens for four months in 1861–62; fell ill and was removed from active service; wrote martial lyrics in defense of Southern cause. Home destroyed in the war. Moved in July 1865 to small farm Copse Hill near Groveton, Georgia, outside Augusta. Eked out a living writing for newspapers and magazines; also did editorial work for the *Atlanta Sun*, *Charleston News*, and other periodicals. Later collections of poetry included *Legends and Lyrics* (1872) and *The Mountain of the Lovers* (1873); *Collected Poems* published 1882. Edited posthumous edition of the poetry of Timrod in 1873.

JOHN HECKEWELDER (March 12, 1743–January 31, 1823) b. John Gottlieb Ernestus Heckewelder in Bedford, England. Son of the Rev. David Heckewelder, Moravian minister. Family moved with other Moravian colonists to settlement at Bethlehem, Pennsylvania, in 1754. Worked at Moravian settlement near Nazareth, Pennsylvania; apprenticed to a cedar cooper. In 1762 joined evangelist Christian Frederick Post in trying to establish mission on Muskingum River in Ohio Territory; attempt interrupted by outbreak of Pontiac war. (Mission, Gnadenhütten, subsequently established by Post and David Zeisberger.) From 1771 served as missionary to converted Delaware in Ohio Territory, initially as assistant to Zeisberger; ordained deacon in 1778. Married Sarah Ohneberg in 1780 in Nazareth, Pennsylvania. Arrested in 1781 by British forces and accused of spying for Americans; summoned repeatedly to Detroit by British commander to defend himself against charges; in his absence a massacre of Moravian Indians occurred. Temporarily resettled the mission in Michigan, and returned to Bethlehem in 1786 because of his wife's failing health. Helped negotiate treaties with various tribes of the Old Northwest, 1792–93. Published *Johann Heckewälders Reise von Bethlehem in Pensilvanien bis zum Wabashfluss* (1797, English translation 1888). Returned to Ohio Territory in 1799, and as agent for Society for Propagating the Gospel surveyed distribution of lands to Christian Indians. After retiring to Bethlehem in 1810, wrote pioneering studies *An Account of the History, Manners, and Customs of the Indian Nations, Who Once Inhabited Pennsylvania and the Neighbouring States* (1819) and *A Narrative of the Mission of the United Brethren Among the Delaware and Mohegan Indians* (1820). Other writings, published posthumously, included glossaries, maps, and journals.

CHARLES FENNO HOFFMAN (February 7, 1806–June 7, 1884) b. New York City. Son of Maria Fenno and Josiah Ogden Hoffman (prominent lawyer). Right leg amputated following accident at age 11. Studied at Columbia College, 1821–23, without graduating; studied law in Albany with Harmanus Bleecker; admitted to New York bar in 1827. With Charles King, co-edited *New York American*, 1830–33; was editor of the first issues of *The Knickerbocker* (1833); early literary associates in New York included William Cullen Bryant, Nathaniel P. Willis, Fitz-Greene Halleck, James Kirke Paulding, Robert Sands, and Gulian Verplanck (Hoffman's uncle). Made western tour, 1833–34, visiting Pittsburgh, Detroit, Chicago, Prairie du Chien, Wisconsin Territory, and St. Louis; journey recounted in *A Winter in the West* (1835). On his return to New York, assumed editorship of *American Monthly Magazine*, 1835–37 and *New-York Mirror* (1837). Journalistic sketches collected in *Wild Scenes in the Forest and Prairie* (1839). Briefly served as associate editor of *The New Yorker* under Horace Greeley before assuming patronage jobs as third chief clerk (1841–43) and deputy surveyor (1843–44) for New York Customs Authority. Published a novel, *Greyslaer: A Romance of the Mohawk* (1840), based on 1828 Beauchamp-Sharp murder case, and three collections of verse: *The Vigil of Faith* (1842), *The Echo* (1844), and *Love's Calendar, Lays of the Hudson, and Other Poems* (1847); also edited anthology *The New-York Book of Poetry* (1837). At request of Henry Rowe Schoolcraft, made verse adaptations of Ojibwa oral poetry printed in Schoolcraft's *Oneóta; or Characteristics of the Red Race of America* (1845). Acquainted with Edgar Allan Poe, Herman Melville, Evert Duyckinck, Rufus Griswold, and other New York literary figures. Editorship of New York *Literary World* (1847–49) interrupted by attack of mental illness. After brief hospitalization, accepted clerkship in State Department; boarded in Washington, D.C., with family of Henry Rowe Schoolcraft; proposed marriage to Schoolcraft's daughter Jane. Following recurrence of mental illness, hospitalized again; ultimately confined to Harrisburg (Pennsylvania) Insane Asylum in 1849, where he remained for the rest of his life.

JOSIAH GILBERT HOLLAND (July 24, 1819–October 12, 1881) b. Belchertown, Massachusetts. Son of Anna Gilbert and Harrison Holland. Childhood impoverished; worked in factory as a boy. After early experience as schoolteacher, attended Berkshire Medical College, graduating 1844. Practiced medicine briefly; worked as daguerrotypist; published *Bay State Weekly Courier* (which failed after six months); worked as educator, becoming superintendent of schools in Vicksburg, Mississippi. Married Elizabeth Chapin in 1845; they had three children. In 1849 returned to Massachusetts to become assistant editor of *Springfield Republican*, under Samuel Bowles. Wrote wide variety of items for the paper, including a series of moralistic letters under the pseudonym Timothy Titcomb. Journalistic writing collected in *History of Western Massachusetts* (1855), *The Bay-Path* (1857), and the widely popular *Timothy Titcomb's Letters to Young People, Single and Married* (1858). After 1857 devoted himself primarily to writing books. Published volumes of poetry—*Bitter-Sweet* (1858), *Kathrina, Her Life and Mine in a Poem* (1867), *The Marble Prophecy* (1872), and *The Puritan's Guest* (1881)—and novels including *Miss Gilbert's Career* (1860), *Arthur Bonnicastle* (1873), *Sevenoaks* (1875), and *Nicholas Minturn* (1877), as well as collections of moral essays. Was a friend of Emily Dickinson, one of a small circle to whom she occasionally showed work. In later years, in addition to literary and editorial work, served as president of New York City Board of Education and chairman of board of trustees of City College. From 1870 until his death he was editor of *Scribner's Monthly*.

OLIVER WENDELL HOLMES (August 29, 1809–October 7, 1894) b. Cambridge, Massachusetts. Son of Sarah Wendell (merchant's daughter) and Abiel Holmes (minister of First Church of Boston). Graduated Harvard 1829; entered Harvard Law School but transferred a year later to private medical school. Poem "Old Ironsides," protesting the impending destruction of the frigate *Constitution*, appeared in *Boston Daily Advertiser* in 1830 and became widely popular. Reputation as writer enhanced by essays under rubric "The Autocrat of the Breakfast-Table" in *New England Magazine*, the first of which appeared in November 1831. After two years of medical study in France (1833–35), and further work at Harvard Medical School, granted M.D. from Harvard in 1836; began practice in Boston. Published first collection of verse, *Poems* (1836). As researcher, awarded three Boyleston prizes by Harvard for essays on medical subjects; taught medicine at Tremont Medical School, of which he was a founder; professor of anatomy at Dartmouth, 1838–40. In 1840 married Amelia Lee Jackson, daughter of Massachusetts supreme court justice; they had three children (the eldest, Oliver Wendell, became a justice of United States Supreme Court, 1902–32). Continued important medical research, including landmark paper on pueperal fever in 1843. Appointed Parkman Professor of Anatomy and Physiology at Harvard Medical School in 1847, a position he held until 1882, when he was named professor emeritus; dean of Harvard Medical School, 1847–53. Was a member of celebrated "Saturday Club" and was considered one of the great conversationalists of his era; friends included James Russell Lowell, Nathaniel Hawthorne, Ralph Waldo Emerson, John Greenleaf Whittier, Henry Wadsworth Longfellow, John Lothrop Motley, and William Dean Howells. In 1853 delivered well-received lecture series on the English poets, and in 1857 resumed his "Breakfast-Table" series for *Atlantic Monthly*, collected in *The Autocrat of the Breakfast-Table* (1858), *The Professor at the Breakfast-Table* (1860), *The Poet at the Breakfast-Table* (1872), and *Over the Teacups* (1891). Published three novels, all originally serialized in the *Atlantic—Elsie Venner* (1861), *The Guardian Angel* (1867), and *A Mortal Antipathy* (1885)—and a variety of other prose including *John Lothrop Motley: A Memoir* (1879), *Medical Essays* (1883), and *Ralph Waldo Emerson* (1884). Poetry collected in *Songs in Many Keys* (1862), *Songs of Many Seasons* (1875), *The Iron Gate* (1880), and *Before the Curfew* (1887).

JOHN HENRY HOPKINS, JR. (October 28, 1820–August 13, 1891) b. Pittsburgh, Pennsylvania. One of 13 children of Melusina Muller and John Henry Hopkins, a prominent lawyer; after conversion experience, father became member of Trinity Episcopal Church, was elected rector in 1823, and soon achieved full clerical standing. Family moved to Cambridge, Massachusetts, in 1831, and the following year to Burlington, Vermont, where father became Episcopal Bishop of Vermont. Hopkins graduated University of Vermont in 1839; served as tutor in Savannah, Georgia, 1842–44; graduated New York General Theological Seminary in 1850, and in the same year was ordained Episcopal deacon. In 1853 founded *The Church Journal*, which he edited until 1868. Active in foundation of dioceses of Pittsburgh in 1865, and of Albany and Long Island in 1868. Ordained priest in 1872; served as rector in Plattsburgh, New York (1872–76) and Williamsport, Pennsylvania (1876–87). Published biography of father in 1873; other writings included

Carols, Hymns and Songs (1863), *The Canticles Noted* (1866), and *Poems by the Wayside* (1883). Died at the home of a friend near Hudson, New York.

GEORGE MOSES HORTON (1798?–1883?) b. into slavery on plantation of William Horton in Northampton County, North Carolina; in childhood moved with his master to Chatham, near Chapel Hill. Belonged in turn to son and grandson of his original owner. Taught himself to read. Worked on campus of University of North Carolina; said to have been paid by students to compose love poems for them. *The Lancaster Gazette*, a Massachusetts newspaper, published three of his poems in 1828, and others appeared in *Freedom's Journal*, *The Liberator*, and *Southern Literary Messenger*. *The Hope of Liberty* (1829), designed to earn his freedom and passage to Liberia, failed to earn enough to do so (subsequently reprinted as *Poems by a Slave* in 1837 and 1838). In the 1830s, the author Caroline Lee Hentz tutored him in poetic composition and transcribed his verses while he learned to write; he read poetry in volumes given him by students. Second book, *The Poetical Works of George M. Horton, the Colored Bard of North Carolina*, published 1845. Wrote letters and otherwise constantly attempted to gain freedom, while working on campus as handyman, waiter, and servant. In 1865 escaped and reached Sherman's army in Raleigh. That same year published final collection, *Naked Genius*. Settled after the war in Philadelphia, where he is believed to have died in about 1883.

RICHARD HOVEY (May 4, 1864–February 24, 1900) b. Normal, Illinois. Son of Harriette Farnham Spofford, an educator, and Charles Edward Hovey, a Civil War general and former president of Normal University of Illinois who later practiced law. Grew up in North Amherst, Massachusetts, and in Washington, D.C. Before college, educated mostly at home by mother. First book, *Poems*, published privately in 1880. Graduated Dartmouth (where he wrote song "Men of Dartmouth") in 1885. Studied art at Art Students' League of Washington, and theology at General Theological Seminary of Episcopal Church in New York City; contemplated taking orders, but did not complete training. In summer 1887 met Canadian poet Bliss Carman and artist Thomas Buford Meteyard, with whom he made walking tour of New England; in Scituate, Massachusetts, met Thomas William Parsons, poet and translator of Dante, whom he regarded as mentor. Corresponded intensively with novelist Amelie Rives, 1888–89. Gave lectures in philosophy, 1888–89, at Thomas Davidson's school in Farmington, Connecticut. In 1890 met Henriette Knapp Russell, wife of actor Edmund Russell and popular proponent of physical training system Delsartism (during stay in London, her friends included Oscar Wilde, James McNeill Whistler, and Madame Blavatsky); began affair with her. Under influence of Sidney Lanier's *The Science of English Verse*, published essays on poetry and poetic technique in *The Independent*, 1891–94. Undertook multi-part verse drama on Arthurian themes titled *Poem in Dramas*; first volume published as *Launcelot and Guenevere* (1891). Went to Europe with Mrs. Russell in 1891; traveled by himself in France, settling in

Giverny. Joined Mrs. Russell in Tours; their son Julian born February 1892. Returned to U.S., leaving son in care of foster mother; visited Bliss Carman in Nova Scotia. Elegy on death of Thomas William Parsons, *Seaward*, published in book form in 1893. In collaboration with Carman, and with Meteyard as book designer, wrote *Songs from Vagabondia* (1894), which achieved enormous popularity. Married Mrs. Russell, recently divorced, in January 1894; worked sporadically as actor; in May the couple sailed for Europe. Worked on translations of Belgian symbolist playwright Maurice Maeterlinck (published *The Plays of Maurice Maeterlinck*, 1894–96); after a year in London went to France in June 1895; met Stéphane Mallarmé and other members of symbolist movement; reunited with son Julian. Returned to U.S. in 1896; settled in New York City. Published another volume with Carman, *More Songs from Vagabondia* (1896), and further installments of poetic drama cycle, *The Birth of Galahad* (1898) and *Taliesin: A Masque* (1899); poetry collected in *Along the Trail* (1898), which included poems in support of Spanish-American War. Began lectureship at Barnard College in 1899. After several years of ill health, died following minor intestinal operation when blood clot lodged in his heart. Posthumously published work included *Last Songs from Vagabondia* (1901), another collaboration with Carman; *The Holy Graal and Other Fragments* (1907), further pieces of Arthurian drama cycle; *To the End of the Trail* (1908); and *Dartmouth Lyrics* (1924).

JULIA WARD HOWE   (May 27, 1819–October 17, 1910)   b. New York City. Daughter of Julia Rush Cutler Ward (an occasional writer of poems) and Samuel Ward (a wealthy banker); sister-in-law of sculptor Thomas Crawford and aunt of popular novelist F. Marion Crawford. In 1843 married reformer Samuel Gridley Howe (18 years her senior) and moved to Boston; they had six children, four of whom survived their mother (children included writers Laura Richards and Maud Howe Elliott). With her husband, published abolitionist newspaper *The Commonwealth* beginning in 1851; their Boston home was frequented by Theodore Parker, Charles Sumner, and other anti-slavery activists. First collection of poetry, *Passion Flowers*, appeared in 1854, followed by *Words for the Hour* (1857) and *A Trip to Cuba* (1860). *Atlantic Monthly* published "The Battle Hymn of the Republic" in April 1862; song became unofficial anthem of Union Army. After the war, Howe campaigned for woman suffrage; was a founder in 1868 of New England Woman Suffrage Association and served as its first president; active from 1869 on in American Woman Suffrage Association; president of Association for the Advancement of Women, 1878–88. Campaigned for world peace; in "Appeal to Womanhood Throughout the World" (1870) called for international women's peace conference; became president (1871) of Woman's International Peace Association. Active in support of prison reform and Greek independence. Was first woman elected to National Academy of Arts and Letters. Marriage strained by husband's objection to many of her public activities (she later wrote, "I have never known my husband to approve of any act of mine which I myself valued"); he died in 1876. Poetry collected in *Later Lyrics* (1866) and *From*

Sunset Ridge: Poems Old and New (1899); other writings included *Sex and Education* (1874), *Modern Society* (1881), *Margaret Fuller* (1883), *Is Polite Society Polite?* (1895), and memoirs *Reminiscences* (1899) and *At Sunset* (1910). Died in Newport, Rhode Island.

WILLIAM DEAN HOWELLS (March 1, 1837–May 10, 1920) b. Martins Ferry, Ohio. Son of Mary Dean and William Cooper Howells (a Welsh-born printer and publisher with wide political and philosophical interests). Little formal schooling; assisted father (who had bought a newspaper in Hamilton, Ohio) as typesetter. Published first poem in 1852 in *Ohio State Journal*, for which father was reporter, and for which Howells himself worked as a typesetter; while working there, formed friendship with John James Piatt. Relocated with family to Jefferson, Ohio; maintained rigorous course of self-education while working full time as printer for *Ashtabula Sentinel*, a newspaper with abolitionist sympathies edited by his father. Periodic nervous collapses led to failure as editor of *Cincinnati Gazette*. Became city editor and columnist of *Ohio State Journal* in 1858. Published poems, stories, and reviews in *Atlantic Monthly*, *National Era*, *Dial*, and other periodicals; first book, verse collection *Poems of Two Friends* (written in collaboration with John James Piatt), published 1860. Wrote Lincoln campaign biography, using proceeds to travel East where he met literary figures including James Russell Lowell, James T. Fields, Oliver Wendell Homes, Nathaniel Hawthorne, Ralph Waldo Emerson, and Henry David Thoreau. Appointed U.S. consul in Venice (1861–64), where he studied Italian, Dante, and Venetian art. Married Elinor Mead in Paris in 1862; they had two daughters and a son. Resigning consulship, briefly joined staff of *The Nation* in New York before moving to Cambridge to serve as assistant editor of *Atlantic Monthly*. Formed close friendships with Mark Twain and William and Henry James. In 1871 succeeded James T. Fields as editor of *Atlantic Monthly*. Published first novel, *Their Wedding Journey* (1871), followed by, among other titles, *A Chance Acquaintance* (1873), *Poems* (1873), *A Foregone Conclusion* (1874), *The Lady of the Aroostook* (1879), and *The Undiscovered Country* (1880). Resigned *Atlantic* editorship in 1881 to write full-time; moved to Boston. Later novels included *Dr. Breen's Practice* (1881), *A Modern Instance* (1882), *The Rise of Silas Lapham* (1885), *Indian Summer* (1886), *The Minister's Charge* (1886), *April Hopes* (1887), *Annie Kilburn* (1888), *A Hazard of New Fortunes* (1890), utopian novel *A Traveler from Altruria* (1894), *The Landlord at Lion's Head* (1897), *The Story of a Play* (1898), *The Kentons* (1902), and *The Son of Royal Langbrith* (1904). Increasingly involved in radical social causes; pleaded for clemency for anarchists unjustly convicted of murder following Haymarket riot of 1887. Older daughter Winifred died in 1889. Contributed regular "Editor's Study" column to *Harper's Monthly*, 1886–92; moved to New York to edit *Cosmopolitan*, but resigned after conflict with its owner over his political views. Encouraged many younger writers including Stephen Crane, Paul Laurence Dunbar, Henry Blake Fuller, Abraham Cahan, and Stuart Merrill. Elected first president of American

Academy of Arts and Letters in 1908; traveled frequently in Europe. Died of pneumonia in New York.

WILLIAM REED HUNTINGTON (September 20, 1838–July 26, 1909) b. Lowell, Massachusetts. Son of Hannah Hinckley and Elisha Huntington, prominent physician and public official. Graduated Harvard, where he was class poet, in 1859. Studied for Episcopal ministry; ordained 1861; accepted position as assistant minister of Emmanuel Church; in 1862 became rector of All Saints Church, Worcester, Massachusetts, and served in that capacity for 21 years. Married Theresa Reynolds in 1863. Read Phi Beta Kappa poem at Harvard in 1870. From 1883, as rector of Grace Church, was a leading figure in the religious and cultural life of New York City. Worked on revised version of Book of Common Prayer (published 1892); interest in church architecture led to involvement with building of Cathedral of St. John the Divine in New York City, of which he was a trustee for 22 years, and where a memorial chapel was dedicated to him. His religious and ecclesiastical ideas were outlined in many works, including *The Church-Idea* (1870), *Conditional Immortality* (1878), *The Causes of the Soul* (1891), *The Peace of the Church* (1891), *Popular Misconceptions of the Episcopal Church* (1891), *The Spiritual House* (1895), *A National Church* (1898), and *Briefs on Religion* (1902). Published two volumes of memoirs, *Twenty Years of a Massachusetts Rectorship* (1883) and *Twenty Years of a New York Rectorship* (1903). Poems collected in *Sonnets and a Dream* in 1899 (second edition 1903).

HELEN HUNT JACKSON (October 15, 1830–August 12, 1885) b. Helen Maria Fiske in Amherst, Massachusetts. Father Nathan W. Fiske taught classics and moral philosophy at Amherst College; when she was 14, her mother, Deborah Vinal, died of consumption. Educated at Ipswich Female Academy in Massachusetts and Abbott Brothers school in New York City. Early friend and schoolmate of Emily Dickinson, with whom she retained lifelong ties. In 1852 married Edward B. Hunt, officer of army corps of engineers; he died in 1863 while testing a submarine device. Of their two sons, one died in infancy, the other in 1865. Moved to Newport, Rhode Island, where she became acquainted with Thomas Wentworth Higginson. With his encouragement, began to contribute poetry and prose to *New York Independent, Hearth and Home, Scribner's Monthly*, and other periodicals, some of them pieces based on travels in Europe from 1868 to 1870. Most of these writings were published anonymously, under pseudonuym "Saxe Holm," or identified only with initials "H. H."; she continued this practice for much of her career. Writing was well received; first collection of poetry, *Verses*, appeared in 1870, and over the next decade she published a variety of sketches, essays, and fiction including *Bits of Travel* (1872), *Bits of Talk About Home Matters* (1873), the poem *The Story of Boon* (1874), *Mercy Philbrick's Choice* (1876), *Hetty's Strange History* (1877), *Bits of Travel at Home* (1878), and a novel for children, *Nelly's Silver Mine* (1878). Traveled West for her health in 1872; while wintering in Colorado Springs met banker and railroad manager

William S. Jackson, whom she married in 1875, settling permanently in Colorado Springs. Developed deep interest in American Indians and in 1881 published *A Century of Dishonor*, influential account of U.S. government mistreatment and deception; sent a copy to every member of Congress at her own expense. In 1882 appointed U.S. Special Commissioner to investigate condition of Mission Indians of California; aside from official report, recorded impressions in *Glimpses of California and the Missions* (1883). Disappointment at inaction in response to her report prompted writing of *Ramona* (1884), popular novel about girl of mixed Indian and Scottish blood set against backdrop of American incursions into Spanish California. Two collections of poetry, *Easter Bells* and *Pansies and Orchids*, also appeared in 1884. Other late publications included three books of cat stories for children, *Letters from a Cat* (1879), *Mammy Tittleback and Family: A Story of Seventeen Cats* (1881), and *The Hunter Cats of Connorloa* (1884); *The Training of Children* (1882), and posthumously published volumes *Zeph* (1885), *Glimpses of Three Coasts* (1886), *Sonnets and Lyrics* (1886), and *Between Whiles* (1887). Soon after publication of *Ramona*, broke her hip in fall that left her crippled; traveled to San Francisco to recuperate, and died there of cancer. Emily Dickinson wrote on learning of her death, "Helen of Troy will die, but Helen of Colorado, never. Dear friend, can you walk, were the last words that I wrote her. Dear friend, I can fly—her immortal reply."

EDWIN JAMES (August 27, 1797–October 28, 1861) b. Weybridge, Vermont. Youngest of 13 children of Mary Emmes and Daniel James. Graduated Middlebury College in 1816; studied botany, geology, and medicine in Albany, New York. Accompanied 1820 expedition of Major Stephen H. Long to explore country between Mississippi and Rocky Mountains; reached summit of Pike's Peak (named James Peak by Long); explored Arkansas, Red, and Canadian rivers. Summarized findings in *Account of an Expedition from Pittsburgh to the Rocky Mountains* (1822–23). Became a U.S. army surgeon in 1823; subsequently stationed at forts Crawford, Mackinac, and Brady. In April 1827 married Clarissa Rogers; they had one son. Studied Indian languages and published various translations, grammars, and studies; with John Tanner (a former captive among the Ojibwa) wrote *A Narrative of the Captivity and Adventures of John Tanner* (1830); with Tanner made first Ojibwa translation of complete New Testament (1833). Resigned from army in 1833; helped edit *Temperance Herald and Journal* in Albany. Served as sub-agent for Potawatomi at Old Council Bluffs, Nebraska, 1837–38. Settled as farmer at Rock Spring, near Burlington, Iowa. Was an ardent abolitionist and assisted in the escape of fugitive slaves.

SARAH ORNE JEWETT (September 3, 1849–June 24, 1909) b. Theodora Sarah Orne Jewett in South Berwick, Maine. Daughter of Caroline Frances Perry and Theodore Jewett, wealthy physician, professor of medicine, and president of Maine Medical Society. Father's patients included fishermen and farmers whose lives she later described. Graduated from Berwick Academy in 1866. First published story appeared in *Flag of Our Union* in 1868; contributed many children's stories to periodicals including *Riverside* and *Our Young Folks*. Series of stories of Maine village life, published in *Atlantic Monthly* with enthusiastic support of its editor William Dean Howells, appeared in book form as *Deephaven* in 1877, achieving considerable success. Children's stories collected in *Play Days* (1878). Father died in 1878. Continued to live and write in South Berwick, but traveled frequently to Boston and New York. As friend of James T. Fields (publisher of *Atlantic Monthly*) and his wife Annie Adams Fields, became part of Boston literary circle including Oliver Wendell Holmes, John Greenleaf Whittier, James Russell Lowell, Harriet Beecher Stowe, and Thomas Bailey Aldrich. Published further collections and sketches—*Old Friends and New* (1879), *Country By-Ways* (1881), *The Mate of the Daylight and Friends Ashore* (1883)—and novel *A Country Doctor* (1884), whose title character was modeled on her father. Following death of James T. Fields in 1881, became close companion of Annie Fields, living with her for much of every year in Boston and Manchester-by-the-Sea, and traveling with her in Europe, Florida, and the Caribbean. On trips to Europe met Christina Rossetti, Alfred Tennyson, Matthew Arnold, George Du Maurier, Henry James, and Rudyard Kipling. Another novel, *A Marsh Island* (1885), was followed by the collections *A White Heron* (1886), *The King of Folly Island and Other People* (1888), *Strangers and Wayfarers* (1890), *Tales of New England* (1890), *A Native of Winby* (1893), and *The Life of Nancy* (1895) and popular history *The Story of the Normans* (1887). *The Country of the Pointed Firs* (1896), based on experiences in the Boothbay Harbor region of Maine, was acclaimed by many as her best book; additional stories dealing with the fictional town of Dunnet Landing were published in *The Queen's Twin and Other Stories* (1899). *The Tory Lover*, a novel of the American Revolution, appeared in 1901. Received honorary degree in literature from Bowdoin in 1901, the first woman so honored. Thrown from a carriage in 1902; suffered spinal damage and stopped writing. In later years formed friendship with Willa Cather. Died in her South Berwick home of a cerebral hemorrhage. Poems appeared posthumously in *Verses* (1916).

FANNY KEMBLE (November 27, 1809–January 15, 1893) b. London, England, into distinguished theatrical family; given name Frances Anne Kemble. Daughter of Maria Thérèse De Camp and Charles Kemble; niece of John Philip Kemble and Sarah Siddons. Grew up mostly under care of aunt Adelaide De Camp; as adolescent spent three years at school in Paris. Made debut as Juliet at Covent Garden (of which her father was manager) in 1829; became overnight stage success. After father, burdened by debt, was forced to cut ties with Covent Garden, accompanied him to the U.S. in 1832 and toured for two years, playing in New York, Philadelphia, Boston, Baltimore, and Washington, and enjoying great popularity; presented to Andrew Jackson; formed close friendship with novelist Catharine Maria Sedgwick and Unitarian minister William Ellery Channing. In June 1834 abandoned stage career to marry Pierce Mease Butler of Philadelphia, heir to large sea-island plantation in Georgia; they had two daughters, one of whom became the mother of novelist Owen Wister. A two-volume record of Kemble's American experiences, *Journal of a Residence in America* (1835), stirred some resentment for occasional criticisms of American life; husband objected to its publication and at his urging she omitted anti-slavery passages. Made six-month visit with husband and daughters to Georgia plantation in December 1838; shocked by first-hand exposure to slavery. (Record of Georgia stay published in England in 1863 as *Journal of a Residence on a Georgian Plantation*, in effort to sway British public opinion in favor of the Union.) Marital strains continued after family returned to Philadelphia and during three-year stay in England beginning in December 1840. Despite her efforts to keep family united, she and husband had increasingly long separations; Kemble often summered in Lenox, Massachusetts, home of Catharine Maria Sedgwick and her circle. *Poems* published in 1844. After final breakup of marriage, returned to London in 1845; the following year relocated to Italy. Published memoir *A Year of Consolation* (1847); the following year Butler sued her for divorce on grounds of abandonment, and she returned to America. In the case, which became notorious, Kemble was represented by celebrated counsel Rufus Choate, although the case never came before a jury; divorce, including custody of children, awarded to Butler in 1849. Kemble established successful career as Shakespearean reader in America and abroad. Purchased cottage in Lenox, Massachusetts. Continued to travel regularly between England and America, and gave readings until 1869. Became close friend of Henry James, whom she met in Rome in 1872. In later years published autobiographies *Records of a Girlhood* (1878) and *Records of Later Life* (1882); *Notes Upon Some of Shakespeare's Plays* (1882); *Far Away and Long Ago* (1889), a novel set in the Berkshires; and *Further Records* (1891), a final volume of memoirs. Returned to England in 1877 and remained in London until her death.

FRANCIS SCOTT KEY (August 1, 1779–January 11, 1843) b. on family estate in Frederick (now Carroll) County, Maryland. Son of Ann Phoebe Charlton and John Ross Key (an officer in American Revolutionary Army). Graduated St. John's College, Annapolis in 1796; studied law, opening practice at Fredericktown in 1801. Married Mary Taylor Lloyd in 1802; they had six sons and five daughters. The family moved to Georgetown in the District of Columbia, where Key practiced law for a time with his uncle, future congressman Philip Barton Key. In 1814, during British withdrawal from Washington, was asked to intervene in plight of an American physician held prisoner aboard a British ship; after arranging his release, witnessed British bombardment of Baltimore. In response to the sight, on the dawn of September 14, of the American flag still flying over Fort McHenry, wrote "The Star-Spangled Banner." Poem published (as "Defence of Fort McHenry") in *Baltimore American* on September 21, it achieved immediate nationwide popularity. As lawyer, practiced extensively in federal courts; served as U.S. attorney for

District of Columbia (1833–41). Died of pleurisy in Baltimore. Poetry collected posthumously in *Poems of the Late Francis S. Key, Esq.* (1857).

SIDNEY LANIER (February 3, 1842–September 7, 1881) b. Macon, Georgia. Son of Mary Jane Anderson and Robert Sampson Lanier, a lawyer. As a child showed precocious musical ability. Graduated Oglethorpe University in Milledgeville, Georgia, in 1860; plans for further study interrupted by outbreak of war. Joined Macon Volunteers in July 1861; the following year fought in Seven Days' Battle near Richmond, Virginia; served as mounted scout along James River, 1863–64. In 1864 captured aboard blockade runner (on which he served as signal officer) and imprisoned for four months at Point Lookout, Maryland. Health deteriorated in prison; contracted tuberculosis. Released February 1865; worked as hotel clerk in Montgomery, Alabama, then as teacher and law clerk in father's office. In 1867 married Mary Day (with whom he had four sons) and published novel *Tiger-Lilies*, based on war experiences. Admitted to Georgia bar in 1869 and practiced for a time in father's law office. Although frequently hindered by chronic tuberculosis (he wrote to Bayard Taylor that "pretty much the whole of life has been merely not dying"), was eventually able to make career in music and poetry. In 1873 named first flutist of the Peabody Orchestra, Baltimore; devoted much study to history of Elizabethan music. Published first poem in *Lippincott's* in 1874. Although only one volume of poetry published during lifetime (*Poems*, 1877), his work appeared in a number of magazines; gained considerable reputation as poet and critic. From 1879 until his death two years later at age 39, lectured on English verse at Johns Hopkins. Wrote series of retellings of medieval tales for children—*The Boy's Froissart* (1879), *The Boy's King Arthur* (1880), *The Boy's Mabinogion* (1881), and *The Boy's Percy* (1882), as well as popular travel guide *Florida: Its Scenery, Climate, and History* (1875). Major critical work, *The Science of English Verse*, appeared in 1880. Died at Lynn, in mountains of North Carolina, where he had gone to recover health. Collected poems, edited by his wife, appeared posthumously in 1884, along with further critical work: *The English Novel* (1883), *Music and Poetry* (1898), and *Shakspere and His Forerunners* (1902).

EMMA LAZARUS (July 22, 1849–November 19, 1887) b. New York City. Daughter of Esther Nathan and Moses Lazarus; father, a wealthy sugar merchant, came from Sephardic family that had been in America at least since 18th century; mother was of German descent; family spent summers in Newport, Rhode Island. Educated by private tutors; little religious training; learned German, French, and Italian at an early age. *Poems and Translations* (1867), published at her father's expense, contained work written between ages 14 and 16. Ralph Waldo Emerson, to whom she sent a copy, wrote to her in February 1868 and they met briefly in April; in an extended correspondence, he served as literary mentor, reading and commenting on her poetry. Also received encouragement from Thomas Wentworth Higginson and Edmund Clarence Stedman; corresponded with naturalist John Burroughs. Second collection, *Admetus and Other Poems*, published 1871; contributed poems frequently to *Lippincott's*, *Scribner's*, *The Galaxy*, *The Century*, and other leading periodicals. Disappointed when Emerson failed to include any of her work in his 1874 anthology *Parnassus*, but made amicable visit to him in Concord in 1876. Published historical novel *Alide: An Episode in Goethe's Life* (1874) and *The Spagnoletto* (1876), verse drama about 17th-century painter Jose de Ribera. Translations of Heine collected in *Poems and Ballads of Heine* (1881); also translated (from German versions) medieval Hebrew poetry of Yehudah HaLevi, Solomon Ibn Gabirol, and Moses Ben Ezra. In response to Russian pogroms of early 1880s, and deeply impressed by 1881 visit (with Reform rabbi Gustav Gottheil) to immigration center at Ward's Island, became prominent worker for Jewish causes; organized refugee relief and contributed articles on Jewish subjects to *The Century*; wrote weekly column "An Epistle to the Hebrews" for *The American Hebrew*, 1882–83 (collected in book form in 1900); in 1882 article espoused creation of a Jewish homeland in Palestine, although not for American Jews; instrumental in founding of Hebrew Technical Institute. In 1882 published *Songs of a Semite*, which included "The Dance of Death," verse drama (based on a work by German writer Richard Reinhard) about 14th-century massacre of German Jews; dedicated "Dance of Death" to George Eliot, whose *Daniel Deronda* she credited with "elevating and ennobling the spirit of Jewish nationality." Wrote sonnet "The New Colossus" in support of fund-raising campaign to build pedestal for Statue of Liberty (poem recited in 1886 at statue's dedication; final lines later embossed on pedestal). Traveled to England and France in 1883; met Robert Browning and William Morris. Ill with cancer, made long visit to Europe, 1885–87; visited the Netherlands, France, and Italy; died less than three months after return to U.S. "By the Waters of Babylon," sequence of prose poems, published in *The Century* in 1887. A posthumous two-volume edition of her works, *The Poems of Emma Lazarus*, edited by sisters Mary and Annie, appeared in 1889.

JAMES MATHEWES LEGARÉ (November 26, 1823–May 30, 1859) b. Charleston, South Carolina. Son of Mary Doughty Mathews and John D. Legaré. Of Huguenot descent on father's side; third cousin of South Carolina statesman Hugh Swinton Legaré. Father edited a farm journal, briefly kept a hotel, and eventually opened an agricultural supply store. Attended College of Charleston, graduating 1841, and St. Mary's College in Baltimore. Eulogized Hugh Swinton Legaré's death in June 1843 in poem "On the Death of a Kinsman." Worked in law office of James L. Petigru in Charleston; wrote poetry; painted (as he would continue to do throughout his life). Fabricated evidence of noble origins of Legaré family, but hoax was exposed in newspapers. Suffered first of recurrent lung hemorrhages. Had his poetry and fiction published by William Gilmore Simms in various periodicals; John James Audubon, an acquaintance of his father, offered to help find a publisher for his poetry. Moved with family in 1846 to Aiken in the South Carolina midlands; father declared bankruptcy two years later. Contributed writing to *The Opal*,

Southern Literary Messenger, the Athens (Georgia) *Weekly Gazette*, *The Literary World*, *Graham's Magazine*, and *The Knickerbocker*. Briefly ran school; taught drawing in Augusta, Georgia, and elsewhere. Initiated long correspondence with Henry Wadsworth Longfellow. Verse collection *Orta-Undis* (1848) published by William D. Ticknor of Boston. Formally confirmed as Episcopalian in 1848. Married Anne C. Andrews in 1850; settled in Aiken. Traveled to New York in 1851, meeting Rufus Griswold and Evert Duyckinck. Served as postmaster of Aiken, 1852–53. Set up a laboratory where he worked for years on a variety of inventions, several of which were eventually patented; most successful were experiments in furniture made from plastic fibers derived from chemically treated cotton; exhibited inventions and paintings at Charleston Industrial Institute in 1856 and 1857. Died of tuberculosis.

CHARLES GODFREY LELAND (August 15, 1824–March 20, 1903) b. Philadelphia, Pennsylvania. Son of Charlotte Godfrey and Charles Leland, a prosperous merchant. Friend from an early age of George Henry Boker, whose father and Leland's were business partners; schoolmate of George McClellan. Early education in Philadelphia (where his teachers included Bronson Alcott, whom he later described as "the most eccentric man who ever took it on himself to train and form the youthful mind") and at Jamaica Plains, Massachusetts. Voracious reader throughout childhood; deeply affected by early reading of Rabelais, of which he later said: "It seems to me now as if it were the great event of my life." Graduated College of New Jersey (later Princeton) in 1845; after graduating, traveled in France and Italy before continuing studies in Heidelberg, Munich, and Paris for two years, 1846–48; became fluent in German; met poet and occultist Justinus Kerner; in 1848 participated briefly in revolutionary upheavals in Paris. Returned to Philadelphia; studied law; admitted to bar, but by 1853 left profession to pursue career in journalism. Contributed book reviews to *Union Magazine* (1849); in New York, assisted Rufus Griswold on *The International Magazine* (1850–52) and on P. T. Barnum's *Illustrated News* (1853). Became staffer on Philadelphia *Evening Bulletin*. Early publications included *Meister Karl's Sketch-Book* (1855), a collection of essays and sketches; *The Poetry and Mystery of Dreams* (1855); and a translation of Heinrich Heine's *Pictures of Travel* (1856). Friends included William Makepeace Thackeray, Lola Montez, Bayard Taylor, and Ole Bull. Married Eliza Belle Fisher in 1856. Briefly edited *Graham's Magazine*, where in May 1857 he published first of his enormously popular Hans Breitmann poems in German dialect. Contributed many articles to *Appleton's Cyclopaedia* (1858–63) under editorship of George Ripley and Charles A. Dana; worked as an editor for *New York Times*; edited *Vanity Fair* (1860–61) and *The Knickerbocker* (1861–62). In 1862 became editor of *The Continental Monthly* (1862–63) in Boston; claimed to have popularized term "emancipation" as alternative to controversial "abolition." Published *Sunshine in Thought* (1862), *The Art of Conversation, or Hints for Self-Education* (1863), and political satire *The Book of Copperheads* (1863). Served in Philadelphia artillery company during Gettysburg campaign, although he saw little action;

formed friendship with fellow soldier Richard Watson Gilder. At close of war, traveled in the West and speculated briefly in coal and petroleum. Became managing editor of Philadephia *Press* in 1866. Partly through influence of James Russell Lowell, awarded honorary M.A. by Harvard in 1867. Upon the death of his father in 1869, was able to give up newspaper work and travel in Europe; eventually settled in London for a decade. Acquaintances in London included Bret Harte, George Eliot, George Henry Lewes, and publisher Nicolas Trübner. *The Breitmann Ballads* (which enjoyed extraordinary popularity in England) were collected in book form in 1871, followed by books on wide variety of topics: *The Music Lesson of Confucius; and Other Poems* (1872), *Egyptian Sketch-Book* (1873), *The English Gypsies and Their Language* (1873), *Fu-Sang, or the Discovery of America by Chinese Buddhist Priests in the Fifth Century* (1875), *English Gypsy Songs* (1875, with Janet Tuckey and Edward H. Palmer), children's book *Johnnykin and the Goblins* (1876), *Pidgin-English Sing-Song; or, Songs and Stories in the China-English Dialect* (1876), *Abraham Lincoln* (1879), *The Minor Arts; Porcelain Painting, Wood-Carving, Stencilling, Modelling, Mosaic Work, Etc.* (1880), *The Gypsies* (1883), *The Algonquin Legends of New England* (1884), *A Dictionary of Slang* (1889, with Albert Barrere), *Etruscan-Roman Remains in Popular Tradition* (1892), *Memoirs* (1893), *Legends of Florence* (1895–96), *The Unpublished Legends of Virgil* (1901), and, in collaboration with John Dyneley Prince, *Kulóskap the Master and Other Algonkin Poems* (1902). Traveled in Egypt with George Henry Boker in 1872. With Walter Besant founded the Rabelais Club. Developed interest in industrial arts education; returned to Philadelphia to promote the idea and wrote a number of manuals. Returned to London in 1884; in later years spent much time in Florence, where he died.

ABRAHAM LINCOLN (February 12, 1809–April 15, 1865) b. near Hodgenville, Kentucky. Son of Nancy Hanks and Thomas Lincoln, a farmer and carpenter. Family moved to Indiana in 1816; mother died in 1818. Received little formal education. In 1830 family moved to Illinois. Worked on flatboat to New Orleans in 1828 and again in 1831. Settled in New Salem, Illinois; worked as storekeeper, surveyor, postmaster; captain of volunteers in Black Hawk War (1832). Served in state legislature, 1834–41, as Whig. Studied law; began law practice in 1836 and moved to Springfield in 1837. Married Mary Todd in 1842 after long, sometimes troubled courtship; they had four sons, two of whom died in childhood. Established law practice with William Herndon as junior partner in 1844. Served one term as Whig congressman (1847–49); opposed Mexican War. Renewed involvement with politics after Kansas-Nebraska Act of 1854 repealed anti-slavery restriction in Missouri Compromise; spoke frequently against it and gained wide recognition. Helped found the Republican Party of Illinois in 1856. Campaigned in 1858 for U.S. Senate seat held by Democrat Stephen Douglas, author of the Kansas-Nebraska Act, and debated Douglas seven times on the slavery issue (debates were published in 1860 in edition prepared by Lincoln). Although Illinois legislature reelected Douglas to the Senate, campaign brought Lincoln national prominence in the Republican party. In February 1860 (after introduction by William Cullen Bryant) delivered address on slavery at Cooper Union in New York City. Received Republican presidential nomination in May and won election in fall with 180 of 303 electoral votes and 40 percent of popular vote; victory led to secession of seven Southern states. In early April 1861 sent naval expedition to provision Fort Sumter in Charleston harbor in South Carolina; when Confederates bombarded the fort, Lincoln called up militia, proclaimed blockade of Southern ports, and suspended habeas corpus. Preliminary and final emancipation proclamations issued September 23, 1862, and January 1, 1863. Delivered address at Gettysburg on November 19, 1863. After long series of command changes, appointed Ulysses S. Grant commander of all Union forces in March 1864. Reelected president; delivered second inaugural address March 4, 1865. Worked for passage of Thirteenth Amendment. Visited Richmond after its capture by Union Army and learned of Appomattox surrender on his return to Washington. Assassinated on April 14 by John Wilkes Booth at Ford's Theatre.

GEORGE CABOT LODGE (October 10, 1873–August 21, 1909) b. Boston, Massachusetts. Son of Anna Cabot Mills Davis and politician and author Henry Cabot Lodge; reared at father's house in Nahant, Massachusetts. In childhood knew Henry Adams, Edith Wharton, John Hay, Theodore Roosevelt, and other members of parents' circle. Graduated Harvard 1895. Continued studies in Romance languages at the Sorbonne in 1895–96, in company with close friend Trumbull Stickney. Began to publish poetry in *Scribner's*, *Harper's*, and other magazines. Briefly returned to Europe in 1897 to study German and philosophy at the University of Berlin. Introduced to Buddhist practices and beliefs by family friend William Sturgis Bigelow. In 1897 went to work in Washington as father's secretary. First book, *The Song of the Wave*, appeared in 1898; saw active service that year in Spanish-American War, participating in capture of Ponce, Puerto Rico. Became interested in "Conservative Christian Anarchy," philosophical position developed with friends Henry Adams and Trumbull Stickney. Verse collected in *Poems 1899–1902* (1902). In 1900 married Elizabeth (Matilda) Frelinghuysen Davis, with whom he had two sons and a daughter. In succeeding years published *Cain, a Drama* (1904), *The Great Adventure* (1905), *Herakles* (1908), and posthumously published *The Soul's Inheritance* (1909). Died following an attack of ptomaine poisoning.

HENRY WADSWORTH LONGFELLOW (February 27, 1807–March 24, 1882) b. Portland, Maine (then part of Massachusetts). Son of Zilpah Wadsworth and Stephen Longfellow, a prominent lawyer. Schooled privately until age 14. After a year at Portland Academy, entered Bowdoin College and graduated in 1825; classmate of Nathaniel Hawthorne; in graduate oration "Our Native Writers" called for a national literature. Appointed to newly instituted Chair of Modern Languages at Bowdoin with stipulation that he first engage in further study abroad; spent three years (1826–29) in France, Spain (where he met Washington Irving), Italy, and Germany. Married Mary Storer Potter in 1831. During his years at Bowdoin, published many textbooks and scholarly articles on Romance languages and literature; in 1833 published a translation of the *Coplas* of the Spanish poet Jorge Manrique; *Outre-Mer*, a prose account of his European journey, appeared in 1835. Appointed Smith Professor of Modern Languages at Harvard (the chair formerly held by George Ticknor) in 1835; went to Europe for year of additional study; visited England, Germany, Denmark, and Sweden; in Holland, Mary suffered a miscarriage and died in November 1835. Spent the winter in Heidelberg, where he met William Cullen Bryant; in Switzerland the following summer met Frances (Fanny) Appleton. He arrived in Cambridge, Massachusetts, in 1836, and the following summer settled into Craigie House, where he would live for the rest of his life. Lectures at Harvard ranged widely over European literature, treating among other subjects Dante, Lope de Vega, Calderón, Moliere, Goethe, Jean Paul Richter, and Anglo-Saxon and Scandinavian literature. Achieved celebrity as poet with publication of "A Psalm of Life" in *The Knickerbocker* in 1838; the following year published first collection of poems, *Voices of the Night*, and the romance *Hyperion*; *Ballads and Other Poems* (1841) included "The Skeleton in Armour," "The Wreck of the Hesperus," and "The Village Blacksmith." Suffering from neuralgia and eyestrain, spent six months in Germany, mostly at Marienberg spa on the Rhine; on return journey met Charles Dickens. Anti-slavery poems collected in *Poems of Slavery* (1842); published verse play *The Spanish Student* (1843), influenced by his study of Spanish drama. In 1843 married Fanny Appleton, who had previously repeatedly rejected his proposal of marriage; they had six children, born between 1844 and 1855. Suffered partial blindness in 1843. Urged by John Greenleaf Whittier in 1844 to run for Congress as abolitionist, but refused on the grounds that "partizan warfare becomes too violent—too vindictive for my taste." In 1845 published verse collections *Poems* and *The Belfry of Bruges and Other Poems* and monumental anthology *The Poets and Poetry of Europe*, containing work from ten modern languages (much of it in Longfellow's own translations). The narrative poem *Evangeline* (1847) went through six editions in its first three months of publication. Daughter Fanny died in 1848. A novel of New England life, *Kavanaugh* (1849), was followed by verse collection *The Seaside and the Fireside* (1849) and verse drama *The Golden Legend* (1851), first published installment of trilogy also including *The New-England Tragedies* (1868) and *The Divine Tragedy* (1871), and later collected as *Christus: A Mystery* (1872). Resigned from Harvard position in 1854 to devote himself entirely to writing. His reading of the Finnish epic *The Kalevala* led to the adoption of its meter for *The Song of Hiawatha* (1855), an enormously popular narrative poem based on American Indian legends he had encountered in the writings of Henry Rowe Schoolcraft. The title poem of *The Courtship of Miles Standish* (1858) incorporated the figures of his mother's 17th-century ancestors John Alden and Priscilla Mullens. Close friends and associates included Nathaniel Hawthorne, James Russell Lowell, Charles Sumner, Charles Eliot Norton, and Louis Agassiz. Wife Fanny died when her dress caught fire in 1861; he was badly burned trying to put the flames out. Devoted himself to translation of Dante's *Divine Comedy* (1865–67) and to series of narrative poems collected in *Tales of a Wayside Inn* (1863). Later poetry published in *Flower-de-Luce* (1867), *Three Books of Song* (1872), *Aftermath* (1873), *The Hanging of the Crane* (1874), *The Masque of Pandora and Other Poems* (1875), *Kéramos* (1878), and *Ultima Thule* (1880–82); juvenilia collected in *The Early Poems* (1878); also edited 31-volume poetry anthology *Poems of Places* (1876–79). Aside from a year in Europe (1868–69), remained in Cambridge. Suffered serious nervous attack in 1881; died the following year of peritonitis. *Michael Angelo* published posthumously in 1883.

JAMES RUSSELL LOWELL (February 22, 1819–August 12, 1891) b. Cambridge, Massachusetts. Son of Harriet Brackett Spence and Charles Lowell (distinguished Unitarian minister); mother suffered from mental illness in later life, and was confined to a hospital for two years. Graduated Harvard 1838 and Harvard Law School 1840; admitted to Massachusetts bar, but within a year abandoned law practice in favor of a literary career. Published poems in *Southern Literary Messenger* and elsewhere; first collection of poetry, *A Year's Life*, appeared 1841, followed by *Poems* (1844). With Robert Carter co-edited *The Pioneer*, short-lived literary magazine of which three numbers (including work by Poe, Hawthorne, and Whittier) were published in 1843. Literary essays serialized in *Boston Miscellany* formed basis of *Conversations on Some of the Old Poets* (1845). Married Maria White (also a poet) in 1844, after long engagement; they had four children, three of whom died in infancy. Under influence of wife's ardent abolitionism, wrote editorials for *Pennsylvania Freeman* and became contributing editor of *National Anti-Slavery Standard*. In his most productive period as a poet published in rapid succession *Poems: Second Series* (1848), *A Fable for Critics* (1848), *The Biglow Papers* (1848), and *The Vision of Sir Launfal* (1848). The Lowells spent the years 1851–52 in Europe; son Walter died in Rome in April 1852. Maria died in October 1853, and two years later Lowell privately published *The Poems of Maria Lowell* for distribution to friends. Lowell delivered lectures on the English poets at Lowell Institute in Boston in 1855; succeeded Longfellow as professor of French and Spanish language and literature at Harvard, remaining there in various capacities until retirement in 1886. Following his appointment spent a year in Europe, studying in Germany, Italy, and elsewhere in preparation for duties at Harvard. In 1857 married Frances Dunlap, governess in whose care he had left daughter Mabel during his absence. Became founding editor of *Atlantic Monthly* (1857–61); contributors during his editorship included Emerson, Whittier, Holmes, Hawthorne, Stowe, Motley, and Longfellow. Second series of *The Biglow Papers*, attacking disunionists and pro-slavery interests, serialized in *Atlantic Monthly* in 1862. From 1864 to 1872 co-edited *The North American Review* with Charles Eliot Norton, contributing articles on the Civil War (in which three of his nephews died) and its consequences (later collected in *Political Essays*, 1888). Delivered widely acclaimed "Ode" at Harvard Commemoration of July 21, 1865, in honor of Harvard men killed in the

Civil War. Published verse collections *Under the Willows* (1869) and *The Cathedral* (1870); essays collected in *Fireside Travels* (1864), *Among My Books* (1870–76), and *My Study Windows* (1871). Made long visit to Europe (1872–75), and was awarded honorary degrees by Oxford and Cambridge. Served as delegate to Republican National Convention and as a presidential elector for Rutherford B. Hayes in 1876. Appointed minister to Spain (1877–80) and Great Britain (1880–85). Frances, after years of failing health and mental illness, died in 1885. In later years published further poetry (*Under the Old Elm*, 1885, and *Heartsease and Rue*, 1888) and literary essays collected in *The English Poets, Lessing, Rousseau* (1888) and *Books and Libraries and Other Papers* (1889).

MARIA WHITE LOWELL (July 8, 1821–October 27, 1853) b. Watertown, Massachusetts. Fourth of nine children of Anna Maria Howard and Abijah White; sister of William Abijah White, who became close friend of James Russell Lowell at Harvard; given name Anna Maria White. Although family was not Catholic, she was sent (as were the daughters of many prominent Protestant families) for primary education to the Ursuline Convent on Mt. Benedict in Charlestown, Massachusetts, where she was among the students forced to flee when the convent was burned by an anti-Catholic mob in August 1834. Later participated in Margaret Fuller's "conversations" (pioneering experiment in women's education), 1839–44. During this period became dedicated to abolitionism and the temperance movement. Became engaged to James Russell Lowell in 1840. Published poetry in third and last number of Lowell's magazine *The Pioneer* (1843); later contributed verse to *The Child's Friend*, *Putnam's Magazine*, *The Knickerbocker*, and to anti-slavery "gift books." Married Lowell in 1844. Support for abolitionism deeply influenced husband; with him, she assisted numerous fugitive slaves. Of their four children, three died in early childhood: Blanche in 1847, Rose in 1849, and Walter in Rome in 1852; only Mabel (b. 1847) survived to adulthood. Traveled with family to Italy in July 1851, remaining until fall of 1852. Health had been frail for years; died at Elmwood, the Lowell house in Cambridge, after protracted illness. Following her death, Lowell arranged for private publication of *The Poems of Maria Lowell* (1855), containing 20 poems.

ROBERT LOWRY (March 12, 1826–November 23, 1899) b. Philadelphia, Pennsylvania. In 1843 joined First Baptist Church after experiencing religious conversion. Enrolled in 1848 at University of Lewisburg, Lewisburg, Pennsylvania (now Bucknell University); graduated 1854. Entered Baptist ministry. Served as pastor in West Chester, Pennsylvania (1854–58); in New York City (1858–61); in Brooklyn, New York (1861–69). In 1869 joined faculty of University of Lewisburg, serving also as chancellor of the university; served concurrently as pastor in Lewisburg. In 1875 moved to Plainfield, New Jersey, and the following year became pastor of the Park Avenue Baptist Church there, holding the position until 1885; served as president of New Jersey Baptist School Union, 1880–86. Wrote many hymns; most famous, "Beautiful

River" (also known as "Shall We Gather at the River"), was written in 1864 during epidemic in Brooklyn and published in collection *Bright Jewels for the Sunday School* (1869). Edited many other collections of religious music devoted in large part to his own songs, including *Chapel Melodies* (1868), *Pure Gold for the Sunday School* (1871), *Hymn Service* (1871), *Royal Diadem for the Sunday School* (1873), *Temple Anthems for the Service of the Sanctuary* (1873), *The Tidal Wave* (1874), *Brightest and Best* (1875), *Welcome Tidings* (1877), *Fountain of Song* (1877), *Chautauqua Carols* (1878), *Gospel Hymn and Tune Book* (1879), *Good as Gold* (1880), *Our Glad Hosanna* (1882), *Joyful Lays* (1884), and *The Glad Refrain for the Sunday School* (1886). Died in Plainfield, leaving a widow, Mary Runyon Lowry, and three sons.

EDWIN MARKHAM   (April 23, 1852 – March 7, 1940)   b. Charles Edward Anson Markham in Oregon City, Oregon Territory. Sixth child of Elizabeth Winchell Markham (wife of Samuel Barzillai Markham, from whom she was separated and who was probably not Markham's father). Grew up on isolated ranch in Suisun, California (between Sacramento and San Francisco); raised by his mother, a member of Campbellite sect Disciples of Christ, who discouraged his interest in literature and treated him severely. Ran away from home for several months in 1867. Attended California College in Vacaville, earning teacher's certificate in 1870; moved with mother (who continued to live with him until her death) to San Jose, where he attended California State Normal School, 1871–72; continued studies at Christian College, Campbellite school in Santa Rosa, 1873–74. Taught high school in Coloma. Married Annie Cox in 1875. Around 1878 became adherent of spiritualist ideas of Thomas Lake Harris, of whose Brotherhood of the New Life he became a nonresident member. Became county superintendent of schools at Placerville in 1879. Began publishing poems in local newspapers; developed interest in socialism and became involved in Grange movement. Affair with Placerville physician Dr. Elizabeth Senter led to divorce from wife Annie in 1884. Forced to give up school position in 1886 because of affair with Caroline E. Bailey, whom he married in 1887; she left him not long after their marriage. Poetry published in *Scribner's* and *The Century*; awarded prize by *The Magazine of Poetry*. Worked as school principal in Hayward (1889) and, from 1890, at Tompkins Observation School of the University of California in Oakland. Mother died in 1891. Formed friendships with Ambrose Bierce, Jack London, and Frank Norris; met Hamlin Garland in 1893 at World's Columbian Exposition in Chicago. Married teacher Anna Catherine Murphy in 1898; their son Virgil was born the following year. Publication of "The Man with the Hoe" in *San Francisco Examiner* in January 1899 made him famous; poem was translated into many languages, and *The Man with the Hoe and Other Poems* (1899) became best seller; family moved to New York City. Commissioned by Republican Club of New York to write Lincoln tribute, published in successful second collection, *Lincoln and Other Poems* (1901). Became regular contributor of newspaper articles on progressive themes to Hearst syndicate. Retired to Staten Island, New York; Sunday salons at his home were regularly attended by literary figures including Theodore Dreiser, Upton Sinclair, Vachel Lindsay, Edwin Arlington Robinson, and Joyce Kilmer. Following death of Thomas Lake Harris in 1906, worked for years on uncompleted official biography. Founded Poetry Society of America in 1910; published influential anthology of new poets, *The Younger Choir* (1910); frequently went on lecture tours. Campaigned against child labor and contributed to the volume *Children in Bondage* (1914). Continued to publish poetry regularly, collecting his verse in *The Shoes of Happiness* (1915), *Gates of Paradise* (1920), *New Poems: Eighty Songs at Eighty* (1932), and *The Star of Araby* (1937). Eightieth birthday celebrated at massive ceremony at Carnegie Hall in 1932. Disabled by stroke in 1938 while on tour to Mexico; died of pneumonia two years later.

CORNELIUS MATHEWS (October 28, 1817–March 25, 1889) b. Port Chester, New York. Son of Catherine Van Cott and Abijah Mathews, a cabinet maker. Attended Columbia College for several years; graduated from newly opened New York University in 1834. Studied law; admitted to New York bar in 1837, but turned to literary career. Strong advocate of American literary nationalism; with Evert Duyckinck and William Gilmore Simms, became part of literary group known as Young America. Contributed to *American Monthly Magazine*, *New York Review*, and *Knickerbocker Magazine*. Published *The Motley Book* (1838) and *Behemoth: A Legend of the Mound Builders* (1839), a novel based on American Indian history and lore. Founded, with Evert Duyckinck, monthly magazine *Arcturus* (1840–42), which Mathews edited and for which he wrote articles and fiction; other contributors included Hawthorne, Longfellow, and Lowell. Wrote play about New York, *The Politicians* (1840); narrative poem on Indian themes, *Wakondah: The Master of Life* (1841); and satirical novel *The Career of Puffer Hopkins* (1842). Chief poetic work, *Poems on Man in His Various Aspects under the American Republic*, appeared 1843, along with a collected volume, *The Various Writings of Cornelius Mathews*. Wrote several more plays, of which *Witchcraft, or the Martyrs of Salem* (1846) was produced with some success, and additional fiction, including the novel *Moneypenny: or, The Heart of the World* (1849). Campaigned for international copyright, and spoke on the subject at dinner in honor of Charles Dickens in 1842. During 1840s and 1850s worked as editor on a number of literary magazines (including *Yankee Doodle*), most of them short lived. After *The Indian Fairy Book* (1855), an anthology based on writings of Henry Rowe Schoolcraft, published no more books, but continued to contribute journalism to *New York Dramatic Mirror*, and to work as an editor on the *New York Reveille*, *The New-Yorker* (1858–76), and *Comic World* (1876–78). Died in New York City.

WASHINGTON MATTHEWS (July 17, 1843–April 29, 1905) b. Killiney, County Dublin, Ireland. Son of Anna Burke and Dr. Nicholas Blayney Matthews. His mother died when he was an infant and his father moved to America, settling in Dubuque, Iowa. Studied at University of Iowa, receiving his medical degree in 1864. Joined army, and served as post surgeon at forts in Montana and North Dakota, 1865–72. Learned Hidatsa; may have had a son by daughter of a Hidatsa chief. Married Caroline Wotherspoon in 1877. Stationed at Fort Wingate, New Mexico, 1880–84; worked at Army Medical Museum in Washington, D.C., 1884–90; again at Fort Wingate until his retirement in 1894. President of American Folk-Lore Society, 1895. Made extensive studies in Navajo language and culture, as well as in physical anthropology. Publications included *Grammar and Dictionary of the Language of the Hidatsa* (1873–74), *Ethnography and Philology of the Hidatsa Indians* (1877), *The Mountain Chant: A Navajo Ceremony* (1887), *Navaho Legends* (1897), and *The Night Chant* (1902).

HERMAN MELVILLE (August 1, 1819–September 28, 1891) b. New York City. Son of Maria Gansevoort (daughter of American Revolutionary hero General Peter Gansevoort) and Allan Melvill (importer and merchant). Father's business failed in financial panic of 1830; family forced to move to Albany; father died January 1832. Educated sporadically at various schools in New York City and in upstate New York. Worked successively as bank clerk, on uncle's farm, as bookkeeper and clerk in brother's fur business, and as teacher in school near Pittsfield, Massachusetts. In 1839 published journalistic sketches as "Fragments from a Writing Desk"; sailed from New York to Liverpool and back as crew member of trading ship *St. Lawrence*. Worked briefly as teacher. Sailed for South Seas on whaling ship *Acushnet* in January 1841; in July 1842 deserted with shipmate Richard Tobias Greene at Nuku Hiva in the Marquesas. After month in Taipi valley, sailed on Australian whaling ship *Lucy Ann*, but was sent ashore at Tahiti as mutineer; escaped and explored Tahiti with friend John B. Troy. Sailed from Tahiti to Hawaii on Nantucket whaling ship *Charles and Henry*, worked at various jobs in Honolulu. In 1843 enlisted in U.S. Navy in Honolulu; sailed to Boston on frigate *United States*; discharged October 1844. Returned to family and worked on *Typee*, fictionalized account of Marquesan experiences, published with great success in 1846; sequel *Omoo* appeared the following year. Married Elizabeth Shaw, daughter of Massachusetts Chief Justice Lemuel Shaw, in August 1847; moved to New York City; they had four children. Published further fiction, *Mardi* (1849), *Redburn* (1849), and *White-Jacket* (1850). Made four-month trip to London and the Continent, 1849–50. In 1850 met Nathaniel Hawthorne, whose work he had previously reviewed; purchased farm Arrowhead near Pittsfield. *Moby-Dick* published 1851; its indifferent reception followed by failure of *Pierre, or The Ambiguities* (1852); failed to recoup reputation with *Israel Potter* (1855) and *The Piazza Tales* (1856). Family gravely concerned about health and mental stability, as Melville suffered recurrent depression. With father-in-law's financial help made year-long trip to Europe and Holy Land; briefly visited Hawthorne in Liverpool; returned to New York 1857. Last published work of fiction, *The Confidence-Man*, appeared in 1857. Between 1857 and 1860 lectured on travels in Rome and the South Seas without success. In 1861 traveled to Washington, D.C., hoping to procure a consular appointment, but failed. Left Pittsfield permanently for New York City in 1863. Visited the front in

Virginia in 1864; collection of Civil War poems, *Battle-Pieces and Aspects of the War*, published in 1866. In December of the same year appointed deputy inspector of customs at port of New York. Oldest son Malcolm died of self-inflicted gunshot wound in September 1867. Long poem *Clarel: A Poem and a Pilgrimage*, based on experiences in Holy Land, published at uncle's expense in 1876. Resigned position as customs inspector in 1885; son Stanwix died in San Francisco the following year. In final years published two small books of poetry in limited private editions, *John Marr and Other Sailors* (1888) and *Timoleon* (1891). Left *Billy Budd, Sailor* in manuscript (first published 1924), along with a number of poems.

ADAH ISAACS MENKEN (June 15, 1835?–August 10, 1868) probably b. Memphis, Tennessee. Menken's origins have long been disputed; she herself gave various accounts of her parentage and place of birth, and later biographers have claimed that she was Jewish or mulatto. Recent research suggests that her parents Richard and Catherine McCord were of Irish origin, and that her given name was Ada McCord. Her father probably died in 1842, after which her mother married Josiah Campbell and moved to New Orleans. At age fifteen said to have given public readings of Shakespeare in Texas; published some poetry. Married musician Alexander Isaac Menken (whose father was a prosperous Cincinnati merchant) in Texas in 1856; claimed Jewish parentage, and received instruction in Judaism from Rabbi Isaac M. Wise, editor of *The Cincinnati Israelite*. Made first stage appearances in Shreveport and New Orleans around 1857; appeared in Cincinnati and Dayton in 1858; made New York City debut in 1859. Published poems and articles in *Cincinnati Israelite*, 1857–59, and *New York Sunday Mercury*, 1860–61. Following break-up of marriage to Menken in July 1859, was married to prizefighter John C. Heenan (known as "The Benicia Boy") in September of the same year. Friendly in New York with Ada Clare, Walt Whitman, Fitz-James O'Brien, and others associated with Charlie Pfaff's beer cellar. Toured in play based on life of Lola Montez. Became world-famous for her ride across stage strapped to the back of a horse in the dramatic version of Byron's "Mazeppa"; first performed the role in June 1861 in Albany, New York; toured frequently, billed as "The World's Delight." Abandoned by Heenan amid public speculation about the legitimacy of her divorce from Menken. Married humorist Robert Henry Newell (known by pseudonym "Orpheus C. Kerr") in September 1862. Traveled with Newell to San Francisco, where she performed in August 1863; met Bret Harte, Charles Farrar Browne ("Artemus Ward"), and other literary figures; divorced Newell. Played Virginia City in March 1864; met Mark Twain. In London (where she opened in *Mazeppa* in October 1864) her salon became a fixture of London society; met Charles Dickens and Charles Reade. Traveled to Paris, where she met Théophile Gautier and George Sand. In Britain again, opened in *The Children of the Sun* in Glasgow and toured England in the role. Returned to New York in March 1866 to be with lover James Paul Barkley, whom she had met while abroad;

acted in New York City and on tour of U.S.; married Barkley in August 1866, but couple separated after three days when Menken departed for Europe; never saw Barkley again (he died the following year). Gave birth to a son in November, of whom Barkley was father; child died in infancy. In Paris, acted in *Les Pirates de la Savane*; notorious for affair with elderly novelist Aléxandre Dumas; photographs of the two of them together circulated widely. Appeared in Vienna in spring of 1867. Returned to London, where she became acquainted with Dante Gabriel Rossetti; in autumn of 1867 apparently had affair with Algernon Charles Swinburne. Gave final performance at Sadler's Wells Theatre in London in August 1868; returned to France but was too ill to perform. Visitors during her last illness included Thomas Buchanan Read and Henry Wadsworth Longfellow. Collected poetry in *Infelicia*, dedicated to Charles Dickens (published days after her death). Died in Paris of cancer.

STUART MERRILL (August 1, 1863–December 1, 1915) b. Stuart Fitz-Randolph Merrill in Hempstead, New York. One of three sons of Emma Fitz-Randolph Laing and George Merrill (a lawyer). In 1866 his father was appointed counselor to the American legation in Paris. Attended boarding school in Vanves, a suburb of Paris, 1875–79; afterward studied at Lycée Fontaines in Paris, where Mallarmé was a teacher of English and classmates included future literary figures René Ghil, Ephraim Mikhael, and Pierre Quillard; graduated in 1884. After family's return to New York, studied law at Columbia. First book, *Les Gammes*, written in French; published in Paris in 1887. Met Walt Whitman in April 1887 in New York City, and presented him with copies of translations that the French poet Jules Laforgue had published of several Whitman poems. Interested in economic ideas of Henry George; defended anarchists sentenced to death in 1886 following Haymarket riot. Father died 1888; with mother, returned to Europe; in London, formed close friendship with Oscar Wilde. *Pastels in Prose* (1890), his only English-language volume (with preface by William Dean Howells), contained translations of Baudelaire, Mallarmé, Huysmans, Villiers de l'Isle Adam, Judith Gautier, Aloysius Bertrand, and other French writers. Returned to New York in 1890, remaining only five months. Returned to Paris in May 1891. Became a manager of the Théâtre d'Art. Apartment on Quai Bourbon became meeting place for writers and artists including Paul Verlaine, Alfred Jarry, Emile Verhaeren, and Guillaume Apollinaire; regular guest at Tuesday evening salon of Stéphane Mallarmé; later had a house at Marlotte in the forest of Fontainebleau. Closely associated with French symbolist school; later volumes of poetry, all written in French, included *Les Fastes* (1891), *Petits Poèmes d'Automne* (1895), *Les Quatre Saisons* (1900), and *Une Voix dans la Foule* (1909); poetry collected in 1897 in *Poèmes 1887–1897*. He contributed to many French periodicals including *La Bazoche*, *Le Décadent*, *Le Scapin*, *Ecrits pour l'art*, *Le Mercure de France*, *La Plume*, and *L'Ermitage*. In Brussels in 1908 married 18-year-old Claire Rion; they settled at Versailles, where he died. *Prose et Vers* published posthumously in 1925.

JOAQUIN MILLER (September 8, 1837–February 17, 1913) b. Cincinnatus Hiner (later spelled Heine) Miller in Liberty, Indiana. Son of Margaret De Witt and Hulings Miller, a Quaker schoolteacher. Family moved from place to place, west along Oregon Trail, settling in early 1853 near what would later be Eugene, Oregon. In 1854, Miller left home and began wandering existence in northern California. Worked as miner and as a cook in mining camps; spent time among Indians near Mount Shasta, and had a daughter, Cali-Shasta, with a woman of the band; involved in several skirmishes among Indians, miners, and soldiers. Returned to Oregon, attending newly opened Columbia College in Eugene, 1858–59. Traveled again to California, where he was briefly jailed for horse theft in July 1859; escaped with cell-mate and again lived with Indians. Studied law in Portland, Oregon, in 1860. Briefly practiced law in Oro Fino, Idaho, before buying interest in a pony express service, riding routes in Idaho, Oregon, and Washington in 1861 and 1862. Used profits from pony express to buy interest in *Democratic-Register* of Eugene in 1862; the same year, the paper was suppressed by federal authorities for supporting Confederacy. Married Theresa Dyer (an aspiring poet who wrote under the name Minnie Myrtle) in September 1862 after brief courtship; they had two children. Edited short-lived *Eugene City Review* under pseudonym "De Weiver" (1862–63). Moved to Canyon City, Oregon, in 1863, where he practiced law; led attack against hostile Indians in 1864, and served as judge of county court, 1866–69. Published two collections of poetry, *Specimens* (1868) and *Joaquin et al* (1869), the title of the latter taken from Miller's poem on Mexican bandit Joaquin Murrieta, whose name he would adopt as his own in 1870. Conducted unsuccessful campaign for Supreme Court Justice in Oregon. After divorce from wife in 1870, custody of children granted to Miller's mother-in-law. In 1870, traveled to San Francisco where he met Bret Harte, Ina Coolbrith, Ambrose Bierce, and other literary figures. Later the same year, traveled to Great Britain, where privately printed *Pacific Poems* (1871) and manners and costume (sombrero, boots, spurs, and buckskin) gained him fame as "frontier poet"; British publisher issued *Songs of the Sierras* (1871) with success. Returned to U.S. in fall of 1871 to find that his popularity did not extend there; traveled in and outside of America, eventually returning to Europe in 1873; stayed chiefly in England and Italy; returned to New York in 1875. Enjoyed some success as playwright with *Forty-Nine* (1882); *The Danites in the Sierras* (first staged 1877; published 1882), a dramatization of his 1875 novel *First Fam'lies of the Sierras*; and *Tally-Ho!* (1883, with music by John Philip Sousa). Published many volumes of verse, including *Songs of the Sun-Lands* (1873), *The Ship in the Desert* (1875), *Songs of Italy* (1878), *Songs of Far-Away Lands* (1878), and *Songs of the Mexican Seas* (1887), and a wide range of prose works, including several novels and the fictionalized memoir *Life Amongst the Modocs* (1873). In 1879, married second wife, hotel heiress Abigail Leland, and settled in New York; they had one daughter, Juanita. First wife, Minnie, died while visiting Miller in New York in 1882. In 1883, moved to Washington, D.C., where he and wife separated, Abigail returning to New York. Returned to San Francisco in 1886, accepting position as editor of *The Golden Era*; in 1887 settled in Oakland on an estate he named The Hights; established a fruit orchard, and planted thousands of trees. Resigned position at *Golden Era* late in 1887. Toured as lecturer in early 1890s, also occasionally working as journalist. Traveled in Klondike as correspondent for Hearst papers, 1897–98; toured briefly with vaudeville show, 1898–99; traveled to China to cover Boxer Rebellion in 1900. *Complete Poetical Works* appeared in London in 1897 (American edition 1900; revised, 1902). Later volumes of poetry included *Chants for the Boer* (1900), *As it Was in the Beginning* (1903), *Light: A Narrative Poem* (1907), and *Panama: Union of the Oceans* (1912). During later years, daughters Maud and Cali-Shasta and her mother lived with him at The Hights; Miller outlived them all. In February 1911, his second wife and their daughter moved to The Hights to care for Miller, whose health was in decline. Died at The Hights.

HARRIET MONROE (December 23, 1860–September 26, 1936)   b. Chicago, Illinois. Daughter of Martha Mitchell and Henry Stanton Monroe, a prosperous lawyer; family's resources severely curtailed as result of Chicago fire of 1876. Graduated from Convent of the Visitation in Georgetown, D.C., in 1879. Returned to live with family in Chicago. Initiated correspondence with Robert Louis Stevenson in 1886; spent summer of 1887 in New York City with mother and sister; met Stevenson. During winter of 1888–89 lived in New York City with sister; frequently attended Sunday evening gatherings at home of Edmund Clarence Stedman, where she met William Dean Howells, Richard Watson Gilder, Elizabeth and Richard Henry Stoddard, and other literary figures; wrote dramatic criticism for the *Herald Tribune*. Returned to Chicago and in 1890 began writing art criticism for *Chicago Tribune*. In 1890 and again in 1897 toured Europe and met literary and artistic figures including Henry James, Aubrey Beardsley, James McNeill Whistler, Thomas Hardy, and Alice Meynell. Associates in Chicago included Albert Pinkham Ryder and Henry Blake Fuller. First collection, *Valeria and Other Poems*, privately printed in 1892. Applied for and received $1,000 commission to write poem for World's Columbian Exposition in Chicago; poem recited by five thousand voices at dedication ceremony in 1892; published as *The Columbian Ode* (1893). In 1896 published biography of brother-in-law John Wellborn Root, the architect who had been one of the chief designers of the Columbian Exposition. *The Passing Show: Five Modern Plays in Verse* appeared in 1903. Worked as freelance journalist; resumed job as art critic for *Chicago Tribune*, 1909–14. Long poem *The Dance of Seasons* published in 1911. With help of close friend Hobart Chatfield-Taylor raised money to launch *Poetry: A Magazine of Verse*; first issue published September 1912. Contributors during Monroe's editorship included Ezra Pound (who served as London editor), Wallace Stevens, William Butler Yeats, William Carlos Williams, Robert Frost, T. S. Eliot, H.D., Marianne Moore, Hart Crane, Vachel Lindsay, Edgar Lee Masters, Amy Lowell, Carl Sandburg, Langston Hughes, Louis Zukofsky, Basil Bunting, Kenneth Rexroth, W. H. Auden, and many others. Verse collection *You and I* published 1914. With Alice Corbin Henderson (assistant editor of

Poetry) edited anthology *The New Poetry: An Anthology of Twentieth-Century Verse in English* (1917). *The Difference and Other Poems* (1924) followed by essay collection *Poets and Their Art* (1926); poetry collected in *Chosen Poems: A Selection from My Books of Verse* (1935). In later years traveled in Mexico and Asia. Died of cerebral hemorrhage in Arequipa, Peru, while returning from literary conference in Buenos Aires, Argentina. Autobiography published posthumously as *A Poet's Life: Seventy Years in a Changing World* (1938).

WILLIAM VAUGHN MOODY (July 8, 1869–October 17, 1910) b. Spencer, Indiana. Son of Henriette Emily Stoy (descendant of early Indiana pioneer family) and Francis Burdette Moody (former steamboat captain). Unsuccessful in business in Spencer, father moved family to New Albany, Indiana, in 1870, where he worked as secretary of an iron works. Father died in 1884, mother in 1886. Graduated Riverview Academy, Poughkeepsie, New York, in 1889, having tutored to support himself. Worked his way through Harvard, which he entered in 1889 on a $400 scholarship. Published verse in *Harvard Advocate* and *Harvard Monthly* (for which he also served as editor); came under influence of George Santayana, then a young instructor. College friends included Robert Herrick, Robert Morss Lovett, Phillip Henry Savage, and other aspiring writers. Spent senior year in Europe, supporting himself as private tutor, 1892–93. Graduated Harvard 1893; continued studies there, completing thesis on Sir Philip Sidney and receiving M.A. in 1894; stayed on as instructor for a year. Taught at University of Chicago (1895–1907), first as English instructor and then as assistant professor. First book, verse drama *The Masque of Judgment* (1900), followed by *Poems* (1901), which included "Ode in the Time of Hesitation," already published in *Atlantic Monthly* the year before. Poetry praised by Harriet Monroe and Edwin Arlington Robinson. *The Fire-Bringer*, second in intended triptych of verse dramas, appeared 1904. Publication of textbook *A First View of English Literature* (1905), written with friend Robert Morss Lovett, enabled him to travel in West and in Europe before settling in New York City. Friends included Edwin Arlington Robinson, Ridgely Torrence, Josephine Peabody, Percy MacKaye, and Edmund Clarence Stedman. Prose drama *A Sabine Woman* produced in Chicago in 1906 and opened on Broadway under new title *The Great Divide* the same year, enjoying a successful run and critical acclaim. Traveled in the spring of 1907 with Ridgely Torrence in North Africa, Spain, and Italy. In 1908 awarded honorary degree at Yale, and elected to American Academy of Arts and Letters. Married Harriet Brainard (divorcée who had been his lover since 1901) in 1909; diagnosed with brain tumor soon afterward. Next play, *The Faith Healer* (1909), failed on Broadway. Traveled to Santa Barbara, California, to Chicago, and to Colorado Springs in effort to regain health. Wrote beginning of third verse drama, *The Death of Eve*, but died at Colorado Springs before it could be completed. Two-volume edition of works published posthumously as *The Poems and Plays of William Vaughn Moody* (1912).

JAMES MOONEY (February 10, 1861–December 22, 1921) b. Richmond, Indiana. Son of Ellen Devlin and James Mooney, Irish immigrants; father died shortly after Mooney's birth. At age 12 determined to learn names and locations of every American Indian tribe. In 1879, without attending college, took job as typesetter and staff writer at *Richmond Palladium*. Active in American branch of National Irish Land League. Began independently to amass ethnographic and linguistic information on American Indians. In 1885 met John Wesley Powell, director of U.S. Geological Survey and of Bureau of American Ethnology; hired by Powell to work for Bureau, remained there for the rest of his life. Did his first fieldwork among Eastern Cherokee, 1885–90. Late in 1890 began investigation of ghost-dance religion in South Dakota and elsewhere; within a year met its messiah, Wovoka, and participated in its ceremonies. From 1894 on spent much time among Plains tribes including the Kiowa, Kiowa-Apache, Arapaho, and Cheyenne, with intermittent visits to the Eastern Cherokee, to Mexico and the Southwest, and to Washington, D.C., to publish his work. Married Ione Lee Gaut in 1897; they had six children. Studied peyote religion, attending peyote ceremonies, and in 1918 helped charter the Native American Church, centered on peyote sacrament. Final years hampered by ill-health and political controversy over his criticisms of government Indian policy and defense of peyotism. Publications included *Sacred Formulas of the Cherokees* (1891), *The Siouan Tribes of the East* (1894), *The Ghost Dance Religion and the Sioux Outbreak of 1890* (1896), *Calendar History of the Kiowa Indians* (1898), *Myths of the Cherokee* (1900), and *The Cheyenne Indians* (1908); contributed over 500 articles to Frederick W. Hodge's *Handbook of American Indians North of Mexico* (1907–10); many of his field notes remain unpublished, including uncompleted studies of Kiowa heraldry and the peyote religion. Died in Washington, D.C. His extensive study of American Indian population before European contact was edited and revised by John R. Swanton and published as *The Aboriginal Population of America North of Mexico* (1928); texts collected in his fieldwork among the Eastern Cherokee were published in *The Swimmer Manuscript: Cherokee Sacred Formulas and Medicinal Prescriptions* (1932).

CLEMENT MOORE (July 15, 1779–July 10, 1863) b. New York City. Son of Charity Clarke (heiress to large tract of land in what is now Chelsea section of Manhattan) and Benjamin Moore (Episcopal bishop of New York, rector of Trinity Church, president of Columbia College). In early youth educated at home; graduated Columbia 1798. Devoted himself to study of Hebrew, and in 1809 published two-volume *A Compendious Lexicon of the Hebrew Language*. In 1813 married Catharine Elizabeth Taylor; they had three daughters. Having come into his inheritance upon his father's death, in 1819 donated land on which General Theological Seminary was built; taught there from 1823 as professor of Biblical studies and later of Oriental and Greek literature. "A Visit from St. Nicholas," originally written in 1822 for his family, was published without Moore's knowledge in *Troy Sentinel* in 1823. It was reprinted frequently thereafter, but Moore was not identified publicly as the author until 1837, when the poem appeared in *The New York Book of Poetry* (edited by Charles Fenno Hoffman). Moore included the poem, along with other verse, in *Poems* (1844); also published a historical work, *George Castriot, Surnamed Scanderbeg, King of Albania* (1850).

GEORGE POPE MORRIS (October 10, 1802–July 6, 1864) b. Philadelphia, Pennsylvania. In his youth worked in printing office. Founded *New-York Mirror and Ladies' Literary Gazette* in 1823, and hired Samuel Woodworth to edit it; after a year took over editorial responsibilities. The weekly magazine included among its contributors William Cullen Bryant, Fitz-Greene Halleck, James Kirke Paulding, and Nathaniel P. Willis (who was contributing editor, 1831–36); Charles Fenno Hoffman and Epes Sargent later played editorial roles as well. Morris's play of the American Revolution, *Brier Cliff*, was successfully produced in 1826. Poem "The Oak" (later known as "Woodman, Spare That Tree!") achieved great popularity upon publication in 1830. First collection of poetry, *The Deserted Bride* (1838), followed by a book of humorous sketches, *The Little Frenchman and His Water Lots* (1839). The *Mirror* failed in 1842, and was revived a few months later as *New Mirror* (with Nathaniel P. Willis as co-editor), but lasted only a year and a half under that title before becoming a daily paper as *Evening Mirror*, with supplement entitled *Weekly Mirror*; contributors included Edgar Allan Poe. (By 1845 the *Mirror* had passed out of the control of Morris and Willis, continuing publication until 1857 under the editorship of Hiram Fuller.) Poetry collected in 1844 as *The Songs and Ballads of George P. Morris*. In 1846, again with Willis, founded the weekly *National Press*, whose name was changed within a few months to *The Home Journal*; paper was very popular, and Morris continued as editor until his death. With Willis, co-edited anthology *Prose and Poetry of Europe and America* (1857). Although he had no military experience aside from a stint in the New York militia, he was generally known as "General Morris." Lived for much of his life with his wife Mary Worthington Hopkins and their children on a country estate near Cold Spring, New York.

JOHN NEAL (August 25, 1793–June 20, 1876) b. Falmouth (now Portland), Maine. Son of Rachel Hall and John Neal, a Quaker schoolmaster. Father died shortly after Neal's birth, and he was raised by his mother. Worked as clerk in dry goods business and itinerant teacher of penmanship. In partnership with John Pierpont, ran dry goods businesses in Boston, Baltimore, and Charleston, 1814–16. Was a member, with Pierpont and Tobias Watkins, of the Delphian Club (founded 1816), literary association that published monthly magazine *The Portico* (1816–18). Studied law and began to write for a living; wrote 150-page critical essay on Byron for *The Portico*. Published series of novels: *Keep Cool* (1817), *Logan, a Family History* (1822), *Seventy-Six* (1823), *Randolph* (1823), *Errata, or the Works of Will Adams* (1823), and *Brother Jonathan* (1825). Other early writings included narrative poems (published under pseudonym "Jehu O'Cataract") collected in *Battle of Niagara, a Poem, without Notes; and Goldau, or, the Maniac Harper* (1818) and verse tragedy *Otho* (1819). Wrote much of Paul Allen's *A History of the American Revolution* (1819); briefly edited *Federal Republican and Baltimore Telegraph* (February–July 1819). Close friendship with John Pierpont broken off following incident in which Neal entered the bedroom of Pierpont's sister-in-law Abby Lord (Neal aggravated the situation by describing the incident in his novel *Randolph*); Neal and Pierpont were later reconciled but were never again as close. Challenged to a duel by Edward Coote Pinkney (whose father he had criticized in *Randolph*), but ignored the challenge; accused of cowardice on handbills distributed by Pinkney. Admitted to bar in 1820, but practiced only briefly; resigned from Delphian Club; affiliation with Quakers formally dissolved following Neal's participation in a street brawl. Went to England in 1823 and began to write articles (initially under pseudonym "Carter Holmes") on American topics for *Blackwood's Magazine*, among them a five-part survey of 135 American authors, the first such overview. Met the utilitarian philosopher Jeremy Bentham in 1825, whose ideas he undertook to promulgate; lodged in Bentham's house for over a year, although their relations were ultimately strained. Returned to the U.S. in 1827; settled in Portland. Practiced law with little success. Married his cousin, Eleanor Hall, in 1828; they had five children. Wrote novel based on witchcraft trials, *Rachel Dyer* (1828), followed by *Authorship* (1830) and *The Down-Easters* (1833). Contributed short fiction, articles, art criticism, and poems to a variety of periodicals, including *The Token* and *The Atlantic Souvenir*; edited *The Yankee* (1828–29), which gave early literary encouragement to Poe, Whittier, Hawthorne, and Longfellow (with whom he formed close friendship); later edited *The New-England Galaxy* (1835), *The New World* (1840), *Brother Jonathan* (1843), and *The Portland Transcript* (1848). Bowdoin College awarded him honorary M.A. in 1836. Campaigned for women's rights; involved in civic life of Portland. In 1850 publicly defended Poe's reputation after attack by Rufus Griswold, stating that Poe "saw farther, and looked more steadily, and more inquisitively into the elements of darkness . . . than did most of the shining brotherhood about him." Last full-length novel, *True Womanhood*, appeared in 1859. Wrote three adventure stories for dime novel publishers Beadle and Adams: *The White-Faced Pacer* (1863), *The Moose-Hunter* (1864), and *Little Moccasin* (1866). Papers destroyed in Portland fire of 1866. Later writings included religious treatise *One Word More* (1854), autobiography *Wandering Recollections of a Somewhat Busy Life* (1869), and *Portland Illustrated* (1874).

JAMES KIRKE PAULDING   (August 22, 1778–April 6, 1860)   b. Great Nine Partners, Putnam County, New York. Son of Catharine Ogden and William Paulding; father and many others in family actively involved in American Revolution. Raised in Tarrytown; moved around 1796 to New York City to live with his brother (who later served as congressman and New York mayor). Worked in a public office and became friendly with Washington Irving and Irving's brother William (who had married Paulding's sister Julia in 1793), collaborating with them on *Salmagundi* (1807–08). *The Diverting History of*

John Bull and Brother Jonathan (1812), a humorous history in the vein of Irving's *History of New York*, was followed by *The Lay of the Scottish Fiddle* (1813), a parody of Scott's *Lay of the Last Minstrel*. Served as major in New York militia during War of 1812. After the war, published other works critical of English politics and culture—*The United States and England* (1815), *A Sketch of Old England by a New-England Man* (1822), and *John Bull in America* (1825)—as well as account of a journey through Virginia, *Letters from the South* (1817), long narrative poem in heroic couplets, *The Backwoodsman* (1818), and unsuccessful sequel to Irving collaboration written by Paulding alone, *Salmagundi, Second Series* (1819–20). Served as secretary of Board of Navy Commissioners under James Madison, 1815–23. In 1818 married Gertrude Kemble (sister of Irving associate Gouverneur Kemble); they had several children. First novel, *Koningsmarke: The Long Finne* (1823), initiated series of fictional accounts of American life, including *The Dutchman's Fireside* (1831), *Westward Ho!* (1832), *The Old Continental* (1846), and *The Puritan and His Daughter* (1849). Also published anti-utopian satire *The Merry Tales of the Three Wise Men of Gotham* (1826); more than 70 stories, some collected in *Tales of the Good Woman* (1829) and *Chronicles of the City of Gotham* (1830); several plays, including *The Lion of the West* (1833) and *The Bucktails* (1847); a biography, *A Life of Washington* (1835); and *Slavery in the United States* (1836), a defense of the Southern view. From 1823 to 1838 served as naval agent for New York City; appointed Secretary of the Navy by Martin Van Buren in 1837. Wife Gertrude died in 1841. Published two more historical novels, *The Old Continental* (1846) and *The Puritan and His Daughters* (1849). After the end of Van Buren's term as president, toured the West with him. Retired to Hyde Park, New York, in 1846.

JOHN HOWARD PAYNE (June 9, 1791–April 9, 1852) b. New York City, one of nine children of Sarah Isaacs and William Payne. Brought up mostly in East Hampton, Long Island, and in Boston, where his father taught school. Showed early interest in the theater, which his father discouraged. Sent to New York to work as counting-house clerk; published theatrical magazine *The Thespian Mirror* (1805–06), which attracted attention of William Coleman, editor of New York *Evening Post*, who for a time was Payne's mentor. Publicized in newspapers and magazines as child prodigy; play *Julia, or The Wanderer* produced in New York in 1806. Formed friendships with Washington Irving, Charles Brockden Brown, James Kirke Paulding, and other literary figures. Contracted numerous debts. With financial support of New York merchant John Seaman attended Union College in Schenectady, New York; published literary magazine *The Pastime* (1807–08). Left school for stage debut in New York City, 1809, in the role of Young Norval in *Douglas* (a role with which he remained permanently identified). Mother died 1807, father 1812. Enjoyed initial acclaim as actor and was called "the American Roscius"; toured Boston, Baltimore, Philadelphia, Richmond, Charleston; first professional American actor to play Hamlet; in Boston, acted with Elizabeth Poe, mother of the poet. Mired in debt, and disappointed at dwindling of celebrity and conflicts with theatrical managers, settled (with financial help of friends and admirers) in England in 1813. Befriended Benjamin West, Washington Allston, Peter Irving (brother of the writer), Samuel Taylor Coleridge, Charles Lamb, and William Hazlitt; acted for a season in provinces; established prolific if largely unprofitable career as playwright in London theater. Drew on variety of sources (including older English work and successful French plays by Pixerecourt, Scribe, and La Beaumelle) to create as many as 60 theatrical pieces. Plays included *Lover's Vows* (1809); *Trial Without Jury* (1815); *Accusation* (1816); *Brutus; or, The Fall of Tarquin* (1818), a successful vehicle for Edmund Kean, stitched together from seven earlier works; *Thérèse; or, The Orphan of Geneva* (1821); *The Two Galley Slaves* (1822); *Mrs. Smith* (1823); *The Fall of Algiers* (1825); *The Lancers* (1827); *Procrastination* (1829); *Oswali at Athens* (1831); *Woman's Revenge* (1832); and *Virginia* (1834). Also published collection of verse, *Lispings of the Muse* (1815). Worked at variety of theatrical jobs, serving as secretary at Covent Garden (1818–19). Leased Sadler's Wells Theatre in 1820, an enterprise that drove him into bankruptcy; imprisoned for debt in Fleet Prison (1820–21); moved to Paris upon release and continued to dodge his many creditors. Wrote the lyrics of "Home, Sweet Home" (with music by Henry Bishop) for inclusion in his play *Clari; or, the Maid of Milan* (1823); the song achieved immediate widespread popularity, but Payne realized little monetary gain from it. Washington Irving spent much time with Payne in Paris, frequently lending him money, and collaborating on a number of plays, including *Charles the Second* (1824) and *Richelieu* (1826). Met Mary Shelley around 1823 and courted her unsuccessfully. Settled in London again in 1826, where he edited and published theatrical newspaper *Opera Glass* (1826–27). Nearly penniless despite prolific output, returned to America in 1832, traveling at expense of friends. A benefit performance of his work, featuring Edwin Forrest and Charles and Fanny Kemble, earned him $10,000. Made plans to publish a magazine of the arts which never appeared, although Payne traveled throughout South securing subscriptions and materials for articles. In 1835 met John Ross, head of the Cherokee Nation, and requested information on tribal history for proposed magazine. As a result of involvement with Ross (at that time resisting state and federal efforts to remove the Cherokee) arrested in Georgia by militia and accused of being an abolitionist; released after 13 days. Published articles describing ordeal and denouncing injustices done to the Indians, and upon his return to New York City, began history of the Cherokee Nation (completed manuscript of first volume is believed lost, although copious notes survive). Maintained connection with Ross in Washington, D.C., assisting him in the preparation of petitions to the federal government; in 1840, following Cherokee removal, traveled with Ross from Washington to his home in Park Hill, Indian Territory (now Oklahoma); met Sequoya, creator of Cherokee alphabet. In 1842, in recognition of his literary talent, and partly through the endeavors of Daniel Webster, President Tyler appointed him American consul at Tunis, where he served from 1843 until his recall by President Polk in 1845. After extensive travels in Europe, returned to America in

1847 seeking a new diplomatic post; eventually relocated to Washington. At gala concert at National Hall in December 1850, attended by President Fillmore and other dignitaries, Jenny Lind acknowledged Payne's presence with a rendition of "Home, Sweet Home," causing great sensation. Returned to Tunis in 1851 after reappointment by Fillmore; died there the following year.

JAMES GATES PERCIVAL (September 15, 1795–May 2, 1856) b. Kensington, Connecticut. Second son of Elizabeth Hart and Dr. James Percival; elder brother Edward was a painter. Sickly in youth; voice permanently damaged by attack of typhoid at age 12. Following father's death in 1807, attended private school where he read extensively but was by his own later account unhappy. At Yale, studied chemistry under Benjamin Silliman; became known as a poet. Graduated 1815; studied botany under Eli Ives in New Haven; subsequent studies at University of Pennsylvania; transferred to Yale Medical Institution, from which he graduated in 1820. Briefly practiced medicine in Charleston, South Carolina. First verse collection, *Poems* (containing long poem "Prometheus"), published in 1821, followed by *Clio I* and *Clio II* (1822) and *Prometheus Part II with Other Poems* (1822); a two-volume collection of his poetry appeared in 1823. Of his circumstances he wrote in 1823: "They are low and sad enough, and they have made my spirits low. I could tell a tale of embarrassments, joined to a bad constitution, injured health, and a neglected orphanage, which would do much to excuse the wrong that is in me." Worked fitfully as newspaper editor, chemistry instructor at West Point, and surgeon in Boston recruiting office. After publication of *Clio No. III* (1827), shifted his ambitions to science, scholarship, and linguistics. Assisted Noah Webster in revising and proofreading *An American Dictionary of the English Language* (1828); translated Malte Brun's *A System of Universal Geography* (1834). In 1835 appointed (along with Charles Shepard) to survey the geology of Connecticut; slow working methods led to difficulties with state government; published *Report on the Geology of the State of Connecticut* (1842). Translated poems from Russian, Serbian, Danish, Hungarian, and other languages, as well as composing original poems in some of these languages; wrote songs in support of William Henry Harrison, published in *The New Haven Whig Song Book* (1840); *The Dream of a Day, and Other Poems*, final collection of poems and translations, appeared in 1843. Lived in seclusion for some years at state hospital in New Haven. From 1851 to 1854 surveyed lead mines in Illinois and Wisconsin for American Mining Company; shortly before his death, appointed state geologist of Wisconsin; traveled throughout Wisconsin, spending time with Winnebago and Ojibwa tribes. Died at Hazel Green, Wisconsin. Two-volume edition of his collected works published posthumously in 1859.

JOHN JAMES PIATT (March 1, 1835–February 16, 1917) b. James' Mills (later Milton), Indiana. Son of Emily Scott and John Bear Piatt; on father's side of French Huguenot descent. Raised in Columbus, Ohio; later attended

Capital University and Kenyon College. As apprentice printer working for *Ohio State Journal* met William Dean Howells in 1852, and the two became close friends. Became editor of *Louisville Journal* shortly after the paper published some of his poetry in 1857. With Howells, published collaborative volume *Poems of Two Friends* (1860). Married poet Sarah Morgan Bryan, herself a contributor to *Louisville Journal*, in 1861; the couple settled in Washington, D.C., where Piatt worked as clerk in Treasury Department until 1867; they had seven children, of whom three sons and a daughter survived to adulthood. In Washington, befriended Walt Whitman. Frequently collaborated with wife in writing poetry; results were published in *Nests at Washington* (1864) and *The Children Out-of-Doors* (1885). Returned to editorial work for *Cincinnati Chronicle* (1867–69) and *Cincinnati Commercial* (1869–78); concurrently served as librarian of U.S. House of Representatives (1871–75), dividing time between Cincinnati and Washington. Appointed U.S. consul in Cork, Ireland (1882–93); became friend of Edmund Gosse, Jean Ingelow, Austin Dobson, Alice Meynell, and others. Afterward retired to North Bend, Ohio; continued to write and work as editor. Piatt's verse collections included *Poems in Sunshine and Firelight* (1866), *Western Windows and Other Poems* (1867), *Poems of House and Home* (1879), *Idyls and Lyrics of the Ohio Valley* (1881), *A Book of Gold, and Other Sonnets* (1889), and *Odes in Ohio and Other Poems* (1897). Disabled by carriage accident several years before his death.

SARAH MORGAN PIATT (August 11, 1836–December 22, 1919)   b. Sarah Morgan Bryan in Lexington, Kentucky. Daughter of Mary Spiers and Talbot Nelson Bryan; grandfather Morgan Bryan was brother-in-law of Daniel Boone and an early settler of Kentucky. Family moved to Versailles, Kentucky, in 1839; mother died in 1844; raised by various relatives and family friends. Graduated Henry Female College in New Castle, Kentucky. Published poetry in Galveston (Texas) *News* and *Louisville Journal* (where editor George D. Prentice encouraged her writing). In June 1861 married John James Piatt; lived successively in Washington, D.C., North Bend, Ohio, and in Cork, Ireland, where Piatt was U.S. consul; they had seven children, of whom three died in childhood. Published many volumes of verse (two of them in collaboration with her husband), including *A Voyage to the Fortunate Isles* (1874), *That New World* (1877), *A Woman's Poems* (1878), *Selected Poems* (1886), *Child's World Ballads* (1887), *An Irish Wild-Flower* (1891), and *An Enchanted Castle* (1893); two-volume collected edition of her poems published 1894. On returning to the United States in 1893, lived in North Bend, Ohio, until husband's death in 1917, after which she lived with son Cecil Piatt in Caldwell, New Jersey.

JOHN PIERPONT (April 6, 1785–August 27, 1866)   b. Litchfield, Connecticut. Second of ten children of Elizabeth Collins and James Pierpont, a clothier. Graduated Yale College 1804, teaching for a short time in an academy at Bethlehem, Connecticut; spent four years as tutor in Colonel William Alston's household in South Carolina. Studied law on his return north. Married

Mary Sheldon Lord in 1810; they had six children. Admitted to bar in 1812, and opened law office in Newburyport, Massachusetts, with little success. Published Federalist political poem *The Portrait* (1812), originally delivered before Washington Benevolent Society of Newburyport. Left the law in 1814 to open dry goods franchises in Boston, Baltimore, and Charleston, in partnership with writer John Neal; the business failed in 1816, and Pierpont was briefly jailed in Baltimore for debt. Decided to enter ministry. *Airs of Palestine* (1816) established reputation as poet; proceeds from book helped defray cost of attending Harvard Divinity School. Graduated 1818, and ordained minister of Hollis Street Unitarian Church in Boston a year later. Friendship with John Neal broken off after 1823 because of incident involving Pierpont's sister-in-law (they reconciled after a few years, but were never again as close). Visited Europe and Palestine, 1835–36. A new edition of his poetry, *Airs of Palestine and Other Poems*, appeared in 1840; in 1843 published *The Anti-Slavery Poems of John Pierpont*. Anti-slavery and temperance views led to long conflict (known locally as "the Seven Years' War") with unsympathetic congregation; in 1845 resigned his position. Went on to serve as pastor of other Unitarian churches in Troy, New York, and West Medford, Massachusetts. Two years after death of first wife, married Harriet Louise Fowler in 1857. Served briefly as army chaplain during the Civil War, but finding the duty arduous resigned to take post as clerk in Treasury Department in Washington, D.C., which he held until his death.

EDWARD COOTE PINKNEY (October 1, 1802–April 11, 1828) b. London, England. Seventh of ten children of Anna Maria Rodgers and William Pinkney of Maryland. Father served in London as U.S. commissioner negotiating claims adjustments under Jay Treaty. After two-year visit to Maryland, family returned to England in 1806 when father was named minister to Britain (served until 1811). In 1815 Pinkney was commissioned as navy midshipman, continuing in navy until father's death in 1822; stationed mostly in Mediterranean; fought pirates in West Indies and received citation for bravery, but frequently was at odds with superiors. In 1823 published the song "Look Out Upon the Stars, My Love" and *Rodolph, A Fragment*. Resigned his commission in 1824 (following a quarrel with his superior officer that nearly resulted in a duel). Practiced law in Baltimore; married Georgiana McCausland, with whom he had one child. Angered by reference to his father in John Neal's novel *Randolph* (1823), challenged Neal to a duel, but was rebuffed; another such challenge was issued to Stephen Simpson, editor of *Philadelphia Mercury*, in response to published statement that Pinkney interpreted as personal slur. Growing reputation as poet furthered by publication of *Poems* (1825). Traveled to Mexico in unsuccessful attempt to gain commission in Mexican Navy; forced to leave country after duel in which he killed his Mexican adversary; became ill. On his return became editor of *The Marylander*, newspaper supporting John Quincy Adams; after a few months, forced to resign due to failing health.

EDGAR ALLAN POE (January 19, 1809–October 7, 1849) b. Boston, Massachusetts. Second of three children of Elizabeth Arnold and David Poe; parents were traveling actors (Elizabeth won acclaim as an actress, while David was regarded as amateurish). Father abandoned family in 1809; mother moved frequently before her death in Richmond, Virginia, in December 1811. Poe and siblings became wards of different foster parents; Poe was taken into home of Frances and John Allan (a Richmond tobacco merchant) but was not legally adopted; name changed to Edgar Allan. Accompanied the Allans to Great Britain; attended schools in London, 1815–20. Family returned to Richmond in 1820; after periods of financial difficulty, Allan became wealthy due to a legacy in 1825. Poe attended private academies in Richmond. Early engagement to Elmira Royster disapproved by Allans and ultimately broken off by her family. Entered University of Virginia in 1826; lost money while gambling and Allan refused to honor debt; returned to Richmond but left household in 1827 after quarrel with Allan. Went to Boston; first book of poetry, *Tamerlane and Other Poems* (1827), published anonymously. Enlisted in U.S. Army under assumed name "Edgar A. Perry" and giving false age; stationed at Fort Independence in Boston harbor; transferred to Fort Moultrie, South Carolina. Partially reconciled with Allan at request of dying foster mother; with Allan's help secured appointment to U.S. Military Academy at West Point. Lived, while waiting for news of appointment, in Baltimore with brother William and aunt Maria Clemm; published second volume of poetry, *Al Aaraaf, Tamerlane and Minor Poems* (1829), favorably reviewed by John Neal. Entered West Point May 1830; dismissed (as he had sought to be) January 1831 for neglect of duty. In New York City, published *Poems by Edgar A. Poe: Second Edition* (1831). Returned to Baltimore and lived with Mrs. Clemm and her eight-year-old daughter, Virginia. Published short fiction in magazines; won recognition in 1833 when "Ms. Found in a Bottle" won competition sponsored by Baltimore *Saturday Visiter*. Through John Pendleton Kennedy obtained editorial position with *Southern Literary Messenger* in 1835; contributed stories, book reviews, and poems. Married Mrs. Clemm's daughter Virginia, then 13 (license taken out in September 1835, probably followed by private ceremony; public marriage in May 1836, after Virginia turned 14). Disputes over salary, editorial independence, and Poe's drinking led to his resignation from the *Messenger*. Moved to New York with Virginia and Mrs. Clemm in February 1837; published *The Narrative of Arthur Gordon Pym* (1838). Moved to Philadelphia in spring or summer of 1838; became co-editor of *Burton's Gentleman's Magazine*, 1839–40; contributed stories including "The Fall of the House of Usher" and "William Wilson." First collection of stories, *Tales of the Grotesque and Arabesque*, published in two volumes in 1839. Left *Burton's*; attempted to start his own periodical, *The Penn Magazine*; corresponded with Thomas Holley Chivers, from whom he attempted to raise money for the magazine. Literary editor of *Graham's Magazine*, 1841–42; contributions included "The Murders in the Rue Morgue," "The Oval Portrait," and "The Masque of the Red Death." Virginia began to show early symptoms of tuberculosis. Met Dickens on 1842 visit to America.

Three poems included in Rufus Griswold's *Poets and Poetry of America* (1842), but subsequent relations with Griswold were poor. Invited by James Russell Lowell to contribute to short-lived magazine *The Pioneer* (1843); contributed "The Tell-Tale Heart" and "Lenore." Won prize in 1843 for "The Gold-Bug"; toured with lecture on "Poets and Poetry of America," 1843–44. Continued to solicit funds for his own magazine, now called *The Stylus*. Moved to New York in 1844; worked on editorial staff of *New-York Evening Mirror* (1844–45), and formed friendship with its co-editor, Nathaniel Parker Willis; with "The Raven," published in the *Mirror* in 1845, achieved fame as poet; published *Tales* (a collection edited by Evert Duyckinck) and *The Raven and Other Poems*. Met Thomas Holley Chivers. Became editor and (on borrowed money) proprietor of *The Broadway Journal* (1845–46); in the *Mirror*, the *Journal*, and elsewhere, launched attack on plagiarisms allegedly committed by Longfellow; attacked in turn by defenders of Longfellow. Published series of sketches on "The Literati of New York" in *Godey's Lady's Magazine* in 1845; successfully sued Thomas Dunn English for libel in 1846 after English (with whom Poe had a fistfight the year before) responded harshly to criticism of him in one of the sketches. A discussion of Poe appeared in the *Revue des Deux Mondes* (1845), followed by translations of a number of his stories; Poe aware of growing French interest in his work. Suffered increasingly from illness and nervous depression. Virginia died of tuberculosis in winter of 1847. Had close relationships with many contemporary women writers, including Fanny Osgood, Elizabeth Ellet, and Sarah Helen Whitman (to whom he briefly became engaged in 1848). In 1848 lectured in New York on "The Universe" and published metaphysical treatise *Eureka*. Returned to Richmond; may have become engaged to childhood sweetheart Elmira Royster (now Elmira Shelton). Stopped in Baltimore on way to New York on literary business and later found in delirious condition there; died four days later. "The Bells" and "Annabel Lee" were published posthumously.

ALEXANDER L. POSEY (August 3, 1873–May 27, 1908) b. near Eufaula, Indian Territory (present day McIntosh County, Oklahoma). One of 12 children of Chickasaw-Creek woman who took English name Nancy Phillips and Lewis Henderson (Hence) Posey (rancher and, later, law enforcement officer of Scotch-Irish descent who claimed to be one-sixteenth Creek). By his own account, spoke little English before age 14. In 1890 enrolled at Indian University at Bacone (near Muskogee, Oklahoma); first poems and prose sketches published in faculty newspaper, where he worked as typesetter. Graduated 1895; elected in the same year to the Creek national legislature; served on many councils and delegations. In 1896, appointed superintendent of Creek Orphanage, Okmulgee, Oklahoma. Married Minnie Harris (of Fayetteville, Arkansas) in May, 1896; they had two children. In early 1898, settled on a farm near Stidham, Oklahoma; appointed administrator of Creek national high schools at Eufaula and Wetumka. Edited *The Indian Journal* (1902–03) at Eufaula, to which he contributed "Fus Fixico Letters," sketches in English-Creek dialect satirizing white injustices to Indians; in 1903, became joint editor of *Muskogee Times*. Became fieldworker for Dawes Commission in 1904, enrolling tribal members in government land-allotment program under Dawes Act. Served as secretary of constitutional convention held in 1905 at Muskogee for proposed Indian state of Sequoyah. Prospered as real estate agent. Shortly before his death resumed editorship of *Indian Journal*; drowned while trying to cross the North Canadian (Creek name Oktahutche) River, Oklahoma, in a small boat. *The Poems of Alexander Lawrence Posey* published posthumously by his wife in 1910.

JOHN WESLEY POWELL (March 24, 1834–September 23, 1902) b. Mt. Morris, New York. Son of Mary Dean and Joseph Powell, English immigrants; father was a Methodist preacher. Family moved frequently, living successively in Ohio, Wisconsin, and Illinois. Studied sporadically at Methodist school in Wheaton, Illinois, and later at Illinois College (in Jacksonville, Illinois), Oberlin, and Wheaton College; he took no degree. Early interest in botany led to his joining Illinois State Natural History Society in 1854, of which he was later elected secretary. Enlisted in army upon outbreak of Civil War; commissioned captain of artillery company which he recruited; lost right arm at battle of Shiloh in 1862; later rose to rank of major of artillery. Married cousin Emma Dean in 1862; they had a daughter. After discharge from army in 1865, became professor of geology at Illinois Wesleyan College in Bloomington; later served as lecturer and museum curator at Illinois Normal University. Organized natural science expeditions in Colorado. Met Ute bands near the White River, 1868–69, and gradually acquired knowledge of Ute and Southern Paiute languages; continued to gather ethnographic information over next several years. In May 1869 led party of 11 men on journey by boat through canyons of the Green and Colorado rivers; emerged from Grand Canyon in August. Conducted further explorations in 1871, 1874, and 1875; results summarized in *Explorations of the Colorado River of the West and Its Tributaries* (1875). Served as director of second division of U.S. Geological Survey of the Rocky Mountain Region, 1875–79, and as overall director, 1880–94; inaugurated series of bulletins, monographs, and atlases, as well as ethnographic studies (beginning in 1877), *Contributions to North American Ethnology*. Directed acquisition of Indian materials for 1876 Philadelphia International Exposition. Undertook comparison of Indian vocabularies gathered by Smithsonian Institution; summarized findings in *Introduction to the Study of Indian Languages* (1877); studies of water and irrigation problems of the West published in *Report on the Lands of the Arid Region of the United States* (1878). From 1879 was director of the newly established Bureau of Ethnology (later Bureau of American Ethnology) under the Smithsonian; oversaw ethnological and linguistic researches of James Mooney, Jeremiah Curtin, James Owen Dorsey, Albert Gatschet, and many others; inaugurated series of annual reports (beginning in 1881) and bulletins (beginning in 1887). Linguistic research summarized in *Indian Linguistic Families of America North of Mexico* (1891). Held title of director until his death, although failing health forced his retirement from active duties. Published philosophical study *Truth and Error, or the Science of Intellection* in 1898. Died at his summer home in Haven, Maine.

STEPHEN POWERS (July 20, 1840–April 2, 1904) b. Waterford, Ohio. Graduated University of Michigan in 1863. Worked as war correspondent for *Cincinnati Commercial* during Civil War. Traveled in Europe in 1866–67, reporting for *The New York Times, The Nation*, and other publications. In January 1869 undertook walking trip across the United States, reaching San Francisco in November. Published an account of his journey in *Afoot and Alone: A Walk from Sea to Sea* (1872). In the summers of 1871 and 1872 devoted himself to the study of California Indians, producing articles that were published serially in *Overland Monthly*, 1872–75. Arranged with John Wesley Powell, director of the Department of Interior's Geographical and Geological Survey of the Rocky Mountain Region, to publish his Indian articles in book form as *Tribes of California* (1877). Left California in 1875 to live on family farm in Ohio. Appointed by Powell as a commissioner to collect California Indian artifacts for the Centennial Exhibition of 1876; returned to California, 1875–76. Later published on agricultural topics. Died in Jacksonville, Florida.

JOHN DYNELEY PRINCE (April 17, 1868–1945) b. New York City. Son of Anne Maria Morris and John Dyneley Prince. Graduated Columbia 1888; studied subsequently at University of Berlin (1889–90) and Johns Hopkins, where he received his Ph.D. in 1892. Married Adeline Loomis in 1889. Accompanied University of Pennsylvania archaeological expedition to Babylonian sites, 1888–89. Professor of Semitic languages at New York University, 1892–1902; later professor of Semitic languages (1902–15) and Slavonic languages (1915–21) and East European languages (1933–37) at Columbia University. Published many articles on Passamaquoddy, Natick, and Pequot tribes; collaborated with Charles Godfrey Leland on *Kulóskap the Master and Other Algonkin Poems* (1902); *Passamaquoddy Texts* published 1921. Other publications included *Mene, Mene, Tekel, Upharsin* (1893), *A Critical Commentary on the Book of Daniel* (1899), *Materials for a Sumerian Lexicon* (1908), *Assyrian Primer* (1909), and *Fragments from Babel* (1939). Served in New Jersey assembly (1906, 1908–09) and the New Jersey senate (1912), and as acting governor of New Jersey in 1912. Appointed ambassador to Denmark by Warren G. Harding in 1921; ambassador to Yugoslavia, 1926–33.

JAMES RYDER RANDALL (January 1, 1839–January 14, 1908) b. Baltimore, Maryland. Son of Ruth Hooper and John Randall, a wealthy merchant; on mother's side, great-great-grandson of René Leblanc, Acadian notary who figures in Longfellow's *Evangeline*. At age ten entered Georgetown College; due to illness left before graduating; traveled in West Indies. On his return worked as printer in Baltimore and shipping clerk in New Orleans. In 1860 appointed professor of English and classics at Poydras College, Creole school in Louisiana. On reading of violence attending passage of 6th Massachusetts Regiment through Baltimore in April 1861, wrote "Maryland, My Maryland." Published in New Orleans *Delta* of April 26, poem quickly achieved popularity throughout the South; set to music (to a tune adapted from the German "Tannenbaum"), became quasi-official battle song of Confederacy. Enlisted in Confederate Army, but ill health caused him to be mustered out almost immediately. In 1866 married Katherine Hammond; they had eight children. Became associate editor of Augusta (Georgia) *Constitutionalist*, and later worked for various other periodicals including Baltimore *Catholic Mirror* and New Orleans *Morning Star*. Served for a time as secretary to several Georgia politicians in Washington, D.C., also acting as correspondent for the Augusta *Chronicle*. Honored by state of Maryland in 1907 on occasion of Jamestown Exposition; collected poems not published until two years after his death.

THOMAS BUCHANAN READ (March 12, 1822–May 11, 1872) b. Chester County, Pennsylvania. After father's death, apprenticed to a tailor; ran away to Philadelphia, where he learned trade of cigar-making. In 1837 went to Cincinnati where he lived with a married sister; supported himself by rolling cigars and painting canal boats. Hired by sculptor Shobal Vail Clevenger (from whom he learned rudiments of sculpting) to chisel engravings on tombstones. Learned trade of sign painter; received sporadic education; published poems in local newspapers. Moved to Dayton, Ohio, where he did theatrical work. Returned to Cincinnati and through generosity of Nicholas Longworth was able to open studio as portrait painter; in 1840, painted portrait of William Henry Harrison, then campaigning for presidency. Moved from town to town, working as portrait painter and sign painter, sometimes giving public entertainments, and occasionally working as cigar-maker. Moved in 1841 to New York and within the year to Boston, where he opened a studio. Befriended Henry Wadsworth Longfellow and Washington Allston. Married Mary J. Pratt (of Gambier, Ohio) in 1843; they had three children. Published poems in Boston *Courier*. Settled in Philadelphia in 1846. Verse collected in *Poems* (1847), *Lays and Ballads* (1849), *The New Pastoral* (1855), *The House by the Sea* (1855), *Sylvia; or, The Last Shepherd* (1857), *Rural Poems* (1857), and other volumes. Visited Europe in 1850; settled in Florence in 1853. In 1855, wife and a daughter died of cholera; Read returned to U.S., and the following year married Harriet Denison Butler (of Northampton, Massachusetts). Spent much time in Philadelphia, Boston, Cincinnati, as well as abroad. During Civil War gave lectures and readings of his war poetry to benefit soldiers; served on the staff of Union general Lew Wallace. Three-volume *Poetical Works* published in 1866. In final years (after 1866) lived mainly in Rome. Painted mythological subjects and portraits of Elizabeth Barrett Browning, Henry Wadsworth Longfellow, and others; also worked occasionally as sculptor, making bust of Sheridan. Later volumes of verse include *The Wagoner of the Alleghanies* (1862), *A Summer Story, Sheridan's Ride, and Other Poems* (1865), and *Good Samaritans* (1867). Died of pneumonia while on a visit to the United States.

LIZETTE WOODWORTH REESE (January 9, 1856–December 17, 1935) b. Huntingdon (now Waverly), Maryland, a suburb of Baltimore. One of four daughters of Louisa Gabler (of German birth) and David Reese (who later served as Confederate soldier). After graduating Eastern High School she became a teacher and continued to teach at various public and private schools in the Baltimore area; taught English at Western High School, 1901–21. Published first poem, "The Deserted House," in *The Southern Magazine* in 1874; first collection of verse, *A Branch of May*, appeared in 1887. Her work was praised by Edmund Clarence Stedman, with whom she formed a close friendship. Her next collection, *A Handful of Lavender* (1891), incorporated the poems of the previous volume with 43 new ones; followed by *A Quiet Road* (1896), *A Wayside Lute* (1909), and *Spicewood* (1920). Sonnet "Tears," published in *Scribner's* in 1899, became widely known. Retired from teaching in 1921. After retirement published verse collections *Wild Cherry* (1923), *Selected Poems* (1926), *Little Henrietta* (1927), *White April* (1930), *Pastures* (1933), and two volumes of prose memoirs, *A Victorian Village* (1920) and *The York Road* (1931). Narrative poem *The Old House in the Country* (1936) and unfinished novel *Worleys* (1936) appeared posthumously.

JOHN ROLLIN RIDGE (March 18, 1827–October 5, 1867) b. in Cherokee Nation near Rome, Georgia. Son of John Ridge and grandson of Major Ridge, Cherokee leaders who helped negotiate 1835 Treaty of New Echota ceding Cherokee lands to the U.S.; mother Sarah Bird Northrup (whom his father met while attending school in Connecticut) was white. Ridge was 11 at time of forced removal of Cherokee to Indian Territory (now Oklahoma). On June 22, 1839, father and grandfather were murdered in retaliation for their involvement with loss of Cherokee lands. Mother moved with children to Fayetteville, Arkansas, where Ridge was educated; briefly attended school in Great Barrington, Massachusetts, but soon returned to Fayetteville, studying Latin and Greek with a missionary to the Cherokee. About 1849 Ridge killed a Cherokee (allegedly in self-defense) who had attacked him as result of the old grievance against his family; fled to Missouri. In 1850, rather than stand trial in Cherokee Nation, immigrated to California with the Gold Rush, leaving a wife, Elizabeth Wilson, and daughter in Arkansas. Worked as miner and trader; in 1853 became deputy clerk, auditor, and recorder in Yuba County, California. Became journalist, writing poems and articles for *Golden Era* and *Hesperian* under pseudonym "Yellow Bird" (literal translation of his Cherokee name Chees-qua-ta-law-ny); sent for family, settling in Marysville, California, and later in San Francisco. In 1854 published *Life and Adventures of Joaquin Murrieta*, novel based on life of Mexican bandit. Edited *Sacramento Bee* in 1857, *California Express* in 1857–58, and *San Francisco Herald* in 1861–63. During Civil War, wrote in support of the Confederacy (with which the Cherokee were allied). After the war, headed one of two rival Cherokee delegations sent to Washington to negotiate peace treaty with federal government; unsuccessfully attempted to gain legal division of the tribe along lines of longstanding political feud that had claimed the lives of his father and grandfather. Returned to California, where he died. *Poems* published posthumously in 1868, although most of the poems were written when he was in his teens.

JAMES WHITCOMB RILEY (October 7, 1849–July 22, 1916) b. Greenfield, Indiana. Son of Elizabeth Marine and Reuben A. Riley (a lawyer and state legislator who later served as Union cavalry captain). Educated at home and at local schools; briefly attended Greenfield Academy in 1870. After leaving school, worked as shoe-store clerk, Bible salesman, house painter. Began publishing poems in local papers in 1870. Started sign-painting business in 1871. From 1872–74, toured Midwest as member of medicine show and as itinerant sign painter; gave solo performances as humorist, 1874–76. Worked briefly in father's law office. Resumed touring in 1876, with Wizard Oil Company medicine show. In 1877 worked as assistant to the editor of *The Anderson Democrat*. In literary hoax, passed off poem "Leonainie" (published in *Kokomo Dispatch* in August 1877) as newly discovered poem by Poe. Regularly contributed poems and sketches to the *Indianapolis Journal*, and in 1879, settling permanently in Indianapolis, joined *Journal* staff as poet and humorist. Humorous verses in Hoosier dialect, written under pseudonym "Benj. F. Johnson, of Boone," became popular and were collected in *The Old Swimmin'-Hole and 'Leven More Poems* (1883). Collection of prose sketches *The Boss Girl* (1885) followed by another volume of verse, *Afterwhiles* (1887). Following successful reading in Boston in 1882, frequently made reading tours of U.S. After 1886 sometimes shared platform with humorist "Bill" Nye; introduced by James Russell Lowell at highly successful 1887 reading at Chickering Hall, New York City, under auspices of International Copyright League. Literary associates included Joel Chandler Harris, George Washington Cable, and Bliss Carman. While continuing as staff writer for *Indianapolis Journal*, continued to publish poetry regularly in collections including *Old-Fashioned Roses* (1888), *Pipes o' Pan at Zekesbury* (1888), *Rhymes of Childhood* (1890), *Green Fields and Running Brooks* (1892), *Poems Here at Home* (1893), *Armazindy* (1894), *A Child World* (1896), *The Rubaiyat of Doc Sifers* (1897), *Home-Folks* (1900), *The Book of Joyous Children* (1902). In addition, due to Riley's wide popularity, earlier work was frequently reissued in illustrated gift editions. Retired from *Indianapolis Journal* in 1888. Visited Scotland and England in 1891. Verse drama *The Flying Islands of the Night* appeared in 1891 but was not well received. Gave final reading tour in 1903. Received numerous honorary degrees; elected to American Academy of Arts and Letters in 1911. Six-volume edition of *The Complete Works of James Whitcomb Riley* was published 1913. Weakened by series of strokes in later years.

EDWIN ARLINGTON ROBINSON (December 22, 1869–April 6, 1935) b. Head Tide, Maine. Son of Mary Elizabeth Palmer and Edward Robinson; descendant of Anne Bradstreet. Grew up in Gardiner, Maine. Studied at Harvard (1891–93); published poems in *Harvard Advocate*. Worked in Boston and

Gardiner for a number of years while devoting himself to poetry. Published *The Torrent and the Night Before* (1896) at own expense; it was followed the next year by *The Children of the Night*. In 1899 worked as confidential clerk to Harvard president Charles W. Eliot before moving in October to New York City. Held variety of jobs, including work as time checker for construction of IRT subway in New York City, 1903–04; began to drink heavily. Encouraged by Edmund Clarence Stedman, who anthologized a number of his poems; introduced by Stedman to poet Ridgely Torrence, who became a close friend; renewed friendship with Harvard acquaintance William Vaughn Moody. Published *Captain Craig* (1902); the book's reviews were poor, although Robinson was defended by Trumbull Stickney in *The Harvard Monthly:* "The honesty and simplicity of his mind, the pathos and kindness of his heart, above all the humor with which his imagination is lighted up continually, have made me begin life over again and feel once more that poetry is part of it, nay the truth of it." Robinson continued to live in obscurity until President Theodore Roosevelt, an admirer of his poetry, offered him job in New York custom house, where he worked from 1905 to 1909. *The Town Down the River* (1910), dedicated to Roosevelt, and *The Man Against the Sky* (1916) gained him wider attention as poet; also published plays *Van Zorn* (1914) and *The Porcupine* (1915). From 1911 spent summers at MacDowell Colony in Peterborough, New Hampshire; assisted, beginning in 1916, by financial stipend donated anonymously by friends. *Merlin* (1917) was first of triptych of book-length Arthurian poems, followed by *Lancelot* (1920) and *Tristram* (1927). Won three Pulitzer Prizes, for *Collected Poems* (1921), *The Man Who Died Twice* (1924), and *Tristram*, whose popular success gave Robinson financial security. Other late books of poetry included *The Three Taverns* (1920), *Avon's Harvest* (1921), *Roman Bartholow* (1923), *Dionysus in Doubt* (1925), *Cavender's House* (1929), *The Glory of the Nightingales* (1930), *Matthias at the Door* (1931), *Talifer* (1933), *Amaranth* (1934), and *King Jasper* (1935). Robinson traveled to England in 1923, his sole trip abroad.

ABRAM JOSEPH RYAN (February 5, 1838–April 22, 1886) b. Hagerstown, Maryland. Parents Mary Coughlin and Matthew Ryan were recent immigrants from Clonmell, Ireland. Family moved to the West in the early 1840s, settling in St. Louis, Missouri, where father eventually opened a general store. Attended Christian Brothers Cathedral school in St. Louis (1853–54); took vows in November 1856. Studied theology at Niagara University, Niagara, New York (1858–59). Ordained September 1860 in St. Vincent's Church, St. Louis. Taught theology at Niagara University and at diocesan seminary in Cape Girardeau, Missouri. In 1862 joined Confederate Army as unofficial chaplain (having been rejected in application for commission); ministered to smallpox victims at Gratiot Prison in New Orleans; wrote two elegies for brother killed in April 1863 while fighting for Confederacy. After the war, edited Catholic newspapers *The Pacificator* and *The Banner of the South* in Augusta, Georgia, and *The Star* in New Orleans. Lived briefly in Mississippi and formed friendship with family of Jefferson Davis; later served as priest in Tennessee, Georgia, and Alabama. During Reconstruction remained spokesman for Confederacy, expressing continuing loyalty to the cause in poems published throughout the 1870s (became known as "The Poet-Priest of the Confederacy"); poems collected in *Father Ryan's Poems* (1879) and *Poems, Patriotic, Religious, and Miscellaneous* (1880); also published devotional work *A Crown for Our Queen* (1882). Lectured in United States, Canada, and Mexico, often as part of fundraising effort for Southern war orphans and widows, and for victims of epidemics. Died at Convent of St. Bonifacius in Louisville, Kentucky.

GEORGE SANTAYANA   (December 16, 1863–September 26, 1952)   b. Madrid, Spain. Son of Josefina Borras de Santayana (widow of American businessman George Sturgis) and Augustin Ruiz de Santayana; christened Jorge Ruiz de Santayana y Borrais. Mother separated from second husband when Santayana was five, and moved to Boston; raised by father in Avila, Spain, until age eight, when they rejoined mother in Boston; father returned permanently to Spain in 1873. Studied at Boston Latin School. Graduated from Harvard 1886, having co-edited the *Harvard Lampoon* (with Ernest Lawrence Thayer and others). Studied in Germany before returning to Harvard for Ph.D. in philosophy, awarded in 1889. Became member of Harvard philosophy faculty (where colleagues included William James and Josiah Royce) and full professor in 1907. Students included T. S. Eliot and Wallace Stevens. Early works included *Sonnets and Other Verses* (1894), first important philosophical work *The Sense of Beauty* (1896), verse play *Lucifer: A Theological Tragedy* (1899), *Interpretations of Poetry and Religion* (1900), and another poetry collection, *The Hermit of Carmel* (1901). *The Life of Reason*, a five-volume study of reason in relation to common sense, society, religion, art, and science, appeared 1905–06; *Three Philosophical Poets*, study of Lucretius, Dante, and Goethe, published 1910. Remained at Harvard until 1912; retired to live off small inheritance from mother, who had died earlier that year. Lived in England and Paris before settling in Rome in 1925. In *Scepticism and Animal Faith* (1923) undertook to reexamine foundations of his philosophy; elaborated on new interpretation in four-volume *The Realms of Being* (1927–40). *Poems, Selected by the Author and Revised* published in London in 1922 (American edition, 1923). Published many other works including *The Genteel Tradition at Bay* (1931) and *The Last Puritan* (1935), a novel about the lingering influence of Calvinism, which became an unexpected bestseller. Autobiography *Persons and Places* appeared in three volumes between 1944 and 1953. During World War II, took refuge in English convent in Rome, remaining there until his death.

EPES SARGENT   (September 27, 1813–December 30, 1880)   b. Gloucester, Massachusetts. Son of Hannah Dane Coffin and Epes Sargent, shipmaster from old Gloucester family. When Sargent was five the family moved to Roxbury, where father worked as merchant before returning to maritime pursuits. Traveled for several months with his father in Russia. Extracts from his letters

describing the journey appeared in the *Literary Journal* published by students of the Boston Latin School, from which Sargent graduated in 1829. Editor and writer on staff of *Boston Daily Advertiser* and *Boston Daily Atlas* (for whom he also served as Washington correspondent). Became involved in Whig politics and wrote *Life and Public Services of Henry Clay* (1842). Wrote a number of fairly successful plays—including *The Bride of Genoa* (1837) and *Velasco* (1839)—and was active as journalist in New York, working for *New-York Mirror* and *The New World*; edited his own short-lived *Sargent's New Monthly Magazine* (1843) and *Modern Standard Drama* (1846). First collection of poetry, *Songs of the Sea with Other Poems*, appeared in 1847. Returning to Boston, edited *Boston Transcript*, 1847–53. In 1848 married Elizabeth Weld of Roxbury. Published prolific quantity of poetry, fiction, plays, travel books, school texts, and miscellaneous anthologies, including *Harper's Cyclopedia of British and American Poetry* (issued posthumously in 1881). Later in life, spiritualism became chief interest, discussed in *Planchette, or the Despair of Science* (1869), *The Proof Palpable of Immortality* (1875), and *The Scientific Basis of Spiritualism* (1880).

HENRY ROWE SCHOOLCRAFT (March 28, 1793–December 10, 1864) b. Albany County, New York. Son of Margaret Rowe and Lawrence Schoolcraft (glassmaker). Studied at public school in Hamilton, New York, Union College, and Middlebury College, where he specialized in geology and mineralogy. Made journey of mineralogical observation in southern Missouri and Arkansas, 1817–18, described in *A View of the Lead Mines of Missouri* (1819). In 1820 served as geologist on Lewis Cass expedition to Upper Mississippi and Lake Superior, publishing *Narrative Journal of Travels through the Northwestern Regions of the United States* (1821). With help of Cass and John C. Calhoun, appointed Indian agent for tribes of Lake Superior region in 1822; the following year married Jane Johnston, a half-blood Ojibwa who had been educated in Europe, granddaughter of Ojibwa chief Waboojeeg. Served in Michigan territorial legislature, 1828–32. Helped found Historical Society of Michigan (1828) and Algic Society of Detroit (1832). Participated in expedition in 1832 that led to what he erroneously believed to be the source of the Mississippi, described in *Narrative of an Expedition through the Upper Mississippi to Itasca Lake, the Actual Source of the Mississippi* (1834). Served as superintendent of Indian affairs for Michigan, 1836–41. Negotiated treaties, including treaty of March 28, 1836, in which the Ojibwa ceded major portion of their territory to the United States. First major study of Ojibwa culture, *Algic Researches* (1839), published in two volumes. Dismissed from position as superintendent for alleged profiteering; moved to New York City. Wife Jane died in 1842; visited Europe. Conducted census of New York Indians in 1845. Further memoirs and compilations of American Indian material appeared as *Notes on the Iroquois* (1842), *Oneóta; or, Characteristics of the Red Race of America* (1845), and *Personal Memoirs of Thirty Years with the Indian Tribes* (1851); also published poem on Indian themes, *Alhalla; or, the Lord of Talladega* (1843). Married in 1847 to Mary Howard of North Carolina. Won congressional funding in 1847 for large-scale survey of American Indians (although most of his material related specifically to the Ojibwa); published in elaborate six-volume edition, illustrated by Seth Eastman and others, as *Historical and Statistical Information Respecting the History, Condition, and Prospects of the Indian Tribes of the United States* (1851–57). Following success of Longfellow's *Song of Hiawatha* (1855), based in large part on Schoolcraft's early work, reissued *Algic Researches* as *The Myth of Hiawatha* (1856). In final years suffered from severe rheumatism. Died in Washington, D.C.

CLINTON SCOLLARD (September 18, 1860–November 19, 1932) b. Clinton, New York. Graduated from Hamilton College 1881; graduate studies at Harvard and Cambridge; formed early friendships with Bliss Carman, Frank Dempster Sherman, Edmund Gosse, Austin Dobson, and Andrew Lang. After traveling in the Near East, became professor of English at Hamilton, remaining there until 1896. Beginning with first verse collections *Pictures in Song* (1884) and *With Reed and Lyre* (1886), published over 40 volumes of poetry, fiction, and essays. Frequent travels were reflected in works such as *Old and New World Lyrics* (1888), *Songs of Sunrise Lands* (1892), and *Italy in Arms and Other Poems* (1915). Wrote *A Southern Flight* (1905) in collaboration with close friend Frank Dempster Sherman, to whose memory he dedicated *Elegy in Autumn* (1917). Married Georgia Brown in 1890; in 1924 they were divorced, and he married poet Jessie B. Rittenhouse. Died at his home in Kent, Connecticut.

EDMUND HAMILTON SEARS (April 6, 1810–January 16, 1876) b. Sandisfield, Massachusetts. Son of Lucy Smith and Joseph Sears, a farmer. Attended Westfield Academy briefly; in 1831 became student at Union College, Schenectady, New York, where he was an editor of college paper and won prize for poetry. Taught at Brattleboro, Vermont; studied theology. Graduated from Harvard Divinity School in 1837 and became missionary for American Unitarian Association, serving mostly in Toledo, Ohio. Subsequently ordained as Unitarian minister in Wayland, Massachusetts. Married Ellen Bacon in 1839, the year of his ordination; they had three sons and a daughter. In 1840 transferred to church in Lancaster, Massachusetts, but due to illness retired after seven years to a small farm in Wayland; health recovered and in 1848 he again became minister in Wayland. Best-known work, the hymn "It Came Upon the Midnight Clear," appeared in anthology *Five Christmas Hymns* in 1852. From 1859 to 1871 was an editor of *The Monthly Religous Magazine*. In 1866 became minister in Weston, Massachusetts. Published numerous theological and devotional writings, including *Regeneration* (1853), *Athanasia; or Foregleams of Immortality* (1858), *The Fourth Gospel, the Heart of Christ* (1872), and *Songs and Sermons of the Christian Life* (1875); also published two works of family history, *Pictures of the Olden Time as Shown in the Fortunes of a Family of Pilgrims* (1857) and *Genealogies and Biographical Sketches of the Ancestry and Descendants of Richard Sears* (1857). In 1874 received serious injuries in a fall from a tree, which led to his death two years later.

LYDIA HUNTLEY SIGOURNEY (September 1, 1791–June 10, 1865) b. Norwich, Connecticut. Daughter of Zerviah Wentworth and Ezekiel Huntley, a groundskeeper. Father employed by Mrs. Daniel Lathrop, in whose home Sigourney was born and to whom she dedicated many poems. Spent much time in Hartford with the family of Daniel Wadsworth, a wealthy art collector. Ran schools in Norwich (1811–12) and Hartford (1812–19). With Wadsworth's help, published *Moral Pieces in Prose and Verse* in 1815. Married Charles Sigourney, Hartford hardware merchant, in 1819 (they had a son and daughter, in addition to a son and two daughters from his previous marriage); despite his initial objections, turned to writing as career in order to supplement family income. Indian epic *Traits of the Aborigines* (1822) published anonymously, as were nearly all of her publications until 1833. Met Lafayette on his 1824 trip to Hartford. Major collection of poems published 1834, revised and reprinted numerous times afterward. Contributed prose and verse to many periodicals, including *The North American Review*, *Graham's Magazine*, and *Southern Literary Messenger*; published 67 books in her lifetime, including *How to Be Happy* (1833), *Letters to Young Ladies* (1833), *Olive Buds* (1836), *Pocahontas and Other Poems* (1841), *Poems, Religious and Elegiac* (1841), *The Voice of Flowers* (1846), *The Weeping Willow* (1847), *Waterdrops* (1848), and *Whisper to a Bride* (1850); illustrated edition of collected poems published by Carey & Hart of Philadelphia in 1848. Widely popular and known as "the American Hemans" (in reference to the popular English poet Felicia Hemans); noted in particular for commemorative poems, which she frequently wrote on request. Traveled to Europe in 1840 where she was introduced to King Louis Philippe of France and made acquaintance of William Wordsworth, Thomas Carlyle, and Samuel Rogers; stirred controversy in England when, on her return, she published without permission a letter from Mrs. Robert Southey detailing the poet's final illness. Following son's early death, published his death-bed journal in *The Faded Hope* (1852). Active in many causes, including higher education for women and temperance. Died in Hartford. Her autobiography, *Letters of Life*, was published posthumously in 1866.

EDWARD ROWLAND SILL (April 29, 1841–February 27, 1887) b. Windsor, Connecticut. Son of Elizabeth Newberry Rowland and Theodore Sill, a physician. After death by drowning of older brother when he was six and death of mother when he was eleven, moved with father to Cleveland. Father died in 1853 shortly after opening office there. Attended Phillips Exeter Academy for two years; returned to Ohio, where he lived with uncle Elisha Noyes Sill in Cuyahoga Falls, and attended Western Reserve Preparatory School for a year and a half. Attended Yale, where he was an editor of *Yale Literary Magazine* and author of class poem. After graduating from Yale in 1861, traveled to California by sea for his health. Worked as postal clerk in Sacramento and at bank in Folsom; desultorily studied law and medicine. Went back East in 1866, stopping in Cuyahoga Falls where in February 1867 he married cousin Elizabeth Newberry Sill (daughter of Elisha Noyes Sill). Briefly attended Harvard Divinity School in spring and summer of 1867 before deciding against ministerial career. (He wrote to correspondent, "On religion, I doubt your ever agreeing with me that the church is a great fraud and nuisance. I am convinced it is doing infinitely more harm than good, every day and week.") Moved to New York, working as journalist for *New York Evening Mail* and as teacher in Brooklyn. In 1868 published *The Hermitage and Other Poems*, only volume of verse publicly distributed in his lifetime. Settled again in Ohio in 1868; served two years as superintendent of schools in Cuyahoga Falls before moving in 1871 to California; taught high school in Oakland. From 1874 to 1882, occupied chair of English at University of California at Berkeley; revolutionized curriculum and pedagogy in his department; acquired reputation as one of the great teachers of his generation. Continued to publish poems in magazines. Retired from teaching in 1882; privately published a second book of poems, *The Venus of Milo* (1883); returned to father-in-law's home in Ohio. Became frequent contributor to *The Century*, *Atlantic Monthly*, *Overland Monthly*, and other journals. Health poor in final years; died unexpectedly in a Cleveland hospital, from syncope following a minor operation.

WILLIAM GILMORE SIMMS (April 17, 1806–June 11, 1870) b. Charleston, South Carolina. Son of Harriet Singleton and William Gilmore Simms, an Irish immigrant. Mother died in 1808; father, a merchant, moved to Tennessee and then to Mississippi Territory, serving as soldier in Indian wars under Andrew Jackson and establishing himself as planter. Simms remained in Charleston under the care of his maternal grandmother, despite repeated urgings by father for the boy to come live with him (father at one point attempted to have son abducted off the street and brought to him in Mississippi); Simms chose to remain with grandmother, although he later said that he regretted the decision. Served apprenticeship to pharmacist; after six years turned to study of law. From age 16 published verse in Charleston press. In 1824 made long visit to father's plantation in Mississippi and to Indian territory west of the Mississippi. Married Anna Malcolm Giles, city clerk's daughter, in 1826; they had a daughter. Admitted to South Carolina bar in 1827 (gave up law practice 1829). In the course of his life published over 30 volumes of fiction, 18 volumes of verse, and a variety of biographies, histories, geographies, political treatises, and literary essays. Early verse publications included *Monody on the Death of Gen. Charles Cotesworth Pinckney* (1825), *Lyrical and Other Poems* (1827), *Early Lays* (1827), *The Vision of Cortes, Cain, and Other Poems* (1829) and *The Tri-Color* (1830). Edited *Southern Literary Gazette* (1828–29) and *Charleston City Gazette* (1830–32); threatened with mob action for opposition to Nullification. Following death of wife Anna in 1832, visited New York, New Haven, and Boston; formed friendships with William Cullen Bryant and Evert Duyckinck. Achieved literary success with novels *Martin Faber* (1833), *Guy Rivers* (1834), and *The Yemassee* (1835).

The Partisan (1835) was first of his best-known series, later known as "the Revolutionary Novels," concerned with South Carolina during Revolutionary War; subsequent volumes in series included *Mellichampe* (1836), *Katharine Walton* (1851), *Woodcraft* (1854), *The Forayers* (1855), and *Eutaw* (1856). Returned to Charleston and in 1836 married Chevillette Eliza Roach, daughter of prosperous plantation owner; they had 13 children. Settled at her family estate Woodlands; gradually took over management and eventually ownership. Continued to publish fiction at rapid rate, including *Richard Hurdis* (1838), *Border Beagles* (1840), *The Wigwam and the Cabin* (1845–46), and *The Cassique of Kiawah* (1859); wrote biographies of Francis Marion, Captain John Smith, Chevalier Bayard, and Nathanael Greene. Later volumes of poetry included *Atalantis* (1832), *Southern Passages and Pictures* (1839), *Donna Florida* (1843), *Areytos; or, Songs of the South* (1846), *Lays of the Palmetto* (1848), *The Cassique of Accabee* (1849), and *The City of the Silent* (1850); poems collected in *Poems: Descriptive, Legendary, and Contemplative* (1853). Edited *The Magnolia* (1842–43), *Simms's Magazine* (1845, subsequently absorbed into *Southern Literary Messenger*), and *The Southern Quarterly Review*, 1849–54. Became ardent defender of slavery; close friend and adviser of South Carolina senator James Henry Hammond; published *Slavery in America* (1838); contributed to *The Pro-Slavery Argument, as Maintained by the Most Distinguished Writers of the Southern States* (1852). Series of pro-slavery lectures in New York state in 1856 canceled after hostile public reaction in Buffalo and Rochester. Wife Chevillette died in 1863. Woodlands (already damaged by a fire in 1862) was destroyed by stragglers from Sherman's army in 1865; fled to Columbia, South Carolina, and witnessed its burning. After the war struggled to support family by fiction and journalistic pieces; edited newspapers *Columbia Phoenix* (1865), *Daily South Carolinian* (1865 66), and *Courier* (1870), and anthology *War Poetry of the South* (1867).

EDMUND CLARENCE STEDMAN (October 8, 1833–January 18, 1908) b. Hartford, Connecticut. Son of Elizabeth C. Dodge (later known as poet and essayist under the name Elizabeth C. D. Stedman Kinney) and Edmund B. Stedman (merchant and army officer). Father died when he was two; raised for next several years on grandfather's farm in Plainfield, New Jersey, passing afterward into care of uncle James B. Stedman in Norwich, Connecticut. Entered Yale 1849, but was expelled in his junior year for "irregularities" and disorderly conduct. Studied law for a time; became part owner of *Norwich Tribunal*. Married Laura Hyde Woodworth in 1853; they had two sons. Dissolved partnership at *Norwich Tribune* and became part owner of *Mountain County Herald* in Winsted, Connecticut, in 1854. Moved to New York in 1855; became partner in clockmaking concern; business failed and Stedman took work as real estate broker. Lived with wife in cooperative "Unitary Home" on East 14th Street. Satirical poem about a society wedding (1859) won him literary reputation furthered by other poems, including "Honest Abe of the West," campaign song for Lincoln. Formed friendships with Bayard Taylor, Richard Henry Stoddard, and Thomas Bailey Aldrich. In 1860 joined staff of

New York *World*, and published first collection of verse, *Poems Lyrical and Idyllic*. Based in Washington during early years of Civil War as correspondent for *World*; often traveled with troops. Assumed position in U.S. attorney general's office in 1862. The following year, returned to New York and entered world of finance with much success, forming his own brokerage company in 1864, and eventually holding a seat on the New York Stock Exchange. Continued to publish volumes of poetry, including *Alice of Monmouth* (1864), *The Blameless Prince* (1869), *Favorite Poems* (1877), *Hawthorne and Other Poems* (1877), and *Lyrics and Idylls* (1879); editions of *Poetical Works of Edmund Clarence Stedman* appeared in 1873 and 1884. First major work of criticism, *Victorian Poets*, appeared in 1875; published pioneering critical study *Poets of America* in 1885. Encouraged many young writers, including Hamlin Garland, Constance Fenimore Woolson, Emma Lazarus, Edwin Arlington Robinson, Ridgely Torrence, Richard Hovey, Lizette Woodworth Reese, Harriet Monroe, William Vaughn Moody, and others. Highly regarded as editor, particularly of American literature; edited 11-volume *A Library of American Literature from the Earliest Settlement to the Present Times* (1889–90); ten-volume edition of the works of Poe co-edited with George Woodberry; *A Victorian Anthology* (1897); and *An American Anthology, 1787–1899* (1900), a major survey of American poetry. Active in wide range of artistic and literary institutions; served as president of American Academy of Arts and Letters (1904–07). Suffered heart attack in 1899, and the following year resigned seat on Stock Exchange.

MATILDA COXE STEVENSON   (May 12, 1849–June 24, 1915)   b. San Augustine, Texas. Raised in Washington, D.C., and educated at Miss Annable's Academy in Philadelphia; intended to become a mineralogist. In 1872 married James Stevenson of U.S. Geological Survey of the Territories, and from 1879 on collaborated with him on his trips to Zuni Pueblo; became expert on domestic rituals from which men were traditionally excluded. In 1887 published *The Religious Life of the Zuñi Child*. Founded Women's Anthropological Society of Washington in 1885. Continued her work after husband's death in 1888; assigned to Bureau of Ethnology in 1889, first woman to be paid as government anthropologist. Conducted studies among the Hopi in 1881; the Sia between 1890 and 1891; and the Taos and Tewa Indians between 1904 and 1910. Work among the Zuni resulted in *The Zuñi Indians: Their Mythology, Esoteric Fraternities, and Ceremonies* (1904). Poor health forced her to return to Washington, D.C., where she died.

TRUMBULL STICKNEY   (June 20, 1874–October 11, 1904)   b. Joseph Trumbull Stickney in Geneva, Switzerland. Son of Harriet Champion Trumbull and Austin Stickney (classics professor). Family lived mostly in Europe; visited U.S. when Stickney was five and nine. Early education at home with father; attended preparatory school in Somerset, England, at age 12, after which the family lived in New York for two years. In 1890, following another stay in Europe, returned to U.S. and entered Harvard in 1891. Worked on *Harvard*

Monthly, to which he contributed many poems (would continue to publish almost exclusively in the *Monthly* for the rest of his life); friends included George Cabot Lodge, William Vaughn Moody, Robert Morss Lovett, and George Santayana; graduated 1895. Spent summer of 1895 with family in Germany; began studies at Sorbonne in Paris. Close friendship with George Cabot Lodge, also resident there. Henry Adams, another friend, wrote of the days when he would "totter about with Joe Stickney, talking Greek philosophy or recent poetry." Had close relationship with Adams' friend Mrs. Elizabeth Cameron. Verse drama "Prometheus Pyrphoros" published in *Harvard Monthly* in 1900; poetry collection *Dramatic Verses* appeared in limited edition in 1902. Studied Sanskrit and collaborated with Sylvain Levi on French translation of *Bhagavad-Gita* (not published until 1938). In 1903 was first American to receive doctorate in literature from Sorbonne; thesis on Greek poetry published as *Les Sentences dans la Poésie Grecque d'Homère à Euripides* (1903). Traveled for three months in Greece in the summer of 1903 before returning to America to teach Greek language and literature at Harvard. Worked on uncompleted translation of Aeschylus' *The Persians,* favorably reviewed Edwin Arlington Robinson's *Captain Craig* for *Harvard Monthly.* Diagnosed with brain tumor in 1904; became blind but continued to write during last months of life. Lodge wrote of Stickney's last days: "He was thirty years old—by far the most promising man I have known, his best work still and surely to come. Under the terrible test of a mortal disease his mind and character rose to higher levels than they had ever touched before." *The Poems of Trumbull Stickney,* edited by Lodge, Moody, and John Ellerton Lodge, published posthumously in 1905.

WILLIAM WETMORE STORY   (February 12, 1819–October 7, 1895)   b. Salem, Massachusetts. Sixth child of Sarah Waldo Wetmore and Joseph Story (Supreme Court justice and leading commentator on American law). When Story was ten, family moved to Cambridge, where Charles Sumner was close family friend; enjoyed early friendship with James Russell Lowell and Thomas Wentworth Higginson. Graduated Harvard in 1838 and Harvard Law School in 1840; began practice as lawyer. Increasingly drawn to artistic career, devoting himself to poetry, music, painting, and sculpture. Contributed regularly to *Boston Miscellany* and formed part of discussion group meeting regularly at home of George Ripley. In 1843 married Emelyn Eldredge; they had four children. During 1840s published two standard works on law and served as a bankruptcy commissioner and court reporter for several federal courts. Delivered Phi Beta Kappa poem "Nature and Art" at Harvard in 1844. Upon father's death in 1845, commissioned by trustees of Mount Auburn Cemetery to execute memorial sculpture; traveled in 1847 to Italy with his family to prepare himself for the task. In Rome, Story and his wife became close friends of Margaret Fuller. While in Europe, prepared two-volume biography of his father, *The Life and Letters of Joseph Story* (1851). Published collections of poems in 1847 and 1856. Eldest son Joseph died in Rome in 1853. Returned briefly to America and to law practice, but in 1856 gave up legal career to devote himself to sculpture; returned to Rome, where he lived for the rest of his life. The Storys settled in an apartment in the Palazzo Barberini, where their neighbors and closest friends were Robert and Elizabeth Barrett Browning. Circle of acquaintances included Christopher Pearse Cranch, Fanny Trollope, William Makepeace Thackeray, Hans Christian Andersen, Charles Eliot Norton, Walter Savage Landor, Elizabeth Gaskell, Russell Sturgis, and John Lothrop Motley; later knew Henry James, who wrote biography *William Wetmore Story and His Friends* (1903). Supporter of Italian independence; acquainted with Mazzini and Cavour. Achieved celebrity as sculptor with exhibition of "Cleopatra" (described at length by Nathaniel Hawthorne in *The Marble Faun*) and "The Libyan Sibyl" at London International Exhibition of 1862; other subjects included Salome, Medea, Alcestis, and Saul; executed posthumous bust of Elizabeth Barrett Browning for her husband; in later years commissioned to create portrait sculptures of Josiah Quincy, Joseph Henry, Edward Everett, James Russell Lowell, Theodore Parker, and John Marshall. During Civil War, contributed letters to London *Daily News* in support of the Union, collected in *The American Question* (1862). Later poetry published in *Graffiti d'Italia* (1868). Wrote series of prose books about Italy, including *Roba di Roma* (1862), *Vallombrosa* (1881), and *Excursions in Arts and Letters* (1891); a novel, *Fiammetta* (1886); and a treatise on art, *The Proportions of the Human Figure* (1866). Made final trip to America in 1877; lectured on art. Served as U.S. Commissioner of Fine Arts to the World's Fair in Paris, 1879. Wife Emelyn died in 1894; he died the next year at his daughter's summer home in Vallombrosa. Sons Thomas Waldo Story and Julian Russell Story were also artists.

JOHN BANISTER TABB (March 22, 1845–November 19, 1909) b. at family estate The Forest in Amelia County, Virginia. Son of Marianna Bertrand Archer and Thomas Yelverton Tabb; family of local distinction, with connections to Washington and Randolph families. Educated at home by private tutors. At outbreak of Civil War, unable to enlist due to poor eyesight; with Major B. F. Ficklin, went to England in 1861 to help arrange transport of supplies to Confederacy. Returning to Charleston, served on blockade runner *Robert E. Lee*, but was not present at its capture in 1863. The following year taken prisoner on board the blockade runner *Siren*, and imprisoned at Point Lookout, Maryland; formed friendship with fellow prisoner Sidney Lanier. Following release in 1865, briefly studied music in Baltimore, intending to become concert pianist, but turned toward religion under influence of Episcopal priest Alfred Curtis. Taught at St. Paul's School in Baltimore and Racine College in Wisconsin. In 1872 formally converted to Roman Catholicism. Entered St. Charles' College in Ellicott City, Maryland, graduating 1875; taught at St. Peter's School, Richmond, and at St. Charles' College. In 1881 attended St. Mary's Seminary, Baltimore, where he completed theological studies; ordained 1884. Became lifelong English teacher at St. Charles' College; students included poet George Sterling. Wrote poetry for many years before private publication of first volume in 1882; first book followed by *An Octave to Mary* (1893) and *Poems* (1894), the latter going through 17 printings.

Popularity of poetry sustained by subsequent collections: *Lyrics* (1897), *Later Lyrics* (1902), *The Rosary in Rhyme* (1904), *Quips and Quiddities* (1907), and *A Selection from the Verses of John B. Tabb* (1907), edited by Alice Meynell. Also published several volumes of humorous verse. Suffered from progressive blindness in later years; forced to retire from teaching in 1907. After his death additional collections *Later Poems* (1910) and *The Poetry of Father Tabb* (1928) appeared.

BAYARD TAYLOR (January 11, 1825–December 19, 1878) b. Kennett Square, Pennsylvania. Son of Rebecca Way and Joseph Taylor (a merchant who later turned to farming); of German and English descent on both sides. Raised in rural Quaker household; educated locally. At 17 apprenticed himself to printer of West Chester *Village Record*. With assistance of Rufus Griswold (then editor of *Graham's Magazine*) published first collection of poetry, *Ximena, or The Battle of the Sierra Morena* (1844) by subscription. Received backing of *Saturday Evening Post, United States Gazette*, and *New-York Tribune* for series of articles on Europe, and set out in 1844 on two-year European journey. Travel account *Views A-Foot: or, Europe Seen with Knapsack and Staff* (1846) went through many editions and made him best-known traveler of the day. After year as proprietor and editor of Phoenix-ville (Pennsylvania) *Pioneer*, returned to New York to work as journalist for *The Literary World* and for Horace Greeley's *New-York Tribune* (whose literary department he ran from 1848 on). Published further collection of poetry, *Rhymes of Travel, Ballads and Poems* (1849). Sent by *Tribune* to California in 1849 to report on Gold Rush; returned by way of Mexico and published *Eldorado, or Adventures in the Path of Empire* (1850), another popular travel book. Delivered Phi Beta Kappa poem at Harvard (1850); given prize by P. T. Barnum for best lyric to be sung by Jenny Lind at New York's Castle Garden. In October 1850 married Mary Agnew, a woman from his hometown in Pennsylvania, although she was seriously ill; she died two months after wedding. Published *A Book of Romances, Lyrics, and Songs* (1851) and, with George Ripley, edited *The Hand-book of Literature and the Fine Arts* (1852). In August 1851 embarked on two years of travel in Africa and Asia; journey took him to Egypt, Abyssinia, the Sudan, Syria, Palestine, Turkey, India, China, and Japan (where he joined Commodore Perry's expedition as master's mate); wrote up adventures in *A Journey to Central Africa* (1854), *The Lands of the Saracen* (1855), and *A Visit to India, China, and Japan, in the Year 1853* (1855). Published best-received verse collection, *Poems of the Orient* (1854), followed by *Poems of Home and Travel* (1855); compiled *The Cyclopaedia of Modern Travel* (1856); went on lecture tours throughout the U.S. In 1856 set off for Europe, producing *Northern Travel* (1858), *Travels in Greece and Russia* (1859), and *At Home and Abroad* (1859–62). In 1857 married Marie Hansen (daughter of a Danish astronomer) in Gotha, Saxony; they had a daughter, Lilian. Returning to the U.S., retired to family farm in Pennsylvania, where he built country home Cedarcroft. Served as Civil War correspondent for *Tribune*; in 1862 went to Russia as secretary of legation in St. Petersburg. Published several novels, including *Hannah Thurston* (1863), *John Godfrey's Fortunes* (1864), *The Story of Kennett* (1866), and *Joseph and His Friend* (1870), and further volumes of poetry, including *The Poet's Journal* (1862), *The Poems of Bayard Taylor* (1864), *The Picture of St. John* (1866), *The Masque of the Gods* (1872), *Lars: A Pastoral of Norway* (1873), *The Prophet* (1874), and *The Echo Club and Other Literary Diversions* (1876). Close friend of many leading writers, including Henry Wadsworth Longfellow, John Greenleaf Whittier, Oliver Wendell Holmes, George Henry Boker, and Charles Godfrey Leland. In the 1860s devoted himself primarily to complete translation of Goethe's *Faust*, which appeared in two volumes in 1870–71. Continued to travel frequently, visiting Germany, Italy, Egypt, and Iceland; later travel books included *Colorado: A Summer Trip* (1867), *Byways of Europe* (1869), and *Egypt and Iceland in the Year 1874* (1874). Gave lectures at Cornell on German literature in 1870; repeated lectures in New York and elsewhere. In 1878 sent to Germany as American minister; died shortly after his arrival in Berlin. *Studies in German Literature* published posthumously in 1879.

ERNEST LAWRENCE THAYER (August 14, 1863–August 21, 1940) b. Lawrence, Massachusetts. Son of Ellen Darling and Edward Davis Thayer, a prominent woolen manufacturer. Attended Harvard, where he studied with William James and developed lifelong interest in philosophy; co-editor of Harvard *Lampoon* with George Santayana (who later recalled Thayer as "a man apart . . . his wit was not so much jocular as Mercutio-like, curious and whimsical, as if he saw the broken edges of things that appear whole"); other college friends included William Randolph Hearst. Graduated Harvard 1885; moved to San Francisco the following year, joining staff of San Francisco *Examiner*, to which he regularly contributed humorous columns and verse. Returned to Worcester, Massachusetts, late in 1887, but continued to contribute to the *Examiner*, which published "Casey at the Bat" on June 3, 1888, under his usual byline "Phin." After 1888, Thayer worked in his father's woolen business for about eight years. Subsequently spent much time abroad; settled in Santa Barbara, California, in 1912, residing there until his death. Studied philosophy on his own; wrote essays but did not publish them. In 1913 married Rosalind Buel Hammett. "Casey at the Bat" widely popularized by comedian De Wolf Hopper in readings throughout the country; Thayer's authorship not publicly established until 1909, when *The Bookman* published an authorized version.

HENRY DAVID THOREAU (July 12, 1817–May 6, 1862) b. Concord, Massachusetts. Son of Cynthia Dunbar and John Thoreau; given name David Henry Thoreau. Father worked successively as farmer, grocer, teacher, and manufacturer of pencils; until 1850s, family frequently in difficult financial straits. After studying at Concord Academy, admitted to Harvard in 1833, barely passing entrance examinations. Met Orestes Brownson and studied German with him; attended lectures on mineralogy, anatomy, and natural history; graduated 1837. Formed close relationship with Ralph Waldo Emerson, who had moved to Concord in 1834, and through him with others associated with Transcendentalist group, including Margaret Fuller, Bronson Alcott, Jones Very, and Theodore Parker. Worked in father's pencil business while beginning (in October 1837) to keep journal which eventually ran to over two million words in 47 manuscript volumes. Taught at Center School, Concord, in 1837, but resigned after being forced by superiors to flog students. With brother John, ran Concord Academy, 1838–41, teaching foreign languages and science. Regularly published poems and essays in *The Dial* (which he helped edit), beginning with first issue in July 1840. Met William Ellery Channing (poet and nephew of Unitarian minister of the same name), who became intimate friend and companion. Shocked by early death of brother John in 1842. Worked in Emerson's household as handyman, 1841–43; continued studies in classical literature; met Nathaniel Hawthorne. In 1845 built a cabin on property of Emerson's at Walden Pond, where he stayed for a little over two years. (During this time maintained active social life in Concord.) Spent a night in jail in 1846 for nonpayment of poll tax; explained his motives (protest against slavery and war with Mexico) in essay "Resistance to Civil Government" (1848, posthumously retitled "Civil Disobedience"). In October 1847 began ten-month residence at Emerson's house, looking after the family while Emerson traveled in Europe. First book, *A Week on the Concord and Merrimack Rivers* (1849), most of it written at Walden Pond, was based on boat trip made in 1839 with brother John; book sold only a few hundred copies. Traveled with Channing to Cape Cod in 1849. Relationship with Emerson became more distant. In 1850s supported himself as surveyor and continued to work in family business, now supplying ground lead for electrotyping. Increasingly involved in abolitionist movement; sheltered escaped slaves en route to Canada. *Walden*, on which he had worked since residence at pond, went through multiple revisions before publication in 1854; it proved unexpectedly successful, selling more than 1700 copies by year's end. Small circle of close friends included William Ellery Channing, F. B. Sanborn, and H.G.O. Blake. On 1856 visit to Brooklyn met Walt Whitman, who presented him with signed copy of *Leaves of Grass*. Met John Brown in 1857, and following Harpers Ferry raid delivered "A Plea for Captain John Brown" in Concord, Boston, and Worcester. Compiled information on relationship of climate to periodic biological phenomena. Worked for many years on projected study of American Indians, compiling thousands of pages of notes and extracts; in 1861 traveled to Minnesota, visiting Lower Sioux Agency at Redwood. Chronic tuberculosis that had flared several times previously became acute in winter of 1860–61. Died at home; his last intelligible words were "moose" and "Indian." *The Maine Woods* (1864) and *Cape Cod* (1865) were published posthumously.

ROSE HARTWICK THORPE (July 18, 1850–July 19, 1939) b. Mishawaka, Indiana. Daughter of Mary Louisa Wight and William Morris Hartwick (a tailor). Family moved to Kansas and eventually settled in Litchfield, Michigan, in 1860; received public education, graduating high school in 1868. "Curfew Must Not Ring To-Night," written when she was in her teens, appeared in Detroit *Commercial Advertiser* in 1870 and achieved wide popularity; illustrated edition published 1882. In 1871 married Edmund C. Thorpe, a carriage maker and writer of German dialect verse; they had two daughters. Contributed regularly to *Youth's Companion, St. Nicholas, Wide Awake,* and other periodicals. Husband Edmund's business failed in 1881, and Thorpe took work editing Sunday school papers in Chicago. After Edmund developed tuberculosis, family moved to San Antonio, Texas, and, in 1886, to Pacific Beach, California. Verse collected in *The Yule Log* (1881), *Temperance Poems* (1887), and *Ringing Ballads* (1887); *The Poetical Works of Rose Hartwick Thorpe* appeared in 1912. Other publications included children's books *Fred's Dark Days* (1881), *The Fenton Family* (1884), *Nina Bruce* (1886), and *The Chester Girls* (1887). Edmund died in 1916; thereafter Thorpe worked for woman suffrage, the YWCA, and the Women's Club of San Diego.

HENRY TIMROD (December 8, 1828–October 7, 1867) b. Charleston, South Carolina. Son of Thyrza Prince (of English and Swiss descent) and William Timrod (bookbinder who had published a volume of poetry in 1814); grandfather Heinrich Dimroth was German immigrant. Father served in Seminole War in 1836; died in 1838; family lived in relative poverty. Attended Christopher Cotes' Classical School in Charleston; established friendships with poet Paul Hamilton Hayne and classicist Basil Gildersleeve. Studied at University of Georgia in Athens, 1845–46; briefly studied law in office of James L. Petigru; worked as private tutor on various plantations in the Carolinas. Contributed to *Southern Literary Messenger, Southern Literary Gazette,* and other magazines and newspapers. As member of literary group associated with Russell's Bookstore in Charleston, received encouragement from William Gilmore Simms; regularly contributed poetry and critical articles (including influential essay "Literature in the South") to *Russell's Magazine* (1857–60). First collection, *Poems,* published by Ticknor and Fields in 1860. Ardent supporter of Southern cause; wrote "Ethnogenesis" in February 1861 to herald birth of Confederacy. Enlisted briefly in militia company in July 1861, but was discharged due to health. Reenlisted in 1862 and served briefly as regimental clerk, and then, while on leave, as war correspondent for *The Charleston Mercury,* in which capacity he witnessed the retreat from Shiloh. Suffering from tuberculosis, once again discharged from service in December 1862. Settled in Columbia, South Carolina, in 1864; worked as associate editor of *The Daily South Carolinian* (in which a benefactor had bought him a part interest). Married Katie Goodwin in February 1864; their infant son Willie died the following year. Lost home and possessions when Sherman's army burned Columbia in February 1865; reduced to extreme poverty. Wrote ode sung at Confederate memorial services at Charleston's Magnolia Cemetery in June 1866. Health failed rapidly; died of tuberculosis after suffering severe hemorrhages of the lungs. Paul Hamilton Hayne edited *The Poems of Henry Timrod* (1873).

JOHN TOWNSEND TROWBRIDGE (September 18, 1827–February 12, 1916) b. Ogden, New York. Son of Rebecca Willey and Windsor Stone Trowbridge. Largely self-educated; published poetry in *The Rochester Republican* when he was 16. Studied at Lockport Academy (1844–45); taught briefly at district schools in northwestern Illinois and in Lockport, New York. Went to New York City in 1847 to pursue writing career; with help of Mordecai Manuel Noah, published stories in *Dollar Magazine* and elsewhere. In 1848 settled in Boston; worked as editor of *Yankee Nation* and, in 1850, of Boston *Sentinel*, for which he wrote controversial editorial opposing Fugitive Slave Act. Published first novel, *Father Brighthopes*, in 1853. Married Cornelia Warren in 1860, with whom he had two children; she died in 1864. Moved to Arlington, Massachusetts, in 1865. Married Sarah Adelaide Newton in 1873; they had three children. Produced some 40 volumes of fiction (much of it for children), poetry, plays, and other writing. Fiction included anti-slavery novels *Neighbor Jackwood* (1857) and *Cudjo's Cave* (1864), and *Coupon Bonds* (1866), popular novella of mercenary New England family which he dramatized in 1876. Verse collections included *The Vagabonds and Other Poems* (1869), *The Emigrant's Story and Other Poems* (1875), and *A Home Idyl and Other Poems* (1881). Published *The South: A Tour of Its Battlefields and Ruined Cities* in 1866. As editor of *Our Young Folks* (1865–73), published work by Charles Dickens, Harriet Beecher Stowe, Bayard Taylor, Rose Terry Cooke, and Louisa May Alcott. Friends included Walt Whitman, Oliver Wendell Holmes, and Henry Wadsworth Longfellow. In 1903 published collected verse, *The Poetical Works of John Townsend Trowbridge*, and autobiography, *My Own Story*.

FREDERICK GODDARD TUCKERMAN (August 10, 1821–May 14, 1873) b. Boston, Massachusetts. Son of Sophia May and Edward Tuckerman, a Boston merchant and importer. Younger brother of botanist Edward Tuckerman; cousin of art critic Henry Theodore Tuckerman. Attended preparatory school of Episcopal bishop John Henry Hopkins and Boston Latin School; entered Harvard 1837; was tutored for a brief period by Jones Very, but left due to eye trouble in 1838. The following year, reentered Harvard, this time in the Law School, from which he graduated in 1842; admitted to Suffolk County bar in 1844. Married Hannah Lucinda Jones of Greenfield, Massachusetts, on June 17, 1847; they had two sons and a daughter. Settled in Greenfield; abandoned law practice to devote himself to study of literature, botany, meteorology, and astronomy; published astronomical observations; recognized as authority on local flora. In 1850 began contributing poems to magazines, eventually publishing in *Atlantic Monthly*, *Putnam's*, and *Littel's Living Age*. Traveled twice to Europe, in the summer of 1851 and in 1854–55; formed close friendship with Alfred Tennyson, with whom he stayed on the Isle of Wight in 1855. Wife Hannah died in May 1857, following the birth of her third child. *Poems* privately printed in 1860; Ticknor & Fields published an edition of the book in 1864. Lived reclusively following wife's death.

MARK TWAIN (November 30, 1835–April 21, 1910) b. Samuel Langhorne Clemens in Florida, Missouri. Third of four children of John Marshall Clemens and Jane Lampton. At age four moved with family to Mississippi River port village Hannibal, Missouri, where father worked unsuccessfully as storekeeper and farmer. Educated locally; after father's death in 1847 worked as apprentice printer. From 1851 published sketches and squibs in papers published by his brother Orion and elsewhere. Worked as journeyman printer (1853–57) in St. Louis, New York, Philadelphia, and elsewhere. In 1857 became cub pilot on Mississippi riverboat; granted pilot's license in 1859; continued to work on river until traffic disrupted by outbreak of Civil War. Accompanied brother Orion (newly appointed Secretary to Nevada Territory) to Carson City, serving as Orion's secretary, speculating in mining stocks, and prospecting; contributed writing to newspapers in Keokuk, Iowa, and Carson City and Virginia City, Nevada. First used pseudonym "Mark Twain" in 1863. In San Francisco contributed to *The Golden Era* and *The Californian*, and began to publish work in eastern publications such as *The Mercury*, the New York *Saturday Press*, and *Harper's*; reported on five-month trip to Sandwich Islands (Hawaii) for Sacramento *Union*. Achieved reputation as public lecturer and humorist. In 1867 sailed on first American cruise ship, the *Quaker City*, for tour of Europe and the Holy Land; published first collection, *The Celebrated Jumping Frog of Calaveras County and Other Sketches*. Account of *Quaker City* tour published with great success as *The Innocents Abroad* (1869). In 1870 married Livy Langdon, with whom he had four children (one of whom died in infancy); settled in Hartford, Connecticut, the following year. *Roughing It*, based on his western experiences, published in 1872. From 1873 traveled frequently with family in Europe, sometimes for years at a time. *The Gilded Age* (1873), written in collaboration with Charles Dudley Warner, followed by novels and travel books including *The Adventures of Tom Sawyer* (1876), *A Tramp Abroad* (1880), *The Prince and the Pauper* (1882), *Life on the Mississippi* (1883), *Adventures of Huckleberry Finn* (1885), *A Connecticut Yankee in King Arthur's Court* (1889), *The American Claimant* (1892), *Tom Sawyer Abroad* (1892), *The Tragedy of Pudd'nhead Wilson* (1894), *Tom Sawyer, Detective* (1895), *Personal Recollections of Joan of Arc* (1896), and *Following the Equator* (1897), based on around-the-world tour, 1895–96. Close literary associates included William Dean Howells, George Washington Cable, and Richard Watson Gilder. Business investments, including establishment of a publishing house (Charles L. Webster & Company) and development of a typesetting machine, led to heavy financial losses. Daughter Susy died in 1896, and wife, Livy, in 1904; daughter Jean suffered from epilepsy and died in 1909. Many later writings, pessimistic treatments of religion and society, remained unpublished; published *What Is Man?* privately and anonymously in 1906. Final years spent at home Stormfield near Redding, Connecticut. *The Mysterious Stranger*, left unfinished, was published posthumously in 1916.

GEORGE BOYER VASHON (July 25, 1824–October 5, 1878) b. Carlisle, Pennsylvania. Father was abolitionist John Bethune Vashon. Family moved to Pittsburgh in 1829; Vashon attended local schools, and became secretary in 1838 of first Juvenile Anti-Slavery Society in America. At 16 entered Oberlin College and in 1844 was its first black recipient of bachelor of arts degree. While still in college taught school in Chillicothe, Ohio, where his students included John Mercer Langston (later dean of Howard Law School and U.S. minister to Haiti). Returned to Pittsburgh after graduation; studied law under Judge Walter Forward. In 1847 application to take bar examination was denied; legal attempts to challenge denial rejected on grounds that as a person of color he was not a citizen. Left Pennsylvania for Haiti; on the way, took bar examination in New York City, and in January 1848 became first black lawyer in the state. Taught college in Port-au-Prince, Haiti, for two and a half years. Upon return to U.S., settled in Syracuse, New York, in 1850, where he practiced law for four years. In 1853, composed "Vincent Ogé," long poem on the hero of the Haitian insurrection of 1790–91. Professor of belles lettres and mathematics at New York Central College in McGrawville, New York, 1854–57. Returned to Pittsburgh and married Susan Paul Smith in 1857; they had seven children. Taught and served as principal in black public schools (1858–63) and taught at Avery College (1864–68); first black to teach at Howard University (1867–68). Contributor to *The Anglo-African Review* and *The New Era*; later writings included articles on black citizenship, history of Nile River, literature, and astronomy, as well as poems "A Life-Day" (1864) and "Ode on the Proclamation of the Fifteenth Amendment" (1870). Briefly associated in 1867 as attorney with the Freedmen's Bureau in Washington, D.C. In 1869 served as delegate at national convention of Colored Men of America, of whose executive committee he became a member in 1870. Final teaching position, beginning in 1874, believed to have been at Alcorn University in Rodney, Mississippi, where he died of yellow fever.

JONES VERY (August 28, 1813–May 8, 1880) b. Salem, Massachusetts. Eldest of six children of Lydia Very and Jones Very (parents were cousins); father was a privateer in War of 1812, and afterward master of Boston ship *Aurelia*. In 1823 accompanied father on board the *Aurelia* to Kronstadt, Russia. The following year, traveled with him to New Orleans; attended school there while father conducted business. After father's death in 1824, continued schooling for three more years. Began work as errand boy for Salem auctioneer; continued to receive tutoring from J. E. Worcester. In 1832 became assistant at Fisk Latin School under direction of Henry Kemble Oliver; while working there, gained academic credits and earned money for tuition, enabling him to enter Harvard as sophomore in 1834. At Harvard, was noted for studious habits, and won a number of academic prizes and honors. Appointed Greek tutor for freshman class (1836–38); began studies at Harvard Divinity School. Around this time, underwent powerful religious experience and began to write poems that he said were "communicated" to him. In

December 1837 delivered essay on epic poetry (originally his Bowdoin Prize Essay at Harvard); Elizabeth Palmer Peabody heard it and recommended Very to Ralph Waldo Emerson as lecturer for Concord Lyceum. Very and Emerson met in April 1838 and formed close relationship. Very's colleagues at Harvard questioned his sanity and requested his withdrawal from academic duties; in September 1838 he entered McLean Asylum in Somerville, Massachusetts, remaining there for a month. Retained ties to Emerson, James Freeman Clarke, and other Transcendentalists, and won attestations of mental health from them; Emerson declared him "profoundly sane." Enjoyed close friendship with Harvard professor Edward Tyrrell Channing. In 1839 Clarke published 27 sonnets by Very in the *Western Messenger*, and Emerson oversaw preparation of *Essays and Poems*, which appeared in September 1839. Poetry won praise from a number of contemporaries, including William Cullen Bryant. Intensity of Very's religious fervor waned after 1840; relationship with Emerson cooled. Returned to Salem; after receiving license to preach from Cambridge Association, served in Eastport, Maine, and North Beverly, Masschusetts, and in Rhode Island. Several of Very's poems were adapted and reprinted in Samuel Longfellow and Samuel Johnson's widely used *A Book of Hymns for Public and Private Devotion* (1846). Continued to preach occasionally for most of his life, and wrote for newspapers; lived with his sisters (one of whom, Lydia Louise Ann Very, also published a volume of poetry).

EDITH WHARTON (January 24, 1862–August 11, 1937) b. Edith Newbold Jones in New York City. Daughter of Lucretia Stevens Rhinelander and George Frederic Jones; parents belonged to old and socially prominent families, with wealth derived from Manhattan landholdings. Family moved to Europe in 1866 following depression in real estate values, and lived successively in England, Italy, France, and Germany. Returned with family to U.S. in 1872, dividing time between New York and Newport, Rhode Island. Educated at home; read extensively in father's library. Private edition of poems published at mother's expense in 1878; one poem published by William Dean Howells in *Atlantic Monthly*. Engagement to Henry Stevens, son of prominent family, broken off by fiancé's family after two years. In 1885 married Edward Wharton, a Harvard graduate interested mainly in outdoor life who lived on an annuity. The Whartons traveled for several months every year in Europe, mostly Italy. In 1889 published poems in *Scribner's*, *Harper's*, and *Century Magazine*; soon began publishing short stories. Bought New York town house and Newport estate; studied art and interior decoration. With architect Ogden Codman wrote *The Decoration of Houses*, published 1897. Suffered mental and physical breakdown in 1898, followed by "rest cure" under supervision of Dr. S. Weir Mitchell. Settled in Washington, D.C., for four months in 1899, and began close friendship with Walter Berry; short story collection *The Greater Inclination* published to great success in the same year; traveled extensively in Europe. In 1901 bought property in Lenox, Massachusetts, and had large house, The Mount, built there. Published second story collection *Crucial Instances* (1901) and historical novel *The Valley of*

Decision (1902). Urged by Henry James to abandon historical subject matter for contemporary material: "*Do New York!* The 1st-hand account is precious." Met Theodore Roosevelt, beginning long friendship. Moved into The Mount. Husband suffered first of series of nervous collapses in 1902. Divided time between Lenox and Europe; toured Sussex with Henry James; at The Mount, house guests included Brooks Adams and George Cabot Lodge. *The House of Mirth* appeared 1905 and was highly successful; adapted for the stage by Wharton and Clyde Fitch. Continued to publish fiction including *Madame de Treymes* (1907), *The Fruit of the Tree* (1907), *Ethan Frome* (1911), *The Reef* (1912), and *The Custom of the Country* (1913). Poems collected in *Artemis to Actaeon* (1909) and *Twelve Poems* (1926). Enjoyed brilliant social life in England and France; friends included Paul Bourget, Howard Sturgis, Percy Lubbock, Henry Adams, and Bernhard Berenson. In 1908 began affair with journalist William Morton Fullerton. The following year, husband admitted embezzling money from Wharton's trust funds; she was granted a divorce in 1913 on grounds of adultery. Traveled in North Africa and Spain in 1914. Following outbreak of World War I, established American Hostels for Refugees; made repeated visits to front; organized Children of Flanders Rescue Committee. Edited *The Book of the Homeless* in 1916 to raise money for refugees, and in the same year was made Chevalier of the Legion of Honor. Bought house in village of St. Brice-sous-Forêt outside Paris. Later fiction included *Summer* (1917), *The Marne* (1918), *The Age of Innocence* (1920), *The Old Maid* (1921), *The Glimpses of the Moon* (1922), *A Son at the Front* (1923), *The Mother's Recompense* (1925), *The Children* (1928), *Hudson River Bracketed* (1929), and *The Gods Arrive* (1932). In 1923 became first woman to receive honorary doctorate of letters from Yale. Autobiography *A Backward Glance* published 1934. Suffered a stroke in June 1937 and died two months later at St. Brice.

JAMES MONROE WHITFIELD (April 10, 1822–April 23, 1871) b. Exeter, New Hampshire. Parents were free blacks about whom little is known. Educated in public grammar schools in Exeter. In 1838, prepared paper for Cleveland convention urging black settlement on borders of California; active thereafter in plans for black emigration and colonization; associates in the 1850s included black nationalists James T. Holly and Martin R. Delany. After a short stay in Boston, relocated in 1839 to Buffalo, New York, working as barber. During late 1840s and 1850s, contributed poems to *The North Star* and *Frederick Douglass' Paper*; verse collection *America and Other Poems* published in Buffalo in 1853. Achieved wide recognition for work with National Emigration Conventions in Cleveland in 1854 and 1856; engaged in controversy with Frederick Douglass over merits of black separatism and emigration; believed to have traveled in 1859 to Central America to investigate possibility of purchasing land there for colonization. Returned to San Francisco in 1861 and, within a year, abandoned emigrationist activities. Worked as barber for remainder of life, mostly in California but also in Oregon, Idaho, and Nevada. Engaged in Masonic activity, serving as grand master of Prince Hall Masons in California

(1864–69) and establishing lodge in Virginia City, Nevada. Active (1869–70) in Elko, Nevada, Republican Club. Later writings included 400-line "Poem Written for the Celebration of President Lincoln's Emancipation Proclamation," and letters and verse contributed to *San Francisco Elevator* and *Pacific Appeal*. Died of heart disease in San Francisco.

ALBERY ALLSON WHITMAN   (May 30, 1851–June 29, 1901)   b. in slavery on a farm near Mumfordville, Kentucky. Mother died in 1862, father in 1863; Whitman became free in 1863. Worked in Kentucky and Ohio as farm laborer, in plough shop, and as railroad construction worker. Attended school for a short period before teaching at Carysville, Ohio, and in Kentucky near his home. Resumed education about 1870, studying for six months at Wilberforce University under Bishop Daniel Alexander Payne, the university's president. First book, *Essays on the Ten Plagues and Miscellaneous Poems*, apparently published in 1871, but no copies are known to be extant; long poem *Leelah Misled* published 1873. By 1877 became pastor of African Methodist Episcopal church in Springfield, Ohio; worked as general financial agent for Wilberforce University. Resigned position at Wilberforce in 1878, then led congregations in Ohio, Kansas, Texas, and Georgia. Published narrative poem *Not a Man and Yet a Man* in 1877, and *The Rape of Florida*, narrative in Spenserian stanzas, in 1884 (revised edition published in 1885 as *Twasinta's Seminoles*). Poetry collected in 1890 under title *Twasinta's Seminoles; Not a Man and Yet a Man; Drifted Leaves: A Collection of Poems*. He and wife, Caddie, had three daughters, Essie, Mable, and Alberta, who later became vaudeville team the Whitman Sisters. In late 1880s, suffering ill health, moved from Midwest to South; served as pastor at St. Philip's African Methodist Episcopal church in Savannah, Georgia; transferred to Allen Temple in Atlanta. In 1893 at World's Columbian Exposition read poem "The Freedman's Triumphant Song" to audience including Frederick Douglass and Paul Laurence Dunbar. Final poetic work, *An Idyll of the South*, appeared in two volumes in 1901. Contracted pneumonia on visit to Alliston, Alabama; died at his home in Atlanta.

SARAH HELEN WHITMAN   (January 19, 1803–June 27, 1878) b. Providence, Rhode Island. Daughter of Anna Marsh and Nicholas Power, a seaman. Father left home when she was ten (he returned after an absence of 19 years and took up residence in a Providence hotel). Educated at private school in Providence; received further schooling at home of an aunt in Jamaica, Long Island. In 1828 married John Winslow Whitman, attorney and inventor; they lived in Boston until his death in 1833, when she returned to mother's home in Providence, where she lived for more than forty years; cared for younger sister Anna, who suffered from mental illness. Published first poem in Sarah Josepha Hale's *American Ladies' Magazine* in 1829; continued to contribute poetry and articles to magazines and newspapers. Formed friendship with Margaret Fuller during her residence in Providence as a schoolteacher (1836–38); other literary associates included George William Curtis, Henry

Wadsworth Longfellow, and Rufus Griswold. In September 1848 met Edgar Allan Poe, who praised her poetry and to whom she had already dedicated a poem; after a few days' acquaintance he proposed marriage; following a stormy courtship, engagement broken off by Whitman in December 1848. (She later said that "had he kept his promise never again to taste wine, I should never have broken the engagement.") Rufus Griswold included a large selection of her poetry in *The Female Poets of America* (1849). Published articles on spiritualism in *New-York Tribune* in 1851; became a medium and held séances. Associated with causes of educational reform, Fourierism, women's rights, universal suffrage, and prevention of cruelty to animals. In 1853 published *Hours of Life and Other Poems*. Defended Poe's reputation in *Edgar Poe and His Critics* (1860); frequently supplied information on Poe to students and biographers. Collected verse appeared posthumously as *Poems* in 1879.

WALT WHITMAN (May 31, 1819–March 26, 1892) b. West Hills, Huntington Township, New York. Son of Louisa Van Velsor and Walter Whitman, a farmer and carpenter; parents descended from early settlers on Long Island. Family moved to Brooklyn in 1823; attended Brooklyn public schools until about 1830. Learned printing trade on Brooklyn newspapers *Patriot* and *Star*; worked as printer until 1836. Taught school on Long Island, 1836–38. Founded and edited newspaper *The Long-Islander* (1838–39) at Huntington, New York; worked on Jamaica *Democrat*, publishing early poetry there; electioneered for Martin Van Buren. Moving to Manhattan in 1841, worked as compositor for *New World*; contributed fiction and journalistic sketches to a variety of newspapers and magazines, including *The Democratic Review*, and published temperance novel *Franklin Evans, or, The Inebriate* (1842). Returning to Brooklyn, worked for the *Star* (1845–46) and *Daily Eagle*, Democratic party newspaper (1846–48); discharged from latter for bias toward Free Soil party. Went to New Orleans; edited *The Crescent* for three months; traveled in Missouri, Illinois, and upstate New York. On his return, founded and edited *Brooklyn Freeman* (1848–49); ran printing, bookselling, and housebuilding business. Published four topical poems in 1850, and the following year addressed Brooklyn Art Union. In 1855 published at his own expense *Leaves of Grass*, collection of twelve poems including what was eventually retitled "Song of Myself." Sent copy to Emerson, from whom he received letter of praise; received visit in Brooklyn from Bronson Alcott and Henry David Thoreau. Enlarged second edition of *Leaves of Grass* published the following year. Edited Brooklyn *Times* (1857–59). Frequented Pfaff's, New York beer cellar known as bohemian meeting place, where associates included Fitz-James O'Brien and Adah Isaacs Menken. Went to Boston in 1860 to oversee third, greatly enlarged edition of *Leaves of Grass* issued by Thayer and Eldridge; met Emerson, who urged him to delete sexually frank passages from "Children of Adam" poems. Continued work as freelance journalist. After outbreak of Civil War visited sick, injured, and wounded at New-York Hospital; visited war front in Virginia in December 1862 upon learning that his brother

George had been wounded. Settled in Washington, D.C., becoming volunteer nurse in military hospitals; supported himself by part-time clerical work in Army Paymaster's office. Returned to Brooklyn on sick leave in 1864. In Washington a year later, appointed to Department of Interior clerkship; fired by Interior Secretary, supposedly because of immorality of his poetry; worked subsequently as clerk in Attorney General's office, 1865–73. Poems of war and its aftermath published in *Drum-Taps* and *Sequel to Drum-Taps* (1865). Reputation defended by close friend William Douglas O'Connor in *The Good Gray Poet* (1866) and by naturalist John Burroughs in *Notes on Walt Whitman as Poet and Person* (1867); *Poems of Walt Whitman*, edited by William Michael Rossetti, published in London in 1868. New editions of *Leaves of Grass* published in 1867 and 1870; prose collected in *Democratic Vistas* (1871) and *Memoranda During the War* (1875); long poem *Passage to India*, inspired by opening of Suez Canal, published 1870. Suffered paralyzing stroke in 1873; left Washington for Camden, New Jersey, where he lived for the rest of his life. "Centennial" edition of *Leaves of Grass* published 1876 (identical to previous edition). Lectured in Philadelphia and New York; traveled to the west as far as Colorado in 1879 and to Canada in 1880. Visited in Camden by Oscar Wilde in 1882. *Leaves of Grass* (1881 edition) withdrawn by publisher James R. Osgood in April 1882 after threat of obscenity charge from Boston district attorney; reprinted in Philadelphia by Rees Welsh & Co. along with prose collection *Specimen Days and Collect*; notoriety led to increased sales. Suffered second stroke in 1888; in the same year published prose collection *November Boughs* and *Complete Poems and Prose*. Poems of his old age, *Good-Bye My Fancy* (1891), followed by final, so-called "deathbed" edition of *Leaves of Grass*. He had prepared an edition of his *Complete Prose Works* before his death in March 1892.

JOHN GREENLEAF WHITTIER (December 17, 1807–September 7, 1892) b. Haverhill, Massachusetts. Son of Abigail Hussey and John Whittier. Raised in devout Quaker household; little formal schooling. William Lloyd Garrison's *Newburyport Free Press* published poem "The Exile's Departure" in 1826; became friend of Garrison. Attended Haverhill Academy, 1827–28. Supported himself as shoemaker and schoolteacher. Edited *American Manufacturer* in Boston (1829) and *Essex Gazette* (1830) in Haverhill before becoming editor of the important *New England Weekly Review* (1830–32); formed friendship with Lydia Huntley Sigourney. Published *Legends of New England in Prose and Verse* (1831) and *Moll Pitcher* (1832). Active in support of National Republican candidates; delegate in 1831 to National Republican Convention in support of Henry Clay, and the following year ran unsuccessfully for Congress. Became deeply involved in anti-slavery movement; in *Justice and Expediency* (1833) urged immediate abolition. Elected as Whig for one term to Massachusetts legislature in 1834; mobbed and stoned in Concord, New Hampshire, in 1835. Moved in 1836 to Amesbury, New Hampshire. Corresponding secretary for American Anti-Slavery Society from 1837. Edited *Pennsylvania Freeman* (1838–40); in May 1838, paper's offices burned and sacked during destruction of Pennsylvania Hall by mob. *Poems*, first authorized collection, published 1838. Split in 1839 with Garrison over the latter's more radical tactics; founded the Liberty party (1840); edited abolitionist gift book *The North Star*, worked on *The American and Foreign and Anti-Slavery Reporter* and *The Emancipator*. Ran for Congress as a Liberty candidate in 1842. Published *Lays of My Home* (1843). Edited *The Middlesex Standard* (1844–45) and *The Essex Transcript* (1845). Lobbied in Washington against the admission of Texas to the Union. Abolitionist verse collected in *Voices of Freedom* (1846); served as corresponding editor of *The National Era* (1847–60), contributing to it much poetry and prose. *The Supernaturalism of New England* published 1847. Collected edition of verse, *Poems by John G. Whittier*, published 1849, followed by *Leaves from Margaret Smith's Journal*, novel about 17th-century Massachusetts. Wrote "Ichabod" in 1850 in response to Daniel Webster's support of Fugitive Slave Law; supported senatorial candidacy of Charles Sumner. Published *Songs of Labor* (1850), *The Chapel of the Hermits* (1853), *The Panorama* (1856), *Home Ballads* (1860), and *In War Time* (1864), as well as prose collections *Old Portraits and Modern Sketches* (1850) and *Literary Recreations and Miscellanies* (1854). Worked for the formation of the Republican party; supported presidential candidacy of John C. Frémont in 1856. *Poetical Works* (1857) published; in same year helped found *Atlantic Monthly*. Close relationship with old friend Elizabeth Lloyd Howell led to consideration of marriage, but in 1859 Whittier decided against it. Was a member of the electoral college for Lincoln. Close friends included Bayard Taylor, Lucy Larcom, and Celia Thaxter. Most popular work, *Snow-Bound*, published 1866 and sold 20,000 copies; followed by *The Tent on the Beach* (1867), *Among the Hills* (1869), *Miriam and Other Poems* (1871), *Hazel-Blossoms* (1875), *The Vision of Echard* (1878), *St. Gregory's Guest* (1886), and *At Sundown* (1890). Campaigned against Massachusetts legislature's censure of Charles Sumner, 1873–74. From 1876 lived most of the time with cousins in Danvers, Massachusetts, while retaining legal residence in Amesbury. Formed close friendship with Sarah Orne Jewett and Annie Fields around 1881. Seventieth birthday dinner in 1877 attended by Ralph Waldo Emerson, Henry Wadsworth Longfellow, Mark Twain, Oliver Wendell Holmes, James Russell Lowell, William Dean Howells, and others. In 1879 received Jubilee Singers of Fisk University at his home, where they sang "Swing Low, Sweet Chariot" and other spirituals. Seven-volume Riverside Edition of his works, *The Writings of John Greenleaf Whittier*, published 1888–89. Corresponded with Helen Keller, 1889–90. Died at Hampton Falls, New Hampshire.

CARLOS WILCOX (October 23, 1794–May 29, 1827) b. Newport, New Hampshire. Father, a farmer, moved to Orwell, Vermont, when Wilcox was four. Health frail from early age; childhood knee injury made him unsuited for farming. Studied at Middlebury College (where he was valedictorian in 1813) and at Andover Theological Seminary, from which he graduated in 1817. Preached in several Connecticut towns, and was ordained pastor of North Church in Hartford in 1824. Only volume of poetry published in his lifetime was *The Age of Benevolence* (1822), self-published book containing first book of projected five-book poem, of which three additional books remained in manuscript at Wilcox's death. In 1824 read poem "The Religion of Taste" before Phi Beta Kappa Society of Yale. Left the pulpit in 1826 due to heart problems; resumed preaching in Danbury after several months of recuperation. The posthumous *Remains* (1828) contained sermons and extracts from later books of "The Age of Benevolence," "The Religion of Taste," and a biographical essay on Wilcox.

ELLA WHEELER WILCOX (November 5, 1850–October 31, 1919) b. Johnstown Centre, Wisconsin. Daughter of Sarah Pratt and Marius Hartwell Wheeler, a teacher of music and dance; parents originally from Vermont. Educated in public schools and (in 1867–68) at University of Wisconsin. Wrote poems, essays, and fiction from an early age, beginning to publish in magazines in her teens; by age 18 was helping to support family with income from writing. Verse collected in *Drops of Water* (1872), *Shells* (1873), and *Maurine* (1875). Achieved notoriety when *Poems of Passion* (1883) was initially rejected by Jansen & McClurg of Chicago on grounds of immorality. Married Robert M. Wilcox, a silversmith, in 1884, and settled with him in Meriden, Connecticut; only child, a son, died shortly after birth in 1887. The couple spent winters in New York City and (after 1891) summers in Short Beach, Connecticut; they traveled widely in Europe and Asia, and developed a deep interest in theosophy and mediumistic séances. Wilcox continued to published many volumes of poetry, including *Poems of Pleasure* (1888), *Poems of Power* (1901), *Poems of Sentiment* (1906), and *Poems of Problems* (1914); for some years wrote daily poem for newspaper syndicate. Also published a novel, *Mal Moulée* (1885), and two autobiographies, *The Story of a Literary Career* (1905) and *The Worlds and I* (1918). During World War I toured army camps in France reciting poems and lecturing on sexual problems; fell ill and returned to United States; died in Short Beach.

RICHARD HENRY WILDE (September 24, 1789–September 10, 1847) b. Dublin, Ireland. Son of Mary Newitt and Richard Wilde. Family arrived in Baltimore, Maryland, in 1797; shortly thereafter father's property, still in Dublin, was confiscated due to business partner's participation in Irish rebellion; family forced to depend upon father's income as ironmonger and hardware merchant. Following father's death in 1802, Wilde moved to Augusta, Georgia, in search of work, and after establishing himself with his older brother Michael, sent for his mother, who joined them in 1803; within two years, she opened a dry goods store with her sons' assistance. The family owned slaves and Wilde would later own several. Assisted by mother, Wilde educated himself; began to write poetry and essays; helped organize Thespian Society and Library Company of Augusta. Studied law privately; admitted to bar 1809; became acting attorney general of Georgia, 1811–13. Elected to House of Representatives, where he served 1815–17; close friend of Henry Clay. Married Caroline Buckle in 1819, with whom he had three sons (one of whom died in infancy);

she died in 1827. Served briefly as mayor of Augusta, 1821–22. Wrote popular lyric "The Lament of the Captive" (frequently known by its first line, "My life is like the summer rose"), an excerpt from an unfinished epic based on adventures of brother James in Florida during Seminole War. The poem was first published without Wilde's permission in 1819; after it became a popular song (having been set to music without Wilde's involvement or authorization), authorship was claimed for Irish poet Patrick O'Kelly, who incorporated the lines in a lyric of his own. Wilde was accused of plagiarism, a charge complicated when friend Anthony Barclay, English consul at Savannah, as a practical joke in 1834 translated the poem into Greek and sent it to a friend, who attributed it to Alcaeus; following newspaper controversy, Wilde declared authorship. Elected to further terms in Congress, 1827–35; opposed Jacksonians and failed to win reelection in 1834; retired from politics. In poor health, traveled to Europe in 1835 and settled in Florence; while in Italy met Horatio Greenough, Hiram Powers, Charles Sumner, and Edward Everett; translated Italian poetry and worked on biography (never completed) of Dante and unpublished study "The Italian Lyric Poets." Engaged in research in libraries and private collections; through his researches, instrumental in 1840 recovery of Giotto's portrait of Dante in the Bargello by removing layer of whitewash. Returned to Augusta in difficult financial straits in 1841; published two-volume study of Italian poet Tasso, *Conjectures and Researches Concerning the Love, Madness, and Imprisonment of Torquato Tasso* (1842), which included translations of Tasso's poems. Worked for years on *Hesperia*, long poem in four cantos, never completed; poem, unpublished during Wilde's lifetime, was eventually edited by his son William Cumming Wilde and published in 1867. Established law practice in New Orleans in 1843; became professor of constitutional law at newly established University of Louisiana (now Tulane University). Died during yellow fever epidemic in New Orleans.

NATHANIEL PARKER WILLIS (January 20, 1806–January 20, 1867) b. Portland, Maine. Son of Hannah Parker and Nathaniel Willis. Grandfather and father both newspaper publishers. Raised in Boston; attended Boston Latin School and Phillips Andover. Published first poems at age 17 in father's newspaper; entered Yale in 1823 and published first book, *Sketches*, volume of Biblical paraphrases in verse, in 1827, the year of his graduation. Embarked on journalistic career, working for Samuel G. Goodrich as an editor of *The Legendary* (1828) and gift book *The Token* (1829) before establishing *American Monthly Magazine* (1829–31) in Boston, writing most of it himself. Continued to build poetic reputation with *Fugitive Poetry* (1829) and *Poems Delivered before the Society of United Brothers* (1831). Moved to New York in 1831; contributing editor on George Pope Morris's *New-York Mirror*, 1831–36; in 1831 went to Europe as foreign correspondent for *Mirror*, detailing travels in Europe and Asia Minor in newspaper pieces eventually collected in *Pencillings by the Way* (1835). Toured western Europe and Middle East; settled in England, where friends and acquaintances included Walter Savage Landor, Charles and

Mary Lamb, Joanna Baillie, Jane Porter, Thomas Moore, and Mary Russell Mitford. In 1835 married Mary Stace, daughter of General William Stace; they had a daughter, Imogen. While in England, came under attack for indiscreet revelations of private conversations in American press; attacked in print by Harriet Martineau and Frederick Marryat. Returned to America in 1836. Two plays were produced in New York, *Bianca Visconti* (1837) and *Tortesa, or the Usurer Matched* (1839), the latter enjoying some popularity. Journalistic pieces and travel sketches collected in *Inklings of Adventure* (1836), *A l'Abri; or, the Tent Pitch'd* (1839), *American Scenery* (1840), *Loiterings of Travel* (1840), and *The Scenery and Antiquities of Ireland* (1842). Collections of poetry included *Melanie* (1835), *Poems of Passion* (1843), *The Lady Jane, and Other Humorous Poetry* (1843), *Poems, Sacred, Passionate, and Humorous* (1844), and *Poems of Early and After Years* (1848). With Dr. T. O. Porter, founded weekly *The Corsair*, 1839–40; after its failure, again entered into partnership with Morris as co-owner and co-editor of *New Mirror* (1843–44), succeeded by *Evening Mirror* and its supplement *Weekly Mirror* (1844–45). Employed Poe on *Mirror*; the two became friends. A year after first wife Mary's death in childbirth in 1845, married Cornelia Grinnell, 20 years his junior; with Cornelia had two daughters and two sons. From 1846, again in partnership with Morris on *National Press* (soon renamed *The Home Journal*). Achieved fame as chronicler of New York fashionable life and writer of light fiction, in the pages of the *Journal* and in such collections as *Lectures on Fashion* (1844), *Dashes at Life with a Free Pencil* (1845), *Rural Letters* (1849), *People I Have Met* (1850), *Life Here and There* (1850), *Hurry-Graphs* (1851), and *Fun Jottings* (1853); characterized in James Russell Lowell's *A Fable for Critics* as "the topmost bright bubble on the wave of the Town." In 1849 published article defending Poe's reputation from the attacks of Rufus Griswold. His work and character came under harsh criticism from sister Sarah Payson Willis, who under pseudonym Fanny Fern satirized him in her novel *Ruth Hall* (1854) for his refusal to give her financial assistance or literary encouragement. Became involved in divorce trial of actor Edwin Forrest, siding with Mrs. Forrest and suffering a physical attack by Forrest (who accused Willis of illicit conduct with his wife) in Washington Square Park. As health declined, traveled in Bermuda and West Indies, writing up journey in *Health Trip to the Tropics* (1853). In 1853 retired with wife and children to country home Idlewild near Tarrytown, New York, not far from Washington Irving's Sunnyside; journalism collected in *Famous Persons and Famous Places* (1854), *Out-doors at Idlewild* (1855), *The Rag-Bag* (1855), and *The Convalescent* (1859). Novel of European-American relations, *Paul Fane* (1857), was unsuccessful. With Morris, edited *The Prose and Poetry of Europe and America* (1857). During Civil War, stayed in Washington as correspondent and enjoyed friendship with Mrs. Lincoln. Following death of Morris in 1864, took on full editorship of *Home Journal*; health failed rapidly. Pallbearers at funeral included Richard Henry Dana, Henry Wadsworth Longfellow, Oliver Wendell Holmes, and James Russell Lowell.

FORCEYTHE WILLSON (April 10, 1837–February 2, 1867) b. Byron Forceythe Willson in Little Genesee, New York. Son of Hiram Willson (teacher who served as local postmaster and operated lumber business). In 1846 moved with family on raft down Allegheny and Ohio rivers; lived in Covington, Kentucky, where his father founded common school system; family settled in New Albany, Indiana, where father died in 1859 leaving comfortable income to family. Studied at Antioch College and then at Harvard, until failing health forced him to withdraw without taking degree. Returned to Kentucky, where he wrote pro-Union editorials for the Louisville *Journal*; also published poems there, of which "The Old Sergeant" became well-known. In 1863 married Elizabeth Conwell Smith, also a poet. Settled in Cambridge, Massachusetts, 1864–66, to supervise his younger brother's education at Harvard. Literary acquaintances included Oliver Wendell Holmes, Henry Wadsworth Longfellow, and William Dean Howells. Developed interest in spiritualism. *The Old Sergeant and Other Poems* appeared in 1867. Died in Alfred, New York.

SAMUEL WOODWORTH (January 13, 1785–December 9, 1842) b. Scituate, Massachusetts. Son of Abigail Bryant and Benjamin Woodworth, a farmer who fought in American Revolution. At 16 went to Boston and apprenticed himself to printer Benjamin Russell (publisher of *The Columbian Centinel*), remaining with him until 1806. From an early age embarked on journalistic enterprises, the earliest of which was *The Fly* (1805–06), a juvenile paper in which John Howard Payne was involved. Went to New Haven, Connecticut; founded *The Belles-Lettres Repository*, which lasted two months; moved to Baltimore, Maryland, where his stay was also brief. In 1809 settled permanently in New York. Early in his career published three volumes of satirical poetry—*New-Haven* (1809), *Beasts at Law* (1811), *Quarter-Day* (1812)—and some popular verses on War of 1812. Married Lydia Reeder in 1810; they had a large family. Continued to work as printer but attempted to augment income through publishing and editing long series of publications, most of brief duration. These included *The War* (1812–14), a weekly devoted to events of War of 1812, *The Halcyon Luminary and Theological Repository* (1812–13), a journal devoted to Swedenborgianism (which Woodworth espoused), *The Ladies' Literary Cabinet* (1819–22), *Woodworth's Literary Casket* (1821), *The New-Jerusalem Missionary* (1823–24), another Swedenborgian publication, and *The Parthenon* (1827). After his friend George Pope Morris founded *New-York Mirror* in 1823, Woodworth became editor, but withdrew after a year. Author of a large quantity of newspaper verse, often published under pseudonym Selim. His best-known poems were "The Bucket" (better known as "The Old Oaken Bucket") and "The Hunters of Kentucky" (both included in *Melodies, Duets, Songs, and Ballads*, 1826). A novel, *The Champions of Freedom* (1819), took the War of 1812 for its background. Wrote a number of plays, including *The Deed of Gift* (1822), *La Fayette* (1824), and *The Forest Rose* (1825), which achieved popularity for the comic Yankee character

Jonathan Ploughboy. Literary and publishing endeavors did not lift him out of poverty; theatrical benefits were given in 1828 and 1829 to provide financial relief. Suffered stroke in February 1837 and was paralyzed for the remainder of his life.

CONSTANCE FENIMORE WOOLSON (March 5, 1840–January 24, 1894) b. Claremont, New Hampshire. Daughter of Hannah Cooper Pomeroy and Charles Jarvis Woolson (stove manufacturer); great-niece of James Fenimore Cooper. Following scarlet fever epidemic in which three of her sisters died, family moved to Cleveland, Ohio, during winter of 1840–41. After early education at Cleveland Female Seminary, sent to Madame Chegary's School in New York, returning to Cleveland following graduation in 1858. Began to write as early as 1862, and devoted herself to it full-time following move to New York after father's death in 1869. In 1870 began to contribute prose sketches, fiction, and verse to *Harper's*, *Atlantic Monthly*, *Lippincott's*, and other periodicals. First volume was children's book *The Old Stone House* (1872), published under pseudonym "Anne March." From 1873 to 1879 spent winters in the Carolinas and Florida in the company of her ailing mother, with St. Augustine as her base. In Florida met Edmund Clarence Stedman, with whom she formed close literary friendship; became friend of South Carolina poet Paul Hamilton Hayne. Published criticism, travel sketches, memoirs, and verse, including book-length poem *Two Women: 1862* (1877), but was best known for fiction, including story collections *Castle Nowhere: Lake Country Sketches* (1875) and *Rodman the Keeper: Southern Sketches* (1880) and novels *Anne* (1883), *For the Major* (1883), *East Angels* (1886), *Jupiter Lights* (1889), and *Horace Chase* (1894). Following mother's death in 1879, moved to Europe, living in England for several years, but ultimately spending most of her time in Italy; visited Greece and Egypt in 1889–90. Met Henry James in Florence in 1880 and they became close friends. Suffered increasingly from deafness and periods of depression. During bout of influenza, died in Venice in fall from balcony. Two further volumes of short fiction were published after her death: *The Front Yard and Other Italian Stories* (1895) and *Dorothy and Other Italian Stories* (1896).

HENRY CLAY WORK (October 1, 1832–June 8, 1884) b. Middletown, Connecticut. Son of Aurelia and Alanson Work. Family moved to Quincy, Illinois, when Work was three years old. In 1841 his father, an active abolitionist, was sentenced to prison in Missouri for his role (as agent of Underground Railroad) in helping fugitive slaves escape. Following father's release in 1845, family returned to Middletown. Received common-school education; apprenticed to a printer; studied harmony in spare time. From 1854 worked as printer in Chicago, while continuing to write songs. First success was "We're Coming, Sister Mary," written for Christy Minstrels. Became popular as songwriter during Civil War, under contract to music publishers Root & Cady; successful topical songs included "Kingdom Coming," "Marching Through Georgia," "Babylon Is Fallen," and "Wake, Nicodemus!" Other songs included "Lily Dale," "My Grandfather's Clock," and the temperance ballad "Father, Come Home!" (featured in play *Ten Nights in a Barroom*). Married in the early 1860s; had three children; wife later suffered from mental illness. Went to Europe in 1865. Relocated to Philadelphia, after publisher was ruined (and plates to Work's songs destroyed) in 1871 Chicago fire; invested savings from songwriting in 150-acre fruit farm in Vineland, New Jersey, which failed. In 1875 returned to Chicago following reestablishment of Root & Cady; enjoyed continued success as songwriter. Was also an inventor; patented a knitting machine, a walking doll, and a rotary engine. Died in Hartford, Connecticut.

Note on the Texts

This volume is an abridged version of the work of the same title edited by John Hollander and originally published in two volumes by The Library of America in 1993. (Publication of the original edition was made possible by grants from the National Endowment for the Humanities and the Lila Wallace–Reader's Digest Fund.) This abridgment is approximately half as long as the original, and contains work by every poet included in the original work (with the exception of some of the translators of American Indian poetry). The selections for this volume were made by John Hollander.

The choice of text for each of the poems selected for inclusion in this volume has been made on the basis of a study of its textual history and a comparison of editions printed within the author's lifetime, along with relevant manuscripts, periodical appearances, contemporary anthologies, and posthumous editions. In general, each text is from the earliest book edition prepared with the author's participation; revised editions are sometimes followed, in light of the degree of authorial supervision and the stage of the writer's career at which the revisions were made, but the preference has been for the authorially approved book version closest to the date of composition. For some popular poems widely disseminated in periodicals, however, the early periodical versions have been preferred. Manuscript sources have been used only when no printed text appears to be authoritative.

Two categories of poems, "19th-Century Versions of American Indian Poetry" and "Folk Songs and Spirituals," are placed in separate sections at the end because the dates of original composition of these pieces are so uncertain that placing them chronologically in the body of the anthology is not feasible. The texts chosen for "19th-Century Versions of American Indian Poetry" are translations or adaptations of American Indian material collected under a variety of circumstances, the details of which in many cases are unknown. Some of these versions have been published in different forms, reflecting alterations made by subsequent editors; the goal in this volume has been to locate the version closest to the transcription of the work from its original language. In reprinting these texts no attempt has been made to duplicate material that accompanied some of them in their original context, such as original-language texts, interlinear commentary, and bracketed glosses (although some of this material will be found in the notes to this volume). For the selections of "Folk Songs and Spirituals," versions have been chosen on the basis both of publication date and of completeness; thus, later versions have sometimes been preferred to earlier ones that are fragmentary or atypical.

A complete list of the sources of the texts can be found in the Notes on the Texts of the original two-volume edition.

The following works have been reprinted with the kind permission of the publishers and institutions listed below:

Joel Barlow. Advice to a Raven in Russia: *Huntington Library Quarterly*, October 1938.

George Henry Boker. *from* Sonnets: A Sequence on Profane Love: Edward Sculley Bradley (ed.), *Sonnets: A Sequence on Profane Love* (Philadelphia: University of Pennsylvania Press, 1929); published with permission of the Manuscripts Division, Department of Rare Books and Special Collections, Princeton University Libraries.

Thomas Cole. A Painter; Lines Suggested by Hearing Music on the Boston Common at Night; The Voyage of Life, Part 2nd, stanzas 1–12; The Dial; Lago Maggiore: Thomas Cole Papers, Manuscripts and Special Collections section, New York State Library.

Stephen Crane. *from* The Black Riders; *from* War Is Kind; "There is a grey thing that lives in the tree-tops"; "Little birds of the night": Fredson Bowers (ed.), *The Works of Stephen Crane, Volume X: Poems and Literary Remains* (Charlottesville: University Press of Virginia, 1975). Reprinted by permission of the University Press of Virginia.

Emily Dickinson. The texts of all poems are from Thomas H. Johnson (ed.), *The Complete Poems of Emily Dickinson* (Cambridge: The Belknap Press of Harvard University Press, 1951). By courtesy of the following publishers: Harvard University Press (reprinted by permission of the publishers and the Trustees of Amherst College from Thomas H. Johnson, ed., *The Poems of Emily Dickinson* [Cambridge, Mass.: The Belknap Press of Harvard University Press]; copyright 1951, 1955, 1983 by the President and Fellows of Harvard College); Houghton Mifflin Company (from Martha Dickinson Bianchi, ed., *Life and Letters of Emily Dickinson*, copyright 1924 by Martha Dickinson Bianchi; copyright renewed 1952 by Alfred Leete Hampson; reprinted by permission of Houghton Mifflin Company; all rights reserved; and from Martha Dickinson Bianchi, ed., *Emily Dickinson Face to Face;* copyright 1932 by Martha Dickinson Bianchi; copyright renewed 1960 by Alfred Leete Hampson; reprinted by permission of Houghton Mifflin Company; all rights reserved), and Little, Brown and Company (from Thomas H. Johnson, ed., *The Complete Poems of Emily Dickinson;* copyright 1929, 1935 by Martha Dickinson Bianchi; copyright renewed 1957, 1963 by Mary L. Hampson; by permission of Little, Brown and Company).

Ralph Waldo Emerson. "Who knows this or that?"; Maia: Ralph H. Orth et al. (eds.), *The Poetry Notebooks of Ralph Waldo Emerson,* (Columbia, Missouri: University of Missouri Press, 1986). Copyright 1986 by the Ralph Waldo Emerson Memorial Association.

Nathaniel Hawthorne. "I left my low and humble home": Nathaniel Haw-
thorne Papers, James Duncan Phillips Library, Peabody & Essex Museum,
Salem, Massachusetts; reprinted by permission.

Sidney Lanier. *from* Hymns of the Marshes; Song of the Chattahoochee;
From the Flats; The Mocking Bird; *from* Street Cries: To Richard Wagner:
Charles R. Anderson (ed.), *The Works of Sidney Lanier (Centennial Edi-
tion)* (Baltimore: Johns Hopkins University Press, 1945).

Abraham Lincoln. My Childhood-Home I See Again: Roy P. Basler (ed.),
The Collected Works of Abraham Lincoln (New Brunswick, New Jersey:
Rutgers University Press, 1953–55).

Herman Melville. *Song from* Mardi: Harrison Hayford, et al. (eds.), *The Writ-
ings of Herman Melville: Mardi* (Northwestern-Newberry, 1970). "The ribs
and terrors in the whale": Harrison Hayford, et al. (eds.), *The Writings of
Herman Melville: Moby-Dick* (Northwestern-Newberry, 1988). The Portent;
Misgivings; The Conflict of Convictions; Shiloh: A Requiem; Malvern Hill;
The House-top: A Night Piece; "The Coming Storm"; "Formerly a
Slave"; America; The Tuft of Kelp; The Maldive Shark; The Berg; After the
Pleasure Party; The Ravaged Villa; Art; Shelley's Vision; In a Bye-Canal:
Robert Ryan, et al. (eds.), *The Writings of Herman Melville: Published
Poems* (Northwestern-Newberry, not yet published). *from* Clarel: Har-
rison Hayford, et al. (eds.), *The Writings of Herman Melville: Clarel,*
(Northwestern-Newberry, 1991). Pontoosuce: Harrison Hayford, et al.
(eds.), *The Writings of Herman Melville: Billy Budd and Other Late Manu-
scripts* (Northwestern-Newberry, not yet published). Billy in the Darbies:
Harrison Hayford and Merton M. Sealts, Jr., eds., *Billy Budd, Sailor* (Chi-
cago: University of Chicago Press, 1962).

Edgar Allan Poe. "Alone"; Israfel; The Haunted Palace; The Bells: Thomas
Olive Mabbott (ed.), *Collected Works of Edgar Allan Poe,* vol. 1 (Cam-
bridge, Massachusetts: The Belknap Press of Harvard University Press, 1969
and 1978). The Conquerer Worm; Dream-Land; Ulalume—A Ballad:
Floyd Stovall (ed.), *The Poems of Edgar Allan Poe* (Charlottesville, Virginia:
University Press of Virginia, 1965).

George Santayana. Sonnet III: "O world, thou choosest not the better
part!"; On a Piece of Tapestry; Cape Cod; On an Unfinished Statue: Wil-
liam G. Holzberger (ed.), *The Complete Poems of George Santayana* (Lewis-
burg: Bucknell University Press, 1979). Reprinted by permission.

Henry David Thoreau. "They who prepare my evening meal below"; "On
fields oer which the reaper's hand has passed"; Fog: John C. Broderick
(general ed.), *The Writings of Henry David Thoreau: Journal, Vol. 1:
1837–1844* (Princeton University Press, 1981). Music: The Pierpont Morgan
Library, New York, MA 920.

Henry Timrod. Dreams; Ethnogenesis; The Cotton Boll: Unpublished proof
sheets, courtesy of the Charleston Library Society, Charleston, South
Carolina.

Frederick Goddard Tuckerman. *from* Sonnets; Third Series; The Cricket: N.
Scott Momaday (ed.), *The Complete Poems of Frederick Goddard Tucker-*

man (New York: Oxford University Press, 1965). Copyright 1965 by Oxford University Press, Inc.; reprinted with permission.

Jones Very. The New Birth; The Morning Watch; The Garden; The Song; The Dead; Autumn Leaves; The Wild Rose of Plymouth: Brown University Library. The Latter Rain: The Historical Society of Pennsylvania, The Gratz Collection. The Cottage: Wellesley College, Special Collections.

Songs and Chants (Southern Paiute): Don D. Fowler and Catherine S. Fowler, eds., *Anthropology of the Numa: John Wesley Powell's Manuscripts on the Numic Peoples of Western North America, 1868–1880* (Washington: Smithsonian Institution Press, 1971).

John Brown's Body (collected, adapted, and arranged by John A. Lomax and Alan Lomax; copyright 1934 [renewed] Ludlow Music, Inc., New York, N.Y.; used by permission): John A. Lomax and Alan Lomax (eds.), *American Ballads and Folk Songs* (New York: Macmillan, 1934).

Dere's No Hidin' Place Down Dere; Joshua Fit de Battle ob Jericho: James Weldon Johnson and J. Rosamond Johnson, eds., *The Book of American Negro Spirituals* (New York: Viking Press, 1925).

Down in the Valley; Frankie and Albert; John Henry; Lonesome Valley: John A. Lomax and Alan Lomax (eds.), *Folk Song: U.S.A.* (New York: Meredith Press, 1947).

Red River Valley: Carl Sandburg, *The American Songbag* (New York: Harcourt, Brace & Co., 1927).

Simple Gifts: Edward Deming Andrews, *The Gift To Be Simple* (New York: J. J. Augustin, 1940), reprinted courtesy Dover Publications, Inc., New York.

This volume presents the texts chosen for inclusion here without change except for the correction of typographical errors, but it does not attempt to reproduce features of their typographic design. For untitled poems, the first line is used as a title. The following is a list of typographical errors in the source texts that have been corrected, cited by page and line number: 9.10, moontide; 48.5, there'e; 48.11, lovely; 82.24, ocean; 219.26, knell; 224.4, you!'); 338.33, Dids't; 496.6, Dark; 616.23, packs; 645.6, touch; 645.31, maryland!; 717.16, Prinelings; 718.4, [comma missing]; 725.7, aflrays; 726.25, Johnnie; 759.7, over-wise.; 783.7, Whom; 787.8, Loon; 791.6, fail; 829.27, him; 834.25, blu; 836.17, me.; 839.16, comanded.

Notes

In the notes below, the reference numbers denote page and line of this volume (the line count includes titles). No note is made for material included in standard desk-reference books, such as *Webster's Ninth New Collegiate Dictionary* or *Webster's Biographical Dictionary*. Quotations from Shakespeare are keyed to *The Riverside Shakespeare* (Boston: Houghton Mifflin, 1974), edited by G. Blakemore Evans. References to the Bible have been keyed to the King James Version.

1.3   *Great Western Canal*] The Erie Canal, extending from Albany to Buffalo and connecting the Hudson River to Lake Erie, opened in 1825.

1.5–6   *Meliusne . . . undas?*] Horace, *Odes* III, 27, lines 42–44, rewritten and metrically rearranged by Freneau. The original passage, from Europa's complaint about having been borne by the bull over the ocean, reads: "*Meliusne fluctus / ire per longos fuit an recentis / carpere floras?*" (Was it better to travel over vast seas or pick fresh flowers?)

1.16   *Holland . . . Spain's*] The struggle for Dutch independence from Hapsburg Spain lasted from 1566 to 1648.

4.4   *December, 1812*] Napoleon's retreat from Russia, begun in October 1812, had by December become a catastrophic rout.

4.17   Neustria] The western part of the Frankish empire in the Merovingian period, located between the Meuse and the Loire.

4.27   Lussian] Portuguese.

4.31   Domingo's . . . India's] Napoleon sent an army to Haiti in 1801 to reestablish French control. After fierce fighting with Haitian rebels and heavy losses to yellow fever, it surrendered to the British in 1803. French forces and their Indian allies were defeated by the British in a series of campaigns, 1799–1801.

5.6   the BAN?] The *ban* was, in the French military system, the portion of the population liable for conscription into the militia or national guard.

5.8   joles] Jaws.

8.1–8   Is dull : . . see.] In Bodman's *Oration on Death*, this stanza is separated from the preceding ones by a prose passage in which Bodman, having addressed the variety of the physical world, proceeds to contemplate the spiritual: "Now, is the pure intellectual world alone destitute of this delightful variety? . . . Has [God] poured out all the various glories of divine art and workmanship in the inanimate and brutal or animal world, and left the higher sort of creatures all of one genius, and turn, and mould, to replenish all the intellectual regions? Surely it is hard to believe it."

9.21–22   *"Integer . . . arcu."*]   Horace, *Odes* I, 22, 1–2: "He who is upright in his life and pure of guilt, needs not Moorish arrows, nor bow." Adams's poem is a strict imitation of the *Ode* from which he takes his epigraph.

9.29   Zara's]   The Sahara Desert.

10.3   Simoon's]   Or simoom; a strong, hot desert wind.

10.11   Bohan Upas]   Tropical Asian tree (*Antiaris toxicaria*) with a poisonous sap which was used for poisoning darts; mere proximity to the tree was popularly believed to be fatal.

13.19   Putnam]   Rufus Putnam (1738–1824), Revolutionary soldier, who helped fortify West Point.

13.26   Arnold]   Benedict Arnold (1741–1801), Revolutionary general and traitor who conspired to betray the Continental forces at West Point.

13.27   André]   Major John André (1751–80), British officer who acted as an intermediary between Benedict Arnold and the British commander Sir Henry Clinton. Captured by the Americans in civilian disguise, he was hanged as a spy.

13.29   The honest three]   The three New York militiamen who on September 24, 1780, stopped and searched Major John André and found papers on him that led them to suspect treason.

16.26   *Donder* and *Blitzen*]   German for Thunder and Lightning.

20.19–21   *Group . . . Vatican*]   Illustrating Genesis 18:1–10; one of a series of frescoes of biblical scenes, designed by Raphael and known as "Raphael's Bible," on the ceiling of Raphael's Loggia.

21.5   *Jacob's Dream*]   Genesis 28:11–16.

21.20   *Luxembourg Gallery*]   The Grand, or East, Gallery of the Luxembourg Palace in Paris contained a series of 24 scenes from the life of Maria de Medicis that Rubens painted for the Gallery; they are now in the Louvre.

23.31   the noble Tuscan]   Michelangelo.

24.3   through Elisha's faith]   Cf. 2 Kings 2:11–12.

26.27   "my hiding-place"]   Cf. Psalm 32:7.

27.7–13   the Eagle . . . Virgin's]   "The constellations, *Aquila*, *Leo*, and *Virgo*, are here meant by the astronomical fugitive." — Pierpont's note.

27.17   Queen . . . free!]   Slavery was abolished throughout the British Empire by the Abolition Act of 1833, which provided for the gradual emancipation of slaves in the West Indies. Emancipation was completed in 1838, a year after Queen Victoria ascended to the throne.

37.22   Pharos]   A lighthouse, one of the Seven Wonders of the World, on the island of Pharos off Alexandria, Egypt.

37.24   Sioux's tower of hunger]   Starved Rock, a cliff along the south bank of the Illinois River where, according to legend, a group of Illinois Indians held out and finally died, besieged by a hostile tribe variously identified as Ottawa or Pottawattomi.

37.25–27   Ugolino . . . Dante]   Conte Ugolino, imprisoned and starved to death in 1289 in the tower of Guaiandi alle Sette Vie at Pisa; he figures as a traitor in Cantos 32 and 33 of Dante's *Inferno*.

37.30–34   modern saint . . . temple]   Joseph Smith (1805–44), Mormon prophet and founder of the Church of Jesus Christ of the Latter-day Saints, in 1839 established the Mormon city of Nauvoo in western Illinois and began the building of a grand temple there, completed after his death.

38.3   "the march of mind,"]   Cf. Edmund Burke's remark in his speech on conciliation with America, March 22, 1775: "The march of the human mind is slow."

38.14   Oolaïtha's]   Daughter of a Sioux chief, who jumped from a high cliff on the shore of Lake Pepin out of disappointment in love, according to Beltrami's *Sources du Mississippi* and Henry Rowe Schoolcraft's *Narrative Journal of Travels through the Northwestern Regions of the United States.*

38.29   Or more Apollo-like]   "West is reported to have said, when he saw the Apollo, 'Good God! how like a young Indian!' "—from Wilde's note. The reference is to the painter Benjamin West's remark on seeing the Apollo Belvedere.

38.35   my countryman]   "Hiram Powers."—Wilde's note. Powers (1805–73) was an American sculptor.

38.36   artist . . . "Divine"]   Michelangelo.

39.13   Chastellux]   François Jean, Marquis de Chastellux (1734–88), French general who fought in the Revolutionary War and author of *Voyages dans l'Amérique Septentrionale* (1786) on travels in America.

39.15   Atala's]   Indian heroine of Chateaubriand's novel (1801) of the same name.

39.20   "Faithful . . . faithless"]   Cf. John Milton, *Paradise Lost*, Book 5, line 896–97: ". . . faithful found / Among the faithless, faithful only he."

39.21   the sinking mountain]   "A few miles below Wabashaw's village, an isolated mountain of singular appearance rises out of the centre of the river to a height of four or five hundred feet, when it terminates in crumbling peaks of naked rock, whose lines of stratification and massy walls, impress forcibly upon the mind the image of some gigantic battlement of former generations."—Henry Rowe Schoolcraft, cited by Wilde.

40.5   Fata Morgana]   Mirage, often visible in the Straits of Messina.

40.17   Ozolapaida]   Legendary Dakota Indian maiden, whose abduction precipitated a feud between warring families of the Assiniboins and the Sioux.

41.3   *Joseph Rodman Drake*]   See biographical note, p. 885.

42.1   *Marco Bozzaris*]   Markos Botsaris (c. 1788–1823) led a Souliot force during the siege of Missolonghi (1822–23). He was killed on August 21, 1823, leading a successful attack on an Albanian force advancing on Missolonghi.

42.14   Suliote]   Souliote; inhabitant of Suli, a mountainous district of northern Greece.

51.3   *Battle of Niagara*]   The battle of Lundy's Lane, fought in Ontario near Niagara Falls on July 25, 1814, during the War of 1812, was claimed as a victory by Americans.

56.3   *Thanatopsis*]   Greek for "contemplation, or view, of death."

57.18   the Barcan desert]   Barka, region in northeastern Libya, in Cyrenaica.

65.3   Cole]   Thomas Cole; see biographical note, p. 879.

67.13   A race . . . away]   For much of the nineteenth century it was widely believed that the mounds such as those that Bryant visited in Illinois were the work of an unknown race unrelated to the American Indians.

67.16   Pentelicus]   Or Pentelikon; a mountain in Greece from which a superior marble was quarried.

71.3   from *Zophiël*]   *Zophiël*, a poem in six cantos based on an episode in the apocryphal Book of Tobit, concerns the unrequited love of the fallen angel Zophiël for the maiden Egla. As with each canto of her poem, Brooks begins the third canto with an Argument synopsizing its narrative: "Midnight.—Zophiël and Phraerion sit conversing together near a ruin on the banks of the Tigris.—Zophiël laments his former crimes; speaks of a change in his designs; dwells on the purity of his love for Egla; and expresses a wish to preserve her life and beauty beyond the period allotted to mortals.—Phraerion is induced to lead the way to the palace of Tahathyam.—Palace and banquet of Gnomes.—Zophiël, by force of entreaty and promise, obtains from Tahathyam a drop of the elixir of life."

74.10   grenadilla]   "The grenadilla is a melon produced from a blossom more rich and beautiful than it is easy to describe. Though much larger, it resembles the cerulean passion-flower so nearly as to seem of the same species; but the leaf of its vine is curled, and of a very different shape."—Brooks's note.

76.24   Maro]   Virgil.

76.30–31   Campbell's war-blast . . . Elsinore]   The reference is to
Thomas Campbell's poem "The Battle of the Baltic," first collected in *Ger-
trude of Wyoming* (1809). The poem describes the naval battle of Copen-
hagen, April 2, 1801.

77.1   *The National Painting*]   John Trumbull's "The Declaration of In-
dependence."

77.6   T*******]   John Trumbull (1756–1843), American painter and
Revolutionary soldier.

77.9   Guido]   Guido Reni (1575–1642), Italian painter.

77.24   S*****d]   Jacob Sherred, a wealthy glazier and painter in New
York City.

79.29–32   Forever float . . . o'er us?]   On Drake's manuscript, the last
four lines are written in the hand of Fitz-Greene Halleck, who with Drake's
approval substituted them for four canceled lines by Drake.

80.28   dog-trees]   Dogwood.

87.4–10   *"Ye blessed* . . . WORDSWORTH]   From William Words-
worth's "Ode: Intimations of Immortality from Recollections of Early Child-
hood," ll. 36–41.

90.1   *The Voyage . . . 2nd*]   In 1839–40 Cole produced a series of four
paintings (commissioned by Lumen Reed) representing "The Voyage of
Life": "Childhood," "Youth," "Manhood," and "Old Age." The present
poem complements the second of these.

94.5   Know'st thou the land]   Cf. the lines about Italy at the opening of
the song in Bk. III, chap. 1, of Goethe's *Wilhelm Meister's Apprenticeship*:
"Kennst du das Land wo die Citronen blühn?" ("Know'st thou the land
where the lemons bloom?")

94.10   vernant]   Flourishing; verdant.

102.3   *Rhea*]   Greek goddess, daughter of Uranus (heaven) and Gaea
(earth), both wife and mother of Kronos, and mother of Zeus and other
Olympians.

104.5   *Uriel*]   One of the seven archangels of Christian legend, whose
name means "fire of God."

104.13   SAID]   Or Sa'adi (Mosharref od-Din ibn Mosleh od-Din Sa'adi, c.
1213–92), Persian poet.

105.26   *Hamatreya*]   Emerson's variant of Maitreya, a figure from *The
Vishnu Parana; a System of Hindu Mythology and Tradition*, translated by
H. H. Wilson in 1840.

105.27 Minott . . . Flint] Founders of Concord.

116.13 evil time's sole patriot] William Henry Channing (1810–84), clergyman and abolitionist, who had been urging Emerson to engage himself more actively in the anti-slavery campaign.

116.32 Contoocook] River in southern New Hampshire.

116.33 Agiochook] Mountain in New Hampshire.

118.31 Cossack eats Poland] Polish nationalists rose against Russian rule in 1830, and their defeat the following year precipitated intense political and cultural repression.

119.4 *Astræa*] Goddess of Justice in Greek mythology; she left the world at the end of the Golden Age and became the constellation Virgo.

122.1 *Merlin*] Here, a legendary Welsh poet of the sixth century.

127.16 *Merops*] From Greek, "articulate speech"; Merops was a soothsayer in the *Iliad*.

127.29 *Saadi*] Cf. note 104.13.

130.7 Dschami's] Jami (Mowlana Nur od-Din 'Abd or-Rahman ebn Ahmad, 1414–92), Persian poet and mystic.

132.22 *Xenophanes*] Greek philosopher (c. 570–480 B.C.) who satirized the anthropomorphizing of divinity and argued for a single god, sometimes interpreted to mean the universe itself.

134.38 the shot . . . world] The fighting at Concord between Massachusetts militia and British regular troops on April 19, 1775, was the first battle of the Revolutionary War.

135.14–15 If . . . slain] Cf. *Katha Upanishad* 2:19–22: "If the slayer thinks he slays, / If the slain thinks he is slain, / Both these have no knowledge, / He slays not, is not slain," or *Bhagavad-Gita* 2:19–22: "Who thinks that he can be a slayer, / Who thinks that he is slain, / Both these have no right knowledge: / He slays not, is not slain." Translations of both works were in Emerson's library.

138.25 *Maia*] "Illusion" in Hindu thought.

147.1 *Swanannoa*] River in western North Carolina; also spelled Swannanoa.

151.2 'Ασπασίη, τρίλλιστος.] "Welcome, thrice (or often) prayed to": the phrase is evidently Longfellow's own.

153.28 Norman's Woe] Dangerous reef off Gloucester Harbor, Massachusetts.

156.7 *Mezzo Cammin*] Italian "mid-journey," from the first line of

Dante's *Inferno*: "Nel mezzo del cammin di nostra vita" ("in the middle of the journey of our life").

164.13   *The Song of Hiawatha*] "This Indian Edda—if I may so call it—is founded on a tradition, prevalent among the North American Indians, of a personage of miraculous birth, who was sent among them to clear their rivers, forests, and fishing-grounds, and to teach them the arts of peace . . . Into this old tradition I have woven other curious Indian legends, drawn chiefly from the various and valuable writings of Mr. Schoolcraft, to whom the literary world is greatly indebted for his indefatigable zeal in rescuing from oblivion so much of the legendary lore of the Indians. The scene of the poem is among the Ojibways on the southern shore of Lake Superior, in the region between the Pictured Rocks and the Grand Sable."—from Longfellow's note.

165.2   Nokomis] Hiawatha's grandmother.

166.34   Ponemah] "Hereafter."—Longfellow's note.

167.2   the beautiful town] Portland, Maine, where Longfellow was born.

167.7   verse . . . Lapland song] Adapted from Johannes Scheffer, *The History of Lapland* (English translation, 1674): "A Youth's desire is the desire of the wind, / All his essaies / Are long delaies, / No issue can they find."

168.11   Deering's Woods] Woods near Portland, Maine, which Longfellow roamed as a child; now preserved as a park.

170.15–16   Bishop . . . Rhine!] A medieval watch-tower on the Rhine, supposedly so named because of the tradition that Archbishop Hatto was devoured there by mice in the 10th century; the story is told in Robert Southey's poem "God's Judgment on a Wicked Bishop."

171.1   *Wayside Inn*] In a letter to Frances Farrer dated December 28, 1863, Longfellow wrote of this poem: "The Wayside Inn has more foundation in fact than you may suppose. The town of Sudbury is about twenty miles from Cambridge. Some two hundred years ago, an English family, by the name of Howe, built there a country house, which has remained in the family down to the present time, the last of the race dying but two years ago. Losing their fortune, they became inn-keepers; and for a century the Red-Horse Inn has flourished, going down from father to son. The place is just as I have described it, though no longer an inn . . . All the characters are real. The musician is Ole Bull; the Spanish Jew, Israel Edrehi, whom I have seen as I have painted him, etc., etc." (Edrehi's first name was actually Isaac.)

176.37   Lethe and Eunoe] Two sides of a stream in Dante's *Purgatorio* XXVIII, 127–32; the waters called Lethe ("forgetfulness") remove the memory of sin and those called Eunoe ("kindly thoughts, remembrance of good") restore the memory of good deeds.

178.1   *Belisarius*] According to legend, the Byzantine general Belisarius (505–65) became a blind beggar after losing favor with Emperor Justinian.

178.21   Ausonian realm] Italy; according to legend, the people of Italy were descendants of Auson, son of Ulysses and Calypso.

178.22   Parthenope] In ancient poetry, a name for Naples; from its legendary founder, the siren Parthenope, who was cast up on its shores.

178.29   Zabergan] Zaberganes, Persian ambassador to Byzantium.

179.3   the Vandal monarch] Gelimer, whom Belisarius defeated in A.D. 534.

179.15   the Monk of Ephesus] Theodosius, the adopted son of Belisarius, became the lover of Belisarius's wife, Antonina; according to the *Anecdota* (*Secret History*) of Procopius, he enrolled himself for a time as a monk at Ephesus in order to avoid danger.

180.1   *Kéramos*] Greek: "potter."

186.4   *Ichabod!*] Hebrew: "inglorious"; a child (I Samuel 4:21) so named by his mother who died giving him birth. Whittier here applies the epithet to Daniel Webster, for his support of the Compromise of 1850, including the passage of a new Fugitive Slave Law.

187.13   *Astræa*] See note 119.4.

187.14–18   *"Jove . . . 1615.*] Cf. Jonson's masque *The Golden Age Restored* (1615), 11–14: "And therefore means to settle / Astraea in her seat again, / And let down in his golden chain / The age of better metal."

188.23   Almeh] An Egyptian dancing-girl.

188.24   Eblis] In Islamic tradition, an equivalent of Satan: a fallen angelic prince, now the devil.

189.1   Mollah] Variant of "mullah."

189.10   Shitan] Form of Arabic *shaitan*, "satan-like."

189.24   raving Cuban filibuster] Pro-slavery expansionists advocated the annexation of Cuba in the years before the Civil War, and had supported two filibustering expeditions in 1850–51.

190.2   Gentoo] Hindu.

193.5   Calendar's horse of brass] Featured in "The Tale of the Third Kalandar" in *The Arabian Nights*.

193.7   Al-Borák] White winged animal, somewhere between a donkey and a mule in height, on which Muhammad is said to have made a journey to the seven heavens.

193.10   Floyd Ireson] In a headnote to this poem added in the Riverside Edition of his collected works (1888), Whittier says: "In the valuable and carefully prepared *History of Marblehead*, published in 1879 by Samuel Roads,

Jr., it is stated that the crew of Captain Ireson, rather than himself, were responsible for the abandonment of the disabled vessel. To screen themselves they charged their captain with the crime."

194.2   Chaleur Bay]   Inlet of the Gulf of St. Lawrence between the Gaspé Peninsula of Quebec and New Brunswick.

195.30   Ramoth hill]   "A hill in South Hampton, N.H., only a few miles from Amesbury, used to be called Ramoth-Gilead." — Samuel T. Pickard, *Life and Letters of John Greenleaf Whittier* (1894).

196.30   Follymill]   ". . . To give the thing a local stand-point, I have introduced the neighboring woods of Follymill, famous hereaway for their mayflowers, or ground laurel." — Whittier to James Russell Lowell, February 18, 1860, in Pickard, *Life and Letters of John Greenleaf Whittier* (1894).

197.27   *Barbara Frietchie*]   "This poem was written in strict conformity to the account of the incident as I had it from respectable and trustworthy sources. It has since been the subject of a good deal of conflicting testimony, and the story was probably incorrect in some of its details. It is admitted by all that Barbara Frietchie was no myth, but a worthy and highly esteemed gentlewoman, intensely loyal and a hater of the Slavery Rebellion, holding her Union flag sacred and keeping it with her Bible; that when the Confederates halted before her house, and entered her dooryard, she denounced them in vigorous language, shook her cane in their faces, and drove them out; and when General Burnside's troops followed close upon Jackson's, she waved her flag and cheered them. It is stated that May Quantrell, a brave and loyal lady in another part of the city, did wave her flag in sight of the Confederates. It is possible that there has been a blending of the two incidents." — Whittier's headnote in the Riverside Edition (1888).

203.30   Amun]   Ram-headed Egyptian deity.

207.2   "The Chief . . . shore."]   A line from "The African Chief" by Sarah Wentworth Morton; the poem was collected in Caleb Bingham's *The American Preceptor*, the "school-book" to which Whittier refers at 207.1.

207.6   Dame Mercy Warren]   Mercy Warren (1728–1814), playwright, poet, historian, and political activist in the American Revolution.

207.12   Memphremagog's]   A lake, largely in Quebec, but extending into Vermont.

207.16   St. François's]   Probably a reference to Lake Saint François (also known as Lake Saint Francis), in southern Quebec to southeast Ontario.

207.24   Salisbury's level marshes]   Marshland adjacent to the town of Salisbury, northeastern Massachusetts, near the coast at the mouth of the Merrimack River.

207.29–30   Boar's . . . Shoals]   Little Boar's Head on the New Hampshire coast and the Isles of Shoals, nine small islands off the Maine and New Hampshire coast.

208.6   Cochecho town]   Dover, on the Cocheco River in New Hampshire, was attacked by Indians on June 28, 1689.

208.17   wizard's conjuring-book]   "I have in my possession the wizard's 'conjuring book' . . . It is a copy of Cornelius Agrippa's *Magic*, printed in 1651 . . . The full title of the book is *Three Books of Occult Philosophy, by Henry Cornelius Agrippa, Knight, Doctor of both Laws, Counsellor to Caesar's Sacred Majesty and Judge of the Prerogative Court*." — from Whittier's headnote to the Riverside Edition (1888).

208.21   Piscataqua]   A river in New Hampshire.

208.33   Sewell's ancient tome]   *The History, Rise, Increase and Progress of the Christian People Called Quakers* (London, 1722) by William Sewell (1654–1720).

208.36   Chalkley's Journal]   Thomas Chalkley (1675–1741), an itinerant Quaker preacher; his *Journal* (1766) was extremely popular among Quakers and often reprinted.

209.28   Apollonius of old]   Apollonius of Tyana (3 B.C.–A.D. 97), Greek philosopher, supposedly a seer and miracle worker.

210.1   White of Selborne's]   Gilbert White (1720–93), English naturalist, author of *The Natural History and Antiquities of Selborne* (1789).

213.31   Pindus]   Range of mountains in west central to northwest Greece; in classical times, the mountains forming the boundary between Epirus and Thessaly.

213.31   Araxes]   Ancient name for the Aras, a river in Turkey. In later editions, Whittier changed "Araxes" to "Aracthus"; his biographer, Samuel T. Pickard, in *Life and Letters of John Greenleaf Whittier* (1894), notes, "Mr. Whittier found that the similarity of names had misled him. It was the Aracthus he had in mind when the poem was written."

214.26   Another guest]   Harriet Livermore (1788–1867). "The portrait of that strange pilgrim, Harriet Livermore, the erratic daughter of Judge Livermore of New Hampshire, who used to visit us, is as near the life as I can give it." — Whittier in a letter to James T. Fields, October 3, 1865. In a headnote added to the 1888 Riverside Edition, Whittier described her as "a young woman of fine natural ability, enthusiastic, eccentric, with slight control over her violent temper, which sometimes made her religious profession doubtful . . . She early embraced the doctrine of the Second Advent, and felt it her duty to proclaim the Lord's speedy coming. With this message she crossed the Atlantic and spent the greater part of a long life in travelling over Europe and Asia."

215.13   Petruchio's Kate]   In Shakespeare's *The Taming of the Shrew*.

215.14   Siena's saint] Saint Catherine of Siena (1347–80), Dominican mystic and diplomat.

215.32   Queen of Lebanon] Lady Hester Lucy Stanhope (1776–1839), eldest daughter of Charles, Viscount Mahon (afterwards 3rd Earl of Stanhope). In 1814, she established a fortified estate at Mt. Lebanon and, adopting Eastern dress, proclaimed a religion that combined Christian and Islamic beliefs. She engaged in intrigues against the British consuls in the district and exercised almost despotic power over the tribal people in the area, who considered her a prophet.

219.6–9   Ellwood's . . . Jews.] Thomas Ellwood (1639–1713), Quaker poet and pamphleteer, author of *Davideis: The Life of King David in Israel, a Sacred Poem* (1712).

219.17   McGregor] Sir Gregory McGregor, Scottish adventurer who arrived in Caracas in 1817 and fought under Bolivar for independence; after this, he made a number of raids around the Caribbean before settling on the Mosquito Coast of Central America and calling himself His Highness, the Cacique of Pogair.

219.19   Taygetos] Mountains in southern Peloponnesus, Greece.

219.20   Ypsilanti's Mainote Greeks] Demetrius Ypsilanti (1793–1832), Greek patriot and commander, successfully defended Argos in a key battle with the Turks.

224.3   knife-grinder . . . Canning] George Canning (1770–1827), English statesman and poet, wrote "The Friend of Humanity and the Knife-Grinder."

230.2   stars . . . such as fall] "Some star which, from the ruin'd roof / Of shak'd Olympus, by mischance, did fall.—*Milton*." — Poe's note.

230.22   Tadmor and Persepolis] Tadmor is a biblical name for Palmyra, ancient city (destroyed A.D. 273) of central Syria, and Persepolis was an ancient city of Persia. "Voltaire, in speaking of Persepolis, says, 'Je connois bien l'admiration qu'inspirent ces ruines—mais un palais erigé au pied d'une chaine des rochers sterils—peut il être un chef d'œuvre des arts!' " — Poe's note.

230.24   O, the wave] "Ula Deguisi is the Turkish appellation; but, on its own shores, it is called Bahar Loth, or Almotanah. There were undoubtedly more than two cities engulphed in the 'dead sea.' In the valley of Siddim were five—Adrah, Zeboin, Zoar, Sodom and Gomorrah. Stephen of Byzantium mentions eight, and Strabo thirteen, (engulphed)—but the last is out of all reason." — Poe's note.

230.28   Eyraco] "Chaldea." — Poe's note.

230.33   Is not . . . loud?] "I have often thought I could distinctly hear the sound of darkness as it stole over the horizon." — Poe's note.

235.28   Porphyrogene]   Greek: "born to the purple," i.e. imperial.

238.12   Eidolon]   An insubstantial image, or phantom.

243.26   *is* there . . . Gilead?]   Cf. Jeremiah 8:22.

243.34   Aidenn]   Eden, here used in the sense of paradise or heaven.

257.3   *Old Ironsides*]   The poem, written in response to the proposal by the Navy Department to scrap the frigate *Constitution*, was published in the Boston *Daily Advertiser* on September 16, 1830, and was widely reprinted; its popularity led to the preservation of the ship, which had captured three British frigates in separate engagements during the War of 1812. Holmes subsequently included it in his Phi Beta Kappa address of 1836, "Poetry, a Metrical Essay," prefacing it with these lines:

> There was an hour when patriots dared profane
> The mast that Britain strove to bow in vain;
> And one, who listened to the tale of shame,
> Whose heart still answered to that sacred name,
> Whose eye still followed o'er his country's tides
> Thy glorious flag, our brave Old Ironsides!
> From yon lone attic, on a summer's morn,
> Thus mocked the spoilers with his school-boy scorn.

258.28   Triton . . . wreathèd horn!]   Cf. Wordsworth, "The World Is Too Much With Us": "Have sight of Proteus rising from the sea; / Or hear old Triton blow his wreathèd horn."

259.20–21   *Georgius* . . . hive!]   George II (1683–1760) succeeded to the throne of Great Britain in 1727; he was of the German House of Hanover.

259.22–23   year . . . gulp her down]   On November 1, 1755, an earthquake destroyed most of the city of Lisbon.

259.24   Braddock's army]   Edward Braddock (1695–1755), British general, commanded British forces in the North American campaign against the French in 1755; on July 9 of that year, French and Indian forces ambushed Braddock's army near Fort Duquesne, Pennsylvania. He lost half of his men, and was himself mortally wounded.

259.30   felloe]   The rim of a wheel.

264.4   DAVID]   Psalm 49:4.

264.6   PSALMS]   Psalm 42:7.

264.8   MILTON]   From "An Epitaph on the Marchioness of Winchester," ll. 55–56.

266.2   Micro-Uranos]   "Little heaven."

267.26–31   Florence . . . Eugene Percy] Children of Chivers.

268.26   Four . . . Death] Chivers' daughter Florence died in October 1842; three other children died within a three-month period in 1848.

270.31   Æonian] Aonia, a district of Boeotia in ancient Greece containing the mountains Helicon and Cathaeron, sacred to the Muses.

272.3   *Wissahiccon*] Wissahickon Creek, in southeastern Pennsylvania.

272.7   White Island's] Albion, oldest name of Great Britain and poetical name for England.

272.18   the river] . The Schuylkill River, Philadelphia.

273.17   *Flaxman*] John Flaxman (1755–1826), sculptor and neo-classic illustrator of Homer and the Greek tragedians.

280.1   *Palais Royal*] The palace and gardens, surrounded by arcades, in Paris, built originally for Cardinal Richelieu in the 17th century.

280.4   "Casta Diva"] Italian: "chaste goddess"; the most celebrated aria in Vincenzo Bellini's *Norma*.

284.8   "Music, Heavenly Maid,"] "When Music, heavenly maid, was young, / While yet in early Greece was sung"—William Collins, "The Passions. An Ode for Music" (1746), lines 1–2.

284.14   Chickerings] A well-known make of piano.

285.20   Pandean flutes] Panpipes.

285.27   Boehm-flutes] Theobald Boehm (1794–1881), German flutist and inventor, produced the prototype for the modern flute in 1847.

288.10   weird bulls . . . tame] In Greek mythology, Medea gives Jason a magic ointment that protects him from the fire-breathing bulls that Aeetes (Medea's father) had commanded him to yoke.

296.3   *Dixie's Land*] An alternate version of the first part of the first stanza appears in the text of the song published in 1859 in *Bryant's Power of Music* (New York: Robert M. De Witt), a booklet containing lyrics without music for songs made popular by the Bryant Minstrel Show: "I wish I was in de land of cotton, / 'Cimmon seed 'an sandy bottom— / CHOR.—Look away— look 'way— away—Dixie Land."

304.12   *"I am . . . tied"*] "I have seen a bunch of violets in a glass vase, tied loosely with straw, which reminded me of myself."—Thoreau's commentary in *A Week on the Concord and Merrimack Rivers*.

310.4   *J.L.M.*] John Lothrop Motley (1814–1877), historian, author of *The Rise of the Dutch Republic* (1856).

310.5   Charmian] Cleopatra's attendant in Shakespeare's *Antony and Cleopatra*.

315.5   Barnaby Rudge] Title character of Dickens' 1841 novel; he had a raven named Grip.

315.11   Mathews] Cornelius Mathews; see biographical note, p. 923 in this volume.

315.31   Melesigenes] Ancient Greek epithet for Homer, from the river Meles in Ionia, near which Homer was said to have been born.

333.4   Laocöon!] The Laocöon group, a famous Hellenistic sculpture from Rhodes, shows the Trojan priest Laocöon and his sons entwined in the coils of a serpent as punishment for warning the Trojans against the wooden horse of the Greeks. It was dug up on the Esquiline hill in Rome in 1506.

333.14   the beautiful Apollo] The Apollo Belvedere, another celebrated classical piece, stands like the Laocöon in a courtyard in the Vatican.

337.37   De Fredis] Felice de Fredis, from whose vineyard the Laocöon group was first excavated.

338.26   Humbled Angelo] Michelangelo went with the architect Sangallo to see the piece while it was still in the ground; he identified the group from Pliny's description of it in *Historia Naturalis*.

342.3   *Leaves of Grass (1855)*] These poems had no titles in this edition. Whitman eventually added the titles that appear in parentheses in the Contents and Index in the present edition.

344.2   entretied] Cross-braced.

346.10   kelson] Keelson: a line of timbers laid over the keel of a ship to steady it.

346.31   Kanuck] Canuck, French Canadian.

346.31   Tuckahoe] Tidewater Virginian.

346.31   Cuff] Negro.

350.34   limpsey] Limp.

354.13   king-pin] Extended spoke of a pilot-wheel.

354.26   jour printer] Journeyman printer.

360.28   fold with powders] Powdered medicine used to be dispensed in folded papers.

361.14   carlacue] Variant of curlicue.

366.28   tilth] The depth to which soil may be cultivated.

370.12   fakes] Coils of a rope.

373.34   omnigenous] Of all kinds.

376.1 life-car . . . slipnoose] Water-tight boat traveling along a rope, to remove passengers from a wrecked ship to the shore.

376.22 bull-dances] A dance in which only men participate; a stag dance.

376.27 musters] Assemblies; here, convivial.

379.2 topples] Overhangs, projections.

379.30 crowded . . . wreck] The *San Francisco* was caught in a gale and wrecked a few hundred miles from New York City in late December 1853; the disaster was reported in the New York *Weekly Tribune* of January 21, 1854.

381.31 tale . . . sunrise] Mexican troops captured about 400 men under the command of Colonel James Walker Fannin near the village of Goliad, Texas, on March 20, 1836, most of whom were volunteers from the southern United States. Having previously decreed that all foreigners caught under arms on Mexican soil would be treated as pirates, President Santa Anna ordered their execution, and about 300 of the prisoners were shot on March 27, 1836.

383.1–2 frigate-fight] Between *Bon Homme Richard*, commanded by John Paul Jones, and the British *Serapis*, September 23, 1779.

385.11 Wallabout] Wallabout Bay, inlet in the East River where American prisoners were held on British prison ships during the Revolutionary War. It later became the site of the Brooklyn Navy Yard.

385.12 Saratoga] Now Schuylerville, on the Hudson River, north of Albany; scene of the surrender of General Burgoyne's British army to the Americans under Major-General Horatio Gates, October 17, 1777.

386.29 Eleves] French: pupils, disciples.

387.25 old topknot] Frontier slang for an Indian.

389.10 Kronos] Or Cronus; a Titan, son of Uranus and Gaea; ruler of the universe until overthrown by Zeus.

389.12 Belus] A legendary ancient king of Egypt.

389.16 Mexitli] Aztec war-god.

390.10 the bull and the bug] E.g., as worshipped by Greeks (bull) and Egyptians (the scarab as an image of the sun god, Khepera).

391.8 tressels] Trestles, here as supporting coffins.

392.29 obis] Obeah, or obi is a form of West African sorcery practiced in the West Indies and in the southern United States. The plural here probably means "obi-men," or sorcerers.

392.34 shasta] Shastras are ancient Hindu sacred texts.

392.36   teokallis] Aztec temples.

394.4   koboo] Or Kubu; native of Palembang, Sumatra.

395.29   sauroids] Huge prehistoric reptiles, mistakenly alleged to have carried their eggs in their mouths.

398.3   chuff] Here, the heel of the hand.

404.6   ennuyees] French: wearied, bored people.

405.10   douceurs] Gifts or bribes.

405.12   cache] This may be used as the French verb, "hide," rather than "hiding-place."

408.27   defeat at Brooklyn] The battle of Long Island, August 27, 1776, at which the British were victorious.

425.32   smouchers] Cheats, pilferers.

438.4   Paumanok] Long Island, in Algonquian (meaning "fish-shaped").

446.31   great star] Venus, as evening star.

457.3   Song from *Mardi*] Sung by the poet Yoomy in Chapter 88: "Then Yoomy, before buried in a reverie, burst forth with a verse, sudden as a jet from a Geyser."

457.8   "*The ribs . . . whale*"] Read from the pulpit by Father Mapple before his sermon in Chapter 9 of *Moby-Dick*.

459.1   *The Conflict of Convictions*] "The gloomy lull of the early part of the winter of 1860–1, seeming big with final disaster to our institutions, affected some minds that believed them to constitute one of the great hopes of mankind, much as the eclipse which came over the promise of the first French Revolution affected kindred natures, throwing them for the time into doubts and misgivings universal." — Melville's note.

459.8–14   fall . . . Mammon] Cf. Milton's *Paradise Lost*, in which the characters Satan, Raphael (an angel), and Mammon (a fallen angel) appear.

460.14   *Iron Dome*] The new dome of the Capitol (built over the older wooden dome), begun in 1856 and completed in 1865.

461.1   Ancient of Days] God, as described in the vision in Daniel 7:9.

462.1   *Shiloh*] A fierce battle was fought near Shiloh Church in southern Tennessee on April 6 and 7, 1862; the combined Union and Confederate losses were over 23,000.

462.23   *Malvern Hill*] In the last engagement of the Seven Days' Battles, Confederate general Robert E. Lee attacked the retreating Army of the Potomac at Malvern Hill, Virginia, on July 1, 1862. The attack was defeated by massed Union artillery, and the Confederates lost over 5,000 men.

462.31   with the cartridge in their mouth] Killed while loading their weapons. The gunpowder used in Civil War muzzle-loading rifles and muskets was contained in paper cartridges; soldiers loaded by biting off the end of the cartridge, pouring the powder down the barrel of the gun, and then ramming the ball down onto the powder.

463.6   Seven Nights and Days] During the Seven Days' Battles, fought outside of Richmond between June 25 and July 1, 1862, Lee succeeded in driving Major General George B. McClellan's forces away from the Confederate capital.

463.26   *The House-top*]   " 'I dare not write the horrible and inconceivable atrocities committed,' says Froissart, in alluding to the remarkable sedition in France during his time. The like may be hinted of some proceedings of the draft-rioters." — Melville's note. More than 100 persons were killed in rioting that broke out in New York City on July 13, 1863, after federal authorities began to draft men under the 1863 Conscription Act. Mobs lynched blacks, attacked Republican newspaper offices, and burned down the Colored Orphans Asylum before the riots were suppressed on July 16.

464.2   parching Sirius] The brightest star in the constellation Canis Major, Sirius (or the Dog Star) was a token of summer heat to the Greeks and Romans.

464.12   Draco] Athenian legislator who, according to tradition, codified the Athenian law around 621 B.C., prescribing the death penalty for most offenses.

464.22   *by S. R. Gifford*] By Robert Swain Gifford (1840–1905), not Sanford R. Gifford.

464.22   *E. B.*] Edwin Booth, Shakespearian actor and brother of John Wilkes Booth.

464.23   *N. A.*] The National Academy of Design in New York City.

465.5   *"Formerly a Slave"*] Elihu Vedder's (1836–1923) painting was listed in the exhibition catalogue as "Jane Jackson, formerly a slave . . . . "

465.24   Berenice's Hair] The constellation Coma Berenices.

467.6   *Clarel*] The four-part poem, in 150 cantos running to nearly 18,000 lines, recounts the pilgrimage through the Holy Land of Clarel, an American divinity student struggling with a loss of faith.

467.32   Siloh's oracle] The pool of Siloam in Jerusalem, site of Jesus' miraculous healing of a blind man; also, "Siloa's brook that flow'd/ Fast by the Oracle of God" (Milton, *Paradise Lost*, I.11).

468.11   titled Rose] The "rose of Sharon" in Song of Solomon 2:1.

468.13–15   Ramleh . . . tower] Or Ramla, a city about 25 miles northwest of Jerusalem; the tower is an ancient minaret.

468.18   Ephraim]   Mountains north of Jerusalem.

468.28–30   Flung . . . Louis]   In the Crusades of 1270 led by Louis IX of France, the Moors defending Carthage were reported to have thrown hot sand into the desert winds so that it would be blown at the Crusaders' army.

468.36   Salem]   A religious and poetic usage for Jerusalem.

470.28   Acra's]   Then the Christian quarter of Jerusalem.

470.32   Olivet]   The Mount of Olives in Jerusalem.

470.39–40   pool . . . Hezekiah's]   Cf. 2 Kings 20:20.

471.32   Vine]   A middle-aged American who is one of Clarel's fellow pilgrims. He is described in I, 29, 31–39.

472.15   Admetus' shepherd]   Apollo served as shepherd to King Admetus of Thessaly after being banished from Olympus for killing the Cyclopes.

472.21   Cecilia]   St. Cecilia, patron saint of music.

472.33   Carthusian]   The Carthusians are one of the strictest monastic orders of Roman Catholicism.

473.13   Sibyl's Golden Bough]   The Golden Bough in Book VI of the *Aeneid*, to which the Cumaean Sibyl directs Aeneas, with instructions to seize it for help in getting to the underworld.

473.15   *Via Crucis*]   "Way of the Cross": the Via Dolorosa, the road in Jerusalem taken by Jesus from the place of judgment to Calvary.

474.30–32   "They wire . . . talk;]   A telegraph cable was laid across the Atlantic in 1858 and used for a few weeks; a permanent transatlantic connection was first achieved in 1866.

474.34   wynd]   A narrow street or passageway.

479.8   Decameron folk]   In Boccaccio's 14th-century work, the seven ladies and three gentlemen who leave plague-ridden Florence for villas outside and tell each other a hundred stories on ten summer days.

480.11   Urania]   A female astronomer, named after the Muse of Astronomy and also after Milton's muse of *Paradise Lost*.

480.21   Albani's porch]   The porch of the Villa Albani in Rome (now Villa Torlonia), containing an important collection of classical sculpture.

481.2   arm'd Virgin]   Athena.

482.11–12   Jacob's . . . angel]   Genesis 32:24–32.

482.13   *Shelley's Vision*]   Presumably a reference to an episode of Shelley's last days when, it is reported, he saw a shadowy vision of himself that inquired of him: "Are you satisfied?" The incident was first described by Thomas Medwin in his *Life of P. B. Shelley* (1847).

482.23   Saint Stephen] First Christian martyr, stoned to death (Acts, chapters 6–7).

483.7   Jael] In Judges 4, Jael kills the defeated Canaanite general Sisera in her tent by driving a tent-peg through his skull.

484.1   *Pontoosuce*] Lake Pontoosuc, north of Pittsfield, Massachusetts.

487.1   *Billy in the Darbies*] At the end of Melville's *Billy Budd, Sailor*, after the hero has been hanged for the killing of Claggart, his shipmates "made some lines which, after circulating among the shipboard crews for a while, finally got rudely printed at Portsmouth as a ballad. The title given to it was the sailor's." Darbies are handcuffs.

487.8   jewel-block] Pulley at the end of the fore and main topsail yards on a square-rigged ship.

489.30   Shiloh] See note 462.1.

489.31   Manassas] Manassas Junction, Virginia, about 30 miles from Washington. Civil War battles fought near the junction on July 21, 1861, and August 29–30, 1862, were generally known in the South as the first and second battles of Manassas, and in the North as the first and second battles of Bull Run. Both were Confederate victories.

490.4   Week of Battles] See note 463.6.

490.13   Fair Oaks and Seven Pines] Fair Oaks and Seven Pines, Virginia, about seven miles from Richmond; scene of a battle (May 31–June 1, 1862) in which McClellan defeated the Confederates under J. E. Johnston.

491.3   Cannæ] In Apulia, Italy; the site of Hannibal's overwhelming victory in 216 B.C. over the Romans.

491.4   Roncesvaux] Or Roncesvalles; mountain pass in the Pyrenees where in 778 the entire rearguard of Charlemagne's army was killed in a battle with Arabs.

491.7   Aceldama] The potter's field said to have been south of Jerusalem, and purchased for the price of Judas Iscariot's bribe; the name means "field of blood" (cf. Acts 1:15–19).

491.24   River of Death] Chickamauga Creek in northern Georgia, where the Confederates defeated Union forces commanded by Major General William Rosecrans, September 19–20, 1863.

491.27   the Great Admiral] Rear Admiral John Dahlgren, who attempted in 1863 to seize Charleston Harbor from the Confederates.

501.22   Caÿster's] Ancient name for a river in Asia Minor, now called Kucuk Menderes River (Turkey); Ephesus was near its mouth.

501.26   Eurotas] A river in Laconia in Greece.

504.4   *Place de la Pucelle*]   Joan of Arc was burned in Rouen in 1431 at the Place du Vieux-Marché, just above the Place de la Pucelle.

510.3   *Sheridan's Ride*]   On October 19, 1864, Confederate troops under Lieutenant General Jubal A. Early attacked Union forces at Cedar Creek, Virginia, and drove them from their positions. Major General Philip Henry Sheridan, who was returning to his command from a conference in Washington, received news of the battle in Winchester, Virginia, and rode to the front on his horse Rienzi, rallying stragglers and directing a successful counter-attack.

515.3   *Vincent Ogé*]   In the original edition, this poem was prefaced by the following note: "Fragments of a poem hitherto unpublished, upon a revolt of the free persons of color, in the island of St. Domingo (now Hayti), in the years 1790–1." Jacques Vincent Ogé (1750–91) was executed at Cap-Français after an unsuccessful attempt to emancipate Haitian slaves.

519.5   Ritter]   Knight.

519.6   Schwillensaufenstein]   Comic place name suggesting drunkenness.

519.15   Gasthaus]   Inn.

519.21   wasser]   Water.

520.18   *"Recessit in Franciam."*]   "He retreats to France": from the medieval Latin scholar's song, *"Huc usque, me miseram,"* *Carmina Burana* no. 126.

520.19–22   *"Et affectu . . . optime."*]   "All must play the harp / and produce the good old songs / and the beating heart / and the body's every gesture / and most of all, scholars / who best love a festival": Lines 3–8 of *"Tempus hoc lititie,"* *Carmina Burana* no. 216.

520.24   Der teufel's los]   "The devil's loose."

520.24   Bal Mabille]   A public dance-hall.

520.27   Orphée aux Enfers]   "Orpheus in the Underworld" (1858), operetta by Jacques Offenbach, which includes the famous "Can-Can" dance music.

521.3   Frankenland]   France.

521.17   cocodettes]   Tarts.

521.19–20   "D'ou vient . . . Dieu!"]   "Where is this great gentleman from? O holy name of God!"

521.26–28   Rond Point . . . Rabelais]   Grand circle on the Champs Elysées in Paris, between the Place de la Concorde and what is now the Etoile, near the rue de Rabelais.

521.36   garçe]   Girl.

522.7   Barriere balls]   Parisian dance halls.

522.12   *l'on s'amuse*]   "A good time is had."

522.15   *gallop*]   Galop.

522.28   Teufel]   Devil.

523.3   *"The Day Is Done"*]   A parody of Longfellow's poem of the same name.

524.17   *Jacob*]   A parody of Wordsworth's "Lucy" poem: "She dwelt among the untrodden ways / Beside the springs of Dove."

525.1   *"When Lovely Woman"*]   A parody of Oliver Goldsmith's song from *She Stoops to Conquer* (1773): "When lovely woman stoops to folly."

527.5   *All or Nothing*]   A parody of Emerson.

528.7   *Camerados*]   A parody of Whitman.

536.28   *Arachne*]   Greek for spider.

548.16   Dodona]   The site in Epirus of the oldest Greek oracle, where a grove of oak trees sometimes delivered the oracles.

549.1   *Ethnogenesis*]   The genesis or beginnings of a race. The Southern Congress (or Convention) in Montgomery, Alabama, was attended by delegates from South Carolina, Georgia, Florida, Alabama, Mississippi, and Louisiana; they met on February 4, 1861, adopted a provisional constitution for the Confederate States of America, and unanimously elected Jefferson Davis as provisional president.

550.14   Moultrie]   Colonel William Moultrie built a fort on Sullivan's Island off Charleston, South Carolina, and successfully defended it against a British naval attack on June 28, 1776; it was later named after him.

550.14   Eutaw]   The battle of Eutaw Springs, South Carolina, September 8, 1781, later celebrated in William Gilmore Simms' novel *Eutaw* (1856).

554.30   The Poet of "The Woodlands"]   William Gilmore Simms, who lived on the plantation "Woodlands" in South Carolina.

558.3   *My Lighthouses*]   The poem is dated "Genoa, November 30."

569.28   Prima]   Prima Ballerina.

578.22   Boanerges]   James and John, sons of Zebedee, called "sons of thunder" (Mark 3:17).

588.13   Sceptic Thomas]   "Doubting" Thomas (John 20:24–29).

599.4   *"Ye cannot enter now"*]   Alfred Tennyson, "Guinevere," l. 168.

599.11   sad Harold, . . . string]   Cf. Byron, *Childe Harold's Pilgrimage*, Canto I, stanza XIII: "He seized his harp, which he at times could string, /

And strike, albeit with untaught melody, / When deemed he no strange ear was listening."

603.3   *Marching Through Georgia*]   Sherman's army left Atlanta on November 16, 1864, and entered Savannah on December 21.

605.3   Prelude]   This poem served as the introduction to Stedman's anthology of American poetry, published in 1900; the "choir" in the first line is comprised of the voices of all the poets included.

606.3   *Statue on the Capitol*]   *Columbia, the Goddess of Liberty* (or *Armed Liberty*) by Thomas Crawford (1814–57) stands 19.5 feet high, surmounting the Capitol's dome, her right hand holding a sheathed sword and her left resting on a shield and holding an olive branch. Her helmet is topped with eagles' plumes. The piece was installed in 1863 during the Civil War.

610.3   *Judith*]   The story of the slaying of the Philistine chief Holofernes by Judith of Bethulia is recounted in the apocryphal book of Judith.

610.8–9   Ashkelon . . . Gaza]   Cf. Jeremiah 47:5. Ashkelon and Gaza were two of the five principal cities of the Philistines.

610.11–13   Baal-perazim . . . Rephaim]   Sites of victories of David over the Philistines in 2 Samuel 5:18–25.

610.18   the seventh angel]   Cf. Revelation 10:7–11.

613.3   *Ode . . . Dec'd.*]   One of the verse "tributes" by Emmeline Grangerford in Chapter XVII of *Adventures of Huckleberry Finn.*

614.9   Everlasting light]   Cf. Isaiah 60:19–20.

615.16   Bill Nye]   Pseudonym of Edgar Wilson Nye (1850–96), popular humorist and lecturer.

616.2   bowers]   Two jacks—of trumps, and of the same color—in the game of euchre.

616.23   twenty-four jacks]   "Jacks" was erroneously printed in the first edition as "packs," and the error has been repeated in many subsequent editions.

618.2   *October 10, 1871*]   The great Chicago Fire burned October 8–10, 1871.

618.13   cry of Macedon to Paul]   Cf. Acts 16:9.

629.3   *Père La Chaise*]   The Père Lachaise cemetery in Paris, where many celebrated people were buried after 1804.

629.6   tomb . . . Eloise]   The monument to Abelard and Heloise (d. 1141 and 1163).

630.7   "bravest . . . brave"]   Marshal Ney (1769–1815), called "bravest of the brave" by Napoleon Bonaparte; he was executed for treason by the restored Bourbon regime following the battle of Waterloo.

630.13   Commune fell]   One of the last Communard strongholds to fall, the cemetery was captured by troops of the Versailles government after bitter fighting on May 27, 1871.

630.16   *Our Golden Gate*]   The strait forming the entrance to San Francisco Bay was so named by Frémont in 1846; the "our" differentiates it from the Golden Gate of Constantinople.

631.33   Gates of Hercules]   More commonly, "Pillars of Hercules"; the Rock of Gibraltar and Jebel Musa, in Ceuta, Morocco, both at the eastern end of the Strait of Gibraltar.

636.16   Pike]   Pike county, Illinois.

638.3–4   *Buddha . . . Hay*]   Adams described the origin of the poem in a letter to John Hay:

"26 April, 1895.

My Dear John:

   Once La Farge and I, on our rambles, stopped for an hour to meditate under the sacred Bo-tree of Buddha in the ruined and deserted city of Anuradjapura in the jungle of Ceylon; and, then, resuming our course, we presently found ourselves on the quiet bosom of the Indian Ocean. Perhaps I was a little bored by the calm of the tropical sea, or perhaps it was the greater calm of Buddha that bored me. At all events I amused a tedious day or two by jotting down in a note-book the lines which you profess to want. They are yours. Do not let them go further.

Ever affectionately,
HENRY ADAMS."

The narrative of "Buddha and Brahma" is derived from an anecdote from *Questions of King Milinda*, as it appeared in F. Max Muller's *Natural Religion*.

638.6   Sakya Muni]   A name for the Buddha, literally "sage of the Sakya" (the Sakya were the tribe Gautama Siddhartha, the Buddha, was born into).

638.24   Eight-fold Way]   The Eight-fold Path of Buddhism, comprising right views, right intention, right speech, right conduct, right livelihood, right effort, right mindfulness, and right concentration.

639.24   Mogadha]   Magadha, an ancient kingdom in northern India and the region in which Buddhism originated.

639.15   Kshatriya]   The warrior or ruling caste into which the Buddha had also been born.

645.8–9   patriotic gore . . . Baltimore]   Twelve citizens of Baltimore were killed by soldiers of the 6th Massachusetts Regiment on April 19, 1861, after a pro-secessionist mob attacked the regiment as it marched through the city.

645.24   Carroll's] Charles Carroll of Carrollton (1736–1832), signer of the Declaration of Independence.

645.25   Howard's] John Eager Howard (1752–1827), officer in the American Revolution who was severely wounded at the battle of Eutaw Springs; he later served as governor of Maryland.

645.32   Ringgold's] Major Samuel Ringgold of Maryland (1800–46), army officer who fought the Seminoles in Florida and was killed at the battle of Palo Alto in the Mexican War.

646.1   Watson's] Colonel William Watson (1808–46), a Marylander and leader of the "Baltimore Battalion" in the Mexican War; he died at the siege of Monterey.

646.2   May] Captain Charles Augustus May (1819–64), born in Washington, D.C., commanded cavalry under Zachary Taylor at the Mexican War battles of Palo Alto, Resaca de la Palma, Monterey, and Buena Vista.

646.10   *Key*] Francis Scott Key, author of "The Star-Spangled Banner," was a Marylander; see biographical sketch, p. 913.

646.17   *"Sic semper",*] In full, *sic semper tyrannis*: "thus be it ever to tyrants," motto of the state of Virginia.

654.17   Antonio] Prospero's antagonistic brother in Shakespeare's *The Tempest*.

654.20   *Glynn*] Glynn County, Georgia; the marshes are near the coastal town of Brunswick.

658.16–17   Habersham . . . Hall] The Chattahoochee River rises in Habersham and Hall counties in northeast Georgia.

664.9–10   The cur . . . lea] A parody of the opening quatrain of Gray's "Elegy Written in a Country Churchyard" (1750): "The curfew tolls the knell of parting day, / The lowing herd winds slowly o'er the lea, / The plowman homeward plods his weary way, / And leaves the world to darkness and to me."

664.25   We, like old Muhlenberg, "care not to stay."] Cf. William Augustus Muhlenberg's (1796–1877) lyric "I Would Not Live Alway": "I would not live alway: I ask not to stay / Where storm after storm rises dark o'er the way."

668.1   *Bartholdi Statue*] Frédéric-Auguste Bartholdi's "Liberty Lighting Up the World," popularly known as "The Statue of Liberty," unveiled in 1886 in New York Harbor.

674.19   brazen giant] The Colossus of Rhodes, one of the Seven Wonders of the World.

675.1   *Venus . . . Louvre*]   The Venus de Milo.

677.6   Gabirol]   11th-century Jewish poet and philosopher of Spain.

693.3   *Twasinta's Seminoles*]   A narrative poem in 251 Spenserian stanzas set against the background of the Seminole wars (1816–42); Twasinta is the Seminole chief in the poem.

694.20   *The Lute of Afric's Tribe*]   The poem is dedicated "To the memory of Dr. J. McSimpson, a colored Author of Anti-Slavery Ballads."

694.21–22   When Israel . . . songs]   Cf. Psalm 137:1–3.

696.4   *Millet's World-Famous Painting*]   *L'Homme à la houe* (1862) by Jean François Millet (1814–75).

698.5   sweet . . . seer]   "Kano Hogai, into whose mouth I put the following summary of Eastern life, was the greatest Japanese painter of recent times, a genius whose penetration to the heart of early oriental ideals seemed like special inspiration. He was for years one of my dearest friends, and in Japanese art my most valued teacher. I have represented him as the reincarnate spirit of oriental art. His death in 1888 was a national calamity." —Fenollosa's note.

698.20   Kásŭga shrine]   "The ancient city of Nara, the capital of Japan in the eighth century, still glories in a grove of mighty pines and cedars which sweep away for a mile to the Eastern mountains, sheltering the dainty buildings of the great Shinto temple, Kásŭga . . . There in the spring and summer of 1886 I spent with Hogai many weeks in delightful study."—from Fenollosa's note.

700.4   Vasubandhu]   "Vasubandhu, the greatest follower of Nagarjuna, and one of the most important patriarchs in the line of esoteric transmission, was a man whose extraordinary spiritual and intellectual endowments enabled him largely to mould the subsequent course of Northern Buddhism, much as St. Paul did that of Christianity. He is the author of numerous works which remain today a cornerstone of Japanese Buddhism."—from Fenollosa's note.

700.19–20   Bodhisats . . . Arhats]   "These are the titles of two degrees in Buddhist saintship. The Arhat, in Northern Buddhism, is one who has attained only subjective purification by withdrawing from the world. He bears marks of the severity of his ascetic discipline. A Bodhisattwa is one who, through the passion of divine love for men, has mingled with the evil of the world and overcome it, thus winning a leadership in the overshadowing army of the good. He is represented as of beautiful face and heavenly mien."—Fenollosa's note.

704.25   Corinna]   In Robert Herrick's (1868–1938) poem "Corinna's Going A-Maying."

704.27   Castara]   Muse of William Habington's *Castara* (1634).

705.5–7   Beau Waller . . . rose]   Edmund Waller; the poem invoked is his song "Go, Lovely Rose."

708.12   Pentelicus']   Mountain in Greece, from which was quarried the marble used for the Parthenon.

710.3   *W. S. M.*]   W. S. Monroe, the poet's younger brother.

713.3   *Chartres*]   The Cathedral of Notre-Dame (consecrated 1260) at Chartres, France.

713.18   cloud of witnesses]   Cf. Hebrews 12:1.

717.26   Denmark's enmity]   Prussia and Austria defeated Denmark in 1864, leading to their joint annexation of Schleswig-Holstein. The two duchies were ceded to Prussia in 1866 after the Austro-Prussian War.

717.28   humble Austria . . . stroke]   The Austro-Prussian War of 1866 lasted seven weeks and ended in the defeat of Austria.

719.18   Zola's friends]   Supporters of Emile Zola, who came to the defense of Captain Alfred Dreyfus, a Jewish staff officer wrongfully convicted of spying for Germany and sentenced to life imprisonment, in the open letter "J'Accuse" (1898); Zola was subsequently convicted of libel and sentenced to a year in prison, but escaped to England.

719.24–25   The Powers . . . Crete]   Fighting between Christians and Muslims in Crete claimed thousands of lives in 1896–97, with both Christian insurgents and Turkish troops committing atrocities. Six European powers (Great Britain, France, Italy, Germany, Austria-Hungary, Russia) eventually imposed a settlement removing Turkish troops and giving Crete autonomy within the Ottoman Empire.

721.21   *Bargello*]   Thirteenth-century Floretine palace celebrated for its art collection.

724.4   Yang-tse Kiang]   Yangtse (Yangzi) River.

724.11   Han-Yang . . . Tchin-Ting]   Han-Yang is a town on the Yang-tese, in east central Hupeh province; Woo-hoo, or Wa-hu, is a former treaty port on the Yangtse, and Tchin-Ting, or Cheng-ting (Zhengding), is located in what is now Hebei province.

724.12   Keou-Kang]   Chiu-chiang (Jiujiang), river-port on the Yangtse, downriver from Han-Yang; a center for porcelain export.

737.10   Pictured Rocks]   Cliffs along the southern shore of Lake Superior in the Upper Peninsula of Michigan.

764.3   *Oktahutchee*]   The North Canadian River in Oklahoma.

766.3   *Tuckanuck*]   Island near Nantucket, where Lodge spent many summers.

769.3 *Ampezzo*] In the Dolomite Alps of northern Italy. The place names are all local; Cristallo is a mountain peak, as is Sorapis.

774.20 Skamander] River rising near Mt. Ida and Troy, and flowing into the Hellespont; the Turkish name is Kucuk Menderes River.

778.1 *Sainte-Marguerite*] A town on the seacoast near St. Nazaire in the Loire-Atlantique.

780.2 *Sunium*] Ancient name for Sounion (also called Colonna), cape southeast of Athens; on its summit is a temple of Poseidon.

780.17 *Mt. Lykaion*] A mountain in Arcadia in the northern Peloponnesus said to have been sacred to Zeus; also spelled Lycaeus. The columns mentioned in the poem are not extant, and ancient accounts of them are based on hearsay.

19TH-CENTURY VERSIONS OF AMERICAN INDIAN POETRY

Unless otherwise indicated, quoted material in the following notes is taken from commentary in the source texts. Tribal names are given in the form adopted by the *Handbook of North-American Indians* (Washington: Smithsonian, 1978–); in a few cases, lack of information in the source texts has made anachronism unavoidable.

783.3–4 *The Song . . . Enemy*] "They sing it in short lines or sentences, not always the whole at one time, but most generally in detached parts, as time permits and as the occasion or their feelings prompt them. Their accent is very pathetic, and the whole, in their language, produces considerable effect."

784.6 I created the spirits] "The figures in the commencement of this long and much esteemed religious song, represent Na-na-bush, the intercessor, the nephew of mankind. They seem designed to carry back the thoughts towards the beginning of time, and have a manifest allusion to a period when this mysterious and powerful being exercised a wish to assume the form of a man. In the second figure he is represented as holding a rattlesnake in his hand, and he calls himself the creator of the mani-toge. The Indians calling invisible and spiritual beings by the same name which they give to the lowest class of reptiles, it is doubtful whether Na-na-bush here claims to have created intelligences superior to man, or only reptiles, and other small creatures, which they commonly call Mani-toag."

784.7 He sat down Na-na-bush] "This figure appears to be descriptive of the first assumption by Na-na-bush of his office, as the friend and patron of men. He is represented as taking a seat on the ground. Fire, with the northern Indians, is the emblem of peace, happiness, and abundance. When one band goes against another, they go, according to their language, to put out the fire of their enemies; therefore, it is probable that in speaking of the perpetual fire of Na-na-bush, it is only intended to allude to his great power."

784.8   Notwithstanding you speak evil] "The fourth figure, which, in the original, is a priapus, indicates that a man takes up the discourse. The circle about his head but descending no lower than his shoulders, shows that his help and his protection are from above, and in the strength thus derived he is able to defy those who speak evil of him, or seek, by the powers of their medicines, to break his life."

784.10   I can use . . . wood] "The business of hunting is one of the first importance to the Indians, consequently, it finds a place in his devotions; indeed, devotion itself having apparently no object beyond the wants and weaknesses of this life, relief in times of hunger, is one of the most important blessings they ever ask for in their prayers. Accordingly, their young men are directed never to use these songs, or to have recourse to the medicine hunt, except in times of the extremest need."

784.12   Of you I think] "The common spicy wintergreen, a stalk of which this figure is intended to represent, is much valued as a medicine by the Indians."

784.14   That which I take is blood] "Here is the figure of a bear lying dead on the ground, and a hand is thrust into the body, to take out some of the blood. The instruction communicated probably is, that when the prayers offered in the preparation for the medicine hunt have been answered, and an animal killed, offerings should be immediately made, by taking some of the blood in the hand, and pouring it on the ground; or, as is more commonly done, by throwing a handful of it towards each of the cardinal points."

784.15   Now I have something to eat] "This figure is that of a lean and hungry man, who, having asked for food, has been heard, and is now proceeding to allay his hunger."

784.16   I cover my head] "The figure is that of a man, probably designed to be represented in a recumbent position, and drawing his blanket over him. His prayer having been answered, his wants supplied, he declares to the spirits his intention to take repose."

784.17   I fill my kettle] "This is the hunter's lodge, and the kettle hanging in it contains the heart of the animal killed in the medicine hunt, of which none but a man and a hunter must venture to taste. Should a woman or a dog even touch this heart, or the blood of the animal, sudden death, or lingering sickness, would follow it. This effect, as well as the dark colour which the Indians say the skin of the females assumes, in instances of the violation of this rule, they attribute to the effect of the medicine applied by the hunter to the heart of the Me-ze-nin-ne-shah. They point out instances of women, formerly distinguished among them for beauty, and particularly for the fairness of the skin, who, by eating of the heart, or touching the blood of an animal killed in medicine hunting, have not only lost that enviable distinction, but have become disgusting and frightful objects, the skin being blackened and covered with ulcers."

785.1   Long ago, in the old time]   "This is the figure of a snake running over the ground; but some are of the opinion that the delineation should be different, namely, an old woman lying down in the middle of the ground. A new speaker is here introduced, which is the mythological personage Me-suk-kum-me-go-kwa, the grand mother of mankind, to whom Na-na-bush gave in keeping, for the use of his uncles and aunts, all roots and plants, and other medicines, derived from the earth. She received, at the same time, especial direction never to leave home, and always to surrender to men the treasures deposited in her bosom, when they should be, in a suitable manner, demanded of her. Hence it is, that the medicine men make an address to Me-suk-kum-me-go-kwa, whenever they take any thing from the earth, which is to be used as medicine."

785.3   I open you for a bear]   "Me-suk-kum-me-go-kwa speaks to one of the medicines whose power she had just acknowledged, by calling them spirits, and says, I disclose, or reveal you for a bear, or to enable the hunter to kill a bear."

785.4   That is a Spirit]   "Here they begin to dance."

785.8   The feather, the feather]   "It sometimes happens that the hunter has wandered far from his lodge, and has neither birch bark on which to delineate his Me-zen-ne-neens, nor o-num-nu, or other powerful medicine, to apply to its heart. In these cases he takes some of the ashes of his fire, and spreading it on a smooth place, he traces in it the figure of the animal; he then takes a feather and sticks it in the ashes, and on this he places the same reliance as on the more common method of treating the Me-zen-ne-neens."

785.9   Who is a spirit?]   "This figure is nearly the same as is given to Na-na-bush, in the beginning of the song, and an allusion is probably intended to the time when this interpreter between mankind and the Supreme Spirit, the Creator of all things, was driven from the presence of his father, to dwell with the meanest things of this world."

785.11   Now they will eat]   "This figure, with open mouth and distended belly, seems to speak the language of human thanksgiving, and gratitude for favors conferred by a superior power."

785.13   This yellow ochre]   "The o-num-mun, a yellowish earth, which they find in many places . . . is a medicine to which they attribute great power. It is a little sack of this which is disproportionately represented in the hand of the figure."

785.14   Now I wish to try my bird]   "The figure is that of a bird's skin, in which his medicine is contained, and it is that, and not the skin itself, he wishes to try."

785.16   I can kill any animal]   "This large bird, whose open mouth indicates the power of his voice, is not one who inhabits the earth, or is ever seen; he lives in the clouds, and his voice is the thunder. He is more commonly called a-nim-me-kee, but here ke-kaun; our loud sounding medicine is strong to give us wind or rain, or whatever state of the air may be needful to ensure success in the hunt."

785.18   I take a bear]   "The allusion is here to the observances respecting the heart and blood of animals killed in medicine hunting, and the sacrifices to be made in the event of success."

786.1   A rattle snake]   "The jealousy of rival hunters is a frequent cause of quarrels and troubles among the Indians. This man boasts that the rattle snake, which always gives notice when danger is near, is on the poles of his lodge, and no evil can come near him without his being informed of it. His life is guarded by a superior power, and he fears not what his enemies can do to him."

786.3   To a Shawnee]   "This is the figure of a man holding in his left hand the four nah-o-bah-e-gun-nun, or sticks, on which this song was recorded, and the authorship is claimed by a Shawnee, from whom the Ojibbeways acknowledge to have received it; and here, it is probable, the performance originally concluded. The remaining figures appear to have been added from other songs."

786.6   I come up from below]   "The design of this figure is to suggest to the mind, that the spirit, to whom prayers in the medicine hunting are addressed, not only knows where animals are on the surface of the ground, but that so great is his power, he can create them where they did not before exist, to supply the wants of those that pray unto him, and can cause them to come up out of the earth."

786.8   I can make an east wind]   "This is sung four times, the north, the west, and the south winds being each, in turn, substituted for the east wind here spoken of. The meaning is, that the spirit has power to give a wind in any direction that may be necessary for the success of the hunter; that he controls all the changes of the atmosphere, and will overrule them in such a manner as to ensure the success of those whose medicine is strong; in other words, whose prayer is effectual. They must therefore regard neither the wind nor the sky, but go forward in confidence of success. The idea of the circle in this figure, into which the winds are represented as rushing, is derived from the apparent form of the visible horizon; the Indians neither know, nor will they believe that the form of the earth is globular."

786.10   Thus I have sat down]   "This is again the figure of Na-na-bush, sitting on the earth, in the same attitude in which he is represented in the first part of the performance. The meaning is, that all who join in these devotional exercises must, throughout their continuance, which is for the greater part of the night, retain immoveably the same attitude, and give a serious attention to the performer, who must observe the same rule; and when all is finished, he, without uttering a word to any of those about him, rises and walks out of the lodge."

786.12   I make to crawl] "Probably the meaning is, that by these observances, and by this prayer, the hunter may cause to crawl (kill) a bear, or any animal. It is to be observed, that a bear is never, in these songs, called by the common name, but always che-mahn-duk."

787.19   *Chant to the Fire-Fly*] Attributed to "the Indian Children."

788.1   *Songs and Chants*] Powell obtained these songs between 1871 and 1873 among the Kaibab band of the Paiute in northwestern Arizona, possibly from Wa-ai´-wints (whom Powell describes as its "poet"), and Chaur-ru-um-pik, a chief.

788.3   *The Home of the River*] "Chaur-ru-um-pik in explanation of this song says that the river comes from the sky and returns by way of the horizon."

791.15   *A Dream*] "The poet said that he had a dream while sleeping on Un-kar-tu-waid-an, a mountain in northern Arizona, that he fell over the cliff and caught by his hand, and hung there trembling with fright. On awakening, he composed the above."

792.1   *Sacred Songs of the Konkau*] Powers heard these songs at the Round Valley Reservation, Mendocino County, California, in 1871 or 1872.

792.2   *Red Cloud*] Mythological figure, father of Oan-koi´-tu-peh.

792.8   *wēk´-wēk*] Kingfisher.

792.13   *The Acorn Song*] "In the acorn song . . . it will be observed that it appears to be spoken by two different persons. The first three verses are attributed by some Indians to Oankoitupeh, and by others to the Red Cloud. The latter would seem to be more poetically correct. Then the last line is evidently spoken by the acorn personified. I have grouped both these together, and called it all the acorn song, but the Indians sing them somewhat confusedly, as indeed they do the other songs more or less. It required a great deal of patient labor to construct order out of their chaos; and even now I am not always positive, for some Indians will attribute a given verse to one of the personages and others to another. Besides that, the interpretation is sometimes a little uncertain, principally, I think, for the reason that a number of the words either belong to an occult, priestly language, or are so antiquated that the modern Indians, in the absence of most of their old men and prophets, are unable to agree absolutely on their meaning."

792.18   *Ki-u-nad'-dis-si*]   An ancient chief who lost most of his tribe in gambling; grandfather of Oan-koi'-tu-peh.

793.1   *Hunter's Song*]   Gatschet obtained this song from Judge G. W. Stidham, a leading citizen of the Creek Nation."

794.1–2   *The Walam Olum, . . . Lenâpé*]   The *Walam Olum* was first published by the botanist Constantine Samuel Rafinesque (1783–1840) in *The American Nations* (1836). Rafinesque asserted that in 1820 he had obtained, from "the late Dr. Ward, of Indiana . . . some of the original Wallam-Olum (painted record) of the Linapi Tribe of Wapihani or White River," but was unable to interpret the pictographs; and that in 1822 "were obtained from another individual the songs annexed thereto in the original language." The transcribed songs were "inexplicable till a deep study of the Linapi enabled me to translate them." The text remained controversial, and has been regarded as fraudulent. In the commentary accompanying his 1885 retranslation, Brinton raises the possibility that Rafinesque may have forged the work, but concludes: "It is a genuine native production, which was repeated orally to some one indifferently conversant with the Delaware language, who wrote it down to the best of his ability. In its present form it can, as a whole, lay no claim either to antiquity, or to purity of linguistic form. Yet, as an authentic modern version, slightly colored by European teachings, of the ancient tribal traditions, it is well worth preservation."

800.13   *The Mountain Chant*]   The Navajo Mountain Chant was part of a winter healing ceremony of nine days duration. Performed at the request of an ill person's family, the ceremony was also intended to aid the tribe as a whole, especially in bringing rain and a plentiful harvest. Hundreds of songs were associated with the ceremony, certain sets of which—"songs of sequence"—were sung only in a specific order. Matthews observed the ceremony on a number of occasions over many years, but specifically describes one held at Niqotlízi (Hard Earth) on the Navajo Reservation in New Mexico, beginning (with the fifth day) on October 24, 1884. "Some songs," he writes, "are self-explanatory or readily understood, but the greater number cannot be comprehended without a full knowledge of the mythology and of the symbolism to which they refer; they merely hint at mythic conceptions. Many contain archaic expressions, for which the shaman can assign a meaning, but whose etymology cannot now be learned; and some embody obsolete words whose meaning is lost even to the priesthood. There are many vocables known to be meaningless and recited merely to fill out the rhythm or to give a dignified length to the song. For the same reasons a meaningless syllable is often added or a significant syllable duplicated."

801.15   *Chinook Songs*]   Boas collected these songs in British Columbia in 1886. He writes: "The Indians are at present in the habit of living part of the year in Victoria, Vancouver, or New Westminster, working in various trades: in saw-mills and canneries, on wharves, as sailors, etc. In the fall they go to Puget Sound hop-picking. At these places members of numerous tribes gather, who use Chinook as a means of communication." The Chinook Jargon, or Oregon Trade Language, combined elements of indigenous languages, English, and French.

803.19   *Pawnee War-Song*] Brinton obtained this song from John Brown Dunbar (1841–1914), a schoolteacher and philologist whose father, John Dunbar, had been a missionary among the Pawnee.

804.1   *The Thanksgivings*] Converse attended the three-day Iroquois Green Corn Festival in September, 1890, at the Cattaraugus Reservation, New York. "The Thanksgivings" comes from a part of this festival called the Great Feather Dance.

804.13   certain timbers . . . fluids] "Referring to the maple."

804.30   our supporters] "Three sisters of great beauty, who delight to dwell in the companionship of each other as the spiritual guardians of the corn, the beans, and the squash. These vegetables, the staple food of the red man, are supposed to be in the special care of the Great Spirit, who, in the growing season, sends these 'supporters' to abide in the fields and protect them from the ravages of blight or frost."

804.33   Ga-ne-o-di-o] Handsome Lake, prophet of the Longhouse religion.

805.7–8   *The Hardening . . . Men*] Addressed by the elder to the younger of the "Beloved Twain," twins who figure prominently in Zuni creation mythology. In Cushing's translation this speech begins in prose: "Brother, behold!"

806.1–2   *The Generation . . . Corn*] Addressed by Paíyatuma (the God of Dew) to the people.

806.28   *Ghost-Dance Songs*] "The great underlying principle of the Ghost dance doctrine is that the time will come when the whole Indian race, living and dead, will be reunited upon a regenerated earth, to live a life of aboriginal happiness, forever free from death, disease, and misery. On this foundation each tribe has built a structure from its own mythology, and each apostle and believer has filled in the details according to his own mental capacity or ideas of happiness, with such additions as come to him from the trance . . . The differences of interpretation are precisely such as we find in Christianity, with its hundreds of sects and innumerable shades of individual opinion. The white race, being alien and secondary and hardly real, has no part in this scheme of aboriginal regeneration, and will be left behind with the other things of earth that have served their temporary purpose, or else will cease entirely to exist.

"There is no limit to the number of these songs, as every trance at every dance produces a new one, the trance subject after regaining consciousness embodying his experience in the spirit world in the form of a song, which is sung at the next dance and succeeding performances until superseded by other songs originating in the same way. Thus, a single dance may easily result in twenty or thirty new songs. While songs are thus born and die, certain ones which appeal especially to the Indian heart . . . live and are perpetuated. There are also with each tribe certain songs which are a regular part of the ceremonial, as the opening song and the closing song, which are repeated at every dance. Of these the closing song is the most important and permanent. In some cases certain songs constitute a regular series, detailing the experiences of the same person in successive trance visions."

806.29   The snow lies there—*ro' răni'!*]   "This is one of the favorite songs of the Paiute Ghost dance. The tune has a plaintive but rather pleasing effect, although inferior to the tunes of most of the ghost songs of the prairie tribes. The words as they stand are very simple, but convey a good deal of meaning to the Indian. It must be remembered that the dance is held in the open air at night, with the stars shining down on the wide-extending plain walled in by the giant sierras, fringed at the base with dark pines, and with their peaks white with eternal snows. Under such circumstances this song of the snow lying white upon the mountains, and the Milky Way stretching across the clear sky, brings up to the Paiute the same patriotic home love that comes from lyrics of singing birds and leafy trees and still waters to the people of more favored regions. In the mythology of the Paiute, as of many other tribes, the Milky Way is the road of the dead to the spirit world. *Ro' răni'* serves merely to fill in the meter."

807.21   Fog! Fog!]   "This song is an invocation of elemental forces. It was composed by an old woman, who left the circle of dancers and stood in the center of the ring while singing it."

807.25   The whirlwind! The whirlwind!]   "This song may possibly refer to the doctrine of the new earth, here represented as white with snow, advancing swiftly, driven by a whirlwind. Such an idea occurs several times in Arapaho songs."

808.8   The rocks are ringing]   "This song was explained to refer to the roaring of a storm among the rocks in the mountains."

809.17   *The Mocking-Bird's Song*]   According to Fletcher, this song was taken down by John Comfort Fillmore from a Tigua girl of the pueblo of Isleta, New Mexico.

810.1   *The Wizard's Chant*]   Translated by John Dyneley Prince.

810.21   Atwuskniges]   "An invisible being who occasionally fells trees with a single blow of his stone axe. This accounted for the fall of an apparently healthy tree."

811.1   *Night Chant*]   The Night Chant is a nine-day healing ceremony, "performed only during the frost weather, in the late autumn and the winter months,—at the season when the snakes are hibernating." Matthews's sources for these texts included *Hatāłi* Natlōi ("Smiling Chanter") and *Hatāłi* Nĕz ("Tall Chanter").

811.3   *Prayer of First Dancers*]   "This prayer is addressed to a mythic thunder-bird, hence the reference to wings; but the bird is spoken of as a male divinity, and is supposed to dwell with other yéi at Tse'gíhi. The prayer is said at the beginning of work, on the last night of the [night chant]. The shaman speaks it, verse by verse, as it is here recorded, and one of the atsā'lei or first dancers, repeats it, verse by verse, after him."

811.4   Tse'gíhi]   "North of the San Juan River, in Colorado and Utah, are a number of cañons abounding in ruined cliff-dwellings. Tse'gíhi is one of these cañons; but the author does not know which. It is often mentioned in the myths as the house of numerous yéi or gods who dwelt in the cliff-houses in ancient days. They are thought to still abide there unseen."

814.14   *Hako*]   Fletcher obtained these texts between 1898 and 1901 from Tahirussawichi, an elder member of the Chaui band of the Pawnee who acted as the *Ku'rahus* or "leader of the ceremony," and translated them in collaboration with James R. Murie, an American-educated Pawnee. *Hako* refers broadly to "all the articles which belong to the ceremony." Suggesting, in Tahirussawichi's words, "the breathing, vibrating tones from the wooden mouth [of a drum]," the term is used because in the course of the ceremony "everything speaks." "With the Hako," he explains, "we are praying for the gift of life, of strength, of plenty, and of peace."

814.16   *Mother Corn Assumes Leadership*]   Sung by six men (the *Ku'rahus* or "leader of the ceremony," his assistant, two doctors, a chief, and a second chief), each stanza of this song was repeated four times.

814.18   Mother . . . now comes,]   Tahirussawichi explains: "As we sing this song we remember that Mother Earth is very old. She is everywhere, she knows all men, she gave life to our fathers, she gives life to us, and she will give life to our children. The ear of corn represents venerable Mother Earth, and also the authority given by the powers above."

814.25   Mother . . . is here]   Tahirussawichi, Fletcher's informant, explains: "As we sing we think that Mother breathing forth life, who has come out of the past, has now started to lead us on the journey we are to take and to the fulfillment of our desire that children may be given us, that generations may not fail in the future, and that the tie may be made strong between the Father and the Son."

815.1   *Song to the Trees and Streams*]   From the second part of the fifth ritual of the Hako. Tahirussawichi comments: "As we are led by the supernatural power in Mother Corn we must address with song every object we meet, because Tira'wa ['the father of all'] is in all things. Everything we come to as we travel can give us help, and send help by us to the Children."

815.14   *Song of the Promise*]   From the second part of the fifth ritual of the Hako. "While we were traveling," Fletcher's informant explains, "we sometimes saw a great cloud of dust rising in the distance. When we saw this cloud rolling up from the earth we knew that is was caused by a herd of buffalo running away from us toward the land of the Children.

"Sometimes a cow and a calf would separate from the herd and come nearer us. We were taught to be mindful of all that we saw upon the journey, for these sights meant the promise of plenty of food for the Children."

816.1   *the A'shiwi*]   "The people, the reference being to the Zunis only."

816.2   *ʾKiäklo*]   An ancestral god appointed to teach the Zuni of their coming to this world.

816.9   Ne'wekwe]   "Galaxy fraternity."

816.22   listening spring]   "The expression has reference to the hearing of voices in the depths of the water."

817.1   Ko'loowisi]   "Plumed serpent."

817.10   the Sha'läko]   "Giant couriers of the rain-makers."

817.12   the place with many springs]   "Named by the Spaniards Ojo Caliente."

817.17   stone-picture place]   "Rocks with pictographs."

817.27   blue-jay spring]   "So named from the blue jays gathering about the spring to drink."

817.34   vulva spring]   "So named because the rock from which the water flows resembles the vulva."

FOLK SONGS AND SPIRITUALS

819.2   *The Cowboy's Lament*]   The origins of "The Cowboy's Lament" can be traced to British broadside ballads of the 18th century taking the form of a deathbed confession and lamentation for a life of dissipation; examples include "The Unfortunate Rake," "The Trooper Cut Down in His Prime," "The Bad Girl's Lament," and many others. The earliest printed version of "The Cowboy's Lament" appeared in N. Howard Thorp, *Songs of the Cowboys* (Estancia, New Mexico, 1908), although this omits a number of familiar elements present in the 1910 Alan Lomax version reprinted here. Some elements of the song later became part of "St. James Infirmary" and other similar variants.

824.1   *Frankie and Albert*]   Although some writers have dated this song back as far as the 1850s, there are no known versions in print before the 20th century; the first known publication of the music was a variation of the familiar melody under the title of "He Done Me Wrong," written and composed by Hughie Cannon and copyrighted 1904 by Howly, Dresser Co., New York. The John Lomax version printed here was gathered from a Texas source in 1909. The transformation of "Albert" into "Johnny" occurred in the 20th century.

831.11   *A Home on the Range*]   The original version of "A Home on the Range" was written by Brewster Higley (1823–1911); the earliest extant published version appeared under the title "Western Home" in 1876 in the *Kirwin (Kansas) Chief*, accompanied with a headnote stating that the poem "was written by B. Higley, of Beaver Creek, Smith County, Kansas, and first published in the KIRWIN CHIEF, March 21st, 1874." Higley's version, which did not become widely known until the song's authorship was investigated as a result of an infringement of copyright suit in 1934, differs in a number of respects from the more familiar folk adaptation collected in John A. Lomax's *Cowboy Songs* in 1910.

833.1   *Jesse James*]   This earliest known printed version of the ballad appeared five years after the shooting of Jesse James by Robert Ford on April 3, 1882.

833.35   Billy LaShade]   Other known variants of the song identify its composer as "Billy Gashade."

834.4–5   *Jim Crack . . . Fly*]   The song apparently formed part of the repertoire of Daniel Decatur Emmett's Virginia Minstrels; it was published in *Old Dan Emmit's Original Banjo Melodies* (second series) (Boston: Keith's, 1844), but it is not known whether Emmett actually composed it. The version printed was published in 1846 by F. D. Benteen of Baltimore, with no author credited; it contains the chorus "Jim crack corn I don't care," missing from the Emmett version.

835.9   *John Brown's Body*]   The song is believed to have originated in the spring of 1861 among the 2nd Battalion, Boston Light Infantry, stationed at Fort Warren near Boston. James E. Greenleaf, the leader of the battalion's choral society, arranged for its publication that year by the publisher C. S. Hall in a version that differs in a number of respects from the later text reprinted here.

843.9   *Michael Row the Boat Ashore*]   Collected by Charles Pickard Ware in the Port Royal Islands, Georgia.

846.1   *Oh My Darling Clementine*]   In the original sheet music (Boston: Oliver Ditson & Co., 1884) the author is identified as Percy Montrose, of whom nothing further is known.

849.9   *Simple Gifts*]   This Shaker hymn exists in various manuscript versions, and is believed to have been composed in the late 1840s.

853.1   *Working on the Railway*]   The song is also widely known under the title "Paddy Works on the Erie."

Index of Titles and First Lines

Index of Poets

Library of Congress Cataloging-in-Publication Data

American poetry : the nineteenth century.
        p.   cm. — (Library of America college editions)
      1. American poetry — 19th century.   I. Series.
ps607.A56   1996
811′.308—dc20
isbn 1–883011–36–1   96-8927
                                                      CIP

About The Library of America

THE LIBRARY OF AMERICA is an award-winning, nonprofit publisher dedicated to preserving America's best and most significant writing in handsome, enduring volumes, featuring authoritative texts. Founded in 1979 with initial funding from the National Endowment for the Humanities and the Ford Foundation, the series, which now numbers nearly 100 volumes, has been called "the most important book-publishing project in the nation's history."

For the first time, the full range of outstanding American writing will be permanently available in uniform, hardcover volumes, priced to reach a wide audience. Each volume contains up to 1600 pages and includes a number of works by our country's foremost novelists, historians, poets, essayists, journalists, philosophers, and statesmen. Authoritative, unabridged, scrupulously accurate texts are a hallmark of the volumes, which also feature a handsomely designed page, high-quality, acid-free paper bound in a cloth cover and sewn to lie flat when opened, a ribbon marker, and printed endpapers. The series includes acknowledged classics and neglected masterpieces, and new volumes are added each year.

Library of America hardcover volumes are available singly or by subscription. A jacketed edition, available in bookstores, is priced between $27.50 and $40.00. A slipcased edition is available by subscription at $24.95.

Library of America College Editions bring these authoritative and comprehensive editions to teachers and students for the first time in an affordable paperback format.

For more information, a complete list of titles, or to place an order, contact The Library of America, 14 East 60th Street, New York, New York 10022. Telephone: (212) 308-3360. Fax: (212) 750-8352. E-Mail: LibAmerica@aol.com.

LIBRARY OF AMERICA COLLEGE EDITIONS

American Poetry: The Nineteenth Century
John Hollander, editor
ISBN 1-883011-36-1 $14.95   1040 pages

Stephen Crane • PROSE AND POETRY
J. C. Levenson, editor
Maggie: A Girl of the Streets; The Red Badge of Courage; Stories, Sketches, Journalism; Poetry
ISBN 1-883011-39-6 $15.95   1379 pages

Frederick Douglass • AUTOBIOGRAPHIES
Henry Louis Gates, Jr., editor
Narrative of the Life; My Bondage and My Freedom; Life and Times
ISBN 1-883011-30-2 $13.95   1126 pages

W.E.B Du Bois • WRITINGS
Nathan I. Huggins, editor
The Suppression of the African Slave-Trade; The Souls of Black Folk; Dusk of Dawn; Essays & Articles from The Crisis
ISBN 1-883011-31-0 $15.95   1334 pages

Ralph Waldo Emerson • ESSAYS AND POEMS
Joel Porte, Harold Bloom, and Paul Kane, editors
Nature; Addresses, and Lectures; Essays: First and Second Series; Representative Men; The Conduct of Life; Poems 1847, May-Day and Other Poems; Uncollected Poems
ISBN 1-883011-32-9 $15.95   1360 pages

Nathaniel Hawthorne • TALES AND SKETCHES
Roy Harvey Pearce, editor
Twice-told Tales; Mosses from an Old Manse; The Snow Image
ISBN 1-883011-33-7 $13.95   1181 pages

Sarah Orne Jewett • NOVELS AND STORIES
Michael Davitt Bell, editor
Deephaven; A Country Doctor; The Country of the Pointed Firs; Stories and Sketches
ISBN 1-883011-34-5 $11.95   937 pages

Edgar Allan Poe • POETRY, TALES, AND SELECTED ESSAYS
Patrick F. Quinn and G. R. Thompson, editors
ISBN 1-883011-38-8 $16.95   1506 pages

Edith Wharton • FOUR NOVELS
R.W.B. Lewis and Cynthia Griffin Wolff, editors
The House of Mirth; Ethan Frome; The Custom of the Country; The Age of Innocence
ISBN 1-883011-37-X $13.95   1156 pages

Walt Whitman • POETRY AND PROSE
Justin Kaplan, editor
Leaves of Grass 1855; Leaves of Grass 1891-92; Supplementary Poems; Complete Prose
ISBN 1-883011-35-3 $16.95   1407 pages

Bookstore orders: Penguin USA, Box 120, Bergenfield, NJ, 07621-0120; tel: (800) 526-0275; fax: (800) 227-9604